T0178127

Lecture Notes
in Business Information Processing　　　517

LNBIP reports state-of-the-art results in areas related to business information systems and industrial application software development – timely, at a high level, and in both printed and electronic form.

The type of material published includes

- Proceedings (published in time for the respective event)
- Postproceedings (consisting of thoroughly revised and/or extended final papers)
- Other edited monographs (such as, for example, project reports or invited volumes)
- Tutorials (coherently integrated collections of lectures given at advanced courses, seminars, schools, etc.)
- Award-winning or exceptional theses

LNBIP is abstracted/indexed in DBLP, EI and Scopus. LNBIP volumes are also submitted for the inclusion in ISI Proceedings.

Yiliu Paul Tu · Maomao Chi

Editors

E-Business

New Challenges and Opportunities for Digital-Enabled Intelligent Future

23rd Wuhan International Conference, WHICEB 2024
Wuhan, China, May 24–26, 2024
Proceedings, Part III

 Springer

Editors
Yiliu Paul Tu ⓘ
University of Calgary
Calgary, AB, Canada

Maomao Chi
China University of Geosciences
Wuhan, China

ISSN 1865-1348   ISSN 1865-1356 (electronic)
Lecture Notes in Business Information Processing
ISBN 978-3-031-60326-6   ISBN 978-3-031-60324-2 (eBook)
https://doi.org/10.1007/978-3-031-60324-2

This Springer imprint is published by the registered company Springer Nature Switzerland AG
The registered company address is: Gewerbestrasse 11, 6330 Cham, Switzerland

If disposing of this product, please recycle the paper.

Preface

The 23rd Wuhan International Conference on E-Business (WHICEB), an AIS-affiliated annual conference, took place from May 24 to 26, 2024, in Wuhan, China. The conference hosts were the School of Economics and Management, China University of Geosciences, Wuhan, China, and Baden-Württemberg Cooperative State University Heidenheim, Heidenheim, Germany. The organizers were The Center for International Cooperation in E-Business, China University of Geosciences, Wuhan, China, the School of Information Management, Wuhan University, China, and the College of Business Administration, Ningbo University of Finance & Economics, China. The conference was sponsored by the Association for Information Systems (AIS), the China Association for Information Systems (CNAIS), the China Information Economics Society, and Wuhan University of Communication.

WHICEB is dedicated to advancing scholarly research and fostering networking opportunities within the e-business sector and related fields. Our goal is to catalyze academic inquiry and business innovation by facilitating discussions on e-business, global finance, and the imperative for ongoing innovation. This conference aims to showcase cutting-edge research, solutions, and methodologies that leverage the Internet as a powerful tool for global commerce. The digital age presents a myriad of challenges, from technological hurdles to behavioral adaptations, marketing strategies to data analytics, and concerns over efficacy to security. In recent years, the ABCD Technology—big data, cloud computing, artificial intelligence, and blockchain—has sparked a new wave of innovation across manufacturing, business, education, and personal life sectors. This digital and intelligent transformation is paving the way for a novel digital economy growth model, redefining "Internet Plus" applications, and enabling businesses to reinvent their models from the ground up. In response to this digital and intelligent trend, companies are actively engaging with new challenges, thereby generating numerous research opportunities.

This year's conference theme, "New Challenges and Opportunities for a Digital-Enabled Intelligent Future," is designed to ignite robust academic and corporate engagement by integrating e-business and information technology in our increasingly digital and intelligent landscape, alongside fresh insights and discoveries in service, marketing, and operational management reform. The conference sought to highlight groundbreaking scientific research in fields enabled by artificial intelligence, foster cross-disciplinary studies, and share experiences from various nations and regions. These proceedings encompass 16 tracks and will be indexed appropriately. The selected best papers from the proceedings will be recommended to international academic journals including but not limited to the following: Electronic Commerce Research and Applications, Electronic Markets, Electronic Commerce Research, Internet Research, Journal of Organizational and End User Computing, Journal of Information & Knowledge Management, International Journal of Networking and Virtual Organizations, and Journal of Systems and Information Technology.

The research papers in these proceedings went through a double-blind peer review process. Papers were accepted based upon a clear research methodology and contributions to the knowledge of e-business including but not limited to case studies, experiments, simulations, and surveys. The efforts made by our track chairs in reviewing submissions are really appreciated, which ensures the quality of the proceedings. On behalf of the conference organization, we thank them for their professional diligence. They are: *Xing Wan, Jiangnan Qiu, and Lin Jia,* Advancing Digital Education; Innovations, Challenges, and Opportunities; *Yaobin Lu, Ling Zhao, and Jiang Wu,* Artificial Intelligence & IoT(AIoT) Enabled Business Innovation; *Yi Wang, Yuan Sun, and Si Shi,* Artificial Intelligence and New Ways of Working; *Guoyin Jiang, Xiaodong Feng, and Wenping Liu,* Computing and Complexity in Digital Platforms; *Dongxiao Gu, Jia Li, and Yiming Zhao,* Data Science and Smart Social Governance; *Zhongyun (Phil) Zhou, Yongqiang Sun, and Xiao-Ling Jin,* Digital Enablement and Digital Governance; *Xiaobo (Bob) Xu, Weiyong Zhang, and Fei Ma,* Digital Innovation and Social Impact; *Ping Wang, Xiuyan Shao, and Cong Cao,* Disruptive Technologies and Digital Transformation; *Xiaoling Li, Lu Wang, and Qing Huang,* E-business Strategy & Online Marketing; *Rong Du, Hongpeng Wang, and Peng Wang,* Emerging e-Commerce Initiatives Enabled by Advanced Technologies; *Shaobo Wei, Xiayu Chen, and Hua Liu,* Emerging Technologies and Social Commerce; *Nannan Xi, Hongxiu Li, Juho Hamari, and Juan Chen,* Engaging Technologies; *Zhaohua Deng, Tailai Wu, and Jia Li,* Healthcare Service and IT Management; *Haichao Zheng, Yuxiang Zhao, and Bin Zhu,* Human-Computer/AI Interactions; *Hefu Liu, Meng Chen, and Zhao Cai,* Information Systems and Operations Management; *Zhao Du, Ruoxin Zhou, and Shan Wang,* Transformative Digital Innovations: Education, Sports, and Entertainment.

This year, we received a total of 354 submissions, from which 107 papers successfully secured acceptance for publication. This results in an acceptance rate of approximately 30.79%. Our proceedings are structured across three volumes. Each paper included in these volumes has undergone a rigorous review process, involving a minimum of three double-blind reviews conducted by members of the Program Committee. Again, we express our sincere appreciation to all members of the Program Committee for their invaluable contributions, unwavering support, and dedicated efforts throughout this process.

April 2024   Yiliu Paul Tu
                                                         Maomao Chi

Organization

Conference Co-chairs

Jing Zhao   School of Economics and Management, China
                                   University of Geosciences, China
Juergen Seitz   Baden-Württemberg Cooperative State University
                                   Heidenheim, Germany
Doug Vogel   Harbin Institute of Technology, China

Publication Chairs and Proceedings Editors

Yiliu (Paul) Tu   University of Calgary, Canada
Maomao Chi   China University of Geosciences, China

Program Committee

Chairs

Weiguo (Patrick) Fan   University of Iowa, USA
Zhen Zhu   China University of Geosciences, Wuhan, China

Members

Yukun Bao   Huazhong University of Sciences & Technology,
                                   China
Zhao Cai   University of Nottingham Ningbo, China
Cong Cao   Zhejiang University of Technology, China
Juan Chen   Anhui University of Finance and Economics,
                                   China
Meng Chen   Soochow University, China
Xiayu Chen   Hefei University of Technology, China
Xusen Cheng   Renmin University of China, China
Zhaohua Deng   Huazhong University of Sciences & Technology,
                                   China
Rong Du   Xidian University, China
Zhao Du   Beijing Sport University, China
Xiaodong Feng   Sun Yat-sen University, China

Dongxiao Gu	Hefei University of Technology, China
Juho Hamari	Tampere University, Finland
Qing Huang	Chongqing Technology and Business University, China
Zhongyi Hu	Wuhan University, China
Lin Jia	Beijing Institute of Technology, China
Guoyin Jiang	University of Electronic Science and Technology of China
Xiaoling Jin	Shanghai University, China
Hongxiu Li	Tampere University, Finland
Jia Li	East China University of Science and Technology, China
Xiaoling Li	Chongqing University, China
Xixi Li	University of Science and Technology Beijing, China
Hefu Liu	University of Science and Technology of China, China
Hua Liu	Anhui University of Finance and Economics, China
Wenping Liu	Hubei University of Economics, China
Yaobin Lu	Huazhong University of Sciences & Technology, China
Fei Ma	Chang'an University, China
Jian Mou	Pusan National University, South Korea
Jiangnan Qiu	Dalian University of Technology, China
Xiuyan Shao	Southeast University, China
Si Shi	Southwestern University of Finance and Economics, China
Yongqiang Sun	Wuhan University, China
Yuan Sun	Zhejiang Gongshang University, China
Yiliu (Paul) Tu	University of Calgary, Canada
Xing Wan	Nanjing University of Finance & Economics, China
Ping Wang	Central China Normal University, China
Fang Wang	Wilfrid Laurier University, Canada
Hongpeng Wang	Lanzhou University, China
Lu Wang	Zhongnan University of Economics and Law, China
Peng Wang	Northwestern Polytechnical University, China
Shan Wang	University of Saskatchewan, Canada
Yi Wang	Southwestern University of Finance and Economics, China
J. Christopher Westland	University of Illinois at Chicago, USA

Qiang Wei	Tsinghua University, China
Shaobo Wei	University of Science and Technology of China, China
Jiang Wu	Wuhan University, China
Tailai Wu	Huazhong University of Science & Technology, China
Nannan Xi	University of Vaasa, Finland
Huosong Xia	Wuhan Textile University, China
Wenlong Xiao	Chang Gung University, Taiwan RoC
Xiaobo (Bob) Xu	Xi'an Jiaotong-Liverpool University, China
Ying Yang	Hefei University of Technology, China
Jinmei Yin	Nanjing University of Aeronautics and Astronautics, China
Ming Yi	Central China Normal University, China
Shuping Zhao	Hefei University of Technology, China
Yiming Zhao	Wuhan University, China
Yuxiang Zhao	Nanjing University of Science and Technology, China
Haichao Zheng	Southwestern University of Finance and Economics, China
Zhongyun Zhou	Tongji University, China
Ling Zhao	Huazhong University of Sciences & Technology, China
Weiyong Zhang	Old Dominion University, USA
Ruoxin Zhou	University of International Business and Economics, China
Bin Zhu	Oregon State University, USA

Session Chairs

Kanliang Wang	Renmin University, China
Jinghua Xiao	Sun Yat-sen University, China
Rong Du	Xidian University, China
Xiangbin Yan	Guangdong University of Foreign Studies, China
Yi Jiang	China University of Geosciences, China

Organization Committee

Chair

Yao Zhang	China University of Geosciences, Wuhan, China

Secretary-General

Fei Wang   China University of Geosciences, Wuhan, China

Members

Jiang Wu   Wuhan University, China
Shangui Hu   Ningbo University of Finance & Economics,
                                         China
Yating Peng   China University of Geosciences, Wuhan, China
Jing Wang   China University of Geosciences, Wuhan, China
Qian Zhao   China University of Geosciences, Wuhan, China

International Advisory Board

Chairs

Joey George   Iowa State University, USA
Robert Kauffman   Copenhagen Business School, Denmark
J. Christopher Westland   University of Illinois at Chicago, USA

Pacific Asian

Patrick Chau   Beijing Normal University-Hong Kong Baptist
                                         University United International College (UIC),
                                         China
Guoqing Chen   Tsinghua University, China
Wei Kwok Kee   National University of Singapore, Singapore
Feicheng Ma   Wuhan University, China
Jiye Mao   Renmin University, China
Michael D. Myers   University of Auckland, New Zealand
Bernard Tan   National University of Singapore, Singapore
Kanliang Wang   Renmin University, China
Nilmini Wickramasinghe   Deakin University, Australia
Kang Xie   Sun Yat-sen University, China
Qiang Ye   University of Science and Technology of China,
                                         China
J. Leon Zhao   City University of Hong Kong, China

North American

Bob Carasik	Wells Fargo Bank, USA
Yili (Kevin) Hong	University of Miami, USA
Zhangxi Lin	Texas Tech University, USA
Ning Nan	University of British Columbia, Canada
Paul A. Pavlou	University of Houston, USA
Arun Rai	Georgia State University, USA
Xinlin Tang	Florida State University, USA
Richard Watson	University of Georgia, USA
Christopher Yang	Drexel University, USA
Han Zhang	Georgia Institute of Technology, USA
Zhongju Zhang	University of Arizona, USA

European

David Avison	ESSEC, France
Niels Bjørn-Andersen	Copenhagen Business School, Denmark
John Qi Dong	Nanyang Technological University, Singapore
Reima Suomi	Turku School of Economics, Finland
Yao-Hua Tan	Vrije Universiteit Amsterdam, The Netherlands
Hans-Dieter Zimmermann	FHS St. Gallen, University of Applied Sciences, Switzerland

Editorial Board of the Proceedings

Yiliu (Paul) Tu (Editor)	University of Calgary, Canada
Maomao Chi (Editor)	China University of Geosciences, China

Advancing Digital Education: Innovations, Challenges, and Opportunities

Xing Wan	Nanjing University of Finance and Economics, China
Jiangnan Qiu	Dalian University of Technology, China
Lin Jia	Beijing Institute of Technology, China

Artificial Intelligence and IoT (AIoT) Enabled Business Innovation

Yaobin Lu	Huazhong University of Science & Technology, China
Ling Zhao	Huazhong University of Science & Technology, China
Jiang Wu	Wuhan University, China

Artificial Intelligence and New Ways of Working

Yi Wang	Southwestern University of Finance and Economics, China
Yuan Sun	Zhejiang Gongshang University, China
Si Shi	Southwestern University of Finance and Economics, China
Jindi Fu	Hangzhou Dianzi University, China

Computing and Complexity in Digital Platforms

Guoyin Jiang	University of Electronic Science and Technology of China
Xiaodong Feng	Sun Yat-sen University, China
Wenping Liu	Hubei University of Economics, China

Data Science and Smart Social Governance

Dongxiao Gu	Hefei University of Technology, China
Jia Li	East China University of Science and Technology, China
Yiming Zhao	Wuhan University, China
Ying Yang	Hefei University of Technology, China
Shuping Zhao	Hefei University of Technology, China
Xiaoyu Wang	First Affiliated Hospital of Anhui University of Chinese Medicine, China

Digital Enablement and Digital Governance

Zhongyun (Phil) Zhou   Tongji University, China
Yongqiang Sun   Wuhan University, China
Xiao-Ling Jin   Shanghai University, China
Zhenya "Robin" Tang   University of Northern Colorado, USA
Qun Zhao   Ningbo University, China
Wei Hu   Tongji University, China

Digital Innovation and Social Impact

Xiaobo (Bob) Xu   Xi'an Jiaotong-Liverpool University, China
Weiyong Zhang   Old Dominion University, USA
Fei Ma   Chang'an University, China

Disruptive Technologies and Digital Transformation

Ping Wang   Central China Normal University, China
Xiuyan Shao   Southeast University, China
Cong Cao   Zhejiang University of Technology, China
Peter Shi   Macquarie University, Australia
Yiran Li   Zhejiang University of Technology, China

E-Business Strategy and Online Marketing

Xiaoling Li   Chongqing University, China
Lu Wang   Zhongnan University of Economics and Law,
        China
Qing Huang   Chongqing Technology and Business University,
        China

Emerging E-Commerce Initiatives Enabled by Advanced Technologies

Rong Du   Xidian University, China
Hongpeng Wang   Lanzhou University, China
Peng Wang   Northwestern Polytechnical University, China

Emerging Technologies and Social Commerce

Shaobo Wei	Hefei University of Technology, China
Xiayu Chen	Hefei University of Technology, China
Hua Liu	Anhui University, China
Jinmei Yin	Nanjing University of Aeronautics and Astronautics, China

Engaging Technologies

Nannan Xi	Tampere University, Finland
Hongxiu Li	Tampere University, Finland
Juho Hamari	Tampere University, Finland
Juan Chen	Anhui University of Finance and Economics, China

Healthcare Service and IT Management

Zhaohua Deng	Huazhong University of Science & Technology, China
Tailai Wu	Huazhong University of Science & Technology, China
Jia Li	East China University of Science and Technology, China

Human-Computer/AI Interactions

Haichao Zheng	Southwestern University of Finance and Economics, China
Yuxiang Zhao	Nanjing University of Science and Technology, China
Bin Zhu	Oregon State University, China
Bo Xu	Fudan University, China
Kai Li	Nankai University, China

Information Systems and Operations Management

Hefu Liu	University of Science and Technology of China, China
Meng Chen	Soochow University, China
Zhao Cai	University of Nottingham Ningbo, China
Yuting Wang	Shanghai University, China
Liangqing Zhang	Chongqing University, China
Yao Chen	Jiangsu University of Science and Technology, China

Transformative Digital Innovations: Education, Sports, and Entertainment

Zhao Du	Beijing Sport University, China
Ruoxin Zhou	University of International Business and Economics, China
Shan Wang	University of Saskatchewan, Canada
Fang Wang	Wilfrid Laurier University, Canada

Best Paper Award and Journal Publication Committee

Chairs

Yiliu (Paul) Tu	University of Calgary, Canada
Maomao Chi	China University of Geosciences, China

Members

Alain Chong	University of Nottingham Ningbo China, China
Chris Yang	Drexel University, USA
Chris Westland	University of Illinois at Chicago, USA
Doug Vogel	Harbin Institute of Technology, China
Patrick Chau	Beijing Normal University-Hong Kong Baptist University United International College (UIC), China
Jun Wei	University of West Florida, USA
John Qi Dong	Nanyang Technological University, Singapore

Weiguo (Patrick) Fan   University of Iowa, USA
Wen-Lung Shiau   Chang Gung University, Taiwan RoC

Sponsoring Journals (alphabetical order)

Electronic Commerce Research
Electronic Commerce Research and Applications
Electronic Markets-The International Journal on Networked Business
Internet Research
Journal of Database Management
Journal of Organizational and End User Computing
International Journal of Networking and Virtual Organizations
Journal of Systems and Information Technology

Contents – Part III

Data Quality, Product Characteristics, and Product Data Pricing in Manufacturing Enterprises

Huiyang Li[1], Meishu Zhang[1,2], Yu Jia[1(✉)], Nianxin Wang[1], and Shilun Ge[1]

[1] School of Economics and Management, Jiangsu University of Science and Technology, Zhenjiang 212003, Jiangsu, China
jiayu@just.edu.cn

[2] Department of Humanities and Social Sciences, Jiangsu University of Science and Technology, Zhenjiang 212003, Jiangsu, China

Abstract. The pricing of data products is a pivotal aspect of the data factor market's construction process, as it holds the key to unlocking the ten-trillion-dollar market potential. Prior studies primarily centered on pricing personal, public, and financial data. In this study, we delve into a novel type of data product, product data, and aim to construct a profit-maximizing pricing model. Specifically, we address the pricing challenge of manufacturing product data and develop a profit-maximizing pricing model tailored to manufacturing product data, considering factors including data quality utility, product characteristics, and the interplay between market supply and demand. To evaluate our findings, we conducted a simulated pricing analysis using a public dataset. Our findings suggest that product competitiveness exerts a more significant influence on pricing than data quality. As such, product data owners must devise strategic pricing plans to achieve optimal profit levels. The model introduced in this study not only supplements the existing theory and methods of data product pricing but also offers novel perspectives on product data pricing strategies.

Keywords: Produce Data Pricing · Data Quality · Product Characterization · Manufacturing Enterprises

1 Introduction

In the digital age, data has emerged as a critical asset for enterprises, with many organizations amassing substantial amounts of market, customer, product, and operational data that may hold significant commercial value for others [1]. Data trading offers enterprises the opportunity to acquire and leverage external data resources, serving as a vital form of inter-organizational collaboration. As stated in a report issued by the Ministry of Industry and Information Technology of the People's Republic of China, China boasts over 50 data exchanges (centers) and a staggering two million commercial enterprises, as of December 2023. Notably, more than 1.5 million of these enterprises are suppliers of data products, constituting over 70% of the total. Incomplete statistics indicate that over

2,000 data products have been listed on prominent exchanges, amassing a cumulative transaction volume approaching 3 billion yuan. It is anticipated that by 2025, the value of China's data trading market will surpass the remarkable milestone of 200 billion yuan. Within this realm, data pricing serves as a pivotal component of data trading [2].

Now that the data has a price tag, we should also consider the field, type and storage of the data and application scenario [3].Currently, research on data pricing spans diverse industries and domains, encompassing finance, the internet, real estate, and numerous others. Despite the extensive research on pricing, there is a notable dearth of studies focusing on data pricing within the context of manufacturing enterprises. In fact, manufacturing enterprises hold a significant amount of high-value data, with product data standing as the most critical. This data contains core information such as product structure design, manufacturing process, manufacturing technology, material management, and production situation, among others [4]. It plays a pivotal role in enterprise decision-making and business development. Currently, many manufacturing enterprises view this data as a "storage burden". However, there are other manufacturing enterprises that have urgent needs for product data. By trading product data, the demand side can shorten the product development cycle, reduce R&D costs and risks, and enhance design, manufacturing, and management levels by digesting and absorbing advanced product data from industry peers. Simultaneously, the owner of the product data can obtain economic benefits from product data transactions.

However, due to the unique characteristics of product data, the pricing approach, strategy, and methodologies for product data differ significantly from those used for standard data products. Therefore, the existing pricing mechanisms cannot be directly applied to the pricing of product data. To address this gap, this paper develops a pricing model tailored for product data. This model is based on the data quality level and product characteristics of product data, and it also takes into account the demanders' utility and willingness to pay while considering the seller's profit maximization objectives. To validate the model's feasibility, a public dataset is used as an example. The utility function is fitted using the random forest regression algorithm, and the proposed profit-maximizing pricing model is applied to simulate pricing analysis. This study provides valuable theoretical support and practical significance for manufacturing enterprises in product data pricing. It also offers insights for establishing standardized pricing mechanisms in the data trading market.

This paper is organized as follows. We first review related studies in Sect. 2. In Sect. 3, we present the problem description and model, including pricing model construction and analysis. In Sect. 4, we present the empirical analysis. In Sect. 5, we discuss the conclusion.

2   Literature Review

2.1   Data Product Pricing

Data, as a by-product of informatization, has long been self-produced and self-used. However, through "assetization", it can form data products that can be applied or traded by business departments of enterprises. Data products are the main form of market circulation of data elements and the subject matter of data prices [5].

At present, research on pricing methods for data products mainly focuses on government public management data, enterprise data, and personal data. Specific data product transaction pricing methods are shown in Table 1.

Table 1. Data Product Pricing Methodology.

Data types	Description	Pricing methodology	Consideration factors	References
Public data	Various types of data generated by government departments in the process of providing public services	Cost pricing	Variable cost; Fixed cost, profit	Jang et al. [6]
		Value pricing	Utility; Application scenario; Data characteristics	Ou Yang et al. [7]
		Market pricing	Prices of similar products; Data quality	Liu et al. [8]
Enterprise data	The data of the survival and development of the enterprise itself and the data generated in the process of production and operation	Option pricing	Data characteristics; Data value	Xiao and Yang [9]
		Market pricing	Data product characteristics; Market environment	Sun and Li [10]
Personal data	Attribute data or behavioral data with individual characteristics	Pricing based on tuple granularity and minimum traceability	Data sources; Attributes	Koutris et al. [11]
		Differential privacy pricing	Privacy elements; Data reference elements and Data aging elements	Li et al. [12]
		Information entropy pricing	Data value; Information content	Shen et al. [13]; Li et al. [14]

Through an examination of existing research on data product pricing methods, it becomes evident that several key issues arise. Firstly, there is a lack of a specific and unified approach to data pricing, with few individuals dedicating efforts to model construction and case simulation studies. Secondly, the current transaction pricing methods have varying focuses. Some methods determine the price of data products based solely on data characteristics or data value, disregarding external factors such as the market's supply-demand dynamics. Thirdly, current data transaction pricing methods tend to be tailored to a single type of data and have limited applicability across various scenarios. They are primarily tailored to enterprises in the Internet, finance, power grids, and other industries, with less attention paid to the pricing strategies for manufacturing enterprises' products data.

2.2 Data Product and Product Data

Currently, there is no widely accepted definition of data products in academia. Huang et al. [15] consider data products as "data sets as products, or information services derived from data sets". Data product is an important new type of enterprise asset with value and profitability. Product data itself is also a data product, usually containing various information related to the product. These data can help enterprises guide their product development and production. However, compared to data products, its connotation is richer, mainly including product, market and other information. There is a close connection between the two, but also some differences. Product data focuses more on the product itself and related information, while data products focus more on products and services built using data, such as data analysis tools, prediction models, etc. There are also differences in factors affecting their transactions. Data products mainly focus on data characteristics, while product data also needs to consider product characteristics. Therefore, on the issue of pricing product data, we can draw on the pricing methods of data products, but at the same time we should also combine the product characteristics of product data.

Data products are derived from data, and this qualitative change of data from self-use to commodity is manifested in data quality [16]. When trading data, the quality of the data and its value must first be quantified and evaluated. It's evident that data quality is a pivotal attribute, as it directly impacts the quality of data products. Regarding the correlation between data quality and value, Yang et al. [17] introduced the concept of the data quality utility function from a data science perspective. They combined this with the objective of maximizing profits for platforms to create a pricing model based on data quality. Low utility data leads to poor decision-making [18], making data utility a crucial factor in assessing data value. Niyato et al. [19] proposed a pricing method based on data utility, which gauges data utility based on its capacity.

In summary, product data is a unique data product endowed with product characteristics. Pricing for product data should consider the quality of the data itself as well as its product characteristics. Therefore, when constructing a pricing model, it's essential to discuss the influence of data quality and product characteristics on the entire model. Additionally, factors like cost and demanders' willingness to pay must be comprehensively considered in formulating the data pricing model. Initially, we must establish a utility function for data quality that reflects its value. This should be combined with product characteristics to factor into demanders' willingness to pay. By creating a data quality utility function that reflects the data's value, incorporating product characteristics into demanders' willingness to pay, and considering the market's supply and demand dynamics, we can ultimately aim for owner profit maximization and derive the optimal price. This offers a valuable reference for establishing a product data pricing mechanism.

3 Problem Description and Model Development

In this study, we assume that the product data trading market is dominated by sellers, where the owner of product data is the manufacturer of a specific product or series of products that enjoys a certain competitive advantage in the market. The demander of product data, on the other hand, is a manufacturer seeking to purchase the data for production purposes. Within this market, the owner has the authority to establish rules aimed at maximizing profits from the sale of product data. Figure 1 illustrated the pricing logic employed.

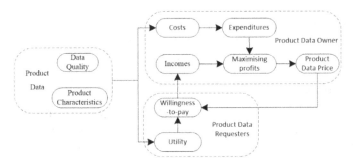

Fig. 1. Pricing mechanism

3.1 Utility Function for Data Quality

Using machine learning methods, this paper represents the data utility by training the accuracy of the model, which in turn reflects the value of the data itself, and only consider the data utility in relation to the data quality, without involving other data dimensions. The accuracy of the set utility function changes with quality throughout the pricing process. Since the exponential data utility function is easier to derive in the optimal pricing model [19], the utility function is defined in this paper:

$$\phi(q) = 1 - ae^{-bq_1} \tag{1}$$

a and b are the fitting parameters. $a > 0, b > 0$. $\phi(q_1)$ is a mapping from data quality to utility, and the function has the following characteristics [19]: (1) $\phi'(q_1) > 0$, the data utility function is increasing; (2) $\phi''(q_1) \leqslant 0$, the data utility function is a marginal decreasing function.

3.2 Demanders' Willingness to Pay

The willingness of demanders to pay typically refers to the highest price that consumers are willing to pay for the goods or services they choose. This paper argues that for product data, demanders' willingness to pay is derived from two factors. On one hand, the characteristics of the data product, specifically data quality q_1, on the other hand, with the characteristics of the product itself, competitiveness q_2. Both factors are positively associated with demanders' willingness to pay, meaning that the stronger the product's competitiveness and the higher the quality of the product data, the higher the demanders' willingness to pay. It is assumed that for a given demander's j willingness to pay w_{ij} for the product data i is a standardized indicator with the value interval of [0, 1], which means that there is no willingness to buy when it takes the value of 0, and the value of 1 means that the data product must be purchased. Therefore, this paper defines the demander's willingness to pay expression as follows:

$$w_{ij} = k_1\phi(q_1) + k_2q_2 \tag{2}$$

k_1 and k_2, are the weight parameters of data quality and product competitiveness in the demander's willingness to pay, respectively $k_1, k_2 \in [0, 1]$, and $k_1 + k_2 = 1, q_1, q_2 \in [0, 1]$. From the functional form of $\phi(q_1)$, $\phi(q_1) \in [0, 1]$.

3.3 Owner's Profit Function

Assume that there are M existing specific manufacturers with potential purchase demand for the product data, where each manufacturer's willingness to pay w obeys a uniform distribution between [0, 1] [17]. A purchase decision is taken only if the manufacturer's willingness to pay is greater than the product data price [20]. Assuming that the average cost per unit of quality level is c, and the transaction price is p, the profit function per unit of data product for the product data owner is:

$$
\begin{aligned}
\pi(p, q_1, q_2) &= pM \int_0^w f(w)dw - cq_1 \\
&= pM \left(\int_0^p f(w)dw + \int_p^w f(w)dw \right) - cq_1 \\
&= pM \left(F(p) + w - p \right) - cq_1
\end{aligned}
\tag{3}
$$

By the definition of the cumulative probability distribution of the demander's willingness to pay $F(p) = P(w \leqslant p)$, since demanders do not make purchase decisions when their actual willingness to pay is less than or equal to the price, it follows that $F(p) = 0$, there is:

$$\pi(p, q_1, q_2) = pM(w - p) - cq_1 \tag{4}$$

4 Results

4.1 Data Selection

To empirically evaluate the proposed pricing model, a real public dataset is employed for simulated pricing analysis. This dataset comprises characteristics of used cars and their associated price data, including variables such as the car's kilometers driven, fuel type, several car-related metrics, mileage, engine type, power index, and seating capacity. The dataset also includes the corresponding price target variable. The data is sourced from a public data platform and divided into training and test sets, with 5710 and 1217 data points, respectively.

For the purpose of pricing data assets of varying quality levels, the data quality levels are initially classified and standardized. By introducing noise to the original dataset, different quality levels are simulated. Assuming that the original training dataset is noise-free and has a quality level of 1, random white noise sequences of varying strengths are added to the unlabeled data vectors of the training dataset to generate training datasets with quality levels of 1, 0.9, 0.8, and so on down to 0.1. Subsequently, target predictions are performed for datasets of varying quality levels using the random forest regression algorithm.

4.2 Data Utility Fitting

Based on the above processing method, 10 groups of data with the quality level of $q_1 > q_2 > ... > q_{10}$ are obtained, and these 10 groups of data are used as the training set, and the same test set of data with the number of 1217 is used to predict the target variables by using the Random Forest Regression machine learning algorithm, and the prediction accuracies are calculated. Table 2 shows the quality level of the 10 groups of training set data and the corresponding prediction accuracy of the test set data:

Table 2. Predictive Accuracy

Quality level	0.1	0.2	0.3	0.4	0.5	0.6	0.7	0.8	0.9	1.0
Predictive accuracy (%)	67.39	68.27	69.83	70.16	70.77	71.41	71.96	73.02	73.82	74.69

In this paper, we use SPSS to fit the above 10 sets of sample points to the true prediction accuracy using a set exponential utility function to obtain the specific utility function as:

$$\phi(q) = 1 - 0.333e^{-0.266q} \tag{5}$$

The R-square of the fitted equation is 0.987, which is a good fit for the equation; therefore, the utility function obtained is used for the determination of the optimal price of the data asset in all the following.

4.3 Determination of Optimal Price

The optimal price for the product data is solved for based on the previously derived demander's willingness to pay, combined with the owner's profit function. For ease of discussion, the price unit of measure is omitted in all cases here.

The willingness to pay of product data demanders is $w_{ij} = k_1\phi(q_1) + k_2q_2$, substituting this into Eq. 3 yields the profit function:

$$\pi(p, q_1, q_2) = pM\left[k_1(1 - ae^{-bq_1}) + k_2q_2 - p\right] - cq_1 \tag{6}$$

Deriving the profit function $\pi(p, q_1, q_2)$ with respect to p and making it 0 gives:

$$p^* = \frac{k_1(1 - ae^{-bq_1}) + k_2q_2}{2} \tag{7}$$

Assume that product data quality and product competitiveness have equal weights, i.e. $k_1 = k_2 = 0.5$. From the previous derivation, $a = 0.333$, $b = 0.266$, and substitute them into Eq. (7). In order to show more intuitively the optimal price with the product data quality and product competitiveness changes, the three-dimensional graph shown in Fig. 2 is drawn: from a single dimension, the optimal price increases with the product data quality or product competitiveness, but the influence of the data quality on the optimal price is much less than the influence of product competitiveness on the optimal price.

Substituting Eq. (7) into the profit function relationship Eq. (6) yields the relationship between the owner's profit and the quality of the data and the competitiveness of the product, that is:

$$\pi(q_1, q_2) = \frac{k_1\phi(q_1) + k_2q_2}{2}M\left[k_1\phi(q_1) + k_2q_2 - \frac{k_1\phi(q_1) + k_2q_2}{2}\right] - cq_1$$

$$= \frac{M}{4}(k_1\phi(q_1) + k_2q_2)^2 - cq_1 \tag{8}$$

Without loss of generality, let us assume that the unit cost of the product data, c, k, m, is the unit cost of the product data. A three-dimensional graph of the profit function is then constructed. As seen in Fig. 3, several noteworthy observations can be made: First, when the data quality remains constant, the owner's profit increases as the competitiveness of the product rises. Second, at lower levels of product competitiveness, an increase in data quality actually leads to a decrease in the owner's profit. Conversely, at higher levels of competitiveness, enhancing data quality boosts the owner's profit. This suggests that when a product's competitiveness is low, its market attractiveness and advantage are also limited. As a result, demanders' willingness to pay for the product data decreases. Consequently, the additional income generated by higher demander payments does not offset the increased cost expenditure, leading to lower profits for the owner when data quality is higher. Third, when data quality is suboptimal, both the utility and price of the data product are correspondingly lower, ultimately resulting in lower profits for the owner of the product data.

In order to visualize the above conclusion, let $q_1 = 0.1$, $q_1 = 0.8$, respectively, obtain the relationship between π and q_2 as shown in Figs. 4 and 5. As well as the relationship between π and q_1 is shown in Figs. 6 and 7 for $q_2 = 0.1$, $q_2 = 0.8$, respectively.

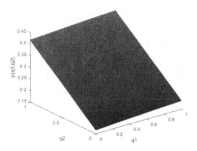

Fig. 2. Changes in the optimal price

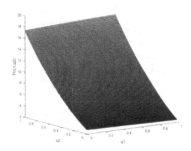

Fig. 3. Profit function

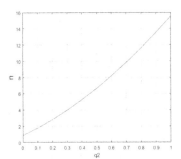

Fig. 4. Relationship between π and q_2 at low q_1

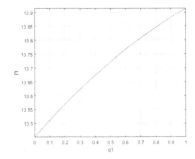

Fig. 5. Relationship between π and q_2 at high q_1

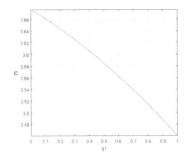

Fig. 6. Relationship between π and q_1 at low q_2

Fig. 7. Relationship between π and q_1 at high q_2

When the level of data quality and product competitiveness is relatively high, it means that data utility and demander's willingness to pay is also high. For product data owners, the cost will also increase. At this time, it will increase their prices appropriately to obtain higher profits, but it can be seen from Fig. 8: First, fixed costs, the increase in price will make the owner's profit. Show the trend of rising first. Second, under fixed prices, the increase in cost has made the owner's profit decline.

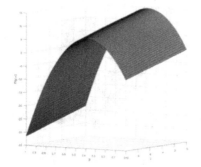

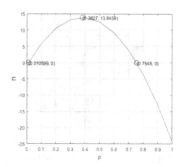

Fig. 8. Profit function on price and cost

Fig. 9. Relationship between product data price and owner profit

To further delve into the impact of price changes on profits, we can make assumptions without loss of generality, so that $k_1 = k_2 = 0.5$, $q_1 = q_2 = 0.8$, $M = 100$. By substituting these assumptions into formula (6), we can obtain the relationship between the price and the profit function, as visualized in Fig. 9. First, it's evident that when the price is relatively low, an increase in price can indeed lead to increased profits. This is because when the price is low, a slight increase in revenue due to the price increase outweighs the reduction in demand caused by the decreased willingness to pay. Therefore, the overall profit enhancement is positive. Second, at higher price levels, the inhibitory effect of price enhancement on profits becomes apparent. A significantly high price can significantly affect the demander's willingness to pay and might even result in losses for the product data owner. As Fig. 8 shows, there exists an optimal price $p^* = 0.3827$, at which the owner's profit is maximized $\pi = 13.8459$. Solving for the critical value when the profit function is 0 shows that the product data owner moves from a profit to a loss position when $p > 0.7548$. This is because while a higher price may increase profit, it also decreases the overall willingness of demanders to purchase. Once the increase in profit is insufficient to offset production losses, profits can decline or even lead to losses.

5 Conclusion

First, the essence of product data production and pricing lies in the factors of data quality and product competitiveness, which have a profound impact on optimal pricing. It's noteworthy that as product data quality or product competitiveness improves, the optimal price rises. Among these two factors, the impact of product competitiveness on the optimal price is generally more significant.

Second, when data quality remains constant, the owner's profit increases with the enhancement of product competitiveness. Put differently, as a product's competitiveness grows, its market demand also rises, leading to higher prices and profits for the product data. Conversely, when a product's competitiveness is low, improving its data quality can actually lead to a decline in profits. When data quality is low, the utility and value of the data product are also limited, resulting in reduced profits for the owner of the product data.

Third, when both data quality and product competitiveness are high, it signifies that the utility of data products and the willingness of product data demanders to pay are also high. However, as prices continue to rise, the willingness of product data demanders to pay will diminish, causing market demand to dwindle and ultimately leading to a decrease in the profitability of product data owners. Therefore, product data owners must carefully balance price increases with maintaining market demand to maximize profits.

The main contributions of this paper are, first, that it narrows the focus of data pricing to specific business scenarios by expanding the scope of the study from finance, government affairs, and healthcare to the manufacturing industry, with a special emphasis on product data in that industry. Second, it introduces a data quality utility function to combine data quality and value from a data science perspective. Third, the mechanism of multidimensional factors is incorporated into the pricing system of manufacturing product data, and a profit-maximizing pricing model is proposed. The impact of product competitiveness on pricing is greater than the impact of data quality on pricing. Therefore, product data owners must develop a strategic pricing plan to achieve the optimal profit level. The model not only complements existing data product pricing theories and methods, but also provides a new perspective for studying product data pricing strategies. In addition, due to the universality of public datasets, while product data is more difficult to obtain. Therefore, this paper initially explores the applicability and effect of the pricing model by utilizing machine learning methods with the help of public datasets, so as to enhance the practical relevance of the research results and provide some pricing guidance for manufacturing product data. In the future, we can continue to improve the pricing model for specific product data, while considering more advanced data analysis and prediction methods, such as deep learning and natural language processing, to improve the accuracy and flexibility of the pricing model. Finally, the construction of an open product data platform can be considered to promote the acquisition and utilization of product data through sharing and cooperation, and to promote the in-depth development of product pricing research in the manufacturing industry.

Acknowledgement. This research is partly supported by the National Natural Science Foundation of China [72372060, 71972090, 72272066, and 71971101], General Project of Philosophy and Social Science Research in Universities in Jiangsu Province [2022SJYB2238], Postgraduate Research & Practice Innovation Program of Jiangsu Province (Product Data Pricing in Manufacturing Enterprises: Pricing by Data Quality and Product Characteristics), Jiangsu University of Science and Technology Youth Science and Technology Innovation Project [1042922212].

References

1. Jones, C.I., Tonetti, C.: Nonrivalry and the economics of data. Am. Econ. Rev. **110**(9), 2819–2858 (2020)
2. Zhai, L.L., Ma, Z.Q., Zhang, S.C.: Review of research on pricing problems of Big Data products. Sci.-Technol. Manag. **20**(06), 105–110 (2018). (**in Chinese**)
3. Fricker, S.A., Maksimov, Y.V.: Pricing of data products in data marketplaces. In: Ojala, A., Holmström Olsson, H., Werder, K. (eds.) ICSOB 2017. LNCS, vol. 304, pp. 49–66. Springer, Cham (2017). https://doi.org/10.1007/978-3-319-69191-6_4

4. Peltonen, H.: Concepts and an Implementation for Product Data Management. Finnish Academy of Technology Helsinki, Finland (2000)
5. Wu, B.Y., Huang, L.H.: The dual dimension of data pricing: from product price to asset value. Price: Theory Pract. (07), 70–5 (2023). (in Chinese)
6. Jang, B., Park, S., Lee, J., et al.: Three hierarchical levels of big-data market model over multiple data sources for Internet of Things. IEEE Access **6**, 31269–31280 (2018)
7. OuYang, R.H., Gong, W.: The pricing mechanism of data elements based on data element value and the contribution of market assessment. Reform **03**, 39–54 (2022). (**in Chinese**)
8. Liu, Q., Tong, Y., Wei, Y.C., et al.: Application of the market approach to valuing Big Data assets. Appraisal J. China **11**, 33–37 (2016). (**in Chinese**)
9. Xiao, X.J., Yang, F.: Valuing data assets in Internet enterprises. Financ. Acc. Mon. **18**, 126–135 (2022). (**in Chinese**)
10. Sun, Z.L., Li, Y.G.: Analysis on the solution path of data product pricing in state-owned enterprises. Appraisal J. China **11**, 46–50 (2023). (**in Chinese**)
11. Koutris, P., Upadhyaya, P., Balazinska, M., et al.: Query-based data pricing. J. ACM **62**(5), 44 (2015)
12. Li, C., Li, D.Y., Miklau, G., et al.: A theory of pricing private data. ACM Trans. Database Syst. (TODS) **39**(4), 1–28 (2014)
13. Shen, Y., Guo, B., Shen, Y., et al.: A pricing model for big personal data. Tsinghua Sci. Technol. **21**(5), 482–490 (2016)
14. Li, X., Yao, J., Liu, X., et al.: A first look at information entropy-based data pricing. In: Proceedings of the 2017 IEEE 37th International Conference on Distributed Computing Systems (ICDCS). IEEE (2017)
15. Huang, L.H., Dou, Y.F., Guo, M.K., et al.: Identifying the features and transaction modes of data products in data markets. Big Data Res. **8**(3), 3–14 (2022). (**in Chinese**)
16. Cai, L., Zhu, Y.Y.: From data quality to data products quality. Big Data Res. **8**(03), 26–39 (2022). (**in Chinese**)
17. Yang, J., Zhao, C., Xing, C.: Big data market optimization pricing model based on data quality. Complexity **2019** (2019)
18. Moges, H.-T., Van Vlasselaer, V., Lemahieu, W., et al.: Determining the use of data quality metadata (DQM) for decision making purposes and its impact on decision outcomes—an exploratory study. Decis. Support Syst. **83**, 32–46 (2016)
19. Niyato, D., Alsheikh, M.A., Wang, P., et al.: Market model and optimal pricing scheme of big data and Internet of Things (IoT). In: Proceedings of the 2016 IEEE international conference on communications (ICC). IEEE (2016)
20. Wertenbroch, K., Skiera, B.: Measuring consumers' willingness to pay at the point of purchase. J. Mark. Res. **39**(2), 228–241 (2002)

Research on the Development of Chinese Industrial Products e-Commerce Based on Text Mining

Zhaoyang Sun[1], Qi Zong[2(✉)], Yuxin Mao[2], and Gongxing Wu[2]

[1] High-Tech Standardization Research Institute, China National Institute of Standardization, Beijing 100191, China

[2] School of Management and E-Business, Zhejiang Gongshang University, Hangzhou 310018, China

18365300981@163.com

Abstract. Policy and report texts related to industrial products e-commerce carry rich and important information, which are crucial for the government to formulate relevant policies and enterprises to plan development paths. In order to study and grasp the development status of China's industrial products e-commerce, 18 industrial e-commerce policy texts and 10 industrial e-commerce reports are deeply mined and analyzed by using text mining methods. Firstly, natural language processing technology is used to pre-process the industrial products commerce-related policy and industry report text data. Then, word frequency statistics and TF-IDF keyword extraction are carried out, and the results of word frequency statistics are displayed visually. Then the feature set is obtained by combining the manual screening method, and the original text corpus is used as the training set using the skip-gram model in word2vec, and the feature words are transformed into word vectors in the multi-dimensional space. Finally, use the k-means clustering algorithm to group the features. The research results based on text mining provide supportive decisions for promoting the development of China's industrial products e-commerce industry.

Keywords: Industrial products e-commerce · E-Commerce platform · Text mining · Policy analysis

1 Introduction

Industrial products refer to products used in industrial production, manufacturing or business operations, etc. According to the purpose of use of the purchaser and the original nature of the product is divided into two categories: one is the purchase of non-productive materials for maintenance, repair and operations; the other is the direct input to the production process of the goods, i.e., production materials. Industrial products e-commerce is a business model that takes enterprises as the main customer group and uses Internet technology to provide a series of services such as trading, logistics, finance,

Y. P. Tu and M. Chi (Eds.): WHICEB 2024, LNBIP 517, pp. 13–24, 2024.
https://doi.org/10.1007/978-3-031-60324-2_2

supply chain and so on for industrial goods producers and consumers. Industrial enterprises use e-commerce technologies, and both parties of transactions complete the entire transaction process through real-time interaction, grasp various market information in a timely manner, and reduce implementation costs [1]. In recent years, the development momentum of the industrial Internet has been strongly influenced by policy promotion, market demand and digital technology progress. China's digital economy has continued to accelerate the development of the industrial products B2B market. In 2022, the scale of China's industrial products e-commerce market reaches 950 billion yuan, a year-on-year increase of 10.46% from 2021. It is expected that the compound annual growth rate of China's industrial products e-commerce market will reach 30% from 2020 to 2025.

In order to address the pain points of industrial development, the government has successively issued relevant policies to integrate the Internet economy with industrialized products, and China's Ministry of Industry and Information Technology (MIIT) has issued a series of policies related to e-commerce of industrial products, including the "Three-Year Action Plan for the Development of Industrial E-Commerce" and the "Special Action Plan for Digital Empowerment of Small and Medium sized Enterprises". These policies explicitly call for further popularizing and deepening the application of industrial e-commerce, encouraging and promoting the joint organization of online trading activities for industrial products by industrial product B2B platforms.

Although in recent years China's industrial products e-commerce industry development is relatively rapid, but the industry as a whole is still in the stage of digital transformation and upgrading, has not yet formed a scale effect and complete system. The development of industrial products e-commerce industry cannot be separated from the support of relevant policies and industry promotion, through in-depth research and analysis of industrial products e-commerce related policies as well as industry reports, it helps to better grasp the current situation of the development of the industry and the characteristics of the law. Based on this, the purpose of this paper is to take industrial products e-commerce related policies and industry reports as the research object, use text mining technology and data visualization methods to carry out quantitative research, and start from high-frequency keywords and topic word clustering to analyze the research hotspots and industry focus areas. The study proves that the text mining process used in this paper helps to reveal the thematic characteristics of China's industrial products e-commerce related policies and industry reports, helps industrial enterprises better understand the focus of China's industrial products e-commerce policies and industries as well as related policies, and also provides quantitative basis for the government to improve the industrial products e-commerce support policies.

2   Related Works

Since the birth of e-commerce, international scholars have used various theories to study its impact on the related fields of industrial product. According to different research focuses, current research can be roughly divided into the following three categories:

(1) Research on e-commerce and its role in the transformation of traditional industrial enterprises. Zhang et al. (2018) [2] proposed the concept of e-commerce embeddedness for the integration trend of e-commerce and manufacturing industry, analyzed

the role of e-commerce on industrial research and development innovation mechanism, and the results showed that e-commerce embeddedness can significantly affect the R&D investment and R&D results of manufacturing enterprises, and also revealed its role in the innovation and upgrading mechanism. Second, the obstacles faced in the development process of industrial e-commerce model. Claycomba et al. (2005) [3] empirically tested different models using overall B2B e-commerce use as the dependent variable and industrial firms' innovation characteristics, environment, channel factors, and organizational structure as predictor variables. The researchers found that factors such as compatibility with existing systems, technological specialization and information technology decision-making facilitated the overall use of B2B e-commerce in industrial firms, which in turn enhanced the value of the firm's performance.

(2) Research on the obstacles faced in the development process of industrial products e-commerce model. Chen et al. (2015) [4] believe that the key factor restricting the large-scale growth of industrial e-commerce is its backward development strategy, such as the conflict between the e-commerce model and the industrial sales model, as well as the lack of professional technical and service support. Thirdly, it is the study of the mechanism of how e-commerce promotes industrialization. Waithaka et al. (2013) [5] identified technical, security, cost, lack of computer knowledge, and environmental issues as obstacles for Kenya's manufacturing industry to adopt the B2B market.

(3) Research on the mechanism of how e-commerce promotes industrialization. Tang Panpan et al. (2014) [6] establish a power model, use the principle of system dynamics to discuss the various factors of e-commerce in the process of promoting industrial development, establish a causal loop diagram and a system flow diagram, and analyze the mechanism of e-commerce's impact on industrial development. Wang (2013) [7] explored how cloud computing and e-commerce affect industrial companies and industries in terms of technology architecture, service model and industry chain.

A review of the literature reveals that text mining research on the industrial products e-commerce is relatively limited. Existing literature mostly focuses on the basic concepts of industrial products e-commerce, the sorting and analysis of model characteristics, and the study of impact mechanisms. There are few quantitative analyzes of industrial products e-commerce from the perspective of text mining. However, for the industrial products industry with many characteristics, there is a gap between the current research results and the actual development needs, and these studies fail to fully combine the characteristics of the industry to further propose solutions, and lack of specific analyses and guidance to support the development of the industry.

Text mining is an increasingly prominent research tool in the field of data mining technology, which aims to reveal hidden patterns and regularities in large-scale text data [8]. Policy texts and industry reports contain a huge amount of information. Compared with traditional manual analyzing methods, text mining technology can effectively deal with problems such as large amounts of text and strong subjectivity. It has more advantages than other data mining techniques, during the process of analyzing the policies and reports related to industrial products e-commerce. Therefore, from the perspective of text mining, research related to the industrial products e-commerce industry has a large amount of explorable space, and future research should dig deeper into the industry's needs.

3 Framework for Industrial Products e-Commerce Text Analysis

With the popularity of big data technology, text mining techniques have been widely used in industrial policy and text reporting. In this context, the design of an effective text mining process becomes crucial. The design of the process involves the planning and organisation of the whole task, and a well-designed process can improve efficiency and ensure the achievement of text mining goals. This study will follow the steps of the flowchart in Fig. 1 to analyse the process in detail.

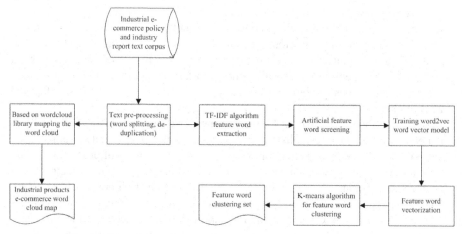

Fig. 1. Flow of text mining related to industrial products e-commerce

(1) Text pre-processing: Text preprocessing is an important step based on policy text corpora, which includes two key steps: text data cleaning and word segmentation. Firstly, unnecessary characters, punctuation, and special symbols are removed through stop word filtering, retaining only key information. Then, split the cleaned text into independent words. Subsequently, optimize and adjust the segmentation results. For example, for overall words like "Made in China", automatic segmentation may split them into two words: "Made in China" and "Made in China". We add new vocabulary through a custom dictionary to maintain word integrity. Finally, perform word frequency statistics and display high-frequency vocabulary in the text through a visual word cloud map.

(2) TF-IDF feature extraction: For the large number of feature words generated after text preprocessing, feature extraction is an indispensable step, which helps to reduce data dimensions and thus alleviate the burden of subsequent model training. The TF-IDF algorithm takes into account two aspects of information: the feature frequency

TF (Term Frequency) and the inverse document frequency IDF (Inverse Document Frequency) [9]. This enables TF-IDF to better reflect the importance of words in the document set, avoiding the limitation of solely relying on word frequency as a feature. In this study, the TF-IDF method is used to calculate the weights of the feature words in the text of the industrial e-commerce, and these feature words are ranked according to the magnitude of their weights, and the words with a TF-IDF value higher than a specified threshold are selected as the final feature words. This step significantly reduces the dimensionality of the text model, providing a suitable model foundation for subsequent semantic similarity calculations.

(3) Feature word vectorisation based on word2vec training: Word2Vec is a word embedding technique used to convert vocabulary into vector representations, which has advantages such as simple models, fast training speed, and the ability to express similarities and analogical relationships between different words effectively. Firstly, a large-scale text corpus needs to be constructed for training the word2vec model. Subsequently, the corpus is preprocessed, and the preprocessed corpus is used to train the word2vec model, where two models, skip-gram and cbow, are used. Skip-gram is based on the idea of taking a word as the centre and trying to predict its surrounding words, and adjusting the word vectors so as to maximise the probability of generating surrounding words from the centre word. CBOW is another training method, which is characterised by the prediction of the centre word using the surrounding words, in contrast to skip-gram [10]. It can be seen that selecting the Skip gram model for word vectorization training results in more predictions, but through optimization of multiple parameters, the final word vector obtained is more accurate. Therefore, skip-gram model is chosen for vectorisation training of feature words in this study.

(4) Text clustering based on k-means: K-means is a simple and classic clustering algorithm with simple algorithm ideas and fast calculation speed, and is suitable for text clustering tasks on large-scale data sets. First, the appropriate k value is determined using the profile coefficient, the excellent samples are selected through the individual profile coefficients of the data objects, and the initial clustering centre is adaptively selected for k-means clustering [11] that optimises the selection of initial clustering centres. Second, each sample is assigned to the cluster to which the nearest clustering centre belongs. Thirdly, the clustering centres are updated by calculating the average value of all the samples in each cluster and using it as the new clustering centre. Fourthly, the second and third steps are repeated and if the distance between the newly calculated clustering centre and the original centre is less than a set threshold, the clustering is considered to reach the desired result and the algorithm stops.

4   Research Findings and Discussion

Based on the text mining method for industrial products e-commerce mining and analysis, in-depth exploration of industrial products e-commerce development status and characteristics of information.

4.1   Data Sources and Data Pre-processing

This research adopts the texts of industry research reports from authoritative organisations and policy-type texts issued by government departments as data sources for the study. Authoritative institutions usually provide in-depth insights and analyses of specific industries through rigorous research methodologies and professional teams, covering industry trends, market conditions, key drivers, etc., which are professional interpretations capable of reflecting the economic and social development. At the same time, a series of policy documents issued by administrative authorities at all levels comprehensively explain the overall goals, key actions and safeguards of industrial products e-commerce and clarify its future development plans and directions, which is also a professional interpretation of the field. Therefore, this study takes into account both the industry reports of authoritative institutions and the relevant policies issued by the government as two important data sources, and further conducts quantitative textual analyses to dig out the thematic focus of the industrial products e-commerce.

The keywords "industrial products e-commerce", "industrial Internet" and "manufacturing e-commerce" were used for searching, and policy texts were obtained by visiting the official websites of the State Council, the Ministry of Commerce, the Ministry of Industry and Information Technology, and other governmental agencies, as well as special policy databases. Policy texts, including notices, plans, guidelines, opinions and other types of policy documents, are obtained by visiting the official websites of the State Council, the Ministry of Commerce, the Ministry of Industry and Information Technology, as well as special policy databases. Meanwhile, industrial products e-commerce research reports are obtained by visiting the websites of e-commerce associations, organisations and market research firms, and downloading relevant documents. The final research data collected after screening mainly includes 18 policy documents related to industrial products e-commerce and 10 research reports from authoritative organisations for the period from 2015 to 2022. Among them, the detailed information of some documents is listed in Table 1 and Table 2.

4.2   Keyword Frequency Analysis

Keyword analysis plays an important role in revealing the core content of policy documents and industry reports. In this study, the jieba library was used to perform the word-splitting process of text data to obtain the keywords and their word frequency distribution. Subsequently, the keyword frequencies of all the documents were summarized and calculated, and the word segmentation results were ranked according to the frequency to generate a word cloud map of the industrial products e-commerce industry, as shown in. Since the samples are industry support policies and market research reports, the document set after word separation may contain high-frequency words such as pronouns,

Table 1. Sample industrial products e-commerce policies

Number	Policy title	Issuing department	Date
1	Guiding Opinions on Deepening the Integration and Development of Manufacturing and the Internet	State Council (PRC)	2016.05.13
2	Three-Year Action Plan for the Development of Industrial E-Commerce	Ministry of Industry and Information Technology	2017.09.11
3	Development Plan for the Deep Integration of Informatisation and Industrialisation under the 14th Five-Year Plan	Ministry of Industry and Information Technology	2021.11.30

Table 2. Sample industrial products e-commerce report

Number	Report title	Research organisation	Date
1	China Manufacturing Industry Internet C2M E-commerce Industry Research Report	Avery Dennison Consulting	2019.05
2	China Industrial B2B Industry Research Report	36Krypton Research Institute	2020.12
3	China Industrial B2B Industry Research Report	Avery Dennison Consulting (China)	2022.07

quantifiers, convergent verbs, etc., which are not substantially helpful for text characterization, so these words are eliminated. Finally, the top 14 effective high-frequency words are organized, as shown in Table 3.

In terms of keyword frequency distribution, "industry", "enterprise", "platform" and 'e-commerce" have the highest frequency. It is inferred that industrial products e-commerce and platforms are important engines for promoting the innovation and development of industrial enterprises. By supporting the key cultivation platforms of industrial products e-commerce, the government and the industry have pushed enterprises to accelerate platform construction.

The frequency of terms "digitalization", "data", and "technology" arranged from high to low shows that the industry is increasingly focused on achieving cost reduction and efficiency improvement in digital transformation, in order to build a sound service system (Fig. 2).

Fig. 2. Industrial products e-commerce word cloud (in Chinese)

Table 3. Frequency of top 14keywords

Keyword	Word frequency	Keyword	Word frequency
industries	2171	procure	828
corporations	1869	industrial product	758
terrace	1526	offerings	705
e-commerce	1194	sector	683
developmental	1103	B2B	610
service	1092	digitisation	608
the Internet	914	numbers	567

4.3 Feature Extraction and Vectorisation

In the process of feature word extraction, we set the threshold value to 0.1, and only feature words with TF-IDF value greater than 0.1 will be selected. Table 4 shows some feature words with high TF-IDF values.

Table 4. Feature word screening and corresponding TF-IDF values

Characteristic word	TF-IDF value
industries	0.404026256
corporations	0.347823617
terrace	0.283990818
e-commerce	0.222205136
developmental	0.205269903
service	0.203222787

4.4 Word Vector Training Results

On the basis of performing feature word extraction, we further train the model using Word2Vec to obtain word vectors. By processing the preprocessed text corpus, a corpus word list is obtained, in which each word corresponds to a 200-dimensional space vector. The industrial products e-commerce feature words correspond to 17 200-dimensional word vectors in this word list.

The effectiveness of the trained word vectors can be evaluated by looking at the similarity between words and the list of related words for a single word. The four word pairs in the policy document are "digitalization" and 'technology", 'manufacturing" and "production", "material" and "platform", and "user" and "Internet" in the policy document, for example, the similarity of each word pair is calculated, and the results are shown in Table 5. Observing the word pair similarity results, it is found that the processing results are consistent with the cognitive logic, which indicates that the Word2Vec training model can generate reasonable and effective word vectors. Therefore, the same operation can be taken for other feature words in the policy text, so as to verify the effectiveness of the word vectors obtained by training.

Table 5. Similarity of related word pairs

Pair of words	Similarity
Digitalisation and Technology	0.83570686
Manufacturing and Production	0.91326806
Materials and Platforms	0.33396235
Users and the Internet	0. 26313045

4.5 Analysis of Clustering Results Based on K-Means

Contour coefficient is a metric used to assess the quality of clustering, which integrates the tightness within clusters and the separation between clusters. After obtaining the feature vectors, the contour coefficients are calculated for different values of k. Observing the trend of the contour coefficients with the change of k values, it is found that the contour coefficients gradually decrease with the increase of k values and fluctuate within the range from 0.06 to 0.44. In the cases where k is equal to 3, 4, and 5, the corresponding contour coefficients are the three largest values among the contour coefficients corresponding to all the values of k, which are 0.4377, 0.2673 and 0.2922. Since the closer the contour coefficient is to 1, which indicates a better clustering effect, we chose to set the value of k to 5, considering that the division into 3 and 4 clusters is not practical.

After determining the value of k, the feature words are clustered using the k-means clustering algorithm, and when k = 5, the feature screening as well as the corresponding categories are shown in Table 6. According to the text mining classification results in Table 6, each cluster class represents a specific topic or related field: cluster 1 is mainly the products and services provided by industrial products e-commerce to meet user needs; cluster 2 mainly reflects the close association of industrial products e-commerce to the development of the Internet and e-commerce; cluster 3 mainly reflects that the B2B model is the most common operation mode in industrial products e-commerce; cluster 4 mainly involves the industrial enterprise development, platform construction, technology application and digital transformation; Cluster 5 is mainly associated with the manufacturing production of industrial products.

Taken together, these clusters involve a number of aspects, including products, services, Internet, B2B, enterprise digitalisation, technology construction, and manufacturing. It can be seen that the construction and policy development of China's industrial products e-commerce is gradually maturing. At present, the industrial products e-commerce has entered from the primary stage of platform construction to the stage of the deep integration of industrial products trading, production and services, while the policy focus has gradually shifted to the smooth flow of all aspects of the supply chain through industrial products e-commerce.

From the viewpoint of the characteristics within the clusters, Cluster 2 and Cluster 3 involve the Internet, industry and e-commerce, indicating that these two clusters are concerned with the interaction between the Internet and industrial products e-commerce in the development of e-commerce. National policies continue to promote the combination of the Internet and the industrial industry, both for the promotion and development of industrial products e-commerce to create a favourable environment, but also prompted the practical application of the industrial Internet platform, the two promote each other to form a virtuous circle. Cluster category 4 contains the most keywords, signalling the further extension of technology application to the industrial side of industrial products e-commerce. The government and the industry are jointly committed to promoting the digital transformation of the supply chain, and the transformation of enterprise management through digital technology has become an important direction in the industrial products e-commerce market competition. Cluster 1 embodies the deepening of services to become the new focus of industrial products e-commerce, with the continued development of the industrial products e-commerce, the improvement of its service system has become an inevitable requirement. Due to the diversity and complexity of industrial products, both supply and demand sides are facing certain problems, and to solve these problems must continue to improve the service system. Cluster 5 is mainly associated with the manufacturing production of industrial products, due to the relative maturity of the manufacturing policy and industry research, so in relation to the industrial Internet and industrial products e-commerce, without too much to expand the text narrative.

Table 6. Feature screening and corresponding categories

Fascicule	Byword
1	Products, Services
2	Internet, Development, Industry, E-Commerce
3	B2B, Industry, Industrial
4	Enterprise, Platform, Construction, Technology, Digitalisation, Data
5	Fabrication

5 Conclusions

This study uses text mining methodology to explore the policies and reports related to industrial products e-commerce and draws the following conclusions:

(1) Platforms are the core of the industrial products e-commerce ecosystem. In the policy-based and report-based text data, the ordering of keywords such as "platform" and "enterprise" shows their high importance, indicating that policies and industries actively promote the innovative development of platforms and continue to empower industrial enterprises. For example, Jiangsu Province's industrial products e-commerce development program emphasizes encouraging large enterprises to build their own collection and marketing platforms, cultivating third-party industrial e-commerce service platforms, upgrading the service capacity of key cultivation platforms, and forming a transparent, efficient, and cost-effective centralized purchasing system on the Internet. The industrial products e-commerce platform is also constantly improving the supply chain finance, warehousing and logistics services and other diversified functions, to meet the needs of enterprises online sales at the same time also bring more value-added benefits for the industrial enterprises to take the initiative to integrate into the new e-commerce business to provide good conditions.

(2) Policy and industry focus on technology application and landing of industrial products e-commerce. From the keyword extraction and clustering results, we preliminarily conclude that the focus of policies and industries has shifted to the combination of technologies with industries and applications, and more attention has been paid to the landing of industrial products e-commerce-related technologies. For example, the Ministry of Industry and Information Technology and many other departments mentioned improving the level of intelligent manufacturing, encouraging the innovation of industrial Internet, 5G, artificial intelligence and industrial APP integration application modes and technologies, accelerating the application innovation and landing, and guiding more enterprises to apply industrial products e-commerce platforms to carry out business. In the traditional industrial supply chain channel, various links including agents, distributors and retailers are actively transforming themselves to adapt to the trend of digitisation, and comprehensively using e-commerce platforms to promote the digitisation process of the entire supply chain.

(3) The industrial products e-commerce has not yet formed a sound policy framework. From the process of collecting policy texts in this paper and the number of valid texts eventually collected, the strategic design and institutional system related to the industrial products e-commerce in China has not yet been perfected, and the degree of protection of the institutional and digital ecosystem is relatively low, and the institutional support provided to the digital transformation of small and medium-sized enterprises (SMEs) is insufficient. The progress of regional and district governments in the implementation of policies involving industrial products e-commerce is relatively slow, and in some areas there is even a lag. Although the state has issued relevant policies, the regions have not yet formulated corresponding implementation rules or policy opinions, resulting in the digital transformation of industrial SMEs lacking a good cluster effect and the formation of a relatively weak e-commerce ecological environment.

Acknowledgement. This research was funded by Basic Scientific Research Business Fees Project "Research on Machine-Readable Standards and Intelligent Application Technologies for the Clothing Industry" (No. 532023Y-10393), Science and Technology Department of Zhejiang Province Program (No. 2021C35128), and Major Humanities and Social Sciences Research Projects in Zhejiang Higher Education Institutions (No. 2023QN077).

References

1. Ocloo, E.C., Xuhua, H., Akaba, S., et al.: The determinant factors of business to business (B2B) E-commerce adoption in small- and medium-sized manufacturing enterprises. J. Glob. Inf. Technol. Manag. **23**(3), 191–216 (2020)
2. Zhang, Y.H., Zhuang, Z.Z., Li, Z.W.: Can E-commerce promote innovative behavior in traditional manufacturing? J. Quant. Techn. Econ. **35**(12), 100–115 (2018). (in Chinese)
3. Claycomb, C., Iyer, K., Germain, R.: Predicting the level of B2B E-commerce in industrial organizations. Ind. Mark. Manag. **34**(3), 221–234 (2005)
4. Chen, M.L., Chen, Y.F., Lin, Q.Y.: Research on industrial control mode of electronic commerce under industry 4.0 background. Manuf. Autom. **37**(04), 146–147+150 2015. (in Chinese)
5. Waithaka, S.T., Mnkandla, E.: Challenges facing the use of mobile applications for e-commerce in Kenya's manufacturing industry. Electron. J. Inf. Syst. Dev. Ctries **83**(1), 1–25 (2017)
6. Tang, P.P., Wu, L.: A research on the effect mechanism of new electronic commerce to the underdeveloped areas of China. Chin. J. Manag. **11**(08), 1143–1149 (2014). (in Chinese)
7. Wang, D.: Influences of cloud computing on e-commerce businesses and industry. J. Softw. Eng. Appl. 06(6), 313–318 (2015)
8. Talib, R., Hanif, M.K., Ayesha, S., et al.: Text mining: techniques, applications and issues. Int. J. Adv. Comput. Sci. Appl. **7**(11), 414–418 (2016)
9. Qaiser, S., Ali, R.: Text mining: use of TF-IDF to examine the relevance of words to documents. Int. J. Comput. Appl. **181**(1), 25–29 (2018)
10. Jin, X., Zhang, S., Liu, J.: Word semantic similarity calculation based on Word2Vec. In: 2018 International Conference on Control, Automation and Information Sciences (ICCAIS), pp. 12–16. IEEE (2018)
11. Krishna, K., Murty, M.N.: Genetic k-means algorithm. IEEE Trans. Syst. Man Cybern. Part B (Cybern.) **29**(3), 433–439 (1999)

The Impact of Digital Innovation Network on Economic Resilience: An Empirical Analysis Based on the Yangtze River Delta Urban Agglomeration

Kaiqi Wang and Qiqing Liu[✉]

School of Information, Central University of Finance and Economics, Beijing, China
liuqiqing516@163.com

Abstract. With the development of digital technology, the mode of lifestyle and the economic pattern have undergone tremendous changes. The rapid updating and iteration of digital technology has increased the frequency of innovation and enhanced the links between groups. Relying on the R&D cooperation of digital technology, a digital innovation network is formed, which makes the member have higher economic resilience, more stable development model, and can cope with the challenges of frequent shocks. Based on the 2008–2019 invention patent data of cities in the Yangtze River Delta from the INCOPAT database, this paper constructs a digital innovation network using social network analysis. The empirical analysis shows that digital innovation network has a significant positive impact on economic resilience, and cities with closer cooperation have higher economic resilience. In order to achieve the goal of high-quality development, we should open up channels for innovation cooperation, realize innovation cooperation and sharing, promote the economic resilience. Big cities should play the radiation role of "innovation center", small and medium-sized cities utilize the cost advantage, to build a closer and more reasonable digital innovation network.

Keywords: Digital Innovation Network · Economic Resilience · SNA · Yangtze River Delta Urban Agglomeration

1 Introduction

With the development of digital technology, economy and society are undergoing profound changes. From the intellectualization of production modes to the individualization of consumption patterns, onto the optimization of economic structure, the pervasive influence of digital technology is evident. At the same time, the occurrence of various black swan events has brought many impacts on economic and social development. In the Proposals for formulating the 14th Five-Year Plan (2021–2025) for National Economic and Social Development and the Long-Range Objectives Through the Year 2035, it was first proposed to promote a new type of people-centered urbanization and build a "resilient city". Withstand disasters through their inherent capabilities, gradually recover and ultimately develop the capacity to adapt to shocks. Improving the economic resilience has emerged as a crucial imperative in the contemporary era.

© The Author(s), under exclusive license to Springer Nature Switzerland AG 2024
Y. P. Tu and M. Chi (Eds.): WHICEB 2024, LNBIP 517, pp. 25–37, 2024.
https://doi.org/10.1007/978-3-031-60324-2_3

In the digital age, the extensive application of digital technology not only accelerates the rate of innovation, but also strengthens the innovative connections among diverse individuals. Relying on the connection function of digital technology R&D, a huge innovation cooperation network has been gradually built. Cities evolve into a community of destiny, sharing resources, risks and pursuing collective development.

Prior to economic shocks, cities boasting advanced levels of digital innovation typically exhibit elevated technological prowess, thereby showcasing stronger economic resilience. The construction of digital innovation network is based on the connection among innovation entities, and forms new innovation achievements through cooperation. The impact of shocks on the digital innovation network will be diffused, enabling the node cities to better cope with the challenges brought by economic shocks. Therefore, from the perspective of the Yangtze River Delta urban agglomeration, this paper adopts the digital innovation network as the framework, focus on the 26 cities in the Yangtze River Delta urban agglomeration as the unit. to study the role of regional digital innovation network in promoting urban economic resilience from 2008 to 2019, offer practical suggestions for resilient cities and digital innovation networks.

2 Literature Review

2.1 Economic Resilience

Resilience has evolved from engineering resilience, ecological resilience to adaptive resilience. An engineering resilience is the ability of a material to return to its original state after being subjected to a force that deforms it. Holling [1] extended the singular concept of engineering resilience to the field of ecology. The ecological resilience denotes the capacity to "absorb" the impact, that is, the system can maintain the original structure, characteristics and state after the impact. Reggiani [2] and Martin & Sunley [3] were among the first to introduce resilience into the field of economics, which was generally recognized by the academic circles. Resilience is defined as both a process and a dynamic adjustment of adaptability[4]. Economic resilience refers to a region's ability to restore its original state post-shock, that is, the region can maintain or restore its original development path after experiencing adaptive changes in economic structure, or transform into a new sustainable development path that can make full and efficient use of economic and social resources.

2.2 Digital Innovation Network and Regional Economic Resilience

With the rapid development of digital technology, innovation has emerged as a pivotal driver for societal progress. Digital innovation networks, serving as the framework for innovation activities, have attracted increasing attention in recent years. The digital innovation network includes the nodes and connections in the network, encompass innovation actors and their interconnections based on digital innovation activities. The main purpose of the Innovation Network is to foster collaboration among members, thereby facilitating innovation cooperation and fostering economic development.

By connecting various innovation entities of digital technology, digital innovation network promotes information sharing, technology transfer. It expedites the translation of innovative achievements into practical applications, enhancing the efficiency and quality of digital innovation. Integrating into the innovation network, acquire advanced technology by establishing links with leading innovation institutions, and promote the improvement of enterprise innovation capability [5, 6]. Furthermore, it helps overcome the obstacles of resource sharing among different innovators and enhance regional innovation capability by establishing intricate connections [7]. Through the digital innovation network, innovators can obtain more technology and knowledge to support innovation activities, enhance cooperation and innovation capability. This promotes regional economic development [8]. When the city suffers from external shocks, it can use technological advantages to respond quickly to the shocks, adjust, and improve [9].

2.3 Theoretical Analysis of Digital Innovation Network Promoting Regional Economic Resilience

Economic resilience is the ability to restore its original state after suffering shocks, to return to its original path after experiencing adaptive changes in economic structure, or to transform into a new path leveraging economic and social resources efficiently. After the economic shock, cities with higher level of digital innovation can use their technological level to find the path to restore quickly. Digital innovation network reflects the innovation cooperation relationship, which can explain the impact of innovation cooperation relationship between node cities on urban economic resilience.

Free Flow of Digital Elements. Long-term innovation collaboration between cities can reduce barriers to the free flow of elements So as to promote the exchange of various elements, especially digital innovation elements. And facilitate joint research of new technologies with innovation cooperation, improve innovation efficiency, finally realize the sharing of innovation benefits. Innovation network can promote the flow of talents, optimize the allocation of talents, and the quality of human resources. It can also promote the flow and sharing of technology [10], the sharing and transmission of information to accelerate the development of urban economy.

When there is information and technology flow among the nodes in the digital innovation network, these nodes can learn, coordinate and cooperate with each other more efficiently in the network, thus forming a closer cooperative relationship [11]. This can help coordinate the allocation and optimization of resources among nodes, accelerate the dissemination of new digital technologies, thus promoting the entire digital innovation network. Therefore, this flow can also help cities adapt to changes in the external environment more quickly, and promote the scale effect by strengthening the interconnection between cities.

Knowledge Spillover of Digital Technology. Knowledge spillover is a kind of unconscious knowledge flow, which can realize the sharing of knowledge and digital technology [12]. The knowledge and technology in the digital innovation network can be transmitted through the cooperation among the nodes, and ultimately promote the innovation of knowledge and technology. On the one hand, the nodes can acquire new knowledge and technology through cooperation and enrich innovation resources. On the other hand, nodes can also promote the development of the whole network by exporting their own knowledge and technology to other nodes. That is to say, the digital innovation network composed of nodes in urban agglomeration can realize knowledge sharing [13], enhance innovation ability through knowledge spillover, thus, improve the economic resilience of the whole urban agglomeration.

Generally speaking, the digital innovation network can integrate and share the resources, promote the flow of knowledge, digital technology, talent and other elements, realize risk diversification and diversification, enhance regional stability and innovation. Based on this, this paper puts forward hypothesis 1:

Digital innovation network is conducive to enhancing urban economic resilience.

The impact of digital innovation network on urban economic resilience will also be affected by urban characteristics and development stages. In the period of better economic development, innovation network can support the production of urban digital innovation achievements and disperse the impact of economic shocks in the period of economic downturn. Simultaneously, urban development varies in scale, development models, and resource endowment, consequently leading to varying impacts of the digital innovation network on economic resilience. Based on this, this paper puts forward hypothesis 2:

Digital innovation network on economic resilience varies in different stages of economic shocks and among cities of different sizes.

The contribution of this paper lies in several aspects. Firstly, most of the current studies on economic resilience regard cities as independent individuals, without considering the links between them, and the impact of the ability of cities to jointly resist and disperse risks on economic resilience after economic shocks. Most of the researches on innovation focus on the quantity of innovation patents, while this paper starts from the perspective of building a digital innovation network, not only considering the innovation itself, but also including the impact of digital innovation spillover on economic resilience. Furthermore, there is little research on economic resilience from the perspective of urban network and urban agglomeration. This paper combines economic resilience, innovation network and urban agglomeration to study the impact of innovation network on urban economic resilience based on the background of urban agglomeration, and provides suggestions for achieving high-quality economic development.

3 Measurement and Analysis of Economic Resilience and Innovation Network

3.1 Scope of Study

The 2008 economic crisis delivered a substantial blow to the national economy and society. This paper treats this event as a pivotal shock, and, in consideration of data availability and scientific rigor, sets the study timeframe from 2008 to 2019. The research scope is defined by the 26 cities in the Yangtze River Delta Urban Agglomeration according to the City Cluster Plan for Yangtze River Delta issued by the National Development and Reform Commission of China in 2016.

3.2 Measurement of Economic Resilience

Martin [14] Based on the sensitivity index method, proposed a shock cycle model for measuring economic resilience. Utilizing Martin's research method as a foundation, based on the core variable method of regional GDP, this paper enhances it by incorporating counterfactual data. Through comparing the actual change in regional GDP with the expected change, the regional economic resilience index is calculated.

$$(\Delta R_i^{t+k})^{\text{expected}} = R_i^t \cdot G^{t+k} \tag{1}$$

$$Resilience_i^{t+k} = \frac{(\Delta R_i^{t+k})^{\text{actual}} - (\Delta R_i^{t+k})^{\text{expected}}}{\left|(\Delta R_i^{t+k})^{\text{expected}}\right|} \tag{2}$$

Among $(\Delta R_i^{t+k})^{\text{expected}}$ anticipation represents the expected change in GDP of region i in [t, t + k], R_i^t denotes the total economic output of region i in year t, G^{t+k} represents the rate of change of GDP of the province in the period of [t, t + k]. Learn from Sun et al. [15] According to the fluctuation of the real GDP growth rate of the Yangtze River Delta economy, the 2008–2009 period is divided into the resistance period, the 2010–2013 period is divided into the recovery period, and the 2014–2019 period is divided into the adaptation period. Regions exhibiting elevated levels of resistance, resilience, and adaptability demonstrate robust economic resilience, experiencing lesser susceptibility to shocks and displaying agility in adjusting and swiftly recovering.

3.3 Measurement of Digital Innovation Networks

Due to disparities in patent quality, the quantity of granted invention patents serves as a reliable metric for assessing the digital innovation capacity of a region, given its correlation with high-quality innovations. Hence, this paper selects the number of authorized joint invention patents to measure the digital innovation network [16]. The specific methodology involves screening invention patents meeting specified criteria with application dates spanning from 2008 to 2019, obtain the cooperation information between cities by manually matching the applicant's address, calculate the number of joint patents between two cities, and the centrality of each city, construct the joint innovation network of the Yangtze River Delta urban agglomeration. Based on the social network analysis (SNA), the relative status of nodes in the network is measured by degree, betweenness and closeness.

The specific measurement method is as follows: the 26 cities are grouped into 676 city pairs, forming a matrix; Match the joint patent data with the city pairs to generate a 2008–2019 digital innovation matrix as shown in formula (3);

$$A_{ij} = \begin{pmatrix} a_{11} & \cdots & a_{1j} \\ \vdots & \ddots & \vdots \\ a_{i1} & \cdots & a_{ij} \end{pmatrix} \tag{3}$$

Treat that innovation cooperation matrix as an undirected matrix; use Ucinet to process undirected symmetric matrix and measure the degree.

4 Empirical Analysis

4.1 Study Design

In order to explore the relationship between innovation network and urban economy, also to eliminate the impact of heteroscedasticity and autocorrelation on estimation, use the generalized least squares method (GFLS) to analyze and construct the benchmark model as shown in formula (4):

$$Resilience_{it} = \beta_0 + \beta_{1,it}centrality_{it} + \theta_{it}\Sigma X_{it} + \gamma_i + \epsilon_t + \mu_{it} \qquad (4)$$

where i Denotes the city and t denotes the time. $Resilience_{it}$ represents the urban economic resilience of city i in year t; $centrality_{it}$ represents the digital innovation network centrality of city i in the urban agglomeration in year t, including degree centrality, closeness centrality and betweenness centrality; ΣX_{it} is a combination of a series of control variables. γ_i represents the fixed effect of the city, ϵ_t represents the time fixed effect, μ_{it} is the random error term.

In order to control the impact of other factors, this study selects science and technology input (rptech), foreign trade level (lnfgcptactmt), Internet development level (lnitbaurnum), financial development level (finance) and infrastructure (perroad) as control variables.

The patent data comes from the INCOPAT database, and the applicant's address information comes from QCCCOM and the official website search of enterprises and institutions. Data for other variables are obtained from China Research Data Service Platform (CNRDS), China Urban Statistical Yearbook and the statistical yearbooks over the years.

4.2 Benchmark Regression

Benchmark Regression of the Impact of Digital Innovation Networks on Economic Resilience. The benchmark regression results of the impact of the innovation network of the Yangtze River Delta urban agglomeration on urban economic resilience are shown in Table 1.. The results of model (1) are positively significant at the 1% level. Models (2), (3) and (4) not only fix the city and time effects, but also add a series of control variables. Furthermore, the analysis introduces three centralities. The impact of these centralities is positive and significant at the level of 1%, indicating that enhancing the city's centrality in the digital innovation network contributes to the city's economic resilience.

Innovation cooperation among cities in the digital innovation network is conducive to the improvement of urban economic resilience. Innovation collaboration facilitates the sharing of knowledge, information, and digital technology among cities through knowledge spillover, thereby enhancing urban resource allocation capabilities and innovation efficiency through the promotion of free factor flow. By promoting digital innovation and realizing their own technological advancements, cities can devise a feasible way in the face of economic shocks with the background of economic downturn, and have higher economic resilience (Table 2.).

Table 1. Benchmark Regression of Digital Innovation Network on Urban Economic Resilience

VARIABLES	(1) Resilience	(2) Resilience	(3) Resilience	(4) Resilience
degree	1.400***	1.154***		
	(3.16)	(5.74)		
closeness			0.337***	
			(3.93)	
betweenness				1.379***
				(5.37)
rptech		−8.787***	−9.906***	−8.778***
		(−10.93)	(−9.20)	(−8.41)
lnfgcptactmt		0.204***	0.201***	0.199***
		(11.44)	(10.01)	(9.15)
lnitbaurnum		0.346***	0.351***	0.292***
		(13.97)	(12.93)	(10.32)
finance		−1.832***	−1.768***	−1.843***
		(−26.51)	(−19.54)	(−21.04)
perroad		0.017***	0.023***	0.020***
		(3.05)	(3.99)	(3.67)
Constant	−0.169	−2.319***	−2.361***	−2.058***
	(−0.92)	(−9.04)	(−7.90)	(−6.76)
Observations	312	312	312	312
Controls	N	Y	Y	Y
City FE	Y	Y	Y	Y
Year FE	Y	Y	Y	Y

Note: ***, ** and * represent $p < 0.01$, $p < 0.05$ and $p < 0.1$ respectively, and the Z statistic is in parentheses

For the specific analysis of different centrality, cities with high degree centrality are in a more central position in the digital innovation network, which can improve innovation efficiency and enhance urban economic resilience through close cooperation. Cities with high closeness centrality have shorter connection paths with other nodes, which can achieve more efficient cooperation and maximize their innovation ability and technological level. Cities with high betweenness centrality have higher control status in the network, and can choose the required nodes for innovation cooperation according to their specific requirements. These cities can capitalize on knowledge spillover through collaboration with high-tech counterparts and engage in cost-effective cooperation with low-tech cities. Use their own control ability to achieve development in the innovation network, which ultimately improves the economic resilience of cities.

Cities with a high level of Internet development can provide channels for digital technology exchange and innovation cooperation among cities, thereby offering important support and impetus for economic development. Science and technology investment shows a negative impact, although science and technology expenditure can improve the level of urban science and technology, but excessive investment may lead to a shortage of resources in other areas; In addition, digital technology research and development is uncertain, solely increasing investment without careful consideration may elevate investment risks.

Periodic Performance of the Impact of Digital Innovation Network on Economic Resilience.   Due to the sample limitation during the resistance period, we opted to regress the recovery period and the adaptation period by stages.

The results show that the cities with high degree centrality have a more significant positive effect in the recovery period, while in the adaptation period, the cities with high degree centrality have a weak positive effect. Digital innovation networks facilitate the redistribution of economic resources, accelerate innovation and technology transfer, promote economic recovery after economic shocks. During the adaptation period, the economic environment is relatively stable, the economic development is more dependent on the long-term development of infrastructure construction and human capital investment. The cities with high closeness centrality have a negative impact in the recovery period and a positive impact in the adaptation period. As closeness centrality also reflects a city's marginal position within the innovation network, marginal cities may struggle to

Table 2. Regression of Digital Innovation Network to Urban Economic Resilience in Different Periods

VARIABLES	(1)	(2)	(3)	(4)	(5)	(6)
	Resilience	Resilience	Resilience	Resilience	Resilience	Resilience
degree	472.912***	17.989*				
	(-2.86)	(1.90)				
closeness			-28.955***	7.889***		
			(−2.71)	(3.05)		
betweenness					−131.472	5.882*
					(−1.48)	(1.67)
Observations	104	156	104	156	104	156
Controls	Y	Y	Y	Y	Y	Y
City FE	Y	Y	Y	Y	Y	Y
Year FE	Y	Y	Y	Y	Y	Y

Note: ***, ** and * represent $p < 0.01$, $p < 0.05$ and $p < 0.1$ respectively, and the Z statistic is in parentheses utilize the innovation network to disperse economic risks in the recovery period. However, they can enhance economic resilience through efficient innovation cooperation during the adaptation period. Betweenness centrality only has a significant positive impact on urban economic resilience at the level of 10% in the recovery period, and improves economic resilience through its core position in the digital innovation network.

4.3 Robustness Test

Substitution of Core Explanatory Variables. To validate the robustness of the benchmark regression results, use Zhao et al. [17] for reference to change the measurement method of economic resilience. Dvalue measures the difference between the annual real GDP growth rate of each city and the benchmark of 2008. If the difference is larger, the resilience is smaller, and vice versa. The specific measurement formula is shown in formula (5):

$$resilience_{it} = \frac{(Dvalue - mindvalue)}{(maxdvalue - mindvalue)} \tag{5}$$

After changing the measurement method of urban resilience, as shown in Table 3., the degree coefficient in the digital innovation network is still positively significant at the level of 1%, that is, the conclusion that the digital innovation network has a significant positive impact on urban economic resilience is robust.

Table 3. Regression Results of Changing Urban Economic Resilience Measures

VARIABLES	(1)	(2)	(3)
	resilience	resilience	resilience
degree	0.090***		
	(5.90)		
closeness		0.081***	
		(3.46)	
betweenness			0.086***
			(5.57)
Observations	312	312	312
Controls	Y	Y	Y
City FE	Y	Y	Y
Year FE	Y	Y	Y

Note: ***, ** and * represent $p < 0.01$, $p < 0.05$ and $p < 0.1$ respectively, and the Z statistic is in parentheses

Elimination of Extreme Values. In order to weaken the impact of extreme values on the empirical analysis, two-sided 1% and 99% tail-shrinking are used, as shown in Table 4.. The impact coefficients are all positive. Except that the impact of closeness centrality on economic resilience is not significant at the level of 10%, the rest are significant at the level of 5%, so the results are robust (Table 5.).

Table 4. Regression Results of Digital Innovation Network on Urban Economic Resilience after Eliminating Extreme Values

VARIABLES	(1)	(2)	(3)
	Resilience _w	Resilience _w	Resilience _w
degree_w	2.099**		
	(2.34)		
closeness_w		0.131	
		(0.63)	
betweenness_w			0.526**
			(2.08)
Observations	312	312	312
Controls	Y	Y	Y
City FE	Y	Y	Y
Year FE	Y	Y	Y

Note: ***, ** and * represent $p < 0.01$, $p < 0.05$ and $p < 0.1$ respectively, and the Z statistic is in parentheses

4.4 Heterogeneity Analysis

Compute the mean permanent population of 26 cities from 2008 to 2019, and categorize the size of cities according to the average number of permanent populations.

The degree centrality of digital innovation network has a significant positive impact on economic resilience in mega-cities, while it has no significant impact in medium-sized cities. The impact of closeness centrality and betweenness centrality on urban economic resilience shows a significant positive impact in mega-cities and a significant negative impact in medium-sized cities, showing an "innovation siphon effect". Digital technology in big cities is more developed, and digital innovation networks can better achieve innovation cooperation and enhance urban economic resilience. However, the advantages of digital innovation network in medium-sized cities are also more vulnerable to the development pressure of technological infrastructure constraints, industrial restructuring and brain drain.

Table 5. Regression Results of Digital Innovation Network on Urban Economic Resilience by City Size

VARIABLES	(1)	(2)	(3)	(4)	(5)	(6)
	Resilience	Resilience	Resilience	Resilience	Resilience	Resilience
degree	0.477 **	1.600				
	(2.25)	(1.27)				
closeness			0.692 ***	−0.380 ***		
			(5.49)	(-2.92)		
betweenness					1.080 ***	−2.403 ***
					(6.24)	(−3.73)
Constant	−2.064***	−2.674***	−2.464***	−2.709 ***	−1.810 ***	−2.811 ***
	(−7.73)	(−4.67)	(−8.84)	(−5.34)	(−6.01)	(−6.13)
Observations	144	168	144	168	144	168
Controls	Y	Y	Y	Y	Y	Y
City FE	Y	Y	Y	Y	Y	Y
Year FE	Y	Y	Y	Y	Y	Y

Note: $***$, $**$ and $*$ represent $p < 0.01$, $p < 0.05$ and $p < 0.1$ respectively, and the Z statistic is in parentheses

5   Conclusions and Recommendations

This study constructs the digital innovation network of the Yangtze River Delta urban agglomeration. Empirical analysis confirms a positive correlation between the digital innovation network and urban economic resilience. Digital innovation network can promote personnel training, scientific and technological development, achieving innovation cooperation are effective measures to enhance economic resilience.

Secondly, the impact of digital innovation network on economic resilience shows heterogeneity in different periods and cities of different sizes. Demonstrate the strong impetus of digital innovation network to economic recovery during the economic recession; The edge cities in the network can't make good use of the risk dispersion mechanism of the digital innovation network.

Finally, the degree centrality has a significant positive effect only in the mega-cities, while the closeness centrality and betweenness centrality have a significant positive effect on the urban economic resilience in the mega-cities and a significant negative effect on the urban economic resilience in the medium-sized cities. Due to the differences in the scale of urban development, there is a certain "innovation siphon effect".

Based on these findings, this paper proposes the following recommendations: Firstly, to build an economically resilient city as the development policy and overall goal. This entails continually enhancing the vibrancy of digital technology innovation, elevating technological prowess through innovation-driven approaches, ultimately fostering high-quality regional economic development.

Secondly, cultivate a good environment for innovation, and provide policy support for the advancement of digital technology and cooperation in digital innovation. Open up digital cooperation channels, and use risk dispersion mechanism to collectively mitigate shocks.

Thirdly, make use of the radiation-driven role of big cities as "digital innovation centers" to promote the innovation level of small cities. This entails harnessing the cost advantages of small cities to enhance their digital technology capabilities. Concurrently, avoid the emergence of a polarized development pattern.

Last, cities tailor their development models and formulate differentiated development policies based on their locations and leading industries. Thereby fostering the smooth operation and healthy development of the economy and society.

References

1. Holling, C.S.: Resilience and Stability of Ecological Systems. Annu. Rev. Ecol. Syst. **4**, 1–23 (1973)
2. Reggiani, A., Graaff., T.D., Nijkamp, P.: Resilience: an evolutionary approach to spatial economic systems. Netw. Spatial Econ. **2**(2) (2002)
3. Martin, R., Sunley, P.: On the notion of regional economic resilience: conceptualization and explanation. J. Geograph. **15**(1), (2015)
4. Boschma, R.: Towards an evolutionary perspective on regional resilience. In: Evolutionary Economic Geography, pp. 29–47 (2017)
5. Delgado-Márquez, B.L., et al.: A network view of innovation performance for multinational corporation subsidiaries. Reg. Stud. **52**(1), 47–67 (2018)
6. Ge, C., Lv., W., Wang, J.: The impact of digital technology innovation network embedding on firms' innovation performance: the role of knowledge acquisition and digital transformation. Sustainability **15**(8), 6938 (2023)
7. Zhao, Y., Lyu, J., Huesig, S.: The impact of innovative city cooperation network on city's innovation efficiency. Evidence from China. J. Knowl. Econ. 1–35 (2023)
8. Wang, C., Zhang, G.: Examining the moderating effect of technology spillovers embedded in the intra-and inter-regional collaborative innovation networks of China. Scientometrics **119**, 561–593 (2019)
9. Holm, J.R., Østergaard, C.R.: Regional employment growth, shocks and regional industrial resilience: a quantitative analysis of the Danish ICT sector. Reg. Stud. **49**(1), 95–112 (2015)
10. Can, Z., Gang, Z., Zefeng, M.: The study of regional innovation network patterns: evidence from the Yangtze River Delta Urban Agglomeration. Prog. Geogr. **36**(07), 795–805 (2017). (in Chinese)
11. Li, J., Ye, S., Wang, S.: Spatial network analysis on the coupling coordination of digital finance and technological innovation. Sustainability **15**(8), 6354 (2023)
12. Schmidt, S.: Balancing the spatial localisation 'Tilt': knowledge spillovers in processes of knowledge-intensive services. Geoforum **65**, 374–386 (2015)
13. Kong, X., Xu, Q., Zhu, T.: Dynamic evolution of knowledge sharing behavior among enterprises in the cluster innovation network based on evolutionary game theory. Sustainability **12**(1), 75 (2020)

14. Ron, M., Peter, S., Ben, G., Peter, T.: How regions react to recessions: resilience and the role of economic structure. Reg. Stud. **50**(4), 561–585 (2016)
15. Jiuwen, S., Chaojun, C., Zheng, S.: Urban economic resilience and its influencing factors in the Yellow River Basin: from the perspective of different types of city. Econ. Geogr. **42**(05), 1–10 (2022). (**in Chinese**)
16. Miao, B., Liang, Y., Suo, Y.: The influence of organizational social network on enterprise collaborative innovation—mediating role of knowledge sharing and moderating effect of digital construction. IEEE Access **11**, 5110–5122 (2023)
17. Chunyan, Z., Shiping, W.: The influence of agglomeration on city economic resilience. J. Zhongnan Univ. Econ. Law **244**(01), 102–114 (2021). (**in Chinese**)

The Impact of Blockchain Traceability Information on Product Sales in e-Commerce Platforms

Mingqian Li and Rong Du[✉]

School of Economics and Management, Xidian University, Xi'an, Shaanxi, China
durong@mail.xidian.edu.cn

Abstract. Blockchain traceability system can address the problem of information asymmetry, thereby influencing consumer purchasing decisions. However, its efficacy within the context of e-commerce platforms remains unclear. To address this issue, we analyzed the impact of blockchain traceability on product sales based on cue utilization theory and using a quasi-natural experiment on the JD Mall e-commerce platform. Empirical analyses show that blockchain traceability information not only promotes product sales growth, but also alleviates consumers' reliance on electronic word-of-mouth. In addition, products with lower brand reputation benefit more from implementing blockchain traceability information. The findings of this study help retailers recognise the potential and application conditions of blockchain traceability information, and provide management insights for e-commerce platforms to adopt blockchain traceability systems.

Keywords: Blockchain traceability information · Electronic word-of-mouth (eWOM) · Brand reputation · Cue utilization theory

1 Introduction

In the rapidly evolving landscape of information technology, e-commerce platforms are leveraging growing network effects to spur business innovation and accelerate sales growth. However, increased heterogeneity in the temporal and spatial aspects of online trading has led to a rise in opportunistic behaviors among merchants on these platforms. Despite the adoption of conventional traceability technologies like Radio-Frequency Identification (RFID) and QR codes, the issue of information asymmetry persists. This challenge is mainly due to the relative ease with which product information can be falsified or altered.

The blockchain, as a distributed data structure built on cryptographic technology, exhibits key characteristics such as decentralization and immutability, which can effectively address numerous vulnerabilities present in traditional traceability systems. Through mechanisms like timestamps and smart contracts, it facilitates comprehensive tracking of the entire supply chain process from manufacturers to consumers, thereby

Y. P. Tu and M. Chi (Eds.): WHICEB 2024, LNBIP 517, pp. 38–49, 2024.
https://doi.org/10.1007/978-3-031-60324-2_4

enabling traceability and real-time visibility [1]. Current literature, on one hand, concentrates on the technological facets, endeavoring to amplify blockchain's applicability in traceability through advancements in system architecture and algorithmic efficiency [2, 3]; On the other hand, research centers on the design of supply chain mechanisms, exploring optimal strategies for decision-makers to implement blockchain traceability in varied market contexts [4, 5]. However, there is a notable gap in research analyzing the effect of blockchain traceability systems on consumer purchasing behavior from a quality disclosure viewpoint. Some scholars have indicated that the traceability and transparency afforded by blockchain technology can bolster product demand downstream in the supply chain [6, 7], and alleviate consumer concerns regarding social welfare[8] and environmental sustainability [9]. Nevertheless, in terms of research methodology, laboratory experiments, system dynamics, etc., are primarily employed to construct realistic scenarios, there remains a dearth of empirical investigations based on objective data pertaining to this subject matter.

In digital contexts, Electronic Word of Mouth (eWOM) serves as a pivotal instrument for consumers to appraise products, demonstrating a heightened trust in user-generated content over seller-generated content. Extensive research has substantiated the influence of eWOM, particularly the volume of online reviews and the valence of online reviews (sentiment conveyed by eWOM), on consumer satisfaction [10], as well as their linear correlation with product sales [11]. In scenarios where an e-commerce platform concurrently presents blockchain traceability information and eWOM as cues of product quality, it becomes imperative to examine the interplay between these two factors.

The effectiveness of blockchain traceability in reducing information asymmetry in online transactions depends not only on its inherent technical attributes like transparency and immutability but also on other quality cues such as origin information and variations in consumer reviews [12]. These cues can either enhance or weaken the impact of blockchain traceability technology on consumer purchasing behavior. Brand reputation, a key quality cues, reflects a consumer's comprehensive assessment and perception of a brand [13]. Although the influence of brand value may diminish in online environments, brand reputation remains crucial in product competitiveness on e-commerce platforms [14]. This is particularly true for highly standardized products where the brand is closely associated with product performance and quality. Consequently, the relationship between brand reputation and the online sales of opened blockchain traceability information products necessitates further exploration and empirical substantiation.

Grounded in cue utilization theory, this paper leverages a quasi-natural experiment on the JD platform to probe into the mechanisms through which blockchain traceability information impacts product sales, taking into account the roles of eWOM and brand reputation. The findings of this research not only enrich the research system of consumer behavior but also furnish a theoretical underpinning and decision-making guidance for the deployment of blockchain in the realm of electronic commerce.

2 Theoretical Foundation and Hypothesis

2.1 Cue Utilization Theory

Cue utilization theory is initially proposed by Cox in the 1960s. The core idea of this theory is that consumers usually analyze a series of cues conveyed by a product in a comprehensive manner, and select the cues that they consider to be more useful as the basis of their purchase decision [15]. Cues can also be subdivided according to their characteristics into internal cues, which are characteristics inherent to the product itself, such as product size, shape, and flavor, and external cues, which are attributes related to the product that are not themselves part of the product [16]. Although internal cues have a higher predictive value, internal cues are not easily available in the online shopping environment where product inaccessibility exists, so consumers tend to utilize external cues to assess product quality [17]. More importantly, the use of external cues is not affected by product factors, and in most cases consumers utilize external quality cues such as brands, product descriptions, and user ratings to make inferences [11].

2.2 Impact of Blockchain Traceability Information on Product Sales

Based on the cue utility theory and the application of blockchain technology in e-commerce, we define blockchain traceability information as external cues. Blockchain traceability systems provide product information that differs from traditional commodity disclosure by acting as a decentralized and distributed digital record of transactions, capturing, sharing, and transmitting trustworthy information between upstream and downstream participants in the supply chain, and storing time-stamped commodity data to each block, thus providing a higher high level of traceability and transparency [1]. In cue utility theory, the trustworthiness of quality information is paramount in consumer decision-making, particularly for high-value or high-risk items. Since product data stored in the blockchain is tamper-proof, consumers develop a more positive perception of quality during the product evaluation process, which increases their willingness to purchase [6]. Moreover, blockchain traceability, by detailedly recording a product's origin and trajectory, mitigates perceived risks linked to the intangibility of products in online contexts [18]. This clarity assists consumers in navigating through the noise of market signals and making more informed choices. We note that, with growing consumer emphasis on product quality, safety, and sustainability [19], blockchain traceability information directly addresses these concerns, thus heightening product appeal and positively impacting purchasing decisions. Hence, the following hypothesis is posited:

Hypothesis 1: Blockchain traceability information exerts a significant positive effect on product sales.

2.3 The Moderating Role of eWOM

eWOM, recognized as an external cue, is frequently scrutinized by consumers to discern potential risks associated with their intended products. A wealth of research indicates that both an elevated average rating and an increased volume of reviews exert a positive effect on product sales [20, 21]. Nevertheless, online reviews have faced criticism for potentially misrepresenting the true quality of products [22, 23], given the possibility of consumer bias or seller manipulation through fabricated reviews. Inconsistent online ratings do not convey uniformly high- or low-quality cues, which creates consumer decision-making difficulties and leads to constraints on the signaling role of eWOM. Blockchain traceability systems, employing mechanisms such as hash functions and consensus algorithms, assure the authenticity of products [24], thereby establishing themselves as robust sources of information with enhanced credibility in assessing product quality [25]. When exposed to multiple quality cues, consumers tend to rank the relative importance of the cues, with more diagnostic cues receiving more weight, thereby diluting the impact of some other cues. Therefore, blockchain traceability information and eWOM might exhibit a degree of substitutability in the conveyance of product quality cues. We further propose the following hypothesis:

Hypothesis 2a: Compared with the opened blockchain traceability information products, review volume of the unopened blockchain traceability information products has a more significant impact on their sales.

Hypothesis 2b: Compared with the opened blockchain traceability information products, review valence of the unopened blockchain traceability information products has a more significant impact on their sales.

2.4 The Moderating Role of Brand Reputation

Brand reputation occupies a pivotal role in influencing consumer decision-making and shaping corporate outcomes. A robust reputation is often synonymous with high product quality, serving to diminish uncertainty and bolster consumer confidence in their purchases [26]. In instances where brand reputation is diminished, consumer trust in the product correspondingly weakens, prompting a greater reliance on alternative, trustworthy quality cues to mitigate perceived risk. Blockchain traceability can bridge this gap by creating cryptographic proofs consisting of digital blocks in the system [27], which effectively inhibit the generation of fraudulent behaviors such as tampering and falsification of product information, thus mitigating the cognitive dissonance of consumers who no longer rely solely on brand reputation to judge product quality. Additionally, a substantial brand reputation cultivates elevated consumer expectations [13], whereas products associated with lower brand reputations are often met with reduced initial expectations. Opening blockchain traceability then provides additional transparency and quality assurance beyond the original consumer expectations, leading to a positive confirmation. This positive difference in expectations is more likely to lead to higher consumer satisfaction and thus increased purchasing behavior. This leads to the formulation of the following hypotheses:

Hypothesis 3: For products with low brand reputation, opening blockchain traceability information increase their sales to a greater extent.

3 Methodology

3.1 Data Collection

We conducted our study using a quasi-natural experiment on the JD Mall. Due to the wide variety of motor oil on the e-commerce platform, and the problems of substandard and fake are common, even if consumers want to identify the authenticity, they can only manually enter the anti-counterfeiting information on the official website of the relevant brand to verify, which is a more cumbersome operation. Addressing this challenge, JD Mall implemented blockchain traceability technology in collaboration with leading manufacturers. Consequently, products included in this authentic traceability initiative were classified as the treatment group. In contrast, comparable products not involved in this program during the same period were designated as the control group. This setup provided a unique opportunity to assess the impact of blockchain technology information on product sales.

In JD Mall, the keyword "automotive motor oil" was searched and sorted by "comprehensive recommendation", and the third-party data collection tool was used to crawl the first 15 pages of product information. After eliminating products with less than 20 accumulated comments, no sales and those unrelated to automotive motor oil, the final 235 SKUs were constructed as a product monitoring list. Taking the event of opening blockchain traceability information for commodities as the baseline, at least 3 months before and after were ensured as the data window period, forming 18 periods of panel data from July 2021 to December 2022. The treatment group contains 37 commodities totaling 342 observations, while 3888 data are obtained as the control group.

3.2 Variables and Measurement

The dependent variable is the online sales of automotive motor oil products, which is directly obtained from a third-party data analysis platform, i.e., the sales of product i in period t. Regarding the setting of independent variables: Review volume is measured by using the total number of new user reviews with textual information every month; Review valence is assessed indirectly by extracting the sentiment polarity from each textual review and substituting the product rating with it using text mining technology. For the same product, the average sentiment value of the monthly retained reviews is the final result. This practice is based on the consideration that average ratings do not necessarily reveal the true product quality or influence consumers' purchasing decisions, and that merchants may incentivize purchasers or hire water armies to generate deceptive scores [28]; Brand reputation, based on professional data provided by ChinaBrand.com, we identified the top 10 brands with the highest evaluation rankings under the motor oil category as high-reputation brands, which were recorded as 1, and the rest were categorized as low-reputation brands and recorded as 0.

In order to accurately estimate the econometric model, we set the retail price of the product as a control variable. In order to control other factors that affect the product brand effect, we employed the number of online stores associated with each brand during the same time frame as an indicator of brand awareness, following the methodology proposed by Tan *et al.* [29].

4 Econometric Specification

Due to the inconsistent time points of policy shocks in the treatment groups, in order to explore the total effect of verifying blockchain traceability information on product sales, this paper employs a Staggered DID model for the assessment of policy effects:

$$\ln Sales_{it} = \beta_0 + \beta_1 BCT_i \times Period_t + \beta_3 Control_{it} + u_i + v_i + \varepsilon_{it} \tag{1}$$

In Eq. (1), $\ln Sales_{it}$ is the natural logarithm of online sales of the product, BCT_i is the policy dummy variable, $Period_t$ is the time dummy variable of blockchain traceability information, and $Control_{it}$ represents the control variable, where $\ln Pri_{it}$ is the natural logarithm of the unit price of the product sales, and $\ln Brd_{it}$ is the brand awareness of the product. u_i denotes the individual fixed effect of product i, and v_i is the time fixed effect. β_1 coefficient reflects the processing effect of opening blockchain traceability information.

The policy effect of blockchain traceability information is clarified, enabling us to further estimate the interaction between two product quality cues, namely eWOM and brand reputation, using the following econometric model:

$$\ln Sales_{it} = \beta_0 + \beta_1 BCT_i + \beta_2 Val_{it} + \beta_3 BCT_i \times Val_{it} + \beta_4 Control_{it} + u_i + v_i + \varepsilon_{it} \tag{2}$$

$$\ln Sales_{it} = \beta_0 + \beta_1 BCT_i + \beta_2 \ln Vol_{it} + \beta_3 BCT_i \times \ln Vol_{it} + \beta_4 Control_{it} + u_i + v_i + \varepsilon_{it} \tag{3}$$

$$\ln Sales_{it} = \beta_0 + \beta_1 BCT_i \times Period_t + \beta_2 BrdRep_i + \beta_3 BCT_i \times Period_t \times BrdRep_i$$
$$+ \beta_4 Control_{it} + u_i + v_i + \varepsilon_{it} \tag{4}$$

In Eqs. (2)–(4), Val_{it}, $\ln Vol_{it}$ are the natural logarithms of review valence and volume, respectively, and $BrdRep_i$ is a dummy variable indicating product brand reputation. β_3 coefficient reflects the interaction coefficients of the two product quality cues with the blockchain traceability information policy.

5 Results

The regression outcomes from our panel data are detailed in Table 1. Analyzing models (1) and (2), we observe that blockchain traceability information exerts a significant positive effect on product sales, irrespective of the control for relevant attribute variables. This finding underscores the strengths of the blockchain traceability system, notably its data immutability and real-time tracking capabilities, which enhance consumer trust and positively influence purchase decisions. Furthermore, our analysis reveals a significant negative correlation between product price and online sales. This suggests that while price is a crucial product quality cue, an emphasis on price reductions may inadvertently erode consumer trust. Consequently, Hypothesis 1 is supported by our data. It is noteworthy, however, that the models exhibit a relatively low goodness of fit. This limitation could stem from the exclusion of certain influential factors, such as advertising investment, promotional activities, etc.

Table 1. Results of Model Regression

Variables	lnSales				
	(1)	(2)	(3)	(4)	(5)
BCT	0.162** (0.029)	0.129* (0.057)	1.469*** (0.000)	0.750*** (0.000)	0.579*** (0.004)
Val			0.801*** (0.000)		
BCT × Val			−1.267*** (0.001)		
BrdRep					omitted
BCT × BrdRep					−0.493** (0.015)
lnVol				0.563*** (0.000)	
BCT × lnVol				−0.123*** (0.000)	
lnPri		−0.517*** (0.000)	−0.672*** (0.000)	−0.546*** (0.000)	−0.596*** (0.000)
lnBrd		−0.028 (0.696)	0.491*** (0.000)	0.290*** (0.000)	7.820*** (0.000)
Constant	5.496*** (0.000)	6.442*** (0.000)	5.113*** (0.000)	4.486*** (0.000)	7.820*** (0.000)
R-squared	0.213	0.223	0.209	0.637	0.209
Number of Obs	4230	4230	4230	4230	4230
Fixed Effect	Yes	Yes	Yes	Yes	Yes

Notes: Cluster-robust standard errors in parentheses; *** $p < 0.01$, ** $p < 0.05$, * $p < 0.1$

In subsequent analysis, models (3) and (4) underwent Hausman tests, with results indicating significance at the 5% level. This suggests the superiority of the fixed effect model over the random effect model in our study context. Consequently, we employed a two-way fixed effects model for regression analysis, incorporating robust standard errors to address heteroskedasticity.

The regression outcomes revealed that the coefficients for the interaction terms between blockchain traceability information and review volume and review valence are −1.310 and −0.126, respectively. Both coefficients are notable at the 1% level. This finding suggests a degree of substitutability between blockchain traceability information and eWOM. Given the relatively stable variation in the number of reviews among products, this substitutability is particularly pronounced in the aspect of review valence. Thus, Hypotheses 2a and 2b are substantiated.

The regression results of model (5) show that the interaction term between blockchain traceability information and brand reputation has a significantly negative effect on product sales ($\beta = 0.493$, $p < 0.05$), i.e., the opening blockchain traceability information for products with low brand reputation has a greater impact on their sales compared to products with high brand reputation, which proves Hypothesis 3.

6   Robustness Check

6.1   Parallel Trend Test

The results of the parallel trend test at 95% confidence interval are shown in Fig. 1. The test results show that before the policy implementation, the policy effect is not significant in most of the periods; while after the policy implementation, the policy effect is shown to be significant, indicating that the parallel trend hypothesis holds for the experimental group and the control group, thus satisfying the prerequisites for the use of the DID model.

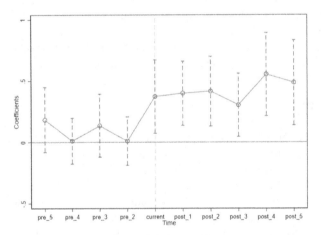

Fig. 1. Parallel Trend Test

6.2   Bacon Decomposition

We used Goodman-Bacon decomposition to calculate coefficient values and weights for each group, thus testing the degree of heterogeneity in treatment effects [30]. As shown in Table 2, the total DID estimation is 0.146, and from the decomposition results, it can be further seen that the weight of the 2X2-DID estimation for the control group of "products with earlier blockchain traceability" is only 1.3%, indicating that heterogeneity of the processing effect exists, but the degree of heterogeneity is relatively mild.

Table 2. Bacon Decomposition Weight

Total estimator	0.146^{***} (0.004)	
2 × 2 DID Grouping Type	Weight	Average DID estimator
Earlier Treatment vs. Later Control	0.011	0.961
Later Treatment vs. Earlier Control	0.013	−0.360
Treatment vs Never treated	0.976	0.144

Notes: *** $p < 0.01$, ** $p < 0.05$, * $p < 0.1$

6.3 Extended Analysis

We note that during the data collection cycle, some products went live with IoT-based authentication technology, which can be considered as traditional traceability information. We treated this event as a policy shock and analyzed it using the Synthetic DID approach [31]. Interestingly, the opening of traditional traceability technology appeared to negatively impact product sales (ATT = −0.292, p = 0.029). Further, we applied the BERTopic model to analyze themes within negative product reviews, and find that "counterfeiting", "quality problems" and "invalid anti-counterfeiting code" are still prominent. This suggests that, compared to traditional traceability methods, blockchain traceability technology is more effective in enhancing consumer purchase decisions [32].

7 Conclusions

This study explores the mechanism of "blockchain traceability information", an emerging quality cue, on product sales in the context of empirical data from the Jingdong platform. The empirical analysis shows that:

Blockchain traceability information can directly affect product sales, which means that retailers who are the first to adopt blockchain traceability systems are more likely to achieve greater profit gains [4]. Scholars have recognized the great potential of blockchain technology to transform supply chain transparency, and they have further explored its potential to provide consumers with accurate information about products and enhance trust in areas such as agricultural products [33], organic food [7], and secondhand luxury goods [34]. Our study extends these insights to new product categories, indirectly affirming blockchain technology's efficacy in aiding consumers to identify authentic products [35].

Blockchain traceability information can partially substitute eWOM. Prior research has also found that consumers may rely less on online reviews for decision-making when more diagnostic cues such as instant communication are available [36]. This indicates that retailers focusing solely on word-of-mouth marketing strategies might not achieve significant returns on investment after implementing blockchain traceability.

The effectiveness of blockchain traceability information varies with product attributes. Particularly, products with lower brand reputations may benefit more. This finding underscores the crucial role of blockchain traceability technology in bridging information gaps, mitigating moral hazards in transactions, and bolstering consumer decision-making confidence, especially when existing quality cues are insufficient.

This paper has some limitations. Firstly, the endogeneity issue within electronic word-of-mouth (eWOM) has not been thoroughly addressed. Future research will aim to control this aspect more effectively, drawing on methodologies from relevant literature. Secondly, our focus was primarily on the moderating roles of eWOM and brand reputation, without delving into other potential mechanisms. For instance, the timeliness of logistics in e-commerce is a critical success factor. Investigating how this, in conjunction with blockchain technology, might enhance consumer perceptions of supply chain credibility and security, thereby influencing purchasing behavior, presents a promising avenue for further research. Lastly, the blockchain traceability systems examined in this paper are predominantly operated by e-commerce platforms. However, in practice, traceability systems may be established by various entities, including merchants themselves or with government support. Future studies will explore how blockchain traceability systems initiated by different stakeholders impact consumer behavior.

Acknowledgement. This research was supported by the National Natural Science Foundation of China under Grant 72171187 and the Fundamental Research Funds for the Central Universities under Grant KYFZ24026.

References

1. Centobelli, P., Cerchione, R., Del Vecchio, P., et al.: Blockchain technology for bridging trust, traceability and transparency in circular supply chain. Inf. Manag. **59**(7), 103508 (2022)
2. Zhu, P., Hu, J., Li, X., et al.: Using blockchain technology to enhance the traceability of original achievements. IEEE Trans. Eng. Manag. **70**(5), 1693–1707 (2021)
3. Arunmozhi, M., Venkatesh, V., Arisian, S., et al.: Application of blockchain and smart contracts in autonomous vehicle supply chains: an experimental design. Transport. Res. Part E: Logist. Transport. Rev. **165**, 102864 (2022)
4. Ji, G., Zhou, S., Lai, K.-H., et al.: Timing of blockchain adoption in a supply chain with competing manufacturers. Int. J. Prod. Econ. **247**, 108430 (2022)
5. Wu W, Han Y, Niu B, et al.: Recent advances in Zizania Latifolia: a comprehensive review on phytochemical, health benefits and applications that maximize its value. In: Critical Reviews in Food Science and Nutrition, pp. 1–15 (2023)
6. Treiblmaier, H., Garaus, M.: Using blockchain to signal quality in the food supply chain: the impact on consumer purchase intentions and the moderating effect of brand familiarity. Int. J. Inf. Manag. **68**, 102514 (2023)
7. Li, Y., Liao, A., Li, L., et al.: Reinforcing or weakening? The role of blockchain technology in the link between consumer trust and organic food adoption. J. Bus. Res. **164**, 113999 (2023)
8. Mangla, S.K., Kazancoglu, Y., Ekinci, E., et al.: Using system dynamics to analyze the societal impacts of blockchain technology in milk supply chainsrefer. Transport. Res. Part E: Logist. Transport. Rev. **149**, 102289 (2021)
9. Köhler, S., Bager, S., Pizzol, M.: Sustainability standards and blockchain in agro-food supply chains: synergies and conflicts. Technol. Forecast. Soc. Chang. **185**, 122094 (2022)
10. Camilleri, M.A., Filieri, R.: Customer satisfaction and loyalty with online consumer reviews: factors affecting revisit intentions. Int. J. Hosp. Manag. **114**, 103575 (2023)

11. Kim, R.Y.: When does online review matter to consumers? The effect of product quality information cues. Electron. Commer. Res. **21**(4), 1011–1030 (2021)

12. Ying, H., Peng, X., Zhao, X., et al.: The effects of signaling blockchain-based track and trace on consumer purchases: insights from a quasi-natural experiment. In: Production and Operations Management (2023)

13. Hollenbeck, B.: Online reputation mechanisms and the decreasing value of chain affiliation. J. Mark. Res. **55**(5), 636–654 (2018)

14. Mu, J., Zhang, J.Z.: Seller marketing capability, brand reputation, and consumer journeys on e-commerce platforms. J. Acad. Mark. Sci. **49**(5), 994–1020 (2021)

15. Cox, D.F.: The measurement of information value: a study in consumer decision-making. Emerg. Concepts Mark. **413**, 21 (1962)

16. Olson, J.C., Jacoby, J.: Cue utilization in the quality perception process. ACR Special Volumes (1972)

17. Miyazaki, A.D., Grewal, D., Goodstein, R.C.: The effect of multiple extrinsic cues on quality perceptions: a matter of consistency. J. Consum. Res. **32**(1), 146–153 (2005)

18. Casino, F., Kanakaris, V., Dasaklis, T.K., et al.: Blockchain-based food supply chain traceability: a case study in the dairy sector. Int. J. Prod. Res. **59**(19), 5758–5770 (2021)

19. Yawar, S.A., Kauppi, K.: Understanding the adoption of socially responsible supplier development practices using institutional theory: dairy supply chains in India. J. Purch. Supply Manag. **24**(2), 164–176 (2018)

20. Dellarocas, C., Zhang, X., Awad, N.F.: Exploring the value of online product reviews in forecasting sales: the case of motion pictures. J. Interact. Mark. **21**(4), 23–45 (2007)

21. Duan, W., Gu, B., Whinston, A.B.: Do online reviews matter?—An empirical investigation of panel data. Decis. Support. Syst. **45**(4), 1007–1016 (2008)

22. De Langhe, B., Fernbach, P.M., Lichtenstein, D.R.: Navigating by the stars: investigating the actual and perceived validity of online user ratings. J. Consum. Res. **42**(6), 817–833 (2016)

23. Siering, M., Janze, C.: Information processing on online review platforms. J. Manag. Inf. Syst. **36**(4), 1347–1377 (2019)

24. Biswas D, Jalali H, Ansaripoor A H, et al.: Traceability vs. sustainability in supply chains: the implications of blockchain. Eur. J. Oper. Res. **305**(1), 128–147 (2023)

25. Das, G., Spence, M.T., Agarwal, J.: Social selling cues: the dynamics of posting numbers viewed and bought on customers' purchase intentions. Int. J. Res. Mark. **38**(4), 994–1016 (2021)

26. Erdem, T., Swait, J., Valenzuela, A.: Brands as signals: a cross-country validation study. J. Mark. **70**(1), 34–49 (2006)

27. Hastig, G.M., Sodhi, M.S.: Blockchain for supply chain traceability: business requirements and critical success factors. Prod. Oper. Manag. **29**(4), 935–954 (2020)

28. Luca, M., Zervas, G.: Fake it till you make it: reputation, competition, and yelp review fraud. Manag. Sci. **62**(12), 3412–3427 (2016)

29. Tan, Y.-C., Chandukala, S.R., Reddy, S.K.: Augmented reality in retail and its impact on sales. J. Mark. **86**(1), 48–66 (2022)

30. Goodman-Bacon, A.: Difference-in-differences with variation in treatment timing. J. Econometrics **225**(2), 254–277 (2021)

31. Arkhangelsky, D., Athey, S., Hirshberg, D.A., et al.: Synthetic difference-in-differences. Am. Econ. Rev. **111**(12), 4088–4118 (2021)

32. Shen, B., Dong, C., Minner, S.: Combating copycats in the supply chain with permissioned blockchain technology. Prod. Oper. Manag. **31**(1), 138–154 (2022)

33. Liu, H., Ma, R., He, G., et al.: The impact of blockchain technology on the online purchase behavior of green agricultural products. J. Retail. Consum. Serv. **74**, 103387 (2023)

34. De Boissieu, E., Kondrateva, G., Baudier, P., et al.: The use of blockchain in the luxury industry: supply chains and the traceability of goods. J. Enterp. Inf. Manag. **34**(5), 1318–1338 (2021)
35. Niu, B., Ruan, Y., Xu, H.: Turn a blind eye? E-tailer's blockchain participation considering upstream competition between copycats and brands. Int. J. Prod. Econ. **265**, 109009 (2023)
36. Tan, X., Wang, Y., Tan, Y.: Impact of live chat on purchase in electronic markets: the moderating role of information cues. Inf. Syst. Res. **30**(4), 1248–1271 (2019)

Population Aging and High-Quality Economic Development: Based on Feature Selection and Empirical Analysis of Provincial Panel Data

Luomeng Zhang[1], Lixin Cui[1], and Lu Bai[1,2(✉)]

[1] School of Information, Central University of Finance and Economics, Beijing, China
`bailu@bnu.edu.cn`
[2] School of Artificial Intelligence, Beijing Normal University, Beijing, China

Abstract. Based on the severe situation of population aging and the requirements for high-quality economic development in China, this paper applies provincial panel data from 2012 to 2021, and uses Lasso and Elastic Net feature selection algorithms to select the variables affecting high-quality economic development. Additionally, this paper measures an indicator of high-quality economic development by entropy method, and empirically tests the impact of population aging on high quality economic development. The results show that, the level of high-quality economic development has declined in time, and the regional heterogeneity has decreased spatially. Through the application of Lasso and Elastic Net regression models for variable selection, the accuracy of measuring an indicator of high-quality economic development is effectively improved, which makes the research results more interpretable. Empirically, this paper finds a significant negative impact of population aging on high-quality economic development, hindering China's progress in this regard. Therefore, China should actively address the issue of population aging to promote high-quality economic development.

Keywords: Machine Learning · Feature Selection · High-Quality Economic Development · Population Aging

1 Introduction

The development of economy and society, and the advancement of technological capabilities, and the improvement of living standards and healthcare levels has led to a continuous decline in birth and death rates, an extension of life expectancy, and an increasingly prominent phenomenon of population aging in China. By the end of 2022, the proportion of the elderly population in China had risen to 14.9%, totaling 210 million people. China has entered a moderately aging society, making it one of the fastest-developing countries in terms of population aging globally.

In recent years, China has put forward the concept of high-quality economic development to enhance the quality and sustainability of its economic growth, emphasizing that high-quality development is the primary task for comprehensively building a socialist modern country. However, the rapid development of population aging in

China has profound implications for various aspects of economic and social life, posing severe challenges to China's high-quality economic development. Therefore, China must proactively address the issue of population aging, enhance the sustainability of economic development, promote high-quality economic development, and construct a modern economic system.

Therefore, against the backdrop of the deepening aging of the population in China, selecting provincial panel data from 2012 to 2021, and combining machine learning algorithms (Lasso and Elastic Net regression models) and econometric models, this study establishes a comprehensive evaluation index system for high-quality economic development in China, and analyzes the impact mechanism of population aging on high-quality economic development through empirical research. The aim is to provide policy foundations for promoting high-quality economic development in China.

2 Literature Review and Theoretical Hypotheses

2.1 Construction of an Evaluation Indicator for High-Quality Economic Development

The content of high-quality development should be more multidimensional and diverse in regional development approaches and paths (Jin, 2018). Economic development, reform and opening up, urban-rural construction, ecological environment, and people's lives should all reach a high-quality level. Therefore, to assess the high-quality economic development of a region, it is necessary to establish a comprehensive and multi-faceted evaluation system for high-quality economic development. Mlachila et al. (2017) measured the quality of economic growth in more than 90 countries from the intrinsic nature and social dimensions of growth. Ma et al. (2019) constructed an evaluation system for high-quality economic development based on high-quality supply, high-quality demand, development efficiency, economic operation, and openness to the outside world. Song and Li (2021) measured the comprehensive indicator of high-quality economic development in various provinces in China, starting from the intrinsic dynamics and external performance of economic development.

2.2 Feature Selection

According to the above analysis, scholars currently primarily evaluate high-quality economic development through econometric models. Traditional econometric methods, however, may not effectively discern the main factors influencing high-quality economic development. Scholars often subjectively select indicators affecting high-quality economic development based on relevant literature theories, without further confirmation, thereby reducing the accuracy of model fitting results. With the advancement of artificial intelligence technology, machine learning methods have gradually been applied to empirical research in economics due to their powerful information processing and excellent predictive optimization capabilities (Athey and Imbens, 2019), effectively improving the accuracy of empirical research results.

Feature selection is a commonly used method in economic research that can identify variables with greater interpretability for the dependent variable. Among them, Lasso and Elastic Net regression models are commonly used feature selection algorithms in economic research. They can effectively address multicollinearity and over-fitting issues in linear regression models (Varian, 2014). In studies predicting oil price volatility, the Lasso and Elastic Net were found to have better predictive performance and higher directional accuracy (Zhang et al., 2019). OLS regression models constructed using variables selected by these two methods also performed better (Zhang et al., 2019) than other single models and combination models (Liang et al., 2020). Moreover, the Lasso and Elastic have also been further developed by integrating structural interactions between features, improving the effectiveness (Cui et al., 2021a; Cui et al., 2021b; Cui et al., 2019).

Therefore, this paper introduces feature selection algorithms from machine learning, specifically the Lasso and Elastic Net regression models. These algorithms are used to select influential factors for high-quality economic development. This approach enhances the interpretability of the high-quality economic development indicator, improves the effectiveness and credibility of studying the impact mechanism of population aging on high-quality economic development, and provides insights into China's high-quality economic development from the perspective of population aging. Hence, the following hypothesis is proposed:

Hypothesis 1: Through the use of Lasso and Elastic Net regression models for the selection of indicator variables influencing high-quality economic development, a more interpretable evaluation indicator for high-quality economic development can be obtained, optimizing the empirical model results for the impact of population aging on high-quality economic development.

2.3 The Impact of Population Aging on High-Quality Economic Development

Regarding the impact of population aging on high-quality economic development, scholars currently do not have a relatively unified viewpoint. This is because high-quality economic development refers to comprehensive economic development. Population aging affects various aspects of the macroeconomy, leading to one influence offsetting another. Therefore, it is challenging to determine the effect of population aging, population aging may have positive effects on the high-quality economic development (Pham and Vo, 2021), and may also have negative effects (Lee and Shin, 2019).

Firstly, the increase in the elderly population directly affects labor supply, leading to a decrease in the number of working-age individuals and a reduction in labor productivity (Zhang and Li, 2022). It also leads to higher labor costs, causing some enterprises, especially labor-intensive ones, to relocate their factories to areas with lower labor costs (Chen et al., 2022), hindering the industrial development of China.

Secondly, compared to younger individuals, the physical and mental abilities of the elderly decline significantly. Their willingness and ability to innovate decrease with age (Fu and Cao, 2021). Learning new knowledge and advanced technology becomes more challenging, reducing the efficiency of research and development (Cao and Xiao, 2022). Moreover, the decrease in the labor force raises labor costs for businesses, leading to a corresponding reduction in R&D investment (Li et al., 2022), which is detrimental to achieving technological breakthroughs and innovation outcomes.

Thirdly, the increase in the elderly population will increase the demand for pension insurance, leading to increased pension insurance expenditures (Song and Gao, 2023), aggravating the financial burden on the government and affecting its support for economic development (Zhang et al., 2019).

Based on the above analysis, it can be observed that population aging plays a role in high-quality economic development from multiple aspects and dimensions. Overall, this paper believes that population aging has a negative impact on high-quality economic development. Therefore, the following hypothesis is proposed:

Hypothesis 2: Population aging has a significant negative impact on high-quality economic development.

3 Construction of a High-Quality Economic Development Indicator

3.1 Selection of Indicators

To comprehensively and scientifically analyze the current state of high-quality economic development in China, it is necessary to integrate numerous relevant economic indicators and establish a multidimensional evaluation indicator system for high-quality economic development. Drawing on the practices of relevant scholars and the Party's directive of "promoting high-quality economic development with the new development philosophy", this paper constructs a comprehensive evaluation indicator system from five aspects of the new development philosophy, including 1 primary indicator, 5 secondary indicators, and 25 representative tertiary indicators, as shown in Table 1. (Direction refers to positive indicators (+) or negative indicators (−)).

3.2 Data Sources and Data Preprocessing

This paper analyzes the level of high-quality economic development in China and its provinces using provincial panel data from 2012 to 2021. The data mainly come from annual publications such as the "China Statistical Yearbook" and the statistical yearbooks of various provinces. Some indicators are converted to Chinese Yuan using the annual average Sino-US exchange rate, and missing data for specific indicators are imputed using the mean value method.

Initially, this paper utilizes Lasso and Elastic Net regression models for feature selection, selecting indicators more relevant to high-quality economic development from the 25 tertiary indicators shown in Table 1. Subsequently, the entropy method is applied to construct a comprehensive evaluation indicator for high-quality economic development based on the selected features.

3.3 Feature Selection Results

This paper explores the construction of an evaluation indicator for high-quality economic development, and the actual per capita GDP of each province in China reflects the regional status of high-quality economic development to a certain extent. Therefore, this

Table 1. An Evaluation Indicator for High-Quality Economic Development

Level 1	Level 2	Level 3	Direction
High-Quality Economic Development	Innovative Development	A1: R&D Expenditure Proportion	+
		A2: Patents per 10,000 People	+
		A3: R&D Personnel Input Intensity	+
		A4: Technology Market Transaction Capability	+
	Coordinated Development	B1: Proportion of Added Value of the Tertiary Industry	+
		B2: Consumption Rate	+
		B3: Investment Rate	+
		B4: Urbanization Rate	+
		B5: Urban-Rural Income Ratio	−
		B6: Urban-Rural Consumption Ratio	−
	Green Development	C1: Industrial Solid Waste per 10,000 GDP	−
		C2: Wastewater per 10,000 GDP	−
		C3: Air Pollutants per 10,000 GDP	−
		C4: Forest Coverage Rate	+
		C5: Greening Rate of Built-Up Areas	+
		C6: Pollution Control Investment Capability	+
		C7: Environmental Protection Expenditure Proportion	+
	Open Development	D1: Foreign Trade Dependence	+
		D2: Foreign Capital Dependence	+

(continued)

Table 1. (*continued*)

Level 1	Level 2	Level 3	Direction
		D3: International Tourism Income	+
	Shared Development	E1: Education Input Intensity	+
		E2: Medical and Health Input Intensity	+
		E3: Social Security and Employment Input Intensity	+
		E4: Per Capita Disposable Income	+
		E5: Unemployment Rate	−

variable is chosen as the dependent variable for Lasso and Elastic Net regression models. The 25 tertiary indicators from Table 1 are used as independent variables to establish Lasso and Elastic Net regression models for feature selection.

The feature values of the independent variables after training with Lasso and Elastic Net regression models are shown in Table 2. Variables with feature values of 0 indicate low correlation with the dependent variable and should be eliminated, while non-zero feature variables should be retained.

From Table 2, it is evident that variables such as R&D expenditure proportion (A1), R&D personnel input intensity (A3), urban-rural consumption ratio (B6), air pollutants per 10,000 GDP (C3), environmental protection expenditure proportion (C7), and medical and health input intensity (E2) have coefficients of 0. These variables are eliminated by both the Lasso and Elastic Net models. The main reasons for this include multicollinearity between R&D expenditure proportion (A1) and R&D personnel input intensity (A3) with patents per 10,000 people (A2) and technology market transaction capability (A4), leading to their elimination. Similarly, the urban-rural consumption ratio (B6) is eliminated due to equivalence with the urban-rural income ratio (B5). Air pollutants per 10,000 GDP (C3) is eliminated due to multicollinearity with industrial solid waste per 10,000 GDP (C1) and wastewater per 10,000 GDP (C2). Environmental protection expenditure proportion (C7) and medical and health input intensity (E2) do not significantly affect the actual per capita GDP of each province, leading to their elimination. The results indicate that the Lasso and Elastic Net regression models can rapidly eliminate variables with low significance and multicollinear variables during feature selection, demonstrating their strong advantages when selecting numerous indicators for the model.

To assess the gap between the predicted values and real values of the models, R^2 and MSE are used to examine the predictive performance of the two models. A higher R^2 indicates a better fit, and a smaller MSE indicates a better fit. In the Lasso model, R^2 is

Table 2. Feature Values of Lasso and Elastic Net Regression Models

Variables	Feature Values		Variables	Feature Values	
	Lasso Model	Elastic Net Model		Lasso Model	Elastic Net Model
Intercept	0.002	0.002	C3	−0	−0
A1	−0.000	−0	C4	−0.046	−0.045
A2	0.100	0.100	C5	0.062	0.061
A3	0	0	C6	−0.027	−0.026
A4	0.058	0.058	C7	−0	−0
B1	−0.121	−0.120	D1	0.023	0.023
B2	−0.062	−0.062	D2	−0.002	−0.002
B3	0.039	0.038	D3	0.013	0.013
B4	0.084	0.084	E1	−0.057	−0.056
B5	0.064	0.063	E2	−0	−0
B6	−0	−0	E3	−0.098	−0.097
C1	−0.039	−0.038	E4	0.771	0.770
C2	−0.103	−0.103	E5	0.006	0.006

0.9739, and MSE is 0.0165. In the Elastic Net model, R^2 is 0.9739, and MSE is 0.0165. Thus, the high R^2 and low MSE values for both models indicate a strong fit, suggesting that the selected indicator variables can effectively construct an evaluation indicator for high-quality economic development.

3.4 Entropy Method for Constructing an Evaluation Indicator of High-Quality Economic Development

This paper simultaneously constructs evaluation indicators for high-quality economic development based on 25 original indicators and those selected through the Lasso and Elastic Net models. The former is denoted as $HQEG_{score1}$, and the latter is denoted as $HQEG_{score2}$. The entropy method is chosen to determine information entropy values and indicator weights. The linear weighting method is then applied to calculate the evaluation indicators for high-quality economic development in each province. Stata 17 statistical software is used to implement the entropy method in constructing these indicators.

To depict the changes in time and space of China's high-quality economic development from 2012 to 2021, this paper analyzes cross-sectional data for the years 2012, 2015, 2018, and 2021. The results are shown in Fig. 1.

Temporal Dynamics. From Fig. 1, it can be observed that in 2015, China's indicator of high-quality economic development decreased compared to 2012. This indicates that hidden risks in China's economic development emerged in 2015, which urgently requires a transformation of the existing economic development mode. In 2018, China's high-quality economic development situation continuously improved significantly, signifying

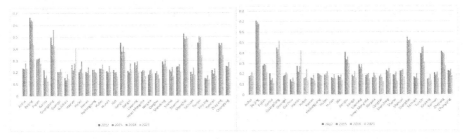

Fig. 1. High-Quality Economic Development ($HQEG_{score1}$ (left) and $HQEG_{score2}$ (right))

a substantial enhancement. This suggests that after proposing the concept of high-quality economic development, various sectors actively worked towards this direction, enhancing the quality and sustainability of China's economic development. However, in 2021, compared to 2012, 2015, and 2018, the level of high-quality economic development in various provinces generally declined. The main reason is the impact of the COVID-19 pandemic on the social and economic development. Therefore, at the current stage, China should stabilize the existing economic development situation and actively promote the transformation and upgrading of the economy.

Spatial Pattern Changes. From Fig. 1, it is evident that in 2012, due to their advantageous geographical location, abundant resources, concentration of talent, and high levels of science, the eastern regions of China had significantly higher levels of high-quality economic development than the central and western regions. The central regions exhibited higher levels than the western regions. These reflect the regional differences in China's socio-economic development. Looking at the high-quality economic development situation in China in 2015 and 2018, the eastern, central, and western regions all showed an upward trend. Although each province still exhibited apparent regional heterogeneity in high-quality economic development, due to the implementation of strategies such as the rise of central China and the western development, the gap between the central and western regions and the eastern regions continued to narrow. This indicates that the policies of support and promotion for underdeveloped areas in China have shown initial effectiveness. From the perspective of 2021, the gap between the eastern, central, and western regions has further narrowed, reflecting the impact of the COVID-19 pandemic on the national economic development, especially its inhibitory effect on the economically developed eastern regions.

4 Empirical Study on Population Aging and High-Quality Economic Development

4.1 Regression Model Specification

Based on the theoretical analysis and research assumptions in the previous sections, to explore and analyze the relationship between population aging and high-quality economic development, this paper constructs the following econometric model:

$$HQEG_{i,t} = \alpha_i + \alpha_1 AGE_{i,t} + \alpha_2 control_{i,t} + \varepsilon_{i,t} \tag{1}$$

Here, i represents the region, t represents the year, the dependent variable $HQEG_{i,t}$ represents high-quality economic development, the core explanatory variable $AGE_{i,t}$ represents population aging, $control_{i,t}$ represents control variables, α_i is the region-specific fixed effect that does not change over time, and $\varepsilon_{i,t}$ is the random disturbance term.

4.2 Variable Selection and Data Sources

Dependent Variable. The dependent variable in this study is High-Quality Economic Development (HQEG), measured as described earlier. Two evaluation indicators for high-quality economic development are obtained using the entropy method. One is the $HQEG_{score1}$, derived solely from the 25 original indicators summarized through literature research without feature selection. The other, $HQEG_{score2}$, is obtained after both referencing relevant literature and feature selection. Regression analyses are conducted on both dependent variables to compare and examine the impact of feature selection on the empirical model's accuracy.

Core Explanatory Variable. The core explanatory variable in this study is Population Aging (AGE). This study selects the proportion of the elderly population, specifically the percentage of the population aged 65 and above in each province, as the indicator for measuring population aging.

Control Variables. Considering that factors other than population aging may influence high-quality economic development in China, the study includes the following control variables: (1) Economic Development Level (gdp), measured using the actual GDP of each province. (2) Industrial Structure (indus), measured using the proportion of the secondary industry's value added to GDP in each province. (3) Government Intervention Capacity (gov), measured using the proportion of local general fiscal budget expenditure to GDP. (4) Foreign Openness Level (fdi), represented by the proportion of foreign direct investment to GDP in each province. (5) Infrastructure Level (inf), represented by per capita urban road area in each province. (6) Human Capital Level (edu), measured by the proportion of people with a college degree or above in each province's population.

This study uses panel data from 30 provinces in China from 2012 to 2021 (excluding Hong Kong, Macau, Taiwan, and Tibet). Data are sourced from the annual "China Statistical Yearbook", "China Population & Employment Statistics Yearbook", " Statistical Communiqué of National Economic and Social Development", and the statistical yearbooks of each province. Some indicators are uniformly converted to Chinese Yuan based on the annual average Sino-US exchange rate. Missing data are imputed using the mean value. Stata17 statistical software is employed for empirical analysis.

4.3 Regression Results and Analysis

The paper conducted descriptive statistics and two rounds of Hausman tests on the relevant variables. Through descriptive statistics, it can be observed that the mean values for most variables exceed the standard deviations, indicating relatively small data dispersion and concentrated distributions, suggesting stability in the data. Through two rounds of

Hausman tests, the statistical p-value are 0.000, which are less than 0.01. Therefore, this paper can reject the null hypothesis that the model is a random effects model. This indicates that a fixed effects model should be chosen for the regression analysis.

Using Eq. (1), this paper performs fixed effects regression on panel data to study the impact of population aging on high-quality economic development and compares the role of feature selection in empirical regression. The regression results are presented in Table 3, where the column (1) represents the regression of population aging on the unselected indicator of high-quality economic development evaluation ($HQEG_{score1}$), and the column (2) represents the regression of population aging on the selected indicator of high-quality economic development evaluation after feature selection ($HQEG_{score2}$).

Table 3. Regression Results

Variables	(1) $HQEG_{score1}$	(2) $HQEG_{score2}$
AGE	−0.912***	−0.867***
	(−4.75)	(−4.36)
gdp	0.000**	−0.000
	(1.98)	(−0.36)
indus	−0.249***	−0.271***
	(−2.92)	(−3.07)
gov	0.059	0.069
	(0.65)	(0.75)
fdi	0.004***	0.005***
	(6.94)	(7.60)
inf	0.001	0.001
	(1.31)	(1.24)
edu	−0.423***	−0.305***
	(−4.00)	(−2.79)
Constant	0.454***	0.460***
	(6.48)	(6.33)
Observations	300	300
R-squared	0.946	0.949
Adjusted R-squared	0.939	0.943
F-statistic	16.79***	19.90***

Note: ***, **, and * indicate significance levels of 1%, 5%, and 10%, respectively.

From Table 3, it can be observed that the R^2 values for models (1) and (2) are 0.946 and 0.949, respectively. The adjusted R^2 values are 0.939 and 0.943, respectively. Model (2) has a better fit, indicating that the indicator of high-quality economic development evaluation obtained after feature selection is more explanatory. This confirms Hypothesis 1 of this study.

Examining the empirical results of models (1) and (2), the coefficients of the Population Aging in both models are significantly negative. This implies a significant negative correlation between population aging and high-quality economic development. In Model (2), with the better fit, for every 1 unit increase in population aging, the level of high-quality economic development decreases by approximately 0.867. This validates Hypothesis 2 of this study.

Regarding the control variables in models (1) and (2), the estimation results for the Economic Development Level are not robust enough, with very small coefficients. This suggests that the impact of actual GDP on high-quality economic development is relatively small, as high-quality economic development involves comprehensive and diversified growth, with GDP being only a part of it. The Industrial Structure has a significant negative impact on high-quality economic development, indicating that the current distribution of industrial structure in China is unreasonable and significantly affects the state of high-quality economic development. Urgent measures are needed to optimize and upgrade the industrial structure. The estimated coefficient for Government Intervention Capacity is positive but not significant, indicating that the fiscal budget expenditure in various provinces is insufficient, and there are shortcomings in certain areas that do not significantly impact high-quality economic development. Further research is needed to identify critical areas that require substantial fiscal support. The Foreign Openness Level can significantly promote high-quality economic development, indicating that foreign direct investment contributes to the inflow and transfer of foreign technology, knowledge, and funds, thereby enhancing China's level of high-quality economic development. China should further open up, relax some restrictions on foreign investment, actively and effectively attract foreign investment, promote international trade, and maintain a fair trade environment. The impact of Infrastructure Level on high-quality economic development is positive but not significant, suggesting that the current level of infrastructure construction in China is gradually losing its driving force for the economy. China should further advance the construction of new infrastructure to provide strong support for high-quality economic development. The Human Capital Level significantly inhibits high-quality economic development, indicating that China not only has fewer high-quality talents with higher education but also lacks sufficient reserves of talents engaged in fields such as technological innovation. This hinders the fulfillment of China's economic development needs. There is a need to enhance the reserve of innovative human capital, increase investment in talents for innovation and high technology education, and meet the requirements of high-quality economic development.

5 Conclusion

Based on the provincial panel data from 2012 to 2021, this paper employs feature selection algorithms to filter indicator variables. It constructs an evaluation indicator for high-quality economic development using the entropy method. Subsequently, the fixed effects model is applied to analyze the role of feature selection algorithms in empirical analysis and the impact mechanism of population aging on high-quality economic development. The research reveals:

First, in terms of measuring the indicator of high-quality economic development, the current level in China has experienced a temporal decline influenced by the pandemic. Spatially, it has been affected by both policy support and the pandemic, leading to a reduction in the degree of regional heterogeneity.

Second, machine learning algorithms have optimized the construction of an indicator for high-quality economic development. This optimization enhances the interpretability of the indicator, consequently improving the fit of regression models in empirical analysis.

Third, population aging has a significant negative impact on high-quality economic development. The increase in population aging is observed to markedly decrease the level of high-quality economic development.

Acknowledgement. This work is supported by the National Natural Science Foundation of China under Grants T2122020, 61602535, and 61976235. This work is also supported in part by the Program for Innovation Research in the Central University of Finance and Economics. This work is also supported by the Emerging Interdisciplinary Project of CUFE.

References

Jin, B.: Study on the "high-quality development" economics. China Ind. Econ. **04**, 5–18 (2018). (in Chinese)

Mlachila, M., Tapsoba, R., Tapsoba, S.J.A.: A quality of growth index for developing countries: a proposal. Soc. Indic. Res. **134**(2), 675–710 (2017)

Ma, R., Zhang, J., Wang, H.: Do S&T talents contribute to high-quality economic development of China?—Empirical test based on effect of S&T talents on TFP. Res. Econ. Manag. **40**(05), 3–12 (2019). (in Chinese)

Song, Y., Li, X.: The theoretical connotation and evaluation system of high-quality economic development under the new development pattern. Guizhou Soc. Sci. **11**, 120–129 (2021). (in Chinese)

Athey, S., Imbens, G.W.: Machine learning methods that economists should know about. Annu. Rev. Econ. **11**(1), 685–725 (2019)

Varian, H.R.: Big Data: new tricks for econometrics. J. Econ. Perspect. **28**(2), 3–28 (2014)

Zhang, Y., Wei, Y., Zhang, Y., et al.: Forecasting oil price volatility: forecast combination versus shrinkage method. Energy Econ. **80**, 423–433 (2019)

Zhang, Y., Ma, F., Wang, Y.: Forecasting crude oil prices with a large set of predictors: can LASSO select powerful predictors? J. Empir. Financ. **54**, 97–117 (2019)

Liang, C., Wei, Y., Li, X., et al.: Uncertainty and crude oil market volatility: new evidence. Appl. Econ. **52**(27), 2945–2959 (2020)

Pham, T.N., Vo, D.H.: Aging population and economic growth in developing countries: a quantile regression approach. Emerg. Mark. Financ. Trade **57**(1), 108–122 (2021)

Lee, H.-H., Shin, K.: Nonlinear effects of population aging on economic growth. Jpn. World Econ. **51**,(2019)

Zhang, C., Li, R.: Population aging, digital economy and high-quality economic development. Econ. Surv. **39**(05), 3–13 (2022). (in Chinese)

Chen, X., Zheng, Y., Yao, D.: Population aging, industrial intelligence, and high-quality economic development. Stat. Decis. **38**(06), 129–132 (2022). (in Chinese)

Fu, J., Cao, X.: Research on the impact of population aging on high-quality economic development in China. Inquiry Econ. Issues **06**, 44–55 (2021). (in Chinese)

Cao, C., Xiao, G.: The impact of population aging on high-quality economic development viewed from the perspective of enterprise innovation. J. Xiangtan Univ. (Philos. Soc. Sci.) **46**(03), 79–84 (2022). (in Chinese)

Li, C., Ge, J., Zhao, S.: Artificial intelligence, population ageing and high-quality economic development. Mod. Econ. Sci. **44**(01), 77–91 (2022). (in Chinese)

Song, J., Gao, C.: Population aging, pension security expenditure and high-quality economic development. Jinan J. (Philos. Soc. Sci.) **45**(02), 98–114 (2023). (in Chinese)

Zhang, K., Chen, Y., Lu, Y.: Research on the growth engine in China's high-quality development stage—analysis from the perspective of population aging. Tianjin Soc. Sci. **04**, 102–110 (2019). (in Chinese)

Cui, L., Bai, L., Wang, Y., Jin, X., Hancock, E.: Internet financing credit risk evaluation using multiple structural interacting elastic net feature selection. Pattern Recogn. **114**, 107835 (2021)

Cui, L., Bai, L., Wang, Y., Yu, P., Hancock, E.: Fused Lasso for feature selection using structural information. Pattern Recogn. **119**, 108058 (2021)

Cui, L., Bai, L., Zhang, Z., Wang, Y., Hancock, E.: Identifying the most informative features using a structurally interacting elastic net. Neurocomputing **336**, 13–26 (2019)

Reform and Practice of "Embedding-Integration" Collaborative Nurturing Mechanism for the Major of Management Science in the Context of New Liberal Arts

Jing Wang, Zhen Zhu$^{(\boxtimes)}$, and Yi Jiang

School of Economics and Management, China University of Geosciences, Wuhan 430074, China
zhuzhen2008@gmail.com

Abstract. Under the background of new liberal arts, the major of management is facing the urgent needs of educational reform and innovation of talent cultivation mode. This paper proposes and discusses the reform and practice of "Embedding-Integration" collaborative nurturing mechanism in the major of management. In the teaching ecology, through the establishment of the three-dimensional embedding concept of "object-tool-activity", we promote the integration and cultivation of students' abilities in five aspects, namely, thinking, curriculum, teaching, and practice and scene, and realize the collaborative cultivation of students' personalized cultivation of the new liberal arts cultivation model. Through the top-level design of teaching programs and models, the development of interdisciplinary knowledge-embedded curricula, the optimization and design of integrated scenarios and practical teaching systems, and the "embedded-integrated" personalized collaborative cultivation, we promote the construction of a new liberal arts major in government, industry, and academia and research for the majors of management sciences. Based on inter-disciplinary cultivation, the integration cultivation idea of "strong foundation, broad vision, and application" has outstanding value for education reform, which can promote the reform of talent cultivation mode of economics and management majors under the background of new liberal arts, provide reform ideas and practical paths for the construction of new liberal arts in other social sciences and liberal arts majors.

Keywords: new liberal arts · collaborative education · embedding-integration

1 Introduction

Since 2018, the construction of new liberal arts in China has gradually emerged. The Department of Higher Education of the Ministry of Education has explicitly put forward the concept of "new liberal arts" within the framework of the "Four New" construction. In November 2020, the Ministry of Education further issued a call for accelerating the construction of new liberal arts, which triggered a wide range of responses and practices among colleges and universities. Many colleges and universities have innovated and explored the new liberal arts from different dimensions, which has brought far-reaching impact on higher education in China. In this context, colleges and universities have begun to actively expand and build the system, which has led to the transformation of the traditional talent cultivation program and teaching mode, provided a diversified choice of paths for the construction of the high-quality development system of new liberal arts [1].

With the large-scale practice of building new liberal arts, China's higher education system is facing a deep reform and innovation. It is not only about the future direction of the development of disciplines, but also a major challenge to the mode of talent cultivation and educational philosophy. With the rapid development of science and technology and the deepening of globalization, the importance of new liberal arts education in cultivating innovative talents is becoming more and more prominent. As an important part of the new liberal arts, the reform and practice of the talent cultivation mode of the management major is of great significance in improving the comprehensive quality of students and adapting to the development of the future society. However, at present, there are problems such as single curriculum, insufficient practical teaching, and insufficient cross-disciplinary integration in the management majors of many colleges and universities, which constrain the comprehensive development of students and affect the quality of talent cultivation. New liberal arts are a key part of the "four new" construction of the Ministry of Education, and collaborative education is regarded as an innovative concept of education. This concept emphasizes "interdisciplinary" and "cross-border cooperation", aims to cultivate all-round development of excellent talents through the deep integration and collaboration among different disciplines [2].

The construction of new liberal arts is not only to promote the cultivation of interdisciplinary talents, but also an educational reform process to build up intellectual and cultural self-confidence in the light of China's current economic practice. This requires keeping close to the economic development, enhancing the connotation of the profession through the new industry-teaching fusion teaching reform by general new technology and new theories adapted to practice, fundamentally improving the teachers' vocational education literacy, perfecting the student training system as well as personalizing the promotion of collaborative parenting construction [3]. The concept of new liberal arts was first put forward by Siloam College in the United States in 2017, and its core idea is to carry out in-depth reconstruction and integration of traditional liberal arts majors, break the inherent boundaries between disciplines and majors, and realize comprehensive learning and cultivation of cross-fields and cross-majors [4].

The hotspots of research on the construction of new liberal arts mainly focus on the refinement of educational concepts and the optimization of disciplinary development. The bibliometric analysis of Huang Kainan and Miao Zikun [5, 6] found that the current educational literature mainly elaborates the manifestation of "new" in the new liberal arts, and summarizes the characteristics of mathematical intelligence, intersectionality, and cultivation system, etc., with the media disciplines pursuing this idea most strongly.

The researcher argues at the theoretical level that the role of the new liberal arts for pedagogical reform can be manifested in two ways:

First, collaborative parenting is an effective educational model. The researcher points out that it can promote cross-fertilization between the new liberal arts and the new engineering disciplines, and through collaborative parenting students can learn and think across disciplines, thus broadening their horizons and thinking abilities, and improving their learning interests and learning efficiency.

Second, innovative integration must be combined with social practice and oriented to social needs. Researchers have found that the use of new technologies in combination with liberal arts education can promote the innovation of teaching mode, make the liberal arts more socially applicable, and allow new technologies such as big data and machine learning to become a new paradigm for the study of "new liberal arts".

In the practice of new liberal arts research and reform, Li Guo [7] put forward a visionary proposal. He advocated that through the careful use of educational resources and international high-level academic exchange platforms, with the synergistic cultivation of the three modules of moral knowledge, and professional knowledge and quality development, we can more effectively cultivate talents with a high degree of comprehensive quality. Eddie Li [8] pointed out that from strengthening students' comprehensive ability, standardizing the reform of the curriculum system strengthening the evaluation system, three aspects of the industry characteristics of the University of Economics and Management personnel training mode construction. Paving the way for the cultivation of economic and management talents in universities with industry characteristics. Yu Haiying [9] examines the inadequacy of the traditional management professional curriculum system from another perspective, in which she advocates the integration of a data science course cluster consisting of basic theories, methods and tools, cases and practice series of courses. The technological empowerment of the management knowledge system using with by modern information technology will undoubtedly help to enhance the data science literacy of management talents and enable them to better cope with today's complex and changing data environment. Ding Qiulei [10] emphasized the importance of breaking through the traditional liberal arts thinking mode. He believes that inheritance and innovation, intersection and integration, synergy and sharing are the main ways to lead the development of humanities and social sciences. These views provide us with a new perspective and lead us to think about how to cultivate talents in the context of new liberal arts. Kuang Cunjiu [11], on the other hand, put forward his insights from a more macroscopic perspective. He believes that we should promote the deep integration of information technology and humanities education, explore the interdisciplinary cross-fertilization mode of talent cultivation. At the same time, it is also crucial to build a "big practice" training system that connects with the society and a mechanism of all-round and whole-process collaborative education, as well as a mechanism for evaluating the quality of the training of talents in the new liberal arts. These views provide us with a comprehensive framework to meet the challenges facing the cultivation of new liberal arts talents.

How to promote the integration of knowledge and the enhancement of ability based on reducing the overlapping of courses in the context of interdisciplinary disciplines is a thorny problem facing the teaching reform. Due to the limited class time and single means of practice, this problem has become the common focus of the cross-fusion teaching reform of different disciplines, and it is the key problem that must be solved to realize the collaborative education and cultivation of the new liberal arts construction.

In addition, because the practical teaching and application training scenarios of management students have long been restricted by teaching resources, enterprise system, business process risks and other factors, there is a large disconnect with the needs of social enterprises, and it is extremely difficult to improve the composite ability and realize personalized learning. Therefore, how to enrich teaching means and expand teaching scenarios is the key path to promote the integration of inter-professional knowledge. The solution of this problem will provide new ideas for the teaching reform of inter-professional integration of new liberal arts, and the reform of cultivation mode will make the major of management science have the natural disciplinary conditions for the integration of new technology, new knowledge and new applications in new liberal arts, and lay the foundation for the design of the "government, industry, academia, and research" four-in-one teaching scenario.

In this paper, we will take the collaborative cultivation of information management and information system and engineering management in the School of Economics and Management of China University of Geosciences (Wuhan) as the teaching reform scenario, combining the "smart construction", "digital economy", "big data" and "digital economy", "Big Data" and "Artificial Intelligence", the training mechanism of the two majors is "embedded-integrated", and innovative exploration is carried out in combination with teaching practice.

2 Teaching Reform and Practice of Management Science and Engineering in School of Economics and Management of China University of Geosciences (Wuhan)

Management science and engineering category (hereinafter referred to as management science category) is the first-level discipline of management, which is characterized by the multidisciplinary intersection of economics, management, civil engineering, computer, mathematics, and other disciplines, and has the natural disciplinary conditions for the fusion of new technologies, new knowledge, and new applications in the new liberal arts. Our information management and information system are a national first-class professional construction point, and engineering management is a first-class professional construction point in Hubei Province. Driven by emerging industry applications such as "Internet+", "big data" and "smart construction", since 2017 China University of Geosciences (Wuhan) School of Economics and Management has been managing the discipline of science class major takes full advantage of the scientific research and industry-academia-research advantages accumulated in recent years, and takes the lead in exploring the collaborative education mechanism of the two majors of information management and information system and engineering management. The research team published a paper in the top journal of engineering education, 《Higher Engineering Education Research》 [12], and the digital teaching reform of engineering management based on the OBE concept has been launched [13]. With the rapid development of engineering digital application, the engineering management program in our university is facing new challenges and opportunities. Under such a trend, the engineering management major needs to keep abreast of the times and integrate the emerging IT technology and big data management thinking, to cultivate talents with digital management ability. At the same time, the information management and information system program also need to deal with the complexity and nested nature of the knowledge system and embed digital and data-based knowledge into limited teaching sessions to meet the needs of industry development. Our reforms and practices optimize the educational contents of engineering management and information management, and information systems majors in the trend of digital application of engineering, improve students' digital management ability, and explore new professional application areas.

2.1 Reform Ideas of Cultivation Mode

The main idea of reform can be summarized as "three-dimensional embedding" in the teaching ecology to drive "five-dimensional integration", and through the scene embedded in the integration of knowledge, teach according to the individual, and promote the personalized collaborative education and training mode of management science majors.

See Fig. 1 for a detailed description of the idea.

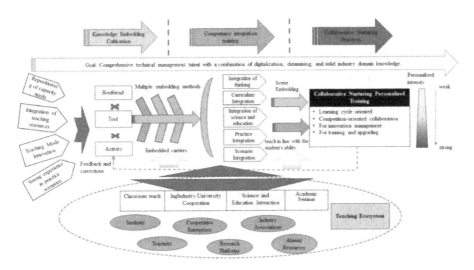

Fig. 1. Reform idea of new liberal arts cultivation model of collaborative education for management science majors

Interdisciplinary knowledge embedding is the core content of the new liberal arts cultivation model of collaborative education, and it is also a boosting force in teaching reform. As an important carrier of knowledge embedding, "ternary embedding" is based on the theory of educational ecology, which regards educational objects (such as teachers and students), educational tools (such as teaching means, technology, and platforms, etc.) and educational activities (such as teaching system inside and outside the classroom) as an organic whole of teaching implementation. By innovatively designing multiple ways of embedding knowledge and realizing digital and data-based knowledge migration, it provides an important and innovative reform to promote the mutual embedding of knowledge in the two undergraduate majors of information management and information systems and engineering management. Knowledge embedding is understood from two perspectives: first, the mutual embedding of knowledge with knowledge, which involves discipline intersection and theoretical innovation; and second, the mutual embedding between the carriers in which knowledge is embedded [14, 15].

Competence integration training is an important process of embedding and solidifying knowledge into new teaching concepts and modes. The process of cultivation is to break the original teaching mode of "specialization-curriculum" and realize the integration of cultivation modes in the five dimensions of "thinking, curriculum, teaching, practice and scene". The focus is to cultivate students' personalized development through the new design of curriculum, teaching, practice, and scenarios by spreading the emerging digital and big data management ideas based on the original specialization. The core of its teaching reform is to provide conditions for the cultivation of students' self-selected ability and achieve the goal of personalized cultivation with the help of novel teaching methods (such as flipped classroom), industry-academia cooperation (joint experimental development), science-education integration (driven by scientific research projects and disciplinary competitions), and international exchanges (lectures and exchanges by international experts).

Scenario embedding is designed to combine the idea of collaborative parenting with tailor-made teaching, to provide diversified training modes geared to students' interests and abilities, and to achieve personalized training in the new liberal arts. The core of scenario-embedded teaching is that experimental design, scientific research, school practical training, and competition coaching are used as the process of integrating abilities, empowering students to learn autonomously and choose appropriate learning modes through diverse learning processes.

2.2 Reform Measures

Relying on our university, information management and information system is a national first-class professional construction point, and engineering management is a first-class professional construction point in Hubei Province. Through the top-level design of teaching programs and modes, the development of interdisciplinary knowledge-embedded courses, the optimization and design of integrated scenarios and practical teaching system, and the "embedded-integrated" personalized collaborative education, we promote the construction of new liberal arts majors of government, industry, academia, and research in the field of management.

Top-Level Design of Teaching Programs and Models

To promote the innovation of "embedded-integrated" collaborative education mechanism for management majors, the top-level design of teaching programs and modes is crucial. The key reform initiatives include: (1) optimizing the knowledge structure of the course cluster, designing the professional course/elective course module shared by the two majors, and opening the knowledge system of knowledge-embedded teaching and learning; (2) innovating the design of the teaching system both inside and outside the classroom, designing a new knowledge-embedded carrier, and optimizing the course system of the carrier.

Cross-disciplinary Knowledge-Embedded Curriculum Development

Efforts have been made to develop cross-disciplinary knowledge-embedded courses to open the base point of curriculum integration with two entry points: information system development and data management. Key reform initiatives include: (1) customizing the system development course to embed engineering management cases as the development object; (2) opening a course on data management and application for engineering applications, realizing the sharing of experimental data between the two majors, and focusing on promoting the data management capability of engineering management; (3) exploring the cooperation of the course internship system according to the direction of the major, with a focus on strengthening the data thinking of the engineering industry; (4) exploring the integration of cross-disciplinary courses under the context of academic affairs, guidance, course instructors and student research incentives. Guidance, course instructors, and the context of student research incentives, explore a composite mentoring model for undergraduates that integrates across majors.

Optimization and Design of Integration Scenarios and Practical Teaching System

Taking science and education interaction, industry-academia cooperation, and international exchange as the resource ties, we design the embedded scenarios of digitalization, data, and engineering management in an all-round way, and take the second classroom and practical teaching system as the breakthrough to strengthen the integration and cultivation of abilities. Key reform initiatives include: (1) making full use of the established BIM studio and the college's big data management laboratory, taking the BIM discipline competition as a hand to play the engineering digitalization competition season; (2) establishing a practical innovation platform for school-enterprise cooperation, and gradually developing engineering management virtual simulation and data-based management experimental courses and scenario platforms with independent property rights; (3) cooperating with leading companies in the industry to cooperate in the development of both cognitive, training and management integrated practical training platform and practical training system; (4) Invite academic lectures of famous experts at home and abroad into the classroom to improve students' ability to conduct academic seminars and track the frontier of the industry.

"Embedding and Integrating" Personalized and Collaborative Education

Teaching students according to their needs and personalized cultivation are important concepts in the construction of new liberal arts. The purpose of the "embedded-integrated" collaborative education mechanism is to provide students with cross-disciplinary personalized learning modes, and to continuously iterate and innovate the cultivation mode. Key reform initiatives include: (1) defining the main modes of personalized cultivation in collaborative education, exploring four types of personalized collaborative education modes, namely, learning cycle, competition collaboration, innovation management, and cultivation and upgrading, and setting up differentiated collaborative education guidance modes; (2) for each type of collaborative education modes, setting up key indicators for short-term composite competence cultivation and long-term career growth, and adjusting the extent and means of knowledge embedding and scenario integration to achieve the goal of "embedding-integration" and to achieve the goal of "integrating". The degree and means of scenario integration are dynamically adjusted to realize the dynamic optimization and adjustment of the collaborative education mechanism, thus generating the iteration and self-growth of the teaching reform. Among them, the short-term cultivation of compound ability includes the cultivation of employment skills (in order to improve the short-term employment ability and employment rate of students) and the cultivation of scientific research ability (to strengthen the ability of students to apply what they have learned and postgraduate research ability, and to improve the motivation and success rate of postgraduate study); and the long-term goal is the enhancement of the comprehensive ability in order to create a high-quality comprehensive ability of the graduates and the space for long-term career growth, and to increase the students' influence on the society of their alma mater and the ability to feed the alma mater.

A diagram of the key reform initiatives and implementation pathways is shown in Fig. 2.

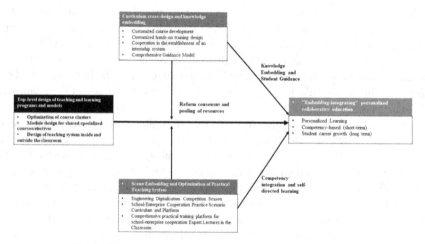

Fig. 2. Key reform initiatives and implementation pathways

3 Conclusion

Under the background of the construction of new liberal arts, this paper has discussed in depth the reform and practice of collaborative cultivation mechanism for the majors of management science to adapt to this trend, we focus on the integrated cultivation mode of management majors, emphasizing the integrated cultivation idea of "strong foundation, broad vision and application", which is of outstanding value for education reform. At the same time, we propose a new liberal arts training model that is adapted to the new liberal arts background and promotes the integration and cultivation of students' abilities in the teaching ecology through the establishment of the concept of "object-tool-activity", and promotes the integration and cultivation of students' abilities in the five aspects of thinking, curriculum, teaching, practice, and scenarios, so as to realize the new model of collaborative education for the personalized cultivation of students. Through the top-level design of teaching programs and models, the development of interdisciplinary knowledge-embedded curricula, the optimization and design of integrated scenarios and practical teaching systems, and the "embedded-integrated" personalized collaborative cultivation, we promote the construction of a new liberal arts major in government, industry, academia, and research for majors in the field of management sciences. Experimental design, scientific research, school practical training, competition coaching, etc., as a process of ability integration, provide conditions for students to choose their own ability cultivation, thus providing a brand-new path to realize personalized cultivation. This reform not only provides a new way of thinking for the development of the major of management science, but also provides a teaching reform model for other majors to explore the integration with digitalization. Through this study, we expect to promote the innovation and development of the education of management major in the context of new liberal arts.

References

1. Lu. X., Wang, D.: Exploring the construction of a high-quality development system for the new liberal arts. Chin. High. Educ. (09), 14–17 (2023)
2. Tian, X., Jiang, S.: The connotation, characteristics, logical evolution and path selection of interdisciplinary collaborative education in the context of the new liberal arts. Educ. Dev. Res. **42**(21), 35–42 (2022)
3. Sheng, S., Qin, Z.: Innovation and practical exploration of the new liberal arts collaborative education system. China Soc. Sci. Daily (007), 05–26 (2022)
4. Loriiv. Designing a model for the new liberal arts Liberal Education. **104**(4), 44–51 (2018)
5. Huang, K., Miao, Z.: A bibliometric analysis of the progress of research on the new liberal arts. New Liber. Arts Theory Pract. **5**(01), 109–123 (2023)
6. Huang, K., Miao, Z.: A bibliometric analysis of the progress of research on the new liberal arts. J. Shandong Univ. (Phil. Soc. Sci. Ed.) **249**(06), 162–171 (2021)
7. Li, G., Li, X., Zhang, X., et al.: Research on the cultivation mode of top innovative talents in management disciplines under the background of the new liberal arts. Tianjin Univ. J. (Soc. Sci. Ed.) **26**(01), 9–16 (2024)
8. Li, Y., Li, F.: Exploration on the cultivation mode of economic and management talents in industry characteristic university based on OBE concept under the new liberal arts. J. Higher Educ. **9**(27), 148–151 (2023)
9. Yu, H., Zhao, J.: Research on the construction of integrated curriculum groups combining data science and management majors in the construction of the new liberal arts. J. Inner Mongolia Finan. Econ. Univ. **21**(05), 1–6 (2023)
10. Ding, Q.: The teaching reform and practice of business administration majors in Northeastern University of Finance and Economics under the background of the new liberal arts. Sci. Vis. (32), 89–91 (2022)
11. Kuang, C.: The reform path and practical requirements of the cultivation mode of new liberal arts talents in Colleges and universities. J. Xinyu Univ. **27**(04), 111–117 (2022)
12. Gong, P., Xiao, T., Sun, J., et al.: The cultivation of engineering management information talents based on knowledge embedding. High. Eng. Educ. Res. **191**(06), 55–61 (2021)

13. Gong, P., Luo, R., Xiong, F., et al.: The reform of BIM practical teaching in engineering management majors based on OBE-CDIO concept. J. Eng. Manag. **34**(03), 153–158 (2020)
14. Chen, C.: The research on knowledge transfer among university research teams from the perspective of knowledge embeddedness. Inf. Sci. (8), 1166–1168 (2009)
15. Xiao, D., Gu, X.: The principle of knowledge embeddedness and the formation of knowledge networks. Inf. Sci. (9), 1311–1317 (2009)

How Review Trust and Digital Reputation Affect Review Adoption: An Expansion of the Elaboration Likelihood Model

Jiali Li[(⊠)] and Liubo Hu

School of Management, Wuhan Donghu University, Wuhan 430212, China
leeqi16@163.com

Abstract. More and more people are getting travel information through various types of travel social sharing platform(TSSP). Digital reputation is an essential trait of social media; the higher the digital reputation, the more likely are TSSP to be trusted by users for social media reviews to be adopted. We used an elaboration likelihood model that measures the impact of peripheral cues (e.g., digital reputation) and corresponding central cues (e.g., review trust) related to social presence on TSSP on travelers' review adoption behavior. We empirically analyzed 539 respondents who adopted travel reviews via TSSP. Our findings suggest that review trust has a positive impact on perceived usefulness, and digital reputation has a positive impact on perceived usefulness. Perceived usefulness has a significant positive effect on travel review adoption. Finally, it was found that TSSP members' perceived level of trust in review and digital reputation varied depending on the level of social presence.

Keywords: Review Trust · Digital Reputation · Review Adoption · Elaboration Likelihood Model · Social Presence

1 Introduction

Similarly to other online market places, the inter-mediation provided by those platforms relies crucially on digital reputation systems based on ratings and reviews voluntarily contributed by users [4]. Through ratings, guests can provide a score for the accommodation and service according to several predefined criteria. Reviews are short, written comments that provide prospective visitors with information about the accommodations, dining, quality of service, and other interactions. This information is crucial for the platform, as we will discuss further in the paper: it builds trust, helps regulate the market, and assists users in deciding whether or not to make a transaction. As such, the review system is neither harmless nor neutral: it influences decisions, impacts prices, provides signals to the platforms' algorithms, creates value, and distributes such value unevenly with remarkable consequences for individuals and places. Social media users reshare (i.e., forward) product information provided by original user-generated product reviews through clippings or provide reviews (i.e., information giving) regarding their usage or experience. Studies have revealed that such a digital reputation has a significant

Y. P. Tu and M. Chi (Eds.): WHICEB 2024, LNBIP 517, pp. 73–84, 2024.
https://doi.org/10.1007/978-3-031-60324-2_7

influence. In IT, a community of practice (CoP) is a group of people informally bound together by shared and distributed information, an example of reciprocal give and take of knowledge sharing [5]. Studies on the influences of digital reputation on social media are being actively conducted in terms of technical adoption [4], information searching and sharing [6], Trust [5], socio-technical approaches [7], information quality, and the influence of the reliability of information sources [10].

A critical characteristic of UGC on social media is that social media generate giving and taking repositories of content as information sharing. However, successful information sharing involves giving and taking. Zhang and Watts (2003, 2008) explained the adoption of advice delivered via email using the theoretical perspective of the dual-process of information processing, a theory of the elaboration likelihood model (ELM) [3]. For this reason, reviews on social media has been proposed as a crucial source for determining tourism decision-making [6]. In other words, it is necessary to consider the taking side (i.e., adoption) of tourism information to understand tourism information search. Therefore, we investigate the travel review adoption of UGC on social media from the viewpoint of the taking side. Drawing on the ELM [3], we compared two alternative influential processes. Reviews trust and digital reputation in motivating the adoption of travel information are moderated through social presence. We also argue that TSSP with a high social presence encourages people to interact more interactively. In short, travel social sharing platform with high-quality review (i.e., review trust) and a high rating scale (i.e., digital reputation) are more likely to lead users to adopt the platform review.

To this end, this study suggests the following research purposes based on the ELM and social influence in adopting travel review. First, to explain the process of travel review adoption of TSSP by users, we set up a study model by applying the ELM, which is explained as two routes of persuasive influences. Second, we intend to examine how the process of information adoption of TSSP by users is affected according to their social presence levels on TSSP. These activities enabled us to empirically analyze the relationships between the factors that affect social media members' travel review adoption according to their social presence levels.

This paper proceeds as follows. We first review the theoretical foundations from previous literature and then advance the research model and hypotheses. Second, we discuss the research methodology, analysis, and results in detail. Finally, we discuss the research findings, limitations, implications, and potential topics for future research.

2 Literature Review and Research Model

2.1 Review Trust

Review trust refers to the persuasive strength of the arguments embedded in an informational message. At the same time, peripheral cues are related to meta-information about the message (e.g., message source) but not the arguments embedded in the message [3]. The relationship between review trust and perceived usefulness has received considerable scholarly attention from the perspective of computer-mediated communication contexts [3]. Bhattacherjee and Sanford (2006) explained how people use the ELM to accept IT, such as a document management system (DMS). They asserted that a vital construct in IT acceptance is usefulness and found that argument quality positively affects the perceived usefulness of DMS [3]. Li (2013) also found a significantly positive relationship between review trust and perceived usefulness in employee information system contexts. In addition, perceived usefulness is considered one of the cognitive responses in the earlier studies [3]. A cognitive response refers to the individual's belief towards a particular object and, thus, represents advantages or advantages, usefulness, ease of use, and need for it [9].

The users exposed to an environment with high-quality and vital information tend to evaluate and think about the information and produce cognitive responses such as whether to perceive the usefulness of the information system [9]. In other words, review trust enhances users' usefulness beliefs regarding information system acceptance and directly affects cognitive judgment [3]. Strong arguments make recipients form a strong attitude regarding the information, and they participate in information activities with cognitive efforts such as carefully scrutinizing and evaluating information (Li, 2013). In this way, high-quality information also enhances an individual's beliefs in the context of information technology acceptance because a strong trust has more influence on their cognitive judgments than affections [3].

Regarding UGC on social media, the travel information adopted among members can be informational. Once the members judge that a specific message is meaningful enough to assist other members – in other words, if the review is high quality – they will perceive that review is a valuable for use. For example, the name of the author who wrote a message, the number of messages that the author has posted, and the number of replies from other members are displayed along with the message, thereby enabling readers to judge the trust of the source, review trust is expected to have a more significant influence on the perceived usefulness of social media. Based on these arguments, we formed the following hypothesis:

H1: The review trust of travel informational messages has a positive effect on members' perceptions of the usefulness of social media.

2.2 Digital Reputation

Digital reputation is that it enforces a system of indirect controls and sanctions for users, which is informal, 'lean,' and extraordinarily cheap [12]. The 'threat' of a negative review encourages hosts and guests to behave well since being reviewed positively is essential to surviving on the platform. From this perspective, a platform like Airbnb may well be considered part of an emerging "surveillance capitalism" that constantly monitors and extracts information from users' interactions not only to monetize them but also to elicit specific behavior [12]. Digital reputation is defined as the extent to which an information source is perceived to be believable, competent, and trustworthy by the information recipient [3]. Digital intermediation platforms have the advantage of allowing for a much richer and more direct flow of information between users but, at the same time, entail problems of trust, reliability, certification, and safety, as they reduce the possibility of hierarchical control and quality assurance. The efforts devoted by OTA platforms to enhancing and communicating a feeling of trust are indeed considerable and the object of a great deal of research. Digital reputation systems act as confidence and responsibility builders; they provide both an augmentation and a certification of the information hosts provide through their listings [15].

In terms of valence, as mentioned above, research shows that 97–98% of social media reviews are positive [13] and that negative experiences are often not reported (Fradkin et al., 2018). Because of this, and given that many platform users do not fully trust the content of reviews [10], their volume may be more critical than their valence. In the context of UGC on social media, perceptions of source credibility play an important role in members' judgments of cognitive authority. Due to celebrity and expert influence on cognitive judgment, such as perceived usefulness, users with high credibility towards the source tend to perceive the usefulness of the information system [3]. Tam and Ho (2005) insisted that people tend to follow rules of thumb and decisions on these rules. In this regard, Bhattacherjee and Sanford (2006) also stated that peripheral cues requiring relatively little effort replace complex cognitive processes and are considered the basis of an information system's usefulness. Thus, digital reputation would be a criterion of users' cognitive judgments. For example, the number of users of the app, e-word of mouth, and app centre rankings so that readers can judge the reliability of the source of information [5]. Li's (2013) study verified the positive effect of digital reputation on a user's cognitive judgments. Therefore, when an information source is credible, the members who adopt the given information will perceive the UGC on social media as a helpful information adoption. Hence, we hypothesize the following:

H2: The digital reputation of travel informational messages has a positive effect on the usefulness of social media.

2.3 Perceived Usefulness

On TSSP, the perceived usefulness can be defined according to how useful it is to adopt the information acquired through UGC on TSSP, with others. Previous studies support that utilitarian considerations (i.e., perceived usefulness) and affective considerations (i.e., attitude) are considered essential predictors and critical determinants of intention [3]. Through UGC on TSSP, social relationships are built by members adopting information from each other (Kim et al., 2011). However, no matter how high the levels of review trust and digital reputation that a specific message has, if the people who intend to adopt the message do not perceive UGC on TSSP, as applicable [3], they will also perceive it as complex to build social relationships with other people by adopting it. TSSP, is defined as a tool that makes users build relationships with known connected or unknown connected people by taking or giving information and, hence, its usefulness information facilitates affective responses and reinforces relationships rigorously with users across the world. Consequently, perceived usefulness can influence the formation of social relationships by mediating review trust and digital reputation.

Further, perceived usefulness is a powerful determinant for building the user's intention to use a new technology or adopt new behavior [3]. Users' performance related to technology is reassured by perceived usefulness (Cheung et al., 2008). If users perceive social media as a helpful space or tool for travel information acquisition, they are more likely to adopt travel information within social media. Hung and Cheng (2013) investigate the relationship between knowledge-sharing intentions and virtual community user perceptions. The study results show that the level of users' perceptions of the usefulness of technology has a positive effect on their intentions to share knowledge in virtual communities. Consequently, the perceived usefulness of UGC on TSSP, leads members to adopt the information. Hence, we propose the following hypotheses:

H3: The perceived usefulness of TSSP, positively affects travel review adoption.

2.4 Moderating the Role of Social Presence

Generally, the ELM theory posits that an informational message is elaborated after the influences of review trust and digital reputation are moderated by the motivation and ability of users. From this point, to measure the latter factors, job relevance or user expertise is generally used as a moderating variable [3]. However, among the members who adopt travel information on UGC on social media, the effects of review trust and digital reputation are influenced by job relevance or user expertise and social presence (Kaplan & Haenlein, 2010). This is because the higher the social presence (e.g., photo, motion, video, etc.), the larger the social influence the social media members have on each other's behavior. Conveying a message varies according to the richness of the information that a member intends to adopt, that is, how a message can be presented and how closely the member exchanges opinions with other members who would use the information. The idea of a social presence is closely related to media richness (Daft & Lengel, 1986). It states that media differ in the degree of richness they possess. That is, rich media (high social presence) enables users to communicate more quickly and effectively than others (low social presence) in resolving ambiguity and uncertainty (Dennis & Kinney, 1998). In addition, Robert and Dennis (2005) indicated that the high-level social presence required by media has less need for the receiver's ability to access the information because receivers are inclined to answer real-time communication quickly. They also insisted that media with a high-level social presence draws more attention to recipients, which helps them form their motivation to react to the message.

On the other hand, receivers using media with low social presence continue thinking or have more time to comprehend the information when they encounter complex, critical, or unimportant information, which is needed for a higher reprocess ability among receivers (Robert & Dennis, 2005). Therefore, in the case of low social presence (low intimacy, low immediacy, and high reprocess ability), such as blogging, the blog (bloggers and readers) has defined interactivity as it is related to the capabilities of a host (blogger) to update the content regularly and also requires blog readers to visit and frequently interact with the site (Hsu & Lin, 2008). Therefore, Mafengwo readers are likely to rely heavily on cognitive judgments rather than heuristic cues in adopting travel information due to their weak interaction with other members, more time, and a higher receiver's reprocess ability of information (Robert & Dennis, 2005). Hence, when blog members are adopting travel information, communication with a higher review trust is likely to engender more information adoption than communication with a lower review trust. Hence, we propose:

H4: Social presence negatively moderates the association between the review trust and the perceived usefulness of social media.

In contrast, in a social media channel with a high social presence, such as Xiaohongshu, its members will share a strong sense of togetherness with other members.

When using a high social presence media, little ability to process information is needed because users respond quickly to the message. Thus, they will rely more heavily on affective and heuristic peripheral cues than relational judgments. Travel information with a high social presence (e.g., photos and videos) allows people to interact more. Xiaohongshu allows its members to communicate detailed and vivid travel information using pictures, videos, and real-time messages. Therefore, these users have less need for and are less likely to consider review trust. In Xiaohongshu environments (mainly friends or friends of friends), digital reputation may directly influence perceived usefulness and social relationships than Mafengwo (e.g., a host blogger and readers), particularly if the posted travel information comes from well-recognized and identified members or trusted travel experts. Based on the above argument, the following hypotheses are proposed:

H5: Social presence positively moderates the association of digital reputation and perceived usefulness of social media.

Based on the ELM and social presence, this study proposed the research model in Fig. 1. The model suggests that the review trust and digital reputation of TSSP are predictors of the members' perceived usefulness. Furthermore, it suggests that the perceived usefulness of TSSP are predictors of the members' travel review adoption. External links attached to the social presence act as a moderating variable.

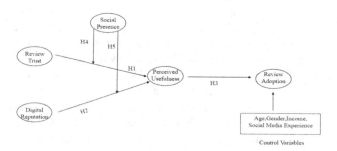

Fig. 1. Research model.

3 Methods

3.1 Measurements

This study's measurements were derived from previous studies about the constructs of review trust, digital reputation, perceived usefulness, and travel review adoption on TSSP. This study adopted multi-measurement items for each construct to overcome the limitations of a single item because a single-item measure is usually particular and thus cannot capture all the attributes of a construct and, consequently, is likely to have a high measurement error rate (Churchill, 1979). Specifically, three review trust items and three digital reputation items associated with review adoption were drawn from previous studies. Three items of the perceived usefulness of TSSP, construct for TSSP, were adopted from previous studies on the use of information technology [1].

Three items were adopted from previous research on information adoption to measure the construct of travel review adoption [1], and the moderator of presence was divided into Mafengwo and Xiaohongshu. These items were measured on a 7-point Likert scale ranging from strongly disagree (1) to agree (7) strongly. Five items related to TSSP (type of TSSP, visiting frequency, time spent, active phase of information adoption, and topic) were generated for general questions. Finally, we added the four demographic variables (see Table 1).

Three academic experts were invited to verify the content validity of the initially generated items. The field experts on TSSP were also asked to indicate whether these measurement items needed to be deleted or reworded and, if necessary, to identify items that should be added. A pretest was also administered to 50 people who had participated in TSSP within the past year. As a result of these three procedures, we decided to delete three of the 12 items generated from the literature mentioned above. Furthermore, ambiguous items associated with digital reputation and perceived usefulness were reworded to ensure clarity.

3.2 Data Collection

We collected data for our study from a top-ranking Internet survey firm Wenjuanxing (www.wjx.cn). This Internet survey firm has a nationwide panel of 650,000 online respondents from whom representative samples are selected. Our study more specifically targeted a sampling group that had focused on the pursuit of travel information more than socialization in TSSP. The Internet survey was collected in June 2023. The participants aged 19 or older who had used social media were primarily screened. For screening, the survey firm selected those who had joined at least one TSSP for travel review adoption during the past year. With this procedure, 539 questionnaires were collected. After checking for outliers, we verified all questionnaires to ensure that the data sets could be coded for analysis. In addition, this study focused on identifying the role of social presence levels of social media and thus divided the respondents based on the study, who insisted that the level of social presence varies with the social media types and indicated that the social presence level of Xiaohongshu is higher than that of Mafengwo. Following this argument, respondents were asked to indicate the most used social media type for travel review adoption: Xiaohongshu or Mafengwo. Based on this question, the respondents were divided into high social presence (Xiaohongshu, N = 299) and low social presence (Mafengwo, N = 240).

Table 1. Demographic characteristics of respondents.

Characteristic		Full group (N = 539)		High social presence group (N = 299)		Low social presence group (N = 240)	
		Frequency	%	Frequency	%	Frequency	%
Gender	Male	232	43.0	110	36.8	122	50.8
	Female	307	57.0	189	63.2	118	49.2
Age	19–29	192	35.6	105	35.1	87	36.3
	30–39	167	31.0	103	34.4	64	26.7
	40–49	93	17.3	58	19.4	35	14.6
	50–59	87	16.1	33	11.0	54	22.5
Education	Middle and high school	86	16.0	47	15.7	39	16.2
	Three years of college	125	23.1	80	26.8	45	18.8
	University	265	49.2	126	42.1	139	57.9
	Graduate school	63	11.7	46	15.4	17	7.1
Occupation	Student	100	18.6	58	19.4	42	17.5
	Office worker	189	35.1	109	36.5	80	33.3
	Services	26	4.8	9	3.0	17	7.1
	Professional	46	8.5	25	8.4%	21	8.8
	Self-employed	48	8.9	28	9.4	20	8.3
	Civil servant	56	10.4	31	10.4	25	10.4
	Homemaker	74	13.7	29	9.7	45	18.8
Monthly income (RMB)	Less than 1000	86	16.0	58	19.4	28	11.7
	1000–3000	96	17.8	49	16.4	47	19.6
	3001–5000	168	31.2	95	31.8	73	30.4
	5001–7000	101	18.7	61	20.4	40	16.7
	More than7000	88	16.3	32	10.7	56	23.3
Type of TTSP	Xiaohongshu	318	59.0	204	114	–	–
	Mafengwo	221	41.0	–	–	106	115

(continued)

Table 1. (*continued*)

Characteristic		Full group (N = 539)		High social presence group (N = 299)		Low social presence group (N = 240)	
		Frequency	%	Frequency	%	Frequency	%
Visiting frequency for tourism review adoption(per week)	Less than one time	69	12.8	30	10.0	39	16.3
	Two times	157	29.1	87	29.1	70	29.2
	Three times	135	25.0	92	30.8	43	17.9
	Four times	35	6.5	16	5.4	19	7.9
	More than five times	143	26.5	62	20.7	81	33.8
Average time spent for each visit	Less than 30 min	93	17.3	52	17.4	41	17.1
	30–1 h	284	52.7	146	48.8	138	57.5
	1–2 h	127	23.6	63	21.1	64	26.7
	More than 2 h	35	6.5	16	5.4	19	7.9
Review adoption phase	Pre-travel	274	50.8	178	59.5	96	40.0
	En-route travel	165	30.6	76	25.4	89	37.1
	Post-travel	100	18.6	55	18.4	45	18.8
Topic	Accommodation	90	16.7	49	16.4	41	17.1
	Attraction	82	15.2	39	13.0	43	17.9
	Destination	78	14.5	32	10.7	46	19.2
	Travel route	82	15.2	37	12.4	45	18.8
	Transportation	75	13.9	30	10.0	45	18.8
	Shopping	25	4.6	13	4.3	12	5.0
	Restaurants	107	19.9	47	15.7	60	25.0
Total		539	100.0	299	100.0	240	100.0

4 Data Analysis and Results

The component-based structural equation modelling technique partial least squares (PLS) was used to evaluate the measurement and structural model. PLS is advantageous because it can work with nominal, ordinal, and interval scaled variables, and makes minimal demands on normal distribution [8].

SmartPLS 3.0 was used in our study as it is preferable for detecting between-group differences when data are non-normally distributed and is best suited for predicting a set of dependent variables from a large set of independent variables.

4.1 Confirmatory Factor Analysis

The composite reliability and Cronbach's α for all constructs exceeded 0.7. Finally, the AVE for each construct was more significant than 0.5. Therefore, the convergent validity of the constructs was supported.

The discriminant validity of the measurement model was verified by comparing the square root of the AVE for each construct with the correlations among the constructs. If the square root of the AVE were more significant than the correlations among the constructs, then this outcome would indicate the discriminant validity of the model (Fornell & Larcker, 1981). As shown in Table 2, the square root of the AVE for each construct exceeded the correlations among the constructs. Therefore, discriminant validity was established.

4.2 Hypothesis Testing – Main Effects

We examined the structural model based on the measurement model to investigate the main effects. The maximum likelihood estimates for the various overall fit parameters.

The squared multiple correlations (R^2: coefficient of determinant) for the structural equations for perceived usefulness, and travel review adoption are shown in Fig. 2. For perceived usefulness, 48.1% of the variance was explained by the direct effects of review trust and digital reputation. Additionally, 42.0% of the variance in travel review adoption was explained by the direct effects of perceived usefulness.

H1–H3 post the structural relationships among argument quality. Review trust had a positive effect on perceived usefulness ($\beta = 0.212$, t-value $= 3.103$) with statistical significance at the $p < 0.01$ level; thus, this result supports H1. The significant positive effect of digital reputation on perceived usefulness supports H2 ($\beta = 0.353$, t-value $= 6.486$, $p < .001$). In addition, perceived usefulness also positively affects travel review ($\beta = 0.566$, t-value $= 12.444$, $p < .01$), supporting H3.

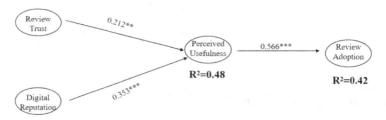

Fig. 2. Estimated model

4.3 Hypothesis Testing – Moderating Effects

We present the moderating effect of social presence and analyze the remaining hypotheses, H4–H5. To compare the research model across social presence groups, we conducted a multi-group analysis using SmartPLS 3.0 by comparing differences in the coefficients of the corresponding structural paths of the two research models. The results indicated that the coefficients from each path among review trust, digital reputation, and perceived usefulness for the high and low social presence groups significantly differed from their corresponding coefficients in the structural model.

In the case of H4, review trust more significantly affected perceived usefulness in the low social presence group (high social presence group:0.042 < low social presence group:0.335, t-value $= -1.931$). In the case of H5, digital reputation more significantly affected perceived usefulness in the high social presence group (high social presence group:0.627 > low social presence group: 0.371,t-value $= 1.879$,). Therefore, the results supported H4 and H5.

5 Discussion and Conclusion

In this study, the factors that affect travel review adoption on TSSP vary according to the level of social presence, and they were analyzed empirically based on the ELM theory. According to the analysis results, H1–H3were supported, verifying all the theoretical arguments established by this study. Moreover, according to the analysis of the moderating effects of social presence, all the hypotheses were supported. Theoretically, our research model provided by the ELM variables (review trust and digital reputation) can be applied to the issue of information adoption on TSSP and the tourism context. In recent literature, Tang, Jang, and Morrison (2012) employed the ELM theory to destination websites. Lee, Reid, and Kim (2014) investigated travelers' intention to share knowledge and found that information-seeking and relationship-building displayed different sharing structures through the identification process. In sum, our research elaborates on TSSP as a persuasive tool in the period of social networking for review adoption based on the ELM theory, depending on the level of social presence.

The study shows that the central and peripheral routes' roles differ based on the social presence level within TSSP. This result is a significant contribution to the field, as it combines the concept of social presence with the present ELM, which has yet to be previously reviewed. In practical terms, this study exhibited the need to employ the findings that the information processing methods of TSSP members would differ according to the social presence levels of media types. In other words, in social media types with low social presence, such as blogs, their members are more likely to make cognitive judgments (Robert & Dennis, 2005), and thus, these media types need to be more substantial in content. Furthermore, in business terms, tourism marketers using such media types should distribute rich content to promote their tourism products, destinations, and attractions to secure stable visiting numbers. In addition, TSSP which want to attract and maintain their readership should provide travel information with rich content.

This study highlights the limitations of using TSSP for review adoption in China, despite its classification as a TSSP with different social presence. Additionally, the study only considered the axis of social presence between the two dimensions of social media proposed by Kaplan and Haenlein (2010). Future studies should review the results of this study in relation to the other axis of self-presentation/self-disclosure.

In summary, this study aims to enhance TSSP, a crucial online travel information source, by providing insights into the factors that affect the adoption of travel information through TSSP. It is important to note that beyond social presence, other differences such as information type, social capital, and member attachment should also be considered.

Acknowledgement. This research was supported by the Youth Foundation Project of Wuhan Donghu University (2023dhsk003) and Party Building - Ideological - Political Work Research Center Project of Private Universities (DJSZY23010).

References

1. Angst, C.M., Agarwal, R.: Adoption of electronic health records in the presence of privacy concerns: the elaboration likelihood model and individual persuasion. MIS Q. **33**(2), 339–370 (2009)
2. Arbuckle, J.L.: Analysis of Moment Structures AMOS (Version 18.0). SPSS, Chicago (2009)
3. Bhattacharjee, A., Sanford, C.: Influence processes for information technology acceptance: an elaboration likelihood model. MIS Q. **30**(4), 805–825 (2006)
4. Celata, F., Capineri, C., Romano, A.: A room with a (re) view. Short-term rentals, digital reputation, and the uneven spatiality of platform-mediated tourism. Geoforum **112**, 129–138 (2020)
5. Chai, S., Kim, M.: What makes bloggers share knowledge? an investigation on the role of trust. Int. J. Inf. Manag. **30**(5), 408–415 (2010)
6. Cheung, C.M.K., Lee, M.K.O., Rabjohn, N.: The impact of electronic word-of-mouth: the adoption of online opinions in online customer communities. Internet Res. **18**(3), 229–247 (2008)
7. Chu, S.-C., Kim, Y.: Determinants of consumer engagement in electronic word-of-mouth (eWOM) in social networking sites. Int. J. Advert. **30**(1), 47–75 (2011)
8. Chin, W.W., Marcolin, B.L., Newsted, P.R.: A partial least squares latent variable modeling approach for measuring interaction effects: results from a monte carlo simulation study and an electronic-mail emotion/adoption study. Inf. Syst. Res. **14**(2), 189–217 (2003)
9. Davis, F.D.: Perceived usefulness, perceived ease of use, and user acceptance of information technology. MIS Q. **13**(3), 319–340 (1989)
10. Gretzel, U., Yoo, K.H.: Use and impact of online travel reviews. In: O'Connor, P., Höpken, W., Gretzel, U. (eds.) Information and Communication Technologies in Tourism 2008, pp. 35–46. Springer Vienna, Vienna (2008). https://doi.org/10.1007/978-3-211-77280-5_4
11. Hair, J.F., Jr., Black, W.C., Babin, B.J., Anderson, R.E., Tatham, R.L.: Multivariate Data Analysis, 6th edn. Pearson Prentice Hall, Upper Saddle River (2006)
12. Inversini, A.: Reputation in travel and tourism: a perspective article. Tour. Rev. **75**(1), 310–313 (2020)
13. Kushcheva, N., Eilola, T.M.: Relevance of social media management in online reputation building in tourism and hospitality: case of Finland. In Online Reputation Management in Destination and Hospitality: What We Know, What We Need to Know, pp. 163–174. Emerald Publishing Limited (2023)
14. Petty, R.E., Cacioppo, J.T.: Communication and Persuasion: Central and Peripheral Routes to Attitude Change. Springer, New York (1986). https://doi.org/10.1007/978-1-4612-4964-1
15. Yaşarsoy, E., Çalişkan, G., Pamukçu, H.: The place and importance of digital reputation management in tourism establishments. Revista Turismo Desenvolvimento **39**, 41–63 (2022)

An Empirical Study on the Spillover Effect of Monetary Incentives on Physicians' Free Knowledge Contribution Behaviors in Online Healthcare Communities

Xuchen Fang[1], Pei Yin[1,2]($\boxtimes$), and Han Yan[1]

[1] University of Shanghai for Science and Technology, Shanghai 200093, China
pyin@usst.edu.cn
[2] School of Intelligent Emergency Management, University of Shanghai for Science and Technology, Shanghai 200093, China

Abstract. Online medical communities often rely on paid online consultations to encourage physicians to provide higher-quality medical expertise, fostering the community's sustainable development. However, the impact of this monetary incentive on physicians' contributions of free knowledge remains uncertain. To address this question, we empirically examine how the introduction of monetary incentives within a healthcare community influences physicians' voluntary knowledge contributions through a natural experiment. Combining propensity score matching with staggered difference-in-differences estimation methods, we find that monetary incentives have a positive and short-term effect on the quantity and quality of physicians' unpaid online contributions. Moreover, our analysis reveals that this positive impact is more pronounced and enduring among physicians in departments which are less suitable for online consultations. Concerning physician titles, the positive spillover effect is more significant for associate and junior physicians compared to chief physicians. In conclusion, our study suggests that monetary incentives are effective in stimulating physicians' free knowledge contribution in the short term. For the long term, tailoring incentives to each department's specific characteristics can be beneficial, especially for physicians who have already established a strong online reputation.

Keywords: Online Healthcare Communities · Monetary Incentives · Physicians' Free Knowledge Contribution Behaviors · Spillover Effect · Natural Experiment

1 Introduction

Online health communities have become prevalent means for public health information access. However, patient-driven social communities often contend with low-quality user contributions, leading to problems like data redundancy and misinformation, impeding patients' accurate comprehension of health issues [1]. In contrast, physician-led healthcare communities offer a more dependable solution. These communities not only integrate medical resources and improve physician-patient communication but also provide a reliable platform for patients to access and share authentic health information, particularly concerning chronic diseases [2]. Consequently, physician-led online healthcare communities have become essential platforms for individuals in search of reliable health knowledge and services.

For the sustainable development of physician-led online healthcare communities, it is crucial to motivate physicians to consistently deliver high-quality medical expertise. Typically, these incentives come in the form of paid online consultations [3]. These paid contributions, initiated by patients and provided reactively by physicians, often involve one-on-one interactions, limiting the broader dissemination of knowledge. On the contrary, physicians voluntarily share free articles online to promote health awareness, catering to a wider audience and integrating various patient concerns with their specialized knowledge.

Despite the crucial role of free knowledge contributions in facilitating patients' access to health information, existing research highlights a significant gap. Few studies differentiate between paid and unpaid contributions by physicians, and the impact of monetary incentives designed to promote paid contributions on physicians' unpaid contributions remains uncertain. Most scholars who make such distinctions in this field tend to focus on paid contributions, examining the external financial incentives associated with knowledge payment [4], and analyzing the motivations influencing physicians' engagement in either paid or unpaid contributions [5, 6].

This paper aims to bridge this research gap by exploring the spillover effect of monetary incentives on physicians' free knowledge contributions in online healthcare communities. Specifically, it addresses the following research questions:

(1) Does the introduction of monetary incentives have a spillover effect on physicians' free knowledge contribution behaviors?
(2) If such a spillover effect exists, how long does it work?
(3) Furthermore, does the spillover effect vary among different groups of physicians, such as those from different departments or with different titles?

2 Literature Review and Theoretical Background

2.1 Physicians' Knowledge Contributions in Online Healthcare Communities

Knowledge contribution in online communities refers to the behavior where users share their knowledge with others in the community, including activities such as sharing ideas, expertise, or assisting in problem-solving [7]. In online health communities, while non-professionals often provide personal experiences and emotional support, motivated by reciprocity, altruism and empathy, professionals typically contribute accurate medical information and treatment advice, driven by reputation and knowledge self-efficacy [8].

In the physician-led online healthcare communities involving both patients and physicians, physicians are the primary contributors of knowledge, with patients or other health information seekers as receivers. The concept of physicians' knowledge contribution encompasses all participatory behaviors, including different forms of consultation services and posting articles online. Consultation services are generally compensated, whereas most of articles are voluntary. Some scholars distinguished between paid and unpaid knowledge contributions by physicians in these communities. Their findings indicate that paid contributions are driven by extrinsic motivation, enjoyment, and professional motivation [5], and professional motivation has a stronger positive effect on the unpaid contributions than material motivation for physicians with high professional and online expertise [6].

2.2 Monetary Incentives and Physicians' Knowledge Contributions

Monetary incentives are commonly used to motivate user contributions in online knowledge communities. Currently, enterprises primarily use internet tools and communities to monetize knowledge by offering products and services, such as paid consultation between doctors and patients on online medical platforms and paid answers between users in Q&A communities. Existing studies on the indirect effect of monetary incentives on free knowledge contribution mainly focus on other types of online knowledge platforms, such as online Q&A communities. For instance, Kuang [9] find that monetary incentives for paid knowledge-sharing activities have a positive effect on motivational participation and spillover into non-motivational online participation behaviors. The spillover effect refers to the impact an organization has on individuals or society outside of the organization when conducting an activity.

Some scholars have verified that the introduction of monetary incentives has a spillover effect on free knowledge contributions in online Q&A communities and they suggest that the underlying mechanism is reputation building [10].

2.3 Motivation Theories Related to Physicians' Knowledge Contribution

As mentioned above, the potential motivations for online knowledge contributions by physicians include material, reputation, professional and interest motivation. These motivations can be further understood from the perspective of self-determination theory, a motivation theory about human behavior proposed by American scholars Deci and Ryan (1975). This theory classifies motivation into intrinsic and extrinsic groups based on the degree of self-determination. The former stems from an individual's autonomy of interest needs, while the latter emphasizes that an individual's actions originate from an external stimulus, often in order to obtain external rewards or to avoid punishment. The concepts of intrinsic and extrinsic motivation have been widely applied in studies of user online participation behavior, such as in the exploration of extrinsic versus intrinsic rewards for online reviews [11].

2.4 Literature Review

Prior research on physicians' knowledge contributions focuses on the motivations behind contributions, with few differentiating between paid and unpaid contributions. Moreover, fewer studies examine the indirect impact of monetary incentives for a compensated activity on users' contribution to another activity for free. In related contexts, such as online Q&A platforms, monetary incentives have shown to have spillover effects on users' unpaid participation behavior. Similarly, in online healthcare communities, physicians' behavior is driven by both internal and external motivations. Therefore, based on motivation theory, monetary incentives may indirectly influence physicians' free knowledge contributions in online healthcare communities through a spillover effect.

3 Hypotheses Development

Drawing from existing theories and previous studies, since the paid contribution and the free contribution are two distinct types of knowledge contribution behaviors, the introduction of monetary incentives may yield two contrasting effects on free knowledge contributions: a positive spillover effect, where a complementary effect exists between paid and free knowledge contributions, and a negative spillover effect, where a substitution effect exists between the two.

The negative spillover effect of monetary incentives on free knowledge contributions may arise from two underlying mechanisms. First, the introduction of monetary incentives in the community leads to an increase in paid contributions. The online resource model suggests that, as contributors shift their focus towards compensated activities, the resources previously allocated for free contributions are reduced, resulting a substitution effect. Second, introducing monetary incentives may cause active contributors to perceive that their pro-social behaviors convert to exchange behaviors, leading to a reduction in their online engagement [12]. Similarly, physicians driven by altruism to make free knowledge contributions may reduce their pro-social behaviors when financial incentives are introduced.

On the contrary, monetary incentives can positively influence physicians' free knowledge contributions for several reasons. Firstly, according to signaling theory, free contributions in Q&A communities, such as educational articles on medical topics, can enhance a physician's reputation, leading to higher earnings and audience growth [10]. Secondly, an increase in the number of offline patients that physicians serve may lead to a higher quantity of articles shared online despite resource constraints [13]. Similarly, a portion of the demand and content of physicians' free knowledge contributions comes from their involvement in paid ones. As the number of paid consultations increases, physicians gain a deeper understanding of patient needs and accumulate practical experience, which form the foundation for their voluntary articles and strengthen their pro-social motivation to help and educate patients. Therefore, a larger volume of paid knowledge contributions may actually lead to more free contributions although there seems to be a crowd-out effect. Third, the trust and recognition physicians perceive from patients' choices can enhance their self-efficacy and reciprocal motivation [14], which may lead to an increase in the volume of free contributions. Fourth, monetary incentives, by raising the number of paid services online, urge physicians to devote more time to the online healthcare community, which may subsequently facilitate additional activities. Creating a positive spillover effect on free knowledge contributions. Lastly, given the limited opportunities for physicians to actively publish contents in the community, articles may serve as a channel to promote services, such as paid consultations.

In summary, the introduction of monetary incentives indirectly influences physicians' free knowledge contributions online. We propose the following hypotheses:

H1: There is a spillover effect of monetary incentives on the quantity of physicians' free knowledge contributions online.

In this paper, the free knowledge contribution by physicians online exemplified by the posting of free medical popular science articles. To capture the impacts of monetary incentives, social norms, and their combined influence on consumers' motivation, Burtch [15] analyzed online reviews using two metrics: the quantity and length. Wang [10] defined the quality of users' free knowledge contributions in the online Q&A community by the average number of characters per answer and the average number of vote-up within a certain period. Building on these methodologies, we plan to measure the quality of physicians' articles by both the number of characters and patient-perceived usefulness. Accordingly, the following hypotheses are proposed.

H2: There is a spillover effect of monetary incentives on the quality of physicians' free knowledge contributions online.

H2a: There is a spillover effect of monetary incentives on the number of characters of physicians' free knowledge contributions online.

H2b: There is a spillover effect of monetary incentives on the patient-perceived usefulness of physicians' free knowledge contributions online.

4   Research Method

4.1   Context and Data

Our empirical setting is Haodf.com, a leading online healthcare community in China. This platform provides services including online medical consultations, appointment referrals, medical information inquiries, and the dissemination of medical knowledge. In November 2016, Haodf launched a subscription-based service named "Private Doctor," which offers personalized one-on-one consultations, maintaining a stable relationship between patients and physicians within a specific period.

We selected physicians from 16 representative departments on the platform and then developed a Python crawler to obtain their data of individual profiles and historical online activities from May 1, 2016 to October 31, 2017. We filtered physicians who had registered online prior to 2017 and matched the collected data with these the platform provided based on physicians' attributed information. Then, we complied a sample of 11,703 physicians, among which 314 physicians were identified as "Private Doctor" from November 2016 to April 2017 by searching for consultations and articles using the keyword of "private doctor". The dataset encompasses the following fields: ① publication date, content and number of "Helpful" received for the free educational articles on medical topics published by the doctor. ② dates of "Private Doctor" behaviors. ③ gender, physician title, department, registration date, hospital ranking and the city of the hospital's location. ④ dates of consultations. These data points are linked via the unique identifiers of physicians. For the subsequent estimation, we constructed a panel dataset with physicians as the cross-sectional unit and months as the time unit.

Given that some variables are highly skewed, we applied a transformation, $\ln(x + 1)$, in the main analysis to minimize the excessive effect of outliers. Definitions of the main variables and their descriptive statistics are presented in Table 1.

Table 1. The main variables and their descriptive statistics

Variable	Description	MEAN	SD	MIN	MAX
ArticleNum_i,t	The quantity of free knowledge contributions. The count of articles contributed by physician i in period t	.06	.28	.00	4.76
ArticleChar_avg_i,t	The quality (number of characters) of free knowledge contributions. The average number of characters per article contributed by physician i in period t	.34	1.50	.00	9.95
HelpNum_i,t	The quality (patient-perceived usefulness) of free knowledge contributions. The count of "Help" received by physician i for contributing articles in period t	.07	.41	.00	7.47
Post_i,t	A dummy variable indicating whether physician i has initiated the "Private Doctor" service by period t (1 if yes, 0 if no)	.01	.09	.00	1.00
OrderNum_i,t −1	The count of paid consultations received by physician i in period t−1	.18	.57	.00	5.83

4.2 Identification Strategy

To identify the spillover effect of monetary incentives on physicians' free knowledge contributions in online healthcare communities, we select the "Private Doctor" service as a monetary incentive and voluntary text articles as the indicator of physicians' online free knowledge contributions, and employ a staggered difference-in-differences (DID) approach, a quasi-experimental design, with data from six months before and after the official service release. The individual shock point is the date when physicians initiate the service. The control group includes individuals who had not yet initiated the service during the experimental period.

However, there could be a self-selection bias leading to an endogeneity problem, as the decision to start the "Private Doctor" service and contribute free articles may be affected by physicians' individual characteristics. To address this issue, we utilize propensity score matching (PSM) to construct comparable treatment and control groups, thereby minimizing differences in the physicians' characteristics between the two groups. The covariates selected for this paper encompass three aspects of physicians' background: personal, online experience, and offline experience. Time-varying variables are derived from the cross-sectional data for November 2016. Ultimately, based on the matching weights retained for the subsequent estimation, our sample consists of 1,604 physicians, with 314 individuals in the treatment group.

The matching process in this study involves several steps. Initially, we estimate the propensity score using a Logit model. Subjects are then randomly reordered and matched in a 1:5 ratio within a 0.05 caliper. The quality of matching is assessed through common support and balance tests. The common support test indicates that the propensity scores of 314 treated physicians and 11,274 out of 11,389 untreated individuals fall within the common value range. Post-matching, the covariate standardized deviation between treatment and control groups is below 10%, indicating the suitability of our variable selection and matching method. Consequently, our final sample for subsequent analysis comprises 1,604 physicians, including 314 in the treatment group (details are reported in the Appendix 1).

4.3 The Empirical Model

We use a staggered DID model with both time and individual effects fixed, as following:

$$y_{it} = \beta_0 + \beta_1 * Post_{it} + \beta_2 * OrderNum_{i,t-1} + \mu_i + \gamma_t + \varepsilon_{it} \tag{1}$$

where y_{it} denotes the quantity or quality of physician i's free knowledge contribution in period t, including $ArticleNum_{it}$, $ArticleChar\_avg_{it}$ and $HelpNum_{it}$. $Post_{it}$ is a dummy variable indicating whether physician i has already started the "Private Doctor" service by period t. The control variable $OrderNum_{i,t-1}$ denotes the volume of physician i's paid orders in period t−1. μ_i captures individual-level fixed effects, γ_t captures time-level fixed effects. According to the staggered DID model, β_1 captures the treatment effect of monetary incentives on physicians' free knowledge contributions in online healthcare communities.

5 Empirical Results

5.1 Main Results

Table 2 reports the estimation of the treatment effect according to Eq. (1). Column (1) of Table 2 presents the regression results for the matched samples with the quantity of contributions as the dependent variable. The coefficient of 'Post' free educational articles on medical topics is positive and statistically significant, indicating that there is a positive spillover effect of monetary incentives on the quantity of physicians' free knowledge contributions in online healthcare communities. **This finding supports Hypothesis 1 (H1).**

Column (2) and (3) of Table 2 present estimation results with the quality of contributions as the dependent variables, including the average number of characters per article and the number of "Helpful" received. The coefficients of 'Post' in both columns are positive and statistically significant, indicating that monetary incentives have a positive spillover effect on the quality of physicians' online free knowledge contributions. Hence, **Hypothesis 2 (H2) is supported.**

Table 2. The main result

PSM weighted matching	(1)	(2)	(3)
	ArticleNum	ArticleChar_avg	HelpNum
Post	0.127***	0.577***	0.126***
	(2.94)	(3.31)	(2.96)
OrderNum	0.077***	0.455***	0.080*
	(2.99)	(2.88)	(1.86)
Constant	0.049***	0.291***	0.049***
	(3.47)	(4.59)	(2.73)
Observations	19,248	19,248	19,248
R-squared	0.401	0.341	0.200
Number of clusters	1604	1604	1604
Doctor FE	YES	YES	YES
Month FE	YES	YES	YES

Note: Robust t-statistics in parentheses. *** $p < 0.01$, ** $p < 0.05$, * $p < 0.1$

5.2 Robustness Checks

We conduct a series of robustness checks based on the model assumptions and model uncertainties, such as event study, placebo test and homogeneity treatment effect. After all the tests, we find that the results are robust (details are reported in the Appendix 2).

6 Empirical Extension

6.1 Heterogenous Analysis

Department. We categorize the sample into two groups based on the physicians' departments. Sample 1 comprises departments associated with chronic diseases, which carry a lower risk and necessitate ongoing communication between physicians and patients, such as Cardiology. These departments are well-suited for online consultations. Sample 2 includes departments that are less suitable for online services. We repeat the estimation for the two groups, respectively and present the results in Table 3. Column (1) and (4) of Table 3 indicate that the positive spillover effects of monetary incentives on the quantity of free knowledge contributions exist regardless of departmental affiliation of the physicians.

Column (2), (3), (5) and (6) of Table 3 report the results regarding the quality of free knowledge contributions. We find that monetary incentives positively influence the average number of characters per article for physicians in both Sample 1 and Sample 2. However, the effect of monetary incentives on the perceived usefulness of the articles is only significant for physicians in Sample 2. This outcome may be attributed to the fact that physicians in Sample 1 already had a relatively high volume of online paid consultations, and thus the introduction of "private doctors" as a marketing approach has marginal impact on them. In contrast, physicians in Sample 2 who initially had fewer online paid consultations, have a greater need to actively contribute free articles to get more public attention, build their reputation and subsequently attract more paid consultations.

Table 3. The result of Heterogeneity in Physician departments

PSM weighted matching	Sample 1			Sample 2		
	(1)	(2)	(3)	(4)	(5)	(6)
	ArticleNum	ArticleChar_avg	HelpNum	ArticleNum	ArticleChar_avg	HelpNum
Post	0.105**	0.589***	0.032	0.149**	0.610**	0.200***
	(2.02)	(3.21)	(0.76)	(2.37)	(2.29)	(3.02)
OrderNum	0.018	0.116	0.006	0.153***	0.881***	0.180**
	(0.84)	(1.15)	(0.15)	(3.56)	(3.14)	(2.47)
Constant	0.052***	0.279***	0.078***	0.044**	0.288***	0.025
	(3.22)	(4.52)	(5.69)	(2.20)	(3.07)	(0.93)
Observations	11,184	11,184	11,184	8,064	8,064	8,064
R-squared	0.320	0.341	0.196	0.452	0.354	0.220
Number of cluster	932	932	932	672	672	672
Doctor FE	YES	YES	YES	YES	YES	YES
Month FE	YES	YES	YES	YES	YES	YES

Note: Robust t-statistics in parentheses. *** p < 0.01, ** p < 0.05, * p < 0.1

Titles. We classify the sample into two groups based on the rank of physicians' title. Sample 1 comprises chief physicians and Sample 2 includes associate physicians and others. We repeat the estimation for the two groups and present the results in Table 4. The result indicates that the positive spillover effects of monetary incentives on the quantity and quality of free knowledge contributions exist regardless of whether the contributors hold the title of chief physician. Moreover, the coefficients of 'Post' free medical popular science articles suggest that monetary incentives have a greater positive spillover effect on free knowledge contribution for contributors whose title is not chief physician.

6.2   Long-Term Effect

In this section, we explore the spillover effect of monetary incentives on physicians' free knowledge contributions from a long-term perspective. Our long panel, spanning from May 1, 2016, to October 31, 2017, encompasses one year after the launch of the "Private Doctor" service. We divide the timeframe into four periods of three months each [10]. Considering the intensity effect of multiple service behaviors, we define a new treatment group consisting of physicians who initiated the service in the first period and engaged in only one service activity throughout the entire year. The new control

Table 4. The result of Heterogeneity in physician titles

PSM weighted matching	Sample 1			Sample 2		
	(1)	(2)	(3)	(4)	(5)	(6)
	ArticleNum	ArticleChar_avg	HelpNum	ArticleNum	ArticleChar_avg	HelpNum
Post	0.104**	0.474***	0.081**	0.196*	0.892**	0.219**
	(2.57)	(3.03)	(2.08)	(1.88)	(2.14)	(2.38)
OrderNum	0.060*	0.344*	0.062	0.078**	0.540**	0.106*
	(1.94)	(1.77)	(1.03)	(1.97)	(2.23)	(1.77)
Constant	0.038**	0.204***	0.035*	0.073***	0.476***	0.079**
	(2.46)	(3.06)	(1.70)	(2.67)	(3.70)	(2.42)
Observations	13,380	13,380	13,380	5,868	5,868	5,868
R-squared	0.454	0.361	0.236	0.343	0.329	0.183
Number of cluster	1115	1115	1115	489	489	489
Doctor FE	YES	YES	YES	YES	YES	YES
Month FE	YES	YES	YES	YES	YES	YES

Note: Robust t-statistics in parentheses. *** p < 0.01, ** p < 0.05, * p < 0.1

group is composed of physicians never starting the service at any point during the year. After PSM, the treatment group includes 116 physicians and the control group includes 506 physicians.

Based on the canonical DID model, our new model specification is

$$y_{it} = \beta_0 + \beta_1 * Treat_i * After1_t + \beta_2 * Treat_i * After2_t + \beta_3 * Treat_i * After3_t + \beta_4 * Treat_i * After4_t + \mu_i + \gamma_t + \varepsilon_{it} \qquad (2)$$

where $After1_t$ equals one in the first three-month period after the cutoff date, $After2_t$ equals one in the second three-month period after the cutoff date, and so on. In this specification, β_1 captures the short-term treatment effect. β_2, β_3 and β_4 capture the long-term treatment effect in their respective periods.

The estimation results are shown in Table 5. Column (1) of Table 5 indicates that the positive spillover effect of monetary incentives on the quantity of physicians' free knowledge contributions decays by the time. As for the quality, column (2) of Table 5 indicates that the effect on the average number of characters per article presents the same trend as the quantity. Column (3) of Table 5 suggests that there is no long-term effect on the perceived usefulness of contributions.

Next, we add the factor of physicians' department and explore whether the long-term effect varies among departments. As the analysis conducted in Sect. 6.1, we divide the sample into two groups by physicians' department and repeat the estimation. Table 6 presents the empirical results, indicating that there is a long-term effect for physicians whose department is less suitable for online services. This finding is consistent with the results of the heterogenous analysis.

Table 5. The result of long-term effect

PSM weighted matching	(1)	(2)	(3)
	ArticleNum	ArticleChar_avg	HelpNum
Treati * *After*_1t	0.208***	1.115***	0.144***
	(3.54)	(4.06)	(2.93)
Treati * *After*_2t	0.089**	0.425*	0.053
	(2.14)	(1.88)	(1.12)
Treati * *After*_3t	0.025	0.129	0.026
	(1.02)	(0.69)	(0.52)
Treati * *After*_4t	0.045	0.196	0.009
	(1.51)	(1.15)	(0.18)
Constant	0.035*	0.258**	0.065**
	(1.73)	(2.10)	(2.40)
Observations	11,196	11,196	11,196
R-squared	0.304	0.328	0.199
Number of cluster	622	622	622
Doctor FE	YES	YES	YES
Month FE	YES	YES	YES

Note: Robust t-statistics in parentheses. *** $p < 0.01$, ** $p < 0.05$, * $p < 0.1$

Table 6. The result of long-term effect between different departments

PSM weighted matching	Sample 1			Sample 2		
	(1)	(2)	(3)	(4)	(5)	(6)
	ArticleNum	ArticleChar_avg	HelpNum	ArticleNum	ArticleChar_avg	HelpNum
$Treat_i$ * $After1_t$	0.158***	0.802***	0.074	0.257**	1.439***	0.222***
	(3.21)	(3.08)	(1.23)	(2.52)	(3.15)	(2.94)
$Treat_i$ * $After2_t$	0.024	0.094	−0.023	0.148**	0.761***	0.129**
	(0.60)	(0.30)	(−0.31)	(2.18)	(2.63)	(2.58)
$Treat_i$ * $After3_t$	−0.020	−0.273	−0.087	0.074**	0.572***	0.140***
	(−0.62)	(−0.95)	(−1.15)	(2.00)	(2.77)	(2.66)
$Treat_i$ * $After4_t$	−0.022	−0.180	−0.072	0.117**	0.610***	0.099
	(−0.74)	(−0.64)	(−0.96)	(2.36)	(3.56)	(1.59)
Constant	0.057***	0.438**	0.107**	0.012	0.057	0.019
	(2.81)	(2.57)	(2.40)	(0.37)	(0.37)	(0.72)
Observations	6,966	6,966	6,966	4,230	4,230	4,230
R-squared	0.318	0.288	0.181	0.313	0.384	0.239
Number of cluster	387	387	387	235	235	235
Doctor FE	YES	YES	YES	YES	YES	YES
Month FE	YES	YES	YES	YES	YES	YES

Note: Robust t-statistics in parentheses. *** $p < 0.01$, ** $p < 0.05$, * $p < 0.1$

7 Discussion and Conclusions

In this study, we explore how monetary incentives influence physicians' voluntary contributions to online healthcare communities, specifically focusing on hdf.com. Our analysis reveals that these incentives initially enhance both the quantity and quality of physicians' free contributions. This includes an increase in the number of medical popular science articles, the average article length, and their perceived usefulness by patients. The impact is notably more pronounced and enduring among physicians from departments less conducive to online consultations. Additionally, the positive spillover effect is more significant in associate and junior physicians than in chief physicians. This trend likely stems from physicians using these free educational articles as a strategy to garner attention and establish their professional reputation.

7.1 Theoretical Contribution

This paper makes two key theoretical contributions. Firstly, it enhances our understanding of the impact of monetary incentives on physicians' online contributions by addressing a gap in existing research. Prior studies have not adequately distinguished between paid and unpaid contributions or explored the direct and indirect financial impacts. Our research differentiates these contribution types and investigates how monetary incentives for paid activities influence unpaid contributions. We also refine the assessment of contribution quality by including metrics such as article length and patient-perceived usefulness. Secondly, the study expands the limited body of literature on the lasting effects of monetary incentives. Within the healthcare context, we analyze the prolonged spillover effect of these incentives, considering variations across different physician groups.

7.2 Management Insights

This study provides valuable insights for managing online healthcare communities. Firstly, it confirms the efficacy of monetary incentives. However, these incentives are primarily short-term motivators, highlighting the need for alternative strategies to sustain community development, especially for physicians with established online reputations. Secondly, special consideration should be given to physicians from departments less suited for online services. Facilitating their active participation and customizing services to department-specific needs could yield significant benefits.

7.3 Limitations and Future Research Directions

This study has certain limitations. Firstly, while it accounts for departmental and positional heterogeneity among physicians, it overlooks their online characteristics. Future research should incorporate factors like patient ratings to deepen understanding of the dynamics in online communities. Secondly, our assessment of article quality, based solely on character count and votes, is narrow. Future studies could benefit from including additional dimensions such as readability and thematic analysis for a more holistic evaluation.

Acknowledgement. This research was supported by Shanghai Philosophy and Social Science Planning Project under Grant 2022ZGL010.

Appendix 1 PSM

The covariates selected for this paper encompass three aspects of physicians' background: personal, online experience, and offline experience. Time-varying variables are derived from the cross-sectional data for November 2016. For instance, the number of historical free knowledge contributions refers to the total number of articles contributed during the six-month period from May to October 2016.

The matching steps are as follows: First, estimate the propensity score by a Logit model; Next, reorder the subjects by random seeds and then conduct a 1:5 matching within 0.05 caliper; Finally, access the matching quality through common support test and balance test.

The result of common support test shows that the propensity score of 314 treated physicians fall within the range of common values, and for the 11,389 untreated individuals, the scores of 11,274 are within this range. The covariate standardized deviation result shows that the post-matching deviations between the treatment and control groups are all below 10% (see Fig. 1). From the kernel density plot of the propensity scores, it can be observed that the lines representing the treatment group and the control group are more closely aligned after matching (see Fig. 2). These results suggest that the selections of matching variables and method employed are appropriate.

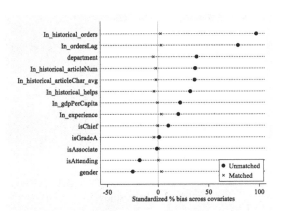

Fig. 1. Standardized % bias across covariates

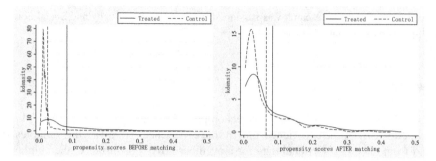

Fig. 2. Propensity scores

Appendix 2 Robustness Checks

We conduct a series of robustness checks based on the model assumptions and model uncertainties, respectively.

Model Assumptions

Parallel Trend Assumption. We use event study to test the parallel trend between the treatment group and control group. The basic period is November 2016, the point when the first "Private Doctor" behavior is observed. From Fig. 3, we find that there is no significant difference in the outcome variables between the treatment group and control group before the intervention, indicating similar development trends. Therefore, the assumption of parallel trends is satisfied.

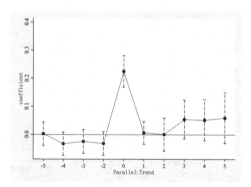

Fig. 3. Event study

No Anticipatory Effects. We conduct the placebo test by setting the placebo cutoff dates to 1–4 months before the real cutoff dates. Figure 4 shows that there is no treatment effect on the outcome variable. Therefore, the assumption of no anticipation effect is satisfied. Meanwhile, our findings are specific to the paid service instead of other spurious trends or failure in the matching procedure.

Homogeneity Treatment Effect. When policies are implemented at different points in time, differences in treatment timing and heterogeneous treatment effects may lead

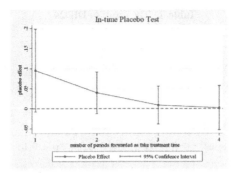

Fig. 4. Placebo test

to biases in staggered DID estimates obtained under two-way fixed effects (Goodman-Bacon, 2021). This paper first performs a Bacon decomposition, and the results show that treatment errors account for only 1.7%.

Regarding the issue of treatment effect dynamics, we use CSDID, based on inverse probability weighting least squares. The double robust DID results are showed in Table 7, and all the outcome variables are significant, consistent with the main results. Then, we use DID2s, a two-step regression method identifying group effects and period effects at the first stage and identifying the average treatment effect by comparing the differences in outcome between the treatment group and the control group in the second stage. From Table 8, the outcome variables are all significant, consistent with the main results.

Table 7. The result of CSDID

VARIABLES	(1)	(2)	(3)
	ArticleNum	ArticleChar_avg	HelpNum
ATT	0.058**	0.419***	0.102***
	(2.32)	(2.73)	(2.99)
Observations	16,764	16,764	16,764

Note: z-statistics in parentheses, *** $p < 0.01$, ** $p < 0.05$, * $p < 0.1$

Model Uncertainties

Model Specification. During the model setting stage, the function form may be uncertain. This paper changes the function form of the model to a Poisson model. From the Column (1), (2) and (3) of Table 9, the outcome variables are all significant, consistent with the main results.

Sample Validity. During the data search stage, the validity of the sample remains to be verified. To reduce the impact of extremely active users, this paper removes physicians whose average monthly number of articles is more than two standard deviations above the mean. From the Column (4), (5) and (6) of Table 9, the outcome variables are all significant, consistent with the main results.

Table 8. The result of DID2s

VARIABLES	(1)	(2)	(3)
	ArticleNum	ArticleChar_avg	HelpNum
1. Post	0.107***	0.601***	0.095***
	(5.67)	(6.02)	(3.30)
Observations	19,248	19,248	19,248

Note: z-statistics in parentheses, *** p < 0.01, ** p < 0.05, * p < 0.1

Table 9. The results of Poisson Model and Excluding Outliers

PSM weighted matching	Poisson Model			Excluding Outliers		
	(1)	(2)	(3)	(4)	(5)	(6)
	ArticleNum	ArticleChar_avg	HelpNum	ArticleNum	ArticleChar_avg	HelpNum
Post	0.673***	0.476***	0.914***	0.137***	0.639***	0.125***
	(34.12)	(25.67)	(29.76)	(2.64)	(3.13)	(2.90)
OrderNum	0.404***	0.424***	0.372***	0.072***	0.422***	0.076*
	(34.08)	(37.56)	(22.28)	(2.68)	(2.69)	(1.68)
Constant				0.044***	0.283***	0.050***
				(2.70)	(4.02)	(2.85)
Observations	8,172	7,932	6,852	18,516	18,516	18,516
R-squared				0.304	0.310	0.185
Number of id	681	661	571			
Log likelihood	−21,459	−99,475	−25,163			
Number of clusters				1543	1543	1543
Doctor FE	YES	YES	YES	YES	YES	YES
Month FE	YES	YES	YES	YES	YES	YES

Note: (1–3) Robust z-statistics in parentheses. (4–6) Robust t-statistics in parentheses. *** p < 0.01, ** p < 0.05, * p < 0.1

Endogeneity. During the model estimation stage, endogeneity should be considered. First, the propensity score matching (PSM) only considers the balance in observable variables between the treatment and control groups. However, there may still be unobservable features leading to self-selection of different physicians for "Private Doctor" service. To address this issue, this paper uses the look-ahead propensity score matching (LA-PSM), limiting the sample to original treatment group physicians. The new treatment group includes physicians who had policy behaviors between November 1, 2016, and January 31, 2017; the new control group includes physicians who had policy behaviors only between February 1, 2017, and April 30, 2017. From Fig. 5, we can see that the lines representing the treatment group and the control group are more closely aligned after matching. From Fig. 6, the post-matching deviations between the treatment and control groups are all below 10%. These results suggest that the selections of matching variables and method employed are appropriate.

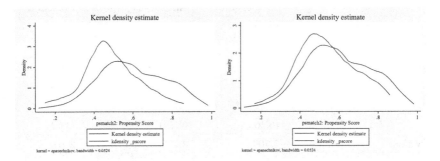

Fig. 5. Propensity scores of LA-PSM

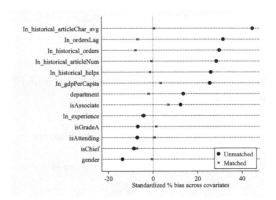

Fig. 6. Standardized % bias across covariates of LA-PSM

Table 10 shows the results after kernel matching, indicating that all outcome variables are significant, consistent with the main results.

Next, we conduct the coarsened exact matching (CEM) and the entropy balance matching (Eblance), respectively. CEM stratifies each variable based on user-defined breakpoints or an automatic binning algorithm and then performs exact matching on the stratified data. Compared to PSM, CEM doesn't make any assumptions about the underlying data generation process, which greatly reduces imbalance, model dependence, and estimation errors. After matching, the L1 statistic measuring overall imbalance decreases from 0.88 to 0.78.

Eblance is a method that simultaneously controls the multidimensional balance of covariates between the treatment and control groups, in order to maximize the exact matching of the two groups of samples. In this paper, the variables for matching include the first moment, second moment, cross moment and third moment of continuous variables of all covariates.

Table 10. The results after LA-PSM

LA-PSM weighted matching	(1)	(2)	(3)
	ArticleNum	ArticleChar_avg	HelpNum
Post	0.261***	1.394***	0.276***
	(6.70)	(7.33)	(3.73)
OrderNum	0.018	0.168*	0.024
	(0.90)	(1.67)	(0.54)
Constant	0.110***	0.528***	0.130***
	(6.36)	(6.22)	(3.60)
Observations	2,709	2,709	2,709
R-squared	0.549	0.427	0.259
Number of clusters	301	301	301
Doctor FE	YES	YES	YES
Month FE	YES	YES	YES

Note: Robust t-statistics in parentheses. *** $p < 0.01$, ** $p < 0.05$, * $p < 0.1$

Table 11 presents the model testing results after CEM and Ebalance weighting, consistent with the main results.

Table 11. The results after CEM and Ebalance

VARIABLES	CEM weighted matching			Ebalance weighted matching		
	(1)	(2)	(3)	(4)	(5)	(6)
	ArticleNum	ArticleChar_avg	HelpNum	ArticleNum	ArticleChar_avg	HelpNum
Post	0.080***	0.468***	0.101***	0.098***	0.553***	0.096***
	(3.93)	(4.24)	(3.74)	(5.67)	(6.06)	(3.49)
OrderNum	0.016	0.031	0.019	0.011	0.112**	0.011
	(1.53)	(0.59)	(1.30)	(1.35)	(2.29)	(0.72)
Constant	0.009***	0.071***	0.009*	0.100***	0.551***	0.120***
	(2.66)	(3.91)	(1.83)	(13.55)	(13.57)	(9.16)
Observations	54,216	54,216	54,216	140,436	140,436	140,436
R-squared	0.164	0.151	0.120	0.456	0.382	0.231
Number of clusters	4518	4518	4518	11703	11703	11703
Doctor FE	YES	YES	YES	YES	YES	YES
Month FE	YES	YES	YES	YES	YES	YES

Note: Robust t-statistics in parentheses. *** $p < 0.01$, ** $p < 0.05$, * $p < 0.1$

References

1. Swire-Thompson, B., Lazer, D.: Public health and online misinformation: challenges and recommendations. Annu. Rev. Publ. Health **41**(1), 433–451 (2020)
2. Liu, Q.B., Liu, X., Guo, X.: The effects of participating in a physician-driven online health community in managing chronic disease: evidence from two natural experiments. MIS Q. **44**(1), 391–419 (2020)
3. Faraj, S., von Krogh, G., Monteiro, E., et al.: Special section introduction—online community as space for knowledge flows. Inf. Syst. Res. **27**(4), 668–684 (2016)
4. Liu, Z., Zhao, Y.C., Chen, S., et al.: Exploring askers' switching from free to paid social Q&A services: a perspective on the push-pull-mooring framework. Inf. Process. Manag. **58**(1), 102396 (2021)
5. Yang, Y., Zhu, X., Song, R., et al.: Not just for the money? An examination of the motives behind physicians' sharing of paid health information. J. Inf. Sci. **49**(1), 145–163 (2023)
6. Zhang, X., Guo, F., Xu, T., et al.: What motivates physicians to share free health information on online health platforms? Inf. Process. Manag. **57**(2),(2020)
7. Cummings, J.N.: Work groups, structural diversity, and knowledge sharing in a global organization. Manag. Sci. **50**(3), 352–364 (2004)
8. Zhang, X., Liu, S., Deng, Z., et al.: Knowledge sharing motivations in online health communities: a comparative study of health professionals and normal users. Comput. Hum. Behav. **75**, 797–810 (2017)
9. Kuang, L., Huang, N., Hong, Y., et al.: Spillover effects of financial incentives on non-incentivized user engagement: evidence from an online knowledge exchange platform. J. Manag. Inf. Syst. **36**(1), 289–320 (2019)
10. Wang, J., Li, G., Hui, K.L.: Monetary incentives and knowledge spillover: evidence from a natural experiment. Manag. Sci. **68**(5), 3549–3572 (2022)
11. Khern-am-nuai, W., Kannan, K., Ghasemkhani, H.: Extrinsic versus intrinsic rewards for contributing reviews in an online platform. Inf. Syst. Res. **29**(4), 871–892 (2018)
12. Sun, Y., Dong, X., McIntyre, S.: Motivation of user-generated content: social connectedness moderates the effects of monetary rewards. Mark. Sci. **36**(3), 329–337 (2017)
13. Wang, L., Yan, L., Zhou, T., et al.: Understanding physicians' online-offline behavior dynamics: an empirical study. Inf. Syst. Res. **31**(2), 537–555 (2020)
14. Fan, H., Lederman, R.: Online health communities: how do community members build the trust required to adopt information and form close relationships? Eur. J. Inf. Syst. **27**(1), 62–89 (2018)
15. Burtch, G., Hong, Y., Bapna, R., et al.: Stimulating online reviews by combining financial incentives and social norms. Manag. Sci. **64**(5), 2065–2082 (2018)

Customer Satisfaction Analysis of Dingxiang Doctor Online Consultation Platform Based on Network Comments

Dengshi Zhao, Chi Fu, Yueqian Liu, Shiqing Qiu, and Jiamin Peng[✉]

School of Management, Guangdong University of Technology, Guangzhou, China
jmctu@163.com

Abstract. With the advantage of the Internet, the online consultation platform provides efficient and convenient consultation services for the general public, and its prosperous development promotes the rational allocation of medical resources and eases the contradiction between the supply and demand of medical resources. Among them, customer satisfaction is crucial to the sustainable development of online medical platforms. At present, for the online medical field, based on the grounded theory, there are few studies on the establishment of the customer satisfaction evaluation model of the online consultation platform by using the network comments as the original data for text analysis.

In view of this, the article selects the dermatology department of online consultation platform Dingxiang Doctor as the research object, after crawling the relevant online comments on the official website, a model consisting of 17 conceptualization categories, 9 initial categories and 5 main categories is constructed based on the grounded theory. It is found that the overall customer satisfaction score of Dingxiang Doctor is 4.10, indicating that the overall satisfaction of patients with Dingxiang Doctor is high, in which the initial category that has the greatest impact on the customer satisfaction score is the doctor's professionalism; whereas the scores of the additional services and the perceived value belong to the medium level, there is still a large space for improvement, and the platform setting and the cost performance have not yet reached the satisfaction of the customers, where the platform need to focus on improvement and enhancement.

Keywords: Healthcare · Online consultation · Customer satisfaction · Online evaluation

1 Introduction

Online consultation services have become an integral part of the healthcare system as it addresses a range of difficulties in medicine, including improving the efficiency of healthcare and enabling the integration and rational allocation of healthcare resources. With the development of online consultation services globally to date, internet medical consultations have been expanding, bringing benefits to most people, but it is worth noting that there are still online healthcare giants that are experiencing sustained losses

© The Author(s), under exclusive license to Springer Nature Switzerland AG 2024
Y. P. Tu and M. Chi (Eds.): WHICEB 2024, LNBIP 517, pp. 104–117, 2024.
https://doi.org/10.1007/978-3-031-60324-2_9

(e.g., Penguin Doctor and Ping An Hao Doctor in China). Taking China as an example, as of December 2022, China's Internet healthcare user base reached 363 million (CNNIC, 2023). The large population base provided an opportunity for the rapid development of such platforms in the early stage, but users use online consultation services mostly just out of curiosity, and the actual user stickiness is low.

Customer satisfaction refers to a customer's perception of whether a product or service has met his or her inner expectations after consuming it, and if the inner expectations are met the customer will be satisfied, and vice versa [1]. In the online environment, customer satisfaction is transmitted through word-of-mouth in a visual way (e.g., online reviews, online ratings, etc.) and further influences other users' service usage intention. Although the importance of customer satisfaction with online consultation platforms for their continued use and for the development of the platforms is well documented, there are still some critical gaps in the existing research. These gaps revolve around two central issues: comprehensively assessing online consultation customer satisfaction and understanding the factors that influence customer satisfaction with online consultation platforms.

Initially, prior studies have typically used either scales or satisfaction assignment scores in assessing customer satisfaction and a combination of the two for a comprehensive assessment. There are many emotion words in the emotion lexicon that can directly express customer satisfaction, and these words can directly express the level of customer satisfaction. However, the fact that different people say the same words does not mean that they are equally satisfied. Therefore, when measuring customer satisfaction, if the satisfaction level is graded only on the basis of basic vocabulary, it is easy to be confused in the process of measurement and judgement.

Secondly, the factors that influence customer satisfaction on online consultation platforms and that can effectively drive users to continue using the platform and to make contributory behaviors beyond the role of the user (e.g., platform recommending behaviors) are still under-discussed from both theoretical and practical perspectives. Therefore, this study addresses these gaps by seeking to answer two fundamental questions from the perspective of the customers of an online consultation platform:

Q1: How do we assess online consultation customer satisfaction?

Q2: What are the factors influencing customer satisfaction on online consultation platforms? Which factors are more significant?

In order to provide valuable insights into the above issues, this study selects the online consultation platform-Dingxiang Doctor as the research object, conducts an in-depth mining of the online review data of Dingxiang Doctor. Through social network analysis methods and grounded theory analysis methods, our research goal is to establish a customer satisfaction evaluation model for online consultation platforms, which provides a theoretical reference for the evaluation of Internet medical patient satisfaction. Based on this, we further propose a satisfaction improvement strategy for online consultation platforms to provide feasible improvement ideas for their subsequent continuous improvement.

2   Literature Review

2.1   Research on User Satisfaction of Online Medical Consultation

Due to the significant development of online consultation services in recent years, relevant research results have also emerged in an endless stream. Among them, a considerable number of literatures combine the unique characteristics of medical and health services to explore users' satisfaction with such services from different perspectives, and investigate the important factors that users consider when using online medical consultation services. Liu Yongmei and other scholars draw lessons from the trust model in mobile commerce, and construct the initial trust model of individual to mobile medical service from four aspects: hospital perceived reputation, individual personality characteristics, structural assurance and information quality [2]. Yan Mengling introduced the theory of 'incentive-health care', and used the mixed research method of qualitative and quantitative analysis to explore the influence mechanism of doctor's information-emotional interaction mode. The results show that the doctor's information interaction mode is the health factor, while the doctor's emotional interaction mode is the incentive factor [3]. Arwa et al. used questionnaires to measure patients' views and attitudes towards the use of electronic consultation through the technology acceptance model (TAM), discovered motivation, trust, attitude, and social influence were significantly related to participants' intention to use e-consultation, while participants' trust in and perception of the usefulness of e-consultations were significant factors in their intention to use e-consultation services [4]. By reviewing the existing literature, it is found that although customer satisfaction with online consultation platforms is obvious to their continued use and the important role in the development of the platform, there are still some critical gaps: a comprehensive assessment of online consultation customer satisfaction and the use of grounded theory based on online reviews to mine the influencing factors of online consultation platform customer satisfaction. Therefore, this study takes online reviews as the raw data, and extracts five main categories that constitute the satisfaction index system through text analysis, including quality perceived value, service perceived value, brand, price and satisfaction. From the perspective of platform, doctors and consumers, this paper comprehensively expounds the formation mechanism of user satisfaction in online consultation service.

2.2   Grounded Theory

Grounded theory is a bottom-up method of constructing entity theory. It defines the basic concepts that reflect the nature of events through effective information, and then uses the links between these concepts to establish corresponding development concepts. Philosophically, it is a research method based on post-positivism paradigm, emphasizing the falsification of constructivism theory [5, 6].

The grounded theory has been widely used in various research fields since it was put forward. In the field of psychology, Yan Yu and other scholars have conducted exploratory research on the concept and structural dimensions of the Buddhist mentality in the work situation through interviews, grounded theory research and questionnaire surveys. The study found that the Buddhist mentality in the work situation includes four dimensions: indifference, contentment with the status quo, friendliness without struggle, and letting nature take its course [7]. In the field of tourism management, from the perspective of tourists' experience, Wu Heng et al. used the grounded theory to dig out the embeddedness dimension and constituent elements of the marketplace culture, and combined with the Kano model to distinguish the demand attribute categories of different elements for tourists [8]. In the field of e-commerce, Reziya and other scholars use grounded theory to encode the interview materials crawled in three stages, and construct a user screenshot behavior model in the social media environment [9]. In addition, the grounded theory is also applied to the study of legal regulation [10], government policy research [11], etc., including the customer satisfaction research mentioned above. This study will use grounded theory to explore the factors that affect customer satisfaction by using online reviews as raw data.

3 Data Collection

Our research data is derived from the online reviews of dermatological patients on the online consultation platform of Dingxiang Doctor, using an efficient web crawler software-octopus collector web crawler software. Since the online reviews with too long-time span cannot reflect the latest status of online consultation, the reviews of the past two years are preferred to ensure the integrity and timeliness of the text. From January 1, 2021 to March 15, 2023, 1821 comments were received.

3.1 Text Preprocessing

In order to extract and analyze the obtained articles to the maximum extent, this research adopted manual screening and further processed the original data with Excel in order to extract and analyze the mixed information. After screening, a total of 1180 valid Chinese comments were obtained.

3.2 Semantic Web Analysis

Semantic network analysis can accurately extract the central idea of the whole text, overcome the subjectivity of traditional content analysis, and reduce the cost of manual coding. In this study, semantic network analysis is used to extract and classify themes, features and internal connections, so as to systematically deconstruct text content [12, 13]. In order to visualize the relationship structure between high-frequency words, this study processes the original data structure with the help of Python, constructs a chain list of data, calculates the coefficients between points. Each point in the figure represents a high-frequency word. The dots are connected with numbers, and the larger the value, the stronger the connection between the dots, and vice versa (Fig. 1).

By analyzing the above social network semantic map of Dingxiang Doctor Dermatology online reviews, a preliminary inference can be made on customer perception that the professionalism and service attitude of the doctor's treatment will most directly affect the patient's evaluation of this experience, and at the same time, this will also pave the way for the grounded theoretical analyses of the subsequent study.

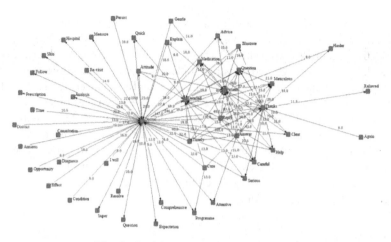

Fig. 1. Social semantic network diagram

4 Model Setup

Based on the previous semantic network analysis, this study will continue to use grounded theory, combined with comments, to encode each comment step by step, and analyze all kinds of empirical data to form a theory according to three procedures: open coding, selective coding and theoretical coding [14].

4.1 Open Coding Phase

In the coding process, the study adheres to the core principles of classical grounded theory. Specifically, two researchers read all the text data together, extract and number the semantic fragments related to the research topic, and arrange the semantic fragments in order during encoding, which are encoded independently by the two researchers. In the initial coding process, the researchers keep an open mind and use the native code as much as possible. After the independent coding, the two researchers then compare and finalize the initial code (see Table 1).

Table 1. Open coding of factors influencing customer satisfaction

Initial categoies(B+)	Related concepts (C+)	Frequency	Cases of comments
Brand impression	Dingxiang Doctor	99	*You can ask for medical advice, it's quite convenient, now I have any problems first come to Dingxiang Doctor to check it, so I don't panic;*
	Online consultation	47	*It really made me appreciate the convenience of online medical care, it's really a great trend;*
Platform setting	Replying times	167	*Two places were consulted. But the doctor's reply didn't make it clear. Because the skin problem is different in both places. I don't know how to use the medication now. But the number of follow up questions ran out;*
	Information protection	26	*Hate the issue of disclosure by default, various checklists contain a lot of personal information that is not willing to be disclosed;*
	APP logging	34	*When I was in the middle of asking a question, I was automatically logged out, and then I couldn't log in, it said something wrong;*
	Complaint channel	11	*Problems are not dealt with and there is no channel for complaints;*

(*continued*)

Table 1. (*continued*)

Initial categoies(B+)	Related concepts (C+)	Frequency	Cases of comments
Doctor's professionalism	Accuracy	783	*This doctor is particularly professional, I think her answers are very different from those 20 or 30 yuan, it is true that she is director level, and then the answers are very professional, the treatment is very practical and right on the money! Effective!*
	Patient reassurance	357	*Did not seek timely medical attention for various reasons. Now my heart is much more stable and some of my anxiety is relieved. Thanks very much for Dr Huang's help, and I will come back for a follow-up consultation*
Consultation timeline	Speed of reply to messages	231	*Very timely help for those who are abroad, especially those with long waiting times for medical care in the US. Special thanks to the doctor!*
Service quality	Attitude	197	*The doctor was kind, analyzed the cause of the disease and gave me some treatment options, and finally recommended the option that best suited me;*
	Level of detail	64	*Doctors really talk in detail, the various causes are analyzed very carefully, compared with the perfunctory attitude of doctors when I go to the hospital is completely different;*

(*continued*)

Table 1. (*continued*)

Initial categoies(B+)	Related concepts (C+)	Frequency	Cases of comments
Additional services	Prescription	88	*Recommended the use of prescription drugs, I applied for and it still do not issue a prescription, resulting in the issue has been closed unable to contact the doctor, and delays in the use of medication, I contact Dingxiang Doctor customer service, actually went to the reunion, depressed;*
	Dispatch	53	*Slow delivery of medicines;*
Cost performance	Cost performance	112	*Felt like it was a waste of my ¥19 to ask for nothing; Since you don't have time, don't respond, your one response is to say you don't have time and then ask me something I described when I asked the question ~ a waste of the patient's opportunity to ask the question, their time and their money!*
Perceived value	Subjective perception	41	*Second consultation, trustworthy;*
Positive attitude	Needs met	48	*The problem that had been bothering me for a long time was finally solved;*
	Positive reputation	53	*This doctor is especially recommended;*

4.2 Selective Coding Phase

By further comparing and summarizing the above 17 initial concepts with the 9 initial categories, five main categories are formed, which are brand, quality perceived value, service perceived value, price, and satisfaction. As a result, the evaluation indexes and index elements of the customer satisfaction model of Dingxiang Doctor's online consultation platform based on online reviews were determined, and the coding results are shown in Table 2:

Table 2. Dingxiang Doctor customer satisfaction index system

Main categories(A+)	Initial categories(B+)	Related concepts (C+)
Brand	Brand impression	Dingxiang Doctor
		Online consultation
Quality perceived value	Platform setting	Replying times
		Information protection
		APP logging
		Complaint channel
	Doctor's professionalism	Accuracy
		Patient reassurance
	Consultation timeline	Speed of reply to messages
Service perceived value	Service quality	Attitude
		Level of detail
	Additional services	Prescription
		Dispatch
Price	Cost performance	Cost performance
	Perceived value	Subjective perception
Satisfaction	Positive attitude	Needs met
		Positive reputation

4.3 Theoretical Coding Phase

Through the above analyses, 17 concepts, 9 initial categories and the finalized 5 main categories were finally extracted. The following is the final stage of grounded theory-satisfaction model construction (Fig. 2).

This study selects the four main categories of quality perceived value, service perceived value, brand and price as the antecedent variables, and selects satisfaction as the result variable, basically covering all the factors affecting customer satisfaction of Dingxiang Doctor. The evaluation model reflects various factors affecting patient satisfaction, including main factors, secondary factors and satisfaction.

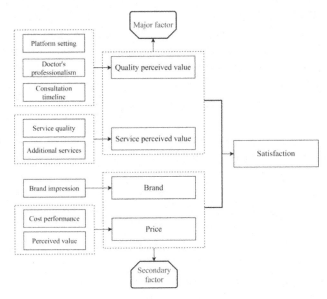

Fig. 2. Customer Satisfaction Evaluation Model for Online Consultation Platform

5 Results

5.1 Subjective Sentence Determination and Assignment

Patient's evaluation of the online consultation through online reviews is the subjective sentence, which are often prone to ambiguity judgment. Therefore, based on the internationally accepted e-commerce customer satisfaction evaluation index, this study scored the subjective sentence by referring to the domestic customer satisfaction evaluation index system construction method and Likert five-level scale scoring method [15]. The scoring criteria are 5, 4, 3, 2, and 1 satisfaction levels.

5.2 Calculate the Initial Category Score

After extracting and assigning values to the subjective sentences, as well as obtaining the scores of the initial categories as shown in the table above, the formula for calculating the satisfaction of each dimension by the weighted average method is:

$$S_{jx} = \frac{\sum_{i=1}^{n} S_{ix}}{n_i}$$

The S_{jx} denotes the satisfaction score of the x_{th} initial category in the j_{th} main category, S_{ix} denotes the total score of the initial category x in the i_{th} main category, and n_i denotes the total number of comments in the i_{th} initial category. In addition to the satisfaction, in order to reflect the importance of each category, the study does a weighting of the initial categories with the following formula:

$$N_{ji} = \frac{n_j}{n_i} * 100\%$$

In the formula, n_j denotes the number of evaluations in the j_{th} initial category, n_i denotes in the i_{th} main category, and N_{ji} denotes the weight of the j_{th} initial category in the i_{th} main category. Based on above tables and formulas, the initial category satisfaction scores and weights were obtained as shown in Table 3.

Table 3. Initial Category Score Table

Coding	Main category	Coding	Initial category	Weighting N_{ji}	Satisfaction S_{jx}
A1	Brand	B1	Brand impression	1	4.15
A2	Quality perceived value	B2	Platform setting	0.13	2.82
		B3	Doctor's professionalism	0.61	4.39
		B4	Consultation timeline	0.25	4.13
A3	Service perceived value	B5	Service quality	0.85	4.28
		B6	Additional services	0.15	3.63
A4	Price	B7	Cost performance	0.44	2.97
		B8	Perceived value	0.56	3.83
A5	Satisfaction	B9	Positive attitude	1	4.04

5.3 Calculate the Main Category and Overall Satisfaction Scores

The satisfaction score of the main category is a weighted sum of the initial category satisfaction scores under each main category and the initial category weights, the formula is as follows:

$$T_j = \sum_{i=1}^{n} S_{ji} * N_{ji}$$

The T_j represents the main category satisfaction score, S_{ji} represents the score of the i_{th} initial category in the j_{th} main category and N_{ji} represents the weight of the i_{th} initial category in the jt_h main category. Similarly the formula for the weight of the main category satisfaction score in the overall sample is as follows:

$$N_j = \frac{n_j}{n} * 100\%$$

The n_j is the total number of subjective sentences in the j_{th} main category, n represents the total number of subjective sentence evaluations, and N_j represents the weight of the j_{th}

main category. Based on the above calculations, the overall satisfaction is then deduced, which is calculated as follows:

$$T = \sum_{j=1}^{n} T_j * N_j$$

The T is the overall customer satisfaction score, T_j is the score of the j_{th} main category, and N_j is the overall weight of the j_{th} main category, and the formula can be used to derive an overall customer satisfaction score of 4.10 for the Dingxiang Doctor online consultation platform, as shown in Table 4.

Table 4. Main category score table

Overall satisfaction T	Coding	Main category	Weighting	Satisfaction
4.10	A1	Brand	0.04	4.15
	A2	Quality perceived value	0.57	4.12
	A3	Service perceived value	0.32	4.18
	A4	Price	0.05	3.46
	A5	Satisfaction	0.02	4.04

6 Conclusion and Discussion

6.1 Factors of Customer Satisfaction

Through previous studies, it was found that the main factors affecting the customer satisfaction of Dingxiang Doctor online consultation platform are as follows:

Firstly, the professionalism of the doctor. The professional strength of doctors is the primary factor affecting customer satisfaction. In practice, if the doctor possesses a higher level of competence and the consultation results are favorable, there will be more comments, which indicates that the doctor is chosen by more users and has been widely trusted by users both in terms of professional competence and service quality.

Secondly, the convenience of information interaction. The online consultation platform has an impact on the information interaction between doctors and patients, and the study found that patients would give doctors bad comments due to the platform's abnormal login, drug prices, delivery speed, etc. At present, the number of doctors on the online consultation platform is far less than the number of patients, resulting the platform doctors' consultation time is significantly different, with a clear head effect.

Finally, the price of platform consultation. Platform consultation price has a significant impact on user satisfaction. Because of the unique characteristics of online consultations, users are not only concerned about the cost of medical consultations, but also consider whether the price set is in line with the value and service capabilities of the doctor they are accessing through the internet.

6.2 Management Implications

According to the above analysis, the following recommendations are drawn:

First, improve the quality of doctors' online services and control the online consultation time. Doctors must have the ability to listen to patients' needs, communicate effectively with users with empathy, and provide personalized diagnostic advice due to a variety of difficulties for doctors to accurately understand the personal characteristics of users and to provide targeted diagnostic information.

Second, improve extended services and standardize charges. In order to further enhance the Internet online consultation extension service, doctors can obtain patients' residential addresses when prescribing medicines according to their conditions. The system suggests co-operative pharmacies selling prescription drugs near the user's address to facilitate the user's selection. When the user selects a prescription, the doctor will confirm the prescription, greatly enhance the convenience of the service.

Thirdly, market regulation should be strengthened. Nowadays, China has introduced many policies to guide the development of online health field. As a major mode and a new industry of health services, it can set up special complaint hotlines and strengthen accountability mechanisms for violations such as misdiagnosis, poor prescribing and overmedication by doctors on the Internet.

6.3 Limitations and Future Works

There are some limitations to this study. On the one hand, in this study, the data collected came from the comment section of the official website of Dingxiang Doctor, but it was not possible to obtain information about the users who commented online, including, but not limited to, age and gender. As a result, there were greater difficulties in analyzing customer satisfaction on a demographic level. Therefore, the subsequent research can improve sampling, combine quantitative research with qualitative research, and maximize sampling sources and reduce random errors by analyzing network texts, questionnaires and in-depth interviews. On the other hand, in the process of building the customer satisfaction model, based on workload considerations and the characteristics of each department, this study only captured the reviews of the dermatology department of Dingxiang Doctor, the sample is not broad enough, and the subsequent model needs to be further improved and optimized.

Acknowledgments. This study is funded by the National Natural Science Foundation of China (71972054), the Philosophy and Social Sciences Planning Project of Guangdong Province (GD24CGL10), and is also a phased research result of the 2024 College Students' Innovation and Entrepreneurship Training Project of Guangdong University of Technology, titled "Research on Customer Satisfaction and Service Optimization Strategy of Online Consultation Platform Based on Online Reviews".

References

1. Cardozo, R.N.: An experimental study of consumer effort - expectations and satisfaction. J. Mark. Res. **2**(3), 244–249 (1965)

2. Liu, Y., Che, X., Wei, X.: Research on consumers' Initial trust for mobile health. China J. Inf. Syst. (01), 15–30 (2014). (in Chinese)
3. Yan, M.L., Zhang, J.Y.: How doctors' informative-emotional interaction modes impact the satisfaction of mobile consultation service: an analysis based on the motivation-hygiene theory. Chin. J. Manag. Sci. **27**, 108–118 (2019). (in Chinese)
4. Althumairi, A., Hariri, B., Aljabri, D., Aljaffary, A.: Patient acceptance and intention to use e-consultations during the COVID-19 pandemic in the eastern province of Saudi Arabia. Front. Public Health **10**, 896546 (2022)
5. Kools, S., Mccarthy, M., Durham, R., et al.: Dimensional analysis: broadening the conception of grounded theory. Qual. Health Res. **6**(3), 312–330 (1996)
6. Corbin, J., Strauss, A.: Techniques and procedures for developing grounded theory. Basics Qual. Res. **63**(2), 201–243 (2008)
7. Yan, Y., Feng, M., Zhang, Y.: Workplace 'Buddha' theoretical construction and empirical test in Chinese organizational context. Acta Psychologica Sinica 1–18 (2024). (in Chinese)
8. Wu, H., Ye, H., Wu, H., et al.: Human fireworks: a study on the element identification and demand attributes of street culture rootedness from the perspective of tourist experience. Tour. Trib. 1–17 (2024). (in Chinese)
9. Aihaiti, R., Zheng, X., Li, S., Fan, H.: Construction of user screenshot behavior model in social media environment: based on grounded theory. Document. Inf. Knowl. 1–12 (2024). (in Chinese)
10. Ql, H., Qu, J.: Comparative research on the policy text of personal information protection in the library website in China and Abroad. J. China Soc. Sci. Tech. Inf. **40**(11), 124–132 (2022). (in Chinese)
11. Gao, C., Peng, W.: Analysis and evolution characteristics of chinese culture and tourism integration policy: grounded theory research based on multiple policy texts. Libr. Inf. Serv. **67**(21), 35–47 (2023). (in Chinese)
12. Newman, M.E.J.: Fast algorithm for detecting community structure in networks. Phys. Rev. E **69**(6), 066133 (2004)
13. Marya, D., George, B.: A semantic network analysis of the international communication association. Hum. Commun. Res. **25**(5), 1468–2958 (1999)
14. Song, B., Xiao, F.: Data investigation and analysis based on grounded theory. J. Phys: Conf. Ser. **1813**(1), 23–25 (2021)
15. Fasanghari, M.: The fuzzy evaluation of E-commerce customer satisfaction utilizing fuzzy topsis. In: International Symposium on Electronic Commerce and Security, pp. 870–874 (2008)

The Concept and Connotation of "AIGC+": A Retrospect and Prospect of AIGC

Jiangping Wan[(✉)], Lianzheng Zhou[(✉)], and Yuge Wang

School of Business Administration, South China University of Technology, Guangzhou 510640, China

csjpwan@scut.edu.cn, 202230383193@mail.scut.edu.cn

Abstract. The explosion of Midjourney and ChatGPT has led to 2022 being dubbed the year of AIGC (Artificial Intelligence Generated Content), followed by a boom in AIGC applications around the world and in various industries for more than a year. Focusing on this hotspot, this paper reviews the origin of the concept of AIGC, its basic elements, and its current development, and then proposes the concept of "AIGC+" based on the discussion of the modals of AIGC and specific application scenarios under the modals, and provides an in-depth outlook on the future development of "AIGC+" in terms of application, industry direction and market impact, which reveals the important position of "AIGC+" as a new type of productivity in the era of digital economy, and predicts that "AIGC+" will have a profound impact on the future development of the digital economy, including business, work and life.

Keywords: Artificial Intelligence Generated Content · AIGC · "AIGC+" · ChatGPT

1 Introduction

In 2023, the General Artificial Intelligence (AGI) technology represented by AIGC has triggered a continuous stirring worldwide. AIGC has experienced three waves of progress in a short period of time: The first wave was the emergence of large models represented by GPT, which made AIGC products known to the public. The second wave was the rapid innovation of AIGC application in productivity scenarios, which transformed intelligence from Chat to Work. The third wave was that AIGC continued the innovation of full-process intelligence in business scenarios to serve the real economy. AIGC is expected to achieve deep integration with a wide range of business scenarios, and to promote a huge change in the industrial production mode. The AGI represented by AIGC will act as a meta-capability engine, deeply impacting all aspects of business, work and life, from the labour market to knowledge development, content creation and collaborative interaction, to enable everyone to enter the future intelligent era of "AI everywhere" [1].

This paper reviews the conceptual origin, development foundation, and current status of AIGC. Then it introduces the concept of "AIGC+" based on "AIGC+modality" and "AIGC+scenario application". Finally, it presents the future development trend of the application layer of AIGC. The organization of this paper is as follows (Fig. 1):

Y. P. Tu and M. Chi (Eds.): WHICEB 2024, LNBIP 517, pp. 118–129, 2024.
https://doi.org/10.1007/978-3-031-60324-2_10

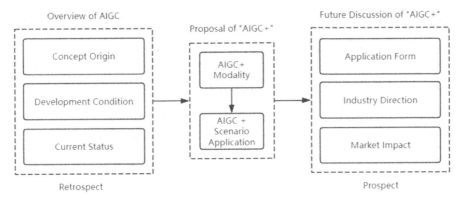

Fig. 1. The organisation of this paper

2 Overview of AIGC

2.1 The Concept of the AIGC

In 1950, Alan Turing proposed the well-known 'Turing Test' in his paper 'Computing Machinery and Intelligence'. The test is an experimental method used to determine whether a machine can be considered 'intelligent' or not. It involves assessing whether the machine can mimic human thought processes and engage in human-like interactions with a person. AI has been expected to be used for content creation since Turing [2]. *Illiac Suite*, the world's first computer-generated musical composition, appeared in 1957. *Eliza*, the world's first human-computer dialogue robot, appeared in 1966. In the 1980s, IBM developed the voice-controlled typewriter *Tangora*. Since 2000, AI content generation technology has made significant progress due to continuous improvements in speech recognition, computer vision, natural language processing, etc. In 2007, the first novel completed by an AI device, *1 The Road*, was published. In 2012, Microsoft demonstrated a fully automatic simultaneous interpretation system that can translate English speech to Chinese speech [3]. In 2014, the emergence of Generative Adversarial Network (GAN) led to the widespread use of deep learning models for intelligent synthesis of text, images, speech, and other content. This is referred to as Generative Artificial Intelligence (Gen AI) in academia.

Currently, both academia and industry define AIGC as a new type of production mode that utilizes AI technology to automatically generate content following PGC (Professional Generated Content) and UGC (User Generated Content). PGC refers to content created by experts or professional teams with qualifications in content-related fields. It is characterized by higher thresholds and costs but guaranteed content quality. Professional video platforms are an example of PGC, where users are more likely to receive and search for video resources to watch. This is similar to the concept of Web 1.0. UGC, which is associated with the concept of Web 2.0, refers to the freedom that users have to upload content. This is evident in platforms such as Twitter and YouTube, where users are not only receivers but also providers of content. This allows the scale of content production to expand greatly, but the quality of the content varies. AIGC involves the use of

AI to replace human beings in content creation. It offers faster production frequency, the ability to customize styles to meet personalized needs, and an unlimited scale of creative inspiration. AIGC is expected to become the main mode of content generation in the future, as it overcomes the shortcomings of PGC and UGC in terms of both quantity and quality [3, 4] (Fig. 2).

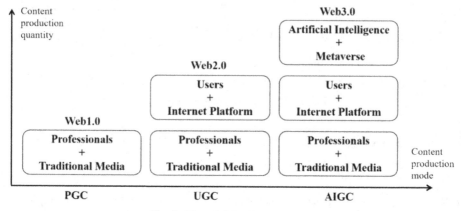

Fig. 2. From PGC, UGC to AIGC

2.2 The Basis of the AIGC

As illustrated in Fig. 3, the foundation of AIGC consists of three key components: data, hardware, and algorithms [4].

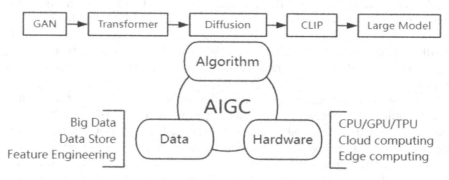

Fig. 3. The three key components of AIGC

Data. High-quality, large-scale datasets are essential for training large models and directly impact the accuracy and stability of generated content. In recent years, the size and diversity of data have increased rapidly with the advent of the Big Data era. Cloud computing and data storage services, such as Amazon S3 and Microsoft Azure Blob storage, provide efficient, secure, scalable, and easy-to-handle solutions for storing and processing massive data. Innovative applications of data management technologies, such as data cleaning, deduplication, labelling, and classification, make data easier to organize and process. These technologies provide a solid foundation for the development of AIGC technology [5, 6].

Hardware. Computational power is another infrastructure of AIGC, and the implementation of large models has a strict dependence on huge computational power. OpenAI (2020) reports that training a GPT-3 XL model with 1.3 billion parameters requires approximately 27.5 PFlop/s-day of computational power. In other words, ChatGPT would take 27.5 days to complete training at a rate of 1 trillion times per second. In recent years, hardware devices designed for deep learning, such as Graphics Processing Units (GPUs) like Nvidia A100, have made significant progress, while cloud and edge computing are providing more convenient and efficient computational power, driving the continued development and application of AIGC [4, 7].

Algorithms. AIGC was developed due to advancements in deep learning models. These models possess features such as generality, fundamentality, multimodality, large amounts of training data, and high and stable quality of generated content, which make them ideal for automated content production. In 2014, Ian Goodfellow proposed the Generative Adversarial Network (GAN) as an early content generation model, which has been widely used to generate images, videos, and 3D object models. Subsequently, other generative algorithms for deep learning, such as the Transformer and Diffusion Model, emerged. The Transformer Model is a deep learning model that uses a self-attention mechanism and is mainly used in Natural Language Processing (NLP). The Diffusion Model was initially developed to eliminate image noise. However, from an optimization standpoint, it has surpassed GAN as the most advanced image generator. Since 2018, AI has entered the era of pre-trained models, which have overcome the challenges of high thresholds for using pre-basic models, high training costs, and simple content generation. In 2021, OpenAI released the cross-modal deep learning model CLIP (Contrastive Language-Image Pre-Training) as open source. With the support of multimodal technology, the pre-training model has evolved from a single model in the early days to multimodal and cross-modal models, including text-generated images, text-generated videos, etc. [3, 8].

2.3 The Status of AIGC

Currently, the AIGC is experiencing a period of rapid development. Large technology enterprises are competing to establish themselves in the field of AIGC, while emerging technology startups are quietly releasing pre-training models in various fields. The popular AIGC application, ChatGPT, has already amassed over 100 million users in just two months, demonstrating the industry's enormous market scale and growth potential. It is clear that the AIGC industry is on the rise and holds great promise [9].

Globally, governments are actively promoting the development of AI technology and have introduced a series of policies and plans. The US government supports the development of AI technology through policies such as the US Innovation and Competition Act, and the European Union plans the development path of AI through documents such as the

EU Artificial Intelligence Strategy. In China, the government attaches great importance to the development of AI technology, listing it as a national strategy and introducing policy documents such as the New Generation Artificial Intelligence Development Plan to promote the integration of AI technology into various industries [10, 11].

Taking the layout of Microsoft and OpenAI as an example, we can get a glimpse of the development status of AIGC: In 2019, Microsoft invested $1 billion in OpenAI to further advance AI technology. While focusing on technology development, Microsoft is actively preparing for the commercialization of OpenAI by integrating its technology with its own products. In 2020, Microsoft planned to use the GPT-3 model in Office, Bing, and other products. In 2021, it deployed OpenAI-developed GPT, DALLE, Codex, and other tools centrally in Azure. In January 2023, Microsoft invested billions of dollars in OpenAI. On 2 February, Microsoft announced that all its products will integrate ChatGPT, providing powerful AI capabilities [2].

3 Proposal of "AIGC+"

3.1 Modals of AIGC

As far as the existing mainstream AIGC products are concerned, AIGC can be mainly divided into four major modal content generation: text, image, audio and video.

AIGC+TEXT: Text generation encompasses structured writing, creative writing, and dialogue writing. Structured writing uses structured data to generate texts for specific scenarios, such as news. Creative writing focuses on generating personalized and creative texts, making it suitable for marketing, social media and blogs. Dialogue writing is mainly used for chatbots, similar to customer service [12].

AIGC+IMAGE: Image generation has two mature landing use scenarios: image editing and picture generation. Image editing functions include removing watermarks, increasing resolution, and applying specific filters. AI painting is a recent development in image generation, which includes creative image generation (random or according to specific attributes to generate paintings) and functional image generation (to generate logos, model drawings, marketing posters, etc.) [7].

AIGC+AUDIO: Audio generation techniques can be categorised into two types: text-to-speech synthesis and speech cloning. Text-to-speech synthesis is used for robotics and voice broadcasting tasks, where it takes text as input and outputs the speech of a specific speaker. On the other hand, speech cloning is used for intelligent dubbing and similar scenarios, where it takes a target speech as input and converts the input speech or text to the target speaker's speech [7].

AIGC+VIDEO: AI technology is not only able to generate images, but also able to compose a complete video by producing sequential frames. It has been used for video clip processing, generating trailers and promotional videos, etc. With the emergence of OpenAI's pre-trained video generation large model Sora in early 2024, AIGC is expected to revolutionize the way video content is generated and marketed [5].

3.2 AIGC Application in Scenarios

AIGC has the potential to revolutionize content generation and relationship building across industries, empowering the shift towards new production modes. Industries with a high level of digitization and strong demand for content are typical application scenarios for AIGC. Currently, the application of AIGC has become increasingly mature in media, film & television, game, e-commerce, etc. Its commercial application in medical, finance, and industry and other sectors is also rapidly developing [13]. The several typical scenarios are descriptions and examples of AIGC applications in the following:

AIGC+Media: The excellence of AIGC text generation technology in structured writing has been widely recognized around the world, with the founders of Narrative Science predicting that by 2030 more than 90% of news will be produced by robots. AIGC technologies play an important role in supporting information gathering, editing, content production, delivery and product innovation in the textual content production process. For example, speech recognition technology can transcribe voice content, effectively reducing the workload of recording and organizing before writing, and improving the timeliness of news. Taking the 2022 Winter Olympics as an example, its intelligent voice recorder is helping journalists to quickly produce a two-minute article through cross-lingual voice transcription. Its intelligent editing tools, such as automatic subtitle generation, video segmentation and task tracking, not only save time and labour costs, but also maximize the value of content rights. AIGC also supports the media industry's widespread use of virtual anchors - digital humans created using artificial intelligence synthesis technology. Through the use of underlying algorithms and real-time voice and character animation technology, virtual anchors can automatically broadcast input text and synchronize voice, facial expressions and lip movements. As the technology improving, AIGCs with stronger cognitive abilities will also be used in the media [13].

AIGC+Film & Television: The film and television industry have a long industrial chain, a long production cycle, slow capital turnover, a shortage of high-quality scripts and high production costs. AIGC technology can stimulate the vitality of script writing, reduce filming costs, improve the quality of post-production and expand the scope of creation. In terms of script creation, AIGC can quickly generate story scripts by analyzing massive script data, such as the short film "Lawyer" created by GPT-3 in 2020. AIGC can also convert text into scripts to reduce the pressure of rewriting, for example, Seahorse Light Sail's Novel-to-Script feature has helped revise more than 80% of film and TV scripts in the industry, including popular films such as Hello, Lee Hwan Young and Wandering Earth. In terms of scene creation, AIGC reduces construction costs through virtual composite scenes and uses real-time rendering technology to preview post-production effects on the set, reducing production time. For example, "Fox Demon Xiao Hong Niang Yue Hong Chapter" uses virtual filming technology to achieve real-time synthesis of live scenes and CG elements. Virtual characters based on reality enhancement technology can interact with real people, bringing new audio-visual experiences to audiences, such as Hunan TV's Xiao Yang and Beijing Spring Festival Gala's virtual Teresa Teng. In post-production, AIGC technology is used not only for image repair and restoration, but also for synthesizing faces to replace specific characters; AI repair technology is used to repair historical images, such as the HD-quality presentation of Leslie Cheung's "Fever" concert; and AI face-swapping technology is used to replace faces; and AI face-swapping technology is used to "digitally resurrect" deceased actors or to replace actors with poor track records, such as the replacement of deceased actors in the film Fast & Furious 7. "Passion 7" in the deceased actor Paul Walker's face [13].

AIGC+Game: There is a classic "impossible triangle" argument in the game industry, that is, "you can only choose between time, cost and quality". However, the maturity of AIGC technology is expected to break this "impossible triangle" and improve the productivity of the game industry. First, AIGC has the technical characteristics of high efficiency production, and has an absolute advantage in repetitive and mechanized content production; second, the trend of AIGC's large model makes its initial cost higher, but the development of AIGC technology is still in line with Moore's Law, and with the maturity of technology iteration and the price of software and hardware equipment, the ultimate goal of reducing cost and increasing efficiency can be achieved; Finally, the performance of the AIGC in the field of content generation, especially in the field of image generation, has been improved by the development of the technology. Finally, the performance of AIGC in the field of content generation, especially in the field of image generation, has reached the average human level and is capable of satisfying a large number of repetitive and trivial art needs in the game industry. Currently, many game developers are already using AIGC technology to create game scenes. For example, Justin Roiland, creator of Rick and Morty, released a game in late 2022 that featured artwork created by Midjourney. In addition, with NPCs as an important part of the game, generative AI can take on a lot of low value work and be more productive during character development, saving more resources and allowing game artists to focus on content creation. In AI world, a meta-universe avatar creation company, is currently experimenting with introducing generative AI technology to the virtual NPC creation process. With the help of Gen AI, the game itself can also get more creative interaction methods, such as Cyber Manufacture Co. Recently released the latest AIGC technology preview Quantum Engine, users can use natural language to interact with NPCs, AI will be based on the user's expression of real-time generation of plot interaction. This application breaks the production relationship of AI technology serving game development, using generative AI as the core of the game to provide users with a truly private and personal gaming experience [14].

AIGC+E-commerce: With the maturity and commercial application of various digital technologies, immersive consumption has become the mainstream development trend of e-commerce, and virtual anchors, 3D online previews, digital exhibitions and other forms have greatly enriched consumers' consumption experience. With the support of AIGC, the virtual human cargo field will usher in a more realistic and immersive digital reproduction, thus creating an immersive consumption experience for consumers. First, the creation of virtual anchors fills the manpower gap, enabling 24-h uninterrupted display and introduction of goods, and with the advancement of NLP, virtual anchors can provide consumers with a more vivid interactive experience. Second is the online display of 3D models of goods, to provide users with a full range of product presentation, and even a virtual use of scene construction, such as Ikea 2022 launched a virtual design tool, so that users can scan their own room or use its virtual showroom for furniture placement, to provide consumers with a more immersive shopping experience. Finally, the shopping scene digital reproduction, through the construction of three-dimensional scenes in two-dimensional space, AIGC technology can achieve low-cost, high-volume construction of the virtual shopping scene, thereby reducing the cost of business to build a 3D scene, and provide consumers with online and offline integration of the consumer experience. In the future, with generative AI and the improvement of perception and cognition of AI technology, the application of AIGC in e-commerce will be more real and sustainable [15].

3.3 Definition of "AIGC+"

In summary, "AIGC+" can be defined as the entire process of generating relevant content based on Artificial Intelligence Generated Content (AIGC) through single-modal or cross-modal generation and applying it to specific services or scenarios to improve their quality and efficiency. "AIGC+" represents the application of AIGC as a new type of productivity and production mode in various fields and industries, similar to "Internet+", which will be an important direction and tool for future industrial upgrading.

"AIGC+Modals" covers the application of AI in single or multiple forms of generated content, such as text, image, audio and video. Extending "AIGC+Modals" to specific service areas, we can get the definition of "AIGC+Scenarios": AIGC is applied to a scene and enables the whole process of improving the quality and efficiency of the scene. More broadly, "AIGC+" represents the application of AIGC in various fields, including but not limited to media, games, film & television, music, e-commerce and other industries. "AIGC+" is not only a technical means, but also a new type of productivity and production mode, which can make the production mode of various industries smarter, more efficient and more innovative by introducing AIGC.

4 The Future of "AIGC+"

4.1 Application Form

Multimodal large models will shape comprehensive applications: Multimodal large models covering linguistic and visual domains have become a hotspot in the current AI field, such as the emergence of OpenAI's GPT-4 Turbo and Google's Gemini2. Multimodal big models continuously strengthen reasoning ability through powerful information perception, expand the service boundary, and improve the comprehensiveness and reliability of application scenarios. These models not only have high information richness and strong learning ability, but also show great inter-actability in intelligent applications. In terms of application empowerment, multimodal large models use massive heterogeneous data to improve efficiency and capability ceiling, and solve complex problems across industries and fields. In terms of user experience, multimodal large models improve the capability and richness of cross-industry applications, solve more AI application problems, and create a wider range of usage scenarios. Overall, multimodal big model can help build a more friendly and rich user interface, push the interaction between applications and people to a situation closer to human habits, it can be integrated with VR/AR, meta-universe and other technologies to create a new experience that is deeper, multi-dimensional and all-encompassing in the future [1].

AI agent will become the mainstream form of big model landing business scenarios: They integrate perception, analysis, decision-making, and execution capabilities, making them ideal AI assistants. AI agents provide rich, diverse, and highly personalized experiences in work, life, learning, entertainment, health, and other aspects, enabling individuals and enterprises to enter the AI assistant era. Enterprises are increasingly adopting AI agents as the ideal mode of productization to meet the growing demand for complex quality improvement and efficiency enhancement. AI agents make 'human-computer collaboration' the new norm to help enterprises to establish theirs intellectualized cores. The AI agent promotes 'human-machine collaboration' as the core of a new mode of intelligent operation, enabling enterprises to achieve greater productivity. Individuals and small organizations can realize their full potential, leading to more innovations with the support of AI agent as the carrier of AIGC applications. The AI agent is transforming enterprise productivity. AIGC will help to atomize and fragment enterprise work tasks, continuously tapping the efficiency and potential of each link through AI to achieve a more efficient collaborative work mode in the future [1].

4.2 Industry Direction

Application innovation is expected to be a significant direction for the development of the AIGC industry in the near future: The general intelligence of large-scale models has the potential to bring about a great transformation in the industry, reflecting a 'force multiplier' effect. Enterprises have already begun investing in and experimenting with AIGC applications. Innovation in applications is considered the primary means for AIGC technology to be implemented and to connect with user value. Large models' general intelligence not only enhances business value but also accelerates the development and deployment efficiency of application software, promoting the multi-point blossoming of AIGC technology. In B-end application scenarios, AIGC will primarily land in productivity and office-related scenarios, as B-end customers have a higher willingness to pay for new AI technologies. However, variations in industries and business scenarios will require identifying the appropriate combination of technologies and scenarios. Regarding technical factors, AIGC has advantages in knowledge management, search, maps, digital assistants, intelligent dialogue, and other scenarios. Concerning industry factors, AIGC's ability to generalize provides companies with more options for production optimization and innovation paths. It will benefit first if the applications closely related to business operations [1].

Medium and large enterprises are likely to develop exclusive self-use models: The future development of large models shows a parallel trend of generalization and specialization. General pre-training large models are not suitable for multi-domain specific tasks, which is why medium and large enterprises prefer to build their own exclusive models. Enterprise demand emphasizes not only the ability of large models to solve universal problems but also their expertise in specific fields. They can provide more accurate and valuable services through the accumulation of industry knowledge. It is expected that more enterprises will build their AI applications on the basis of private, proprietary models. Enterprises are increasingly focusing on constructing proprietary large models in order to enhance the intrinsic ability of AIGC applications. It is important for these enterprises to cultivate their internal teams to achieve this goal. It is crucial for B-side customers to have access to proprietary models that are trained based on specific tasks and domain knowledge in the future. Medium and large enterprises are expected to take the lead in building proprietary big model services, which will promote the enhancement of industry ecology and customer usage [1].

The eco-industry is continuously improving: The ecosystem is becoming more refined through standard specifications, technology research and development, content creation, industry application, and asset service. The ecosystem surrounding standard specifications, technology research and development, content creation, industry application, and asset service is becoming more refined. This refinement will enable the upgrading of related industries. The standard specification establishes a comprehensive and integrated system for the AIGC ecosystem, covering technology, content, applications, services, and supervision. The aim is to encourage the healthy development of AIGC within the bounds of reasonable compliance and legality. As core technology continues to evolve and key capabilities are significantly enhanced, AI algorithms with improved performance and smarter logic will be applied to AIGC. Continuous innovation in technological research and development will strongly promote the creation of content, improve its quality, and bring it closer to human intellectual and aesthetic standards. This content is applicable to various scenarios across all industries. The successful development of AIGC will promote asset services. The complete ecological chain of AIGC includes rapid follow-up, compliance assessment of generated content, asset management, property rights protection, and trading services. This chain aims to reshape the value of AIGC and fully release its commercial potential. The development of 5G, cloud computing, VR, AR and other advanced technologies, along with the R&D and innovation of new-generation intelligent terminal equipment, has led to the creation of the complete AIGC ecosystem. This ecosystem is a driving force for releasing the dividends of data elements, promoting the upgrading of traditional industries, facilitating the development of the digital economy, and constructing the integration of the digital and real economies [2].

4.3 Market Impact

AIGC is becoming more inclusive: The innovation of business models has led to opportunities for rapid promotion of AIGC applications. The huge business prospects and rapidly iterative technology are reducing the marginal cost of AIGC, creating a positive market competition pattern. This will ultimately benefit small-medium enterprises and the general public. AIGC's innovative business models continue to emerge under the wave of intelligence. These models range from the extension and derivation of traditional business links to industry-customized API services, industry AI tool platforms, and customized application development. AIGC aims to promote the generation of new business models throughout society, foster healthy competition among technology, products, and businesses, and make AI more inclusive in the future. In the context of the growing AI industry, the threshold for commercialization by individual creators and developers is expected to decrease. This will enable SMEs to reduce costs and increase efficiency, while it will be also driving growth in the service market. A continuous refinement of business models will lead to a positive development pattern for the AI market. This process will further activate the vitality of the AIGC ecosystem, enabling AIGC to empower a wider range of users and enterprises [14].

AIGC requires appropriate security measures: AIGC, an emerging technology, is driving a new trend in AI. However, it is also accompanied by predictable and unpredictable risks, such as privacy concerns, loss of control of results, and data leakage, which have raised concerns from various parties. The social, economic, and ethical issues brought about by AIGC should not be ignored. For instance, efficiency gains may wipe out traditional jobs, generate new professional orientations, and trigger new social, economic, and ethical problems. All parties must take effective measures to ensure the safety and reliability of AIGC applications for human using. As a result, countries worldwide have become concerned with the constraints on AIGC in terms of laws, regulations, ethics, and morality. Governments have introduced regulations to regulate the development, application, and service process of AIGC. Each practice body must take legal compliance seriously and practice in a compliant manner. This includes standards the data domain, AI products, personal services, and industry applications. It is important to adhere to laws and regulations [14].

5 Conclusion

Looking back at the history of AIGC, we see that from the "Turing Test" to today's sophisticated technology, AIGC is no longer a conceptual abstraction, but a practical product supported by powerful data, high-performance computing and advanced algorithms. The multimodal applications of AIGC provide rich innovation opportunities for various industries, and AIGC drives industrial upgrading and digital transformation. Meanwhile, the concept of "AIGC+" has drawn a broader blueprint for the future development of AIGC. We highlight the gradual universalization of AIGC and the need for appropriate security measures for industrial direction and market impact of AIGC. From the rise of multimodal large-scale models to the AI agent as the mainstream form of landing business scenarios, AIGC is gradually penetrating various industries, and application innovation has been identified as an important direction for the development of the AIGC industry, while a perfect ecosystem will also promote the in-depth development of AIGC.

Acknowledgement. This research was supported by Guangzhou key industrial technology project modern industrial technology under Grant 201802010035.

References

1. IDC: Ding Talk: Top 10 Trends in the AIGC Application Layer (2024). (in Chinese)
2. Xu, X., et al.: Next generation artificial intelligence technology (AIGC): development evolution, industrial opportunities and prospects. Ind. Econ. Rev. **4**, 5–22 (2023). https://doi.org/10.19313/j.cnki.cn10-1223/f.20230705.001. (in Chinese)
3. Cai, Z., Wei, H.: Evolution of artificial intelligence generated content (AIGC) and its application scenario of library intelligent service. Libr. J. **42**(4), 34-43–135-136 (2023). https://doi.org/10.13663/j.cnki.lj.2023.04.004. (in Chinese)
4. Wu, J., et al.: AI-Generated Content (AIGC): A Survey. http://arxiv.org/abs/2304.06632 (2023)

5. Foo, L.G., et al.: AI-Generated Content (AIGC) for Various Data Modalities: A Survey. http://arxiv.org/abs/2308.14177 (2023)
6. Zhang, C., et al.: A Complete Survey on Generative AI(AIGC): Is ChatGPT from GPT-4 to GPT-5 All You Need?. http://arxiv.org/abs/2303.11717 (2023)
7. Gu, R., et al.: Innovative Digital Storytelling with AIGC: Exploration and Discussion of Recent Advances. http://arxiv.org/abs/2309.14329 (2023)
8. Cao, Y., et al.: A Comprehensive Survey of AI-Generated Content (AIGC): A History of Generative AI from GAN to ChatGPT. http://arxiv.org/abs/2303.04226 (2023)
9. Guo, D., et al.: AIGC challenges and opportunities related to public safety: a case study of ChatGPT. J. Saf. Sci. Resil. 4(4), 329–339 (2023)
10. Li, X., et al.: AIGC in China: Current Developments and Future Outlook. http://arxiv.org/abs/2308.08451 (2023)
11. Wang, Y., et al.: A survey on ChatGPT: AI–generated contents, challenges, and solutions. IEEE Open J. Comput. Soc. 4, 280–302 (2023). https://doi.org/10.1109/OJCS.2023.3300321
12. Du, Y., Zhang, Z.: AIGC: The Era of Intelligent Creation. Chinese Translation Press, Beijing (2023). (in Chinese)
13. Guo, Q., Zhang, J.: AI+Humanities: development and trends of AIGC. Journal. Enthusiast. 3, 8–14 (2023). https://doi.org/10.16017/j.cnki.xwahz.2023.03.004. (in Chinese)
14. China Academy of Information and Communications Technology, JD Exploration Research Institute: Artificial Intelligence Generation Content (AIGC) White paper (2022)
15. Zhan, X., et al.: Application scenarios and development opportunities of AIGC in the digital intelligence integration environment. Libr. Intell. Knowl. 40(1), 75–85+55 (2023). https://doi.org/10.13366/j.dik.2023.01.075. (in Chinese)

From Code to Carbon Cuts: A Province-Level Analysis of Digital Finance's Impact on Emission Reduction in China

Yuekun Ma[✉]

Beijing Foreign Studies University, No. 2, North Road, West 3rd Ring, Beijing, China
mayuekun@bfsu.edu.cn

Abstract. To address the challenges of global warming, China has proposed the dual carbon target, and digital finance, as an emerging phenomenon, will play a pivotal role in promoting energy conservation and emission reduction. Drawing on panel data from 30 provinces in China from 2011 to 2019, this study empirically examines the impact of digital finance on carbon emissions. The findings from a two-way fixed effect model reveal that the influence of digital finance on carbon emissions follows an environmental Kuznets curve pattern, exhibiting an inverted U-shaped relationship, and the digitalization level of inclusive finance exhibits the highest efficacy. Moreover, its impact on technological innovation demonstrates a U-shaped trend. Results obtained through the SDM model indicate that digital finance also effectively decreases coal-related emissions and facilitates the transition towards cleaner energy sources such as natural gas. Heterogeneity analysis further reveals that the effect of digital finance on carbon emissions is most pronounced in western regions while being less significant in areas with lower energy quality. Therefore, it is imperative to expedite the development of digital finance and surpass the turning point at the earliest opportunity while simultaneously paying attention to tailoring strategies based on local conditions. Facilitate green innovation and digital transformation among enterprises while harnessing the enabling power of digital finance to serve real needs. Fully leverage its potential in advancing clean energy adoption for structural change.

Keywords: Digital Finance · Carbon Emissions · Technological Innovation · Clean Energy Adoption

1 Introduction

Excessive carbon dioxide emissions are a significant contributor to climate change. Greenhouse gases such as carbon dioxide emitted by human activities contribute to global warming, exacerbate the instability of the climate system, and lead to frequent extreme weather. In response to the increasing severity of global climate challenges, there is unanimous support across diverse sectors for promoting low-carbon development. As a developing country, China has been trying to address climate change, striving to peak carbon dioxide emissions before 2030 and achieve carbon neutrality before 2060.

© The Author(s), under exclusive license to Springer Nature Switzerland AG 2024
Y. P. Tu and M. Chi (Eds.): WHICEB 2024, LNBIP 517, pp. 130–142, 2024.
https://doi.org/10.1007/978-3-031-60324-2_11

Digital finance generally refers to using digital technology by traditional financial institutions and Internet companies to realize financing, payment, investment, and other new financial business models. China's digital finance has developed rapidly in the past decade, exerting a broad impact on the real economy, traditional financial market, and online lending market.

In addition, many scholars have demonstrated the critical role of digital finance in energy conservation and emission reduction. This study focuses on the impact of digital finance on carbon emissions. The following arrangements are made for this paper: firstly, a literature review is conducted, and on this basis, research hypotheses are proposed. Then, the variables, data sources, and econometric models used in the empirical analysis of this paper are introduced, including the two-way fixed effect model and the SDM model. Then, the four parts of raw coal total, crude oil total, natural gas total, and cement are studied to explore the role of digital finance in energy transition. Then, heterogeneity analysis is conducted according to the geographical location and energy resource endowment, and finally, a summary and suggestions are made. Under the condition of controlling other factors, the study confirms the inverted U-shaped characteristics of digital finance on carbon emissions and innovatively discovers its essential role in promoting the use of clean energy (such as the policy of replacing coal with gas), which has practical significance for both governments and enterprises.

2 Literature Review and Research Hypothesis

2.1 Digital Finance and Carbon Emissions

The Environmental Kuznets Curve (EKC) suggests that as a country or region experiences economic growth, primarily measured by per capita income, the initial level of pollutant emissions gradually increases, leading to a deterioration in environmental quality. However, once economic growth surpasses a certain developmental threshold, emissions of significant pollutants peak and subsequently decline. Dinda (2004) [1] systematically summarized relevant research on the EKC, attributing its formation to advancements in economic development, such as the transition from a clean agricultural economy to a polluting industrial economy and then to a clean service economy, as well as to an increase in people's Income and corresponding preference for better environmental quality.

Specifically, in the context of China, Yan et al. (2016) argued that the impact of financial development on carbon intensity exhibits an inverted U-shaped relationship [2]. On the one hand, higher financial development leads to higher technological advancements, resulting in lower carbon dioxide intensity. On the other hand, a higher level of financial development also correlates with a higher economic growth rate, leading to increased energy consumption and carbon dioxide emissions. There is a tradeoff between these two opposing effects.

Furthermore, numerous studies have confirmed that the development of the digital economy has a significant spatial spillover effect, influencing the carbon emission levels of neighboring regions (Xu et al., 2022) [3]. Based on this, many scholars believe this spillover effect exhibits an inverted U-shaped pattern, initially increasing and then decreasing. For instance, Li et al. (2022) empirically demonstrated from both theoretical and empirical perspectives that, in the short term, the digital economy's promotion of carbon emissions is primarily due to increased energy use and non-green technological advancements [4]. However, in the long term, the digital economy's suppression of carbon emissions is primarily attributed to green technological advancements and industrial structural upgrades.

Based on the above analysis, this study proposes Hypothesis 1: The impact of digital finance on carbon emissions exhibits an inverted U-shaped pattern, initially increasing and then suppressing emissions. Additionally, this study hypothesizes that digital finance has a spillover effect on carbon emissions in neighboring regions. Hypothesis 2: Digital inclusive finance utilizes digital technologies to provide enterprises with more prosperous financing channels, increasing the proportion of renewable energy consumption and reducing carbon emissions.

2.2 Digital Finance and Technological Innovation

Most studies suggest that digital finance can reduce carbon emissions by promoting technological innovation in enterprises. The development of digital finance mainly promotes enterprise innovation through two channels. Firstly, digital finance improves bank competition and credit supply, promoting enterprise innovation (Zhang et al., 2023) [5]. Secondly, digital finance helps to lower credit barriers and encourage enterprises to invest in research and development for innovation (Zhu et al., 2022) [6]. From the perspective of enterprises, the development of digital finance promotes technological innovation by diversifying risks and reducing costs, enabling energy production sectors to improve pollution emission efficiency and thereby reduce carbon emissions (Shahbaz et al., 2013) [7]. Based on previous research, this study proposes Hypothesis 3: Digital finance has the potential to stimulate green innovation within enterprises, thus achieving emission reduction effects.

2.3 Heterogeneity in the Impact of Digital Finance

Additionally, studies are exploring the regions where digital finance is more effective in reducing carbon emissions. From the perspective of financial development, Deng et al. (2021) used panel data from 285 cities in China from 2012 to 2018 to argue that the emission reduction effect of digital finance is more pronounced in cities with lower economic and financial development levels [8]. From the perspective of financial regulation, Zheng et al. (2022) examined geographical locations and environmental pollution, proposing that the development of digital finance has a more significant emission reduction effect in cities in central and northeastern China, which have less environmental pollution and lower financial regulatory intensity [9]. From the income perspective, Acheampong (2019) demonstrated differences in the direct and indirect impacts of financial development on carbon emissions among different income groups, and domestic financial development measures have no linear impact on carbon emissions in low-income countries [11]. Based on these insights, this study proposes Hypothesis 4: The impact of digital finance on carbon emissions exhibits heterogeneity across different regions.

3   Materials and Methods

The core explanatory variable, carbon emissions, is derived from the CEADs database by Guan et al. (2021), encompassing four components: raw coal, crude oil, natural gas, and cement [12]. The core explanatory variables are sourced from The Peking University Digital Financial Inclusion Index of China by Guo et al. (2020) [13]. This index system for digital inclusive finance is constructed based on three dimensions: the breadth of digital finance coverage, the depth of digital finance utilization, and the level of digitization in inclusive finance. Considering the multitude of factors influencing carbon dioxide emissions, this study introduces relevant variables to control for the accuracy of the impact of digital finance on emissions. Additionally, take logarithms to mitigate heteroscedasticity.

Per Capita Income (lnincome): This variable uses residents' per capita disposable income. The affluence level of residents in a region reflects the economic development level of that region. Previous research indicates that income growth contributes to increased CO_2 emissions in China (Zhang et al., 2014) [9].

Population Size (lnpop): This variable is measured by the region's total population. Studies suggest that concerning CO_2 emissions, higher population density corresponds to higher emissions (Zarco-Perinan et al., 2021) [14].

Industrial Structure Upgrading (lnIS): Numerous scholars posit that the industrial structure plays a pivotal role in influencing carbon emissions. In this study, the degree of industrial structure upgrading is quantified by the ratio of the output value of the tertiary industry to that of the secondary industry, as proposed by Yu (2015) [15].

Urban road (lnroad): Following the findings of Timilsina et al. (2009) [16], urban areas emerge as the primary contributors to CO_2 emissions, with road transportation emissions constituting a significant portion. Consequently, this study adopts per capita urban road area as a metric to gauge the level of development in urban road transportation. Furthermore, according to Li et al. (2021) [17], control variables encompass Foreign Direct Investment (FDI), representing the proportion of total investment by foreign-invested enterprises to GDP, and Government Intervention Level (gov), denoting the ratio of local fiscal general budgetary expenditure to GDP (Table 1).

3.1   Two-Way Fixed Effects Model

Building upon the theoretical framework discussed above, this paper employs a two-way fixed effects model as the initial empirical approach to address the endogeneity concerns related to omitted variables when examining the impact of digital economic development on carbon emissions. The baseline model is defined as follows. $lnCO_{2it}$ represents the carbon dioxide emissions for the i-th city in the t-th year.

$$ln\,CO_{2it} = \alpha + \beta_1 ln\,DE_{it} + \beta_2 ln\,DE_{it}^2 + \sum_{j} \beta_j control_{it} + \mu_i + \gamma_t + \varepsilon_{it} \qquad (1)$$

Table 1. Variable description

	Variable name	Describe	Source
Dependent variable	carbon dioxide emissions (lnCO$_2$)	carbon dioxide emissions	China Emission Accounts and Datasets (CEADs)
Independent variable	digital finance index (lnDE)	construct based on three dimensions: the breadth of digital financial coverage, the depth of digital financial usage, and the degree of inclusiveness in digital finance	The Peking University Digital Financial Inclusion Index of China
Control variables	Income (lnincome)	The per capita disposable income of all residents	National Bureau of Statistics of China
	population Size (lnpop)	The total regional population	National Bureau of Statistics of China
	industrial structure upgrading (lnIS)	the ratio of the output value of the tertiary industry to that of the secondary industry	National Bureau of Statistics of China
	the level of urban road transportation (lnroad)	per capita urban road area	National Bureau of Statistics of China
	government support (lngov)	The ratio of local fiscal general budgetary expenditure to GDP	National Bureau of Statistics of China
	foreign direct investment (lnFDI)	The proportion of the total investment by foreign-invested enterprises to GDP	National Bureau of Statistics of China

3.2 Spatial Durbin Model

To investigate the spatial spillover effects of the digital economy on carbon emissions, spatial interaction terms are incorporated into the baseline regression. A spatial Durbin model is established to analyze the spatial dependency of the data in geographic space.

$$\ln CO_{2it} = \alpha + \rho W \ln CO_{2it} + \beta_1 \ln DE_{it} + \beta_2 \ln DE_{it}^2 + \varphi_1 W \ln DE_{it} + \varphi_2 W \ln DE_{it}^2$$
$$+ \beta_3 control_{it} + \varphi_3 W control_{it} + \mu_i + \gamma_t + \varepsilon_{it} \quad (2)$$

Provinces that are geographically closer exhibit spatial correlation in carbon emissions. However, neighboring regions may not necessarily share similar levels of economic development. Therefore, the weight W in Formula 2 utilizes an economic-geographic distance weight matrix. Building upon Lin et al. (2005) [18], economic distance is measured as the difference in per capita GDP between regions, while geographic distance is computed as the reciprocal distance based on latitude and longitude. The GDP data has been adjusted to exclude the impact of inflation. The final calculation method is expressed in Formula 3. Q_i represents the mean per capita GDP of region i, and d_{ij} denotes the square of the distance between regions i and j.

$$W = \begin{cases} \dfrac{|Q_i - Q_j|}{d_{ij}^2} & i = j \\ 0 & i \neq j \end{cases} \tag{3}$$

4 Results and Discussion

4.1 The Result of Baseline Regression

Table 2. The result of baseline regression

Variables	$lnCO_2$				
	(1)	(2)	(3)	(4)	(5)
lnDE	0.719***a	0.642***	1.381	0.618**	0.565***
	(2.840)	(2.86)	(1.30)	(2.67)	(2.84)
lnDE²	-0.074**	-0.062**	-0.184	-0.059**	-0.053**
	(-2.56)	(-2.56)	(-1.47)	(-2.35)	(-2.33)
	(1)	(2)	(3)	(4)	(5)
Indigitization_level					-0.156**
					(-2.59)
lnincome		-0.099	0.634	-0.126	-0.555
		(-0.74)	(1.20)	(-0.22)	(-0.96)
lnpop		1.240**	0.523**	1.329**	1.597***
		(2.06)	(2.39)	(2.23)	(2.84)
lnroad		0.145	0.360	0.138	0.127
		(1.36)	(1.24)	(1.29)	(1.36)
lnIS		0.131	-1.397***	0.221	0.269
		(0.52)	(-3.14)	(0.80)	(1.15)
lngov		0.146	1.445	0.168	-0.113
		(0.20)	(0.59)	(0.22)	(-0.16)
lnFDI		0.037	-0.277	0.050	0.029
		(0.55)	(-1.67)	(0.68)	(0.40)
intercept	2.704***	-6.201	-6.745	-6.740	-3.597
	(4.78)	(-1.58)	(-1.02)	(-0.96)	(-0.55)
province fixed effect	NO	YES	NO	YES	YES
year fixed effect	NO	NO	YES	YES	YES

a: *, **, and *** indicate statistically significant at the10%, 5%, and 1% levels

The regression results indicate that, after controlling for fixed effects of provinces and years, the coefficient for the linear term is 0.618, and the coefficient for the quadratic term is -0.059, both significant at a 5% level. This suggests that digital finance exhibits an inverted U-shaped relationship with carbon emissions, characterized by an initial increase followed by a subsequent decrease. The three dimensions of the digital financial index were decomposed and sequentially included in the regression. The results indicate that the regression coefficient for the level of digitization in inclusive finance is more significant compared to the breadth of digital financial coverage and the depth of digital financial utilization. Hypothesis 1 has been validated (Table 2).

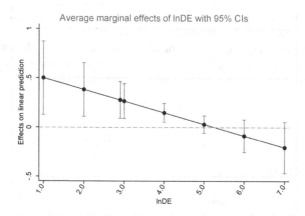

Fig. 1. The marginal effect coefficient of digital finance on carbon emissions

Figure 1 depicts the marginal effect coefficient of digital finance on carbon emissions, which is also the slope of the inverted U-shaped curve. After the logarithm of the digital finance index exceeds 5.0, the marginal effect shifts from promoting to inhibiting. In the early stages of digital finance development, enterprises must invest significant resources and labor in digital transformation. During this period, the development of digital finance lags behind the real economy, and the emission reduction effects are not prominent. As digital finance advances to a certain level, the effects of emission reduction become apparent. Scale effects and positive externalities come into play, effectively reducing costs and lowering carbon emissions.

4.2 The Result of the Durbin Model

SDM Model: Spillover Effects of Digital Finance on Carbon Emissions

Before using the SDM model, an LR test is performed to determine whether the control time fixed effect or the individual effect. The results show that the bidirectional fixed effect is reasonable (Table 3).

In the results obtained from the Spatial Durbin Model (SDM), the impact of digital finance on carbon emissions continues to exhibit an inverted U-shaped pattern. Moreover, the spatial coefficient is −0.297, which is significant at a 5% level, indicating that local carbon emissions may be influenced by the development of digital finance in neighboring regions. The hypothesis that digital finance has spillover effects on carbon emissions has been validated.

SDM Model: Digital Finance on the Different Components of Carbon Emissions.

China's carbon emissions primarily stem from the combustion of fossil fuels in the power and heating sectors, with coal constituting the predominant source of these fossil fuels. To further elucidate the causal pathway, the carbon emissions were decomposed. The provincial-level carbon dioxide emissions inventory in China from the Carbon Emission Accounting Database (CEADs) adopts an apparent emission accounting method, encompassing four components: raw coal total, crude oil total, natural gas total, and cement (Table 4).

Table 3. Spillover effects of digital finance on carbon emissions

Variables	(1)	(2)	(3)
	Main	Wx	Spatial
lnDE	0.647***	0.417	
	(0.167)	(0.482)	
$lnDE^2$	−0.0610***	−0.0394	
	(0.0195)	(0.0584)	
rho			−0.297**
			(0.132)
control variables	YES	YES	YES
province fixed effect	YES	YES	YES
year fixed effect	YES	YES	YES

Table 4. Regression on the emission ratio of the natural gas sector

Variables	Natural gas					
	Main	Wx	Spatial	LR_Direct	LR_Indirect	LR_Total
lnDE	−0.181***	−0.303***		−0.190***	−0.407***	−0.597***
	(0.0377)	(0.108)		(0.0393)	(0.145)	(0.160)
$lnDE^2$	0.0188***	0.0250*		0.0194***	0.0342**	0.0536***
	(0.00441)	(0.0131)		(0.00463)	(0.0171)	(0.0188)
rho			0.187*			
			(0.0998)			

Table 5. Regression on the emission ratio of the raw coal sector

Variables	Raw coal					
	Main	Wx	Spatial	LR_Direct	LR_Indirect	LR_Total
lnDE	0.170***	0.364**		0.168***	0.338**	0.506***
	(0.0632)	(0.169)		(0.0651)	(0.158)	(0.169)
$lnDE^2$	−0.0176**	−0.0357*		−0.0174**	−0.0332*	−0.0507**
	(0.00743)	(0.0203)		(0.00768)	(0.0189)	(0.0201)
rho			−0.104			
			(0.122)			

Initially, the proportions of these four emission components relative to the total emissions were calculated. This was utilized as the dependent variable, and SDM was employed to investigate the individual effects of digital finance on each proportion. The SDM outcomes for crude oil total and cement are not statistically significant and are therefore not included due to space constraints (Table 5).

For natural gas, the first-order coefficient is -0.181, and the second-order coefficient is 0.0188, both statistically significant at a 1% level. This suggests that the influence of digital finance on the proportion of carbon emissions from natural gas follows a U-shaped pattern. Additionally, it indicates the presence of a spillover effect, signifying that in the early stages of digital finance development, there is a restraining effect on natural gas consumption, followed by a subsequent promotion of consumption in later stages. The indirect spatial effects, calculated through the partial derivative method by Pace and Lesage (2009) [19], are shown in the LR_Indirect column. The first-order and second-order coefficients are statistically significant at a 5% significance level, indicating that the development of digital finance in adjacent regions has a spillover effect, affecting the local proportion of natural gas use.

For Raw coal, the first-order coefficient is 0.17, and the second-order coefficient is -0.0176, both statistically significant at 1% and 5% significance levels, respectively. This implies that digital finance's impact on the proportion of carbon emissions from raw coal follows a U-shaped pattern, in contrast to the inverted U-shaped pattern observed for natural gas. This reflects changes in energy structure. The underdeveloped nature of the digital finance market in the early stages hampers the innovation of renewable energy technologies. Renewable energy innovation faces challenges such as project uncertainty and uncertain investment returns. As digital inclusive finance develops, the consumption ratio of renewable energy to total energy consumption increases.

These outcomes affirm the empowering role of digital finance in the natural gas industry chain. Hypothesis 2 has been validated. Natural gas is a low-carbon fossil energy source with tremendous growth potential, but China's infrastructure is still imperfect. Additionally, the financial repression theory posits that delayed financial development can inhibit the potential for green transformation in regions or industries. Therefore, there was no significant increase in natural gas consumption in the early stages of digital finance development. After reaching a certain level of development, the development of digital inclusive finance can help stakeholders, including enterprises, governments, and residents, expand their financing channels. In the downstream sector, the evolution of digital finance prompts a shift in focus towards data value exploration in transaction pricing and other aspects, making the coal-to-gas project environmentally and economically beneficial.

4.3 Digital Finance and Technological Innovation

Suppose the quantity of domestic patent applications granted is used as a proxy variable for technological innovation, with digital inclusive finance and its quadratic term as explanatory variables. In that case, the relationship between digital inclusive finance and technological innovation exhibits a U-shaped pattern, characterized by initial suppression followed by promotion, as indicated by the regression equation.

$$inpat = -24.184 - 0.703 ln\, DE + 0.087 ln\, DE^2 + 3.569 ln\, income + 0.018 ln\, pop$$
$$+\ 0.216\, ln\, road - 1.43 ln\, IS + 2.077 ln\, gov + 0.194 ln\, FDI \qquad (4)$$

The regression equation indicates that the coefficients of lnDE and lnDE^2 are significant at a 10% significance level, while lnincome and lnIS are significant at 5% and 1%, respectively. The coefficient before lnDE is -0.703 and before lnDE^2 is 0.087, suggesting a U-shaped relationship between digital finance and domestic patent applications. Hypothesis 3 has been validated. During the initial stages of development in digital inclusive finance, companies need to reset various production equipment and consume a substantial amount of energy to increase output and achieve technological innovation, leading to environmental degradation and increased carbon emissions. As digital inclusive finance matures, the output of enterprises gradually stabilizes, and technological and scale effects effectively reduce costs, resulting in a significant reduction in carbon emissions.

5 Heterogeneity Analysis

Table 6. Heterogeneity analysis

Variables	Geographic classification			Energy quality classification		
	Eastern	Central	Western	High	Middle	Low
	lnCO$_2$	lnCO$_2$	lnCO$_2$	lnCO$_2$	lnCO$_2$	lnCO$_2$
lnDE	0.279	0.773**	24.567**	0.123	0.429	−1.258*
	(1.14)	(2.00)	(2.30)	(0.33)	(1.29)	(−1.68)
lnDE^2	−0.032	−0.070	−2.132**	−0.014	−0.033	0.127*
	(−1.05)	(−1.55)	(−2.30)	(−0.33)	(−0.78)	(1.72)
intercept	−9.041	−6.567	−76.611**	−35.792*	0.952	−2.564
	(−1.32)	(−0.77)	(−2.42)	(−1.83)	(0.12)	(−0.48)
control variables	YES	YES	YES	YES	YES	YES

5.1 Geographic Classification

From an economic perspective, there exists an imbalance in the development between China's eastern and western regions. Currently, the developed coastal regions in the east occupy less than 5% of the national land area but account for one-third of the total population and contribute to nearly half of the GDP. Therefore, it is necessary to categorize the country into three parts—eastern, central, and western—for heterogeneity analysis, as illustrated in Table 6. The results indicate that the inverted U-shaped pattern of digital finance's impact on carbon emissions is most significant in the western region. The relatively backward development of digital finance in the western region has a more significant marginal effect on optimizing energy structures and promoting green transformation of enterprises, thus leading to a more significant emission reduction effect.

5.2 Energy Quality Classification

With its vast territory, China exhibits diverse endowments of energy resources, leading to varying energy-related challenges and disparities in development levels among different provinces. Tang et al. (2023), considering primary indicators such as energy supply security, energy consumption, energy structure, and energy technology, have constructed a provincial-level monitoring system for high-quality energy development and provided rankings for all 31 provinces nationwide [20]. Building upon this ranking, the current study categorizes the provinces into high, medium, and low energy quality regions for heterogeneity analysis.

The results in Table 6 indicate that regression coefficients are insignificant in both high and medium-energy quality regions, while they exhibit a U-shaped pattern in low-energy-quality regions. In regions with low energy quality, where energy reserves are unstable, per capita energy consumption is high, clean energy utilization is limited, and insufficient human capital innovation, digital finance seems less effective. Addressing these fundamental issues in areas with scarce resources is essential for digital finance to play a more effective role in carbon reduction. Hypothesis 4 has been validated.

6 Conclusions

The regression results indicate that the impact of digital finance on carbon emissions follows the inverted "U-shaped" pattern described by the Environmental Kuznets Curve. It is imperative to expedite the development of digital finance and surpass the turning point at the earliest opportunity. Considering the significant role played by the digitalization level of inclusive finance, expediting the construction of new financial infrastructure is essential. Simultaneously, banks should comprehensively increase their technological investments, promote adopting digital inclusive financial products, and lower customer entry barriers.

Digital finance can contribute to reducing carbon emissions by fostering corporate innovation. For enterprises, engaging in green innovation activities is characterized by a lengthy cycle and high costs. However, the development of digital finance can facilitate convenient financing and lending for businesses, thereby supporting enterprises in undertaking green transformations.

Further breakdown of the calculated results for apparent carbon emissions indicates that digital finance plays a significant role in the coal-to-gas conversion process. The extensive use of coal energy has supported China's economic growth but has also led to severe environmental pollution. In 2013, the State Council introduced measures to accelerate the coal-to-gas project. However, this policy faces difficulties, such as increasing economic burden on residents and financial pressure on the government due to subsidy policies. The development of digital finance effectively addresses this challenge. The advancement of big data enables banks to assess the creditworthiness of relevant enterprises more conveniently. Additionally, financial technology can be employed to establish environmentally beneficial affiliated funds.

References

1. Dinda, S.: Environmental Kuznets curve hypothesis: a survey. Ecol. Econ. **49**(4), 431–455 (2004)
2. Yan, C., Li, T., Lan, W.: Financial development, innovation, and carbon emission. Financ. Res. **2016**(01), 14–30 (2016). (in Chinese)
3. Xu, W., Zhou, J., Liu, C.: The impact of digital economy on urban carbon emissions: based on the analysis of spatial effects. Geogr. Res. **41**(01), 111–129 (2022). (in Chinese)
4. Li, Z., Wang, J.: The dynamic impact of digital economy on carbon emission reduction: evidence city-level empirical data in China. J. Clean. Prod. **351**, 131570.1-131570.12 (2022)
5. Zhang, P., Wang, Y., Wang, R., Wang, T.: Digital finance and corporate innovation: evidence from China. Appl. Econ. **56**, 615–638 (2023)
6. Zhu, D., Zhang, X.: Environmental effects and mechanisms of china's digital financial development. Collected Essays Finan. Econ. **283**(03), 37–46 (2022). (in Chinese)
7. Shahbaz, M., Tiwari, A.K., Nasir, M.A.: The effects of financial development, economic growth, coal consumption, and trade openness on CO_2 emissions in South Africa. Energy Policy **61**, 1452–1459 (2013)
8. Deng, R., Zhang, A.: Research on the environmental effect of digital finance development in China and its influence mechanism. Res. Sci. **43**(11), 2316–2330 (2021). (in Chinese)
9. Zhang, C., Zhao, W.: Panel estimation for income inequality and CO_2 emissions: a regional analysis in China. Appl. Energy **136**, 382–392 (2014)
10. Zheng, W., Zhao, H., Zhao, M.: Is the development of digital finance conducive to environmental pollution control? Concurrently discussing the regulatory impact of local resource competition. Ind. Econ. Res. **2022**(01), 1–13 (2022). (in Chinese)
11. Acheampong, A.O.: Modelling for insight: does financial development improve environmental quality? Energy Econ. **83**, 156–179 (2019)
12. Guan, Y., et al.: Assessment to China's recent emission pattern shifts. Earth's Future. https://doi.org/10.1029/2021EF002241. https://agupubs.onlinelibrary.wiley.com/doi/full/. Accessed (2021)
13. Guo, F., Wang, J.Y., Wang, F., et al.: Measuring the development of digital financial inclusion in China: index compilation and spatial characteristics. China Econ. Q. **19**, 1401–1418 (2020). (in Chinese)
14. Zarco-Perinan, P.J., Zarco-Soto, I.M., Zarco-Soto, F.J.: Influence of population density on CO_2 emissions eliminating the influence of climate. Atmos. **12**(9), 1193 (2021)
15. Yu, B.: Economic growth effects of industrial restructuring and productivity improvement——analysis of dynamic spatial panel model with Chinese city data. China Ind. Econ. **12**, 83–98 (2015). (in Chinese)
16. Timilsina, G.R., Shrestha, A.: Transport sector CO_2 emissions growth in Asia: underlying factors and policy options. Energy Policy **37**, 4523–4539 (2009)
17. Li, J., Chen, L., Chen, Y., He, J.: Digital economy, technological innovation, and green economic efficiency—empirical evidence from 277 cities in China. Manag. Decis. Econ. **43**, 616–629 (2021)

18. Lin, G., Long, Z., Wu, M.: A spatial analysis of regional economic convergence in China: 1978–2002. China Econ. Q. (S1), 67–82 (2005). (in Chinese)
19. LeSage, J., Pace, R.K.: Introduction to Spatial Econometrics. Chapman and Hall/CRC (2009)
20. Tang, B., Wu, Y., Zou, Y., et al.: Research on China's energy economic index: based on the industry perspective. J. Beijing Ins. Technol. (Soc. Sci. Edn.), **23**(02), 9–16 (2021). (in Chinese)

The Impacts of Characteristic Factors on Learning Satisfaction: An Empirical Study in Gamification Virtual Simulation Systems

Jun Yin, Aoxue Qiu$^{(\boxtimes)}$, Lulu Li, and Shilun Ge

School of Economics and Management, Jiangsu University of Science and Technology, Zhenjiang, China

qax_just@163.com

Abstract. Virtual simulation technology has become one of the indispensable technologies in the field of teaching. However, the application of virtual simulation experiments and the embedding of corresponding gamification elements do not always show the enhanced learning effect. In order to effectively guide the application of virtual simulation experiments, we combined the adaptive structure theory for individuals and self-determination theory, and through a controlled experiment of 2 (task complexity: high vs. low) × 2 (field cognitive styles: field independent vs. field dependent) + 1 (control group), we firstly verified the effectiveness of the application of the gamification virtual simulation system, and at the same time, focused on the factors of task characteristics and individual characteristics, to explore how these two constructs can influence students' learning satisfaction by affecting intrinsic motivation. Our findings suggest that gamification virtual simulation systems are more effective in enhancing students' learning experiences. And setting high-complexity tasks better reinforces intrinsic motivation (autonomy needs, competence needs, and relationship needs) fulfillment, which in turn effectively enhances learning satisfaction. Compared to students with field-dependent cognitive styles, students with field-independent cognitive styles were able to achieve higher learning satisfaction by obtaining higher competence needs and relationship needs in a gamification virtual simulation system, but there was no significant difference between the two in terms of autonomy need.

Keywords: Gamification Virtual simulation · Adaptive Structuration Theory of Individuals · Self-determination theory · Task complexity · Field cognitive style

1 Introduction

In recent years, the development of virtual simulation technology has brought a profound impact on university laboratory teaching [1]. The improving technical features and the continuing reduction in application costs of virtual reality technology have made it one of the six key educational technologies predicted by the 2022 Higher Education Horizon Report [2]. As online virtual simulation experiments are increasingly being adopted by universities, many innovative approaches are being integrated into regular university laboratory courses for various forms of blended laboratory teaching attempts [3], and scholars have proposed various interventions including gamification [4], but the results have been mixed, with the embedding of gamification elements not always showing enhanced learning effects. Some evidence suggests that gamification may lead to negative experiences such as increased stress, over-engagement and negative emotions [5], due to the fact that the effectiveness of gamification depends not only on its design itself, but also on the user's perception of the gamification experience [6]. Indeed, many studies have sought an answer to the question, "How to rationally apply virtual simulation teaching experiments to enhance student practice and satisfaction"? However, existing research focuses more on the selection of game elements and the design of game mechanics for game-based learning [7], and lacks attention to the impact and mechanisms of the effects of characteristics factors in the application of extant well-established gamification systems.

Therefore, this paper proposes a student-centered approach, guided by ASTI and SDT theories, to first validate the effectiveness of the application of gamification virtual simulation systems through empirical research, and at the same time focusing on the task characteristics and individual characteristics factors, to explore how these two constructs can affect students' learning satisfaction by affecting intrinsic motivation, and then to open up a new avenue for the future research on the effective use of gamification virtual simulation system.

2   Theoretical Background and Research Hypothesis

2.1   Adaptive Structuration Theory for Individuals

ASTI was developed from the AST (Adaptive Structuration Theory) to explain the interactions between individual users, information technology, and social structures [8]. This theory identifies Structured inputs are antecedent drivers of the adaptive technology use process and include technology characteristics, task characteristics, and individual characteristics. This study explored the effects of task complexity and field cognitive style, where task complexity is precisely the structural feature of the task that Desanctis and Poole [9] were most concerned with when proposing the AST theory; field cognitive style is considered to be an important personality factor influencing students' learning outcomes [10]; and since this study applies a mature and well-established gamified virtual simulation teaching system and was not involved in the technical design or personalization and modularization introduction of the system, the structured inputs of the technical features that ASTI theory focuses on are only validated in this paper and are not talked about as antecedent variables.

2.2   Self-Determination Theory

Guided by the ASTI theory, this study employs a more microscopic theory to explain in detail the specific adaptation process from an intrinsic motivation perspective. Self-Determination Theory (SDT), a comprehensive theory of human behavioral motivation proposed by the American psychologist Deci [11], is one of the most established theoretical frameworks in the study of gamification and game motivation. Self-Determination

Theory suggests that when an individual's three basic psychological needs (autonomy needs, competence needs, and relationship needs) are supported in activities, their motivational regulation tends to be more autonomous and regulated, which in turn translates into intrinsic motivation, motivating them to use the experiment proactively and ultimately to achieve better learning outcomes.

Based on the theoretical guidance of ASTI and SDT, the research model was constructed in this study, as shown in Fig. 1.

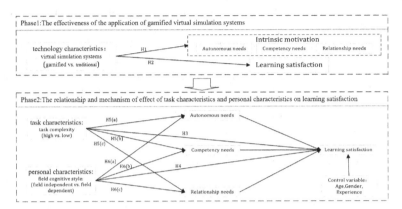

Fig. 1. Research model

2.3 The Effectiveness of the Application of Gamification Virtual Simulation Systems

Intrinsic motivation and learning satisfaction of participants are important indicators of the effectiveness of gamified learning. According to existing studies, it can be found that the application of gamification elements has a positive impact on students' intrinsic motivation and learning satisfaction [12]. The gamification virtual simulation system promotes independent and collaborative learning by introducing gamified elements such as competition and rewards, which fully stimulate students' deep intrinsic motivation and enhance the learning. This leads to the following hypothesis:

H1. The application of gamification virtual simulation system can inspire students' intrinsic motivation to learn.

H2. The application of gamification virtual simulation system can improve the learning satisfaction of students.

2.4 The Influence of Task Complexity and Field Cognitive Style on Learning Satisfaction with the Application of Gamification Virtual Simulation Systems

Task complexity is a direct reflection of the difficulty of the teaching content of virtual simulation experiments, and existing research has confirmed the positive impact of high task complexity on learning outcomes [13]. For college students, they may prefer to encounter tasks that are challenging and correspondingly rewarding in virtual simulation experiments, which not only improve their abilities, knowledge and skills, but provide a better learning experience. This leads to the following hypothesis:

H3. High task complexity has a positive impact on learning satisfaction of students who apply gamification virtual simulation systems.

For individuals, cognitive style, as an important individual difference variable, influences their cognitive processes, such as attentional and memory activities, and is one of the most important factors affecting learning effectiveness [14]. And existing research has confirmed the positive impact of field-independent cognitive style on learning outcomes [15]. Gamification virtual simulation system adds a variety of gamified tips and learning aids for users through gamified elements, and field-independent learners are able to utilize these resources more autonomously for better knowledge acquisition, learning, and empowerment. This leads to the following hypothesis:

H4. Field-independent cognitive style has a positive effect on learning satisfaction of students who apply gamification virtual simulation system.

2.5 Mediation Effect of Intrinsic Motivation

Setting up high-complexity tasks in a gamification virtual simulation system, as well as using a variety of gamified elements (avatars, badges, etc.) to give timely feedback and assistance to students during the learning process, can provide individuals with a feeling of being able to freely participate in the learning and better strengthen the fulfillment of the needs for autonomy; and compared with low-complexity tasks, completing high-complexity tasks with the help of various gamification elements in virtual simulation experiments is more likely to enable students to obtain competence enhancement and perception, which in turn enhances the interaction and communication between students and between students and the system, and thus increases the students' learning satisfaction. This leads to the following hypothesis:

H5a. Autonomy needs mediate the effect of task complexity on learning satisfaction.
H5b. Competency needs mediate the effect of task complexity on learning satisfaction.
H5c. Relationship needs mediate the effect of task complexity on learning satisfaction.

Learners with different cognitive styles have different tendencies to process information. Compared with field-dependent cognitive styles, field-independent learners are better able to stick to themselves, autonomously seek and utilize the needed gamification elements to better satisfy their own needs and are better able to obtain the enhancement of competence and sense of competence, which in turn strengthens the communication links between students and between students and the system, and thus enhances the students' learning satisfaction. This leads to the following hypothesis:

H6a. Autonomy needs mediate the effect of field cognitive style on learning satisfaction.
H6b. Competency needs mediate the effect of field cognitive style on learning satisfaction.
H6c. Relationship needs mediate the effect of field cognitive style on satisfaction with learning.

3 Method

3.1 Sample Selection

To increase the credibility of the study and ensure the diversity of the sample data, this study selected the sample of subjects by class, invited a total of 164 recent graduates of a university in their senior year to participate in the experiment, informed the specific content of the experiment, the time and duration needed, and the way to participate, and confirmed that each student could participate in the experiment.

3.2 Research Scenario Design

(1) Research Scenario Design for Phase 1

To verify the effectiveness of the gamification virtual simulation experimental appliance, two experimental projects with the same content are selected for the phase 1 of the study: an experiment on material procurement management in manufacturing enterprises. And the similarities and differences between the two are shown in Table 1.

Table 1. Similarities and differences between the two types of virtual simulation experiments

	Conventional experiments	Gamification Virtual Simulation Experiment
Similarity	(i) Tasks are identical: the same task operations can be performed	
	(ii) Identical operational processes: the tasks in the experiment have the same operational processes	
	(iii) The experimental content is the same: the purpose, knowledge, needs, and content of each task are the same	
Difference	(i) Objective and task elements (with clear objectives and tasks) (ii) Resource elements (provides a manual for operating the system's experiments as a guidance)	(i) (ii) same as Conventional experiments (iii) Situational elements: creating story situations, problem situations and management situations for students using music, animations, game images, etc. (iv) Communication elements: providing space and guidance for communication (v) Evaluation elements: positive feedback is given to users through points, badges, lighting processes, progress bars, etc

(2) Research Scenario Design for Phase 2

To explore how task characteristics factors can influence students' learning satisfaction by affecting intrinsic motivation in the gamification virtual simulation experiments. The second phase of the study selected two system operation tasks that were both significantly different in task complexity and highly related in task content: the two experiments are material procurement management and material procurement process optimization. The specific processes of the two tasks are shown in Table 2.

Table 2. Basic information about the two experimental tasks

Mission complexity	Mission name	Mission content	Mission features
Lower	Procurement management	(i) Procurement tasking (ii) Request for quotations for procurement (iii) Material audit (iv) Procurement contract entry (v) Procurement contract review	(i) Low information content (ii) A fixed single path for task operations (iii) Has fixed marked answers
Higher	Procurement process optimization	(i) Procurement process research and modelling (ii) Interviews and analysis of procurement process issues (iii) Procurement process optimization	(i) High level of information (ii) Need for graphical analysis skills (iii) Task operations and options are not unique (iv) The results of the analysis are open-ended

3.3 Organization of Experimental Groupings

In this study, 164 students from a school of economics and management were invited as the subjects of the study. 77 students studied using the conventional virtual simulation system as the control group, and 87 students studied using the gamification virtual simulation system, as the experimental group. Before the experiment began, students in the experimental group were assessed for their field cognitive styles using the "Cognitive Style Mosaic Graphic Test" revised by Professor Houchong Zhang of Beijing Normal University, of which 41 students tended to have a field-dependent style and 46 students tended to have a field-independent style. Then they are randomly assigned for low-complexity and high-complexity tasks respectively.

3.4 Experimental Procedure

First, one or two experimental assistants were set up for each group in this study, and the duration of the experiment was 45 min. The specific flow is shown in Fig. 2.

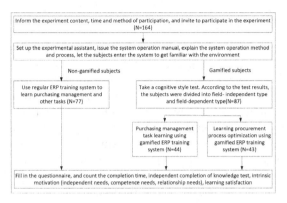

Fig. 2. Experimental flow chart

3.5 Measurement of Intrinsic Motivation and Learning Satisfaction

Based on the self-determination theory, this paper refers to the studies of Suh et al. [16] and Jang et al. [17], and combines the specific scenarios of users using the virtual simulation system to measure the intrinsic motivation of the users in terms of three basic psychological needs (autonomy, competence, and relational needs). Learning satisfaction is a comprehensive judgment of whether the user's experience is consistent with learning expectations. According to the situation of gamification virtual simulation system, based on the study of Aparicio et al. [18], a scale of respondents' satisfaction with the use of the system was constructed and adapted, namely, the learning satisfaction scale. All the questions are shown in Table 3.

4 Empirical Results and Analysis

Excluding responses with missing values left 138 valid questionnaires, including 77 participants using the conventional virtual simulation system and 61 participants using the gamification virtual simulation system.

4.1 Questionnaire Reliability and Validity Analysis

The reliability and validity of the questionnaire were assessed by confirmatory factor analysis before statistical analysis of the data. As shown in Tables 3 and 4, the factor loadings of individual question items, Cronbach's alpha and CR values for all indicators were greater than 0.7; the AVE values of all indicators are greater than 0.5, so the scale has good reliability, structural validity and convergent validity. And the square root of AVE for each construct is larger than the correlation of that construct with all the other constructs, ensuring the discriminant validity of the constructs. In a word, the questionnaire used in this study passed the tests of reliability and validity.

4.2 Common Method Bias

In this study, the anonymity and confidentiality of personal information was purposely emphasized to the respondents during the questionnaire survey, and it was promised that the data of the questionnaires would be used for academic research only, to ensure that more authentic information would be obtained. Meanwhile, this study used the validated factor analysis of Common Marker Variable. A common method factor is added and the path coefficient between it and other question items is set to a to construct the control model; by testing the chi-square difference between the four-factor model and the control model, the results illustrate that the chi-square difference between the two models was 2.167, which did not reach the significant level ($p = 0.141 > 0.05$), so there is no significant common methodological bias in this study.

4.3 Regression Analysis

Validity of the Gamification Virtual Simulation Experimental Appliance.
In this study, the PSM method was used to eliminate the problem of non-randomness and imbalance of the sample data. Independent samples t-tests were first performed on the control variables, which showed that age and experience were significantly different between the two groups and were therefore used as covariates to calculate the propensity score. The sample was subjected to PSM with 1:1 caliper range of 0.05, the sample size of successful matching was 117 and the results show that the standardized bias after matching is 0%, which satisfies the criterion that it must be less than 10%, meanwhile, the results of the independent samples t-test showed that there was no significant difference in covariates between the two groups after matching, which satisfied the balance assumption. Figure 3 shows the kernel density comparison between the propensity score values of the experimental group and the control group before and after PSM matching. Through observation, it can be intuitively found that the overlap of the two kernel density curves of the experimental group and the control group is significantly higher after matching compared with that before matching, which satisfied the common support assumption. Therefore, it indicates that the gap between the characteristic variables of the two groups of samples is greatly reduced after matching, and the effect of PSM is significant.

Based on applying the PSM with 1:1 caliper range of 0.05 and calculating the corresponding propensity values of the individuals involved in the pairing, the average treatment effect (ATT) of the experimental group was obtained in this study. As shown in Table 5, the use of a gamified virtual simulation system showed a significant positive effect on students' acquisition of intrinsic motivation as well as on their perceived level of learning satisfaction. Therefore, H1 and H2 hold.

Table 3. Reliability and validity of the learning experience questionnaire

Latent variable	Subject matter	Factor loading	Cronbach's alpha	CR	AVE
Autonomous needs	AN1: I feel no pressure from the outside world during the use of gamification virtual simulations	0.834	0.913	0.9146	0.7815
	AN2: What I learned during the use of the gamification virtual simulation was of interest to me	0.913			
	AN3: During the use of gamification virtual simulations, task manipulation interests me intensely	0.903			
Competency needs	CN1: I feel empowered in the use of gamification virtual simulations	0.852	0.895	0.8950	0.7396
	CN2: In using the gamification virtual simulation process, I feel I am up to the task	0.861			
	CN3: The use of gamification virtual simulations has allowed me to progress in my abilities	0.867			
Relationship needs	RN1: I feel supported by others in the use of gamification virtual simulations	0.860	0.902	0.9024	0.7553

(*continued*)

Table 3. (*continued*)

Latent variable	Subject matter	Factor loading	Cronbach's alpha	CR	AVE
	RN2: In using the gamification virtual simulation process, I feel I have been valuable to others	0.916			
	RN3: In using the gamification virtual simulation, I felt a sense of belonging in connection with others	0.829			
Learning satisfaction	US1: The gamification virtual simulation system can fully support my learning about virtual simulation	0.862	0.929	0.9296	0.7676
	US2: Gamification virtual simulation system improves learning efficiency compared to pre-use expectations	0.877			
	US3: Gamification virtual simulation systems improve learning compared to pre-use expectations	0.902			
	US4: How satisfied are you with the gamification virtual simulation system in general?	0.863			

The Effects of Task Complexity and Field Cognitive Style on Learning Satisfaction. The results of the regression analysis using data from the 61 samples before matching in the experimental group was shown in Models 1–3 of Table 6. The results show that task complexity can positively affect the learning satisfaction of the gamification virtual simulation system at a significance level of 0.05 ($\beta = 0.7191$, $p < 0.05$); and field

Table 4. Discriminant validity and correlation of constructs

Variable	Autonomous needs	Competency needs	Relationship needs	Learning satisfaction
Autonomous needs	0.884			
Competency needs	0.831[c]	0.860		
Relationship needs	0.778[c]	0.830[c]	0.869	
Learning satisfaction	0.804[c]	0.785[c]	0.817[c]	0.876

Notes: Square root of AVE for each latent construct is given in diagonals; [a] $p < 0.1$, [b] $p < 0.05$, [c] $p < 0.01$.

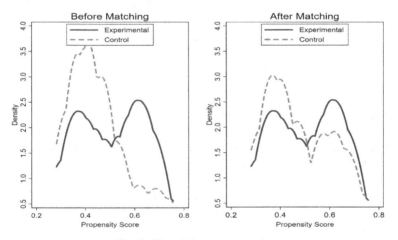

Fig. 3. Kernel density comparison

Table 5. Propensity value matching estimation results

	Intrinsic motivation			Learning satisfaction
	Autonomous needs	Competency needs	Relationship needs	
ATT	0.6063[b]	0.5688[b]	0.7319[c]	0.6352[c]

Notes: t statistics in parentheses; [a] $p < 0.1$, [b] $p < 0.05$, [c] $p < 0.01$.

cognitive style can positively affect the learning satisfaction of the gamification virtual simulation system at a significance level of 0.1 ($\beta = 0.6553$, $p < 0.1$). learning satisfaction ($\beta = 0.6553$, $p < 0.1$). Therefore, H3 and H4 hold.

Table 6. The effects of task complexity and field cognitive style on learning satisfaction

	Learning satisfaction						
	Model 1	Model 2	Model 3	Model 4	Model 5	Model 6	Model 7
task complexity		0.7191[b]			0.8095[b]		
		(2.3021)			(2.6194)		
field cognitive style			0.6553[a]				0.7028[a]
			(1.9957)				(1.9823)
Controls	YES	YES	YES	YES	YES	YES	YES
_cons	10.0284[b]	9.0417[a]	7.7682[a]	7.6377	5.8845	9.7723	9.1755
	(2.0842)	(1.9506)	(1.7251)	(1.2480)	(1.0249)	(1.3135)	(1.3243)
N	61	61	61	58	58	54	54
r2_a	−0.0199	0.0489	0.0306	−0.0477	0.0410	−0.0456	0.0156

Notes: t statistics in parentheses; [a] $p < 0.1$, [b] $p < 0.05$, [c] $p < 0.01$.

The Mediation Effect of Intrinsic Motivation.
The results of mediating effect are shown in Table 7 and Fig. 4. The results show that autonomy needs, competence needs, and relational needs all play a fully mediating role in the effect of task complexity on learning satisfaction, the proportion of mediating effect is 88.19%, 85.02%, 87.05% respectively, so H5a, H5b, and H5c hold.; and competency needs, relationship needs all play the full mediating role in the effect of field cognitive style on learning satisfaction, the proportion of mediation effect is 83.6%, 83.82%, and autonomous needs have no mediation role in the effect of field cognitive style on learning satisfaction, so H6b, H6c hold and H6a does not.

4.4 Robustness Check

In this paper, we use the control variables in the baseline regression as covariates, and the PSM method is used to test the robustness of the regression results. 58 samples were obtained after deleting the unmatched samples with task complexity as the grouping condition, and 54 samples were obtained after deleting the unmatched samples with field cognitive style as the grouping condition. Independent samples t-tests were conducted respectively, and the results showed that none of the covariates were significantly different and satisfied the balance assumption. Further robustness tests were conducted to

Table 7. Mediation Analysis (N = 61)

Type of effect	path	Effect	BootSE	BootLLCI	BootULCI	%Percentage of mediating effects
Mediating effects of intrinsic motivation	task complexity → Autonomous needs → Learning satisfaction	0.6342	0.2667	0.1395	1.1941	0.8819
	task complexity → Competency needs → Learning satisfaction	0.6114	0.2574	0.1488	1.1578	0.8502
	task complexity → Relationship needs → Learning satisfaction	0.6260	0.2713	0.1336	1.2013	0.8705
	field cognitive style → Autonomous needs → Learning satisfaction	0.3806	0.2821	−0.1176	0.9848	——
	field cognitive style → Competency needs → Learning satisfaction	0.5481	0.2771	0.0258	1.1200	0.8360
	field cognitive style → Relationship needs → Learning satisfaction	0.5493	0.2809	0.0158	1.1363	0.8382
total effect	task complexity → Learning satisfaction	0.7191	0.3177	0.0275	0.0827	
	field cognitive style → Learning satisfaction	0.6553	0.3290	0.0513	−0.0037	

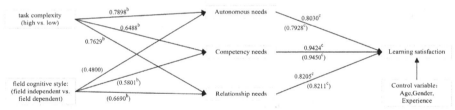

Notes: The mediating effect of intrinsic motivation in the influence of field cognitive style on learning satisfaction in parentheses; [a] $p < 0.1$, [b] $p < 0.05$, [c] $p < 0.01$

Fig. 4. Result of the mediation analysis

influence the path study, and the results are shown in Models 4–7 of Table 6, Table 8, and Fig. 5. The results show that after using the PSM method to eliminate the non-randomness and imbalance problem of the sample data and to some extent the endogeneity problem, the results are consistent with the results of the regression test and the mediation effect test, indicating that the results are robust.

Table 8. Robustness check of Mediation Analysis

Type of effect	path	Effect	BootSE	BootLLCI	BootULCI	%Percentage of mediating effects
Mediating effects of intrinsic motivation	task complexity → Autonomous needs → Learning satisfaction (N = 58)	0.6797	0.2694	0.2135	1.2713	0.8397
	task complexity → Competency needs → Learning satisfaction (N = 58)	0.6750	0.2632	0.2141	1.2457	0.8338
	task complexity → Relationship needs → Learning satisfaction (N = 58)	0.7055	0.2823	0.2059	1.2979	0.8715
	field cognitive style → Autonomous needs → Learning satisfaction (N = 54)	0.3759	0.2900	−0.1551	0.9921	——
	field cognitive style → Competency needs → Learning satisfaction (N = 54)	0.5784	0.2882	0.0444	1.1673	0.8230
	field cognitive style → Relationship needs → Learning satisfaction (N = 54)	0.5822	0.2975	0.0299	1.2047	0.8284
total effect	task complexity → Learning satisfaction (N = 58)	0.8095	0.3305	0.0177	0.1466	
	field cognitive style → Learning satisfaction (N = 54)	0.7028	0.3468	0.0482	0.0059	

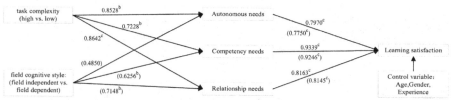

Notes: The mediating effect of intrinsic motivation in the influence of field cognitive style on learning satisfaction in parentheses; [a] p < 0. 1, [b] p < 0.05, [c] p < 0.01

Fig. 5. Result of the robustness check of the mediation analysis

5   Research Conclusion and Enlightenment

5.1   Findings and Conclusions

The results show that: First, the application of gamification virtual simulation system can enhance students' intrinsic motivation and learning satisfaction, which confirms its effectiveness. Second, the application of gamification virtual simulation system in the high-complexity task is more likely to improve learning experience by motivating students' intrinsic motivation. Third, we found that students with field-independent cognitive styles were able to achieve higher learning satisfaction by obtaining higher competence needs and relationship needs in a gamification virtual simulation system, but there was no significant difference between the two in terms of autonomy need. And one possible explanation is that students of both field cognitive styles learn in simulation experiment environments with a strong sense of being controlled, and therefore have the same perception of autonomous need satisfaction.

5.2 Contributions

In terms of theoretical contributions, 1) the study explains the influencing factors of the application effectiveness of gamification virtual simulation system with the help of ASTI theory, and explores the influencing paths with the help of SDT theory, which enriches the research of the gamification virtual simulation system, and provides a strong support for future applications of gamification in the information field of educational places; 2) in terms of research methodology, this study adopts a multi-research methodology of experiment + questionnaire, where the controlled experiment provides an immersive and objective environmental for participants to fill out the questionnaire to ensure the authenticity and validity of the information in the questionnaire. In addition, it responds to chen et al. [5]'s call for research on using multiple research methods to explore the impact of gamification on online learning.

In a practical sense, the results of this study suggest that the possible effects of system, task, and individual characteristics on students' behavior can be investigated from the perspective of ASTI theory to enhance the quality of student-centered design, strengthen the satisfaction of students' intrinsic needs, and timely and accurately adjust the controllable factors to achieve the maximum effect of the application.

5.3 Limitations and Future Research Directions

This study also has certain limitations: the virtual simulation experiment of a university's school of economics and management is selected as the research object, and the scope is only limited to one university, and the number of samples is small. In the future, the scope and number of samples could be expanded to carry out further research. Secondly, for the mechanism of student satisfaction, only task complexity and field cognitive style have been explored without in-depth research on system characteristics and other factors in the task and individual characteristics; therefore, the mechanism of the three characteristics and their interactions on the learning effect could be explored more comprehensively in the future in order to guide the effective application of the gamification virtual simulation system in a more detailed way.

References

1. Ministry of Industry and Information Technology. White Paper on the Development of Virtual Reality Industry. Radio and Television Information (4) (2016). (in Chinese)
2. Wang, Y.W., Li, Y.S., Jiang, S.X., Li, X.D.: Trends in digital transformation of higher education in the context of the epidemic-interpretation and insights from the U.S. horizon 2022 report (teaching and learning edition). China Educ. Inf. **28**(05), 13–20 (2022). (in Chinese)

3. Xing, B.B., Liu, C., Zhao, L.I., et al.: The impact of blended laboratory teaching on students learning effectiveness and learning experience in higher education: an example of "basic chemistry" course. Mod. Educ. Technol. **32**(2), 99–108 (2022). (in Chinese)

4. Santhanam, R., Liu, D., et al.: Research note—gamification of technology-mediated training: not all competitions are the same. Inf. Syst. Res. **27**, 453–465 (2016)

5. Chen, G.Q., Li, J.C., Deng, H.S.Y., et al.: Research on the impact of gamification competition on online learning user behavior. J. Manage. Sci. **23**(02), 89–104 (2020). (in Chinese)

6. Hanus, M.D., Fox, J.: Assessing the effects of gamification in the classroom: a longitudinal study on intrinsic motivation, social comparison, satisfaction, effort, and academic performance. Comput. Educ. **80**, 152–161 (2015)

7. Clark, D.B., Tanner-Smith, E.E., Kilingsworth, S.S.: Dital games, design, and leaning a systematic review and meta-analysis. Rev. Educ. Res. **86**(1), 79–122 (2015)

8. Schmitz, K.W., Teng, J., Webb, K.J.: Capturing the complexity of malleable it use: adaptive structuration theory for individuals. MIS Q. **40**(3), 663–686 (2016)

9. Desanctis, G., Poole, M.S.: Capturing the complexity in advanced technology use: adaptive structuration theory. Organ. Sci. **5**(2), 121–147 (1994)

10. Strickland, C.: Tools for High-Quality Differentiated Instruction: An ASCD Action Tool. ASCD, Alexandria (2007).

11. Deci, E.L., Ryan, R.M.: The general causality orientations scale: self-determination in personality. J. Res. Pers. **19**(2), 109–134 (1985)

12. Jahn, K., et al.: Individualized gamification elements: the impact of avatar and feedback design on reuse intention. Comput. Hum. Behav. **119**(2), 106702 (2021)

13. Robinson, P.: Task Complexity, Cognitive Resources, and Syllabus Design. A Triadic Framework for Examining Task Influences on SLA, pp. 287–318. Cambridge University Press, Cambridge (2001)

14. Messick, S.: The nature of cognitive styles: problems and promise in educational practice. Educ. Psychol. **19**(2), 59–74 (2009)

15. Chang, J.-J., Lin, W.-S., Chen, H.-R.: How attention level and cognitive style affect learning in a MOOC environment? Based on the perspective of brainwave analysis. Comput. Hum. Behav. **100**, 209–217 (2019)

16. Suh, A., Wagner, C., Liu, L.: Enhancing user engagement through gamification. J. Comput. Inf. Syst. **58**(3), 204–213 (2016)

17. Jang, H., Reeve, J., Ryan, R.M., et al.: Can self-determination theory explain what underlies the productive, satisfying learning experiences of collectivistically oriented Korean students? J. Educ. Psychol. **101**(3), 644–661 (2009)

18. Aparicio, M., Oliveira, T., Bacao, F., et al.: Gamification: a key determinant of massive open online course (MOOC) success. Inf. Manage. **56**(1), 39–54 (2019)

Prediction of Banking Customer Churn Based on XGBoost with Feature Fusion

Zhongyi Hu[1(✉)], Fangrui Dong[1], Jiang Wu[1], and Mustafa Misir[2]

[1] Wuhan University, Wuhan 430072, China
Zhongyi.hu@whu.edu.cn
[2] Duke Kunshan University, Kunshan 215316, China

Abstract. With the increasing competition in the banking industry, accurate prediction of banking customer churn has become an important way in managing customer relationships. To explore efficacy features, enhance the generalization performance of customer churn prediction, this study proposed a XGBoost model with feature fusion for banking customer churn prediction. At first, a feature fusion model based on improved RFM and Affinity Propagation clustering was proposed to extract features representing the long-term and dynamic behavior of customers. By integrating different types of features, a XGBoost model was proposed to predict customer churn. Experimental results demonstrate the superior performance of the proposed model in comparison to other benchmark models.

Keywords: Customer churn prediction · XGBoost · Feature fusion

1 Introduction

In the post-pandemic era, with the volatile global economic environment and the rapid development of financial technology, the banking industry is facing unprecedented competitive pressure. Banks are constantly innovating and improving the quality of their products and services to retain existing customers and attract new ones. However, the cost of acquiring new customers is more than five to six times that of retaining existing customers [1]. Therefore, being able to accurately predict churned customers, which enables banks to precisely provide personalized services to improve customer satisfaction and retention rates, has become a matter of paramount importance.

Over the years, various studies have investigated machine learning techniques to predict customer churn in different fields, including telecom, retail, e-commerce, and others [2–5]. On one hand, some scholars have proposed to build customer churn prediction models by adopting and improving traditional machine learning techniques, such as decision tree, logistic regression, naïve bayes, and support vector machine [4–7]. While those single model-based predictions do not produce satisfactory performance, some studies switched the attentions to ensemble models. By aggregating predictions from multiple models, ensemble learning models can balance the biases and variances of individual models, resulting in improved generalization ability. Recently, several types of ensemble learning techniques, such as random forest, Gradient boosting, AdaBoost,

© The Author(s), under exclusive license to Springer Nature Switzerland AG 2024
Y. P. Tu and M. Chi (Eds.): WHICEB 2024, LNBIP 517, pp. 159–167, 2024.
https://doi.org/10.1007/978-3-031-60324-2_13

have been successfully applied to predict customer churn [2, 3, 8]. Instead of improving the prediction of customer churn with different kinds of machine learning techniques, some researchers have also tried to extract highly efficient features to enhance the prediction of customer churn. Generally, the recency, frequency, and monetary (RFM) model is widely applied as a basis model to extract features in predicting customer churn. Depending on the scene, additional features such as customer satisfaction [9], social network influence [10], and time-varying features [11], have been proposed to build prediction models in conjunction with RFM features.

To accurately predict churned customers in the banking industry, this study proposed a XGBoost model with feature fusion. Firstly, a feature fusion model, incorporating an improved RFM model and AP clustering algorithm, was proposed to extract customer long-term behavioral and dynamic change features in the banking industry. Then, the XGBoost model was proposed to predict customer churn. The effectiveness of the proposed model was verified by comparing it with several benchmark features and prediction models. The results demonstrate the superior performance of the model in extracting features and identifying potential churned customers.

The remainder of the paper is organized as follows. We present the proposed model in Sect. 2. Section 3 overviews the dataset and describes data preprocessing and feature engineering. Section 4 details the experimental results with interpretation of the findings. Finally, we conclude in Sect. 5.

2 Proposed Model

To accurately predict churned customers in the banking industry and provide valuable understandings of the prediction model, this study proposed a XGBoost model with feature fusion. Figure 1 shows the flowchart of the model.

As shown in Fig. 1, the real-world dataset is firstly preprocessed by handling those missing values, outliers, and non-numerical features. Then, in the stage of feature engineering, a feature fusion model is proposed by integrating RFM model and AP clustering to extract both long-term behavioral and dynamic features. Finally, a XGBoost model is proposed for churn prediction.

In the following subsections, we will briefly introduce related models, such as RFM model, AP clustering algorithm, and XGBoost algorithm.

2.1 RFM Model

The RFM model is an important method in customer relationship management for the purpose of assessing customer value. The model utilizes three indices, namely R, F, and M to characterize customer's consumption behavior. The variables respectively represent the recency of the last purchase (Recency), the frequency of purchases (Frequency), and the monetary value of purchases (Monetary). In the area of banking, customer identity (Identity) is also an important factor of customer churn, so the RFMI that incorporates Identity into RFM model is considered in this study.

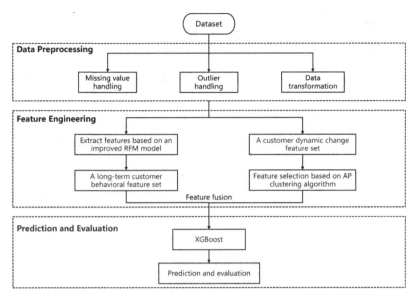

Fig. 1. Flowchart of the proposed model

2.2 AP Clustering Algorithm

The Affinity Propagation (AP) Clustering, an unsupervised clustering algorithm, was first introduced by Brendan J. et. al. in 2007 [12]. The algorithm takes a similarity matrix as input, which represents the pairwise similarities between data points. It then facilitates the exchange of real-valued messages that consider two types of competition among the data points: availability and responsibility. Through multiple iterations, the algorithm determines the final set of cluster centers and their corresponding cluster assignments, accomplishing the clustering task.

Unlike other clustering algorithms, the AP clustering method does not require the prior specification of the final number of clusters and is not sensitive to the selection of initial cluster centers. Besides, the resulting cluster centers generated by this algorithm are the original data points in the dataset, rather than newly generated data points. Given these advantages, in this study, AP clustering is applied for feature selection, in which the features are grouped into several clusters and their centers are regarded as selected features.

2.3 XGBoost Algorithm

XGBoost, short for Extreme Gradient Boosting [13], is a machine learning algorithm that is derived from the gradient boosting decision tree (GBDT) technique. In recent years, the XGBoost algorithm has been demonstrated excellent performance in Kaggle data competitions due to its scalability across diverse scenarios. Compared to the GBDT algorithm, XGBoost integrates a regularization term into the loss function to enhance the generalization capability of the model. In addition, it also utilizes the second-order Taylor expansion to estimate the error, resulting in improved performance.

3 Data Processing

3.1 Dataset

The data used in this study were obtained through sampling from the customer database of a bank in China during the third quarter of 2019. It includes end-of-month asset, behavioral, and deposit information in July, August, and September. The identity information and dates of some activities for customers are also available.

According to the requirements of the bank, the customers are classified into three groups: -1, 0, and 1, representing churned customers, risky customers (i.e., those who have not churned during the prediction period but still have a potential risk of churn), and non-churned customers, respectively. Hence, the task addressed in this study is a three-class classification problem.

3.2 Data Preprocessing

Since the dataset is organized in multiple tables, we integrated those different features based on the distinct customer ID. To distinguish between features with the same name but occurring in different months, a feature named X in July, August, and September was correspondingly labeled as X_m7, X_m8, and X. While those features with a missing rate exceeding 50% were removed from the dataset, other missing values were filled by using mode imputation, mean imputation, forward filling, and backward filling, depending on specific properties of each feature. Correlation analysis was also applied eliminate highly redundant features. Finally, a dataset comprising 67 features and 63,926 samples was obtained.

The distribution of the data for different classes is presented in Table 1.

Table 1. Distribution of different classes

Class	-1	0	1
Number	9693	14769	39711
Proportion	15.1%	23.0%	61.9%

3.3 Feature Engineering

This study investigates customer behavior from two perspectives, namely macro and micro. From the macro perspective, long-term customer behavior is examined by analyzing the average values of asset and deposit data. From the micro perspective, dynamic changes in customer behavior are investigated by examining the monthly fluctuations in asset and deposit data. By combining these two perspectives, the study aims to provide a more comprehensive understanding of customers and improve the accuracy of prediction. Consequently, the process of feature engineering encompasses four stages:

constructing long-term behavioral features based on an improved RFM model, constructing dynamic change features of customers, selecting dynamic features using the AP clustering algorithm, and feature fusion.

(1) Constructing long-term customer behavioral features based on an improved RFM model. In addition to the traditional R, F, and M indicators, customer identity information also has a significant impact on the predictive outcome. Thus, the RFM model was extended to RFMI by incorporating the I factor, which represents identity information including gender and age. Finally, the RFMI feature set, which includes 19 features based on R, F, M, and I indicators, was obtained.

(2) Constructing Dynamic change features of customers. The dataset in this study includes asset data, behavior data, and deposit data for the months of July, August, and September. The monthly fluctuations in asset and deposit data are deemed to be more informative in capturing customer churn compared to the original feature. Dynamic changes are measured in both absolute change and relative change rate.

(3) Feature selection based on AP clustering algorithm for customer dynamic features. Because the customer dynamic feature set contains many features, to prevent the curse of dimensionality and overfitting, we employed the AP clustering algorithm for feature selection. The AP clustering algorithm is capable of effectively partitioning features into different clusters by maximizing intra-cluster similarity and inter-cluster dissimilarity. Consequently, the utilization of the AP clustering method results in the grouping of features that possess similar patterns into cohesive clusters. Moreover, the cluster centers are regarded as representative features. As a result, the collection of representative features from all clusters serves as the result of feature selection. A total of 18 cluster centroids were obtained, resulting in the creation of a new feature set called AP feature set.

(4) Feature fusion. The feature set constructed based on the improved RFM model primarily consists of average values of asset and deposit variables. These features provide an overview of customers' assets and deposits, and offer insights into their long-term behavioral patterns. The features obtained by AP clustering primary emphasis on the monthly fluctuations in assets and deposits, which represent the dynamic changes exhibited by customers. Relying just on a single group of features is insufficient to achieve satisfactory predictive performance. Therefore, a fusion of these two types of features was performed to create a new feature set, namely RFMI_AP feature set, by removing duplicate features, resulting in a dataset containing 35 features.

4 Results

This section presented evaluation of proposed model by using five metrics were applied. They are accuracy, Kappa coefficient, precision, recall, and F1 score.

4.1 Comparison of Different Features

To validate the effectiveness of the proposed feature fusion model, another five group of features were considered as baselines.

(1) Original features, which includes only preprocessed data;
(2) Difference features, which are extracted by calculating the monthly differences or growth of both asset and deposit data;
(3) Ratio features, which are extracted by calculating the monthly growth rate of asset and deposit data;
(4) AP features, which are obtained based on AP clustering;
(5) RFMI features, which are extracted based on the improved RFM model;
(6) RFMI_AP features, which are obtained by proposed fusion model.

The above six groups of features are independently used as inputs for constructing the customer churn prediction model based on the XGBoost algorithm. The dataset was divided into training and testing sets by 7:3, where the training set and testing sets are separately used for model training and evaluation. The performance based on different groups of features are presented in Table 2.

Table 2. Performance comparison of different features

Features Metrics	Original features	Difference features	Ratio features	AP features	RFMI features	RFMI_AP features
Accuracy	0.693	0.696	0.699	0.662	0.662	**0.709**
Precision	0.663	0.669	0.675	0.626	0.62	**0.686**
Recall	0.693	0.696	0.699	0.662	0.662	**0.709**
Kappa	0.361	0.385	0.387	0.292	0.247	**0.409**
F1	0.659	0.67	0.674	0.626	0.604	**0.687**

As shown in Table 2, both the difference features and the ratio features exhibit superior performance compared to the original features across all metrics. These two sets of features show equal levels of performance. As illustrated in Fig. 2, both the difference features and the ratio features have fewer features compared to the original features. This indicates that the churn prediction model based on the proposed dynamic features is more effective than the original features.

Furthermore, the performance of the feature sets extracted using the AP clustering algorithm and the improved RFM model is comparatively lower than that of the original features. However, as shown in Fig. 2, the features derived from the AP clustering algorithm and the improved RFM model comprises 18 and 19 features, respectively, while the original features contain 67 features. The relatively lower performance of these two features may be attributed to their smaller number of features, which may not comprehensively capture customer characteristics. Therefore, it is highly necessary to integrate these two features.

Table 2 also shows that the best performance is generated based on the fusion features, which combines features extracted by the AP clustering algorithm and the improved RFM model. It has an accuracy of 0.709, which is 4.7% higher than the AP-based features and RFMI features. The Kappa coefficient is 0.409, which is 0.117 higher than AP-based features and 0.162 higher than RFMI features. Therefore, the fusion of customer dynamic

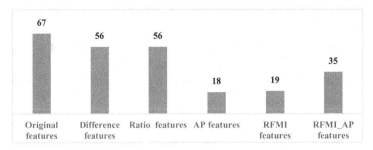

Fig. 2. Number of features in different features

features and long-term behavioral features proves effective in enhancing the predictive performance of the model. Compared to the original features, the fusion features reduce the number of features by nearly half while achieving a noticeable improvement in model performance. In conclusion, the fusion features constructed based on the improved RFM model and AP clustering algorithm demonstrates superior performance in predicting customer churn in the banking industry.

4.2 Comparison of Different Models

To evaluate the effectiveness of the XGBoost-based model for predicting customer churn in the banking industry, four commonly used tree-based machine learning techniques were selected as benchmark models. These models include Decision Tree, Random Forest, LightGBM, and AdaBoost. Like XGBoost, Random Forest, LightGBM, and AdaBoost are ensemble learning techniques based on Decision Tree, and they have shown promising performance in previous research across various domains.

The fusion features were used as the input for building customer churn prediction models based on the five techniques. The dataset was divided into training and testing sets with a ratio of 7:3, where the training set is used for model training and the testing set is used for model evaluation. The experimental results are shown in Table 3.

According to Table 3, XGBoost has superior performance in comparison to other models in terms of all evaluation metrics. The performance of LightGBM and Random Forest is comparable with each other, while the AdaBoost model performs worse than the other three ensemble models. The Decision Tree model exhibits the lowest performance compared to all the other models. For example, the accuracy of XGBoost is 0.709, which is 10 % higher than Decision Tree and 4.2% higher than AdaBoost. And its Kappa coefficient is 0.409, which is 0.204 higher than LightGBM and 0.108 higher than Random Forest. This can be attributed to the fact that the Decision Tree model is a single model, which is prone to overfitting or underfitting. In contrast, ensemble models such as LightGBM, XGBoost, and Random Forest leverage the aggregation of multiple models, thereby enhancing the generalization performance of the models.

In summary, the proposed customer churn prediction model, which combines feature fusion with the XGBoost algorithm, is effective in predicting customer churn. It not only reduces the dimensionality of features and identifies relevant features, but also improves the prediction performance of the model.

Table 3. Comparison of performance among different models

Models Metrics	XGBoost	Decision Tree	Random Forest	LightGBM	AdaBoost
Accuracy	**0.709**	0.609	0.701	0.703	0.667
Precision	**0.686**	0.612	0.676	0.676	0.624
Recall	**0.709**	0.609	0.701	0.703	0.667
Kappa	**0.409**	0.282	0.391	0.385	0.278
F1	**0.687**	0.611	0.678	0.673	0.618

5   Conclusion

In real-life scenarios, the customers of banks are characterized by complicated and diverse dimensions. Screening useful information from a massive amount of information to identify customer churn is challenging. To explore effective features, improve the generalization performance of customer churn prediction, and effectively explain the prediction mechanism of the model, this study proposed a XGBoost model with feature fusion. Experimental verification was conducted using samples from a bank in China. The results showed that the proposed feature fusion based on the improved RFM model and AP clustering algorithm effectively identifies useful features for the prediction model. Finally, compared to other machine learning algorithms, the prediction model built upon the XGBoost algorithm achieved better prediction performance.

Acknowledgement. This work was supported by the Major Research Project of the Ministry of Education on Philosophy and Social Sciences (20JZD024), and the 2022 WHU-DKU Joint Seeding Program (XXWHUDKUZZJJ202303).

References

1. Hadden, J., Tiwari, A., Roy, R., Ruta, D.: Computer assisted customer churn management: state-of-the-art and future trends. Comput. Oper. Res. **34**(10), 2902–2917 (2007)
2. Janssens, B., Bogaert, M., Bagué, A., Van den Poel, D.: B2Boost: instance-dependent profit-driven modelling of B2B churn. Ann. Oper. Res. (2022). https://doi.org/10.1007/s10479-022-04631-5
3. Liu, Y., Fan, J., Zhang, J., Yin, X., Song, Z.: Research on telecom customer churn prediction based on ensemble learning. J. Intell. Inf. Syst. **60**(3), 759–775 (2023)
4. Amin, A., Adnan, A., Anwar, S.: An adaptive learning approach for customer churn prediction in the telecommunication industry using evolutionary computation and Naive Bayes. Appl. Soft Comput. **137**, 110103 (2023)
5. Kurtcan, B.D., Ozcan, T.: Predicting customer churn using grey wolf optimization-based support vector machine with principal component analysis. J. Forecast. **42**(6), 1329–1340 (2023). https://doi.org/10.1002/for.2960
6. Sebastiaan, H., Eugen, S., Bart, B.: Broucke seppe vanden, and verdonck tim, "profit driven decision trees for churn prediction." Eur. J. Oper. Res. **284**(3), 920–933 (2020)

7. Eugen, S.: Vanden broucke seppe, antonio katrien, baesens bart, and snoeck monique, "profit maximizing logistic model for customer churn prediction using genetic algorithms." Swarm Evol. Comput. **40**, 116–130 (2018)
8. Xie, Y., Li, X., Ngai, E.W.T., Ying, W.: Customer churn prediction using improved balanced random forests. Exp. Syst. Appl. **36**(3 Part 1), 5445–5449 (2009)
9. Wu, Z., Jing, L., Wu, B., Jin, L.: A PCA-AdaBoost model for E-commerce customer churn prediction. Ann. Oper. Res. 1–18 (2022)
10. Zhuang, Y.: Research on E-commerce customer churn prediction based on improved value model and XG-Boost algorithm. Manag. Sci. Eng. **12**(3), 51–56, 3 (2018)
11. Mena, G., Coussement, K., De Bock, K.W., De Caigny, A., Lessmann, S.: Exploiting time-varying RFM measures for customer churn prediction with deep neural networks. Ann. Oper. Res. (2023). https://doi.org/10.1007/s10479-023-05259-9
12. Frey, B.J., Dueck, D.: Clustering by passing messages between data points. Science **315**(5814), 972–976 (2007)
13. Chen, T., Guestrin, C.: XGBoost: a scalable tree boosting system, vol. 1603. arXiv e-prints arXiv:1603.02754 (2016)

Technological Traps and Governance Strategies in the Digital Transformation of Education

Shuai Liu[✉]

Nanjing University of Finance and Economics, Nanjing 210023, China
liushuai1106@163.com

Abstract. The digital transformation of education has become a common goal in educational reforms worldwide. The ultimate purpose of educational digitization is to promote human development. However, this process is hindered by technological traps, and calls for corresponding governance strategies. This paper tries to establish a simple model incorporating the traps and governance strategies by investigating the case of a university F. The findings show that technologies traps mainly consist of technological biases, a detachment from digital competency, and an inclination towards "entertainment". In order to overcome these traps and enhance the efficacy of digital transformation in education, it is imperative to integrate rational tools and values, empower teachers with digital skills, and create new educational forms.

Keywords: Digital transformation of education · Technological traps · Governance strategies · Educational forms

Accompanied by the development of digital technologies such as 5G, artificial intelligence, and big data, social development has entered the "digital era". The digitization of education, as an important strategy to promote sustainable development and maintain international competitiveness, has become a shared goal of education reforms worldwide. The 19th National Congress of the Communist Party of China pointed out the need to promote digitalization in education. The digitization of education has had a positive impact on educational equity, lifelong learning, student-centered teaching models, and high-quality education. It has also borne the hopes of further transformation. Against the backdrop of these educational aspirations and the sweeping influence of digital technologies driven by top-down national strategies, from basic education to higher education, digital transformation has become a new focus in educational theory and practice. Digital technologies have gradually permeated every aspect of education and teaching, leading education from the industrial age to the digital age. In this process, while digital technologies have continuously driven educational reforms to go deeper, the risks they bring have also quietly emerged. This article takes the research data of University F as an example to explore the traps and governance strategies brought about by digital technologies in the process of promoting educational transformation.

1 The Fundamental Purpose of the Digital Transformation of Education

The value of technology lies in serving and liberating people. In most fields, the higher the degree of digitization, the lower the degree of human involvement, and the more accurate and successful the digital transformation. However, education is a form of human interaction, involving the connection of thoughts and emotions between individuals, and it cannot and should not be separated from human existence. The ultimate goal of technology-based educational transformation is to serve teachers and students, promote better teaching and learning, and ensure that the outcomes of educational digitization are reflected in human development. Therefore, educational digitization is not simply about applying digital technology to education, but a revolutionary reshaping of education based on digital concepts and technology, integrating digital technology into various levels of the education field, advocating for the deep integration of technology and educational instruction, promoting all-round innovation and transformation in teaching paradigms, teaching processes, evaluation methods, and forming an education model adapted to the digital age [1].

2 Technological Traps in the Digital Transformation of Education

Digital technology is rapidly integrating into various fields of educational instruction. Terms such as digital education, flipped classrooms, smart classrooms, and massive open online courses (MOOCs) are continuously emerging, outlining the ongoing digital transformation in education. Traditional education has been deeply marked by the "digital age" and has caused a series of chain reactions. The continuous infiltration of digital technology into education is creating a brand new educational space, but the risks associated with technology cannot be ignored.

2.1 The Technological Tool Bias in Educational Digitization

In his book "The Erosion of Rationality," founder of the Frankfurt School Max Horkheimer wrote, "Instrumental reason" mainly concerns the applicability of means to achieve purposes that are considered natural or self-evident, without considering whether the purposes themselves are rational. "Instrumental reason" pursues the efficiency of tools, only concerned with how to do it, rather than whether it should be done, treating technology as a tool that can solve all problems and simplifying complex issues [2]. In the process of educational digitization, the technological tool bias mainly manifests in using technology as the core driving force for educational transformation and excessively relying on technological tools to solve educational problems, neglecting the objectives and values of education itself. The pursuit of reason has led to the release of irrationality [3]. In addition, behind digital technology is a set of simple and precise mathematical algorithms. As Erwin Schrödinger said, "When a mathematical model is derived, it suddenly brings order to a field it has never intended to enter or think about." Because of this, digital transformation can bring the risk of simplifying education. Simplification may reduce the uncertainty of education, but uncertainty is precisely where the important attributes and values of education lie. Although some scholars emphasize that without information technology, education will not be able to construct itself, if technology is worshipped too much, education will construct itself incorrectly. This is a trap that education needs to be wary of in digital transformation.

So far, digital education is mainly centered around technology. Its main characteristics are as follows:

Firstly, it emphasizes the application of technology, while neglecting human development. It focuses on the use of digital technology in education to improve the functionality and efficiency of existing education, but rarely studies its impact on individual development. F University has introduced an intelligent teaching system, which requires teachers to utilize it for course design and assignment management. However, due to insufficient training and practice in operating the system, teachers are compelled to spend extensive amounts of time dealing with technical issues. As a result, their preparation workload intensifies, consequently reducing the time available for improving teaching methods and engaging with students.

Secondly, it focuses on technological functions rather than educational functions. It focuses on applying existing technology to educational scenarios, rather than being guided by educational needs and focusing on how to educate and teach. This was also found in the study of F University in Nanjing. Students often feel isolated when they encounter difficult problems on the online platform and cannot find timely human guidance or peer discussion support, despite the platform providing rich video tutorials and practice questions.

Thirdly, it emphasizes existing conditions rather than educational transformation. It focuses on the application of technology based on existing educational scenarios, teaching conditions, and teaching models. It adds to traditional education rather than creating new educational forms and scenarios to promote educational innovation and transformation.

Fourthly, it emphasizes "big data" and neglects "small data". Similar to the application of digital technology in other scenarios, most current digital education is also based on the mindset of big data. It has not deeply explored the inherent needs of personalized development, lacks the collection, mining, and use of multidimensional, individualized "small data." Yuan refers to this phenomenon as "digital + education," which is "cold digital education." He pointed out that education is a human-centric activity aimed at cultivating talents for the nation and promoting individual development. It is an activity filled with emotions, values, and warmth. Digital education needs to transform into "education + digitalization" and develop digital education with warmth [4].

2.2 The Disconnection of Teachers' Digital Competence

Digital competence is the ability to effectively and critically use digital technology [5]. The widespread application of digital technology in the educational field will undoubtedly require teachers and students, as users, to have the corresponding digital literacy. In the process of educational digitization, students need to acquire digital skills, use digital tools, and adapt to the new digital learning. As digital natives of the digital age, students are generally proficient in using smartphones, computers, and other smart learning devices. Compared to teachers who need to master the concepts and methods of digital technology and use them to reconstruct teaching content and modes, students face fewer obstacles in using digital technology for learning. Therefore, the burden of technology brought about by digital transformation mainly falls on the teachers' side. The demand for teachers' digital competence in educational digitization mainly manifests in three aspects.

Firstly, lack of digital educational ideology. There is a need for conceptual transformation, which involves conducting educational instruction guided by digital teaching concepts. The reality is that the skilled use of traditional teaching methods by teachers has led to fixed behavioral patterns and comfortable zones, making it difficult to accept the vision and promises brought by new technologies. Many teachers adopt a wait-and-see attitude towards the digital transformation of education, lacking the motivation to update their concepts. Additionally, digital technology concepts need to be integrated with educational concepts and laws in order to have a positive impact on teaching. This requires teachers to engage in more educational research and reforms, further increasing the burden of updating their thoughts and beliefs. Teachers who are accustomed to traditional lecture-style teaching are generally less willing to use digital teaching tools. According to the survey conducted at F University in Nanjing, after the end of the pandemic prevention and control measures, as the education resumed to normal gradually, the usage rate of digital teaching platforms and tools significantly decreased. Based on the data from a certain online education platform of the university, the total number of student activities on the platform decreased from 441,693 times in the second half of 2022 to 195,910 times in the first half of 2023, and the number of active users decreased significantly.

Secondly, insufficient skills in digital pedagogy. There is a need for method application, which involves acquiring digital literacy such as digital resource acquisition and digital application ability. In this aspect, the lack of teacher capacity is also widespread. Although many technologies for advanced thinking instruction are available, very few teachers use computers for advanced thinking instruction in the classroom, with most of the focus still on communication and exchange [6]. Currently, teachers lack a necessary digital competence training system for mastering digital technology. Many teachers are at a stage of self-learning and exploration motivated by a spirit of reform. There are obstacles to teachers' enhancement of digital literacy.

Thirdly, technological burden, namely the introduction of digital technology, has led to an increase in the burden on teachers. The constant introduction of new platforms, software, and other technological advancements has left teachers exhausted from learning and adapting to constantly evolving tools, and drained from fulfilling the new educational expectations and responsibilities brought about by new technology. In terms of teaching, there is a need to handle a wider range of teaching resources with richer sources, as well as higher demands for personalized classroom instruction. In terms of assessment, there is a need to face the abundance of digitally formatted student work and handle a significant amount of process-oriented and personalized assessment data. In terms of teacher-student interactions, teachers are faced with students who may have more extensive digital experiences, making intergenerational interaction more challenging. Teachers are currently experiencing technological "overload," as the digital transformation of education is placing an increased workload on them [7].

2.3 The "Entertainment" Tendency in Educational Digitization

Neil Postman argued in his book "Amusing Ourselves to Death" that the main contribution of television to the philosophy of education is its idea that teaching and entertainment cannot be separated. The entertainment value of educational television programs makes traditional classrooms seem dull and uninteresting, giving students the misconception that learning is an easy and enjoyable process. If we replace television with digital technology, we find that it corresponds to some problems in the integration of digital technology and education. In the process of educational digitization, although digital technology has brought changes to teaching tools and techniques, the full integration of digital technology and education has not yet led to substantial changes. Digital technology is often only used in a simple manner in educational scenarios, and it may even bring about an "entertainment-oriented" tendency in teaching, which may disrupt the core objectives and values of education. Specifically, this trend can be seen in the following three aspects:

Firstly, superficialization of knowledge. There is a simplification of content, with some digital educational content being overly simplified and lacking depth and challenge. University F introduced a mathematics learning application with the initial goal of helping students grasp mathematical concepts through gamification. However, in order to attract and retain users, the application incorporated excessive game elements and reward mechanisms, resulting in students spending a significant amount of time on the game but only acquiring superficial mathematical knowledge.

Secondly, fragmentation of knowledge. There is fragmentation of knowledge, with systematic knowledge being fragmented into isolated teaching videos, existing in a scattered and disordered manner. Research in modern psychology suggests that the duration of student's classroom attention spans is approximately 10–20 min. In order to make the most of this optimal period of knowledge acquisition, knowledge is being fragmented into short videos lasting around 10–20 min each, resulting in the loss of its systematic nature.

Thirdly, entertainment elements overshadow the main educational objectives. In order to stimulate students' interest in learning, excessive entertainment elements are incorporated into the teaching process, resulting in entertainment elements dominating, overshadowing the learning objectives and failing to achieve the intended learning outcomes. For example, a teacher at F University uses humorous videos and jokes to interpret historical events in the teaching of modern Chinese history in order to enhance the attractiveness of the class. Although this may attract students' attention temporarily, in the long run, it weakens the seriousness of history and prevents students from obtaining comprehensive and accurate historical knowledge.

The presence of "entertainment" elements in digital teaching is undoubtedly intended to enhance teaching effectiveness and make learning as easy as possible. However, if they do not directly align with teaching objectives and exceed the necessary limits, the negative impact is that teaching becomes a form of "entertainment." Once these "entertainment" elements are lacking, students' attention easily drifts away from the current learning tasks, and the presentation of knowledge becomes more fragmented and decentralized, sacrificing systematicity and making deep learning difficult to achieve. In fact, acquiring knowledge is a difficult task, and learning requires effort, endurance, and sweat.

These risks clearly contradict the purpose of educational digitization and may become key factors that restrict the high-quality development and effectiveness of educational transformation (Fig. 1).

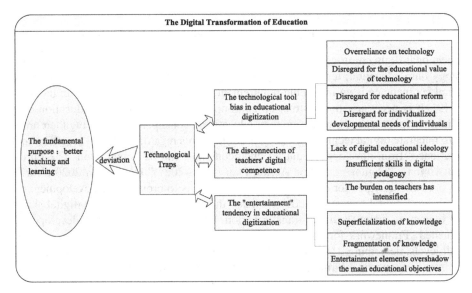

Fig. 1. The purpose and deviation of educational digital transformation

3   Governance Strategies for Technological Traps in Educational Digitization

3.1   Value Integration: Returning to the Original Intention of Educational Digitization

Instrumental rationality considers the applicability of means to achieve purposes that are considered natural or self-evident, without considering whether the purposes themselves are rational. Value rationality focuses on the value of behavior itself, regardless of means and consequences [8]. Instrumental rationality often assumes that people are in a "rational" state. The biggest paradox of modern society lies in the pursuit of rationality, which leads to non-rationality [3]. If the understanding of applying digital technology to educational instruction remains at the level of instrumental rationality, it often simplifies digital technology as a physical tool and overlooks its deeper educational influences, such as on emotions, cognition, and relationships between individuals. In the process of educational digitization, it is important to integrate instrumental rationality and value rationality and focus not only on the effectiveness of tools but also on human development, thus achieving the fundamental goal and ultimate purpose of promoting human development through educational digitization. Specifically, it is necessary to follow the laws of educational development, correctly handle the relationship between education and technology, and change the current situation where technological use is only seen as a means and only focuses on efficiency. Digital technology must establish its foundation on caring for individual lives, deeply integrate with education, and pay more attention to the impact on individuals' emotions, values, attitudes, and other spiritual aspects.

3.2 Empowerment of Subjects: Enhancing Teachers' Digital Competence

Educational digitization cannot be limited to simple superimposition of digital technology onto education; teachers are the leaders of teaching, and enhancing teachers' digital competence is an inevitable requirement of educational digitization in the new era [9]. It is necessary to construct an appropriate system for teacher education and training, helping teachers transition their educational concept and enhancing their ability to integrate digital technology and education. In this regard, beneficial practices and experiences from developed countries and economies can be drawn upon. The European Union's "Digital Education Action Plan (2021–2027)" released in 2020 clearly sets out two strategies for digital education: the first is to promote the development of a high-level digital education ecosystem, and the second is to strengthen digital skills and literacy to adapt to digital transformation. The European Union has developed a dedicated "Framework for Digital Competence for Educators" for education workers at all levels, describing 21 competencies that individuals need to possess in the digital age from five aspects: information and digital literacy, communication and collaboration, digital content creation, safety, and problem-solving. This provides a reference for learners to comprehensively understand digital skills. In addition, the European Union has developed an online self-assessment tool called "SELFIE" for teachers. This tool helps teachers identify their strengths and weaknesses in digital competence, reflect on and improve how digital technology is used in teaching, learning, and evaluation, in order to better cultivate teachers' digital skills and accelerate educational digitization [10]. In our country, the age and academic composition of teachers are relatively complex, and there is a large disparity in digital competence, which hinders the deep advancement of digital education. Therefore, it is necessary to quickly establish our own digital competence framework, focusing on strengthening the cultivation of teachers' digital competence, and incorporating systematic digital teaching skill training courses in the training of normal students and in-service teachers. Universities should establish systems and mechanisms for the development of teachers' teaching abilities, allowing teachers to have the energy and motivation to study and explore digital teaching. F University has established a Teacher Development Center, constructing a training system for teachers' digital literacy, including new teacher training, teacher professional skills training, and master's studios. Teachers must undergo a certain number of digital skills training hours before being eligible for promotion, effectively enhancing the willingness and motivation of teachers to improve their digital literacy.

3.3 Transformation of Education: Creating New Forms of Education

Creating new forms of education is the deep implication of educational digitization. Educational digitization is not just about making adjustments and improvements within the framework of existing teaching models; the functions of digital technology go beyond enhancing the "entertainment" aspect of the knowledge acquisition process. It requires creating new forms of education, as the integration of digital technology and education will force significant changes in traditional teaching and learning modes. Digital technology should lead to changes in the organizational form of education, the relationships between individuals in education, and various behaviors in teaching and learning on social, cultural, and psychological levels. It is a transformation of the overall teaching model [11]. To achieve this, education needs to break free from reliance on existing paths, focus on the core areas of educational transformation, reconstruct itself in terms of teaching and learning, and fully leverage the power of educational digitization. In terms of teaching, teachers need to change their mindset and use digital technology as a means to create educational contexts, reorganize teaching content, and reconstruct classroom structures, expanding teaching time and space, and focusing on inquiry-based, immersive, and interactive teaching. Students should be actively involved in the classroom. In terms of learning, educational digitization helps transform traditional education's single teaching content and methodological focus, addressing the shortcomings of exploring individual potential and meeting personalized needs. It makes "providing suitable education for everyone" possible; the human-computer interaction, knowledge interconnection, and data sharing brought about by digital transformation meet students' personalized and precise learning needs, providing the necessary technical spirit for transformative education. As emphasized by constructivist learning theory and situational learning theory, with the support of technology (such as 3D, VR/AR, mobile terminals), the acquisition and creation of learning contexts become easier, which allows for the use of various methods to solve complex problems in the real world, guiding learning to occur through dialogue, collaboration, and communication in authentic tasks, thereby deepening the understanding of the connections between knowledge [12]. F University pays attention to the construction of educational infrastructure based on digital technology. It was one of the first universities in the province to launch 5G, completing the smart transformation of more than 180 classrooms and establishing 16 virtual simulation courses. It has also purchased digital teaching resources to create conditions for digital teaching. With smart classrooms and virtual simulation laboratories, teachers actively carry out interactive, immersive, and inquiry-based teaching. Through the smart teaching platform, they have reformed student evaluation methods, strengthened process-oriented and personalized evaluation, and improved student learning outcomes (Fig. 2).

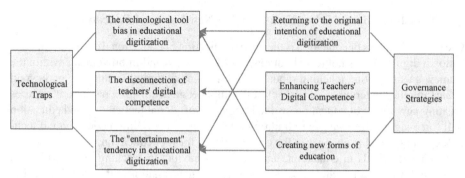

Fig. 2. Technological Traps and Governance Strategies in the Digital Transformation of Education

4 Conclusion

This paper takes F University as a case study, analyzing the technological pitfalls and their impact on teaching in the process of educational digital transformation, and puts forward corresponding governance strategies. The research findings support the view of instrumental rationality of technology in promoting educational change [13], which means that technology should be seen merely as a tool [14]. In fact, learning is a human activity, and technology should focus on the teaching activity itself. The main factors determining teaching effectiveness are human thoughts, emotions, and will2. The research deepens the understanding of the risks of educational digital transformation. It discusses the technological pitfalls in the process of promoting educational change from three dimensions: technological tool orientation, digital literacy, and entertainment orientation. It points out that the existence of these problems deviates from the original purpose of educational digitization. The application of information technology and the reshaping of teaching methods are not the fundamental goals. Education is a process of cultivating individuals, and the ultimate value of educational digital transformation lies in promoting human development.

This study serves as an inspiration for teachers and educational administrators in properly responding to the challenges and opportunities presented by digitizing education. For teachers, the transformation of mindset is the first step in aligning with the trend of digitizing education. Updating teaching philosophies in a timely manner and integrating the concept of digital technology with educational principles will reconstruct teaching methods. In the process of implementing teaching practices, not only should the instrumental value of digital technology be considered, but also its impact on students' development. For educational administrators, it is crucial to establish a sound training system for teachers, enhance their digital competency, and avoid transforming the process of digitizing education into a top-down administrative task. Providing policy guidance, hardware support, and other environmental factors for digital teaching can effectively alleviate the problems that arise during the transformative process.

Although the successful transformation of education through digital means relies largely on technological support, the interaction between technological functionalities and educational subjects means that the journey towards future digitizing education will inevitably not be smooth sailing. The emphasis on the risks associated with digital technology does not negate the transformation of digitizing education, but rather hopes for a more scientific and comprehensive approach in addressing the current challenges. It urges caution and efforts to mitigate these risks, ultimately returning to the original intention of the transformation.

As education is still going through the process of digitizing transformation and has yet to form a mature educational ecosystem, the process of empowering education through technology will undoubtedly continue to bring forth new issues that require attention and resolution. Furthermore, due to the nature of being a single case study, there are limitations to the representativeness of the discussed issues and governance strategies in this paper. Therefore, these aspects should be continuously monitored and improved in future research endeavors.

Acknowledgement. This research was supported by the National Social Science Foundation of China (grant no. 21BGL033).

References

1. Man, Z., Hanteng, L., Sipan, S.: An education literature review on digitization, digitalization, datafication, and digital transformation. In: Proceedings of the 6th International Conference on Humanities and Social Science Research (ICHSSR 2020). https://www.atlantis-press.com/proceedings/ichssr-20/125939327. Accessed 15 Jan 2024
2. Li, M.: Critique on the "instrumental rationality" of educational technology. Educ. Res. (5) (2008). (in Chinese)
3. Weber, M.: Economy and Society, p. 101. University of California Press, Berkeley (1978)
4. Yuan, Z.: Education digital transformation: what to transform, how to transform. J. East China Normal Univ. (Educ. Sci. Ed.) (3) (2023). (in Chinese)
5. Ribble, M., Bailey, G.: Digital citizenship in schools, p. 21. International Society for Technology in Education, Washington (2007)
6. OECD. Global Teaching Insights:A Video Study of Teaching. https//www.oecd.org/education/global-teaching-insights20d6f36b-en. Accessed 10 Jan 2024
7. Zhao, J.: Teacher burden in the technological era: understanding a new perspective on education digital transformation. Educ. Res. (11) (2021). (in Chinese)
8. Wang, K.: Instrumental rationality and value rationality: understanding max weber's sociological thought. Gansu Soc. Sci. (1) (2005). (in Chinese)
9. Tay, H.L., Low, S.W.K.: Digitalization of learning resources in a HEI-a lean management perspective. Int. J. Prod. Perform. Manag. **66**(5) (2017)
10. European Commission. Digital Education Action Plan (2021–2027). https://ec.europa.eu/education/education-in-the-eu/digital-education-action-plan_en. Accessed 16 Jan 2024
11. Lu, J.: Network society, people, education. Jiangsu High. Educ. (1) (2000). (in Chinese)
12. Xiao, R., Xiao, H., Shang, J.: Artificial intelligence and educational transformation: prospects, difficulties, and strategies. China e-Educ. (4) (2020). (in Chinese)
13. Zhang, H.: The integration of instrumental rationality and value rationality: a realistic reflection on the development of educational technology. Educ. Res. (11) (2016). (in Chinese)
14. Borgmann, A.: Technology and the Character of Contemporary Life: A Philosophical Inquiry, pp. 14–20. The University of Chicago Press, Chicago (1984)

Boosting Sales for Agricultural Products Through Live Streaming: The Role of Product Distance, Scene Type and Streamer Type

Nan Wang[1(✉)], Gong Chen[1], and Xiabing Zheng[2]

[1] School of Information Management, Wuhan University, 299 Bayi Road, Wuhan 430072, China
nanwang@whu.edu.cn

[2] School of Public Affairs, University of Science and Technology of China, Hefei 230026, China

Abstract. Live streaming has become an important role for the sales for agricultural products. While live streaming of agricultural product has unique characteristics, this paper addresses how three less investigated live streaming designs which are product distance, scene type and streamer type affects sales for agricultural products. Based on dual-process theory, we further classify the impact of these three factors on sales into product path and non-product path. A dataset of live streaming of agricultural products on the TikTok platform is analyzed to test our hypotheses. Results show that all these three factors have significant impact on sales for agricultural product. Further, by comparing the relative impact of product path and non-product path on sales based on dominant analysis, we found that product distance representing product path is more important than non-product path. Both theoretical and practical implications are discussed.

Keywords: Agricultural Products · Live Streaming · Dual-Process Theory · Product Distance · Scene Type · Streamer Type

1 Introduction

The live e-commerce industries have experienced rapid development in recent years. The emerging sector of agricultural products live e-commerce has gradually evolved into a promising new model with immense potential. The "2023 Harvest Festival TikTok E-commerce to Help Farmers Data Report" released by TikTok E-commerce pointed out that the live streaming of agricultural products from January to September 2023 led to a year-on-year increase of 137 percent in agricultural product sales, and the number of agricultural goods merchants with million-dollar sales exceeded 24, 000. Sales of key boosted products such as edible mushrooms and woody oilseeds reached 850 million yuan, with sales increasing by 173% year-on-year [1].

Due to the critical role of live streaming for agricultural product sales, previous studies investigate factors to boost sales for agricultural products in the live streaming context which are mainly divided into three categories: product factors [2], live streamer factors [3] and technical factors [4]. However, fewer studies have considered the specific designs of live streaming of agricultural products and explored the impact of these designs on sales. We contend that live streaming of agricultural products has three specific characteristics and designs. First, consumers have higher uncertainty about the quality of agricultural products as there is a lack of uniform quality evaluation standards. Consumers need to observe products to evaluate product quality more carefully. Hence, product distance, that is, the horizontal distance of the product from the screen (consumer) in the live streaming screen [5], is a crucial design factor which impacts agricultural product sales. Second, from the live streamer design perspective, apart from the professional steamer, farmers can also be the live streamers to introduce agricultural products as farmers know more about their products. However, the relative impact of farmer streamers to professional streamers on agricultural product sales has yet to be discovered. Third, From the technical design perspective, the scene type, which refers to where the live streaming takes place, can be designed differently. Rural scenes can be used in live streaming, such as product planting scene and product packing scene. However, the relative impact of scene types has yet to be discovered. In summary, we will explore the impact of three live streaming designs which involve product distance, streamer types and scene types on sales.

To answer our research questions, we adopt dual-process theory as the theoretical basis, dividing the impact of three factors into two different paths, namely the product path and non-product path. Moreover, we compare the impact of the two paths on sales using a dominance analysis. Our study has both theoretical and practical contributions. Firstly, we investigate three live streaming designs, product distance, streamer types and scene types, which have yet to be explored in previous studies. Second, we compared the impact of two paths, which can extend the understanding and application context of the dual process theory. Last, from practical perspective, our findings can guide the design of live streaming for agricultural products to boost sales.

2 Theoretical Background

2.1 Dual-Process Theory

Evans & Wason proposed the "dual-process theory" to explain human mental processing [6]. The basic idea of dual-process theory is that humans have two sets of relatively independent cognitive systems. Chaiken explains that the process of individual information behaviour consists of heuristic and systematic paths [7]. When using the systematic process, people use enough cognitive resources to evaluate the cognitive object systematically. In contrast to the systematic approach, the heuristic approach focuses more on external cues other than the message ontology. One of the more widely agreed views about the influence mechanism of dual-process theory is that the two processes work together to influence behaviour [8].

Dual-process theory is a well-established theory applied in the study of consumer purchase intention. We believe that Chaiken's dual-process theory can be used to explain the information processing process of consumer's purchase in the process of live-streaming e-commerce. This study calls the systematic process the product path and the heuristic process the non-product path. Meanwhile, product and non-product path influence consumers' final purchase behaviour of live agricultural products. Moreover, this process is synchronous and parallel. Therefore, we introduce the dual-process theory to divide the product distance, scene type and streamer type into two action paths, product path and non-product path, in order to explore how the three affect the consumers' purchase of live agricultural products and how the two paths differ from each other.

3 Research Model and Hypothesis Development

Given that our research question is about how the design of live streaming affects the sales of agricultural products. Based on dual-process theory, we treat product distance as the product path, while scenes and live streamers are the non-product path. Specific hypotheses are as follows.

3.1 Product Distance and Sales

Chu et al. proposed that spatial distance is the horizontal distance between the consumer and the displayed product [5] and Chu et al. related spatial distance to product brand image and proposed that the closer the spatial distance, the more favorable the consumer attitude and the higher the intention to pay [5]. Based on this definition, we define product distance in live streaming as the distance between the consumer and the product displayed in the live streaming.

Product distance, as an influencing factor of the product path, reflects consumers' judgement of the commodity factors in live streaming. Product distance affects whether consumers can observe the goods clearly through the live streaming screen and thus judge the quality of the goods. Live streaming shopping, as a form of online purchasing transaction, where sellers control the information provided to buyers, and buyers do not have access to product quality information as they would in traditional product selection, that can lead to two information asymmetry problems which are adverse selection and moral hazard. The former can lead buyers to misvalue the product, and the latter can lead to buyers' distrust of the seller, affecting the formation of the transaction [9]. The closer the product distance is, the more product information consumers can obtain through the live stream, thus reducing the information asymmetry between buyers and sellers. When there is less information asymmetry between buyers and sellers, consumers have correct estimation of the product quality by the consumers and the enhancement of their trust in the seller, thus promoting the purchase of the product by the consumers. Therefore, we propose hypothesis 1:

H1: The more proximal the product distance is, the sales will be higher.

3.2 Scene Type and Sales

Previous studies have shown that a suitable shopping environment attracts consumers to browse for more extended periods, helping them find the products they need and increasing their desire to buy [10]. In the live e-commerce environment, consumers will be influenced by the characteristics of the scene. Previous study proved that live streaming scenes closer to reality are more likely to win consumers' trust [11].

Unlike the sale of agricultural products in shopping malls, the live streaming room can set the live streaming location anywhere and will not be limited to the typical shopping mall indoor environment. Second, the origin and processing of agricultural products often reflect the quality and standardization of the product. Given these two points, many live streaming set the scene as the planting scene of agricultural products, packing scene and indoors scene. Therefore, we make hypothesis 2:

H2: Product planting scene and product packing scene lead to higher sales compared to indoors scene.

3.3 Streamer Type and Sales

Yoo & Jin. Proposed that the live streamer's image should match the product's characteristics [12]. Sengupta et al. found that the higher the spokesperson's image matches the product, the more positive the consumer's attitude towards the product [13]. Based on the viewpoint of a live streamer-product match, we use streamer type as an indicator of a live streamer-product match. In the study of the impact of different types of Netflix on live sales, scholars summarized three types of live streamers, namely entertainment live streamers, skill live streamers and marketing live streamers [14]. Concerning the classification of live streamer, we classify the live streamer into farmer streamers and professional streamers.

Compared to professional streamers, farmer streamers have no professional marketing dialogue and a more straightforward introduction to commodity logic. However, the characteristics of the farmer streamer are closer to the agricultural products, which aligns with the current situation of the consumer's pursuit of commodity transparency. Farmers, as live streamers, promote the agricultural products they plant which will increases consumers' trust in the live streaming content, thus increasing sales performance. Therefore, we propose Hypothesis 3:

H3: Farmer streamers have a greater impact on sales compared to professional streamers.

4 Data Collection and Data Analysis

4.1 Data Sources

The TikTok platform (https://www.douyin.com/) contains rich live data on agricultural products, so we chose it as our data source. The "2023 Harvest Festival TikTok E-commerce Data Report" released by TikTok E-commerce indicates that TikTok E-commerce platform had 4.73 billion single agricultural product e-commerce orders from September 2022 to September 2023 and the total number of hours of live e-commerce lectures on agricultural products reaches 37.78 million hours [1].

Considering that different agricultural products have different ripening seasons and different popular degrees on the TikTok platform, the orange and tangerine agricultural products ranked the third highest among the most popular types of agricultural products on TikTok, and at the same time, we captured the data from the middle of November to the first half of December, which is the time when navel oranges are abundantly harvested and marketed in various places. Hence, we chose navel oranges as the type of agricultural products for the study.

4.2 Measurement

Measurement of variables are presented in the Table 1.

Table 1. Measurements of all variables

Function	Variable	Measurement
Dependent variable	LnSale	Logarithmic form of sales for this live streaming
Independent variable	Product distance	Distance of the product in the live streaming from the screen (Proximal distance = 1, Distal distance = 0)
	Scene type	Type of scene in the live room, three types of scenes $(x1, x2) = (1, 0)$: product planting scene; $(x1, x2) = (0, 1)$: product packing scene; $(x1, x2) = (0, 0)$: indoors scene
	Streamer type	Type of live streamer (professional streamer = 0, farmer streamer = 1)
Control variable	Price	The unit price of products
	Follower number	Number of live streamer fans
	View number	Number of live streaming audience
	Like number	Number of Likes on Live streaming
	Time	Duration of the live streaming
	Product type	The product type, selected as navel oranges, its value is taken as 1

4.3 Dependent Variable

Sales performance is dependent variable. We measure the sales of a live stream by the cumulative sales of produce from the start of a stream to the moment of recording. We begin with the Douchacha platform (https://www.douchacha.com/). There will be real-time sales data in the live streaming room of the TikTok platform. After we crawled that sales data, we preprocessed the raw data and used it as the initial dependent variable of the model. The variance of the sales volume (487079.9) is much larger than the mean (449.2492), presenting an over-discrete nature (coefficient of dispersion $\alpha > 0$ and the confidence interval does not contain 0), we take the logarithmisation of the sales volume to explain its skewed distribution, and the processed dependent variable conforms to a normal distribution ($p = 0.6335 > 0.05$). Therefore, following logarithmic processing, the sales (LnSale) is the dependent variable in the model.

4.4 Independent Variable

Independent variables include product distance, scene type and streamer type. We use a crawler program on the TikTok platform to capture the real-time data of the live streaming room, including sales (LnSale), price, view number, like number, and follower number. At the same time, the live room screen is saved, and the product distance, scene type and streamer type are identified manually.

After selecting the agricultural products as navel orange, we started to crawl the data and collected a total of 1, 697 pieces of data, and further eliminated the products that did not belong to the navel orange category by the product name. To ensure the validity of the data, we eliminated the data with a live stream duration of less than 25 min, as well as cumulative sales of less than 3. In addition, since independent variables are category variables, we also considered the number of reciprocities of different categories in the variables when selecting the live streams to ensure effective comparisons. Finally, proximal distance samples are 167, and distal distance samples are 146. Product planting scene samples are 107, product packing scene samples are 105 and indoors scene samples are 101. Farmer streamer samples are 167 and professional streamer samples are 146. Finally, we get 313 valid samples for further analysis.

According to our definition of product distance, product distance can be categorized into proximal and distal distance. Consumers can see the details of the product through the live stream screen when the product is in the proximal place. They cannot see the details of the product when the product is in the distal place. We took several screenshots of the selected live stream room's screen, comprehensively compared the clarity of navel oranges in the screen, and finally gave the labelled values.

The scene type is the scene environment factor of the live room. In the data collection process, we first meticulously define the live stream scenes involved in each piece of data; on this basis, we merge and categorize similar scenes. Finally, we divide the live streaming scenes into three categories. The three scene types are consistent with the process of agricultural products from planting to processing, packing, and finally to selling, which is divided into the product planting scene, product packing scene, and indoors scene. There are two dummy variables used to represent the scene type variables. $(x1, x2) = (1, 0)$ when it is the planting scene, $(x1, x2) = (0, 1)$ when it is the packing scene, and $(x1, x2) = (0, 0)$ when it is the indoors scene.

The streamer type is the live streamer who carries the products in the live streaming, which is also a feature that distinguishes agricultural products live streams from ordinary live streams. When the streamer type is 1, it means that it is a farmer streamer, and 0 means a professional streamer. After repeatedly collecting live stream data, we found that farmers will appear in the form of live streamers in the live stream to promote their own products, and a variety of agricultural products will also use this kind of marketing means live stream. Therefore, we classify farmer streamers and professional streamers by live streamer characteristics such as live streamer image and live discourse characteristics. After several rounds of labelling and checking, we classify the live streamers into farmer streamers and professional streamers.

4.5 Control Variable

First, we control for the effect of product type, and only one product type, navel oranges in this study. Second, since product unit price affects sales, we crawled the prices and pounds of agricultural products sold in the live streaming rooms to calculate the corresponding amount per pound as the commodity unit price. In addition, we introduced the control variable of live streaming duration to control the role of live streaming time. The live streaming duration is measured by subtracting the time difference obtained from the point in time when the instant sales were recorded from the point in time when the live streaming started as the live streaming duration. Finally, we capture metrics that reflect the difference between live streams such as the number of fans, viewers, and likes of the live streaming.

4.6 Descriptive Analysis and Correlations

Descriptive statistics and variables correlations are measured first. All correlation coefficients were less than 0.7 (David et al.), indicating that multicollinearity was not a significant problem [15]. The variance inflation factor for each variable was less than 3, indicating that there was no multicollinearity between the variables (Hair et al.) [16].

5 Results

5.1 Main Models

As shown in Table 2, we take a stepwise regression approach by adding control variables (Model 1) to the model and then adding the three independent variables of main effects (Model 2). The results of Model 1 show that price ($\beta = -0.168$, $p < 0.05$), time ($\beta = 0.221$, $p < 0.01$), view number ($\beta = 0.00142$, $p < 0.01$) and follower number ($\beta = 0$, $p < 0.01$) have a significant effect on sales performance. The results of Model 2 showed that the significance of the control variables did not change with the addition of the three independent variables. Product distance ($\beta = 0.752$, $p < 0.01$) has a significant positive effect on sales performance, supporting H1. Both Product planting scenes ($\beta = 0.608$, $p < 0.01$) and product packing scenes ($\beta = 0.523$, $p < 0.01$) have a significant positive effect compared to indoors scenes, supporting H2. Streamer type ($\beta = -0.299$, $p < 0.05$) has a significant negative effect on sales performance, H3 is not supported.

5.2 Path Dominance Analysis

We further compare the different contributions of the two paths to sales to understand the core design elements of the live streaming. Therefore, we introduced dominance analysis (Budescu) in the subsequent analysis, which is based on the principle of determining the extent to which different explanatory variables in a linear regression contribute to R2 as a way of ranking the different explanatory variables in terms of their importance. Referring to previous approaches in the literature, we conducted further dominance analysis of the variables in Model 1 and Model 2 [17]. Model 1 is the relative ordering of control variables, which shows that live streaming duration (Time) is the most important control

Table 2. Stepwise regression and moderating regression

Variable	Model 1	Model 2	Model 3	Model 4	Model 5
	LnSale	LnSale	LnSale	LnSale	LnSale
Price	−0.168**	−0.159**	−0.152**	−0.160**	−0.152**
	(0.0682)	(0.0658)	(0.0665)	(0.0659)	(0.0668)
Time	0.221***	0.203***	0.205***	0.202***	0.203***
	(0.0320)	(0.0304)	(0.0304)	(0.0303)	(0.0303)
Viewer number	0.00142***	0.00140***	0.00137***	0.00140***	0.00136***
	(0.000287)	(0.000277)	(0.000288)	(0.000277)	(0.000290)
Follower number	0.000***	0.000***	0.000**	0.000***	0.000**
	(1.39e−06)	(1.30e−06)	(1.33e−06)	(1.31e−06)	(1.33e−06)
Like number	1.68e−06	1.93e−06	2.07e−06	1.93e−06	2.01e−06
	(4.10e−06)	(3.67e−06)	(3.75e−06)	(3.67e−06)	(3.76e−06)
Product distance		0.752***	0.614**	0.790***	0.664**
		(0.133)	(0.255)	(0.197)	(0.281)
Streamer type		−0.299**	−0.295**	−0.260	−0.207
		(0.123)	(0.123)	(0.194)	(0.201)
x1		0.608***	0.487*	0.605***	0.440*
		(0.147)	(0.250)	(0.147)	(0.257)
x2		0.523***	0.415	0.523***	0.402
		(0.153)	(0.266)	(0.153)	(0.263)
Pd_x1			0.223		0.298
			(0.320)		(0.328)
Pd_x2			0.185		0.205
			(0.320)		(0.315)
Pd_St				−0.0715	−0.156
				(0.239)	(0.250)
Constant	4.499***	3.976***	4.030***	3.966***	4.015***
	(0.289)	(0.307)	(0.333)	(0.316)	(0.339)

Note: Robust standard errors in parentheses, *** $p < 0.01$, ** $p < 0.05$, * $p < 0.1$

variable explaining the dependent variable, and the rest are, in order, view number, follower number, like number, and price. Model 2 adds three independent variables on the basis of Model 1, and the overall ordering of the variables has also changed. The time of live stream is still the most important variable, the product distance of the product become the second most important variable, followed by view number and follower number in descending order, scene type is ranked fifth, like number and price follow, and Streamer type becomes the last variable in the ranking. The relative order of the three independent variables is product distance, scene type, and streamer type in that order. It can be seen that product distance occupies a higher position and is dominant among the variables, both in the relative ranking among the independent variables (ranked first) and in the importance ranking of the plenary variables (ranked second), suggesting that the product path is more important relative to the non-product path.

5.3 Robustness Check

In order to test the robustness of the main model results, we use three different robustness tests to analyze the main effects regression results further.

First, we adopt the approach of using the sale volume of a live streaming as the new dependent variable, which have similar economic meanings with sales. It can be seen that the main effect of product distance ($\beta = 0.863$, $p < 0.01$), scene type ($\beta = 0.691$, $p < 0.01$, $\beta = 0.492$, $p < 0.01$) and streamer type ($\beta = -0.357$, $p < 0.01$) are consistent with the primary model in terms of significance and coefficient relative size relationship, indicating that the results are reliable. Second, the Bayes Bootstrap method sampling with three different sample sizes was used to obtain the standard errors and confidence intervals of the variable coefficient estimates, and the results are shown that product distance ($\beta = 0.752$, $p < 0.01$), scene type ($\beta = 0.608$, $p < 0.01$, $\beta = 0.523$, $p < 0.01$) and streamer type ($\beta = -0.299$, $p < 0.01$). It can be seen that the coefficients of the variables in the three samples change very little compared to the main model, indicating that the results of the sampling test are robust. Third, potential outliers check. To eliminate the effect of outliers on the regression results, we use two types of winsorisation on the top and bottom of the dependent variable. Two different percentages of winsorisation, 1% and 2.5%, are used. The regression results of the model after two different winsorisation treatments do not change significantly in terms of the relationship and significance of the parameters compared to the main model, indicating that the results are reliable and robust.

6 Discussion

6.1 Key Findings

This study has the following key findings. Firstly, product close design will increase the sales of agricultural products. Second, the professional live streamer is more effective to sell agricultural products in live streaming than farmer live streamers. Third, the agricultural products planting scene and the agricultural products packing scene are more likely to increase the sales of agricultural products than ordinary indoors scenes. Moreover, the planting scene has the best effect on promoting sales, followed by the packing scene. Fourth, according to the dominance analysis of the variables, the impact of product distance is stronger than scene type, and scene type is more important than streamer type. Although there is no apparent moderating effect of product distance on both scene type and streamer type, we found that product distance exhibits a significant positive effect on agricultural product sales in different contexts through further stratification, which is in line with the performance of the variable dominated by product distance. Thus, this study found that product distance design is the most important influencing factor among the three designs, and the product path is the more important acting path among the two paths.

6.2 Theoretical and Practical Implications

This study has theoretical implications. Firstly, this study focuses on product distance, scene type, and streamer type. Fewer previous studies have focused on these live streaming factors. The results could rich theoretical understanding of related fields. Second, this study applies the dual-process theory in the live streaming context for agricultural products, which extends the research context of the theory. This perspective is less common in previous studies. Third, the study further compared the relative impact of two paths on sales. The results could strengthen the understanding of the relative impact of two paths in different research contexts.

The findings provide practical guide for boosting sales for agricultural products through live-streaming. Firstly, from the perspective of live streaming design, they can focus on the proximal display of products in product design. For example, the agricultural products can be placed closer to the camera to narrow the distance between the agricultural products and consumers so that the details can be presented. Secondly, regarding the scene type design, the merchants can place the scene type close to the venues that display more information about the growth and production of agricultural products, such as the fields for planting agricultural products and the warehouses for boxing and packing agricultural products. Third, professional live streamers can be hired from the streamer type. Fourth, when farmers' live streaming budget is limited, they can prioritize the investment from the design of creating a proximal distance of the product.

6.3 Limitations and Future Research

Firstly, the data used in the study came from a single live streaming platform. In future studies, multiple live streaming e-commerce platforms to increase the diversity of data sources and enhance the generalizability of the conclusions. Secondly, we did not consider the superposition of the scenes, which can be used as one of the scene types in future research. Finally, we investigate the product category of navel orange. However, whether the results are consistent for other types of products can be explored.

Acknowledgement. This study is supported by Grants from the National Natural Science Foundation of China (Project No. 71904149), and Featured Social Science Fund of University of Science and Technology of China (Project No. FSSF-A-230109).

References

1. 2023 Harvest Festival TikTok E-commerce to help farmers data report. TikTok E-commerce (2023). https://trendinsight.oceanengine.com/arithmetic-report/detail/1004
2. Yang, L.: Modelling the factors influencing the purchase intention of agricultural products under the mode of "live streaming + e-commerce." Mod. Bus. **35**, 84–86 (2021)

3. Zhu, D., Chang, Y.: Unprofessional or admirable: the effect of county governors' live streaming with goods on purchase intention. Nankai Manag. Rev. **26**(02), 177–187 (2023)

4. Yue, X., Zheng, F., Chen, W.: The effects of technology availability and live streamer characteristics on consumers' willingness to purchase agricultural products. Rural Econ. **11**, 104–113 (2021)

5. Chu, X.-Y.,Chang, C.-T., Lee, A.Y.: Values created from far and near: influence of spatial distance on brand evaluation. J. Mark. **85**(6), 162–175 (2021)

6. Evans, J.S.B.T., Wason, P.C.: Rationalization in a reasoning task. Br. J. Psychol. **63**, 205–212 (1976)

7. Chaiken, S.: Heuristic vs. systematic information processing and the use of source vs. message cues in persuasion. J. Pers. Soc. Psych. **39**(5), 752–766 (1980)

8. Leavitt, K., Fong, C.T., Greenwald, A.G.: Asking about well-being gets you half an answer: intra-individual processes of implicit and explicit job attitudes. J. Organ. Behav. **32**(4), 672–687 (2011)

9. Mavlanova, T., Benbunan-Fich, R., Koufaris, M.: Signaling theory and information asymmetry in online commerce. Inf. Manag. **49**, 240–247 (2012)

10. Pine, B.J., Pine, J., Gilmore, J.H.: The Experience Economy: Work is Theatre & Every Business a Stage. Harvard Business Press (1999)

11. Schouten, A.P., Janssen, L., Verspaget, M.:Celebrity vs. influencer endorsements in advertising: the role of identification, credibility, and product- endorser fit. Int. J. Adv. **39**(2), 258–281 (2019)

12. Yoo, J.-W., Jin, Y.J.: Reverse transfer effect of celebrity-product congruence on the celebrity's perceived credibility. J. Promot. Manag. **21**(6), 666–684 (2015)

13. Sengupta, J., Goodstein, R.C., Boninger, D.S.: All cues are not created equal: obtaining attitude persistence under low-involvement conditions. J. Consum. Res. **23**(4), 351–361 (1997)

14. Meng, L., Liu, F., Chen, S., et al.: Can I arouse you - a study on the influence mechanism of information source characteristics of different types of live netroots on consumers' purchase intention. Nankai Manag. Rev. **23**(01), 131–143 (2020)

15. David, R.A., Dennis, J.S., Thomas, A.W., Jim, F., Eddie, S.:Statistics for Business and Economics, 13th edn. Cengage Learning (2006)

16. Hair, J.F., Black, W.C, Babin, B.J., Anderson, R.E., Tatham, R.L.:Multivariate Data Analysis. Prentice Hall (1998)

17. Budescu, D.V.: Dominance analysis: a new approach to the problem of relative importance of predictors in multiple regression. Psychol. Bull. **114**(3), 542–551 (1993)

An Empirical Study of the Effect of Leadership Style on Project Performance in Open Innovation Communities from the Perspective of Online Collaboration

Zijie Ma[1], Pei Yin[1,2(✉)], and Li-Ke Zhang[1]

[1] University of Shanghai for Science and Technology, Shanghai 200093, China
pyin@usst.edu.cn

[2] School of Intelligent Emergency Management, University of Shanghai for Science and Technology, Shanghai 200093, China

Abstract. Analyzing factors impacting project performance is crucial for open innovation success, with a particular focus on the relatively unexplored influence of leadership in online collaboration. This research empirically investigates the effects of technical and social leadership styles on project performance within the Gitee open innovation community, utilizing a zero-inflated negative binomial regression model for open-source projects analysis. It classifies leadership styles according to leadership behavior theory and examines the moderating role of team size using situational leadership theory. The findings indicate that in the technical aspect, such as project leaders' expertise, technical processing efficiency, and problem-solving skill, positively affect project success, while a variety of technical interests can be detrimental. As for the social aspect, including affiliations with professional groups, community reputation, quality of social interactions, and team cohesion, positively contribute to project outcomes, although centrality in social networks does not. The research also underscores team size as a significant moderator of leadership effectiveness, emphasizing the need to consider both leadership styles and team size in managing open innovation projects. This study offers valuable insights into project management and leadership strategies tailored for project development through online collaboration in open innovation community.

Keywords: Open Innovation Community · Leadership Behavior Theory · Leadership Style · Innovation Performance · Online Collaboration

1 Introduction

With the rapid advancement of the digital economy and information technology, open online collaboration is transforming traditional cooperative models. Unlike conventional offline collaboration, which is constrained by time and space, open online collaboration transcends these barriers, enabling innovation activities to operate free from geographical and temporal limitations, thereby becoming a new catalyst for innovation. The emergence of open innovation communities exemplifies this shift. In these communities, contributors from around the globe leverage their collective intelligence to collaboratively develop innovative and efficient products. However, not all open innovation projects achieve their anticipated success. Therefore, investigating the factors that influence the performance of open innovation is crucial for understanding and fostering this form of innovation.

The metrics for assessing the performance of open innovation vary with the nature of the innovation. For instance, in the case of open-source software, its success depends not only on the number of users but also on the degree of user engagement, specifically whether they transition into contributors to the project. This shift from users to developers not only enhances the value of the innovative product but also aligns fully with the fundamental principles of open innovation.

Existing research on innovation performance has notable gaps. Ghapanchi and Aurum (2012) examined the positive effects of factors identified in dynamic capability theory, while Chen et al. (2017) investigated the influence of user participation motivation and cultural identity. However, these studies often lack empirical data from actual platforms, which constrains the generalizability of their conclusions. Crucially, the impact of leadership within open innovation teams, which typically feature non-hierarchical structures and more egalitarian, free-flowing member relationships, remains underexplored. Specifically, the role and impact of the team initiator's leadership style on project performance require deeper investigation.

Traditional leadership research typically classifies leaders by styles such as inclusive, authentic, and transformational [3]. Within open innovation communities, leadership is predominantly distinguished between task-oriented and social-oriented styles [4], reflecting the value placed on technical expertise ("governance by the wise") and the crucial role of social leaders in organizing and coordinating efforts. In these knowledge-rich settings, leadership effectiveness hinges on a blend of technical and social competencies. However, previous studies have not further broken down the impact of specific behaviors under the two styles on program performance, but rather assessed the two leadership styles in general. But in reality, there are good and bad behaviors within the same leadership style, and not all behaviors may be beneficial. Therefore, this study further breaks down the research granularity of leadership style to specific behaviors to analyze its influence on program performance. Moreover, the impact of leadership varies with team size, as situational leadership theory suggests that a leader's effectiveness is situation-dependent, influenced by their ability to adapt their management approach to different contexts.

Therefore, this paper focuses on open-source software projects aims to address the following questions:

1. How do the leadership styles of open-source software project initiators affect project performance?
2. Does team size play a moderating role in this relationship?

This paper explores the impact of technical and social leadership styles on project performance, thereby broadening the application of leadership behavior theory to virtual teamwork and guiding leaders in choosing effective strategies to improve project outcomes. By integrating leadership behavior theory, the management of open innovation communities can become more professional and systematic.

2 Literature Review and Theoretical Background

2.1 Research on Open Innovation Performance

In an open innovation community, the project performance as a result of collaborative team innovation can be regarded as innovation performance. Regarding the conceptual definition of innovation performance, academic interpretations have evolved from the abstract to the concrete. Cohen and Levinthal (1990) initially considered innovation performance as the ability of a team to achieve outcomes through innovative ideas, methods and processes. Entering the 21st century, the definition becomes the extent to which a team achieves its innovation goals in terms of time, quality, cost, and innovativeness. In recent years, studies have emphasized the objective measurement and quantification of innovation performance.

The influences on open innovation performance are a hot topic of academic research. Prior studies have focused on the effects of leadership style, knowledge integration, and team membership composition on innovation performance. Research on the impact of leadership style on innovation performance covers a variety of types, with transformational and transactional leadership being the most representative. Studies on knowledge integration pointed out that invisible knowledge exchange and knowledge sharing among members are crucial for new technology development. As for team membership composition, studies have focused on the impact of individual differences in gender, age, occupational background, knowledge and skills on innovation performance.

2.2 Leadership Behavior Theory

Whether it is a traditional physical organization or an online virtual organization, the commonly accepted definition of leadership is "the ability of an individual to contribute to the effectiveness and success of an organization by influencing and motivating others" [6]. In the context of open innovation research, this paper defines leaders as project initiators who have the authority to manage projects, including conducting code reviews, processing contribution requests and so on.

Behavioral theory states that leaders are able to influence their employees through specific behavioral patterns, which in turn lead to desired performance. Back in 1945, Stogdill and Shartle analyzed over 1,000 factors describing leadership behaviors and attributed leadership behaviors to two main dimensions: rule making and caring [7]. Based on these perspectives, behavioral theory distinguishes between two main leadership styles: task-oriented and relationship-oriented [8]. Task-oriented leaders focus on task execution and completion, emphasizing goal setting, work assignment, supervision and performance evaluation. In contrast, relationship-oriented leaders focus on the emotional needs of employees, relationship building and communication, as well as enhance employee satisfaction and team cohesion. With the rise of online virtual organizations, behavioral theories have begun to be applied to the study of online platforms. Dahlander and O'Mahony (2011) showed that while technical contributions were initially important, coordination was more significant in the later stages of the project. Ziegert and Dust (2021) used role ambiguity to examine the formal versus shared leadership relationship.

3   Research Hypotheses and Theoretical Model

3.1   Impact of Technical Leadership Style on Program Performance

Technical leaders are task-oriented at their core and typically provide critical technical guidance and support within teams and projects [11]. Particularly in knowledge-intensive environments like open innovation communities, they take on important technical tasks, therefore play an indispensable role [12]. As a result, technical leaders are effective in four main ways: technical expertise, high efficiency in response processing, excellent problem-solving skills, and a broad interest in the technical field.

In addition, users in the community usually have a deep admiration for individuals who are highly skilled [13]. The technical qualities of project leaders attract many users who are eager to improve their abilities. By collaborating with highly skilled leaders, these participants were able to realize self-improvement in their abilities [9]. Ultimately, this interaction and collaboration contributes to the success of open innovation projects. Therefore, this paper hypothesizes:

H1a: Technical expertise of project sponsors has a positive effect on project performance.

Efficient response processing accelerates the review and merging of project contributions. This can move projects forward in a short time and improve overall development efficiency. Meanwhile, Rapid response processing may help promote teamwork [4]. Timely processing of contributions can enhance a collaborative team atmosphere and may motivate more developers to increase their participation in the project [14]. Therefore, this paper hypothesizes:

H1b: response processing efficiency of project sponsors has a positive effect on project performance.

Technical leaders' deep understanding of technology and extensive experience with the technical difficulties of a project enable them to make quick decisions and provide effective solutions when faced with technical challenges [15]. This ability not only helps teams overcome technical difficulties [12], but also attracts developers who are eager to work in challenging technical environments [14]. Problem solving capability is also reflected in the efficiency of response in dealing with problems [9]. Leaders' quick response demonstrates their commitment and motivation to the project. This commitment can attract more users to participate [14] and contribute to the project, which is more conducive to the success of the project. Therefore, this paper hypothesizes:

H1c: The problem solving ability of project sponsors has a positive effect on project performance.

Technical leaders are more inclined to focus on technical knowledge, emphasize the accumulation of technical experience, and possess diverse technical competencies [16]. In addition, they tend to be highly self-driven and self-managed to learn new skills and knowledge on their own. Meanwhile, this openness to new technologies can motivate them to introduce new concepts and methods into the project [17], thus stimulating team members' sense of creativity. Therefore, this paper hypothesizes:

H1d: Project sponsors' broad interest in technology has a positive impact on project performance.

3.2 Impact of Social Leadership Style on Program Performance

Social leaders promote teamwork, communication, and cohesion primarily by strengthening interpersonal relationships [17]. They play a critical bridging role within the team, connecting different participants and programs. The keys to this leadership style are participating in group organizations, building social networks, maintaining community reputation, keeping quality social relationships, and enhancing team cohesion.

The open-source software community characterized by high mobility, team members are more fluid, but stable groups headed by well-known brands or companies still exist [9]. Socially oriented leaders tend to join these groups to expand their social circle and build strong relationships [17]. This approach not only provides social leaders with stable social resources, but also attracts independents who wish to join the group to contribute to the project as a way to gain access. In addition, being a member of a group organization is an honor in itself if the organization enjoys a high reputation [13]. Therefore, this paper hypothesizes:

H2a: Project initiators' participation in professional group organizations has a positive impact on project performance.

A number of studies have shown that centrality in social networks is a key indicator of social resources [18]. A social network is a social structure consisting of a large number of individuals ("nodes") that are connected to each other through a variety of social relationships. In this network, individuals at the center allows them to access a variety of resources, information, and opportunities for collaboration [14], which can lead to new possibilities for their teams. Therefore, this paper hypothesizes:

H2b: A project initiator's social network centrality of an open-source community has a positive impact on project performance.

Leaders with a good reputation in the open-source community are effective in attracting users to participate in project development [14]. Highly reputable leaders are able to build strong relationships of trust among team members. Meanwhile, these community-respected leaders are more likely to be recognized and welcomed by other developers who are willing to collaborate and share resources with them [17]. Therefore, this paper hypothesizes:

H2c: The community reputation of project initiators has a positive effect on project performance.

The value of social resources is not only in the quantity, but also in the quality of social relationships. The high-quality social connections not only increase the project's resource pool, but also raise the overall technical standards [11]. Meanwhile, these leaders form a higher-level network of relationships which is critical for projects to gain support, increase exposure, and find partners in the broader community, thus greatly enhancing the project success. Therefore, this paper hypothesizes:

H2d: the quality of a project sponsor's social connections has a positive impact on project performance.

Social leaders are proficient at creating strong cohesion within their teams. They help members feel a strong sense of belonging by proactively communicating and interacting with them during projects [16]. This leadership style fosters strong bonds among team members [9], stimulates knowledge sharing, and enhances mutual cooperation and support. Therefore, this paper hypothesizes:

H2e: The team cohesion ability of project sponsors has a positive effect on project performance.

3.3 Moderating Effects of Team Size

Situational leadership theory states that leaders should adapt their leadership styles and management approaches to the changing organizational environment and the varying needs of their team members [19]. This suggests that the effectiveness of leadership styles can vary in different organizational environments [12]. Team size as a key organizational context factor can significantly influences the effectiveness of leadership style.

When team sizes are small, communication links are shorter, and information is transferred more efficiently. In this case, the leader can be more directly involved in the technical aspects without having to spend too much effort on the management. At this point, the technical leadership style is more effective than the social leadership style. However, as the size of the team increases, leaders need to focus more on effective teamwork and project management rather than just individual technical contributions. As a result, social leadership styles show more advantages as team size grows. Therefore, this paper hypothesizes (Fig. 1):

H3a: Team size negatively moderates the role of technical leadership style in project performance.

H3b: Team size positively moderates the role of social leadership style in project performance.

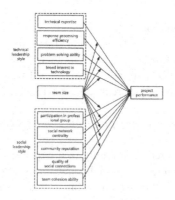

Fig. 1. Theoretical framework model

4 Methodology

4.1 Data and Sample

In this paper, we choose "Gitee" open-source community as the research platform, which provides a series of development tools and services such as code hosting, collaborative development, project management and continuous integration. As of July 2023, Gitee has 10 million registered users and 25 million code repositories, making it the largest code hosting platform within China.

Recommended items from a wide range of domains were collected using python crawler technology and screened for items published in the name of an individual rather than a group, totaling 872 items. Among them, project attribute data, member communication data, leader's homepage and its social network data, and attribute data of leader's participation in other products were collected. And a database was set up for storage, totaling more than 250,000 data.

4.2 Measurement

Dependent Variable. The performance of an open innovation project is quantified as the number of Pull Requests for the project as the dependent variable. The Gitee community adopts a distributed co-development model based on Pull-Request, which allows any peripheral person who wants to participate in the contribution but does not have the permission to modify the code to clone the project into his/her own space through 'fork'. The contributor pushes the updated code to the original project in the form of a Pull-Request, and the person in charge of the project decides whether or not to agree to the code merge after approval and testing. The number of Pull Requests a project receives represents the level of involvement of users in the project, from users to developers.

Independent and Moderating Variables. Technical expertise can be measured by the number of commits the leader has made in the project. Because commits are considered as technical contributions. Response processing efficiency is categorized by the pull request efficiency and issues efficiency, taking into account to calculate the average processing time, which is obtained by subtracting the response time of each response from the posting time and averaging it. Problem solving capability is measured by the number of the project's issues. Diversity of technical interest is quantified using the number of items in the leader's collection which named star.

Professional organization is measured by the number of projects published by the team which represents a higher level of team reputation and professionalism. For social network centrality, we choose Closeness Centrality as the calculation index. The higher the Closeness Centrality of node generally plays the role of a gossiper and is willing to pass messages between different groups of people. Community reputation is measured by the number of followers of the leader. Social relationship quality is quantified by the average number of forks of all projects that the leader has contributed. Team cohesion is measured by the strength of the socialization between the leader and the members in the project, quantified by counting the amount of communication between him/her and the members in the project issues. The moderator variable team size is measured by the number of contributors to the project.

Control Variables. For the project performance, the influencing factors are not only leader attributes but also project attributes, which have been used many times as a research variable in open innovation. In the Gitee community, users can 'star' projects of interest; 'watch' projects to get pushes on subsequent project developments; 'fork' projects to modify the code at will on a copy; 'branch' and 'tag' to represent different development lines of a project; 'release' to show different versions of a software development; and programming 'language' is categorized into Java, Python, C, and other languages; the domain is categorized into 17 types according to community labels.; According to previous studies, open source licenses are categorized into three strengths: 3 refers to strong open source(including GPL, AGPL, etc.); 2 refers to medium open source (including LGPL, PL, etc.); 1 refers to low open source (including Apache, BSD, etc.). Variables overview in the Appendix Table 1.

4.3 Analytical Methods and Results

The dependent variable Pull Request is a non-negative natural number and is too discrete. Meanwhile, there are a large number of zero in the dependent variable, we did the Vuong test, which yielded a value greater than 1.96, proving that the use of zero-inflated negative binomial regression is more appropriate. In order to mitigate skewness, all numeric variables in this paper were log-transformed by adding 1 before transformation. The data were analyzed using StataMP 17. Descriptive statistics for all variables used in this paper are shown in Appendix Table 2.

Table 1 contains the regression results for the five models. In model 1, which contains control variables and all variables of social leadership style, was used to test H2a--H2e. Social leaders' participation in professional group ($\beta = 0.001$, $p < 0.05$), reputation ($\beta = 0.489$, $p < 0.01$), quality of social relationships ($\beta = 0.284$, $p < 0.01$) and Team cohesion ($\beta = 0.715$, $p < 0.01$) are all positive and significant, **thus the H2a, H2c, H2d and H2e hypotheses are all valid.** Social leaders being at the center of asocial network ($\beta = -10.455$, $p < 0.01$) is significant but negative, **thus the H2b hypothesis is not supported.** Since project initiators usually have both technical and social leadership behaviors, the variable of social leadership style is controlled along with other control variables in Model 2 to test H1a—H1c. Technical expertise of technical leaders ($\beta = 0.086$, $p < 0.01$) is positive and significant, **thus the H1a hypothesis is valid.** The efficiency of solving problem ($\beta = -0.152$, $p < 0.01$) and diverse technical interests ($\beta = -0.132$, $p < 0.01$) are significant but negative, **thus the H1b and H1c hypotheses are not supported.**

Models 3–4 were used to test the moderating effect of team size on technical and social leadership styles. In Model 3, the joint effort between team size and technical leadership style are all significant, and the diversity of technical interests ($\beta = 0.036$, $p < 0.05$) turns negative to positive. In Model 4, the joint effort between team size and social leadership style are all significant, too. But the coefficient is as positive or negative as it is alone.

Table 1. Regression results

Variables	Model1	Model2	Model3	Model4
watch	1.177***	1.571**	0.164	0.081
	(2.71)	(2.10)	(0.50)	(0.26)
star	−2.404***	−2.417*	−1.277***	−0.887**
	(−3.56)	(−1.70)	(−2.64)	(−1.96)
fork	−0.879*	−0.829	−0.684*	−0.669*
	(−1.90)	(−0.62)	(−1.75)	(−1.78)
branch	0.006	−0.441	0.042	0.002
	(0.01)	(−0.57)	(0.18)	(0.01)
tag	0.088	0.320	0.022	0.056
	(0.35)	(0.89)	(0.13)	(0.37)
release	−0.605	−0.271	0.122	0.080
	(−1.37)	(−0.51)	(0.62)	(0.45)
language	−0.036	−0.172	0.018	0.014
	(−0.19)	(−0.60)	(0.14)	(0.12)
domain	0.073*	0.161**	0.027	0.015
	(1.69)	(2.17)	(0.84)	(0.50)
licenses	0.218	−0.044	0.035	0.049
	(1.00)	(−0.14)	(0.22)	(0.33)
commit	−0.621***	0.196	−0.021	0.128
	(−3.01)	(0.72)	(−0.13)	(0.82)
technical expertise		**0.086***	0.022	−0.060
		(2.88)	(0.18)	(−0.62)
response processing efficiency(issues)		−0.045	−0.019	−0.037
		(−1.54)	(−0.26)	(−0.55)
response processing efficiency(pulls)		**−0.152***	0.612***	0.598***
		(−7.38)	(6.61)	(6.81)
problem solving ability		**0.428***	−0.516***	−0.658***
		(12.68)	(−3.36)	(−4.43)
broad interest in technology		**−0.132***	0.170	0.134
		(−3.04)	(1.56)	(1.35)

(*continued*)

Table 1. (*continued*)

Variables	Model1	Model2	Model3	Model4
participation in professional group	**0.001****	0.001*	−0.000	−0.000
	(2.24)	(1.66)	(−0.23)	(−0.06)
social network centrality	**−10.455*****	−6.408**	−2.201	−6.479
	(−3.11)	(−2.30)	(−0.32)	(−1.02)
community reputation	**0.489*****	0.361***	0.021	0.090
	(6.38)	(5.87)	(0.15)	(0.66)
quality of social connections	**0.284*****	0.193***	−0.125	−0.000
	(6.01)	(4.73)	(−1.23)	(−0.00)
team cohesion ability	**0.715*****	0.104	−26.419	−27.048
	(3.76)	(0.74)	(−0.00)	(−0.00)
size × technical expertise			**0.039*****	
			(3.60)	
size × response processing efficiency(issues)			**0.050*****	
			(5.22)	
size × response processing efficiency(pulls)			**−0.045*****	
			(−5.63)	
size × problem solving ability			**0.102*****	
			(8.48)	
size × broad interest in technology			**0.036****	
			(2.18)	
size × participation in professional group				**0.000****
				(2.25)
size × social network centrality				**−3.853*****
				(−2.87)
size × community reputation				**0.101*****

(*continued*)

Table 1. (*continued*)

Variables	Model1	Model2	Model3	Model4
				(3.91)
size × quality of social connections				**0.112*****
				(6.50)
size × team cohesion ability				**0.090****
				(2.07)

z-statistics in parentheses *** p < 0.01, ** p < 0.05, * p < 0.1

4.4 Robustness Check

In order to strengthen the robustness of the empirical results, the representation of the dependent variable program performance is replaced with the number of stars which has been used in a large number of previous empirical studies as a measure of project success, and the results are consistent. Regression results in the Appendix Table 3.

5 Discussion and Conclusions

Based on empirical results from open-source projects on the Gitee platform, we find that technical expertise is conducive to project success, whereas problem-solving skills and diversity of technical interests are detrimental to project success. Social leaders' membership in professional group, community reputation, quality of social relationships and team cohesion are all conducive to project success, while being at the center of a social network is detrimental to project success. In addition, team size did have a moderating effect on leadership effectiveness.

Drawing some conclusions that are just the opposite of the research hypothesis may have the following reasons. First, the efficiency of technical leaders in handling pull requests for projects is not the faster the better. Because the faster the pull request is processed, the less time and effort is spent to ensure the validity and format consistency of the contributed code, which is not conducive to the success of the project. This also indicates that short lines or simple code logic of contributed code, and do not help much. Secondly, technical leaders have diverse technical interests, which for the leader is an enhancement of personal ability and development. However, in terms of the overall benefits of the team, too much attention to other projects leads to the dispersion of their energy, thus is not conducive to the success of the project.

Team size does not change the direction of the influence of social leadership behavior on project performance, while it makes the influence of diverse technical interests on project performance change from negative to positive. This suggests that as team size increases, the influence of social leaders on project performance does not change much while the disadvantage of technical leaders will be transformed into an advantage that is more conducive to project success.

5.1 Theoretical Contribution

The theoretical contribution is reflected in three aspects. First, it contributes by high-lighting that technical expertise among leaders positively influences project success. This nuanced understanding challenges a simplistic assumption that faster processing of pull requests or highly efficient technical leaders always leads to better project outcomes. This adds depth to the understanding of the leadership behavior theory [8]. Second, the finding that being at the center of a social network is detrimental to project success provides a nuanced understanding of the dynamics within social leadership. Third, the influence of leadership behavior has changed as team size increases, this finding adds nuance to the understanding of how team dynamics, specifically size, interact with different leadership styles, which contributes to the situational leadership theory [19].

5.2 Management Insights

This study provides critical insights into project management and leadership strategies within the context of online collaboration in open innovation communities. Firstly, it underscores the significance of leadership style, highlighting that technical and social leader behaviors distinctly influence project success. Secondly, it reveals that technical expertise positively affects project success, guiding technical leaders to enhance their skills for improved project outcomes. Thirdly, the research suggests that social leaders can maintain project success by engaging in professional organizations and nurturing social relationships, particularly as team sizes increase. This implies that platforms should encourage leaders to fortify community connections and develop comprehensive social skills. Fourthly, the study identifies a moderating effect of team size on leadership behavior: while the influence of social leaders remains stable with team expansion, the diversity of technical interests becomes more advantageous to project success. Finally, it notes that the diverse technical interests of technical leaders can negatively impact project success, indicating a need for leaders to balance their interests carefully. Additionally, project participants should consider the characteristics of project leader, as their behavior can directly influence project performance.

Acknowledgement. This work was supported by Humanities and Social Science Foundation of Ministry of Education (23YJCZH281), Shanghai Philosophy and Social Science Planning Project (2022ZGL010), Key Lab of Information Network Security, Ministry of Public Security) (C23600). The financial support is gratefully acknowledged.

References

1. Ghapanchi, A.H., Wohlin, C., Aurum, A.: Resources contributing to gaining competitive advantage for open source software projects: an application of resource-based theory. Int. J. Project Manage. **32**(1), 139–152 (2014)
2. Chen, X.H., Zhou, Y., Probert, D., et al.: Managing knowledge sharing in distributed innovation from the perspective of developers: empirical study of open source software projects in China. Technol. Anal. Strategic Manag. **29**(1), 122 (2017)

3. Yukl, G.: Effective leadership behavior: what we know and what questions need more attention. Acad. Manag. Perspect. **26**(4), 66–85 (2012)

4. Baldwin, C., von Hippel, E.: Modeling a paradigm shift: from producer innovation to user and open collaborative innovation. Organ. Sci. **22**(6), 1399–1417 (2011)

5. Cohen, W.M., Levinthal, D.A.: Absorptive capacity: a new perspective on learning and innovation. Adm. Sci. Q. **35**(1), 128–152 (1990)

6. House, R.J., Hanges, P.J., Javidan, M., Dorfman, P.W., Gupta, V. (Eds) Culture, Leadership, and Organizations: The GLOBE Study of 62 Societies. Overview of GLOBE, pp. 9–28 (2004)

7. Lord, R.G., Day, D.: V: leadership in applied psychology: three waves of theory and research. J. Appl. Psychol. **102**(3), 434–451 (2017)

8. Stogdill, R.M.: Leadership, membership and organization. Psychol. Bull. **47**(1), 1–14 (1950)

9. Dahlander, L., O'Mahony, S.: Progressing to the center: coordinating project work. Organ. Sci. **22**(4), 961–979 (2011)

10. Ziegert, J.C., Dust, S.B.: Integrating formal and shared leadership: the moderating influence of role ambiguity on innovation. J. Bus. Psychol. **36**(6), 969–984 (2021)

11. Bock, G.W., Ng, W.L., Shin, Y.: The effect of a perceived leader's influence on the motivation of the members of nonwork-related virtual communities. Trans. Eng. Manag. **55**(2), 292–303 (2008)

12. Mu, W., Bian, Y., Zhao, J.L.: The role of online leadership in open collaborative innovation evidence from blockchain open source projects. Ind. Manag. Data Syst. **119**(9), 1969–1987 (2019)

13. Wasko, M.M., Faraj, S.: Why should I share? Examining social capital and knowledge contribution in electronic networks of practice. MIS Q. **29**(1), 35–57 (2005)

14. Dahlaner, L., Magnusson, M.G.: Relationships between open source software companies and communities: observations from nordic firms. Res. Policy **34**(4), 481–493 (2005)

15. Iansiti, M., Lakhani, K.R.: The truth about blockchain. Harv. Bus. Rev. **95**(1), 118–127 (2017)

16. Daniel, S., Stewart, K.: Open source project success: resource access, flow, and integration. J. Strateg. Inf. Syst. **25**(3), 159–176 (2016)

17. Luther, K., Bruckman, A.: Leadership and success factors in online creative collaboration. IEEE Potentials **30**(5), 27–32 (2011)

18. Linton, C.: Freeman: centrality in social networks conceptual clarification. Soc. Netw. **1**(3), 215–239 (1978)

19. Hersey, P., Blanchard, K.: Management of Organizational Behavior: Utilizing Human Resources. USA (1969)

A Critical Review of Research on Live Streaming of Agricultural Products: Status, Trends, and Mechanisms

Nan Wang[✉], Yanan Zhao, and Shenyao Wang

Wuhan University, Wuhan 430072, Hubei, China
nanwang@whu.edu.cn

Abstract. In recent years, live streaming of agricultural products has gradually become an essential driving force to promote the development of the rural economy in China. Although live streaming of agricultural products has become a research hotspot, there is a lack of a critical review to understand research status and trends on this research topic. Following PRISMA, we search literature on live streaming of agricultural products though Web of Science database and CNKI database. Then, we use CiteSpace software to conduct an overall analysis of current research. Further, we analyze all the empirical studies, and summarized key mechanisms affecting the purchase of agricultural products through live streaming. Both theoretical and empirical contribution are discussed.

Keywords: Live Streaming of Agricultural Products · Status · Trends · Empirical Studies · Mechanisms

1 Introduction

In recent years, live streaming e-commerce has developed rapidly. As of June 2023, the scale of live e-commerce users in China reached 526 million, an increase of 11.94 million people in December 2022, accounting for 48.8% of the overall netizens [1]. Among them, the transaction scale of agricultural products live streaming is larger. The live streaming of agricultural products provides an unprecedented platform for agricultural sales, reducing the distance between farmers and markets, enabling distinctive agricultural products from rural areas to be sold further and more effectively [2]. Live streaming of agricultural products is gradually becoming a significant driving force for rural economic development. The total number of live e-commerce companies in China is 5,732,000, and the number of rural online businesses (online stores) has reached 17,303,000, accounting for 33.1% [1].

In addition to the practical significance of agricultural product livestreaming, there are also distinct theoretical differences between agricultural product livestreaming and general livestreaming of other products. Firstly, agricultural products possess unique attributes such as freshness, seasonality, regional specificity, and safety [3]. Secondly, agricultural product livestreams are in diverse categories, including celebrities, internet

Y. P. Tu and M. Chi (Eds.): WHICEB 2024, LNBIP 517, pp. 202–213, 2024.
https://doi.org/10.1007/978-3-031-60324-2_17

celebrities, government officials, entrepreneurs, and farmers [4]. Thirdly, agricultural product livestreams may take place outdoors, such as in fields, orchards, or farms, or indoors in packaging and shipping sites. Different livestreaming scene might yield different effects [5]. Therefore, the study of agricultural product livestreaming holds both theoretical and practical value.

The boom in live streaming of agricultural products has also triggered extensive attention from scholars. Previous studies on this topic can be categorized into non-empirical and empirical studies. Non-empirical studies focused on the advantages of live streaming of agricultural products, marketing strategies [6], development problems and countermeasures [7], while empirical research focuses on the purchase intention of agricultural products [8]. However, fewer scholars have systematically reviewed the research in the field of live streaming of agricultural products to reveal this field's current status, hotspots, and development. Furthermore, we further subdivide previous research on whether it is an empirical study and summarize mechanism on agricultural products purchase through live streaming as we contend that empirical research has a profound impact on subsequent research as most of their propositions are empirically proved.

This study adopts a bibliometric approach to comprehensively examine relevant studies on the rise of live streaming of agricultural products from 2017 to 2023. Then, this study selected empirical research on purchasing agricultural products via live streaming based on research hotspots, and thoroughly analyzed the mechanism affecting purchase intentions. All the research processes and result analyses strictly followed PRISMA. Overall, this study provides an overall analysis on research on live streaming of agricultural products as well as deep analysis on the empirical research on live streaming of agricultural products, which provide strong support for the related fields and can provide practical guidance for selling agricultural product through live streaming.

2   Overall Analysis of the Literature on Live Streaming of Agricultural Products

2.1   Data Sources

We chose China National Knowledge Infrastructure (CNKI) as the source for Chinese literature and Web of Science for English literature. The research process and analysis of results strictly followed the PRISMA. We conducted the search in CNKI using "直播助农" "农村直播" "乡村直播" "农产品直播", and in Web of Science using "farm product live streaming" and "agricultural products live streaming". The search was conducted in December 2023. No time limit was set to ensure an exhaustive search of the extant literature. As shown in Fig. 1, We retrieved 726 papers based on title, keywords, and abstract in CNKI, and 41 papers based on topic in Web of Science. After manual screening to exclude duplicated literature, literature with unrelated research topic, and other types of literature such as dissertations, conference papers, newspapers, etc., 449 Chinese papers and 14 English papers are included for further analysis.

2.2   Research Methodology

We import Chinese literature bibliographic record in "Refworks" format and English literature bibliographic record in "plain text file" format into CiteSpace 6.2.R6 software.

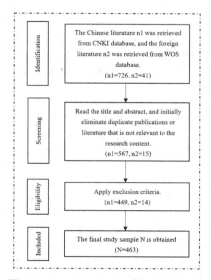

Fig. 1. Literature Retrieval and Selection

Then we analyze the data after converting the literature format, and then draw keyword co-occurrence map, keyword clustering and timeline map, keyword burst map, author cooperation network map, and institutional cooperation network map. The time interval selected is from 2017 to 2023, with a time slice of 1 year.

A node in the graph represents a research object (author/institution/keyword), the circle's size represents the research object's frequency, the connecting line between the circles reflects the cooperation relationship and the degree of closeness, and the different colors represent the different appearing years. In the keyword correlation analysis, the semantically identical keywords are merged. For example, "网络直播" is merged into "直播" and "purchase intention" is merged into "customer purchase intention".

2.3 Results of the Overall Analysis of the Literature on Live Streaming of Agricultural Products

Literature Quantity Distribution. The overall number of Chinese literatures shows a rapid upward trend. In 2017, the first Chinese literature on live streaming of agricultural products emerged. The number of literatures remained stable from 2017 to 2019, with no more than 10 pieces per year. In 2020, various regions in the country introduced support policies for the live streaming industry, leading to an explosive growth in the number of publications. From 2022 to 2023, the number of literatures remained at a high level, with over 100 pieces each year. This indicates that the field of agricultural live streaming is gradually receiving widespread attention and research. However, English literature appears in 2022, with 7 papers published in both 2022 and 2023. This may be due to the rapid development of China's livestreaming industry, research primarily focused on the livestreaming of agricultural products in China.

Research Hotspots and Trends

Keyword Word Frequency Statistics. The key words are the highly refined literary information content by the author. When the same key words appear frequently in a period of time, it can be considered as the hotspots and research trends commonly concerned by scholars in this field. The high-frequency keywords of agricultural products' live streaming research from 2017 to 2023 are shown in Table 1. The keywords with a frequency greater than or equal to 20 in the keyword map of Chinese papers are "农产品""乡村振兴""电商直播""直播带货""直播""直播助农""购买意愿""对策" and "营销策略", indicating that consumer purchase intention, countermeasures to live streaming of agricultural products and marketing strategy are the core research contents in Chinese literature. Since there are fewer English pieces of literature and fewer keywords, keywords with a frequency ≥2 are selected as an agricultural product, purchase intention, experience, live streaming, fresh agricultural products and technology acceptance, which shows that consumer purchase intention, fresh agricultural products, and technology acceptance are the core topics in the foreign literature.

Table 1. High-Frequency Keywords

Frequency	Year	Keywords	Frequency	Year	Keywords
151	2019	农产品	4	2022	Agricultural Product
109	2021	乡村振兴	3	2021	Purchase Intention
105	2020	电商直播	2	2022	Experience
96	2020	直播带货	2	2023	Live Streaming
43	2019	直播	2	2021	Fresh Agricultural Products
40	2020	直播助农	2	2022	Technology Acceptance
25	2021	购买意愿			
23	2020	对策			
22	2020	营销策略			

Keyword Clustering Analysis. We summarize and analyze the core research themes through keyword clustering mapping, and characterize the changes of research hotspots in this field in terms of period with the help of keyword clustering time zone map. Based on the keyword co-occurrence, the clustering adopts the LLR algorithm to form regions and cluster identifiers with different research characteristics. The smaller number of cluster represents the more keywords the cluster contains, and the block color of a cluster indicates the year when the keyword co-occurrence relationship in the cluster first occurred. Nine clusters were obtained for Chinese literature and six clusters were obtained for foreign language literature (see Fig. 2). The cluster module values (Q) of both Chinese and English literature were greater than 0.3, which indicated that the clustering structure was significant, and the average profile values (S) were greater than 0.7, suggesting that the clustering results were credible.

Fig. 2. Keyword Clustering

Based on the clustering keywords for theme summarization, as shown in Table 2, Chinese literature can be divided into (1) research on consumers' purchase intention, including research on anchor, emotional identity, and other influencing factors. (2) research on live streaming of agricultural products for helping farmers, including marketing mode, development strategy, talent training, implementation path, etc. (3) research on marketing strategy of live streaming of agricultural products. The foreign literature can be divided into (1) research on consumer purchase intention for fresh or green agricultural products, including research on influencing factors such as social proximity, altruism, etc. (2) research on countermeasures for the sustainable development of live streaming of agricultural products. (3) research on government subsidies for live streaming of agricultural products.

For Chinese literature, the hot topics in 2017 mainly focused on #2 Rural Live Streaming, which is the initial stage of research on live streaming of agricultural products and stage of relevant concepts proposed. The research mainly focused on the concept and characteristics of rural live streaming and discusses it in combination with traditional rural e-commerce. The research at this stage points out that live streaming of agricultural products is the inevitable development of the times. Overall, the research topics in this stage are relatively single, the research method is mainly based on conceptual description, and the study of live streaming of agricultural products has not received extensive attention from the academic community.

In 2019, more attention is paid to the optimization strategy of live streaming of agricultural products, and the hot topics are focused on #4 Consumers and #8 Agricultural products. In 2020, the study of live broadcasts of agricultural products continues to improve and enrich, and there are a variety of hot topics in the study. On the one hand, it focuses on the marketing mode of live streaming with goods (e.g. #0 live streaming with goods, #1 live streaming e-commerce, and #7 marketing strategy). On the other hand, it focuses on the development status quo, problems and countermeasures of live streaming to help agricultural products (e.g. #3 live streaming to help agricultural products). In 2021, the hot topics focus on the study of live streaming of new media under the background of rural revitalization (#2 live streaming of the countryside) and the influencing factors of the consumer's willingness to buy (#4 consumer and #6 purchase intention). The hot topics in 2022–2023 focus on #5 digital economy and #6 purchase intention. In the English literature, the hot topics for 2022–2023 focus on #0 purchase intention and #5 government subsidies (Fig. 3).

Top 15 Keywords with the Strongest Citation Bursts

Keywords	Year	Strength	Begin	End	2017 - 2023
乡村直播	2017	1.95	2017	2019	
直播	2019	2.45	2019	2020	
电商	2020	1.57	2020	2021	
问题	2020	1.31	2020	2020	
建议	2020	1.19	2020	2020	
脱贫攻坚	2020	1.19	2020	2020	
直播营销	2020	0.99	2020	2021	
营销模式	2020	0.92	2020	2020	
供应链	2020	0.9	2020	2020	
农村电商	2017	2.02	2021	2021	
电商平台	2021	1.01	2021	2021	
主播	2021	0.82	2021	2021	
东方甄选	2022	0.76	2022	2023	
抖音	2021	0.76	2022	2023	
感知价值	2022	0.73	2022	2023	

Top 15 Keywords with the Strongest Citation Bursts

Keywords	Year	Strength	Begin	End	2021 - 2023
sor theory	2021	0.63	2021	2021	
live broadcasting	2021	0.63	2021	2021	
social presence	2021	0.63	2021	2021	
fresh agricultural products	2021	0.56	2021	2021	
purchase intention	2021	0.49	2021	2021	
experience	2022	0.48	2022	2023	
technology acceptance	2022	0.48	2022	2023	
delone	2022	0.24	2022	2023	
e commerce	2022	0.24	2022	2023	
dimensions	2022	0.24	2022	2023	
internet	2022	0.24	2022	2023	
green purchase intention	2022	0.24	2022	2023	
germination	2022	0.24	2022	2023	
impact	2022	0.24	2022	2023	
adoption	2022	0.24	2022	2023	

Fig. 3. Keyword Bursting

Keyword Burst Analysis. The top 15 keywords were selected and analyzed according to the year of emergence. Keywords such as TikTok, perceived value, and "green purchase intention" have emerged in recent years, suggesting that these directions are future research trends in the field. For example, how to improve the perceived value of products and enhance consumers' willingness to buy has become a hot topic in agricultural products live streaming. Consumers are not only concerned about the function and price of the product, but also about whether the product can meet their emotional and psychological needs. Besides, as a social media platform, TikTok has been rapidly rising at home and abroad in recent years, and more and more people have begun to carry out marketing activities on TikTok. In addition to TikTok, there are other platforms where live streaming can be carried out. Therefore, the impact of different platforms on the sales of agricultural products live streaming has become an important direction for future research. How live streaming of agricultural products affects consumers' green purchase intention and how to develop effective green marketing strategies are also hot topics for future research.

3 Mechanisms for Empirical Research on Live Streaming of Agricultural Products

Based on the overall analysis of agricultural products' live streaming, we found that agricultural products' live streaming purchase behavior is a research hotspot. Thus, we further screened empirical studies on this topic and sorted out the mechanisms affecting the shopping of live streaming of agricultural products.

3.1 Literature Search and Selection

The search process and analysis of the results strictly followed PRISMA. Under the guidance of experts in the field of e-commerce and through a preliminary pilot search, this study was searched in CNKI using ("农产品" OR "助农" OR "农村" OR "乡村") AND

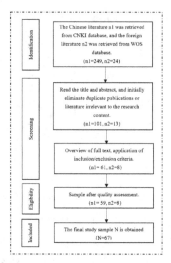

Fig. 4. Literature Screening

("直播" OR "网络直播" OR "在线直播") AND ("购买意愿" OR "购买行为" OR "消费者意愿") as the search formulas, and the search was carried out using ("Agricultural products" OR "farm produce") AND ("Live streaming" OR "Live broadcast" OR "Online streaming") AND ("Purchase intention" OR "Buying behavior" OR "Consumer willingness") retrieved in Web of science. The searches were conducted in December 2023. To increase the comprehensiveness of the search, no time limit was imposed on the included papers.

The exclusion-inclusion criteria are shown in Table 2. These criteria were used to screen the literature in two stages. In the first stage, we only read the titles and abstracts of the literature to avoid omissions. Therefore, if any of the criteria in Table 2 were met, the literature would be included in the second stage for full-text assessment. Drawing on the quality assessment criteria by NIDHRA S [9], this study developed the five quality assessment criteria, QA 1 (Is the topic discussed in the paper relevant to the factors influencing consumer purchase intention in live produce streaming?), QA 2 (Is it clear in what context this study was conducted?), QA 3 (Is the research methodology adequately described?), QA 4 (Is the process of data collection clearly explained?), and QA 5 (Does it accurately evaluate the method of data analysis?). Score 2 points if an article fully meets a particular criterion, 1 point for partial compliance, and 0 points for complete non-compliance.

Duplicate papers and irrelevant studies were removed by reading the titles and abstracts of the literature, leaving 101 papers in Chinese and 13 papers in English. Then, the papers were selected according to the inclusion/exclusion criteria in Table 2, leaving 61 papers in Chinese and eight papers in English. Thus, the sample before the quality assessment contained 69 studies on the factors influencing the willingness to purchase agricultural products live. Based on the quality assessment criteria, we scored the articles (maximum 10 points), and those with scores lower than six were defined as low-quality and deleted, and 2 Chinese papers were deleted. Finally, 67 papers were included.

Table 2. Inclusion/Exclusion Criteria

Inclusion Criteria	Exclusion Criteria
1. The Papers study the influencing factors of consumers' purchase intention in livestream of agricultural products	1. Papers that mention live streaming of agricultural products but do not examine the factors influencing their willingness to buy
2. Peer-reviewed journal articles	2. Conference papers, dissertations, book reviews, editorials, moderator's introduction
3. Papers with full-text access	3. Papers for which the full text is not available

Figure 4 shows the overall literature search and refinement process. The included studies were published between 2021 and 2023. Next, we will analyze and discuss the basic features of these studies in depth.

3.2 Basic Characteristics

Among these studies, various theories and models have been utilized, primarily the "Stimulus-Organism-Response" model (SOR) model (n = 30) and the stereotype content model (n = 2). SOR is a model that is used to describe how the environmental stimulus affects the individual's psychological state, which in turn affects the individual's behavior. Individual behavior. The stereotype content model is used to describe how people process and remember information. Theories such as the trust transfer theory, the theory of planned behavior, the customer value theory, the theory of heat flow experience, and the classic 4Ps theory in marketing were used in the study to explain the consumers' willingness to buy in the live streaming of agricultural products.

The majority of the studies utilized quantitative research methods (n = 61), with a smaller number of quantitative studies (n = 3), and only four studies employed a combination of qualitative research and qualitative-quantitative methods (n = 4). A total of 65 studies used questionnaires. Most of these questionnaires were collected online (n = 33), reflecting the digital nature of the live produce audience. Taking into account the differences between audiences, a combination of online and offline methods was also used (n = 9). The sample size of the questionnaire ranged from 98–1124. Interview methods (n = 3) and web ethnographies (n = 2) were used less frequently. Future research can consider using longitudinal studies or experimental designs to validate causality, as well as qualitative or mixed-methods research, to provide more in-depth insights into the drivers of consumers' purchase intentions in live streaming of agricultural products, and to provide a more comprehensive rationale for the mechanisms of consumers' purchase intentions. Most of the studies did not specify the research platform (n = 62), and only five studies explored the factors influencing consumers' purchase intention on specific platforms, including Jitterbug (n = 2), Taobao, and Jitterbug (n = 2), and Taobao, TikTok, and Pinduoduo (n = 1). Future studies can focus on different platforms as each platform has unique features, mechanisms influencing consumers' willingness to buy may differ.

3.3 Psychological Mechanisms Influencing Live Shopping of Agricultural Products

Trust Mechanism. Trust generally refers to the degree of confidence that viewers have in the various aspects involved in the process of live shopping for agricultural products, including the anchor, the products, and the platform [10]. In agricultural product live streaming, consumers lack control over certain information, affecting trust, but the visual experience and detailed displays enhance reliability compared to traditional e-commerce. Xiaoxu Dong et al. demonstrated that the utilization of high-quality live-streaming e-commerce platforms results in an augmentation of consumers' trust in environmentally sustainable practices, consequently bolstering their intention to engage in green purchasing behaviors [11].

Values Mechanism. Value refers to the consumer's perception of the value received through live streaming shopping [12]. When consumers are satisfied with the live streaming of agricultural products, they believe that the quality of agricultural products is good and the price is reasonable. Thus, they can gained enough information and value from the live streaming and are more likely to have a willingness to buy. Yan Zhou et al. confirmed that the interactivity, spatial presence, professionalism, and quality of live agricultural product streaming enhance the perceived value of agricultural products, thus influencing purchase intention [13].

Risks Mechanism. Risk refers to the uncertainty perceived by live-streaming audiences during the live-streaming shopping decision-making process or the possibility of causing economic, psychological, and other losses after purchase [12]. Risk is prominent in live streaming of agricultural products due to unique challenges, contributing to consumer concerns. Hongpeng Guo et al. confirmed that perceived risk hurts purchase intention and mediates between live characteristics of fresh produce and purchase intention in live streaming of agricultural products [14]. Zhou Ying et al. found that the behavior of anchors in the mode of live streaming to help farmers can change the level of risk perception of live audiences and thus affect their willingness to buy [13].

Emotional Experience Mechanism. Among the emotional experiences that influence consumers' willingness to buy in live streaming, positive emotion is the degree to which consumers generate perceptions of psychological pleasure under the influence of external stimulate [8]. Arousal is a change from a feeling of tiredness, sleepiness, or boredom to a feeling of excitement, stimulation, alertness, or activity [15]. From the perspective of irrational consumption, Xia Zhihua et al. argued that positive emotions promoted consumers' willingness to buy and pointed out that the professionalism of anchors and the marketing strategy of limited-time and limited-priced promotions play a crucial role in stimulating consumers' positive emotions [8]. Xiaolin Li found that arousal can be stimulated to promote consumers' willingness to buy, especially in the emergency of scarcity promotions, where consumers are more likely to rely on emotions to make decisions, and perceived time and competitive pressures increase consumers' arousal, limiting the allocation of attention to impulse purchases [15] (Fig. 5).

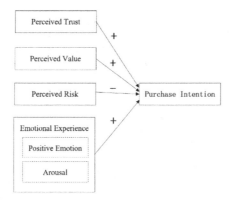

Fig. 5. Mechanisms Influencing Consumers' Purchases Intention

4   Conclusions and Discussion

4.1   Key Findings

A two-part study was conducted in this research, i.e., an overall analysis and an analysis of the empirical literature. Based on the overall literature analysis, this study uses biblio-metric methods to outline and summarize the literature on the study of agricultural prod-ucts' live streaming purchase intention and mainly obtains the following conclusions. Firstly, agricultural products live streaming literature began to emerge in 2017, and the number of articles issued increased rapidly after the introduction of live streaming indus-try support policies in many parts of the country in 2020. Secondly, Regarding the core theme, the research background of both Chinese and English literature is the live stream-ing of agricultural products in China. China is far ahead in the live streaming industry. The research mainly centers on the countermeasures to the problems of live streaming of agricultural products and the marketing strategy, focusing on exploring topics such as purchase intention, fresh agricultural products, and technology acceptance. Thirdly, regarding the evolution of research hotspots, early research in agricultural products' live streaming has a single theme, mainly focusing on the concept and characteristics of agri-cultural products' live streaming. With the evolution of time, research in this field has developed rapidly, the research content is more affluent, and the method is more diver-sified. In the past two years, the research hotspots mainly focus on the willingness to buy and the digital economy, and these directions are also future research trends. Based on the analysis of empirical literature, this study summarizes four main mechanisms that affect the sales of agricultural products which are perceived value mechanism, trust mechanism, emotional mechanism and perceived risk mechanism.

4.2   Limitations and Future Research

First, only Web of Science and the CNKI were used as the search source. Second, there may be omissions of the relevant literature due to the bias of the judgment or the inclusion of the database literature, etc. In addition, the CiteSpace analysis software was used to analyze the keywords rather than the complete text, so there may be omissions or biases in detecting the article as a whole. Last, only peer-reviewed journal articles were considered in the sample to review the mechanisms of live purchasing of agricultural products. Future studies can include papers published in other venues.

5 Contributions

This study has theoretical contributions. First, this study reveals the hotspots and trends of the research in this field. Second, this study proposes future direction of live streaming of agricultural products, which provides a trend reference for subsequent research. In addition, this study offers a model that includes four dimensions (perceived value, perceived trust, emotional experience, and perceived risk) influencing the willingness to purchase agricultural products through live streaming, providing theoretical contribution to research on live agricultural products purchase behavior. Regarding practical contributions, based on the analysis of empirical research, four mechanisms are proposed to promoting live agricultural products purchase behavior through livestreaming. Thus, practice can be done by augmenting perceived value, enhancing the establishment of trust within the live streaming environment, minimizing the risks and stimulating an emotional experience for the consumer during the live broadcast.

Acknowledgement. This study is supported by Grants from the National Natural Science Foundation of China (Project No. 71904149, 71974148, 71921002), and the Major Projects of Ministry of Education Humanities and Social Sciences Key Research Base (Project No. 22JJD870002).

References

1. The 52nd Statistical Report on China's Internet Development (2023). https://cnnic.cn/n4/2023/0828/c199-10830.html. (in Chinese)
2. Zhu, B., Xu, P., Wang, K.: A multi-group analysis of gender difference in consumer buying intention of agricultural products via live streaming. Res. World Agric. Econ. 4(1), 25–35 (2023). https://doi.org/10.36956/rwae.v4i1.789
3. Tao, W., Yiming, C.: Integration and development of digital economy and agriculture: practice models, realistic obstacles, and breakthrough paths. Issues Agric. Econ. 7, 118–129 (2020). https://doi.org/10.13246/j.cnki.iae.2020.07.011. (in Chinese)
4. Yiwu, Z., Changjiang, M., Lili, L., et al.: Value reconstruction of live e-commerce and upward pricing of agricultural products: mechanism and implementation path. Issues Agric. Econ. 2, 108–117 (2022). https://doi.org/10.13246/j.cnki.iae.20210909.002. (in Chinese)
5. Jianping, D., Wenping, L.: Key pathways to enhance user stickiness in agricultural product live broadcasting scenarios. China Bus. Market 36(5), 30–41 (2022). https://doi.org/10.14089/j.cnki.cn11-3664/f.2022.05.003. (in Chinese)
6. Wang, Z.: How "Live Streaming + E-commerce" Helps Rural Revitalization. People's Forum, (15 vol), pp. 98–99 (2020). (in Chinese)
7. Guo, H., Qu, J.: Research on the sustainable development of live streaming sales helping agriculture. People's Forum (20), 74–76 (2020). (in Chinese)
8. Zhihua, X., Weiyi, L.: Study on the factors influencing consumers' purchase intention of agricultural product e-commerce live streaming attributes. China Bus. Rev. 11, 5–9 (2023). https://doi.org/10.19699/j.cnki.issn2096-0298.2023.11.005. (in Chinese)

9. Nidhra, S., Yanamadala, M., Afzal, W., et al.: Knowledge transfer challenges and mitigation strategies in global software development—a systematic literature review and industrial validation. Int. J. Inf. Manage. **33**(2), 333–355 (2013). https://doi.org/10.1016/j.ijinfomgt.2012.11.004

10. Yu, Z., Zhang, K.: The determinants of purchase intention on agricultural products via public-interest live streaming for farmers during COVID-19 pandemic. Sustainability **14**(21) (2022). https://doi.org/10.3390/su142113921

11. Dong, X., Zhao, H., Li, T.: The role of live-streaming e-commerce on consumers' purchasing intention regarding green agricultural products. Sustainability **14**(7) (2022). https://doi.org/10.3390/su14074374

12. Ying, Z., Zhou Haiyan, Y.: Mechanism of host behavior in live broadcasting mode affecting audience purchase decision under the live broadcast aid agricultural model. Bus. Econ. Res. **19**, 96–99 (2021). (in Chinese)

13. Zhou, Y., Lu, L., Liu, L., 等. The innovation path of agricultural products e-commerce marketing mode under the background of "live broadcast + short video". Appl. Math. Nonlinear Sci. (2023). https://doi.org/10.2478/amns.2023.2.00452

14. Guo, H., Sun, X., Pan, C., 等. The sustainability of fresh agricultural produce live broadcast development: influence on consumer purchase intentions based on live broadcast characteristics. Sustainability **14**(12) (2022). https://doi.org/10.3390/su14127159

15. Li, X., Guo, M., Huang, D.: The role of scarcity promotion and cause-related events in impulse purchase in the agricultural product live stream. Sci. Rep. **13**(1) (2023). https://doi.org/10.1038/s41598-023-30696-8

Decoding Policy Directives: An Empirical Study on the Influence of Central Policy Signals on Local Environmental Regulation Behavior

Chen Wang, Huijun Wang, Jiabao Pan[(✉)], Jin Li[(✉)], and Xi Wang

Central University of Finance and Economics, Beijing 100098, China
jiabaop@cufe.edu.cn, jinli7lijin@163.com

Abstract. Central policy texts are crucial instruments utilized by the central government for communicating policy directions, guiding behavior, and administering societal affairs. Analyzing central policy texts helps the public to understand policies and attribute real-world issues. Prior studies draw conclusions mainly based on statistics of word frequency while lacking consideration of the semantics content of these texts. This study employs text mining techniques, specifically Whole Word Masking (WWM)-BERT, to analyze 348 central government documents from 2016 to 2018, which enables the extraction of latent semantic meanings from the policy texts. Aligned with signaling theory, our research investigates the roots of environmental policy implementation disparities, examining aspects such as intensity, clarity, and credibility/reliability of communication. The findings indicate that document signals, such as issuing department, wording intensity, and clarified regulatory targets of policy documents significantly enhance local governments' environmental regulation behaviors. Meanwhile, the absence of standardized benchmarks for ecological environmental administrative penalties may exert negative impact on the effectiveness of credible threats in shaping environmental regulation outcomes.

Keywords: WWM-BERT · Signaling Theory · Policy Implementation Disparities · Policy Text · Text Mining

1 Introduction

The ecological environment exerts a significant impact on the improvement of the economy, taxes, and various other aspects, all of which are intricately linked to the foundation of a state. As the economy and technology continue to advance, the importance of environmental protection is gaining prominence. This is particularly evident in China, where the government places a strong emphasis on environmental protection. The construction of an ecological civilization has been elevated to a national strategy since the 18th National Congress of the Communist Party of China. This commitment is further reinforced by the establishment of the Central Environmental Protection Inspection System, which aims to enhance the performance of local governments in environmental protection.

Y. P. Tu and M. Chi (Eds.): WHICEB 2024, LNBIP 517, pp. 214–225, 2024.
https://doi.org/10.1007/978-3-031-60324-2_18

While the Chinese government has implemented numerous measures to address environmental protection issues, a noticeable phenomenon persists. The execution of environmental policies by local governments often deviates from the expectations and initial conceptions set by the central government, leading to what is termed as the environmental/green policy implementation disparities [1]. The presence of an environmental implementation disparities exerts a detrimental influence on environmental protection efforts, which contributes to the persistent emergence of what is commonly referred to as the "environmental governance paradox" or "green paradox" [2].

The causes of the environmental policy implementation disparities, according to current research, predominantly revolve around issues within the system design. Scholars argue that the relatively unreasonable institutional arrangement constrains the enthusiasm of local governments for environmental governance, thus contributing to the implementation disparities [1]. To address these disparities, researchers have explored solutions from various perspectives, including signaling theory, the central-local relation perspective, and others [1, 3]. Among these studies, there is a relative scarcity of research based on signaling theory. However, within the paradigm of central-to-local transmission of policy signals for regional environmental regulation, signaling theory offers insights into the role of policy signals released by the central government from the perspective of information transmission in local environmental regulation. This can provide valuable references for policy formulation and environmental problem-solving. Moreover, scholars studying disparities in environmental policy implementation from this perspective currently face challenges due to the timeliness of research data, necessitating more timely information support. Furthermore, within the realm of investigations into Chinese policy text, the employed research methods have been somewhat constrained. Scholars apply varying research methods in the context of Chinese policy text mining, such as content analysis [4], machine learning [5], and, to a lesser extent, deep learning models [6]. However, current research predominantly relies on simple word frequency statistics and superficial textual analysis, lacking in-depth consideration of the semantics of policy texts. Such approach often fails to capture the profound meanings and implications embedded in policies, thereby limiting the genuine problem-solving capabilities concerning social, economic, and environmental issues.

This study employs text mining methods, utilizing the BERT language model based on whole-word masking (WWM) technology, to delve into the semantic information within Chinese policy texts. Such approach aims to address text recognition issues and extract features indicative of policy signals. Drawing upon signaling theory, we further investigate how central signals influence local environmental regulation behavior, aiming to provide insights for narrowing the disparities in environmental policy implementation.

2   Related Work

2.1   Focus of Environmental Policy Implementation Disparities

Disparities in environmental policy implementation are contingent upon the central policies and local environmental governance. Existing research tends to attribute disparities to the failure of local environmental governance, suggesting a lack of recognition of environmental laws at the local level. Moreover, it posits that the ineffective enforcement of central environmental policies is due to the opposition or circumvention by local government officials [7].

This research approach overlooks the institutional reasons behind the disparities in environmental policy implementation and the responsibilities of the central government in environmental management. Lieberthal [8] noted that local governments, under immense pressure to prioritize economic development and endowed with significant autonomy, have limited space for implementing environmental policies. Environmental agencies operate under the leadership of local governments focused on short-term economic growth rather than long-term sustainability.

So an analysis of environmental governance issues from a more macroscopic government governance perspective is needed [9]. This paper aims to explore the role of the central government in local environmental governance, and to examine in detail the environmental governance policy texts issued by the central government, in order to explore ways to crack the implementation disparities of environmental policies.

2.2 Signaling Theory in Addressing Real-World Questions

Signaling theory was first proposed by Spence [10] and originates from the study of market interactions in situations of asymmetric information between buyers and sellers. Its core idea is that due to the asymmetry of information, the informed party needs to send signals to the receiving party, which will understand and react to the received signals. It is an important component of information economics.

For the past century, research on management decision models has been based on the basic assumption of complete information, overlooking the important role of asymmetric information in management practice [11]. The emergence of signaling theory has led researchers to focus on the significant role of asymmetric information in decision-making. Its application in management practice has also become increasingly common, prompting managers to pay more attention to the quality of information transmission, namely, whether one party can fully understand the characteristics of the other party, in order to reduce information asymmetry. For example, in corporate governance, CEO reports on company earnings can serve as favorable quality information transmitted to potential investors or the board of directors [12]; in human resource management, the identification and screening of signals are increasingly applied in talent recruitment [13]; in strategic management, improving the communication network of signals within the organization can better convey the voice of employees, thereby facilitating the coordinated development of the entire organization [14].

In the field of environmental regulation, a perspective based on signaling theory reveals a phenomenon of asymmetric information, where the central government acts as the information sender and the local government as the information receiver, but the determination of the central government in environmental regulation is not fully reflected in information transmission. Therefore, the central government needs to fully convey high-quality signals of environmental protection through central policy documents. This study focuses on exploring how the central government can improve the quality of its signals to enhance the performance of local governments in the implementation of environmental policies, thereby addressing local environmental regulation issues.

2.3 Knowledge Mining for the Recognition of Chinese Policy Documents

In terms of the analysis of Chinese policy texts, content analysis emerges as a prominent method across various studies. For instance, Liu employed a content analysis approach to gauge the policy sentiment within the China Monetary Policy Implementation Report by assessing the frequency of specific word categories, thereby examining its impact on market confidence [4]. Ge's focus on government innovation involved a multi-case text analysis of the OPSI Case Library. By employing an encoding approach within content analysis, Ge extracted crucial textual information and transformed qualitative data into quantitative data using deductive and inductive logic. This approach offers experiential insights to government departments, facilitating more effective innovation [15]. Furthermore, machine learning techniques play a significant role in such research endeavors. Zhong utilized text mining technology to enhance urban biodiversity governance through K-means unsupervised classification, which extracts semantic information from policy texts and suggests potential strategies for improving governance effectiveness [5].

In summary, the majority of research concerning Chinese policy texts relies on conventional word frequency statistical analysis methods or machine learning techniques utilizing static word embeddings, with limited exploration into deep learning approaches. Consequently, there exists a challenge in thoroughly uncovering the semantic nuances within policy texts to effectively address underlying practical issues.

3 Method

3.1 Data

Given the pivotal role of policy texts in signaling environmental regulation behavior, our study centers on the analysis of 348 policy documents obtained from the Legal Information Centre of Peking University. These documents were extracted using key search terms for "environment," "pollution," and "industry," covering the period from 2016 to 2018. Additionally, we gathered environmental indicators from the China City Statistical Yearbook spanning from 2017 to 2019, encompassing data from 295 Chinese cities across 31 provinces, to reflect the environmental regulation behavior of municipal governments.

3.2 Text Mining

To facilitate the application of text recognition, we initiated a preprocessing stage for policy documents. This involved segmenting text using periods, employing Chinese regular expressions to remove non-Chinese characters, and integrating jieba with HIT's stop word list to filter out irrelevant terms. Given the unique nature of Chinese words, which are not composed of independent symbols like letters, we opted for WWM-BERT [16]. This BERT model, based on whole word masking strategy, no longer divides words into small segments, thus overcoming the limitation of only blocking a portion of the entire word. During the pre-training stage, this model masks an entire Chinese vocabulary, significantly enhancing the application capacity of language models in Chinese scenarios. Moreover, leveraging dynamic word embedding technology, the BERT model can grasp semantics based on context, enabling it to effectively mine signal features within policy documents.

Building on Li's research [1], our aim is to identify 26 features within the document. Among these, three feature recognition tasks involve simple frequency statistics, which we used traditional encoding methods. For 14 features presenting low recognition difficulty, we employed keyword matching processing. However, for the nine features requiring semantic-level analysis, we utilized deep learning technology to construct classifiers for recognition. This approach facilitates multi-label classification of policy texts, encompassing a total of nine labels. These 9 features of policy signals, identified through deep learning, are illustrated in the measurement items depicted in Fig. 1. Other features were not elaborated on in detail due to space limitations.

To solve the problem of multi-label classification, we transform it into several simpler single-label classification problems [17]. Specifically, it is further converted into 9 distinct binary classification problems.

Table 1. The performance of deep learning model on 9 categories.

Category[a]	# of data	% of data	AUC	F1-score	Precision	Recall
II	1510	10.07	0.847	0.846	0.854	0.846
CLG	372	2.48	0.823	0.825	0.852	0.829
CE	1052	7.01	0.811	0.805	0.838	0.810
CTLG	704	4.69	0.821	0.818	0.835	0.820
CTE	2608	17.39	0.813	0.811	0.822	0.812
PE	1088	7.25	0.812	0.803	0.845	0.809
RCS	978	6.52	0.903	0.902	0.911	0.903
OPT	1064	7.09	0.828	0.826	0.847	0.828
CRB	5624	37.49	0.688	0.663	0.767	0.691

[a]II stands for Incentive institutions, CLG for commitments for local governments, CE for commitments for enterprises, CTLG for credible threats for local governments, CTE for credible threats for enterprises, PE for polluting enterprises, RCS for Responsibility of civil society, OPT for Other policy targets and CRB for clarity of regulation behavior.

We utilized the aforementioned 348 policy documents as a corpus and established a WWM-BERT pre-training model. Subsequently, we fine-tuned this model and appended a fully connected layer and batch normalization to create nine corresponding classifiers for recognizing text features. The training dataset comprised 13,210 labeled texts curated by domain experts. To address class imbalance, we employed undersampling for negative classes and integrated 5-fold cross-validation. In assessing classifier performance, we employed metrics such as AUC, F1-score, precision, and recall, as delineated in Table 1. Ultimately, we deployed these nine classifiers to process the remaining text, yielding a dataset comprising 55,091 data points.

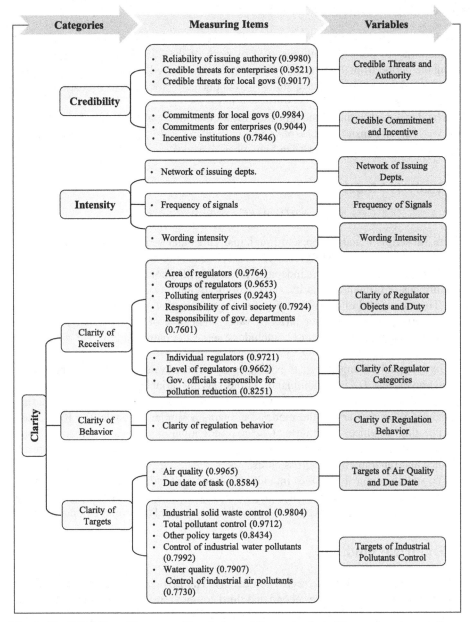

Fig. 1. Final Variables of Document Signals through Factor Analysis (The numbers in parentheses following each measuring item represent the corresponding factor loadings. Since KMO is 0.467, no principal component could be extracted for the dimension of intensity)

3.3 Variable Measurement

Based on both the classification results and traditional coding outcomes, we calculated the quantities of policy signals received by each of the 295 cities under 26 features during the period from 2016 to 2018. These quantities served as measurement items for the independent variable. Subsequently, we conducted factor analysis to distill the final 10 core independent variables, as illustrated in Fig. 1.

The dependent variable encompasses local environmental regulation behavior. For this, we sourced density of absorptive fine particulates (AFP) data with a one-year lag from 295 cities via the China Urban Statistical Yearbook.

4   Analysis Model

$$y_{ct+1} = \alpha D_{ct} + \beta C_{ct} + \mu_p + u_{ct} + \varepsilon_{ct} \tag{1}$$

Where subscripts c and t represent municipal cities and years, the lagged dependent variable y_{ct+1} denotes ln(AFP) (change ratio for density of absorptive fine particulates) for city c in year $t + 1$. The core independent variables D_{ct} comprises 10 variables across three dimensions (intensity, clarity, and credibility/reliability), serving as document signals. The anticipated effect of α is negative, signifying that a higher quality of central signals corresponds to a lower ln(AFP) value, indicative of improved environmental regulation behaviors. The vector C_{ct} includes a series of control variables to account for city-specific characteristics.

Given that all document signals exhibit nearly identical values for all signal recipients within a given year, D_{ct} is predominantly a time-varying variable with minimal individual discrepancies. This equivalence allows for controlling the time-fixed term, rendering its inclusion unnecessary in the model. Following a similar rationale, the RE model, incorporating provinces fixed terms (μ_p) and individual(city) random effect (u_{ct}) and estimated using Generalized Least Squares (FGLS), considers both fixed effects for each province and random effects across cities.

The specific control variables include: (1) number of industrial enterprises, (2) per capita regional GDP, (3) growth rate of regional GDP, (4) the proportion of the secondary industry to GDP, (5) fiscal revenue-to-expenditure ratio, and (6) average population.

5   Empirical Findings

Table 2 displays the complete regression results. The first column presents the results of the baseline regression. The second and third column represent robustness checks to ensure the robustness and reliability of the results.

5.1 Basic Regression Results

Column-1 shows the FGLS results of independent variables to ln(AFP), which measures the annual environmental regulation behaviors of municipal governments. The results show that the central environmental regulation signals can significantly affect the local governments' regulation behaviors.

Table 2. Regressions results on key independent variables and municipal environmental regulation behaviors (Robust standard errors clustered by individuals in parentheses).

	ln(AFP) (1)	ln(ISWU) (2)	ln(AFP) (3)
Intensity			
networks	−0.021***	0.028*	−0.021***
	(0.00)	(0.02)	(−5.12)
frequency	0.021**	−0.064**	0.022***
	(0.01)	(0.03)	(2.60)
wording	−0.001***	−0.001	−0.001***
	(0.00)	(0.00)	(−4.27)
Clarity			
objects	0.700***	−1.627*	0.715***
	(0.20)	(0.85)	(3.57)
regulator	0.941***	−1.487*	0.937***
	(0.22)	(0.83)	(4.22)
pollutants	−0.192**	0.632*	−0.190**
	(0.09)	(0.36)	(−2.16)
due	−0.323*	0.219	−0.358**
	(0.18)	(0.39)	(−2.07)
acts	0.000	0.001***	0.000
	(0.00)	(0.00)	(1.57)
Credibility			
threats	1.626***	0.415	1.635***
	(0.57)	(1.33)	(2.95)
commitments	0.089	−0.393	0.039
	(0.22)	(0.56)	(0.18)
Constant	9.469***	−0.650	9.697***
	(1.67)	(4.73)	(5.91)
Control Variables	Yes	Yes	No
Provinces Fixed Effect	Yes	Yes	Yes
Observations	885.000	885.000	885.000

* $p < 0.1$, ** $p < 0.05$, *** $p < 0.01$

In dimension of intensity, the coefficient of network of issuing departments is -0.021, $p < .01$, which indicates that the network of issuing departments can significantly improve local governments' environmental regulation behaviors. The explanation lies in China's governance system, which allows central government departments to directly mobilize corresponding local government departments. Increased participation of central departments in document issuance leads to greater mobilization of local government departments, resulting in more impactful overall regulation behaviors by local governments. Wording intensity's coefficient is -0.001, $p < .01$, which shows that wording intensity can improve local governments' environmental regulation behaviors, but the effect is limited. It is worth noting that signals' frequency (measured by the number of annually issued documents), with a coefficient of 0.021, $p < .05$, cannot improve local governments' regulation behaviors. It comes to the conclusion that if documents do not contain such information about wording intensity, enough network of issuing department and regulation targets, despite the high volume of policy document output, transforming it into a corresponding implementation is challenging.

Clarity can significantly affect the regulation behaviors of provincial governments. The coefficients of clear target of industrial pollutants control, air quality and due date are -0.192, $p < .05$; -0.323, $p < .1$, indicating that they can effectively enhance the environmental regulation behaviors of cities. However, the definition of the receivers – regulator objects and duty, and regulator categories cannot significantly improve provinces' behaviors. This can be explained by the fuzzy theory of policy implementation and the existing empirical researches. Relatively vague central policies can provide local governments with space to adapt to local conditions [18], which will have unexpected positive impacts on local environmental regulation behavior.

In the credibility/reliability dimension, the coefficients of the credible threats is 1.626, $p < .01$, This finding may appear contrary to previous studies focusing period from 2000 to 2015 [1]. However, it is essential to note that the earliest regulatory norms in the field of ecological environmental governance were outlined in the "Opinions on Standardizing the Discretionary Power of Environmental Administrative Penalties," issued by the former Ministry of Environmental Protection (now the Ministry of Ecology and Environment) in March 2009 (Huanfa [2009] No. 24). This document played a crucial role in mitigating the issues of arbitrariness and non-standardization in penalties. Despite the initial success, subsequent practical implementation faced challenges such as inconsistent texts, inert execution, and inflexible discretion [19]. In response to these issues, the Ministry of Ecology and Environment introduced the "Guiding Opinions on Further Standardizing the Application of Discretionary Power in Environmental Administrative Penalties" (Huanzhifa [2019] No. 42) in 2019, aiming to enhance the standardization of discretion benchmarks. Our research findings indirectly underscore the necessity of this introduced document.

5.2 Robustness Checks

Initially, we conducted robustness testing by replacing the dependent variable, it involves altering the dependent variable to the ratio of industrial solid waste utilized (ISWU), a direct reflection of local government environmental regulation behaviors. Column-2 displays the results. The significance of core independent variables for the new dependent variable aligns with basic regression results in Column-1, yet the direction is opposite, suggesting that higher central signal quality corresponds to a higher ratio of industrial solid waste utilized.

Furthermore, we performed robustness testing by excluding control variables, eliminating external interference and validate the stability of research findings. The Column-3 represents the results, revealing that the significance of these core explanatory variables aligns with the benchmark results in Column-1. Moreover, their direction and coefficient magnitude remain consistent. This suggests that the quality of policy signals, rather than control variables, are influencing change ratio for density of absorptive fine particulates.

6 Discussion and Conclusion

Research has discovered that central policy documents play a crucial role in environmental governance, but there are certain disparities in their actual implementation. However, signaling theory provides a unique way to solve problems. From the perspective of signaling theory, the central government is regarded as the signal sender, while local governments are regarded as the signal receivers. The signal initiators send high-quality signals to alleviate information asymmetry, enabling the signal receivers to understand and respond to the received signals, narrowing the disparities in environmental policy implementation and improving local regulation behavior.

By analyzing the results of the study, this study suggests that the central government should improve wording intensity, network of issuing department and regulation targets when issuing environmental policy documents to improve the quality rather than the number of documents issued. At the same time, appropriately reducing the clarity of environmental policy documents can offer local governments more space to adapt the policies to local conditions and thus have a positive impact. Ultimately, the standardized advancement of threats in environmental policies is crucial for local governments to narrow disparities in environmental implementation. Further regulation of discretionary powers in environmental administrative penalties is necessary.

This study employed Dynamic Word Embedding Technology WWM-BERT for policy text recognition. The whole word masking method of this model, utilized during pre-training, can mask entire Chinese words rather than just parts of them, enhancing BERT's adaptability to Chinese scenarios and facilitating the exploration of semantic features in Chinese environmental policy texts. By incorporating environmental policy texts from 2016 to 2018 into the model's corpus, its applicability across the field is broadened, offering potential solutions to similar environmental policy text recognition challenges and facilitating deeper exploration of practical issues. The findings of this study highlight the significant impact of signals such as the network of issuing department, wording intensity, and clarity of regulation targets in enhancing local environmental regulation behavior. The methodology proposed here enables a more effective application of signaling theory in environmental regulation, introducing a fresh perspective to address the disparities between China's environmental policies and their implementation.

The limitations and future work of this study are as follows: Firstly, due to the data spanning only three years, the duration of sample is relatively brief. With the inclusion of more data in future research, innovative discoveries may emerge. Secondly, the WWM-BERT pre-trained language model used in this study only considered samples within the period of 2016 to 2018 and did not encompass all policy texts in the environmental regulation field. The addition of more data could potentially enhance the robustness, portability, and other relevant performance aspects of the language model.

Acknowledgement. This work was supported by the National Natural Science Foundation of China under Grants 72104260; Central University of Finance and Economics under the Program for Innovation Research; The Program for Innovation Research in School of Government, Central University of Finance and Economics.

References

1. Li, J.: Signalling compliance: an explanation of the intermittent green policy implementation gap in China. Local Gov. Stud. **49**, 492–518 (2023). https://doi.org/10.1080/03003930.2021.1997743
2. Wen, H., Li, F.: The mechanism and typical mode of atmospheric environment policy implementation gap from the perspective of configuration — fuzzy set qualitative comparative analysis based on 61 cases. J. China Univ. Geosci. (Soc. Sci. Ed.) **21**, 70–81 (2021). https://doi.org/10.16493/j.cnki.42-1627/c.2021.05.007. (in Chinese)
3. Chen, Y., Yan, Q., Wang, L.: Research on regional environmental policy implementation deviation from the perspective of intergovernmental relation—based on game model. J. Beijing Inst. Technol. (Soc. Sci. Ed.) **21**, 56–64 (2019). https://doi.org/10.15918/j.jbitss1009-3370.2019.6414. (in Chinese)
4. Liu, P., An, P.: Research on the impact of central bank communication on market confidence: based on the intermediate target of monetary policy. Huabei Finance 1–11 (2023). (in Chinese)
5. Zhong, L., Yang, R., Fu, Y.: Research on the progress of urban biodiversity governance in China based on policy text analysis. Chin. Landscape Archit. **38**, 51–56 (2022). https://doi.org/10.19775/j.cla.2022.09.0051. (in Chinese)
6. Shen, S., et al.: ChpoBERT: a pre-trained model for Chinese policy texts. J. China Soc. Sci. Tech. Inf. **42**, 1487–1497 (2023). (in Chinese)
7. Economy, E.: The River Runs Black: The Environmental Challenge to China's Future. Cornell University Press (2004)
8. Lieberthal, K.: China's governing system and its impact on environmental policy implementation. Tiao-kuai (1997)
9. Ran, R.: Political incentives and local environmental governance under a "pressurized system". Comp. Econ. Soc. Syst. 111–118 (2013). (in Chinese)
10. Spence, M.: Job market signaling. Q. J. Econ. **87**, 355–374 (1973). https://doi.org/10.2307/1882010
11. Stiglitz, J.E.: Information and the change in the paradigm in economics. Am. Econ. Rev. **92**, 460–501 (2002)
12. Zhang, Y., Wiersema, M.F.: Stock market reaction to CEO certification: the signaling role of CEO background. Strateg. Manag. J. **30**, 693–710 (2009)
13. Suazo, M.M., Martínez, P.G., Sandoval, R.: Creating psychological and legal contracts through human resource practices: a signaling theory perspective. Hum. Resour. Manag. Rev. **19**, 154–166 (2009)
14. Taj, S.A.: Application of signaling theory in management research: addressing major gaps in theory. Eur. Manag. J. 338–348 (2016)
15. Ge, L.: Causes, processes and effects of government innovation—multiple case text analysis based on the OPSI case library. Sci. Technol. Dev. **19**, 785–792 (2023). (in Chinese)
16. Cui, Y., Che, W., Liu, T., Qin, B., Yang, Z.: Pre-training with whole word masking for Chinese BERT. IEEE/ACM Trans. Audio Speech Lang. Process. **29**, 3504–3514 (2021). https://doi.org/10.1109/TASLP.2021.3124365
17. Li, D., Yang, Y., Meng, X., Zhang, X., Song, C., Zhao, Y.: Review on multi-lable classification. J. Front. Comput. Sci. Technol. 1–16. (in Chinese)

18. Synthesizing the implementation literature: the ambiguity-conflict model of policy implementation. J. Public Adm. Res. Theory (1995). https://doi.org/10.1093/oxfordjournals.jpart.a037242.
19. Cheng, C.: The dilemma and solution of China's ecological environment administrative penalty discretion benchmark system. Jianghuai Tribune 106–114 (2023). https://doi.org/10.16064/j.cnki.cn34-1003/g0.2023.03.010 (in Chinese)

The Impact of Experts' Voting on the Fundraising Performance of Crowdfunding Projects

Jinmou Hu, Weijia You[✉], and Bojin Chen

Beijing Forestry University, Beijing 100083, China
wjyou@bjfu.edu.cn

Abstract. Crowdfunding offers an effective means of gathering small amounts of funds from a substantial number of backers. This study seeks to examine the impact of the experts' voting and comments on the fundraising performance of crowdfunding projects. Utilizing data from 7358 crowdfunding projects and employing the Heckman model, our study indicates that crowds often tend to align with expert evaluations, perhaps driven by the herding effect and the expert endorsement mechanism. Moreover, the comments from experts in the voting process have the potential to mitigate information asymmetry issues. Lastly, we also found that the impact of expert evaluations varies across project categories. The findings provide important managerial implications. Firstly, fundraisers should closely monitor the votes and evaluations of experts as these factors can influence the behavior of crowdfunding investors. Secondly, platform administrator should actively invite more experts to participate in the review process as it can help to disclose more information, assisting investors in making better investment decisions.

Keywords: Crowdfunding · Experts' voting · Information Asymmetry

1 Introduction

Crowdfunding stands as an innovative method that empowers entrepreneurs to secure financial support from the public by presenting their creative ideas on online platforms to raise funds for their products or services (Mollick, 2014). Despite experiencing rapid growth in recent years, crowdfunding projects still face a remarkably low success rate[1]. Consequently, numerous scholars have dedicated themselves to researching the factors influencing the funding performance of crowdfunding projects. Understanding the key factors affecting funding performance not only assists high-quality projects in raising more funds but also helps the crowdfunding market attract more investors, thereby promoting the overall development of crowdfunding. While numerous scholars have extensively researched factors influencing crowdfunding performance in terms of project characteristics and fundraisers, there is limited understanding regarding the impact of platform efforts, such as inviting experts to vote before the fundraising begins.

---

[1] https://www.kickstarter.com/help/stats?ref=global-footer.

The voting process here refers to the process that the crowdfunding platform invites experts, characterized by their heightened professionalism or extensive experience in investment, to evaluate the crowdfunding projects before the crowdfunding campaign launches. The experts who have received invitations voluntarily engage in the review process, expressing their support or opposition by casting votes for crowdfunding projects. They provide reasons for their votes and may also offer professional opinions and insights into the project. Fundraisers voluntarily opt in this voting process. Although many scholars have discussed the voting mechanism or the role of experts in various aspects, such as the study about expert reviews' impact on future traveler ratings (Zhang et al., 2016), its influence in the context of crowdfunding is yet to be explored. This study focuses on the role of experts in the crowdfunding market and investigates the impact of the experts' voting on a project's fundraising performance, thereby contributing to the literature on determinants of project funding and voting mechanisms in the crowdfunding context.

As the impact of experts' votes in the crowdfunding context remains unclear, we are motivated to explore some intriguing research questions. Firstly, what is the approval rate of these experts' votes on fundraising outcomes? Secondly, how does the number of experts involved in the voting process influence fundraising performance? Are these effects consistent across different categories?

2 Literature Review and Hypotheses Development

2.1 The Impact of Experts' Approval on the Funding Performance of Crowdfunding Projects

For conventional financial products, the process of securing funds, whether from financial institutions or the public, is subject to rigorous oversight from pertinent regulatory bodies. Fundraisers are obliged to adhere to strict guidelines, ensuring comprehensive disclosure of potential risks to investors. However, the landscape differs in crowdfunding, where fundraisers secure financial support from backers prior to bringing the product to market, without the stringent supervision typical in traditional markets. Consequently, fundraisers often possess a more comprehensive understanding of the anticipated product quality compared to backers, resulting in an information asymmetry issue between the two parties (Kim et al., 2022; Wei et al., 2021). This information asymmetry provides fundraisers with the opportunity to exaggerate the quality of their product, potentially leading to misleading backers in an effort to boost their fundraising performance. Therefore, the information provided by fundraisers may not be reliable.

In this context, addressing the challenge of information asymmetry becomes imperative for investors. To mitigate this issue, investors actively seek additional insights into crowdfunding projects by analyzing the decisions of their peers (Zhang & Liu, 2012). Specifically, investors exhibit a proclivity to mimic the decisions of their counterparts and demonstrate a heightened interest in projects characterized by a larger support base, which indicates that the project is of better quality (Li et al., 2022). This phenomenon is referred to as the "Herding Effect," and it is observed that there is a positive relationship between the cumulative lending amount from experienced individuals and the lending amount of a successor in lending crowdfunding (Chen et al., 2022). Based on previous researches, we infer that if the crowdfunding platform provides experts, characterized by their heightened professionalism or extensive experience in investment, the opportunity to evaluate projects before project fundraising commences, it is natural that crowds will tend to herd, i.e., to follow the evaluations put forth by these experts.

Moreover, experts' vote in favor of a project may enhance the project's perceived reliability—a phenomenon termed "Trust Endorsement." Empirical evidence supports the notion that expert trust endorsement exerts a positive influence on mitigating consumers' perceived risk or improving their trust on projects (Biswas et al., 2006; T. Kim & Yoon, 2023). The higher the rate of experts who vote yes, the more pronounced the positive effects of this trust mechanism. Hence, we propose:

H1: The higher the rate of experts who vote yes, the more favorable the funding performance of the project will be.

2.2   The Impact of the Number of Experts Involved on the Funding Performance of Crowdfunding Projects

As elucidated earlier, the inclination of crowds to follow expert evaluations arises from the herding effect or the trust placed in these experts. Furthermore, in the expert voting process, experts not only convey their attitudes toward the project but also provide detailed opinions, which drive fundraisers to disclose more details about the project. For instance, in our dataset, one expert remarked, "This drone product looks very impressive, but I'm uncertain about its wind resistance." The fundraiser quickly responded, stating, "The wind resistance of the drone is at level 5–6", while this information can't be found in the project descriptions. Consequently, this process compels fundraisers to share more pertinent project information, because if fundraisers fail to address experts' concerns, backers may perceive issues with the project. Building upon this phenomenon, we posit that the greater the number of experts participating in the project's voting process, the more information backers can obtain, which may alleviate the information asymmetry problems, reducing backers' perceived risk and enhancing the project's fundraising performance. Hence, we propose:

H2: The greater the number of experts involved in the voting process is, the better the funding performance of the crowdfunding project will be.

2.3   The Impact of Experts' Voting on Different Project

In reward-based crowdfunding, backers' decisions to pledge money are influenced by a combination of intrinsic and extrinsic factors (Bretschneider & Leimeister, 2017; Zhang & Chen, 2019). Projects utilize various rewards to attract diverse backers, and the nature of these rewards varies across different crowdfunding project types. This variation leads to distinctions in the number of intrinsically and extrinsically motivated backers. Investors with different motivations exhibit distinct preferences for product features, and the same feature may have varying effects on investors with different motivations (Gong et al., 2021; Li & Wang, 2019). For example, Gong et al. (2021) suggested that the lottery option is more appealing to intrinsically motivated backers (donors) compared to their counterparts (rewardees). Therefore, we infer that the impact of the experts' voting may vary across different project categories.

To verify our hypotheses, we have specifically chosen three highly representative categories: Technology, Donation, and Design. Technology projects are characterized by the inclusion of numerous innovative ideas and functionalities. Investors are primarily motivated to invest in technology projects due to the innovativeness inherent in these endeavors, showing their inclination to be early adopters and experience the novel features introduced by technological products. Consequently, investors of technology projects exhibit a heightened concern for the successful development of these products and the prospective returns they may generate. Thus, they demonstrate increased sensitivity to the risks associated with the potential success of the project. Moreover, technology projects are inherently more complex and variable, resulting in higher-risk endeavors (Kim et al., 2022). As a consequence of these characteristics, we hypothesize that investors who prefer technology projects are more inclined to rely on the opinions of experts when making investment decisions. Therefore, we propose the following hypothesis:

H3a: The funding performance of technology projects is significantly influenced by experts' approval rate.

In the donation project, which centers on soliciting funds to aid individuals in impoverished areas, investors contributing to this cause receive local specialties from these areas in return for their charitable contributions. Consequently, we infer that the donation project holds significant appeal for intrinsically motivated backers, who exhibit lower sensitivity to risks compared to their counterparts (Gong et al., 2021). As a result, they are inclined to rely less on expert opinions when making investment decisions. Therefore, we propose the following hypothesis:

H3b: The funding performance of donation projects is unaffected by the influence of experts' approval rate.

The design project primarily focuses on funding for artworks or culturally related products. For instance, in our dataset, there is a design project dedicated to promoting the culture of the Forbidden City. Investors supporting this project receive a T-shirt featuring elements from the Forbidden City's culture as a reward. Given the ubiquity of T-shirts in daily life, investors contribute to this project more for the appreciation of the Forbidden City culture rather than the utilitarian aspects of the T-shirt itself. The assessment of design projects is highly subjective, given the inherent difficulty in quantifying the value of art or culture. Furthermore, culture is a domain where expert opinion traditionally plays an important role. If a cultural project garners contributions from expert backers, it tends to attract additional support and enhance the project's likelihood of success (Petit & Wirtz, 2022). From this view of point, we deduce that assessing the quality of design projects poses a challenge for crowds relying solely on their own knowledge. Investors, therefore, exhibit a tendency to depend more on expert opinions when making investment decisions in design projects. Consequently, we propose the following hypothesis:

H3c: The funding performance of design projects is significantly influenced by experts' approval rate.

3   Data

To verify the research hypotheses, this paper conducts empirical research based on data collected from JD Crowdfunding, one of the largest reward-based crowdfunding platforms globally. Our dataset includes 7358 projects, with 1409 projects participating in the voting process provided by the platform. To answer our research questions, we construct these variables, as shown in Table 1. Then Table 2 presents their summary statistics.

Table 1. Variable Descriptions

	Symbol	Definition
Key variable	Approvals$_i$	The number of experts who support project i
	Experts$_i$	The total number of experts who participated in the voting process for project i
	Approval_rate$_i$	The number of experts who support project i, divided by the total number of experts participated in the voting process for project i
Fundraising performance	Raised$_i$	The total funds raised for project i
	Backer$_i$	The total number of investors support for project i
Control variable	Goal$_i$	The fundraising target of project i
	Duration$_i$	The total days of fundraising of project i
	Startercreate$_i$	The number of projects created by the fundraiser before the focal project i
	Starterfocus$_i$	The number of projects that had been focused on by the fundraiser of project i
	Discussion$_i$	The total number of discussions of the project i
	Price$_i$	The mean price of all funding options within project i
Project quality	Follower$_i$	The number of investors who follow project i
Instrumental variable	IV$_i$	The ratio of all projects participating in the voting process before the commencement of project i

4   Results

4.1   The Effect of the Rate of Experts Who Vote Yes in Crowdfunding Market

In our dataset, not every project engages in the expert voting process. Relying solely on the subsample comprising projects participating in the voting process introduces a selection bias problem. Specifically, experts' evaluations are only observed in projects opting to partake in the voting process, resulting in missing data for projects that abstain

Table 2. Summary Statistics of Key variables

Variable	Observations	Mean	Std	Min	Max
Approvals	1409	74.207	53.773	2.000	911.00
Experts	1409	77.031	54.322	2.000	911.000
Approval_rate	1409	0.957	0.070	0.507	1.000
Raised	7358	253,057	2,039,194	1.000	118,632,715
Backer	7358	530.983	1,755.546	1.000	55,709.000
Follower	7358	576.232	1,089.147	0.000	31,908.000
Goal	7358	76,562.280	201,861.200	5.000	10,000,000
Duration	7358	35.280	10.657	6.000	180.000
Startercreate	7358	4.891	11.738	1.000	110.000
Starterfocus	7358	1.040	3.088	0.000	34.000
Discussion	7358	51.843	104.208	0.000	2,794.000
Price	7358	2,977.911	9,761.510	5.000	362,253.300
IV	7358	0.074	0.086	0.000	0.220

from participation. This situation may introduce bias when investigating the influence of expert reviews on the funding performance of crowdfunding projects. To address this concern, we employ the Heckman Two-Stage Model as a methodological approach.

In the first stage, we estimate the probability of each project participating in the expert evaluation process through Probit model, subsequently generating a new variable IMR (Inverse Mills Ratio). Model (1) represents the first stage model, where the independent variable is *If_judge,* which indicates whether the project participates in the voting process, the dependent variable γ_i encompasses variables influencing the decision to participate in the expert evaluation, including *Goal, Duration, Startercreate, Startersupport and Price.* The symbol μ_i refers to unobservable characteristics of projects, assuming they follow a normal distribution. Besides, to address endogeneity issues, we also introduce an instrumental variable *IV* in Model (1) based on the potential existence of learning effects (the definition of variable *IV* presented in Table 1, we have verified the validity of instrumental variable *IV,* its coefficient is 1.417 and the t value is 28.001). Model (2) provides the equation for calculating the variable IMR, where ϕ denotes the probability density function, and Φ represents the cumulative distribution function. Leveraging the estimation results from Model (1), we employ Model (2) to obtain the variable IMR. In the second stage, we introduce the new variable IMR into the regression model, resulting in the construction of Model (3). It is worth noting that we use the variable *Follower* to control for project quality, excluding the potential explanation that the high quality of projects contributes to the better funding performance. This helps ensure that the better funding performance is a result of experts' approval rate rather than project quality.

Given the right-skewed distribution of variables, we apply a logarithmic transformation, adjusted by adding one to address zeros.

$$Probit(If\_judge_i) = \alpha\gamma_i + \beta IV_i + \mu_i \tag{1}$$

$$IMR = \lambda(-\omega_i\gamma) = \phi(-\omega_i\gamma)/[1 - \Phi(-\omega_i\gamma)] \tag{2}$$

$$\begin{aligned} Ln(Performance_i) = {} & \beta_0 + \beta_1 key\_variable_i + \beta_2 Ln(Goal_i) \\ & + \beta_3 Ln(Duration_i) + \beta_4 Ln(Startercreate_i) \\ & + \beta_5 Ln(Starter\,support_i) + \beta_6 Ln(Discussion_i) \\ & + \beta_7 Ln(Price_i) + \beta_8 Ln(Follower) + \beta_9 IMR + \varepsilon_i \end{aligned} \tag{3}$$

To test Hypothesis H1, we use the variable *Approval_rate* as the key variable, the estimation result is shown in Table 3.

As Table 3 shows, the coefficients of *Approval_rate* are significantly positive at the 1% significance level on dependent variable *Raised* and *Backer* (Columns 2–3). This statistical significance implies that the funding performance of crowdfunding projects, as assessed by the total funds raised and backers supported, exhibits a positive correlation with the approval rate of experts, the higher the expert approval rate, the better the funding performance. This outcome substantiates the notion that crowds exhibit a proclivity to follow expert evaluations. Consequently, Hypothesis H1 is supported.

4.2 The Effect of the Number of Experts Involved in Crowdfunding Market

To investigate the effect of the number of experts who participated in the voting process on project's funding performance and test Hypothesis H2, we use the variable *Experts* as the key variable, the estimation result is shown in Table 4.

In Table 4, the coefficients of variable *Experts* exhibit significant positive effects on the dependent variables *Raised* and *Backer* (Columns 1–2). This implies that an increased number of experts participating in the voting process is associated with improved funding performance for the project. Within the voting process, experts not only express attitudes regarding the quality of projects but also offer specific reviews. This prompts fundraisers to disclose more relevant information about the project. Consequently, increased participation of experts in the voting process effectively mitigates information asymmetry issues. This, in turn, facilitates enhancements in the fundraising performance of their projects. This empirical observation substantiates Hypothesis 2.

4.3 The Effect of the Experts' Approval Rate on Different Project

To investigate the impact of experts across different project categories and examine Hypotheses H3, we opted for three paradigmatic project classifications: technology projects, characterized by investors displaying heightened sensitivity to risks; donation projects, recognized for efficiently drawing intrinsically motivated investors with lower risk sensitivity compared to their extrinsically motivated counterparts; and design

Table 3. The Effect of Approval_rate on Project's Funding Performance

	First Stage	Second Stage	
	Probit(If_judge)	Ln(Raised)	Ln(Backer)
Approval_rate		4.006***	2.373***
		(0.697)	(0.534)
Ln(Goal)	0.198***	0.088	0.035
	(0.021)	(0.063)	(0.049)
Ln(Duration)	0.248***	0.370**	0.639***
	(0.066)	(0.188)	(0.147)
Ln(Startercreate)	0.057***	0.345***	0.189***
	(0.022)	(0.062)	(0.048)
Ln(Startersupport)	0.014	0.098	0.073
	(0.026)	(0.067)	(0.053)
Ln(Discussion)		0.671***	0.705***
		(0.045)	(0.035)
Ln(Price)	0.008	0.169***	−0.173***
	(0.014)	(0.036)	(0.028)
Ln(Follower)		0.272***	0.226***
		(0.035)	(0.027)
IV	6.678***		
	(0.242)		
IMR		0.979***	0.935***
		(0.153)	(0.119)
Intercept	−4.604***	−2.690**	−4.341***
	(0.333)	(1.313)	(1.016)

Standard errors in parentheses.* $p < 0.1$, ** $p < 0.05$, *** $p < 0.01$.

projects, challenging for crowds to evaluate due to their inherent value intricacies. The estimations for the three subsamples are delineated in Table 5.

For technology projects, the coefficient of *Approval_rate* has a statistically significant positive effect on the dependent variable *Raised* and *Backer* (Columns 1–2).This outcome implies that the voting process by experts may not only attract more investors, but also induce investors to contribute more substantially to technology projects, thereby enhancing the overall funding performance of technology project. This finding supports Hypothesis H3a.

In the donation projects, the coefficients associated with *Approval_rate* exhibit no statistically significant impact on the dependent variables *Raised* and *Backer* (Columns 3–4). This outcome indicates that the funding performance of donation projects is unaffected by experts' evaluations. The intrinsically motivated investors support donation projects for their social benefits, and their behavior appears to be independent of experts' perspectives. This finding lends support to Hypothesis H2b.

Table 4. The Effect of the Number of Experts Involved on Project's Funding Performance

| | The Second Stage of Heckman Model | |
	Ln(Raised)	Ln(Backer)
Experts	0.002*** (9.0e−04)	0.001** (6.0e−04)
Ln(Goal)	0.026 (0.062)	−0.001 (0.048)
Ln(Duration)	0.417** (0.188)	0.666*** (0.147)
Ln(Startercreate)	0.368*** (0.062)	0.202*** (0.049)
Ln(Startersupport)	0.111 (0.068)	0.081 (0.053)
Ln(Discussion)	0.657*** (0.046)	0.698*** (0.035)
Ln(Price)	0.172*** (0.036)	−0.172*** (0.028)
Ln(Follower)	0.222*** (0.035)	0.196*** (0.027)
IMR	0.891*** (0.159)	0.877*** (0.123)
Intercept	1.798* (0.996)	−1.661** (0.772)

Standard errors in parentheses.* $p < 0.1$, ** $p < 0.05$, *** $p < 0.01$. The result of the first stage of Heckman model is same with result present in Table 3.

In the context of design projects, the coefficients of the variable *Approval_rate* manifest statistically significant positive effects on the dependent variables *Raised* and *Backer* (Columns 5–6). This result shows that investors are inclined to align with the evaluations provided by experts in the domain of design projects. The funding performance of design projects experiences substantial enhancement through the experts' voting. Thus Hypothesis H3c is supported.

Table 5. The Effect of Experts' Approval_rate across Different Project Categories

	Technology		Donation		Design	
	Ln(Raised)	Ln(Backer)	Ln(Raised)	Ln(Backer)	Ln(Raised)	Ln(Backer)
Approval_rate	3.220***	1.651**	−4.761	−6.373	7.662***	5.511***
	(1.013)	(0.702)	(11.98)	(7.627)	(1.582)	(1.129)
Ln(Goal)	0.102	−0.0625	−1.796	−1.513**	0.0966	−0.00183
	(0.124)	(0.0930)	(1.115)	(0.710)	(0.145)	(0.107)
Ln(Duration)	0.264	0.741***	1.575	1.217	0.113	0.267
	(0.316)	(0.240)	(1.688)	(1.075)	(0.406)	(0.299)
Ln(Startercreate)	0.268*	0.304***	−1.937	−1.200	0.234	0.259**
	(0.149)	(0.112)	(1.795)	(1.143)	(0.157)	(0.115)
Ln(Startersupport)	0.0894	0.204**	0.262	0.163	0.175	0.00225
	(0.123)	(0.0950)	(0.608)	(0.387)	(0.149)	(0.110)
Ln(Discussion)	0.807***	0.758***	0.152	0.258	0.682***	0.635***
	(0.0762)	(0.0545)	(0.403)	(0.257)	(0.0935)	(0.0671)
Ln(Price)	0.0773	−0.233***	0.275	−0.175	0.00471	−0.232***
	(0.0588)	(0.0456)	(0.389)	(0.248)	(0.0799)	(0.0592)
Ln(Follower)	0.328***	0.219***	0.416	0.350*	0.375***	0.359***
	(0.0588)	(0.0422)	(0.323)	(0.205)	(0.0804)	(0.0579)
IMR	0.753***	1.113***	−4.115	−2.620	1.025***	0.992***
	(0.238)	(0.176)	(3.142)	(2.001)	(0.288)	(0.210)
Intercept	−1.314	−2.776*	31.90	25.75*	−4.869*	−5.840***
	(2.085)	(1.535)	(21.89)	(13.94)	(2.798)	(2.031)

Standard errors in parentheses.* p < 0.1, ** p < 0.05, *** p < 0.01. For brevity, we omit the estimation results in Model (1) (First stage).

5 Robustness Check

To further validate our results, we also use the variable *Approvals* instead of variable *Approval_rate* as the key variable, the estimation result is shown in Table 6.

As Table 6 shows, the results are similar with those in Table 3. It indicate that the higher the number of approvals, the more pronounced the herding effect and expert endorsement mechanism, contributing to an enhanced fundraising performance.

Table 6. The Effect of Approvals on Project's Funding Performance

	First Stage	Second Stage	
	Probit(If_judge)	Ln(Raised)	Ln(Backer)
Approvals		0.003***	0.001**
		(9.0e−04)	(0.0006)
Ln(Goal)	0.198***	0.033	0.002
	(0.021)	(0.063)	(0.048)
Ln(Duration)	0.248***	0.414**	0.664***
	(0.066)	(0.188)	(0.147)
Ln(Startercreate)	0.057***	0.372***	0.205***
	(0.022)	(0.062)	(0.049)
Ln(Startersupport)	0.014	0.109	0.079
	(0.026)	(0.068)	(0.053)
Ln(Discussion)		0.656***	0.696***
		(0.045)	(0.035)
Ln(Price)	0.008	0.170***	−0.173***
	(0.014)	(0.036)	(0.028)
Ln(Follower)		0.225***	0.198***
		(0.035)	(0.027)
IV	6.678***		
	(0.242)		
IMR		0.930***	0.902***
		(0.160)	(0.124)
Intercept	−4.604***	1.657*	−1.754**
	(0.333)	(0.999)	(0.775)

Standard errors in parentheses.* $p < 0.1$, ** $p < 0.05$, *** $p < 0.01$. The result of the first stage of Heckman model is same with result present in Table 3.

6   Conclusion and Discussion

The primary objective of this study was to examine the impact of experts' vote in crowdfunding. From the perspective of the information asymmetry, our findings indicate that crowds tend to align with experts' evaluations of projects, manifesting the herding effect and expert endorsement mechanism, which contribute to the fundraising performance of projects. Moreover, during the voting process, experts not only express opinions on project quality but also provide specific reviews. This encourages fundraisers to disclose more information about the project. Our results demonstrate that increased participation of experts in the voting process effectively alleviates information asymmetry issues, thereby facilitating project's fundraising performance. Finally, we observed that the influence of experts' approval rate varies across project categories. Specifically, the expert's approval rate significantly impacts technology and design projects but does not influence the fundraising performance of donation projects.

There are two managerial implications derived from our study. Firstly, experts' opinions during the voting process are crucial; therefore, fundraisers should seek maximum support from these experts. A relatively higher rate of experts voting in favor significantly improves the project's funding performance, as backers often align with the evaluations provided by experts. Secondly, crowdfunding platforms should actively encourage more experts to participate in the voting process. Proactively involving experts compels fundraisers to disclose additional information about their products, effectively mitigating information asymmetry and thereby contributing to the enhanced fundraising performance of projects.

Acknowledgement. This research was supported by Fundamental Research Funds for the Central Universities under Grant 2021SRY05 and Beijing Social Science Foundation under Grant 22GLB023.

References

Biswas, D., Biswas, A., Das, N.: The differential effects of celebrity and expert endorsements on consumer risk perceptions. The Role of Consumer Knowledge, Perceived Congruency, and Product Technology Orientation. J. Advertising **35**(2), 17–31 (2006)

Bretschneider, U., Leimeister, J.M.: Not just an ego-trip: Exploring backers' motivation for funding in incentive-based crowdfunding. J. Strateg. Inf. Syst. **26**(4), 246–260 (2017)

Chen, D., Huang, C., Liu, D., Lai, F.: The role of expertise in herding behaviors: evidence from a crowdfunding market. Electron. Commer. Res. 1–49 (2022)

Gong, J., Pavlou, P.A., (Alvin) Zheng, Z.: On the use of probabilistic uncertain rewards on crowdfunding platforms: the case of the lottery. Inf. Syst. Res. **32**(1), 115–129 (2021)

Kim, K., Park, J., Pan, Y., Zhang, K., (Michael) Zhang, X.: Risk disclosure in crowdfunding. Inf. Syst. Res. **33**(3), 1023–1041 (2022)

Kim, T., Yoon, H.J.: The effectiveness of influencer endorsements for smart technology products: the role of follower number, expertise domain and trust propensity. J. Prod. Brand Manag. (2023)

Li, G., Wang, J.: Threshold effects on backer motivations in reward-based crowdfunding. J. Manag. Inf. Syst. **36**(2), 546–573 (2019)

Li, Y., Liu, F., Fan, W., Lim, E.T.K., Liu, Y.: Exploring the impact of initial herd on overfunding in equity crowdfunding. Inf. Manag. **59**(3), 103269 (2022)

Mollick, E.: The dynamics of crowdfunding: an exploratory study. J. Bus. Ventur. **29**(1), 1–16 (2014)

Petit, A., Wirtz, P.: Experts in the crowd and their influence on herding in reward-based crowdfunding of cultural projects. Small Bus. Econ. **58**(1), 419–449 (2022)

Wei, X., Fan, M., You, W., Tan, Y.: An empirical study of the dynamic and differential effects of prefunding. Prod. Oper. Manag. **30**(5), 1331–1349 (2021)

Zhang, H., Chen, W.: Backer motivation in crowdfunding new product ideas: is it about you or is it about me? J. Prod. Innov. Manag. **36**(2), 241–262 (2019)

Zhang, J., Liu, P.: Rational herding in microloan markets. Manage. Sci. **58**(5), 892–912 (2012)

Zhang, Z., Zhang, Z., Yang, Y.: The power of expert identity: how website-recognized expert reviews influence travelers' online rating behavior. Tour. Manage. **55**, 15–24 (2016)

Social Network Services and Loneliness: A Comparative Study Between the Urban Solitary Youth and the Elderly

Muduo Qu[1], Shan Wang[2(✉)], Yang Chen[3], and Fang Wang[4]

[1] Beijing 101 Middle School, 11 Yiheyuan Road, Beijing 100091, China
[2] University of Saskatchewan, 25 Campus Drive, Saskatoon, SK S7N 5A7, Canada
wang@edwards.usask.ca
[3] Beijing Foreign Studies University, 19 Xisanhuan North Road, Beijing 100089, China
[4] Wilfrid Laurier University, 75 University Avenue West, Waterloo, ON N2L 3C5, Canada

Abstract. People are using Social Network Services (SNSs) more and more in today's digital and mobile world to communicate with the outside world rather than going face-to-face with it. While providing the convenience of connectivity, SNS use has a profound impact on psychological well-being. Prior research on the effects of SNSs on psychological well-being has not yet produced resounding findings. Focusing on one aspect of psychological well-being, loneliness, this study hypothesizes and compares three mediating mechanisms of SNS use on loneliness (i.e., offline social support, online social capital, and meaning in life) among different types and between elderly and young adults. A sample of 207 elderly and 310 young adults was collected to validate the hypotheses. The elderly group comprises 94.7% of the respondents who are older than 50. Of the respondents in the sample of young adults, 97.1% are between the ages of 20 and 35, and all of them are single and reside in a city other than their hometown. The result of PLS-SEM analysis shows no direct effect of SNS use on loneliness. The mediating effects vary between elderly and urban solitary youth, as well as among types of SNS. Elderly people place a high value on seeking offline social support and meaning in life, which helps them alleviate loneliness, while young adults prioritize expanding online social capital which exacerbates their loneliness. This study contributes theoretically to social network theories and developmental psychology, as well as practical implications for SNS design.

Keywords: Social Network Services · Loneliness · The urban solitary youth · The elderly

1 Introduction

Single-living households are becoming more and more common due to the trend of social mobility; in China and South Korea, this percentage surpasses 25% and 30%, respectively. Urban solitary youth are the youngers who live alone in big cities away from their hometowns. A term "empty nest family" is used to describe a family in which children have grown up and moved out, leaving only the old couple in their hometown. Loneliness is reported to be a common phenomenon for people who live alone, regardless of age. It is often associated with a higher risk of both physical and mental health issues and is harmful to people's well-being. Many theories have suggested that human has an innate motivation for maintaining social bonds. In a digital society, most people connect with others through Social Network Services (SNSs). Can the use of SNSs alleviate loneliness among individuals living alone? Does SNS use exert the same influence on urban solitary youth and the elderly as both are somewhat detached from society? Are the strengths of different types of SNSs in meeting the needs of single people equal?

Abundant research has explored the effects of SNS use on loneliness, but no consensus has been reached. Our literature review suggests that the discrepancy among the results has been interpreted by the attributes of users, or the purpose, timing, and activities of SNS use. However, the studies on age differences and the divergent effects among various types of SNSs are still inadequate.

This study intends to resolve the inconsistent results from the perspectives of the age difference and the divergent effects of SNS types. We chose to compare the urban solitary youth and the elderly because both experience some level of social isolation. The comparison can better illustrate the differential power of age differences on the impact of using SNSs on loneliness. The results contribute to not only SNS design for specific users, but also social network theory and developmental psychology.

2 Literature Review

SNS (e.g. Facebook, Twitter, TikTok) is a subset of ICTs that support interpersonal communication and collaboration, and allow individuals to post and exchange self-generated content on their social pages in social media networks [1].

Loneliness is a personal and negative emotion in which a person feels disconnected, isolated, or unwelcome due to the mismatch between what he desires and the actual perceived quantity and quality of social relationships [2].

Many studies have shown the significant benefits of SNSs, such as enhanced life satisfaction, reduced depressive symptoms, decreased social isolation, and reduced loneliness [3]. In contrast, some studies do not find a significant association between SNS use and loneliness, or well-being [4]. Some studies even link SNS use to undesirable outcomes such as envy, social comparisons, addiction [5], and loneliness [2].

Some user factors, including genders, ages, races, regions, personality traits, living situations, economic conditions, and social network elements, have been investigated in previous studies to explain the variance among the results [6]. For example, the literature review by Musetti et al. [5] highlights that negative outcome of SNSs use may depend on users' attachment types. Another study shows that for users who are shy and have low social support, using SNSs helps to compensate for the lack of social support in real life [2]. Users with low self-esteem and high levels of social anxiety will suffer from problematic use of SNSs due to fear of negative social evaluation from others [7].

As for the age differences, prior research has either studied the elderly or the young SNS users, and studies comparing between them are lacking. Comparing the effects of different Facebook activities on life satisfaction between older and younger users, Kem and Shen [6] found that older users were more satisfied with Facebook than younger users. They find that older adults are more likely than young adults to engage in and benefit from those direct communication activities that build bonding capital.

In their literature review, Cotton et al. [3] suggest that instead of treating SNS use as monolithic, it is necessary to distinguish the type, amount, purpose, and timing of SNS use. Some examine the comparative effects of different types of user behavior on user loneliness [8]. Yang and his coworkers [9] find that active use could attenuate loneliness by obtaining a higher level of online social support, while passive use leads to a higher degree of loneliness through upward social comparison. A meta-analysis by Meier and Reinecke [10] shows that time spent on SNS and content consumption behaviors may negatively affect human well-being, whereas the number of friends and behaviors such as messaging or commenting may positively affect well-being.

Our literature review suggests some research gaps. Firstly, The impact of SNS use on loneliness is still inconclusive. Secondly, although there are many studies of older or younger adults separately, there are not enough studies that specifically compare older and younger adults living alone. Thirdly, the mechanism linking SNS use and loneliness can vary depending on the distinct structures and features of different types of SNSs, but few prior studies have differentiated the effects of different types.

To explain the inconsistent effects of SNS use on loneliness, this study intends to investigate the mechanism of age difference and different modes of SNSs, through three major motivations of SNS use, including obtaining social support, online social capital, and finding meaning in life.

3 Theoretical Background

3.1 Social Convoy Model (SCM)

Kahn and Antonucci have proposed SCM [11] to explain the sources and patterns of social support in a dynamic lifespan process. The model uses convoy as a metaphorical term to depict a person moving on the journey of life, accompanied and supported by a set of people to whom he is related. The composition and support structure of the convoy is changing across the life span, triggered by a series of events in life, like leaving parents' home, employment, birth of children, divorce, retirement, etc.

According to the SCM, a person's requirements for social support are determined jointly by his personal properties and situational properties. Afterward, together with the latter two, the requirements determine the structure of his convoy (size, connectedness, stability, etc.). Thereafter, the convoy structure, combined with personal properties and situational properties, will determine one's adequacy perception of social support, which will in turn affect one's well-being.

3.2 Socioemotional Selectivity Theory (SST)

Some studies show that old people report more positive emotions than young people [12]. The improved emotion seems to be inconsistent with the shrinking social network size of the elderly. To explain the inconsistency, SST [13] has been proposed from the time and motivation perspectives. In youth, there is a long future to be prepared, people are likely to pursue expansive goals such as acquiring novel information, new skills, or new social contacts. However, as the endpoint of life is predictable, the elderly begin to focus on deriving meaning and satisfaction from present life. They would rather pursue those emotionally meaningful goals than expansive goals.

The motivational shift with aging leads to concentrating energy on emotional meaning and reducing weak-tie connections from their networks. For regulating one's emotions, the intimacy of social interaction is more useful than social network size. For example, trying to contact a stranger often causes anxiety, while calling a close old friend usually makes people feel better. Older people can gain more from experiencing these close relationships and achieve more positive emotional states with a shrinking network.

3.3   Uses and Gratifications Theory (UGT)

According to UGT, SNS use and its psychological effects are determined by users' goals and motivations [14]. Many studies have identified various motivations for SNS use, such as maintaining existing relationships and creating new relationships [15], building and expanding personal identity, networking, communicating, surveillance (cognitive or information seeking), and diversion (relief from boredom, entertainment) [14].

The contradictory conclusion on the effect of SNS use can be attributed to the diverse types of SNSs. SNSs can vary by theme, access, visibility, connectedness, etc. Therefore, SNSs differ in their abilities to gratify different use motivations. Some are good at direct communication or maintaining existing relationships, such as WeChat and WhatsApp. Some are good at expanding weak ties, such as Weibo and Twitter. Some are good at cognition and information seeking, such as Quora, YouTube, and Zhihu. Some are good at entertaining users or escaping such as Kiktok, or providing all kinds of online games. Rae and Lonborg [15] find that motivations can moderate the impact of Facebook use on human well-being.

4   Research Model and Hypothesis

Based on SCM, SST, and UGT, we propose a research model to compare the effects of using different types of SNSs among users of different ages.

The urban solitary youth and elderly are quite different in personal properties and situational properties, which affect each stage of SCM. According to SCM and SST, motivations for using SNSs are different between the urban solitary youth and the elderly. Different motivations can affect their selection of SNSs, and different types of SNSs help users form personal networks with different structures (i.e., the structure of one's convoy).

Based on UGT, we identify three motivations for SNS use, namely offline social support (OSS, gaining social support from real-world relationships), online social capital (OSC, gaining resources from the virtual-world network), and meaning in life (MIL, seeking meaningful things or relief from boredom). Different personal networks formed from using different SNSs have their advantages in meeting the aforementioned motivations. The perception of motivation gratifications can predict users' well-being.

Figure 1 shows the research framework. In the framework, we propose that SNS use patterns, including elderly use vs solitary youth use, and the use of different types of SNS, affect user gratifications (OSS, OSC, and MIL), which in turn affect users' perception of loneliness.

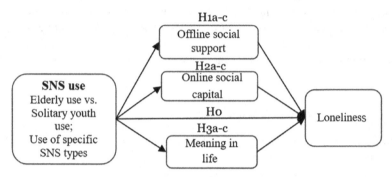

Fig. 1. The Research Model

4.1 The Direct Effect of SNS Use on Loneliness

SNSs offer a means to connect with others and therefore contribute to intervening loneliness. Many studies have reported a negative association between SNSs and loneliness [16]. Therefore, we may propose the following hypothesis:

H0. SNS use has a direct impact on loneliness.

4.2 The Mediate Effect of Offline Social Support

Social support refers to one's perception of the availability of support from his/her social network. There are three types of social support: emotional (liking, love, empathy, appraisal), instrumental (aid in goods or services), and cognitive and informational support [17]. According to SCM, social support includes expressing positive affect, affirmation, and giving aid or assistance. To identify the preferred sources of social support between elderly and young people, we defined offline social support as support from their real-world networks. It includes emotional supports (affect and affirmation) and instrumental supports (giving aid or assistance) but excludes cognitive and informational support.

Not only old people but also young people who live alone may suffer from loneliness due to the shrinking social connections. A meta-analysis determines the important role of social support in attenuating loneliness [18]. Another meta-analysis supports that social support mediates SNS use and alleviates loneliness [16].

According to SST, the elderly prioritize retaining close ties to satisfy their emotional goals, but young people would not because of an expansive future time to expect. For the elderly, the main purpose of using SNSs is to interact with friends in real life. The emergence of SNSs can facilitate the elderly to receive and offer emotional support [3], thereby causing less feeling of loneliness [9]. The elderly might prefer those SNSs that excel at direct communication. For example, Using WeChat will make it easier for older people to get offline social support.

However, the effect of SNS use on loneliness among young people living alone may be quite different. Orben and Przybylski [4] find no association between SNS use and adolescent well-being. Some study finds that SNS use predicts a higher level of online social support, while others relate it to a higher level of stress [8]. To resolve stress or frustration, young people usually use SNSs to "escape" from passive moods. They would prefer to select entertaining or informational SNSs such as Microblog, Twitter, TikTok, etc., to satisfy their surveillance and diversion motivations.

Therefore, we hypothesize that:

H1a. For the elderly, OSS mediates the relationship between SNS use and loneliness.

H1b. For the urban solitary youth, OSS does not mediate the effect of SNS use on loneliness.

H1c. SNSs that support direct communication or maintaining strong relationships can better help the elderly obtain social support, which in turn reduces loneliness.

4.3 The Mediate Effect of Online Social Capital

Social capital refers to a particular kind of resource coming about through changes in social relations and related to social structure [19]. Williams [20] differentiated between online and offline social capital (OSC). The Internet has destroyed some of the real-world social capital and reconstructed it into new social capital in the online virtual world, known as OSC. Some types of SNS are particularly good at helping users maintain their existing social network and obtain OSS, while some are good at expanding new ties and supporting OSC [21]. SNS use predicts a higher level of well-being when maintaining existing relationships, but a lower level of well-being when establishing new relationships [15].

Different SNSs will satisfy different user motivations and have different strengths in creating OSC [21]. Those SNSs used as direct communication tools can transfer social capital from offline to online. Those used for entertainment, like video streaming, online games, etc., might impair social capital. For example, one can expand new ties more easily on Twitter than on Facebook or Friendster, since there is no need for approval or reciprocal relationships. Thus, the use of Twitter leads to a high level of online bridging capital but not online bonding capital [21], while Facebook can not only generate online bridging capital but also keep offline bonding capital.

Based on SST, the elderly benefit less from bridging networks and more from bonding social capital, while young adults are the opposite [7]. They might just select those SNSs used for maintaining existing close relationships when offline interaction becomes unrealistic. Therefore, they may not be capable of enhancing online social capital. On the contrary, young people might choose SNSs which facilitate the expansion of new networks and the access to novel things, therefore broadening online bridging social capital.

Therefore, we hypothesize:

H2a. For the elderly, OSC does not mediate the relationship between SNS use and loneliness.

H2b. For the urban solitary youth, OSC mediates the relationship between SNS use and loneliness.

H2c. SNSs that support expanding social networks can better help the urban solitary youth generate OSC, thereby reducing loneliness.

4.4 The Mediate Effect of Meaning in Life

MIL serves as a safeguard against feelings of loneliness or diminished psychological well-being. It refers to "the extent to which people comprehend, make sense of, or see significance in their lives, accompanied by the degree to which they perceive themselves to have a purpose, mission, or over-arching aim in life" [22]. People could obtain MIL by personal achievement, self-acceptance, helping others, maintaining social relations, and a sense of belonging [23]. SNSs provide a platform for social connection and engagement. They can assist people in developing their sense of self, reality, and worldview. They can also boost their self-assurance and sense of control over the world, which leads to the creation of meaning in life. Giving life meaning can help to counter loneliness [23].

Many people think that older adults feel they matter less, but empirical studies show that older adults report more MIL than younger adults [24]. According to SST, when people get old, they usually have a more positive understanding of their current and past life experiences than young adults. Meanwhile, the elderly desire to seek meaning in new roles when they face retirement or declining physical capacity.

Because the elderly don't interact with others as much, SNSs assist them in maintaining healthy relationships, engaging in activities they enjoy, getting help from health professionals, and rebuilding meaningful relationships. Such assistance is more important for the elderly than young people to explore meaning and belongings during the process of their social role transformation. In contrast, young adults who live alone typically do so to pass the time after demanding workdays with entertainment or leisure activities. They would like to play online games or browse short videos. These activities substitute meaningful interpersonal interaction and social engagement, leading to a sense of emptiness among young adults.

Therefore, we may assume the following hypothesis:

H3a. For the elderly, MIL mediates the relationship between SNS use and loneliness.

H3b. For the urban solitary youth, MIL does not mediate the relationship between SNS use and loneliness.

H3c. SNSs that are good at maintaining meaningful relationships, or engaging in meaningful activities can better help the elderly feel more MIL, which in turn leads to reduced loneliness.

5 Methodology

A survey method was used to validate the hypotheses. The following provides an overview of the measurements and the sources of constructs. Loneliness (LL), MIL, and OSC are measured using five-point Likert scales ranging from 1 (strongly disagree) to 5 (strongly agree). To measure Loneliness, six items are adapted from Hays and Dimatteo's ULS-8 scale [25]. To measure OSC, four items are adapted from Hofer and Aubert [21]. MIL was measured by five items adapted from Steger et al. [26].

OSS includes instrumental support (SSI) and emotional support (SSE). We adapt Kessler et al. [27]'s scale to measure OSS, asking respondents to identify the sources of aid or assistance, and the sources of comfort or concern when encountering difficulties, from nine options including "spouses, family, friends, relatives, colleagues, affiliated units, official or semi-official organizations, unofficial organizations, others". The values of OSS are the total number of selected items. Overall SNS use is measured by the total duration of daily SNS use. Specific SNS use is measured using a matrix item, the rows include 6 types of SNSs, and the column includes five frequency options.

To collect data, we used a paper questionnaire and an online questionnaire created with Credamo.com. To achieve elderly respondents, we first shared an online questionnaire to three WeChat groups for retirees and several WeChat groups in which members fill out questionnaires on behalf of their parents. 99 online questionnaires were collected. Then, we distributed paper questionnaires in several communities and parks in Beijing, and 108 elderly respondents answered. The younger respondents are all achieved through WeChat. The final dataset consists of 207 elderly and 310 young adults. 94.7% of the elderly respondents are above 50 years old and 97.1% of the young respondents range from 20 to 35 years old. 72.5% of the elderly have retired. 60.2% of them living alone or living with their spouse. 100% of the youth live in a city away from their hometown, 39.7% of them live alone and 60.3% share a suite with others.

6 Data Analysis

6.1 Measurement Model Assessment

The latent variables LL, OSC, and MIL are measured using reflective indicators. The Cronbach's alpha and CR are over 0.7, and the Average Variance Extracted (AVE) is over 0.5, which shows good reliability. The factor loadings for each construct are over 0.7 (except for the loadings of two indicators, such as "feel sad" in LL, and "fight against injustice" in OSC, which are over 0.6), demonstrating satisfying convergent validity. The square root of AVE for each construct is larger than its correlation with other constructs, demonstrating sufficient discriminant validity. OSS is measured using two formative indicators because SSE and SSI are different dimensions for OSS. The correlation coefficient among the two indicators is 0.587, and the VIF is less than 3.3, which passes the formative construct quality assessment.

6.2 Common Method Bias

The highest correlation among constructs is 0.567, and all the items have extracted 5 common factors and the highest factor explained no more than 40% of the variance among all items. That demonstrates is no symptom of common method bias, because the common method bias would result in extremely high correlations.

6.3 Structural Model Assessment

Table 1 demonstrates the results of structural assessment (i.e., the path "Y" means for the urban solitary youth, the path "E" means for the elderly).

Table 1. The direct and indirect path coefficients for overall and specific SNS.

Path	Overall	Wechat	Microblog	Zhihu	TikTok	Games	Dating
Y: SNS-LL	−0.072	−0.185***	−0.058	0.023	0.098	0.078	0.089
E: SNS-LL	−0.026	−0.007	−0.121	−0.048	−0.144	−0.081	0.078
Y:SNS-OSS-LL	−0.009	−0.042*	−0.009	0.003	−0.009	−0.001	−0.005
E:SNS-OSS-LL	−0.066*	−0.146**	−0.067*	−0.035	−0.013	0.058	−0.047
Y:SNS-OSC-LL	0.044*	0.048*	0.054*	−0.006	0.000	0.051*	0.059*
E:SNS-OSC-LL	0.074	0.054	0.052	0.021	0.031	−0.006	0.016
Y:SNS-MIL-LL	0.011	−0.018	−0.004	0.024	0.001	−0.003	−0.027
E:SNS-MIL-LL	−0.130***	−0.259***	−0.195***	−0.079*	−0.047	0.066	−0.002

(*, $p < 0.05$; **, $p < 0.01$; ***, $p < 0.001$).

In the model for the elderly, the direct effects of SNS use on loneliness are not significant, no matter the overall SNS use or every type of SNS. However, for young people, using communication apps (e.g. WeChat) has a significant negative impact on loneliness, but the effect of overall SNS use and using other types are not significant.

The mediating mechanisms through gratifying the motivations of OSS, OSC, and MIL are quite different between young and old users. OSS and MIL can mediate overall SNSs use and loneliness for elderly people, but OSC cannot. While for young people, the mediating effects of OSS and MIL are not valid for overall and most types of SNS use, but OSC has a significant positive mediating effect.

The mediating mechanisms through gratifying the motivations of OSS, OSC, and MIL are different among types of SNSs. For elderly people, the mediating effect of OSC is not significant for all types of SNSs, but the mediating effects of OSS are confirmed for direct communication apps (e.g. WeChat), and microblogs (e.g. Sina microblog and Twitter), are not supported for Knowledge Sharing (e.g., Zhihu), Live broadcast (e.g., TikTok), Game and Dating Apps. And the mediating effect of MIL are not supported for Live broadcast (e.g., TikTok), Game and Dating Apps. In the model for young people, the mediating effects of OSS and MIL are not valid for most types of SNS use and loneliness, only using WeChat results in reduced loneliness through more OSS. But OSC has a significant positive mediating effect, except for Zhihu and TikTok.

7 Conclusions and Discussion

In this study, using most types of SNSs has no direct impact on loneliness, not only for young adults but also for the elderly. The use of WeChat is an exception. For the urban solitary youth, using WeChat takes up a lot of their time to get their work done and contact friends. Therefore, using WeChat means that one never has time to feel lonely. Previous studies have obtained contradictory results concerning the relationship between SNS use and the feeling of loneliness. Some discover a large positive impact, others a negative one, and still others find no discernible impact. Orben [4] proposes that the correlations between SNS use and loneliness need further investigation because a third factor can affect their relationship. In this study, no direct correlation may be because several mediators suppress each other.

The mediating mechanisms through gratifying the motivations of OSS, OSC, and MIL are different between young and old users as well as among types. The differences are interesting and reasonable. It can be inferred that a suppressing effect may occur due to age differences and differences among SNS types.

As suggested by UGT, different motivations lead to engagement in different SNSs, and thereby yield different psychological effects between old and young users. Our research posits that using WeChat and Microblog can help elderly people gain more OSS and feel more MIL, thereby alleviating loneliness. The result is not in accordance with the previous study of Kim and Shen [6]. They find that the elderly engage in and benefit more from those direct communication activities on SNSs, which promote bonding capital. However, the activities promoting bridging social capital do not affect loneliness. Usually, Microblog is good at promoting bridging capital. But if the elderly use Microblog to obtain OSC, or to improve MIL, the use will help mitigate loneliness. Social support may come from both bonding and bridging networks.

Using TikTok, games, and dating services cannot mitigate loneliness through OSS, MIL, and OSC. Seeking cognitive goals by using Zhihu can mitigate loneliness by providing MIL rather than OSS and OSC. The goals for the elderly using TikTok, games, and dating apps are usually for entertainment and passing time. They cannot provide OSS and MIL for the elderly. The results are in accordance with SST. As the elderly have limited future time, they focus their energy on deriving meaning from the present life. Expanding OSC (both bonding and bridging) is not useful and meaningful to them.

Unlike the elderly, the urban solitary youth's use of SNSs, except for WeChat, cannot alleviate the lonely feeling by assisting them in obtaining more OSS and enhancing their sense of MIL. In addition, although using SNS (e.g. WeChat, Microblog, game, and dating apps) helps urban solitary youth expand their OSC, it makes them feel a higher level of loneliness. This result is in accordance with the previous study of Utz and Breuer [8]. They find that SNS use is effective for enhancing online social support, but online social support predicts a higher level of stress. The finding for online social support is similar to that for OSC. The result is in accordance with SST. Individuals with expansive prospects (i.e., the urban solitary youth) prioritize expansive motivations broadly including expanding new relationships, escaping from negative emotions, entertainment, passing time, and seeking novel information. Unlike the elderly, the urban solitary youth are proficient in using various SNSs (i.e. WeChat, Microblog, game, and dating apps) to establish a novel network and expand social capital from the virtual world. The superficial relationships in OSC have less affection and commitment and will interfere with maintaining real-world relationships. This might make people feel more vacuity and lonely. The use of Zhihu and TikTok is an exception. Because Zhihu and TikTok are used for cognitive or entertainment goals; they are not good for obtaining online social support.

Therefore, inconsistent with Kem and Shen [6], the differences in activities and connectedness in not the determinants of SNS use differences across the lifespan. The key points are the needs or motivations of users. Young and older users have different motivations and accordingly select particular types of SNS capable of gratifying certain motivations which result in preferred structural features of personal networks.

Our study reveals several interesting implications both for theory and practice. First, the results of this study offer managerial implications for the design of SNSs. Designers might investigate the needs and motivations of the elderly and young people. Second, by identifying different users' motivations and strengths in gratifications among various types of SNS, this study validates and extends UGT in the field of SNSs. Third, by comparing elderly and urban solitary youth, this study validates and extends developmental psychology theories such as SST. It is not activities and connectedness but the SNS use motivations that cause the differences in SNS use across lifespan. Fourth, by testifying the sequential associations from motivation across the lifespan, the selection of different types of SNSs, and their psychological outcomes, this study contributes to the theory of SCM.

References

1. Kane, G., Alavi, M., Labianca, G.: What's different about social media networks? A framework and research agenda. MIS Q. **38**(1), 275–304 (2014)
2. Song, H., et al.: Does Facebook make you lonely? A meta-analysis. Comput. Human Behav. **36**, 446–452 (2014)
3. Cotten, S.R., Schuster, A.M., Seifert, A.: Social media use and well-being among older adults. Curr. Opin. Psychol. **45**, 101293 (2022)
4. Orben, A., Przybylski, A.K.: Screens, teens, and psychological well-being: evidence from three time-use-diary studies. Psychol. Sci. **30**(8), 682–696 (2019)
5. Musetti, A., Manari, T., Billieux, J., Starcevic, V., Schimmenti, A.: Problematic social networking sites use and attachment: A systematic review. Comput. Human Behav. **131**, 107199 (2022)
6. Kim, C., Shen, C.: Connecting activities on Social Network Sites and life satisfaction: a comparison of older and younger users. Comput. Human Behav. **105**, 106222 (2019)
7. Naidu, S., Chand, A., Pandaram, A., Patel, A.: Problematic Internet and social network site use in young adults: the role of emotional intelligence and fear of negative evaluation. Pers. Individ. Dif. **200**, 111915 (2023)
8. Utz, S., Breuer, J.: The relationship between use of social network sites, online social support, and well-being: results from a six-wave longitudinal study. J. Media Psychol. **29**(3), 115–125 (2017)
9. Yang, S., Huang, L., Zhang, Y., Zhang, P., Zhao, Y.C.: Unraveling the links between active and passive social media usage and seniors' loneliness: a field study in aging care communities. Internet Res. **31**(6), 2167–2189 (2021)
10. Meier, A., Reinecke, L.: Computer-mediated communication, social media, and mental health: a conceptual and empirical meta-review. Communic. Res. **48**(8), 1–28 (2020)
11. Kahn, R.L., Antonucci, T.C.: Convoys over the life course: atachment, roles, and social support. Life-span Dev. Behav. **3**, 253–286 (1980)
12. Park, Y., Gordon, A.M., Mendes, W.B.: Age differences in physiological reactivity to daily emotional experiences. Affect. Sci. **4**(3), 487–499 (2023)

13. Carstensen, L.L.: Socioemotional selectivity theory: social activity in life-span context'. Annu. Rev. Gerontol. Geriatr. **11**, 195–217 (1991)
14. Smith, S.A., Watkins, B.: Millennials' uses and gratifications on Linkedin: implications for recruitment and retention. Int. J. Bus. Commun. **60**(2), 560–586 (2023)
15. Rae, J.R., Lonborg, S.D.: Do motivations for using Facebook moderate the association between Facebook use and psychological well-being? Front. Psychol. **6**, 771–779 (2015)
16. Gilmour, J., Machin, T., Brownlow, C., Jeffries, C.: Facebook-based social support and health: a systematic review. Psychol. Pop. Media **9**(3), 328–346 (2020)
17. Berkman, L.F., Glass, T., Brissette, I., Seeman, T.E.: From social integration to health: durkheim in the new millennium. Soc Sci Med **51**(6), 843–857 (2000)
18. Zhang, X., Dong, S.: The relationships between social support and loneliness: A meta-analysis and review. Acta Psychol. (Amst) **227**, 103616 (2022)
19. Coleman, J.S.: Social capital in the creation of human capital. Am. J. Sociol. **94**, 95–120 (1988)
20. Williams, D.: On and off the net: scales for social capital in an online era'. J. Comput. Commun. **11**, 593–628 (2006)
21. Hofer, M., Aubert, V.: Perceived bridging and bonding social capital on Twitter: differentiating between followers and followees. Comput. Human Behav. **29**(6), 2134–2142 (2013)
22. Steger, M.F.: The pursuit of meaningfulness in life. In: Lopez, S.J. (ed.) Handbook of Positive Psychology, 2nd ed., Oxford University Press, Oxford (2009)
23. Wang, X., Sun, Y., Kramer, T.: Ritualistic consumption decreases loneliness by increasing meaning. J. Mark. Res. **58**(2), 282–298 (2021)
24. Steger, M.F., Oishi, S., Kashdan, T.B.: Meaning in life across the life span: levels and correlates of meaning in life from emerging adulthood to older adulthood. J. Posit. Psychol. **4**(1), 43–52 (2009)
25. Hays, R.D., Dimatteo, M.R.: A short-form measure of loneliness. J. Pers. Assess. **51**(1), 69–81 (1987)
26. Steger, M.F., Frazier, P., Oishi, S., Kaler, M.: The meaning in life questionnaire: assessing the presence of and search for meaning in life. J. Couns. Psychol. **53**(1), 80–93 (2006)
27. Kessler, R.C., Price, R.H., Wortman, C.B.: Social factors in psychopathology stress, social support, and coping processes. Ann. Rev. Psychol. **36**(1), 531–572 (1985)

User Behavior Analysis in Online Health Community Based on Inverse Reinforcement Learning

Yaqi Zhang[1], Xi Wang[1], Zhiya Zuo[2], and Dan Fan[1(✉)]

[1] School of Information, Central University of Finance and Economics, Beijing, China
fandan@cufe.edu.cn

[2] Department of Information Systems, City University of Hong Kong,
Kowloon Tong, HKSAR, China

Abstract. With the rapid development of the Internet, online health communities (OHCs) have gradually become an important platform for the public to seek medical services. User behavior research, an interesting research topic in OHCs, has garnered widespread academic attention in information management. While traditional quantitative and qualitative studies remain foundational, a growing number of scholars have shifted their focus toward harnessing machine learning techniques to delve deeply into OHC user behaviors, aiming to extract actionable insights for community refinement and decision-making. Given the substantial data volume of OHCs, there remains a gap in employing reinforcement learning for relevant studies. This paper embarks on a detailed analysis and predictions of user behaviors in breast cancer OHCs using inverse reinforcement learning. Research findings suggest that users are more likely to initiate new discussions, respond to others, and self-reply after receiving peer replies. Moreover, the rewards obtained through inverse reinforcement learning serve as compelling features for predicting future user behavior. The F1 value of the prediction increased by 13% and 24% in the dataset with time windows of 3 years and 5 years. The findings may contribute to the effective management and sustainable development of OHCs.

Keywords: Inverse reinforcement learning · Online health community · User behavior analysis · Churn prediction

1 Introduction

The rapid development of the Internet and advancements in information have significantly enriched how the general public acquires health knowledge. Platforms specifically designed for patients to consult with doctors and seek medical advice, such as "Haodf.com," forums like the "DXY Forum" tailored for interaction among patients, and global initiatives like the "Global COVID-19 Practical Sharing Plat-form" created for knowledge exchange in the fight against the pandemic, exemplify the diverse landscape of OHCs. Popular messaging apps like "WeChat" and "QQ," which allow the creation of groups for disseminating medical information, also fall under the umbrella of OHCs.

Y. P. Tu and M. Chi (Eds.): WHICEB 2024, LNBIP 517, pp. 250–259, 2024.
https://doi.org/10.1007/978-3-031-60324-2_21

The development of OHCs has given rise to a wealth of user data. By employing artificial intelligence techniques to collect and analyze this data, valuable and shareable knowledge can be generated. This strengthens patient communication and assists hospitals and related industries in expanding their services and collaborations.

To ensure the long-term stability and development of OHCs, scholars have undertaken multidimensional research on user behavior within these communities. Among them, users' participation motivation and activeness are research focuses of the OHCs. Particularly, the motivations for patient users are more diverse, driven by the desire to gain knowledge, emotional support, and a stronger sense of belonging [1, 2]. Current studies either utilize machine learning methods to establish predictive models or simulation models for user engagement or employ econometric modeling approaches to build models explaining user behavior. Most of these computational methods are rooted in existing theoretical frameworks, defining variables and con-ducting model fitting. There is relatively less exploration from a purely data-driven perspective. Additionally, research integrating artificial intelligence algorithms into analyzing user behavior still needs further development. In the field of OHC, there is currently a gap in the literature regarding the use of reinforcement learning to study user behavior. There is a lack of clarity in defining the reward function and establishing mechanisms for reinforcement learning in OHC. Therefore, this paper proposes using reinforcement learning models to fit user behavior and predict behavioral patterns within OHCs.

This study employs Inverse Reinforcement Learning (IRL) methods to analyze user behavior in an OHC focused on breast cancer. As an exploratory study, this study selects user responses (including responses to others and self-replies), initiates discussions, and receives replies as indicators of user engagement. The results indicate that users are more inclined to initiate new discussions, respond to others, or self-reply after receiving different types of replies from other users. Furthermore, by utilizing the reward values obtained through IRL, the proposed predictive model outperforms the benchmark feature sets and algorithm combinations. The proposed model is expected to apply to the design and decision-making processes of OHCs, offering predictive insights into user attrition and facilitating sustainability.

2 Literature Review

2.1 Social Support

Social support, a foundational element of OHCs, underpins their formation and on-going utility. Social support in the context of OHCs refers to establishing and strengthening social connections by two or more users through social media plat-forms, where providers can contribute to the well-being of recipients [3]. Existing studies categorize social support into different types based on various criteria. Generally, social support is classified into informational support, emotional support, companionship, and instrumental support [4]. Current research has employed various methods to categorize social support into different types. Text mining, topic induction classification, and quantitative content analysis are widely used to distinguish different types of social support. After distinguishing different kinds of social support, studies have found that various forms impact users in OHCs differently.

Social support, a crucial factor distinguishing OHCs from regular online communities, is directly associated with user engagement behavior. Existing research indicates that the social support users receive reinforces their participation in OHCs [5]. Moreover, studies have showed that users who receive more informational support, seek more emotional support, or are offered more companionship tend to spend more time engaging in OHC activities. Conversely, users seeking or receiving more informational support are often more prone to leave [6].

2.2 User Churn Prediction

User engagement refers to the behavior of users posting, commenting, or participating in various activities within OHCs. In online communities, user engagement is driven by motivations such as seeking and providing information, relaxation and entertainment, social interaction, and self-fulfillment [7]. The active time of users in OHCs is measured by the time difference between their last and first posts on OHCs. When users exhibit a decrease in short-term activity or remain inactive for an extended period within the OHCs, researchers often interpret this as user churn. The substantial loss of users can lead to the community falling behind or even terminating.

The factors influencing user engagement are diverse. In addition to social support, peer participation positively impacts user engagement, to some extent moderating the relationship between social support and user participation behavior [8]. Users who make new friends in online communities and establish connections with other community members are less likely to leave the community [9]. In addition to social support and social networks, factors such as the richness of perception channels, perceived effectiveness, user concerns about privacy disclosure and community gamification can all influence user participation [5, 10, 11].

2.3 Inverse Reinforcement Learning

Reinforcement Learning (RL) and Inverse Reinforcement Learning (IRL) together form a symbiotic framework within the field of artificial intelligence. In essence, IRL can be viewed as an extension or application of RL, seeking to uncover the latent objectives that drive decision-making in a given environment. RL focuses on mapping situations to actions to maximize digital rewards. An agent observes the state of the environment, takes actions and receives rewards or penalties for each action. Through continuous learning, the agent identifies actions and strategies that maximize rewards [12].

In RL, an agent has a reward function used to achieve a given objective. However, the form of the reward function is unknown in many cases, such as a robot learning to navigate an unfamiliar environment. IRL is a specialized category of RL. IRL aims to estimate the reward function that leads an agent to take actions in specific states. This estimated reward function is then used to interpret the reasons and motivations behind the agent's actions. The actions observed by the agent are represented as its historical trajectory. Therefore, the main difference between RL and IRL lies in whether the reward function is known and whether the action trajectory is part of the agent's observations.

IRL has the ability to understand and predict users' real behaviors, and it is currently widely applied in the research of online communities. In the context of recommendation systems, the IRL model, by observing user behaviors, can extract adaptive reward functions. This allows the inference of user preferences on social networks or streaming platforms, predicting how individuals interact with various types of web platforms. Additionally, it can automatically generate recommendation strategies based on certain user behaviors that best align with user interests [13, 14].

IRL is also applied to research user behavior motivation within online communities. Dantas et al. found that social psychological feedback, such as receiving comments or likes, drives user participation in online social communities [15]. By utilizing learned user behavior motivations, IRL can be widely employed to distinguish between different types of users. In a study on Twitter, Luceri et al. differentiated ordinary users from those disrupting the Internet order by learning the reward values associated with user posting behavior [16]. Similarly, Likmeta et al. used IRL to analyze the focus and motivations of users reposting posts, distinguishing between regular users and spam users. The research indicates that the efficiency of user classification using IRL is generally higher than that of machine learning and other regression models [17].

In the OHC context, there is still a gap in research using IRL for user behavior analysis and prediction. Therefore, this study employs IRL for user behavior analysis, aiming to predict user engagement and attrition behaviors by fitting real-world data.

3   Method

3.1   Data

This study collected data from an online health community (Breastcancer.org) for breast cancer survivors as the research data source. The dataset comprises all publicly available posts and basic user profile information from 2002 to 2019, involving a total of 74,149 users and 4,574,264 posts. This study focuses on two time windows of three and five years, examining their participation behaviors. The two time windows are from September 2016 to 2019 and from September 2014 to 2019.

In terms of data preprocessing, user entries meeting the following criteria, starting from the first week since posting message upon entering the OHC, will be excluded from the dataset:

- Users with a posting frequency of three or fewer messages, indicating low activity.
- Users who initiated discussions but never received any replies.
- Users who have never initiated any discussions.

After data preprocessing, the dataset for the 3-year time window includes a total of 2390 eligible users with a related post count of 24,500. For the 5-year time window, the dataset consists of 2873 eligible users with a related post count of 37,584. In order to establish a user churn predictive model, this study has created distinct feature sets for these filtered users, including an IRL-based feature set and the original feature set without IRL.

3.2 Features Based on IRL

In this study, each user is considered an agent. Due to the vast number of users in OHCs, the model represents a system with multi agents. Like most studies in IRL, this paper considers the breast cancer OHC as the environment within the model. In RL models for online communities, the "state" is generally defined as various indicators influencing user engagement. In this study, the user's reception of replies from other users is selected as a passive state for investigation. Additionally, based on the types of social support and the text of the posts, it is further segmented into received emotional support, informational support, and companionship. The "action" typically refers to user-initiated participation behaviors in the OHC. In this study, actions are defined as three types of user engagement behaviors. The agent observes users from the first post they send upon entering the OHC and records the state-action scenarios for the first week, forming the state-action trajectory for each user.

In the specific application, we establish the model as follows:

- State: Indicates whether a user has received replies from other users in the OHC. The values are binary. Based on the types of social support, the state is further refined into three types: (1) User receives informational support from other users. (2) User receives emotional support from other users. (3) User receives companionship from other users. In the model, only direct replies from other users under discussion threads initiated by the user are considered. Indirect replies received under discussion threads undertaken by other users are not considered.
- Action: (1) Whether the user initiated a new discussion thread. (2) Whether the user replied to other users. (3) Whether the user self-replied.
- Transition: State-action pairs (state1, state2, state3, action1, action2, action3) constitute the agent's state-action trajectory. For each action taken by the user, observe the current state, forming the current state-action pair. The transition probabilities are calculated based on the occurrences of state-action pairs.
- Reward: A unique IRL model is developed for each user. The IRL method outputs a scalar value associated with the state-action combinations for each user, as mentioned above. Each value represents the reward for the user executing a specific action in a particular state. High reward values for state-action pairs (s, A) indicate that the user is highly motivated to perform action A in state s, while low reward values suggest the opposite. In this study, the analysis will focus on whether there is motivation for users to initiate new discussion threads, post replies to other users, and self-reply in different types of receiving replies from other users.

This study observes user behavior during the first week after entering the OHC. Through the analysis of these behaviors, it aims to predict whether users will post in the following week. The reward values obtained through IRL from the users' state-action trajectory in the first week will be used as a features set.

3.3 Alternative Feature Sets

The above IRL model utilizes whether the user initiated a new topic, replied to others, self-reply, received emotional support, informational support, and companionship as states and actions. Meanwhile, the six features without undergoing IRL can serve as an alternative feature set. This study takes the quantity of these six features from users during the first week of posting in the OHC as a benchmark model. Based on whether users post in the next week, users can be classified into active and inactive categories.

Subsequent classification predictions are conducted, and the results are compared with those obtained after applying IRL.

4 Results

4.1 Reward Analysis

Using the filtered users as intelligent agents, the model takes the state-action trajectories of each user during the first week after entering the OHC as input. The output results depict the reward function, as shown in Figs. 1 and 2, representing the average reward values for all users. Figure 1 displays the reward values for single factors, and Fig. 2 illustrates the reward values for multi-factor joint effects, both presented in 4 × 4 matrices. The horizontal axis represents actions, the vertical axis represents states, and the color legend on the right indicates increasing reward values from light to dark. In each corresponding block, a darker color indicates a higher reward value.

Figure 1 illustrates single-factor reward values, the horizontal axis from left to right represents *not posting, initiating a new discussion, replying to others, and self-replying.* The vertical axis from top to bottom represents *not receiving replies, receiving companionship, receiving informational support, and receiving emotional support.* The research results indicate that reward values for initiating new topics and self-replies are the highest in the state of receiving emotional support. This suggests that users receiving emotional support are motivated to initiate new topics and engage in self-replies. Additionally, receiving informational support or companionship is more effective in encouraging users to reply to others compared to other states. This aligns with existing research on user behavior, where receiving replies is often considered one of the factors influencing user participation, impacting engagement in OHCs [18].

Figure 2 illustrates multi-factor reward values, the horizontal axis is consistent with that in the single-factor case. The vertical axis from top to bottom represents *users receiving companionship and informational support, companionship and emotional support, informational support and emotional support, and all three types of social support.* Since each of the three types of social support as a single factor has a promoting effect on users replying to others, their joint effects are also significant. In addition, the research findings indicate that the combined impact of receiving informational support, emotional support, and companionship significantly promotes self-replying and initiating new discussion threads. This new finding indicates that the combined effect of social support has an impact on user engagement.

4.2 Churn Prediction

The results of predicting user posting behavior in the next week using different feature sets are shown in Table 1. A total of 11 algorithms were employed, including

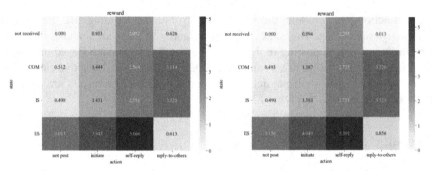

Fig. 1. Single-factor reward values (three years on the left and five years on the right)

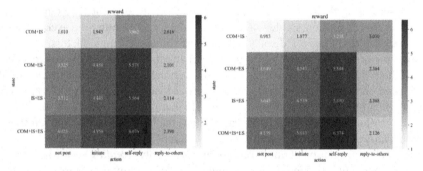

Fig. 2. Multiple-factor reward values (three years on the left and five years on the right)

Bernoulli Naive Bayes (BNB), Logistic Regression (LR), Support Vector Machine (SVM), k-Nearest Neighbors (KNN), Radom Forest (RF), eXtreme Gradient Boosting (XGBoost), Adaptive Boosting (AdaBoost), Gradient Boosting Decision Trees (GBDT), Multi-Layer Perceptron (MLP), Long Short-Term Memory (LSTM) and Gated Recurrent Unit (GRU). Furthermore, the quantity of user-initiated new topics, replies to others, self-replies, and received emotional, informational, and companionship support during the first week were used as benchmark features. The results indicate that, for the 3-year time window, the highest F1 score obtained using IRL-derived reward values as features is 85.71%, while the highest benchmark F1 score is 72.26%. In the 5-year time window, the highest F1 score achieved with IRL-derived reward values as features is 86.63%, while the highest benchmark F1 score is 62.94%. Therefore, the effectiveness of predicting future user behavior using reward values obtained through IRL is superior to using the original features without IRL. Particularly, to further enhance prediction accuracy, the study added features based on the reward values obtained through IRL, including expressions of gratitude, seeking social support, and providing social support. The results show only a slight improvement in prediction accuracy, specifically with the AdaBoost algorithm (from 0.83 to 0.85).

Table 1. Classification Results Evaluation

Algorithm	IRL-3 years				Benchmark-3 years			
	Accuracy	Precision	Recall	F-1	Accuracy	Precision	Recall	F-1
BNB	60.00%	62.91%	79.73%	70.73%	60.63%	62.28%	85.64%	72.12%
LR	53.89%	60.65%	63.90%	62.23%	57.74%	62.00%	74.74%	67.78%
SVM	59.46%	59.46%	81.19%	68.12%	60.67%	67.57%	65.10%	66.31%
KNN	72.55%	74.98%	80.79%	77.78%	58.74%	62.39%	77.06%	68.95%
RF	64.85%	64.03%	93.31%	75.95%	61.34%	61.67%	54.12%	57.91%
XGBoost	84.64%	85.83%	81.70%	83.88%	61.80%	65.12%	76.99%	70.56%
AdaBoost	71.00%	72.58%	82.34%	77.15%	61.13%	62.76%	85.15%	72.26%
GBDT	84.77%	84.94%	86.49%	**85.71%**	61.17%	61.41%	77.55%	70.37%
MLP	58.62%	64.04%	84.03%	70.71%	62.34%	65.17%	78.75%	71.32%
LSTM	63.00%	64.11%	82.92%	72.18%	58.70%	56.41%	65.64%	60.68%
GRU	62.19%	64.26%	87.69%	74.47%	58.40%	56.46%	62.41%	59.28%
Algorithm	IRL-5 years				Benchmark-5 years			
	Accuracy	Precision	Recall	F-1	Accuracy	Precision	Recall	F-1
BNB	55.12%	55.64%	67.67%	61.07%	59.02%	61.90%	52.98%	57.10%
LR	51.17%	53.43%	55.82%	54.60%	55.82%	54.60%	68.06%	60.95%
SVM	55.50%	56.36%	64.06%	59.96%	58.29%	63.67%	44.11%	52.12%
KNN	85.83%	85.83%	84.40%	85.11%	55.54%	56.51%	59.00%	57.72%
RF	76.43%	74.65%	82.80%	78.51%	56.86%	56.41%	71.18%	62.94%
XGBoost	87.22%	86.98%	86.28%	**86.63%**	57.59%	60.28%	51.56%	55.58%
AdaBoost	84.02%	83.56%	83.02%	83.29%	58.70%	61.68%	52.17%	56.52%
GBDT	85.31%	85.46%	83.60%	84.52%	58.39%	60.43%	54.60%	57.46%
MLP	60.31%	61.15%	65.00%	63.01%	58.25%	60.43%	54.67%	57.41%
LSTM	83.61%	85.01%	80.72%	82.32%	59.01%	56.75%	65.42%	60.78%
GRU	84.03%	85.79%	80.63%	83.32%	44.88%	44.82%	58.61%	50.79%

5 Discussion and Conclusion

This study employs IRL to establish a multi-agent model to explore the latent motivations behind user engagement behaviors. Firstly, based on the rewards obtained through IRL, this study found that users who receive emotional support are more motivated to initiate new topics and self-reply. In situations where users receive emotional, informational, and companionship support simultaneously, there is a higher incentive for users to engage in these two behaviors. Secondly, users who receive informational support or companionship are more motivated to reply to others. The findings above may be due to the fact that when users receive different types of social support, they establish connections with other users in the OHC or realize the benefits of staying in the OHC, so their participation in the OHC will increase. Thirdly, we use the reward values as features to predict users' future behavior. Compared to the benchmark model without IRL, it can predict more accurately. IRL can conduct a more detailed analysis based on users' past behaviors. Analyzing past trajectories forms personalized reward for each user, thereby improving predictive performance.

This study can be applied to the field of OHC. The ongoing exploration of user behavior motivations in OHCs and the prediction of user engagement and churn behaviors provide intervention recommendations for managers. The findings can assist OHC managers in maintaining user engagement, preventing churn, and improving users' health status through the OHC platform. Regarding research methodology, the application of IRL in management studies, particularly in online community management, remains relatively unexplored. This study pioneers the application of IRL to research and manage OHCs, actively exploring user behaviors within communities.

However, the model has certain shortcomings and limitations. In this IRL model, the state only considers the three types of social support a user receives from other users, excluding other factors that may influence user behavior, such as the level of intimacy and closeness between users. In text processing, the quality of posts that a user receives is not considered within the model. Demographic features are vital indicators for explaining user behavior, but in this model, the user's personal information has been excluded from registration time and user ID. Therefore, incorporating demographic factors such as age, location, and gender, obtained from users' filled-out profiles and personal signatures, could enhance model performance.

Acknowledgements. This work was supported by the National Natural Science Foundation of China under Grants 72104261, 72201221, and 72274230; Central University of Finance and Economics under the Program for Innovation Research.

References

1. Mo, P.K.H., Coulson, N.S.: Online support group use and psychological health for individuals living with hiv/aids. Patient Educ. Couns. **93**(3), 426–432 (2013)
2. Zhang, Y., He, D., Sang, Y.: Facebook as a platform for health information and communication: a case study of a diabetes group. J. Med. Syst. **37**, 1–12 (2013)
3. Price, S.L., et al.: Maternal knowing and social networks: understanding first-time mothers' search for information and support through online and offline social networks. Qual. Health Res. **28**(10), 1552–1563 (2018)
4. Barrera, M., Jr., Ainlay, S.L.: The structure of social support: A conceptual and empirical analysis. J. Commun. Psychol. **11**(2), 133–143 (1983)
5. Mirzaei, T., Esmaeilzadeh, P.: Engagement in online health communities: channel expansion and social exchanges. Inf. Manage. **58**(1), 103404 (2021)
6. Wang, X., Zhao, K., Street, N., et al.: Analyzing and predicting user participations in online health communities: a social support perspective. J. Med. Internet Res. **19**(4), e6834 (2017)
7. Laeeq Khan, M.: Social media engagement: What motivates user participation and consumption on youtube? Comput. Human Behavior **66**, 236–247 (2017)

8. Wang, J., Yao, T., Wang, Y.: Patient engagement as contributors in online health communities: the mediation of peer involvement and moderation of community status. Behav. Sci. **13**(2), 152 (2023)

9. Yao, Z., et al.: Join, stay or go? A closer look at members' life cycles in online health comunities. Proc. ACM Hum.-Comput. Interact. **5**(11), 1–22 (2021)

10. Feng, B., Li, X., Lin, L.: Valenced social identities and the digital divide in online health communities. Comput. Hum. Behav. **122**, 106812 (2021)

11. Ouyang, P., Wang, J.-J., Ali, U.: The impact of gamification on the patient's engagement in the online health community. Aslib J. Inf. Manage. **74**(6), 1196–1213 (2022)

12. Kaelbling, L.P., Littman, M.L., Moore, A.W.: Reinforcement learning: a survey. J. Artif. Intell. Res. **4**, 237–285 (1996)

13. Panjasuchat, M., Limpiyakorn, Y.: Applying reinforcement learning for customer churn prediction. In: Journal of Physics: Conference Series, vol. 1619, p. 012016. IOP Publishing (2020)

14. Das, S., Lavoie, A.: The effects of feedback on human behavior in social media: An inverse reinforcement learning model. In: Proceedings of the 2014 International Conference on Autonomous Agents and Multi-agent Systems, pp. 653–660 (2014)

15. Dantas, A.P.R.R.S.: Inferring user preferences by analyzing their behavior on streaming platforms using inverse reinforcement learning (2022)

16. Luceri, L., Giordano, S., Ferrara, E.: Detecting troll behavior via inverse reinforcement learning: a case study of Russian trolls in the 2016 us election. In: Proceedings of the International AAAI Conference on Web and Social Media, vol. 14, pp. 417–427 (2020)

17. Likmeta, A., Metelli, A.M., Ramponi, G., Tirinzoni, A., Giuliani, M., Restelli, M.: Dealing with multiple experts and non-stationarity in inverse reinforcement learning: an application to real-life problems. Mach. Learn. **110**, 2541–2576 (2021)

18. Wang, X., High, A., Wang, X., Zhao, K.: Predicting users' continued engagement in online health communities from the quantity and quality of received support. J. Assoc. Inf. Sci. Technol. **72**(6), 710–722 (2021)

User Experience of VR Sports: A Uses and Gratifications View

Hong Chen[✉]

Tampere University, Kalevantie 4, 33100 Tampere, Finland
hong.chen@tuni.fi

Abstract. Virtual reality (VR) sports have become a new phenomenon in sports. We have witnessed an increase in VR sports among individual participants in their casual lives during and after the COVID-19 pandemic. However, there is a lack of a deep understanding of the user experience in VR sports usage in casual life at the individual participant level. To address the above research gap, this research explores the user experience of VR sports based on a uses and gratifications perspective via interviews among twelve VR sports users. The present research provides a deep understanding of the user experience of VR sports usage by identifying four gratifications in VR sports usage that meet users' psychological needs. The four gratifications are hedonic gratification, utilitarian gratification, technology gratification, and social gratification.

Keywords: User experience · VR sports · Digital Sports · Uses and gratifications theory

1 Introduction

Immersive wearable technology such as virtual reality (VR) has been increasingly applied in people's daily lives including shopping, tourism, and sports, especially during and after the COVID-19 pandemic. Compared with traditional 2D esports such as websites or video esports, VR sports provide users with immersive, realistic, and interactive sports experience in a 3D environment via VR technology (Harris et al., 2021). Some scholars also verified that VR sports could even activate users in their daily lives to prevent mental and physical illness (Westmattelmann et al., 2021). The previous VR sports literature has researched VR sports from the views of sports professionals, such as athletes and coaches (Bum et al., 2018; Müller et al., 2022). Some recent studies have also investigated VR sports from the views of spectators or individual participants in a leisure time context (Harris et al., 2021; Oagaz et al., 2022; Seong & Hong, 2022), aiming to understand their VR sports behavior.

In the existing literature, scholars have applied various theories to investigate VR sports usages at the individual participant level, such as the technology acceptance model (TAM) (Seong & Hong, 2022), flow theory (Lee & Oh, 2022), emotion theories (Dirin & Laine, 2023), and benefits and risks theory (Westmattelmann et al., 2021). VR sports could facilitate individual participants' needs for sports with the convenience of time

© The Author(s), under exclusive license to Springer Nature Switzerland AG 2024
Y. P. Tu and M. Chi (Eds.): WHICEB 2024, LNBIP 517, pp. 260–272, 2024.
https://doi.org/10.1007/978-3-031-60324-2_22

and without the limitation of space. However, previous studies have examined the user experience of VR sports with a focus on VR technology features, user cognition, and emotions, and few studies have attempted to study how VR sports could meet users' psychological needs and motivate their usage of VR sports.

Uses and gratifications theory (U&G) is a nomological theoretical framework to understand how media could satisfy individuals' needs without offering a predefined research construction. It has been applied to explain how information technologies could meet individuals' psychological needs and motivate their technology usage in different technology contexts. Extant research has studied different gratifications in technology use based on U&G, such as content, process, utilitarian, hedonic, social, and technology gratifications. The literature shows that U&G could be an appropriate theory to understand how VR sports could meet individual participants' psychological needs and motivate their usage of VR sports. However, little research has examined how VR sports could satisfy users' psychological needs based on user experience from the view of gratifications.

To address the above research questions, the current study examines the gratifications users have experienced in their VR sports usage with interview data collected among VR sports users. Specifically, drawing on U&G, this study identified four gratifications in VR sports usage, including hedonic, utilitarian, technology, and social gratifications, which encourage users to participate in VR sports. The current study enriches the literature on VR sports by identifying the four gratifications in VR sports use that satisfy individuals' psychological needs. The four gratifications identified from the VR sports user experience could also provide VR sports developers with some practical guidelines on how to enhance VR sports users' gratifications and meet their psychological needs from a technological design view.

2 Literature Review

2.1 VR Sports

VR sports is a kind of digital sport rendered by VR technology and an alternative to real sports and sports competitions (Hutchins, 2008). Specifically, VR sports could facilitate physical movements and players must obey tournaments or competitions' rules (Filchenko, 2018). Compared with the traditional 2D static presentation of the Internet or mobile phones, VR headsets could provide users with a vivid 3D presentation of the virtual environment and realistic simulation of physical movements to involve users in the virtual sports environment, spurring users' multiple senses in the VR sports usage (Jang & Park, 2019). Thus, VR headsets have great potential in transforming kinetic sports such as baseball, golfing, and fishing and leisure fitness sports such as dancing and aerobics in the virtual digital environment.

In the previous research on VR sports, some studies have examined the user experience for sports professionals, such as coaches and athletes (Bum et al., 2018). VR provides a realistic simulation of the sports environment and movements, assisting athletes to track the movements of their sport such as motions, pitch, and performance. Müller et al. (2022) examined how to incorporate the visual anticipation of VR simulator design in VR sports to improve athletes' skills and performance.

In the VR leisure sports field for casual sports users, VR sports can simulate physical movements of sports and offer a mixed experience of entertainment and exercise (Seong & Hong, 2022). Various digital sports have been developed based on VR technology for people's leisure lives, such as VR tennis (Oagaz et al., 2022), VR golfing (Harris et al., 2021), and VR baseball (Seong & Hong, 2022). VR sports have become an alternative to exercise in the offline avenues when there is inconvenient time or a lack of partners and opponents (Uhm et al., 2022). Some studies have researched VR sports system design (Nunes et al., 2014) and sports content design (Oagaz et al., 2022) to provide users with a mixed experience of sports and entertainment (Seong & Hong, 2022; Uhm et al., 2022). Meanwhile, some scholars have explored individual users' VR sports participation. For example, Westmattelmann et al. (2021) have investigated user perceptions of the benefits and risks of using VR sports platforms that influence their intention to adopt VR sports. However, few studies have examined individual users' gratifications in VR sports usage and how their participation in VR sports could satisfy their psychological needs.

2.2   Uses and Gratifications Theory

U&G was first proposed in media research to explore how particular media could satisfy audiences' psychological needs (Katz et al., 1973). U&G defines human goals as psychological needs generating a series of motivations, which have an influence on humans' use of media and determine different users' cognition and behaviors (Katz et al., 1974). U&G has been applied to explain what psychological gratifications motivate humans' selection and participation in media platforms (Luo et al., 2023) and social media (Leung, 2013). Meanwhile, U&G, as a nomological theoretical framework without offering a predefined research construction, could be developed, and extended with various intrinsic and extrinsic motivations based on various research contexts (Gan & Li, 2018; Nohutlu et al., 2023). In information system (IS) field, some studies have employed U&G to understand users' usage of technologies, such as the Internet (Leung, 2013), live streaming (Bawack et al., 2023), mobile phones (Leung & Wei, 2000), AI (Cheng & Jiang, 2020), VR-based tourism (Rather et al., 2023) and augmented reality (AR) learning (Tom Dieck et al., 2023).

As Table 1 shows, prior IS research has categorized various gratifications in different technologies usage based on U&G. Users usually attempt to adopt technologies to fulfill psychological needs, such as task performance, entertainment, companionship, and personal identity (Tom Dieck et al., 2023; Leung & Wei, 2000). A study based on U&G demonstrated content gratification (e.g., usage of messages, information sharing, and self-document in social media) and process gratification deriving from enjoyment and passing time motivated individuals' usage of social media (Stafford & Stafford, 2001). Some scholars argued that users have social gratification in using online communities since users could have a self-personal identity stemming from social interaction in online communities (Luo et al., 2023; Nohutlu et al., 2023). Some IS scholars found that users have hedonic gratifications such as fun/entertainment, and enjoyment (Leung, 2013; Luo & Li, 2023), utilitarian gratifications such as information or education needs (Leung, 2013) and social gratifications such as relationship interaction, status and reciprocity (Leung & Wei, 2000; Luo & Li, 2023) in using different IS. Rather et al. (2023)

stated that users also have technology gratification in their VR use (e.g., VR-based content, characters, technologies).

Table 1. A summary of prior research based on U&G in the IS field.

References	Contexts	Gratifications
Stafford (2001)	Websites	Content gratification: Utility of media Process gratification: Enjoyment
Leung (2013)	Facebook, blogs, and forums	Social gratification: Interacting with friends or families, sharing interests or recent situation Recognition gratification: Promoting expertise and establishing self-identification Hedonic gratification: Entertainment, relaxation, passing time Cognitive gratification: Broadening knowledge, refining thinking
Luo et al. (2023)	Information-sharing virtual communities	Hedonic gratification: Enjoyment Utilitarian gratification: Relative advantage Social gratification: Reputation, horizontal/vertical relationship
Leung & Wei (2000)	Mobile phone	Technology gratification: Immediacy, mobility, instrumentality Sociability gratification: Status Hedonic gratification: Entertainment, reassurance, relaxation Utilitarian gratification: Acquisition, time management
Cheng & Jiang (2020)	AI chatbot	Hedonic gratification: Entertainment Utilitarian gratification: Information Social gratification: Social presence (psychological connection) Technology gratification: Media appeal

(continued)

Table 1. (*continued*)

References	Contexts	Gratifications
Rather et al. (2023)	VR-based tourism	Technology gratification: VR identification (e.g., the sense of belonging to VR-based apps, content; technology as part of me; personal meaning)
Nohutlu et al. (2023)	Online communities	Cognitive gratification: Learning Social gratification: Establishing ties with others Personal gratification: Self-efficacy, reputation Hedonic gratification: Fun, enjoyment
Tom Dieck et al. (2023)	AR learning	Hedonic gratification: Enjoyment, fantasy, escapism, flow Utilitarian gratification: Information seeking, personalization Sensual gratification: Immersion, presence Modality gratification: Curiosity, novelty, coolness

In sum, U&G is an appropriate lens to understand individuals' usage of IS and could be applied in this study to understand individuals' participation in VR sports. In addition, the different gratifications identified in the literature based on U&G provide a good theoretical base to understand the gratifications in VR sports use that fulfill users' psychological needs.

3 Research Method

3.1 Data Collection

The current study conducted semi-structured interviews among 12 casual VR sports users, including five VR sports users using HTC-Vive headsets and seven using Oculus Quest 2 headsets. The researcher who conducted the interviews played VR sports and invited a couple of VR sports players the author has played with in VR sports to join in the interviews. Seven interviewees were recruited, and they also recommended five VR sports players to join in the project. The interviews were conducted via telephone or social media.

The interviews were organized in English. The twelve participants were asked about their use experience regarding VR sports, who are fluent with English. The interview questions are listed as follows and the interview was conducted in English:

1. What is your favorite VR sports item?
2. What are your experience /feelings when playing VR sports?
3. Why do you want to use VR sports/what are your needs for using VR sports?
4. Do you meet with a virtual character/player/familiarity in a VR sports scenario?
5. What are your feelings when you interact with the virtual robot/multiplayer?
6. Do you like interacting with multiplayer (or virtual robot or friends) in the virtual world or with your friends in the real world? why?
7. How much do you rely on digital technology in your life, such as mobile phones, social media, or the Internet?
8. How is your feeling different from other technology use, such as mobile phones or the Internet?

Table 2. The demographic characters of the interviewees.

Participant	Age	Gender	VR devices	VR sports use frequency
1	26–30	Male	Oculus quest2	1–2 times per week
2	< 26	Female	Oculus quest2	Occasionally
3	> 35	Female	HTC-Vive	1–2 times per month
4	26–30	Female	HTC-Vive	Occasionally
5	26–30	Male	HTC-Vive	1–2 times per year
6	< 26	Male	HTC-Vive	1–2 times per month
7	30–36	Male	Oculus quest2	Everyday
8	30–36	Male	Oculus quest2	1–2 times per week
9	26–30	Male	HTC-Vive	Everyday
10	30–36	Female	Oculus quest2	1–2 times per month
11	30–36	Male	Oculus quest2	Occasionally
12	26–30	Female	Oculus quest2	1–2 times per week

The consent from each interviewee was obtained at the beginning of each inter-view to ensure that they understood the purpose of this study and that they agreed to participate in the interview voluntarily. Each interview lasted for about 30 min. The details of the 12 interviewees are listed in Table 2. For example, the interviewees' age range is 25 to 36, five are female (n = 5, 42%) and seven are male (n = 7, 58%). All interviewees' data were recorded and kept anonymous and confidential. Meanwhile, the transcription of the interviews can only be accessed by the study's authors.

3.2 Data Analysis

The transcripts of the twelve interviewees were analyzed to identify users' gratification in VR sports in their daily lives via using content analysis method (Duriau et al., 2007). The definitions of hedonic gratification, utilitarian gratification, social gratification, and technology gratification based on the literature were applied in the content analysis to identify different factors associated with the four gratifications in VR sports usage (See Table 3). For example, hedonic gratification of VR sports stems from emotional experience such as killing time as leisure and fun; VR sports' utilitarian gratification stems from task performance and content-related factors including VR sports courses, clear visual and aesthetic appealing contents and background music; technology gratification of VR sports could be mapped from easy and convenient controllers, 3D, multiple senses and immersive presence, realistic simulation and map of VR sports, and avatars. Also, a humanoid virtual social robot and various social interaction in different ways would contribute to users' social gratification of VR sports, such as experiencing interesting online activities and scenarios with friends and maintaining relationships with familiarities in the far distance.

Table 3. The definitions of the four gratifications of U&G

Gratifications	Definitions	References
Utilitarian gratifications	Satisfy users' cognitive utility needs especially using VR sports contents, accomplishing VR sports tasks, and improving sports skills	Stafford (2001); Cheng & Jiang (2020)
Hedonic gratifications	Users can obtain or achieve enjoyable emotional support, entertainment, or negative emotional expression in VR sports usage	Abu Shawar & Atwell (2007); Leung (2013)
Social gratifications	Users engage in social interaction in VR sports, such as social presence (psychological connection with other users) and social interaction	Luo et al., (2023); Nohutlu et al., (2023)
Technology gratifications	The ability of VR technology renders users with some functions	Tom Dieck et al. (2023)

4   Findings

Four gratifications were identified including hedonic gratification, utilitarian gratification, technology gratification, and social gratification, which encourage users to use VR sports and satisfy their psychological needs. Seven interviewees played single-player mode of VR sports such as Beat saber (n = 4, 33%) and Pingpong eleven (n = 3, 25%). Five inter-viewees reported their usage experiences when playing the multiplayer mode including fishing (n = 1, 8%), exploration (n = 1, 8%), dancing (n = 1, 8%), and mini golf (n = 2, 16%).

4.1 Hedonic Gratification in VR Sports

Hedonic gratification is one important motivator for users to participate and engage in VR sports either with single-player or multiplayer modes. Ten interviewees reported their emotional experience to gain hedonic gratifications, such as killing time as leisure (P2, 4, 9 and 10), searching for the thrill (P2 and 6) and relaxation (P8 and 12), and experiencing fun (P3, 11 and 12), entertainment (P3 and 7), fantasy (P3 and 11), interesting (P9 and 10) and isolated but not lonely (P12) in VR sports usage. For example, participant 11 demonstrated emotional experience and feelings when playing VR Pingpang Eleven with an Oculus Quest 2 headset.

*"Balls show suddenly, the levels 1–2 are easy, and high levels are harder and intense exercise. I think the VR game is **more enjoyable than PC ones**. I can feel more mobile and realistic. I can engage in the virtual world." (P11).*

*"Various natural backgrounds and surroundings are easy to engage, **enhance the experience, and have a lot of fun and exciting** than others." (P11).*

*"It is also immersive and inspires **interest, entertainment of sports**. I can easily have a sense of accomplishment." (P7).*

"I use VR to have leisure time and explore the universe, trying to see, and explore what it is inside and how to move…That is different, interesting, exciting, wow it is interesting. I can also get something new, inspiring me to use it." (P10).

4.2 Utilitarian Gratification in VR Sports

The current study applies the definition of utilitarian gratification as users' cognitive utility needs especially using VR sports contents, accomplishing VR sports tasks, and improving sports skills (Stafford & Stafford, 2001; Cheng & Jiang, 2020), and the current study identified content-related factors in VR sports to explain how utilitarian gratification motivates users to apply VR sports. Nine interviewees reported their VR sports experiences from the content-appealing view.

Four streams of users' utilitarian gratifications were identified in VR sports. 1) Users explore different VR sports courses to master skills such as scratching and growing up (P2, 3, and 11 reported); 2) The quality and aesthetic contents appeal to users, encouraging them to participate in VR sports (P3, 5, 6, 10 and 12 re-ported); 3) Background music or spatial audio guide users to conduct VR sports such as dancing and golfing (P8 and 9 reported); 4) Clear visual content assists task conduction in VR sports (P8 reported). Examples are shown as follows:

*"I can immerse in the virtual scene and have a realistic interaction with scenes and others. I also **enjoy some combat courses** while playing games." (P3).*

*"**Elegant contents** appeal to me, and **thrill courses** appeal to me, I think my good and immersive experiences stem from **the great content** no matter with the headsets, because I think the quality of the headsets is fine which does not bother my sense of the scenes." (P9).*

*"...less intense sports than (beat saber), where mini golf has a lot of relax, which does not need a lot of effort. **Spatial audio is easy to use voice and guide multiplayer.**" (P8).*

4.3 Technology Gratification in VR Sports

In our data analysis, technology gratification is another reason for individuals' usage of VR sports in their daily lives. Technology gratification stems from VR technology-related elements including control of VR handlers, realistic and immersive VR sports environment, simulation of sports and navigation, and virtual avatar, which is a unique VR technological feature rendering users a realistic presence and identity in the VR sports world.

In the VR sports context, VR technology provides users with 1) easy and convenient control of handlers (P1, 2, 3, 7, 8, and 9 mentioned); 2) immersive and 3D vivid presence in VR sports (P1, 2, 3 and 7 mentioned); 3) realistic simulation of sports (P7 mentioned); 4) realistic map to navigate (P8 and 11 mentioned) and 5) multiple senses invoked: handlers' vibration or blowing wind in the virtual environment (P9 mentioned). Examples are intercepted from participants 2, 7, 8 and 9:

*"I can **easily control the virtual world**. Comfortable **3D images** provide me with a safe private space. And I can have virtual, various but **immersive experience**." (P2).*

"Realistic simulation of Ping pang, the VR environment is easy to control and immersive to inspire my interest." (P7).

"I have intuitive controllers, and realistic maps and clear directions help me navigate in VR mini golf." (P8).

*"The handler is easy to control. Multiple senses invoked, my hands **are shaking via handlers** and **a cool breeze blowing my face and body** in the scene." (P9).*

Moreover, five interviewees (P1, 5, 6, 10, and 12) mentioned the virtual avatar in their VR sports usage brought technology gratification to them. As participant 1 said, a virtual avatar customized by himself helps him get involved in the VR sports because the virtual avatar embedded in the virtual scene enhances the user's presence, and the user can physically move in the virtual sports world via the virtual identity. Examples are shown as follows:

*"**High presence of embedded avatar** assists me to physically move in the virtual world." (P1).*

*"**Avatars appear to present in the space**, turn in the right direction and time." (P10).*

4.4 Social Gratification in VR Sports

The current research identified social gratification in VR sports usage. Different types and features of social interactions among social relationships such as with virtual social robots, colleagues, and friends are observed to appear in the VR sports usage, and users have different social gratification gained in the VR sports usage.

Specifically, the current study found that 1) a humanoid virtual social robot that is happy and friendly in the scenario provides a good social connection with users, cultivating users' social confidence and skills as well as accompanying the users (P2 mentioned); 2) Users make social interaction with other players in different ways in the virtual world, such as sharing interesting things to friends, watching and experiencing bizarre scenes with friends and other players, enriching social interaction which might be hard to experience in the real world for some users (P2 and 9 mentioned); 3) Maintaining and developing social ties with familiarities such as friends and colleagues in VR sports (P2, 8, 9, 10, and 12 mentioned).

*"It was also interesting when I was dancing with the robot, **it seemed very happy and friendly**, also very encouraging. I guess it can help people to **construct confidence in real socializing**. The virtual robot is like a mental health consultant and makes me more comfortable with 3D images because the VR glasses build this safe and private space for you. Although I know the virtual robot is not a real man, it makes me familiar with the virtual world and makes me **feel accompanied by someone** so that I am not nervous and feel safe." (P2).*

*"We could **dance and move with rhythm** such as swinging, crouching, and shaking. Sometimes, there is shaking ground, and a cool breeze blows my face and body, seeming to **dance in the forest and valley**…. I dance together with my partners, we have two avatars in the scene and **collaborate to finish tasks together**, which is so interesting, especially since **I get a lot of encouragement** when we do a good job and get a great mark." (P9).*

*"Colleagues: we have **informal, formal, random discussions, connecting to the aspect of work and team social**, or some daily topics just what is recently doing. For friends: I can gain **a lot of fun and company** in the VR minigolf." (P12).*

5   Discussion and Conclusion

The current study identifies four gratifications to elaborate on users experience in VR sports usage based on U&G, including hedonic gratification, utilitarian gratification, technology gratification, and social gratification.

In particular, the current study exploited positive emotional experiences in VR sports such as fun/entertainment/exciting/interesting and killing time as leisure activity contributes to users' hedonic gratification. The results are consistent with other IS research that IS could bring users with hedonic gratifications, such as the Internet (Leung, 2013) and social media (Cheng & Jiang, 2020). Moreover, in this study, it is interesting to find that although VR headsets isolate users from the physical world, the participants did not feel lonely because they engaged in the VR sports tasks and experienced a sense of flow, which partly contrasts with the result of some other digital sports based on PC, which found that users experience temporary loneliness after they use the digital sports for a couple of days (Luo et al., 2023).

In the current research, some sports content-related factors identified in VR sports, such as challenging or thrilling courses of VR sports, aesthetic content, and visual or spatial audio guidance satisfied users' utilitarian needs, and users gain utilitarian gratifications when they master sports skills and finish related tasks in VR sports. Specifically, challenging/thrill courses in VR sports help users master their sports skills such as scratching and crouching in the current study. Meanwhile, the current study found the high quality and aesthetic design positively encourage users to join in VR sports by satisfying utilitarian gratification, or vice versa no matter what VR headsets the participants have used. Moreover, clear visual content or audio guidance in the VR sports background would assist users in accomplishing sports tasks and improving their sports performance in consistent with prior research evidence that high-quality of sensory cues help users conduct VR shopping (Morotti et al., 2021).

Technology gratification stemming from VR sports experience includes 1) easy control of handlers; 2) immersive and 3D vividness; 3) realistic simulation of sports; 4) realistic map to navigate 5) multiple senses invoked and 6) virtual avatars driving users to participate in VR sports. The evidence of easy control of handlers based on technological ease of use has been supported by prior VR technology research to positively affect the adoption of the technology (Seong & Hong, 2022). And vividness, immersion, and presence enhanced by the virtual avatar of VR technology have been examined by prior research (Jang & Park, 2019). Multiple senses from VR sports applications might also motivate users to conduct VR sports, which is consistent with the result that multiple senses could activate users' gestures and movements in a VR shop (Speicher et al., 2017). Moreover, the findings show that incorporating realistic simulations of movements and maps in the virtual sports world to navigate sports activities motivate users to employ VR sports and contribute to their technology gratification in VR sports usage. The reason might be that these features of VR sports could activate further users' movements and involve them in the virtual world.

Different types and features of social interactions with virtual social robots, friends, and colleagues in virtual world in VR sprots make sports participants feel a sense of social gratification. The current study found that VR sports provide a digital platform for people to keep connected with their friends and colleagues who also play VR sports and enrich their social activities in the virtual VR sports environment, such as diving and watching bizarre scenes that are hard to experience in the real world. Besides, in VR sports context, the reasons for social interaction with friends differ from those with colleagues. The former social interaction owes to users' need to relax and search for fun with friends, while the latter one is mainly due to the motivation to maintain team relationships via informal and formal communication when playing VR sports. Interestingly, the current study found that a humanoid and friendly virtual social robot in VR sports generates a series of positive VR sports experience such as accompanying users and helping users cultivate social skills. The finding extends and is partly consistent with prior research on virtual characters, clarifying that humanoid virtual agents have a high presence and enhance consumers' perceived trust and experience with such agents (Zhu et al., 2023).

In sum, the current study contributes to the VR sports literature by providing an understanding of users' gratifications in participating in VR sports. The four gratifications identified in this study based on U&G bring new insights into user experience in VR sports research from the U&G view and explain how VR sports could meet users' various psychological needs. This study also provides a deep understanding of the four gratifications by exploring the explanations for the four gratifications based on the features of VR sports. The current study also bears some practical implications for VR sports developers. For example, the identified four gratifications in VR sports could guide VR sports developers to improve their VR sports design to meet users' psychological needs from the views of utilitarian, hedonic, social, and technology gratifications, and consider both VR technology and sports content in their design.

6 Limitations and Future Work

The current study has its limitations. First, this study focuses on VR-based sports, and cautious should be taken when generalizing the research's findings into other VR usage contexts such as VR shopping. Second, cultural bias might occur in the current research. Future work could take the cultural backgrounds of participants into consideration. Third, the current study explored the user experience in VR sport usage without consideration of user group. Future research could compare users' gratifications and experience in VR sport usage among different user groups. Fourth, the current study applied semi-structured interviews in data collecting. In future work, mixed research methods could be applied to understand the user experience of VR sports, such as secondary data or surveys to explain how VR sports could meet users' psychological gratifications.

References

Bawack, R.E., Bonhoure, E., Kamdjoug, J.-R.K., Giannakis, M.: How social media live streams affect online buyers: a uses and gratifications perspective. Int. J. Inf. Manage. **70**, 1–15 (2023)

Cheng, Y., Jiang, H.: How do AI-driven chatbots impact user experience? Examining gratifications, perceived privacy risk, satisfaction, loyalty, and continued use. J. Broadcast. Electron. Media **64**(4), 592–614 (2020)

Dirin, A., Laine, T.: The influence of virtual character design on emotional en-gagement in immersive virtual reality: the case of feelings of being. Electronics **12**(10), 1–19 (2023)

Duriau, V.J., Reger, R.K., Pfarrer, M.D.: A content analysis of the content analysis literature in organization studies: research themes, data sources, and methodological refinements. Organ. Res. Methods **10**(1), 5–34 (2007)

Filchenko, M.: A comparison between esports and traditional sports. Introduction to Games Studies, 1–10 (2018)

Gan, C., Li, H.: Understanding the effects of gratifications on the continuance in-tention to use WeChat in China: a perspective on uses and gratifications. Comput. Hum. Behav. **78**, 306–315 (2018)

Harris, D.J., et al.: Exploring sensorimotor performance and user experience within a virtual reality golf putting simulator. Virtual Reality **25**(3), 647–654 (2021)

Hutchins, B.: Signs of meta-change in second modernity: the growth of esports and the world cyber games. New Media Soc. **10**(6), 851–869 (2008)

Jang, Y., Park, E.: An adoption model for virtual reality games: the roles of presence and enjoyment. Telematics Inform. **42**, 1–9 (2019)

Katz, E., Blumler, J.G., Gurevitch, M.: Uses Gratifications Res. **37**(4), 509–523 (1973)

Leung, L.: Generational differences in content generation in social media: the roles of the gratifications sought and of narcissism. Comput. Hum. Behav. **29**(3), 997–1006 (2013)

Leung, L., Wei, R.: More than just talk on the move: uses and gratifications of the cellular phone. J. Mass Commun. Quart. **77**(2), 308–320 (2000)

Luo, C., Li, H., Luo, X., Cui, X.: Exploring the effects of sense of membership on information sharing virtual communities. J. Electron. Commer. Res. **24**(2), 107–126 (2023)

Morotti, E., Stacchio, L., Donatiello, L., Roccetti, M., Tarabelli, J., Marfia, G.: Exploiting fashion x-commerce through the empowerment of voice in the fashion virtual reality arena: Integrating voice assistant and virtual reality technologies for fashion communication. Virtual Real. 1–14 (2021)

Nohutlu, Z.D., Englis, B.G., Groen, A.J., Constantinides, E.: Innovating with the customer: co-creation motives in online communities. Int. J. Electron. Commer. **27**(4), 523–557 (2023)

Oagaz, H., Schoun, B., Choi, M.-H.: Real-time posture feedback for effective motor learning in table tennis in virtual reality. Int. J. Hum. Comput. Stud. **158**, 1–12 (2022)

Rather, R.A., Hollebeek, L.D., Loureiro, S.M.C., Khan, I., Hasan, R.: Exploring tourists' virtual reality-based brand engagement: A uses-and-gratifications perspective. J. Travel Res. 1–19 (2023)

Seong, B.-H., Hong, C.-Y.: Decision making in virtual reality sports games ex-plained via the lens of extended planned behavior theory. Int. J. Environ. Res. Public Health **20**(1), 1–18 (2022)

Stafford, T.F., Stafford, M.R.: Identifying motivations for the use of commercial Web sites. Inf. Resour. Manag. J. **14**(1), 1–9 (2001)

Tom Dieck, M. C., Cranmer, E., Prim, A., Bamford, D.: Can augmented reality (AR) applications enhance students' experiences? Gratifications, engagement and learning styles. Inf. Technol. People 1–41 (2023)

Westmattelmann, D., Grotenhermen, J.-G., Sprenger, M., Rand, W., Schewe, G.: Apart we ride together: the motivations behind users of mixed-reality sports. J. Bus. Res. **134**, 316–328 (2021)

Zhu, S., Hu, W., Li, W., Dong, Y.: Virtual agents in immersive virtual reality environments: Impact of humanoid avatars and output modalities on shopping experience. Int. J. Hum.–Comput. Interact. 1–23 (2023)

Research on the Influence Mechanism of Privacy Concerns on Online Behavioral Advertising Acceptance

Yixuan Yao and Li Li[(✉)]

School of Economics and Management, Nanjing University of Science and Technology,
Nanjing 210094, China
lily691111@126.com

Abstract. Online behavioral advertising is a product of the combination of Internet advertising and big data technology, which has become the main means of advertising and marketing nowadays with its unique advantages such as accurate targeting, but at the same time, it has also triggered people's concern about information privacy and security. In order to study the influence mechanism of users' privacy concern level on the acceptance of online behavioral advertisements, this study collects data through questionnaire survey method, empirically analyzes and explores the causal complexity of the influence mechanism of privacy concern and advertisement acceptance by using the Structural Equation Modeling (SEM) and fsQCA methods. mechanism. The results of the study show that: (1) privacy concern has a direct positive effect on perceived risk; perceived risk, perceived gain and perceived ad usefulness jointly act on user attitudes to influence online behavioral ad acceptance, in which perceived gain plays a partially intermediary role; Subjective norms directly influence perceived usefulness; privacy invasion experience plays a moderating role between perceived usefulness and behavioral willingness; (2) the driving paths of ad acceptance can be classified into comprehensive-driven, revenue-driven, and effect-driven. The findings of the study help e-commerce enterprises and platforms to rationally optimize their advertising strategies, and provide theoretical and practical insights into how to effectively improve users' attitudes and willingness to use online behavioral advertisements.

Keywords: Privacy Concerns · Online Behavioral Advertising · Structural Equation Modeling · fsQCA

1 Introduction

Emerging communication technology has revolutionized advertising. Big data analytics notably propels Online Behavior Advertising (OBA)—now a dominant advertising tool [1]. OBA relies on clandestine tracking of digital footprints for user insights [2], leading to concerns about privacy. This brought about Privacy Concern, a measure of consumer unease towards personal data handling [3]. In China, internet and OBA usage surges, paralleled by increased privacy and data security issues. Research on the impact of privacy concerns on OBA acceptance is, however, lacking, indicating an important area for investigation. Users' perceptions of online behavioral ads violating privacy can result in negative attitudes, brand avoidance, and redressive behavior. Tucker [4] found that when users perceive personal data control, they respond more positively to ads. Zhao Jiang [5] demonstrated, based on 258 empirical data samples, that awareness of potential privacy risk leads to negative attitudes towards ads and advertisers, directly influencing user demands, willingness, and leading to reluctance in ad engagement, resistance, and avoidance [6].

However, existing studies, both globally and domestically, oversimplify the interactive relationship of model variables, ignoring mediators and moderators. Addressing this oversight, this paper utilizes the Technology Acceptance Model (TAM), introducing subjective norms as an independent variable, perceived risk as mediator, and privacy invasion experience as moderator. This adds complexity to the model and corrects the overlooked influencers. It will construct an innovative, China-contextual theoretical model, overcoming gaps in the domestic privacy concern scale. Meanwhile, in order to reveal the multiple concurrent causal relationships between the variables and their asymmetrical effects on overall ad acceptance, as well as the multiple equivalent scenarios that lead to a high willingness to click on ads, Structural Equation Modeling (SEM) and fsQCA methods were used to deepen the relationship between privacy issues and ad acceptance.

2   Research Hypotheses and Modeling

2.1   Subjective Norms

Fishbein and Ajzen introduced the concept of subjective norms in the Theory of Reasoned Action (TRA), defining them as the degree of pressure an individual perceives on an important reference person to agree or disagree with his or her behavior when he or she performs a certain behavior [7]. Combined with the object of this study, this paper defines subjective norms as the influence of people who are important to individuals when they are exposed to online behavioral advertisements. Davis supplemented and improved the Technology Acceptance Model (TAM) by proposing the TAM2 model in 2000 and confirmed that subjective norms will positively influence behavioral intentions and perceived usefulness [8]. Accordingly, this study proposes the following hypotheses.

H1: Subjective norms will positively influence perceived ad usefulness.

2.2   Privacy Concerns

Online behavioral advertising's effectiveness is intrinsically linked to user data processing. User privacy concerns, correlating positively with perceived risk, surge when personal information is used, thus impacting potential ad benefits [9-11]. Safety concerns around personal privacy while interacting with online behavior-based advertisements further inflate these risks. Accordingly, the following hypotheses are proposed in this study.

H2: Privacy concerns will positively affect perceived risk.
H3: Privacy concerns will negatively affect perceived benefits.

2.3 Perceived Risk, Perceived Benefit and User Attitudes

Building on social exchange and privacy computing theories, this paper defines 'perceived benefit' in online behavioral advertising as a user's evaluation of potential positives, such as efficient search, personalized information, and satisfaction from tailored services [12]. 'Perceived risk' encompasses concerns over misuse of private data for unfair pricing or unauthorized third-party access, negatively impacting users' assessments of potential privacy-related losses.

Despite individual differences and attitudes towards online behavioral advertising, users generally follow a "benefit maximization" principle. This entails assessing perceived risks and benefits, with an inverse relationship existing between them, thus affecting their actions. These form our study's hypotheses.

H4: Perceived risk will negatively affect users' attitudes toward online behavioral advertising.
H5: Perceived benefits will positively influence users' attitudes toward online behavioral advertising.
H6: Perceived risk will negatively affect perceived benefits.

2.4 Technology Acceptance Model

This study utilizes the technology acceptance model to analyze users' approach and intentions towards online behavioral advertising [13]. Users' attitudes and perceived ad utility positively influence behavioral intent, which subsequently leads to system usage. Ad utility pertains to the improvement in search and shopping efficiency, while attitude reflects users' consistent psychological tendency towards such ads. This lays the foundation for our hypothesis.

H7: Perceived ad usefulness will positively influence user attitudes.
H8: Perceived ad usefulness will positively influence users' behavioral intentions.
H9: User attitudes will positively influence behavioral intentions.
Perceived ad usefulness enhances users' perceived benefits, signaling potential rewards from online behavior-based ads. Accordingly, the following hypotheses are proposed.
H10: Perceived ad usefulness will positively affect perceived benefits.

2.5 Mediating Effects of Perceived Benefits and Perceived Risks

When users have a high level of privacy concern, they will pay extra attention to the risks they may face in the process and reduce their perceived benefits from online behavioral advertising, and at the same time, a high level of privacy concern will also directly reduce users' perceived benefits.In addition, perceived benefits can somewhat weaken the negative effect of perceived risk on user attitudes and enhance the positive effect of perceived ad usefulness on user attitudes. Accordingly, the following hypotheses are proposed.

H11: Perceived risk partially mediates the effect of privacy concerns on perceived benefits.
H12: Perceived benefits partially mediate the effect of perceived risk on user attitudes.
H13: Perceived gain partially mediates the effect of perceived ad usefulness on user attitudes.

2.6   The Moderating Role of Experiences of Privacy Violations

Individuals' past experiences will have an impact on their values and behavioral norms, which in turn will influence their behavior [14]. Users' previous negative privacy experiences (e.g., identity theft, financial loss, etc.) can lead to an elevated level of concern with privacy issues. It has been shown that information privacy concern acts as a moderating variable between perceived usefulness and user intention to use [15, 16]. Accordingly, the following hypotheses are proposed.

H14: Privacy violation experiences have a significant moderating role in the effect of perceived ad usefulness on behavioral intentions.

2.7   Theoretical Modeling

Based on the above assumptions, the research model is shown in Fig. 1.

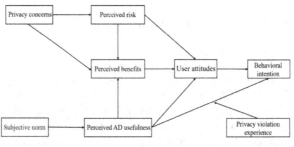

Fig. 1. Study model

3   Methodology

3.1   Measurements

The main part of the survey questionnaire in this study measured users' privacy experiences, privacy concerns, perceived trust, perceived risk, perceived benefit, perceived usefulness, attitudes toward online behavioral advertising, and behavioral intentions, which were categorized using a seven-point Likert scale that classified users' approval of the question items as 1-strongly disagree, 2-comparatively disagree, 3-somewhat disagree, 4-undecided, 5-somewhat Agree, 6- Comparatively Agree, and 7- Strongly Agree.

The sources of the variables in this study are shown in Table 1:

3.2   Data Collection

This study employed both online and offline methods for questionnaire distribution. Online platforms such as social media and shopping groups were utilized alongside physical deployment in a bustling Nanjing subway station. Of the 437 collected responses,

Table 1. Sources of research variables

Variable	Mark	Source	Variable	Mark	Source
Privacy concerns (Collection, Control, Awareness, Policy effectiveness)	PC(CL, CT, AW, PE)	Malhotra (2004) Smith et al. (1996) Hong et al. (2013)	Subjective norm	SN	Park J et al. (2014) Taylor & Todd (1995)
Perceived risk	PR	Lim (2003)	User attitude	ATT	Davis (1989) Gao et al. (2013)
Perceived benefit	PB	Bleier (2015) Smith (2011)	Behavioral intention	BI	Ajzen & Fishbein (1975)
Perceived AD usefulness	PAU	Davis (1989)			

382 were online and 55 were paper-based. Questionnaires with inconsistent answers (e.g., reverse question BI5) and those completed in under 100 s were excluded. Post data cleansing, 380 valid responses were used for the empirical study, presenting an 86.9% validity rate.

3.3 Descriptive Statistics

Our study's descriptive statistics reveal a female-majority participation with 36.84% and 63.15% for males and females respectively. Predominant age bracket was 18–30 years at 83.9%. As for education, 45.53% had bachelor's degrees while 50% had master's degrees. 97.37% of the sample frequently interact with online behavioral ads, noting broad experience with e-commerce and online shopping. These insights reflect their psychological responses to such ads, affirming data credibility.

4 Results

4.1 SEM Results

Reliability and Validity Analysis. This study used SPSS 21.0 to conduct factor analysis on the model, which validated the model with KMO value of 0.829 and Bartlett's test's p-value being less than 0.001. Table 2 exhibits the fitness parameters, indicating the model's applicability and the questionnaire's appropriateness.

The results of the reliability and validity tests are shown in Table 3, where the Cronbach's α for most of the variables reached 0.9, thus the questionnaire sample has good reliability. The standardized factor loadings of the 39 indicator variables on their corresponding latent variable dimensions were all above 0.578 (greater than 0.5); the average variance extracted (AVE) for the seven latent variables (AVE) were all greater

Table 2. Model fitting results

Norm	χ^2/df	RMSEA	GFI	AGFI	CFI	IFI	TLI
Model value	1.900	0.049	0.848	0.825	0.946	0.947	0.942
Reference standard	<3	<0.08	>0.8	>0.8	>0.9	>0.9	>0.9

Table 3. Results of reliability and validity tests

Variable		Cronbach's Alpha		CR	AVE
Privacy concerns	Collection	0.749	0.906	0.9297	0.5251
	Control	0.812			
	Awareness	0.757			
	Policy effectiveness	0.755			
Perceived risk		0.825		0.8522	0.542
Perceived benefits		0.909		0.9045	0.6558
Perceived AD usefulness		0.948		0.9165	0.7855
Subjective norm		0.924		0.9453	0.7759
User attitude		0.936		0.9284	0.7219
Behavioral intention		0.939		0.9367	0.7876

than 0.5 and the combined reliability (CR) were all greater than 0.8, thus the measurement model has good convergent validity.

As shown in Table 4, the value of the square root of AVE for each latent variable is higher than the absolute value of the correlation coefficient between that variable and the other latent variables, and the measurement model has good discriminant validity.

Table 4. Result of discriminative validity tests

	PC	PR	PB	SN	PAU	ATT	BI
PC	**0.930**						
PR	0.519	**0.852**					
PB	−0.272	−0.299	**0.905**				
SN	−0.198	−0.196	0.749	**0.917**			
PAU	−0.012	0.055	0.36	0.426	**0.945**		
ATT	−0.17	−0.315	0.695	0.717	0.354	**0.928**	
BI	−0.223	−0.296	0.641	0.7	0.309	0.806	**0.937**

Furthermore, the problem of multicollinearity among the variables was tested by calculating the variance inflation factor (VIF). The result shows that the VIF ranges from 1. 08 to 2.43 which are less than 5.

Therefore, there is no multicollinearity among the independent variables. Taken together, the test results show that the measurement model has a good fit and good reliability and validity, so it is possible to conduct structural equation modeling based on the sample data as well as this measurement model to test the paths of the potential variables as well as the mediating and moderating effects.

Hypothesis Testing. In order to further analyze whether the assumptions of the path relationships in the theoretical model of the mechanism of influence of privacy concerns on the acceptance of online behavioral advertisements are valid, this paper uses AMOS 21.0 for structural equation modeling.

Table 5. Results of path coefficient

Hypothesis	Path	Coefficient	S.E	C.R	P-value	Result
H1	SN→ PAU	0.433	0.056	8.071	***	Support
H2	PC → PR	0.516	0.106	8.388	***	Support
H3	PC → PB	0.119	0.078	−1.409	0.159	Not Support
H4	PR → ATT	−0.141	0.056	−3.306	***	Support
H5	PB → ATT	0.311	0.062	4.689	***	Support
H6	PR → PB	−0.137	0.071	−2.725	0.006	Support
H7	PAU → ATT	0.471	0.064	7.077	***	Support
H8	PAU → BI	0.25	0.058	4.711	***	Support
H9	ATT → BI	0.626	0.062	11.421	***	Support
H10	PAU → PB	0.732	0.053	14.132	***	Support

According to Table 5, in the theoretical model constructed in this study, all the hypotheses except privacy concern → perceived benefit are verified, and the user's level of privacy concern is more likely to directly affect the assessment of the associated risks than the consideration of potential benefits.

We tested if perceived risk and return mediate our model using AMOS's Bootstrap method with a 95% confidence interval across 2,000 samples. Results are in Table 6.

The results show that none of the upper and lower bounds of the 95% confidence intervals in the above paths contain 0. Therefore, the three mediation effects of perceived benefits and user attitudes are all significant, and the mediation effect is verified.

In the theoretical model constructed for this study, privacy invasion experiences moderated the effect of perceived ad usefulness on the inter-intention of user behavior. Therefore, this study chose to use Hayes' (2013) SPSS macro program PROCESS (Model 5) to conduct a moderated mediation effect test, the results of which are shown in Table 7 and Fig. 2.

Table 6. Standardized bootstrap mediation effects tests

Path	Efficiency value	SE	Percentile 95% CI			Result
			Lower	Upper	P	
PR → PB → ATT	−0.043	0.019	−0.086	−0.011	0.009	Support
PAU → PB → ATT	0.228	0.063	0.113	0.355	0.001	Support
PAU → ATT → BI	0.295	0.067	0.169	0.436	0.001	Support

Table 7. Moderating effects tests

	Behavioral intention			
	Coefficient	SE	t-value	p-value
Constant	0.2911	0.4732	0.6153	0.5387
PAU	0.4044	0.1088	3.7155	0.0002
ATT	0.4573	0.0397	11.5256	0.0000
PPIR	0.7630	0.3713	2.0551	0.0406
PAU x PPIE	−0.1728	0.0823	−2.1008	0.0363
R-sq	0.248			
F	41.251			

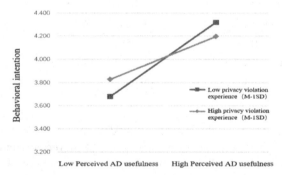

Fig. 2. Moderating role of privacy violation experiences in the relationship between perceived ad usefulness and behavioral intention

The results show that while perceived ad usefulness x privacy invasion experience has a significant effect on the dependent variable behavioral intention (p = 0.0363 < 0.05). Therefore, privacy invasion experience has a moderating role in the mediation model consisting of perceived ad usefulness, user attitude, and behavioral intention, moderating the path of perceived ad usefulness → behavioral intention.

4.2 fsQCA Results

Data Calibration and Necessity Analysis. In this paper, user's behavioral intention towards online behavioral advertisements is taken as the outcome variable and other variables are taken as the antecedent variables and the data is calibrated according to Ragin C C's calibration methods to improve the interpretability of the results.

After data calibration, the fsQCA software was used post-data calibration for analyzing single antecedent variables, revealing no necessity for the outcome variable, with all consistencies less than 0.9. No singular antecedent could induce the outcome variable, prompting further analysis on grouping paths for online ad acceptance.

fsQCA Results Regarding Consumers' Willingness to Click on Ads. In this paper, fsQCA software is used to analyze the conditional grouping that generates the willingness to click on online behavioral advertisements, as shown in the table, the combinatorial consistency is 0.81, which is higher than the set threshold; the coverage rate is 0.82, which means that it covers 82% of the samples, and it has a high explanatory power for the outcome variables.

Table 8 shows that the results of the analysis of the grouping that generates the willingness to click on online behavioral advertisements can be categorized into three patterns: integrated-driven, revenue-driven, and effect-driven. The synthesis-driven pattern is presented by histogram H1, with low privacy concern, high perceived gain, and high perceived ad usefulness as the core conditions. Regardless of how the perceived risk, subjective norms and user attitudes change, as long as the user has low privacy concerns and perceives that online behavioral advertisements are beneficial to him/her, he/she is likely to generate a willingness to click on the advertisements. The path also corroborates the important role that privacy concerns play in the mechanism of influence on users' acceptance of online behavioral advertisements; the revenue-driven model is presented by the grouping states H2a and H2b, with high perceived revenue and high user attitudes as the core conditions, and low privacy concerns and high subjective norms as the auxiliary conditions triggering advertisements willingness to click on the advertisements, which is mainly due to the user's The main reason is that users expect to reap potential benefits from online behavioral ads or receive influence from others; the effect-driven model is represented by the groupings H3a and H3b, with high perceived ad usefulness and high user attitudes as the core conditions, and the main motivation is that users believe online behavioral ads can help to improve the efficiency of searching or shopping.

The analysis shows that three of the five grouping paths have low privacy concern as a core or auxiliary condition to trigger users' willingness to click on online behavioral advertisements, and the coverage is high, which confirms the previous conclusion that privacy concern has a significant effect on the acceptance of online behavioral advertisements.

fsQCA Results Regarding Consumers' Unwillingness to Click on Ads. At the same time, this study examines factors influencing users' non-clicking inclinations towards ads. Four primary scenarios revealed are: (1) NH1, with low perceived benefit and negative user attitude towards ads, users gain no willingness to click, regardless of privacy concerns. (2) NH2 and NH3 denote high perceived risks coupled with low perceived

Table 8. Configurations leading to consumers' willingness to click on ads

Casual Condition	Solution				
	H1	H2a	H2b	H3a	H3b
PC	⊗	⊗			⊗
PR			•	•	⊗
PB	•	•	•		
PAU	•			•	•
SN			•	•	
ATT		•	•	•	•
Consistency	0.86	0.87	0.93	0.92	0.89
Raw coverage	0.66	0.68	0.43	0.44	0.58
Unique coverage	0.03	0.03	0.01	0.02	0.02
Solution Consistency			0.81		
Solution Coverage			0.82		

benefits and usefulness, discouraging ad clicking. (3) NH4 suggests high privacy concerns along with low benefit and usefulness perception discourage ad engagement, hence elevating advertising content requirements.

Robustness Test. The robustness of fsQCA, examined via adjustments to calibration and consistency thresholds as well as case frequencies, validates this study. Raising the consistency threshold from 0.8 to 0.85 and 0.9 doesn't significantly alter the intermediate and simple solutions' consistency and coverage, affirming the robustness of our findings.

5 Discussion and Implications

5.1 Conclusions of the Study

This study explores the influence of users' privacy concerns on online behavioral advertisement acceptance using questionnaires and integrating relevant theories with the TAM model. The results found that (1) the higher the level of privacy concern of users, the more they will pay extra attention to their privacy leakage and other related risks in the process of contacting online behavioral advertisements. (2) Perceived risk and perceived usefulness of advertisements have a direct impact on perceived benefits, and all three play a role in users' attitudes and have an impact on the acceptance of online behavioral advertisements, with perceived benefits playing a partly intermediary role, that is to say, perceived risk plays a direct role in the users' attitudes towards online behavioral advertisements, and is also affected by the perceived benefits, and the negative impact is weakened accordingly if the perceived benefits are high. diminishes accordingly if the perceived benefit is high. Similarly, perceived ad usefulness directly contributes to user attitudes in a positive way, and further strengthens this positive contribution by affecting the level of perceived benefits. (3) Subjective norms have a direct impact on the perceived usefulness of ads. If people around them have a positive attitude towards online behavioral ads or use them frequently, then users themselves will recognize the extent to which online behavioral ads improve the efficiency of searching or shopping. (4) The hypothesis of the moderating role of privacy invasion experience between perceived ad usefulness and behavioral intention was tested. This suggests that privacy invasion experiences inhibit the extent to which perceived advertising usefulness contributes to behavioral intentions. (5) The grouping paths that drive ad acceptance can be categorized as integrated, revenue-driven, and effect-driven.

5.2 Managerial Implications

Enterprises need to explicitly inform users about their data tracking practices, collection purposes, and retention scope and period. Post-collection, information needs ethical protection and can't be sold for profit. Ad strategies should be enhanced to boost ad usefulness perception and acceptance.

Regulators need to amplify personal info regulations such as business regulations on personal data utilization and collection, establishing registration for e-commerce operators, and enhancing data security controls. Online platforms involved in privacy protection need regulation, as does supervision of e-commerce platforms, network operators, and IT service providers. An industry self-regulation mechanism regulating data collection, application processes, and method use needs to be developed to bolster industry self-regulation..

5.3 Limitations and Future Research Directions

In addition, there are some limitations of this study. The distribution of educational attainment in the final sample questionnaire results of this study is more concentrated, in which 95.5% of the samples have bachelor's degree or above. Therefore the representativeness of the sample is limited, and the lack of representativeness of the sample and the concentration of the distribution may have a certain impact on the results of the study and the scope of application of the study.

References

1. Varnali, K.: Online behavioral advertising: an integrative review. J. Mark. Commun. **27**, 93–114 (2019)
2. Jiang, Y., Zhang, H., Jia, J., et al.: Research on behavioral targeted advertising (OBA) and consumer privacy concerns in the context of big data. Manag. World, 182–183 (2015).

3. Smith, J.H.: Milberg: information privacy: measuring individuals' concerns about organizational practices. MIS Quart. **20**(2), 167–196 (1996)
4. Tucker, C.: Social networks, personalized advertising, and privacy controls. Soc. Sci. Electron. Publ. **51**(5), 546–562 (2013)
5. Zhao, J., He, S.: Mechanism of consumer privacy attitude on behavioral intention in targeted advertising. J. Syst. Manag. **30**(2), 373–383 (2021)
6. Mpinganjira, M., Maduku, D.K.: Ethics of mobile behavioral advertising: antecedents and outcomes of perceived ethical value of advertised brands. J. Bus. Res. **95**, 464–478 (2019)
7. Fishbein, M.: A theory of reasoned action: some applications and implications. Nebraska Sympos. Motivat. **27**, 65 (1980)
8. Venkatesh, V., Davis, F.D.: A theoretical extension of the technology acceptance model: four longitudinal field studies. INFORMS (2000).
9. Youn, S.: Determinants of online privacy concern and its influence on privacy protection behaviors among young adolescents. J. Consumer Affairs **43**(3)+ (2009)
10. Liao, C., Liu, C.C., Chen, K.: Examining the impact of privacy, trust and risk perceptions beyond monetary transactions: an integrated model. Electron. Comm. Res. Appl. **10**(6), 702–715 (2011)
11. Malhotra, N.K., Kim, S.S., Agarwal, J.: Internet users' information privacy concerns (IUIPC): the construct, the scale, and a causal model. Inf. Syst. Res. **15**(4), 336–355 (2004)
12. Smith, J.H.: Dinev: information privacy research: an interdisciplinary review. MIS Quart. **35**, 989 (2011)
13. Davis, F.D.: Perceived usefulness, perceived ease of use, and user acceptance of information technology. MIS Quart. **13**(3), 319–340 (1989)
14. Lippert, S.K., Forman, H.: Utilization of information technology: examining cognitive and experiential factors of post-adoption behavior. IEEE Trans. Eng. Manag. **52**(3), 363–381 (2005)
15. Zhang, H., Yi, K., Tang, Z.: The impact of information privacy concerns on users' use of social media - a contextual analysis of the "privacy debunking" in China. J. Intell. **35**(1), 161–166 (2016)
16. Tan, X., Qin, L., Kim, Y., Hsu, J.: Impact of privacy concern in social networking web sites. Internet Res. **22**(2), 211–233 (2012)

Task Delegation from AI to Humans: The Impact of AI Transparency on Human Performance

Yunran Wang[1], Yiwei Jiang[1], Jian Tang[1(✉)], and Xinxue Zhou[2]

[1] School of Information, Central University of Finance and Economics, Beijing, China
`jiantang@cufe.edu.cn`
[2] School of Business, Guangxi University, Nanning, China

Abstract. This study examines the effects of AI transparency in AI-human task delegation. According to the principal-agent theory (PAT), increasing transparency can help address the problem of hidden action. Through a between-subjects experiment with three conditions (AI advantage information, AI function information, vs. no information), we explore the impact of AI transparency on human task performance and consider the mediating effect of human epistemic uncertainty and AI trust. Results show that AI function information enhances accuracy, while AI advantage information encourages more task completion. Epistemic uncertainty fully mediates the relationship between transparency and task performance (both accuracy and image number), while AI trust only mediates the effect on image number. The results have implications for the future work of the design of AI transparency in human-AI collaboration.

Keywords: AI-human delegation · agent transparency · human-AI collaboration · task performance · principal-agent theory

1 Introduction

The widespread use of Artificial Intelligence (AI) and the adoption of AI-based Information Systems (AI-based IS) are fundamentally changing the way humans live and work. AI exhibits features like efficiency, accuracy, and reliability, and in some domains (e.g., financial sectors), its capabilities approach or even surpass human levels. Humans, on the other hand, have the advantage of adapting quickly to new situations by using their metaknowledge. AI-human collaboration can leverage their respective strengths and achieve a synergy effect. In previous human-AI collaborations, AI often plays the role of assistant or parallel working partner [1]. The increasingly autonomous AI artifacts can guide human actions and even change the task delegation directions. Task delegation from AI to humans becomes an emerging and productive method of AI-human collaboration, because compared to humans, AI can better assess existing knowledge and execute delegation, leading to higher collaborative performance [2]. Delegation involves one party transferring the right and responsibility to execute a task to another party [3].

In real life, many fields (e.g., image classification, content auditing, language translation) have adopted AI for its advantages, but there are always cases in which AI cannot complete tasks and delegate them to humans. For instance, in image classification tasks in scientific crowdsourcing, AI-human delegation allows the AI to quickly recognize images, and when it comes to rarer species, tasks will be delegated to human experts to categorize to maximize efficiency and accuracy. Existing research primarily focuses on scenarios where humans delegate tasks to AI, exploring factors influencing the willingness to delegate tasks, such as attitudes towards AI, trust, perceived usability, etc. [4]. Limited research has investigated AI delegating tasks to humans [5].

AI transparency is a key information design element in AI-human delegation. When AI delegates tasks to humans, humans often do not know the reasons and principles of AI-human delegation decisions. The lack of information can result in negative outcomes, such as losing human attention and triggering negative emotions, which harm the overall performance of human-AI collaboration [6]. Therefore, when AI delegates tasks to humans, how to design transparency of AI information is of great importance. Using principal-agent theory (PAT) as a theoretical lens, this study investigates the effects of AI transparency on human task performance in the context of AI-human delegation. Specifically, this study addresses the following research questions: (1) Does AI transparency affect human task performance in AI-human delegation? (2) What are the underlying mechanisms?

2 Literature Review

2.1 Human-AI Collaboration and Task Delegation

The collaboration between humans and AI can be initiated in many ways. One of the most common forms is the AI taking the role of providing suggestions and support in collaboration, and humans have the right to make the final decision. How to design AI to enhance human decision-making has been a concern of previous research. Wang and Yin [7] assessed the effectiveness of four common explanatory models on different prediction tasks from the perspective of AI interpretability, revealing significant differences in the impact of AI interpretability on decision-making among individuals with different levels of professional knowledge. Besides the AI-assisted decision-making pattern, delegation initiated by the AI model has attracted increasing research interest. Fügener et al. [2] discussed human-AI collaboration on the task instance level, and they suggested that humans and AI have complementary knowledge. They examined four human-AI collaboration patterns: human alone, AI alone, human delegating to AI, and AI delegating to humans. The research found that humans and AI working together will improve combined performance, and the AI-human delegation pattern performs the best.

To sum up, the AI-human delegation pattern shows advantages in improving task performance. Past studies mainly focused on exploring the influences of this pattern on human trust, satisfaction, and task performance. Limited research paid attention to enhancing human performance by designing AI transparency [5].

2.2 Agent Transparency in Human-AI Collaboration

Agent transparency refers to the ability of the information systems that enable humans to "understand the intent, performance, plans, and reasoning processes of intelligent agents" (p.2) [8]. In the context of human-AI collaboration, agent transparency specifically refers to AI providing information through interactive interfaces to support collaboration between humans and AI, therefore, this research refers to it as AI transparency.

Previous research has focused on the design and implementation of transparency, demonstrating its impact on trust, epistemic uncertainty, perceived control, and task performance. Mercado et al. [9] found that operators' trust and perceived usability increased when presenting basic, logical, and predictive information. Kizilcec (2016) discovered that providing either too much or too little transparency will negatively affect trust. Liu [10] manipulated AI's explanation types as transparency and found that transparency can reduce uncertainty and enhance trust, but the effect varies with AI types. Past studies have investigated the effects of transparency on task performance and found that it could improve humans' decision accuracy. For instance, compared to only displaying basic information, algorithms have a higher hit rate when they display both basic and logical information [11].

In general, previous research has investigated different types of AI transparency and their effects on human perceptions and performance. However, scholars have not reached a conclusion about what kind of information should be presented in the AI-human delegation condition to enhance collaboration.

2.3 Principal-Agent Theory

Principal-agent theory (PAT) is used to deal with cooperation and conflicts between agentic entities working together. There are two contractual parties: the principal and the agent. The principal delegates decision-making authority to the agent, who acts on behalf of the principal. However, in the contractual relationship, neither is fully aware of the other's motives and behavior, and tends to maximize their own interests. Hence, phenomena of information asymmetry and conflicts of interest often arise, leading to two significant problems in principal-agent relationships: hidden information and hidden action. Hidden information arises pre-contractually and describes the principal's difficulty in determining whether an agent has the qualities and skills to perform a task in their interest, while hidden action happens post-contractually and refers to the agent's activities that may be in their own but not the principal's interest [12].

While principal-agent theory is traditionally applied to situations involving humans on both sides, recent research has expanded it to examine the relationships between humans and AI. Some studies focus on the relationship that humans as the principal and AI as the agent. Candrian and Scherer [4] explored the impact of AI process transparency and the social risk premium on humans' willingness to delegate tasks to AI. Recently, several studies have started exploring AI as the principal and delegate tasks to humans and proved that hidden information and hidden action problems are still in AI-human delegation relationships [13]. In the AI-human delegation context, hidden information refers to AI lacking understanding of the situation and the human agents, leading to suboptimal delegation. Hidden actions refer to the possibility that humans may not follow AI's suggestions and expectations when executing tasks. Furthermore, Guggenberger et al. [13] pointed out that humans' attitudes toward AI as the principal should also be considered as a new perspective that may lead to principal-agent problems, because humans who have a negative attitude toward AI may refuse to collaborate with it. In general, in the AI-human delegation context, information asymmetry, conflicts of interest, and human attitudes toward AI are recognized as three causes of hidden information and action.

3 Hypotheses Development

In the AI-human delegation, the AI has been extensively trained on big data and pre-set delegation rules based on human information. The way to reduce the hidden information problems may be by enhancing its knowledge about human partners. This research is not concerned with improving AI's ability (e.g., algorithm optimization, adaptive learning), hence, the hidden information problems are not addressed currently. We tend to alleviate human agents' hidden actions to improve their performance in the AI-human delegation context. According to Guggenberger et al. [13], information asymmetry, conflicts of interest, and human attitudes toward AI may lead to humans' hidden actions in the context of AI-human delegation. In most human-AI collaborations, the most critical problem is the lack of AI-related information and humans have no information about AI mechanisms and performance. This will cause their distrust and further lead to bad performance. Therefore, designing AI transparency can alleviate the information asymmetry problems by reducing humans' epistemic uncertainty toward AI. Furthermore, when humans have more information about AI, they may adjust their attitudes and build trust toward the AI principal. Through influences on human perception of the AI, it will further impact their task performance. We also included common control variables, such as gender, age, education, AI experience, and task experience. Besides, we added human prior attitudes toward AI as a control variable for it is an important factor that needs to be considered in the AI-human delegation pattern. Figure 1 illustrates our theoretical framework, and we will detail our reasoning below.

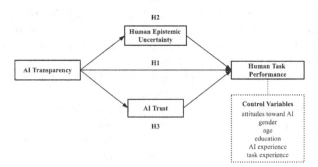

Fig. 1. Research model.

3.1 Effects of AI Transparency on Human Task Performance

Task performance refers to the effectiveness of people in completing their core work or responsibility [14]. In human-AI collaboration, the measurement of human task performance is often related to the accuracy [2]. Before tasks are delegated, humans often want to know information about the AI, such as its goal, operating process, and advantage. Hence, many researchers tried to design different levels of AI transparency to investigate human performance and found that human task performance is highly related to the current situation and transparency [11]. Previous research also proves that providing AI transparency will increase the ability of humans to observe and perform tasks [4]. Therefore, we suppose that:

H1: AI transparency will positively influence human task performance.

3.2 The Mediating Effect of Human Epistemic Uncertainty

The term uncertainty derives from the field of statistics, and is applied to examine risk quantification, system evaluation, etc. Uncertainty can be divided into two types: (1) aleatoric uncertainty, also named irreducible uncertainty, and (2) epistemic uncertainty, also known as reducible uncertainty, subjective uncertainty, and knowledge uncertainty. Among them, only epistemic uncertainty can be reduced by providing more information and knowledge. In the AI-human delegation condition, humans always hold a high level of epistemic uncertainty toward the AI partner because they have no information about it. Previous research suggests that explanatory knowledge is the most direct way to reduce epistemic uncertainty [15]. In this study, we anticipate that providing humans with AI transparency will make them know more about the AI principal, and then decrease their epistemic uncertainty toward it. Furthermore, epistemic uncertainty is proven to be associated with reduced performance. When humans have a high epistemic uncertainty toward the AI partner, they may spend more time understanding AI's behavior and distract their attention from performing tasks. They may even reject AI's delegation because they don't know how to collaborate with AI. In this study, we propose that when providing AI transparency, humans' epistemic uncertainty toward AI decreases, they may be more willing to collaborate with AI and their performance on tasks will increase accordingly. Hence, we propose the following:

H2: Human epistemic uncertainty mediates the relationship between AI transparency and human task performance.

3.3 The Mediating Effect of AI Trust

Trust is the willingness of a party to be vulnerable to the actions of another party in the expectation that the other will perform a particular action important to the trustor [16]. In the AI-human delegation condition, trust refers to the extent to which humans are confident in and willing to act according to the delegation decisions of the AI. Hence, in this study, we intend to examine humans' trust in AI (i.e., AI trust). Previous research generally agrees that trust and transparency are closely linked. Kizilcec [17] pointed out that the design of agent transparency is important to the user experience, and it is crucial to balance the level of transparency to enhance the trust of users. Furthermore, trust has been a crucial antecedent to task performance in human-AI collaboration research. Previous research suggests that increasing users' trust in AI will lead to better task performance because they believe AI is capable of completing tasks and tend to take their roles in the collaboration [18]. Hence, we anticipate that:

H3: AI trust mediates the relationship between AI transparency and human task performance.

4   Methodology

4.1   Stimulus

This research is embedded in the context of AI delegating image classification tasks to humans. We chose the image classification task for two reasons: 1) it does not need any professional skills or training to make human performance similar to that of AI, as well as the AI and human classification accuracy of images can be calculated, and 2) humans and AI have complementary knowledge and, thus, the potential to reach complementary team performance [2]. Therefore, we believe that image classification is a suitable delegation task. Previous research has not reached a consensus on whether providing AI advantage (e.g., AI's high accuracy and efficiency) and function transparency (e.g., AI model, working process) is beneficial for human task performance [13]. We conducted a between-subject experiment has three conditions (AI advantage information vs. AI function information vs. no information).

Before the formal experiment, we conducted a pilot study to assess manipulations and questionnaires. We recruited 55 participants from Credamo, a Chinese company similar to Qualtrics in the United States. Based on the results, we improved our experiment procedures and revised the questionnaires.

4.2   Procedure

During experiments, participants were first asked to finish the questionnaires about attitudes toward AI and then were guided to the developed AI image classification platform. After finishing the image classification tasks delegated by AI, humans would return to the questionnaire platform to finish the rest of the questions. In the AI image classification platform, participants would receive AI advantage information or function information if they were in AI transparency conditions (see Table 1.), while in the control group, they had no information about the AI partner. Across all conditions, participants would receive task assignments. After reading the information, participants would receive AI-delegated image classification tasks, which we selected according to Fügener et al. [2]. To calculate human image classification accuracy, we required participants to complete 11 image classifications at least, and the remaining 19 image classifications were voluntary. To reinforce the AI-human delegation scenario to participants, we mentioned that 'The AI delegated this image to you for classifying' when the AI delegated the task, as well as inserted pages to show that the AI also classified images itself.

4.3 Measurements

We anticipate that when humans are willing to accept the AI-human delegation, they intend to do more tasks and be more conscientious when accomplishing tasks [2]. Hence, we collected the number (N_{image}) and accuracy ($acc = N_{correct}/N_{image}$) of images that participants classified to reflect participants' task performance. Besides, we measured AI trust, epistemic uncertainty, and attitudes toward AI by adapting mature measurements, and measured with multi-items (1 = strongly disagree; 7 = strongly agree). Four items of AI trust are adapted from Perrig et al. [19], and two items of epistemic uncertainty are adapted from Ferris [20]. Measurements of attitudes toward AI are adapted from the general attitudes toward artificial intelligence scales (GAAIS) [21].

Table 1. Examples of AI transparency treatments.

AI advantage information	AI function information
Hi, I am the AI Classifier on this platform, do you know my **advantages** in image classification?	Hi, I am the AI Classifier on this platform, do you know my **function** of image classification?
1. I use one of the **best-performing** models for image classification	1. I use the **convolutional neural network** model GoogLeNet Inception v3
2. I can differentiate **1000** image categories and can complete the classification at **30 ms/image**	2. I train on millions of known images to extract **classification features**
3. I have an average of **77%** correct classification of images	3. Based on these features, I calculate the **similarity** between the new and the known image to get the classification result

4.4 Manipulation Check

For the AI advantage and function information conditions, participants were asked manipulation check questions after they returned to the questionnaire platform. The statements were 'I saw the AI advantage information' and 'I saw the AI function information', and were measured on a 7-point Likert scale ranging from 1(strongly disagree) to 7 (strongly agree). Using paired-samples T-test, we find that our manipulation was successful both in AI advantage ($M_{adv} = 5.92, M_{fun} = 3.68, t = 11.14, p < 0.001$) and AI function ($M_{adv} = 4.25, M_{fun} = 6.17, t = -11.07, p < 0.001$) groups. For the control group, we asked the same questions as experimental groups but required participants to answer yes or no. Participants passed the manipulation check when they answered the two questions correctly.

4.5 Results

A total of 160 participants were invited to the study on the Credamo. We excluded participants from data analysis if 1) they failed to pass the screening attention check during the study, 2) the duration was too short, or 3) they didn't pass the manipulation

Y. Wang et al.

check. On these grounds, 15 participants were excluded, resulting in 145 valid (N_{adv} = 50, N_{fun} = 48, N_{con} = 47).

The participants consisted of 52.4% females and 47.6% males. The age range of participants was appropriate to the situation in this study. 95.2% of them had a college or higher education. And 94.6% of participants are under 30 years old. In addition, more than 66.2% of participants use AI (e.g., chatbot, ChatGPT) more than four times a week. 89% of participants had not done image classification tasks before, which we assumed that they had average experience with our tasks. Therefore, the respondents' understanding of the questionnaire and the results are convincing.

We analyze the reliability and validity by using SPSS 26 and SmartPLS4.0 (see Table 2.). Firstly, the KMO value is 0.78 and Bartlett's test passed the test at the significance level of 0.001. All Cronbach's alpha and composite reliability (CR) results were above the acceptable value of 0.75. All AVE values were significantly larger than 0.50 and each item was loaded on its designated factors with all items' values being greater than the acceptable value of 0.40, and all HTMT ratios were lower than 0.60. Besides, the variance inflation factors (VIF) of human epistemic uncertainty, AI trust, and attitudes toward AI are all below 3.0, which means that there is no serious multicollinearity problem. Thus, the research model demonstrated satisfactory reliability and validity.

Table 2. Results of discriminant validity, reliability and convergent validity analysis.

	HEU	AT	ATA	AVE	Cronbach's α	CR
HEU	0.850			0.722	0.835	0.840
AT	0.531	0.838		0.703	0.903	0.903
ATA	0.192	−0.033	0.761	0.579	0.782	0.788

Note(s): Numbers on the diagonal are the positive square roots of the average variance extracted (AVE) values; Off-diagonal values are the estimates of inter-correlation between the latent constructs.
HEU = Human Epistemic Uncertainty, AT = AI Trust, ATA = Attitudes toward AI.

To test H1, we first examine the effect of AI transparency (i.e., AI advantage information and AI function information) on human task performance (i.e., number and accuracy of images). Subsequently, we conducted an analysis of variance (ANOVA). The results are shown in Fig. 2. After adding the control variables (i.e., attitudes toward AI, gender, age, education, AI experience, task experience), the results reveal a significant difference between AI transparency and accuracy (M_{adv} = 0.58, M_{fun} = 0.65, M_{con} = 0.55, $F(2, 142)$ = 6.64, p = 0.002) and the image number(M_{adv} = 20.96, M_{fun} = 18.48, M_{con} = 16.89, $F(2, 142)$ = 3.23, p = 0.042). Besides, we find that the accuracy of the AI function information group is significantly higher than the control group (p = 0.001), as well as it is higher than the advantage group (p = 0.053). The image number of the advantage function condition is significantly higher than the control group (p = 0.039). Besides, attitudes toward AI showed no significant impact on task performance. Hence, H1 is supported by the finding that AI function information will positively influence human accuracy and AI advantage information positively impacts the number of images finished.

Based on bootstrapping procedures on Hayes [22]'s mediation test method, we verified the mediating role of AI trust and epistemic uncertainty on task performance using 5000 bootstrap samples. Results are shown in Table 3.. In both advantage and function information groups, it can be found that the indirect effect of epistemic uncertainty excluded zero ($CI_{adv-acc}$: [0.008, 0.105], $CI_{fun-acc}$: [0.010, 0.125], $CI_{adv-imn}$: [0.152, 0.800], $CI_{fun-imn}$: [0.187, 0.948]), and direct effects do not exist. Therefore, epistemic uncertainty fully mediates the relationship between AI transparency and task performance (both accuracy and image number). AI trust has a full mediation effect from AI advantage and function AI transparency to the image number ($CI_{adv-imn}$: [−0.345, −0.003], $CI_{fun-imn}$: [−0.357, −0.006]). Thus, H2 and H3 are supported.

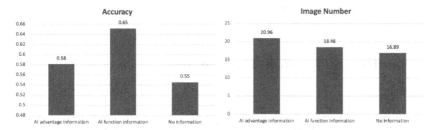

Fig. 2. Effects of AI advantage, function, and no information on accuracy and image number.

Table 3. Results of mediating effect testing.

Path	Direct effects			Indirect effects			
	Effect	LLCI	ULCI	Path	Effect	LLCI	ULCI
ADV → ACC	−0.019	−0.094	0.055	ADV → EU → ACC	**0.0533**	0.008	0.105
				ADV → AT → ACC	0.0004	−0.023	0.021
FUN → ACC	0.043	−0.036	0.123	FUN → EU → ACC	**0.065**	0.010	0.125
				FUN → AT → ACC	0.0004	−0.025	0.025
ADV → IMN	2.431	−1.562	6.424	ADV → EU → IMN	**0.448**	0.152	0.800
				ADV → AT → IMN	**−0.131**	−0.345	−0.003
FUN → IMN	−1.558	−5.808	2.690	FUN → EU → IMN	**0.543**	0.187	0.948
				FUN → AT → IMN	**−0.153**	−0.357	−0.006

*Note(s): Significant mediation effect in **bold**. The baseline is the control group.*
ADV = AI advantage information condition, FUN = AI function information, ACC = accuracy,
IMN = image number.

5   Discussion

The purpose of this study is to examine the design of AI transparency influencing human epistemic uncertainty, AI trust, and task performance. Our empirical results supported the majority of hypotheses.

First, AI transparency positively influences human task performance, and different types of information have different effects on human performance. We find that conveying human the AI function information will increase their image classification accuracy. This could be attributed to the fact that, after reading the information about AI functions, humans can acquire insights about AI classification methods, aiding them in more effectively categorizing images. Besides, humans are willing to do more tasks when they receive the advantages information of AI. This finding coincides with previous research that when humans know the AI task delegation is good and beneficial, the hidden actions will not occur immediately and they tend to collaborate more frequently with AI [13].

Second, AI transparency influences human task performance by influencing AI trust and epistemic uncertainty. Coinciding with past studies, transparency will lower people's epistemic uncertainty toward the AI partner, and enhance trust toward it [23]. Specifically, whether providing AI advantage or function information, epistemic uncertainty has a fully mediating effect on both human accuracy and image number, suggesting its crucial role in human-AI collaboration.

6 Theoretical and Practical Implications

The current work makes three theoretical contributions to the research. First, this research aims at improving human task performance in the AI-human task delegation context and measures task performance by the image number and accuracy humans did. Past research about AI-human delegation mainly focused on human acceptance, and only used accuracy as the measure of performance [2]. As the AI-human delegation showed the potential for better performance, observing more outcomes will help to enhance the adoption of the AI-human delegation pattern. Second, our study extends the application of PAT theory in the AI-human delegation context. While Guggenberger et al. [13] explore AI-human delegation from the theoretical lens of PAT, we apply PAT in the AI delegating image task context to investigate the relationship and problems between humans and AI empirically. We designed the transparency of AI to reduce the hidden actions of humans in AI-human delegation and proved it is applicable. Third, this research investigates and compares two types of transparency (i.e., AI advantage and function information) together, which have not been studied before. It offers insights that AI transparency needs to be designed according to the goal of task performance.

As for practical contributions, for AI-related information system designers, it is of great importance to design and present AI transparency to users. Different kinds of information will have different effects on user perception and behavior. Hence, they should figure out the goal and design transparency toward it. As for the managers, before carrying out the AI-human delegation pattern, they should figure out related problems that may be confronted and solve them. By conducting surveys and interviews, they can get an understanding of their users' features, such as their attitudes toward AI, previous experience, current situation, etc., and personalize the AI. Based on the understanding, the AI-human delegation pattern can be used more effectively and efficiently.

7   Limitations and Future Directions

In evaluating the results of this study, some limitations need to be noted. First, the problem of conflicts of interest in PAT has not been investigated in our research because we considered transparency would not significantly influence it. We believe it will be meaningful to examine it in the AI-human delegation context. Second, our study focuses on the AI advantage and function information, we suggest that other types of transparency can be designed and tested in the AI-human delegation. For instance, previous research proposed that presenting explanations, and uncertainty scores will have impacts on human performance. Third, we conducted this study in the image classification tasks. AI-human delegation also exists in contexts like news detection, financial audits, etc. It will be interesting to investigate delegation in these fields.

Acknowledgement. This work was partially supported by the Social Science Fund Research Base Project of Beijing (19JDGLB029).

References

1. Jiang, J., Karran, A.J., Coursaris, C.K., Léger, P.M., Beringer, J.: A situation awareness perspective on human-AI interaction: tensions and opportunities. Int. J. Hum. Comput. Interact. **39**(9), 1789–1806 (2022). https://doi.org/10.1080/10447318.2022.2093863
2. Fügener, A., Grahl, J., Gupta, A., et al.: Cognitive challenges in human-artificial intelligence collaboration: investigating the path toward productive delegation. Inf. Syst. Res. **33**(2), 678–696 (2022)
3. Baird, A., Maruping, L.M.: The next generation of research on IS use: a theoretical framework of delegation to and from agentic IS artifacts. MIS Q. **45**(1), 315–341 (2021). https://doi.org/10.25300/MISQ/2021/15882
4. Candrian, C., Scherer, A.: Rise of the machines: delegating decisions to autonomous AI. Comput. Hum. Behav. **134**, 107308 (2022)
5. Hemmer, P., Westphal, M., Schemmer, M., et al.: Human-AI collaboration: the effect of AI delegation on human task performance and task satisfaction. In: Proceedings of the 28th International Conference on Intelligent User Interfaces (2023)
6. Afzal, S., Arshad, M., Saleem, S., et al.: The impact of perceived supervisor support on employees' turnover intention and task performance: mediation of self-efficacy. J. Manage. Dev. **38**(5), 369–382 (2019)
7. Wang, X., Yin, M.: Are explanations helpful? a comparative study of the effects of explanations in AI-assisted decision-making. In: 26th International Conference on Intelligent User Interfaces (2021)
8. Chen, J.Y., Procci, K., Boyce, M., Wright, J., Garcia, A., Barnes, M.: Situation awareness-based agent transparency (No. ARL-TR-6905). Aberdeen Proving Ground, MD: U.S. Army Res. Lab. 1–29 (2014)
9. Mercado, J.E., Rupp, M.A., Chen, J.Y., et al.: Intelligent agent transparency in human–agent teaming for multi-UxV management. Hum. Factors **58**(3), 401–415 (2016)
10. Liu, B.: In AI we trust? Effects of agency locus and transparency on uncertainty reduction in human–AI interaction. J. Comput.-Mediat. Commun. **26**(6), 384–402 (2021)

11. Stowers, K., Kasdaglis, N., Newton, O., et al.: Intelligent agent transparency: the design and evaluation of an interface to facilitate human and intelligent agent collaboration. In: Proceedings of the Human Factors and Ergonomics Society Annual Meeting. SAGE Publications Sage CA: Los Angeles, CA (2016)

12. Fayezi, S., O'Loughlin, A., Zutshi, A.: Agency theory and supply chain management: a structured literature review. Supply Chain Manage. Int. J. 17(5), 556–570 (2012)

13. Guggenberger, T., Lämmermann, L., Urbach, N., Walter, A.M., Hofmann, P.: Task delegation from AI to humans: a principal-agent perspective. In: ICIS (2023)

14. Conway, J.M.: Distinguishing contextual performance from task performance for managerial jobs. J. Appl. Psychol. 84(1), 3 (1999)

15. Charles, R., Berger, J.J.B.: Language and social knowledge: Uncertainty in interpersonal relations. Lond Edward Arnold. Lang. Soc. 13(1), 87–90 (1984)

16. Mayer, R.C., Davis, J.H., Schoorman, F.D.: An integrative model of organizational trust. Acad. Manag. Rev. 20(3), 709–734 (1995)

17. Kizilcec, R.F.: How much information? Effects of transparency on trust in an algorithmic interface. In: Proceedings of the 2016 CHI Conference on Human Factors in Computing Systems (2016)

18. Zhang, Y., Liao, Q.V., Bellamy, R.K.: Effect of confidence and explanation on accuracy and trust calibration in AI-assisted decision making. In: Proceedings of the 2020 Conference on Fairness, Accountability, and Transparency (2020)

19. Perrig, S.A., Scharowski, N., Brühlmann, F.: Trust issues with trust scales: examining the psychometric quality of trust measures in the context of AI. In: Extended abstracts of the 2023 CHI Conference on Human Factors in Computing Systems (2023)

20. Ferris, K.R.: Perceived uncertainty and job satisfaction in the accounting environment. Acc. Organ. Soc. 2(1), 23–28 (1977)

21. Schepman, A., Rodway, P.: The general attitudes towards artificial intelligence scale (GAAIS): confirmatory validation and associations with personality, corporate distrust, and general trust. Int. J. Hum. Comput. Interact. 39(13), 2724–2741 (2023)

22. Hayes, A.F.: Introduction to mediation, moderation, and conditional process analysis: A Regression-Based Approach. Guilford Publications (2017)

23. Bhatt, U., et al.: Uncertainty as a form of transparency: measuring, communicating, and using uncertainty. In: Proceedings of the 2021 AAAI/ACM Conference on AI, Ethics, and Society, (2021)

The Spillover Effect of Doctor's Knowledge Sharing on Their Online Consultation Volume

Li Chen, Qianru Lai, Shuang Geng$^{(\boxtimes)}$, Jie Wang, Yuxi Lin, and Yuefeng Qian

College of Management, Shenzhen University, Shenzhen 518060, China
gs@szu.edu.cn

Abstract. Doctors' online knowledge sharing enhances patients' access to medical knowledge and interactions between doctors and patients. Given its importance, previous studies have discussed the impact of doctors' knowledge sharing on patient choice. However, these studies mainly focus on the relationship between knowledge sharing and patients' choices within a single platform (i.e. online consultation platform). Very few studies notice the cross-platform spillover effect of doctors' knowledge sharing and compare the difference between the within-platform spillover effect and cross-platform spillover effects. Drawing on the theory of trust transfer, this study investigates the difference between the within-platform and cross-platform effects of doctors' knowledge sharing on patients' consultation choices. We analyzed a panel dataset generated between 2017 and 2023 and found that doctors' knowledge has both with-in-platform and cross-platform spillover effects on the patient's choice. In addition, the within-platform spillover effect is stronger than the cross-platform spillover effect. The findings in this study provide vital managerial insights for knowledge-sharing platforms and healthcare platforms in their function management.

Keywords: Health knowledge sharing · Spillover effect · Trust transfer

1 Introduction

With the emergence of online medical platforms, patients can consult doctors online anywhere and anytime. The COVID-19 pandemic also witnesses a surge in the usage of online medical consultation services. So far, 15% of patients in China used these platforms for diagnosis, treatment, and information about healthcare [1]. Online health consultation services have shifted the way people seek medical care.

Despite its convenience, patients sometimes find it challenging to find the target doctor among a variety of doctor options online although patients can specify their disease department. Moreover, the brief introduction of doctors cannot provide sufficient information for patients to make their choices. In the past few years, the emergence of social media platforms, such as Douyin, enables doctors to share patient-concerned health information outside the medical platforms. For example, doctors can release health science videos on social platforms (Fig. 1) based on their experience and expertise. After the posting, viewers can also interact with doctors through these videos, such as clicking likes (e.g., Fig. 1(A)), commenting, and collecting. According to the "Douyin Health Science Popularization Data Report" in 2023, over 35,000 certified doctors have created 4.43 million pieces of health science content [2].

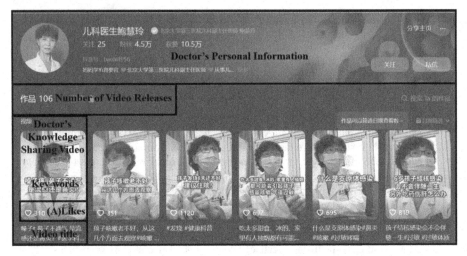

Fig. 1. A Doctor's Video Page on Douyin

Since viewers can interact with doctors through these videos, these social media platforms serve as a new channel for communication between patients and doctors. These platforms offer multiple benefits for doctors and patients. Doctors can enhance their online reputation and image by sharing professional knowledge while building strong relationships with patients [3]. By continuously creating and sharing high-quality medical knowledge, patients can obtain more information about the doctors, and their search friction for doctors is probably reduced [4].

While some social media platforms simply offer the functions of creating and sharing knowledge content, some platforms attempt to provide multiple types of services including online health consultation. Taking Xiaohe Health doctor as an example, viewers on Douyin can click on the doctor poster's image jump to the doctor's consultation page, and register for online consultation. Thus, video viewers can be transformed into consulting patients within the platform. By contrast, when the social media platform does not offer consultation services, viewers may not choose to consult or may shift to other medical platforms to consult doctors. Prior studies have noticed the spillover effect within healthcare service platforms that enables doctors to create and share knowledge content, which benefits their online reputation and enhances their consultation volume [5]. However, few studies notice the trust transfer within social media platforms and from social media platforms to healthcare service platforms. Therefore, we investigate the following research questions in this study:

Q1: Whether the health science video viewers can be transformed into consultation patients within social media platforms (within platform spillover effect)?

Q2: Whether the health science video viewers can be transformed into consultation patients outside the social media platforms (cross-platform spillover effect)?

To answer the above questions, we collect doctors' videos and consultation service records on Douyin [2], Xiaohe Health [6], and Haodf Online [7], from 2017 to 2023. Panel regression analysis shows that doctors' health knowledge sharing has both a positive direct spillover effect and a positive indirect spillover effect on cross-platform consultations. Within platform spillover effect is relatively stronger than cross-platform spillover effect.

2   Literature Review

2.1   Doctors' Health Knowledge Sharing Behavior

Doctors' health knowledge sharing can be categorized into two types: general knowledge sharing and specific knowledge sharing [8]. General knowledge sharing involves doctors offering free health information through public channels such as articles and videos. Specific knowledge sharing is private and tailored to patients' needs through face-to-face consultations or paid online consultations [8]. Previous research has demonstrated that doctors' behavior in sharing knowledge within online health communities impacts the online consultation volume. Specifically, both free and paid knowledge sharing can lead to increased consultation volume [9]. General knowledge sharing increases doctors' online reputation [5], thus has a positive impact on doctors' consultation volume. Current studies on doctors' health knowledge-sharing behavior mainly focus on within-platform effects drawing on the signaling theory, while the cross-platform effect is rarely noticed, not to mention the comparison between these two types of effects.

2.2   Trust Transfer Theory

According to McKnight's trust theory, the personal qualities and online reputations of doctors [10] significantly impact patient choices. Trust can be transferred when there is a strong connection between a trusted party and an unknown third party. Trust transfer theory encompasses two types: within-platform and cross-platform [11]. Within-platform trust transfer refers to the process by which trust, initially placed in a specific entity such as a location or institution, is subsequently transferred to another associated entity within the same platform. Conversely, cross-platform trust transfer occurs when trust in one platform is transferred to another platform [10, 11]. For instance, mutual trust between community members can transform into trust in virtual communities (within-platform) [12]. It is also found that customers tend to transfer their trust from offline to online stores (cross-platform trust) [13].

Existing studies on doctor-patient trust transfer mainly focus on the transfer of patient trust between online platforms and offline hospitals [14], while little has been done on the transfer of patient trust between different online platforms.

2.3 Spillover Effect

Spillover effects are the unintended effects of events in one environment on other individuals in a different, indirectly related environment [15]. Previous studies on spillover effects related to social interaction are mostly conducted in the fields of politics, economy, culture, and education, and there are also studies on consumer conversion within social platforms. These studies have focused on the spillover effect of social media platforms, which can improve content conversion [15], strengthen the impact of advertising [16], promoting trusting behaviors within communities [17] or between online and offline environments [18].

3 Research Model

Health knowledge sharing helps improve people's life quality and health level, through the dissemination of health medical knowledge. On social platforms, doctors can make full use of their professional medical knowledge, to share diverse health science content, such as graphics, audio, and video, as a way to demonstrate their professional qualities, enhance their online reputation and performance [19], and potentially achieve higher financial returns through positive emotions [20].

Simultaneously, people use social media to access medical information and knowledge and seek medical advice and social support during disease management. In the above process, users can choose their preferred communication style with doctors, such as following doctors' social accounts, liking, commenting, collecting, and forwarding the content released by doctors. This facilitates doctor-patient communication and trust-building. For doctors, gaining patients' initial trust helps attract potential patients.

Drawing on the trust transfer theory, we assume that trust in health knowledge sharing on social platforms can be successfully transferred to the within-platform consultation service as well as the external consultation platform (cross-platform trust). Specifically, viewers' interaction with doctors through social function helps build their initial trust for the doctor, and this trust may be directly transferred to the consultation service within-platform. At the same time, patients may also transfer trust generated based on the former platform to cross-platform consultation (cross-platform trust), through Internet search and other means. Thus, a positive direct spillover effect based on trust transfer is hypothesized:

H1. Doctors' health knowledge-sharing behavior on social platforms will have a positive direct spillover effect on the doctors' consultation within the platform.

On the other hand, based on the concept of cross-platform trust, the impact of doctors' health knowledge sharing on patients' medical choices can also extend beyond within-platform transformation. Social media platform users who browse health knowledge-sharing content are often motivated by health management and seeking treatment advice. When these users build initial trust for doctors, their trust may be transferred to other healthcare service platforms. This becomes a positive indirect spillover effect between the social media platform and the healthcare service platform. Therefore, we hypothesize that:

H2. Doctors' health knowledge-sharing behavior on social platforms will have a positive indirect spillover effect on online health service platform.

4   Research Methodology

4.1   Research Context and Data Collection

We collect data from the short-video platform Douyin, its healthcare consultation page named Xiaohe Health, and the healthcare service platform Haodf Online. Douyin is a large short-video social platform in China with 680 million monthly active users, accounting for 67.3% of the total mobile Internet users. Haodf Online is a leading online consultation platform. Our data collection process is as follows. First, on Douyin, we searched for "doctor" to gather information on the doctor accounts, including their videos' release time and amount, likes, comments, collects, forwards, count, and whether they opened a merchandise window. After obtaining the doctor list on Douyin, the consultation data is collected from the Xiaohe page, including doctors' online consultation volume, time, job title, professional title, city level, gender, hospital, and service score. We also collect the consultation information of these doctors on the Haodf Online platform. After doctor information cross-checking, we retained data only from doctors who were registered and certified on all three platforms or functional modules simultaneously. At last, we obtained a sample of 468 doctors and 30,624 balanced panel data from June 2017 to January 2023. Monthly data serves as the unit for statistics, matching, screening, and logarithmic processing.

4.2   Model Specification

For Xiaohe Health (within-platform), the regression model (1) is used to analyze the impact of knowledge sharing on Xiaohe health's consultation volume:

$$
\begin{aligned}
XiaoheConsultation_{it} = {} & \alpha_0 + \alpha_1 releases_{it} + \alpha_2 likes_{it} + \alpha_3 collects_{it} + \\
& \alpha_4 comments_{it} + \alpha_5 forwardings_{it} + \alpha_6 controls_{it} + \lambda_t + D_i + \varepsilon_{it}
\end{aligned}
\tag{1}
$$

where i stands for doctor and t for month. The explained variable $XiaoheConsultation_{it}$ refers to the doctor i's consultation volume in the Xiaohe health in month t. Core explanatory variable $releases_{it}$, $likes_{it}$, $collects_{it}$, $comments_{it}$, $forwards_{it}$ indicates the number of releases, likes, collects, comments and forwards of doctor i's health videos in month t, respectively. To control other factors affecting consultation volume, we introduce control variables $controls_{it}$ including city level, job title, professional title, gender, whether the doctor opens a merchandise window, online consultation price, and service score. D_i, λ_t, ε_{it} are doctor fixed effect, time fixed effect and random error terms, respectively. α_0 is a constant term.

For Haodf online platform, we replaced the explained variables using the consultation volume on this platform on the basis of model (1) and adopted the regression model (2):

$$
\begin{aligned}
HaodfConsultation_{it} = {} & \beta_0 + \beta_1 releases_{it} + \beta_2 likes_{it} + \beta_3 collects_{it} + \\
& \beta_4 comments_{it} + \beta_5 forwards_{it} + \beta_6 controls_{it} + \lambda_t + D_i + \varepsilon_{it}
\end{aligned}
\tag{2}
$$

where i stands for doctor and t for month and year. The explained variable $HaodfConsultation_{it}$ refers to doctor i's online consultation volume on Haodf Online in month t. $releases_{it}$, $likes_{it}$, $collects_{it}$, $comments_{it}$, $forwards_{it}$, $controls_{it}$, D_i, λ_t, ε_{it} are same as baseline model (1). β_0 is a constant term.

5 Results

We first conducted the Hausman test, sequence correlation test, and heteroscedasticity test, respectively. To eliminate the common influence of sequence correlation and heteroscedasticity, we adopted the "Heteroscedasticity – sequence correlation" clustering robust standard error, to obtain the empirical results.

5.1 Results of Xiaohe Health

Table 1 presents the results of regression analysis that examines the impact of doctors' Douyin health sharing on consultation volume in Xiaohe Health. Controlling for city, job title, professional title, gender, whether merchandise window opened, online consultation price, and service score, we found that the number of doctors' videos releases ($\beta = 0.194$, $p < 0.01$) and the number of videos collects ($\beta = 0.796$, $p < 0.001$) had a positive impact on consultation volume in Xiaohe health. However, the number of videos forwards had a negative effect ($\beta = -0.552$, $p < 0.001$). Besides, there was no significant relationship between the number of likes or comments on doctors' Douyin videos and online consultations in Xiaohe Health. It shows that doctors' knowledge-sharing behavior has a positive direct spillover effect on the volume of within-platform online consultations (Xiaohe Health), which is, partially consistent with hypothesis 1.

5.2 Results of Haodf Online

Table 1 also shows the impact of doctors' health video release on Haodf Online's consultation volume, controlling for city level, doctor job title, professional title, gender, whether to open a merchandise window, online consultation price and service score. We found that the number of doctors' videos collects ($\beta = 0.110$, $p < 0.05$) had a positive impact on online consultations in Haodf Online. However, the number of releases, likes, comments, and forwards of Douyin videos had no significant relationship with Haodf Online's consultation volume. It shows that doctors' knowledge sharing behavior has a positive indirect spillover effect on cross-platform consultation volume (Haodf Online), indicating that hypothesis 2 is supported.

Overall, regression results show that knowledge sharing behavior has a greater impact on within-platform patient consultation choices (Xiaohe health) compared to cross-platform patient consultation choices (Haodf Online).

Table 1. Empirical results

	Xiaohe	Haodf
$lnreleases_{i,t}$	0.194** (0.038)	0.040 (0.053)
$lnlikes_{i,t}$	−0.243 (0.026)	−0.098 (0.034)
$lncomments_{i,t}$	0.121 (0.029)	0.146 (0.043)
$lncollects_{i,t}$	0.796*** (0.031)	0.110* (0.042)
$lnforwards_{i,t}$	−0.552*** (0.028)	−0.030 (0.038)
city	−0.023	0.174
job title	−0.031	0.058
professiona title	0.015	0.086
gender	0.033	−0.016
window	0.009	−0.038
price	−0.021	0.001
service score	0.042	0.165
$R - square$	0.1210	0.0408

6 Discussion

This study presents new findings and reveals some important insights into the patients' consultation decision-making. First, empirical results show that the more doctors' health videos were released and collected, the more within-platform consultations happened. This suggests that the knowledge-sharing behavior of doctors has a positive direct spillover effect on within-platform consultation. Another finding is that the more doctors' videos were forwarded, the fewer within-platform consultations were conducted, which is contrary to our initial expectation. One possible explanation is that video viewers prefer consultation over other platforms that have larger doctor groups and higher popularity through search engines. Their forward behavior is more likely a marking behavior for future searches. Therefore, the increase in the number of forwards of health videos may lead to fewer within-platform consultations. In addition, the more doctors' health videos were collected, the more cross-platform consultations were conducted. This suggests doctors' knowledge sharing has a positive indirect effect on cross-platform consultations.

This paper makes several theoretical contributions. This paper complements the research on the mechanism of spillover effects of doctors' knowledge-sharing behavior within- and cross-platform. Prior studies focus on within-platform spillovers or other application domains, but this study focuses on the trust transfer and spillover effects in the healthcare domain using a large-scale dataset from multiple platforms. It provides convincing evidence for the spillover effect within and outside multi-function social platforms, which enriches the research scope in health knowledge dissemination and patient choices.

The paper also provides insights for social media platforms and online consultation platform managers. For those social media platform managers, it suggests that platform operators should maintain their self-operated consultation function module and add personalized interactive features. They can encourage doctors to use various knowledge dissemination channels and engage in frequent peer-to-peer interactions, such as live streaming. These interactions further improve their patient trust and help the platform to attract more consultation users. For online health consultation platforms, platform operators should strengthen cooperation with social platforms and encourage doctors to disseminate knowledge in diversified forms, such as video, voice, text, and pictures.

The study has limitations that should be considered. Firstly, we only have access to doctors' information on limited platforms. Future research should explore a broader range of platforms. Second, more robustness tests should be conducted to validate the results. Third, the study does not consider the impact of video types on the spill-over effect. Future studies need to investigate the impacts of video types, viewer characteristics, and platform criteria such as popularity on the spillover effects.

7 Conclusion

This study investigates the spillover effect of knowledge-sharing behavior of doctors on social media platforms. Two types of spillover effects were examined: within- and cross-platform spillover effects. Results show that doctors' knowledge-sharing behavior has a positive direct spillover effect on within-platform consultation, and a positive indirect spillover effect on consultation outside the platform. The findings provide insights into patients' medical choice behavior and suggest that managers of social media and consultation platforms should collaborate to convert video viewers into paying patients.

Acknowledgement. This study was supported by the National Natural Science Foundation of China (71901150 and 72334004), Guangdong Basic and Applied Basic Research Foundation (2022A1515012077), Guangdong Philosophy and Social Science Planning Project (GD23XGL113), and Guangdong Province Innovation Team (2021WCXTD002).

References

1. Jiang, J., Yang, M., Kiang, M., Cameron, A.F.: Exploring the freemium business model for online medical consultation services in China. Inf. Process. Manage. **58**(3), 1–24 (2021)
2. Douyin Homepage. https://www.douyin.com/note/7219193337868340535. Accessed 27 Jan 2024
3. Wu, H., Deng, Z., Wang, B., Wang, H.: How online health community participation affects physicians' performance in hospitals: empirical evidence from China. Inf. Manage. **58**(6), 103443 (2021)

4. Kraft, T., Valdés, L., Zheng, Y.: Consumer trust in social responsibility communications: the role of supply chain visibility. Prod. Oper. Manag. **31**(11), 4113–4130 (2022)

5. Meng, F., Zhang, X., Liu, L., Ren, C.: Converting readers to patients? From free to paid knowledge-sharing in online health communities. Inf. Process. Manage. **58**(3), 102490 (2021)

6. Xiaohe Health Homepage. https://www.xiaohe.cn. Accessed 27 Jan 2024

7. Haodf Online Homepage. https://www.haodf.com. Accessed 27 Jan 2024

8. Zhang, X., Guo, F., Xu, T., Li, Y.: What motivates physicians to share free health information on online health platforms? Inf. Process. Manage. **57**(2), 102166 (2020)

9. Ma, D., Zhang, C., Hui, Y., Xu, B.: Economic uncertainty spillover and social networks. J. Bus. Res. **145**, 454–467 (2022)

10. Gong, Y., Wang, H., Xia, Q., Zheng, L., Shi, Y.: Factors that determine a patient's willingness to physician selection in online healthcare communities: a trust theory perspective. Technol. Soc. **64**, 101510 (2021)

11. Lu, Y., Yang, S., Chau, P.Y., Cao, Y.: Dynamics between the trust transfer process and intention to use mobile payment services: a cross-environment perspective. Inf. Manage. **48**(8), 393–403 (2011)

12. Shi, Y., Sia, C.L., Chen, H.: Leveraging social grouping for trust building in foreign electronic commerce firms: an exploratory study. Int. J. Inf. Manage. **33**(3), 419–428 (2013)

13. Lee, K.C., Chung, N., Lee, S.: Exploring the influence of personal schema on trust transfer and switching costs in brick-and-click bookstores. Inf. Manage. **48**(8), 364–370 (2011)

14. Lu, J., Bai, J., Zhao, H., Zhang, X.: The effect of "offline-to-online" trust transfer on the utilization of online medical consultation among Chinese rural residents: experimental study. J. Med. Internet Res. **25**, e43430 (2023)

15. Zhao, K., Lu, Y., Hu, Y., Hong, Y.: Direct and indirect spillovers from content providers' switching: evidence from online livestreaming. Inf. Syst. Res. **34**, 1526–5536 (2022)

16. Geng, S., Yang, P., Gao, Y., Tan, Y., Yang, C.: The effects of ad social and personal relevance on consumer ad engagement on social media: the moderating role of platform trust. Comput. Hum. Behav. **122**, 106834 (2021)

17. Iacono, S.L.: Does community social embeddedness promote generalized trust? An experimental test of the spillover effect. Soc. Sci. Res. **73**, 126–145 (2018)

18. Libai, B., Muller, E., Peres, R.: The role of within-brand and cross-brand communications in competitive growth. J. Mark. **73**(3), 19–34 (2009)

19. Wang, L., Yan, L., Zhou, T., Guo, X., Heim, G.R.: Understanding physicians' online-offline behavior dynamics: an empirical study. Inf. Syst. Res. **31**(2), 537–555 (2020)

20. Geng, S., et al.: The association between linguistic characteristics of physicians' communication and their economic returns: mixed method study. J. Med. Internet Res. **26**, e42850 (2024)

Chatbot with Resilience: The Impact of Repair Strategies on Customer Satisfaction in Conversational Breakdowns

Jia Zeng[1], Dan Fan[1(✉)], Xinxue Zhou[2], and Jian Tang[1]

[1] School of Information, Central University of Finance and Economics, Beijing, China
fandan@cufe.edu.cn

[2] School of Business, Guangxi University, Nanning, China

Abstract. When chatbot is used in customer service, conversational breakdowns are common. Repairing from conversational breakdowns is a key step in service recovery. Drawing upon grounding in communication theory, this paper explores the impact of three repair strategies (i.e., keyword confirmation explanation, confirmation, and top response) on customer satisfaction. We formulate a research model to compare how repair strategies impact customer satisfaction through two pathways: perceived intelligence and customer participation. We further introduce AI attitude as an individual difference variable, which moderates the pathway. Through the online between-subjects laboratory experiments, we gathered data from 244 participants. Our findings indicate that the keyword confirmation repair strategy can influence customer satisfaction through perceived intelligence and customer participation. The paper discusses both theoretical and practical implications.

Keywords: Chatbot Resilience · Conversational Breakdown · Repair Strategy · Common Ground Theory · Customer Satisfaction

1 Introduction

Chatbots have many advantages when it comes to customer service. However, conversational breakdowns are also common because chatbots cannot understand users' service inquiries [1, 2]. From the perspective of Common Ground Theory [3], both individuals in a conversation have to coordinate on content. For customers, the chatbot is a "black box". Customers struggle to comprehend the tasks the chatbot can or cannot perform or how to recover from conversational breakdowns. If the chatbot does not respond appropriately, customers will give up and switch to human customer agents. As a result, increasing instances of handovers will result in an escalation of companies' operational costs. Therefore, designing appropriate repair strategies for chatbots is crucial to mitigate the negative impact of conversational breakdowns.

Repair refers to the actions and measures taken to correct defects in the service process, such as rephrasing, simplifying language, and providing additional information [4]. Some companies will use structured message templates or highlighting designs to

© The Author(s), under exclusive license to Springer Nature Switzerland AG 2024
Y. P. Tu and M. Chi (Eds.): WHICEB 2024, LNBIP 517, pp. 306–317, 2024.
https://doi.org/10.1007/978-3-031-60324-2_26

improve the efficiency of information communication, such as setting up hyperlinks and bolding keywords. Others avoid having chatbots directly acknowledge a conversation breakdown because this false signal can cause the customer to close the conversation directly. Existing research predominantly concentrates on customers' preferences for various repair strategies in the context of conversational breakdown. Lee et al. explored the attitudes of individuals with distinct characteristics concerning strategies such as apologies, compensation, and providing choices [6]. Based on the Common Ground Theory , Ashktorab explored users' preferences for eight repair strategies [4]. The eight repair strategies differ in terms of whether the evidence of breakdown is available, whether the repair is initiated by the system or the self (i.e., the human), and whether the self-repair is assisted by the system. Although the prior research explored users' preferences for repair strategies, it is still uncertain how these strategies function to influence customer satisfaction and what is the underlying mechanism.

In this study, we explored how and why three distinct repair strategies (i.e., keyword confirmation explanation, confirmation, and top response) influence customer perceptions and behaviors [4]. The interaction between chatbots and customers can be considered as the process of forming consensus in the conversation. When the conversation is breakdown, both parties need to continue to communicate and confirm until they understand each other. The keyword confirmation explanation repair and confirmation repair strategies both provide evidence of breakdowns in the conversation. This manipulation can quickly grab the customer's attention and participation. On this basis, the keyword confirmation explanation highlights the key words that it understands and provides an explanation. It is an effective method to assist the customer in better reformulating by revealing the underlying logic of the system. On the other hand, the Top Response Repair strategy ignores uncertainty and takes action by selecting the intent with the highest confidence. This requires the customer to notice by themselves and correct. We posit that diverse chatbot repair strategies can impact customer satisfaction through a dual pathway: perceptual and behavioral. On one hand, existing research emphasizes that repair efforts by chatbots contribute to heightened customer evaluations of the perceived intelligence and satisfaction. On the other hand, revealing system status or providing evidence of conversational breakdown can capture customers' attention and increase their willingness to participate. However, increased participation may pose the risk of deviating from customer expectations, potentially resulting in more adverse effects and diminishing evaluations of customer satisfaction [6]. We further explore individual differences in AI attitudes. We believe these variances can influence customers' choices during the repair process [6].

Our theoretical framework and findings contribute to the understanding of chatbot repair strategies and customer service in several ways. Firstly, our study contributes to the existing literature on chatbot repair by investigating the mechanisms through which repair strategies influence customer behavior. Secondly, we clarify the dual pathways through which repair strategies affect customer service and reveal their marginal conditions. Thirdly, the study's conclusion offers practical insights for designing repair strategies for chatbots.

2 Theoretical Development and Hypotheses

2.1 Grounding in Communication with Chatbot

Common Ground Theory is a framework that views communication as a form of collaborative action, describing the process of achieving grounding in communication [3]. This theory can also be applied in human-computer interaction [9]. People need to be able to seek evidence that they have been understood and to provide evidence of their intentions. In human-computer interaction, obtaining the necessary evidence for achieving grounding is more challenging, and users and chatbots often need to exert additional effort to achieve mutual understanding. This is the grounding problem in human-computer interaction [9]. Therefore, to adhere to the principle of the least collaborative effort and common ground theory , we specifically focus on the characteristics of how chatbots communicate with customers and their impact on the service experience. Below we discuss breakdowns and repairs based on common ground theory.

Breakdowns. Chatbots typically use intent probability models to define breakdown in the dialogue agent. Chatbot processes and analyzes the freely inputted content from customers [1]. If the predicted confidence of the chatbot exceeds the specified threshold, it provides the correct response to the customer. Conversely, when the predicted confidence is low or there are multiple similar confidences, the chatbot is unable to offer relevant answers to the user, indicating a conversational breakdown [2]. As research progresses, there is increasing attention to the reasons and methods for conversational breakdowns in chatbot interactions [5]. Conversational breakdowns can trigger negative emotions in customers while decreasing customer satisfaction, trust, and continuation intention [4]. Researchers have found that rapid conversational breakdowns can lead to the failure of interaction between the chatbot and the customer, resulting in a poor experience for the customers [1]. Customers may seek help from human customer service with negative emotions. This undoubtedly increases the operational burden on enterprises.

Repair. "Repair" is defined as "replacing the wrong with the right" [10]. Even in human conversations, misunderstandings are common [3]. Therefore, a more realistic objective for conversational design is to facilitate efficient repair when the conversation is at risk of breaking down. Chatbots are considered to need to take more proactive efforts in repair. This means that developers must consider appropriate improvement strategies that allow chatbots and users to repair misunderstood statements or ambiguous vocabulary in the design of conversations. Based on common ground theory, conversation repair can firstly be divided based on whether breakdown evidence is provided [4]. Repairing without evidence of a breakdown implies that the system overlooks uncertainty and opts for the most probable intent to act. Top response repair is a typical type of repair, requiring users to initiate the correction of the error response after encountering it. A repair with evidence of breakdown means that the chatbot identifies potential breakdown and confirms with the customer, such as the confirmation Strategy. This repair strategy can gain more attention and action from customers [8].

On the other hand, certain strategies for assisted self-repair have garnered attention. These strategies aid customers in the repair process by incorporating additional prompts on the page. Ashktorab's findings suggest that exposing the system model of the chatbot and providing detailed explanations about the system's state (i.e., The keyword confirmation explanation repair) can be effective methods to assist customers in rephrasing [4]. Researches emphasizes that by increasing transparency in the system, customers consciously modify input to improve conversation outcomes. Several studies argued that the system needs to explain the utility of its behavior to users (such as keyword-based), which will increase user understanding of the system and feedback willingness. Benner suggests that by explaining situations, providing potentially useful messages, or offering feedback on errors, conversation agents can help customers understand their skills and potential shortcomings [2]. This repair strategy may lead to higher acceptance. Therefore, our study considers top response repair, confirmation repair, and keyword confirmation explanation repair as comparative strategies, delving into the construction and design of these repair strategies and their distinct impacts on conversation repair.

2.2 Chatbot Repair Strategies and Dual Pathways

Because the focus of this article is on the repair strategies of chatbots, we will limit the rest of the theoretical development to the processing of chatbot responses and discuss how it affects customer satisfaction through a dual process: one is perceptual, and the other is behavioral.

Satisfaction is considered as the customer's evaluation of a particular service experience or the overall experience [7]. It is a decisive factor and a key predictive indicator for cultivating customer loyalty. Enterprises believe that improving customer satisfaction can achieve an increase in operational profits and market share [12]. Positive and effective service repair is the expectation of every customer. Previous research has found that customer satisfaction is directly related to the degree to which a business answers questions, expresses warmth and friendliness, and responds to customer needs. If consumers perceive a higher level of expertise and intelligence, satisfaction will be higher [7].

Chatbots communicate information related to decisions, procedures, and organizational performance to stakeholders. These elements play a significant role in shaping customer experience and assessing the service repair process. The disclosure of additional information empowers individuals to better understand the service process, fostering enhanced control and confidence in service utilization [14]. Moreover, there is a perception that chatbots can intelligently process customer input and deliver more effective information to accomplish tasks. This alleviates the psychological burden on customers during conversation repair in turn, thereby enhancing their perception of the chatbot. The keyword confirmation ex-planation repair exposes the chatbot's comprehension mechanism. Through high-lighting keywords, customers can readily identify instances and the underlying mechanism of conversational breakdown, thereby enhancing their perception of the intelligence level of the chatbot service agent. The keyword confirmation ex-planation repair unveils the chatbot's comprehension mechanism. By emphasizing keywords, customers can easily recognize instances and the underlying mechanism of conversational breakdown, thereby increasing their Perceived Intelligence of the chatbot.

Hypothesis 1 (Positive Mediation Through Perceived Intelligence): Comparing with the confirmation and top response strategies, the keyword confirmation explanation strategy increases a customer's perceived intelligence, which, in turn, enhances customer satisfaction.

Customer participation refers to the act and magnitude of investment of a customer's own tangible assets effort or time in their actions. Customers are more likely to resolve their needs when they invest additional effort in interacting with the chatbot and adjusting their questioning approach. Previous research suggests that when customers encounter more transparent and disclosing responses [13], they are more inclined to invest effort in communicating with the chatbot. This heightened participation and remediation effort can lead to increased customer satisfaction [15].

Therefore, we assert that customer repair efforts play a crucial role in human-computer interactions during conversational breakdown scenarios. Simultaneously, according to expectancy theory, after a service failure, customers who invest more effort may become more dissatisfied with the service and the organization. Such a negative violation of expectations leads to lower service evaluations [5]. As a result, customer participation may also moderate the effects of repair strategies on customer satisfaction [7].

Hypothesis 2 (Negative Mediation Through Customer Participation): Comparing with the confirmation and top response strategies, the keyword confirmation strategy increases customer participation, thereby reducing customer satisfaction.

2.3 The Moderating Effect of AI Attitude

Research suggests that individuals' general attitudes toward AI play a significant role in shaping their acceptance of the technology. Scholars comprehensively evaluate individuals' attitudes towards AI, taking into account various dimensions, including the technical aspects of AI, its convenience in daily life, usage habits, and cultural influences [6]. The chatbot has become an indispensable part of daily life as a recent innovation in artificial intelligence technology. Previous studies have found that consumers' AI attitudes toward influence their behavior and perception in human-computer interaction scenarios. The individual customer factors are closely linked to their actual perceptions and behaviors.

In our study, customers with positive attitudes toward chatbots are likely to harbor higher expectations. These individuals are more inclined to participate with the chatbot to address conversation issues. They are likely to give greater recognition to the chatbot's performance. Conversely, customers with a negative AI attitude toward may resist and be averse to the use of AI agents for service repair. They may perceive that the chatbot is unable to resolve issues, resulting in their unwillingness to actively participate in conversation repair. Individuals with a lower AI attitude are also likely to provide lower service evaluations. In summary, we posit that when customers hold more positive AI attitudes, repair strategies will positively impact customer satisfaction. Conversely, for customers with more negative AI attitudes, this positive effect may be weakened or even reversed. Our final hypothesis is formulated as follows:

Hypothesis 3 (Moderation by AI Attitude): The keyword confirmation strategy has a positive impact on customer satisfaction for those with positive AI attitudes. In contrast, for those with negative AI attitudes, such an effect is either non-existent or even reversed.

Figure 1 shows the complete research framework.

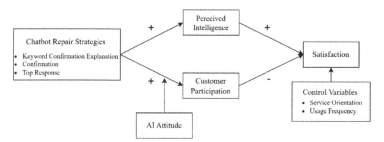

Fig. 1. Research Framework

3 Pretest

Before the main experiments, we conducted a pretest using a between-subjects design by varying the chatbot's repair strategy while keeping all other aspects of the interaction consistent. In this pretest, our emphasis was on the effectiveness of manipulating the chatbot repair strategy and conducting reliability and validity tests for the questionnaire scale. During the study, participants took part in a hypothetical customer service task and interacted with a chatbot via virtual chat to resolve a service-related issue. After the chat, participants evaluated the effect of the chatbot repair, perceived intelligence, AI attitude, satisfaction, and control variables (service orientation and usage frequency).

3.1 Stimulus Materials

We selected the e-commerce industry as the context, given its frequent use of virtual chat for customer communication. To address a service-related issue, we focused on one of the most common requests in the online retail sector: modifying shipping and door-to-door delivery times.

We developed a mobile version of experimental platform, where a chatbot service agent is implemented to deal with customer requests. Our overall design primarily follows the guidelines outlined in Ashktorab [4]. In the keyword confirmation explanation repair, the chatbot confirms its understanding to the participants by highlighting the recognized keywords in red and providing an explanation enclosed in parentheses at the end of the response. All replies under confirmation repair maintain the same content as the keyword confirmation explanation repair without further highlighting or explanation. In the top response strategy, the chatbot directly responds to the participant with the highest confidence, without confirming with the participant. Participants are required to actively identify conversational breakdowns and initiate repairs. We illustrate the three repair strategies in Fig. 2.

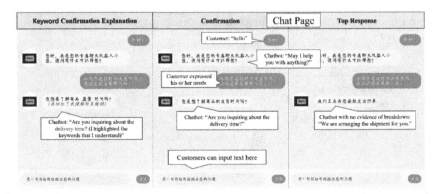

Fig. 2. Repair Strategies

3.2 Pre-test Procedure

Participants were initially asked to read a scenario description: "Meow is currently running a New Year's promotion. You've pre-purchased a refrigerator for your new home. However, your new home is still under renovation, and you haven't moved in yet." Subsequently, participants were instructed to use the chatbot to complete two tasks: "1. Delay the delivery by three months" and "2. Schedule weekend delivery." After reading the instructions, participants followed them to the experimental platform. To better simulate a real shopping scenario, we designed an order page where participants could access the conversation window by clicking "Contact Customer Service". The chat was then initiated on a new screen, where participants started chatting with the chatbot. The chatbot responds based on rules that read keywords when a customer makes a request. The conversation continued till the participants requested for transferring a human agent. Then, participants were directed to the questionnaire link. To identify outliers and ensure subject quality, participants were also asked to answer two attention check questions related to the experimental scenario.

3.3 Pre-Test Results

Forty-four participants from China (21 females) took part in the pretest, who were randomly assigned to one of three conditions. First, we tested the construct for reliability by examining the Cronbach's α value for each construct which was high (Satisfaction = 0.8, Perceived Intelligence = 0.90; AI Attitude = 0.82). Furthermore, the AVE for all factors exceeded 0.50 and the CR for all factors exceeded 0.80, indicating convergent validity.

Next, we conducted a manipulation check for the repair strategy manipulations. Analysis revealed that participants perceived strategies differently across the three strategies ($F(2, 44) = 22.011, p < 0.001$). According to manipulation check question "The chatbot customer service confirmed with me whether it understands my question correctly", Top repair was considered to be less efficient than the confirmation ($M_{Top} = 2.79$ versus $M_{Confirmation} = 5.18, SD = 1.63$ and $SD = 0.98, t(23) = 4.3, p < 0.001$) or Keyword Confirmation Explanation ($M = 5.79, SD = 1.23, t(31) = 6.05, p < 0.001$), but the difference between the latter two did not reach significance. Similarly for Manipulation question "The chatbot customer service told me what keywords it understood in my question", Keyword Confirmation Explanation repair is considered to highlight keywords more than Confirmation ($M_{Keyword} = 6.32$ and $M_{Confirmation} = 3.73$, $SD = 0.75$ and $SD = 1.35$, $t(23) = 6.80$, $p < 0.001$) or top ($M_{Top} = 2.64$, $SD = 1.22, t(53) = 8.44, p < 0.001$). Thus, our manipulation of three sets of repair strategies was successful.

4 Study

4.1 Procedure and Measures

Two hundred and forty-four people (150 female) from China participated in the study. Participants were randomly assigned to one of the three treatment conditions. The cover story and procedure were identical to those of the pretest. Participants were first asked to answer questions about AI attitudes and service orientation. After interacting with the chatbot, participants performed individual difference measures of attention check and manipulation check.

We used Schepman's (2023) 3 items to assess participants' AI attitudes [6] (e.g., "I'm interested in using chatbot"). Additionally, we gauged participants' perceived intelligence and satisfaction levels following service interactions, utilizing methods outlined by Moussawi [11] (e.g., "The chatbot agent can understand my commands") and Han [7] (e.g., "How well did this service experience with the chatbot meet your needs? (extremely poor/extremely well"). The number of conversation-turns each participant had with the chatbot was used to measure the mediating variable of customer participation. To mitigate the interference of other individual characteristics, we incorporated the service orientation and usage frequency mentioned [4, 10] as control variables.

4.2 Results

We conducted a one-way ANCOVA using the three repair strategies as between-subjects factors and frequency of use and service orientation as covariates. Overall, the three types of repair strategies had a significant effect on satisfaction levels ($F(4, 239) = 5.76, P < 0.001$). Multiple comparisons show that there is a significant difference in satisfaction between the keyword confirmation explanation repair and the other two groups of repairs ($M_{Keyword} = 2.67$ vs $M_{Confirmation} = 2.30$, standard deviations are 1.47, 1.45, $p = 0.76$) or ($M_{Top} = 2.14, SD_{Top} = 1.60, p = 0.15$). However, there is no significant difference in satisfaction between the confirmation and the top response repair ($P < 0.5$).

To explore if the effect of three types of repair strategies on satisfaction is mediated. Compared to the top response strategy, the results show that the keyword confirmation explanation repair significantly increases customers' perceived intelligence ($\beta = 0.87$, $t(241) = 3.54, p < 0.001$). Increased perceived intelligence can further lead to higher satisfaction ($\beta = 0.64, t(241) = 16.06, p < 0.001$). The indirect effect test (Table 1) shows that the keyword confirmation explanation repair has a significant indirect positive impact on satisfaction. However, no mediating effect of perceived intelligence was observed in confirmation strategies. These results provide direct evidence for the positive mediating path of perceived intelligence hypothesized in H1. On the other hand, compared to the top response repair, the keyword confirmation explanation repair significantly increased customer participation ($\beta = 1.31$, $t(241) = 3.072$, $p = 0.024$) and further reduced the level of satisfaction ($\beta = 0.423$, $t(241) = 1.93$, $p = 0.054$). The indirect effect test confirmed that keyword confirmation explanation repair and confirmation repair have small negative indirect effect on satisfaction through customer participation. These results support the proposition proposed in H2 that customers participation in negative cognitive pathways to satisfaction in the context of repair failure. Table 1 shows the analysis of mediation effects.

Table 1. Analysis of mediation effects.

Path	Direct effects		Indirect effects		Analysis results
	Effect(t-value)	CI	Effect(BootSE)	CI	
Key → PI → SAT	**0.020(0.119)**	**[−0.2571, 0.2969]**	**0.548(0.167)**	**[0.2872, 0.8352]**	**Full mediation**
ConF → PI → SAT	0.013(0.978)	[−0.2568, 0.2824]	0.152(0.148)	[−0.0897, 0.2894]	No mediation
Key → CP → SAT	**0.524(2.430)***	**[0.1679, 0.8797]**	**−0.099 (0.055)**	**[−0.1990, −0.0210]**	**Partial mediation**
ConF → CP → SAT	**0.244(1.138)**	**[−0.1101, 0.5976]**	**0.052(−0.093)**	**[−0.1880, −0.0200]**	**Full mediation**

Notes: N = 244. Significant effects in bold. * p < 0.1, ** p < 0.01, *** p < 0.001; two-tailed test = Bias-corrected 90% confidence interval (5,000 bootstrap samples). Base group = top response repair; Key = keyword confirmation explanation repair, PI = Perceived Intelligence, SAT = Satisfaction, CP = Customer Participation, ConF = the confirmation repair

In order to test the moderating effect proposed in H3, we first used Stata 16 to conduct a regression test with repair strategies as the between-subject factor, AI attitude as the continuous moderator, and service orientation and usage frequency as control variables. The results show that the keyword confirmation explanation repair has a significant impact on satisfaction compared with the other two strategies ($\beta = 0.444$, $t(241) = 2.09$, $p = 0.038$)) compared to the top response repair, which is consistent with our findings when conducting variance analysis. The two control variables, service orientation ($\beta = 0.09$, $t(241) = 1.05$, $p < 0.3$) and usage frequency ($\beta = 0.044$, $t(241) = 0.42$, $p < 0.7$) have no impact on satisfaction. Significantly. At the same time, the interaction term between repair strategies and AI attitude is significant ($\beta_{Keyword} = 0.335$, $t(241) = 2.19$, $p = 0.029$; $\beta_{Confirmation} = 0.260$, $t(241) = 2.19$, $p = 0.093$). Overall, AI attitude significantly moderates the impact of repair strategies on satisfaction levels.

To explore the pattern of this interaction, we performed a simple slope analysis and examined the marginal effect of repair strategies at one standard deviation above the mean of the AI attitudes [8]. For individuals with positive AI attitudes (AA_{High} is 5.77, 1 standard deviation higher than the mean), the keyword confirmation explanation repair has a significant positive impact on satisfaction ($\beta = 0.868$, $t(241) = 3.02$, $p = 0.003$). On the other hand, for individuals with negative AI attitudes (AA_{Low}=2.97, 1 standard deviation below the mean), the keyword confirmation explanation repair has a negative impact on satisfaction ($\beta = -0.070$, $t(241) = -0.22$, $p < 0.9$), but it is not significant. We found similar results for the confirmation repair. When the individual's AI attitude is positive(AA_{High} is 5.77, 1 SD higher than the mean), the confirmation repair has a significant positive impact on satisfaction($\beta = 0.522$, $t(241) = 1.73$, $p = 0.085$). When the AI attitude is negative ($AA_{Low} = 2.97$, , 1 SD below the mean), the confirmation repair has a non-significant effect on satisfaction ($\beta = -0.207$, $t(241) = -0.68$, $p < 0.5$) negative impact. Collectively, these findings suggest that the influence of repair strategies on satisfaction depends differs by individuals' AI attitudes, thereby supporting H3.

5 General Discussion

Building on common ground theory, we examined the effects of three chatbot repair strategies aimed at improving customer satisfaction when conversations are breakdown and repair efforts are unsuccessful [7]. Our research sheds light on how individuals cognitively and behaviorally respond to chatbots' repair strategies in conversational breakdowns. In comparison with the top repair, both the keyword strategy and confirmation strategy significantly increased customer participation. However, only the keyword confirmation explanation repair showed notable inter-group differences in perceived intelligence and satisfaction. In summary, the repair strategy enhances satisfaction by boosting customers' perceived intelligence. However, in the case of repair failure, the increase in customer participation simultaneously has a negative impact on satisfaction. Additionally, a positive AI attitude positively moderates the effect, whereas a negative AI attitude exerts a negative influence on customer satisfaction.

5.1 Theoretical and Practical Implications

Theoretical Implications. We employed the theoretical framework of grounding in communication to guide the design choices of the repairs studied, which view conversations as collaborative actions. Our research results suggest that adopting a proactive approach and providing more information about the underlying operational status during the repair process contributes to increased customer satisfaction with the service. Specifically, the confirmation explanation repair, emphasizing the customer's keywords and providing a detailed explanation of its functioning, is deemed the most effective. This information-centric design is poised to help customers comprehend exactly why conversational breakdowns occur [4]. The confirmation repair also enhances customer participation, but it leads to an increase in conversational turns. The repetition of confirmations may be perceived as redundant, potentially affecting customers' evaluations of the chatbot's perceived intelligence [13].

In the top response repair, the chatbot does not provide evidence of conversational breakdown and system status information. Although it appears more concise, it requires customers to proactively initiate repairs. Such a repair may be perceived as lacking resources to resolve breakdowns. Our study adds to the existing literature in the field of chatbot repair by exploring the mechanisms through which repair strategies influence customer behavior. We elucidate the dual pathways through which repair strategies impact customer service and unveil their marginal conditions.

Practical Implications. The findings of our study offer practical guidance for designing chatbot services, especially for e-commerce companies. We found that enhancing the visibility and transparency of chatbot systems, such as by explaining principles, can effectively improve customer participation and perception, leading to higher service evaluations. Repair strategies are particularly effective for customers with positive AI attitudes but for customers with negative AI attitudes, excessive customer participation may adversely impact their service experience. Thus, enterprises can improve interaction by providing information on chatbot operation, using different visual cues, and enhancing efficiency [13]. Allowing chatbots to take an active role in conversation repair is recommended, but companies should avoid forced or prolonged interactions that may backfire.

5.2 Limitations and Future Research

Firstly, our manipulation of different repair strategies can be extended to more situations. E-commerce platforms often seek efficient and concise conversations to fulfill corresponding tasks. However, the applicability of our conclusions in other interactive scenarios warrants further exploration, such as banking, finance, medical services, psychological counseling, and others. Second, the visual expression of repair strategies, such as text color, size, or emojis, may impact customer perceptions and behaviors.

Additionally, our experimentally manipulated chatbot ultimately failed to resolve the problem and directed customers to a human agent. If the repair is successful, the customer's assessment of the time and cost of the action may change, and their expectations may differ significantly. Investigating the impact of repair outcomes points an interesting avenue for future research.

Thirdly, apart from the moderating role of AI attitudes, other boundary conditions merit further exploration. For instance, individuals who dislike chatbots may alter their behavior patterns due to anthropomorphism or more empathic responses from the chatbot. The integration of empathic expressions from chatbots with efficient repair strategies has the potential to further enhance customer satisfaction.

Acknowledgement. This work was funded by the National Natural Science Foundation of China (No: 71904215), the Young Talents Support Program from the Central University of Finance and Economics (No: QYP2211).

References

1. Følstad, A., Taylor, C.: Investigating the user experience of customer service chatbot interaction: a framework for qualitative analysis of chatbot dialogues. Q. User Experience **6**(1), 1–17 (2021)

2. Benner, D., Edona, E., Sofia, S., Andreas, J.: What do you mean? A review on recovery strategies to overcome conversational breakdowns of conversational agents. In: In International Conference on Information Systems (ICIS), pp. 1–17. (2021)
3. Clark, H.H., Brennan, S.E.: Grounding in communication. In: Perspectives on Socially Shared Cognition, pp 127–149. American Psychological Association, Washington, DC (1991)
4. Ashktorab, Z., Mohit, J.: Resilient chatbots: repair strategy preferences for conversational breakdowns. In: Proceedings of the 2019 CHI Conference on Human Factors in Computing Systems, pp. 1–12. (2019)
5. Lee, M.K., Sara, K., Jodi, F., Siddhartha, S., Paul, R.: Gracefully mitigating breakdowns in robotic services. In: 2010 5th ACM/IEEE International Conference on Human-Robot Interaction (HRI), pp. 203–210 (2010)
6. Zhang, Y., Luo, X., Shao, B., Benitez, J.: Technology-driven mandatory customer participation: a new recovery strategy to promote customers' online post-recovery satisfaction. Eur. J. Inf. Syst. 1–19 (2022)
7. Han, E., Yin, D., Zhang, H.: Bots with feelings: should AI agents express positive emotion in customer service? Inf. Syst. Res. 34(3), 1296–1311 (2023)
8. Schepman, A., Rodway, P.: Initial validation of the general attitudes towards artificial intelligence scale. Comput. Hum. Behav. Rep. 1, 100014 (2020)
9. Brennan, S.E.: The grounding problem in conversations with and through computers. Social and Cognitive Approaches to Interpersonal Communication, pp. 201–225. Psychology Press (2014)
10. Liao, Q.V., Davis, M., Geyer, W.: What can you do? Studying social-agent orientation and agent proactive interactions with an agent for employees. In: Proceedings of the 2016 ACM Conference on Designing Interactive Systems, pp. 264–275 (2016)
11. Moussawi, S., Koufaris, M., Benbunan-Fich, R.: The role of user perceptions of intelligence, anthropomorphism, and self-extension on continuance of use of personal intelligent agents. Eur. J. Inf. Syst. 32(3), 601–622 (2023)
12. Bhattacherjee, A.: Understanding information systems continuance: an expectation-confirmation model. MIS Q. 25(3), 351–370 (2001)
13. Khurana, A., Alamzadeh, P., Chilana, P.K.: ChatrEx: designing explainable chatbot interfaces for enhancing usefulness, transparency, and trust. In: 2021 IEEE Symposium on Visual Languages and Human-Centric Computing (VL/HCC), pp. 1–11 (2021)
14. Han, E., Yin, D.D., Zhang, H.: Implementing Choices in Chatbot-initiated Service Interactions: Helpful or Harmful? In: ICIS 2022 Proceedings (2022)
15. Zhu, Z., Nakata, C., Sivakumar, K., Grewal, D.: Fix it or leave it? Customer recovery from self-service technology failures. J. Retail. 89(1), 15–29 (2013)

Predicting Startup Success Through a New Graph Convolutional Neural Network Approach

Yue Zhang, Xiaoyi Tang, and Hu Yang[✉]

School of Information, Central University of Finance and Economics, Beijing 100098, China
hu.yang@cufe.edu.cn

Abstract. Venture capital (VC) is a high-risk, high-return capital injection for emerging or small and medium-sized enterprises with growth potential. Accurately predicting the success of startup is critical for venture capital institutions. Previous studies have used data-driven approaches to explore the many factors that influence startup success, but have often failed to delve deeper into the heterogeneous topological information in investment relationships. In fact, graph convolutional neural networks have been shown to be effective for binary classification problems. In this paper, to model the relational embedding of co-investment networks and investment relationship networks, a novel graph convolutional neural network approach, named VC-HGCN, is employed to effectively capture the complex interactions in investment networks by integrating the learned node attributes and network topology information. The results show that VC-HGCN performs better in predicting startup success compared to the benchmark model, and also demonstrates the value of using the two investment networks in combination. Our study improves the accuracy of startup success prediction and provides a powerful tool for venture capitalists to find high-potential startups.

Keywords: Venture Capital · Prediction · Graph Neural Networks · Startups

1 Introduction

Startups are innovative firms with high growth potential and high growth risks, which tend to adopt a disruptive innovation approach, unlike existing firms that use incremental innovation. Startups have not only become an important engine of economic growth, but also have a significant impact on innovation and the technological revolution [1]. Moreover, venture capital (VC), as a key driver of innovation and business development, is particularly critical for early-stage startups [2]. Venture capital institutions expect to provide financial support to emerging or small and medium-sized enterprises with great growth potential through venture capital investment in order to acquire a certain percentage of shares or control of the enterprise. Ultimately, they will receive a high return on their investment through an initial public offering (IPO) or mergers and acquisitions [3]. However, due to the complex environment in which startups grow, almost 90% of startups end up failing [4], and more than half of venture capital activities are loss-making [5]. With the increase in venture capital activity, the uncertainty of startup success and investment risks have further increased. As a result, accurately identifying startup success has become a major challenge.

As the amount of available data grows, data-driven approaches are commonly used for investment decisions in the financial industry. Prior research has revealed a variety of key factors influencing startup success by analyzing historical data, focusing primarily on the correlation between individual characteristics and entrepreneurial success for prediction [6–8]. However, it fails to take into account the complex network of investment relationships between startups and investment institutions, and the information embedded in the network is crucial for understanding and predicting the success of startups, as has been demonstrated by complex network analysis methods [3, 9].

In the investment events of startups, there exists a large amount of historical investment data that can be utilized, including the heterogeneous topological information in the investment relationship network and the co-investment topological information of investment institutions [10]. Among them, not only individual features but also network structures are covered. And graph convolutional neural networks show great advantages in processing graph-structured data, especially in representation learning and node prediction. We believe that the success of startups can be predicted more accurately by deeply mining the structural information and node features in co-investment networks and investor relationship networks.

The research in this paper aims to predict the success of startups through deep learning methods to help venture capital stakeholders evaluate and select investment projects more scientifically. By innovatively applying the VC-HGCN model, the structure of the two types of investment networks as well as the heterogeneous node attributes can be taken into account, and the topological information as well as the heterogeneous node characteristics can be fully integrated to achieve the prediction of startup success. The contributions of this paper are: (1) A novel graph convolutional neural network approach (VC-HGCN) for venture capital investment prediction is proposed, specifically designed to capture and analyze the complex and heterogeneous relationships between startups and investment institutions, which is significantly higher than the benchmark model on the dataset. (2) Innovatively embedded both investment relationship network and co-investment network, and experimentally verified their effectiveness. The remaining contents of this paper are arranged as follows: the Sect. 2 introduces the related literature and research progress; the Sect. 3 describes the network construction and model design process of this paper; the Sect. 4 presents the experimental results of the dataset and the model; and the Sect. 5 provides the summary.

2 Related Studies

Predicting startup success can be equated to predicting venture capital success. As defined by most scholars, regarded as a firm making a merger and acquisition (M&A) or making an initial public offering (IPO) [3]. Early research involved more internal and empirical information [8, 11, 12], and while having more information is helpful, the asymmetric nature of venture capital events and the "financial cracks" caused by pandemic factors make it increasingly difficult to obtain critical data [13].

Since the prediction problem can be viewed as a binary classification problem of "0" and "1", classification algorithms in machine learning can be applied. Early causal studies and the explosion of investment events in recent years provide powerful inputs for forecasting using statistical or machine learning models. This approach can effectively improve the efficiency and accuracy of venture capital investments through feature engineering of real business datasets, and can even outperform the decisions of human investors under the same circumstances [14]. Popular classification algorithms include Logistic Regression, k-Nearest Neighbors, Decision Trees, Support Vector Machine (SVM), etc. However, such algorithms may miss rich network information and ignore interactions between different entities due to the influence of manual feature inputs and the unique network structure in investment events.

Inspired by deep learning algorithms in recent years, convolutional neural networks, recurrent neural networks, and Transformer models have been expanding their applications in the field of prediction. Data trends can be accurately predicted by training multilayer neural networks to model and learn complex patterns of data. Convolutional Neural Networks (CNNs) are suitable for image recognition and video analysis. Recurrent Neural Networks (RNNs) and its variants such as LSTM and GRU are suitable for processing sequential data. For graph-structured data, Graph Neural Networks (GNNs) have proven to be the most effective deep learning method, and the main representatives include Graph Convolutional Networks (GCNs), Graph Attention Networks (GATs), Graph Autoencoders (GAEs), etc. [15].

The graph convolutional network (GCN) proposed by Thomas N. Kipf and Max Welling [16] maps nodes to the vector representation of low-dimensional space by stacked convolution operations, which can effectively realize the supervised node classification task. Obviously, from the perspective of data types and prediction purposes, it is very appropriate to apply graph neural networks to predict the success of startups. However, there are heterogeneity challenges in using the GCN methodology to predict the success of startups. Specifically, GCN is applicable to homogeneous networks, and the entities involved in networks include one type of node. Therefore, this paper aims to construct a graph neural network model that can be used for heterogeneous networks to predict the success or failure of startups. This method overcomes the limitations of heterogeneous nodes by aggregating information from first-order and second-order neighborhood nodes, and applies its successfully to predict the success of startups.

3   Methodology

3.1   Graph Convolutional Networks

Graph Convolutional Network (GCN) [16] is a deep learning model designed for analyzing graph-structured data, and the research in this paper is based on the seminal work on graph convolutional neural networks. For a graph $G = (V, E)$, defined by its node set $V = \{v_1, v_2, ..., v_n\} \in \mathbb{R}^n$ and edge set $E = \{e(v_i, v_j) : 1 \leq i, j \leq n\} \in \mathbb{R}^{n \times n}$. The corresponding adjacency matrix is denoted as $A \in \mathbb{R}^{n \times n}$, and the feature matrix of nodes is $X \in \mathbb{R}^{n \times F}$, where n is the number of nodes and F is the dimension of features. Define normalized Laplacian matrix is $\hat{L} = I - D^{-\frac{1}{2}} A D^{-\frac{1}{2}}$, D is the diagonal matrix with $d_{ii} = \sum_j a_{ij}$, $a_{ij} \in A$, and I is the identity matrix.

Each layer of GCN updates the features of the nodes based on their neighbors, so the operation of each layer can be understood as a process of aggregation of neighbor information [17]. By considering higher-order neighbors, the model can fuse node information at greater distances and express itself using information from more distant neighboring nodes. The update of the node embedding of 2-layer GCN can be expressed as,

$$\hat{A} = \tilde{D}^{-\frac{1}{2}} \tilde{A} \tilde{D}^{-\frac{1}{2}} \tag{1}$$

$$H^{(2)} = \sigma\left(\hat{A}H^{(1)}W^{(1)}\right) = \sigma\left(\hat{A}\sigma\left(\hat{A}XW^{(0)}\right)W^{(1)}\right) \tag{2}$$

where $\tilde{A} = A + I$, $\tilde{D}$ is the degree matrix of $\tilde{A}$, $\sigma(\cdot)$ is activation function, $W^{(0)}$ and $W^{(1)}$ are the learnable parameters.

3.2 New Graph Convolutional Networks for Heterogeneous Networks

For a heterogeneous graph G = (V, E, T, S), including a set of node types T and a set of edge types S, where $|T| + |S| \geq 2$. Each node $v \in V$ satisfies $\phi : V \rightarrow T$, and each edge $e \in E$ satisfies $\phi : E \rightarrow S$. Clearly, there exists more than one type of nodes and edges for heterogeneous graph. Since different types of nodes and edges may have completely different semantics and importance, a single aggregation strategy for GCN cannot adequately capture effective information.

The modeling of startup success prediction in this paper is based on historical investment events. Since the network contains two types of nodes and two types of investment relationships, the percentage of the two types of networks will affect the strength of the heterogeneous attribute of the network, and affects the proportion of nodes belonging to the same class. Therefore, this paper introduces the model proposed by J Zhu et al. [18] to design a model to improve the performance of GCN on heterogeneous graphs, which can better adapt to networks with different levels of heterogeneity. It is improved by combining the research in this paper and named as VC-HGCN model (Fig. 1).

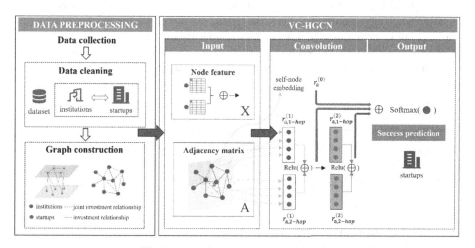

Fig. 1. The overview of proposed model

Model Inputs. Since the proposed model requires graph-structured inputs, it is needed to first model the network of historical investment events, including the network of investment relationships between investment institutions and startups, and the network of co-investments between investment institutions, and build the appropriate representations for these different types of nodes and relationships. Consider figure $G = (V, E, X, T, S)$ is composed of a set of nodes $V \in \mathbb{R}^{n \times n}$, a set of edges $E \subseteq V \times V$, a set of features on nodes $X \in \mathbb{R}^{n \times F}$, a set of node types $T = \{T_{in}, T_{st}\}$, T_{in} represent the investment institution node, T_{st} represent the startup node, a set of edge types $S = \{S_{in}, S_{co}\}$, S_{in} represent investment relationships, S_{co} represent co-investment relationship. Each node $v \in V$ satisfy $\phi : V \rightarrow T$, Each edge $e \in E$ satisfy $\phi : E \rightarrow S$. For investment institutions to invest in startups, a set of edges $E_{invest} = \{(v_i, v_j) \in E | S(v_i, v_j) = S_{in} \wedge T(v_i) = T_{in} \wedge T(v_j) = T_{st}\}$. For investment institutions to invest in the same round in the same firm, a set of edges $E_{co-invest} = \{(v_i, v_j) \in E | S(v_i, v_j) = S_{co} \wedge T(v) = T_{in}\}$.

The corresponding adjacency matrix is denoted as $A \in \mathbb{R}^{n \times n}$, and the feature matrix of nodes is $X \in \mathbb{R}^{n \times F}$, where n is the number of total nodes and F is the dimension of features.

$$A = \begin{bmatrix} A_{in \times in} & A_{in \times st} \\ A_{st \times in} & A_{st \times st} \end{bmatrix} \tag{3}$$

where $A_{in \times in} \in \mathbb{R}^{q \times q}$ is a sub-matrix denoting the co-investment relationship. $A_{in \times st} \in \mathbb{R}^{q \times p}$ is a sub-matrix denoting the relationship of the investment institutions in the startups. $A_{st \times in} \in \mathbb{R}^{p \times q}$ and $A_{st \times st} \in \mathbb{R}^{p \times p}$ are meaningless sub-matrix. The total number of investment institutions are q, the total number of startups are p.

The features of investment institutions and startups are in f_{in} and f_{st} dimensions, respectively. For the following convolution, setting $F = \max(f_{in}, f_{st})$, a feature transformation layer is defined to map the two types of node features to the same feature space.

Convolutional Layer. Since GCN directly aggregates information about itself and its neighbors when aggregating messages, the characteristics of the learned nodes are similar to those of its neighbors. Therefore, in order to learn the heterogeneous graph better, this model separates self-embedding from neighbor node embedding. From the spectral perspective, layer propagation can be understood as the spectral filtering process of features. In the model proposed in this paper, low and high-frequency components can be captured simultaneously by concatenating self-embedding with neighbor node embedding, so that nodes can be better represented.

For node v, the $i - hop$ neighborhood is defined as $\overline{N}_i(v)$, denoted as the set of nodes whose shortest path is i of node v. To reduce the amount of computation, the function of $i - hop$ neighborhood of nodes is calculated by a sparse matrix.

The feature embedding of the node itself is denoted as,

$$r_v^{(0)} = \sigma(x_v W_e) \tag{4}$$

where $x_v \in X$ is the features of node v itself and W_e is the learnable weight matrix.

The representation of v for the kth round of iteration is that,

$$r_v^{(k)} = Relu\left(r_{v,1}^{(k)} \| r_{v,2}^{(k)}\right) \text{ and } r_{v,i}^{(k)} = AGGR\{r_u^{(k-1)} : u \in \overline{N}_i(v)\} \tag{5}$$

where $\|$ denotes the concatenation. Our model works best at $k = 2$.

Throughout the training process of the model, the loss is calculated using the cross-entropy loss function. The gradient is calculated by back propagation algorithm and Adam optimizer to update the model parameters to minimize the loss function.

Model Output. In the output part of the model, we concatenate all the representations learned by the model as inputs to the final output layer. After concatenating, the model is classified by a fully connected layer, and node labels are predicted using softmax($\cdot$).

$$R_v = \left[r_v^{(0)} \| r_v^{(1)} \| r_v^{(2)} \right] \tag{6}$$

$$\hat{y} = \mathrm{softmax}(R_v \cdot W_c + b_o) \tag{7}$$

where W_c and b_o are the learnable parameters, $\hat{y}$ is the output. The final output of the model is a binary categorization result with a label of 1 for "business success" and 0 for "business failure".

4 Experiment and Results

4.1 Experimental Dataset

The data used in this paper comes from Zero2IPO database, which is the data set of venture capital investment from Private Equity Venture Capital Events Database, the dataset of investment institutions from Venture Capital Institutions Database, and the dataset of Exit Events Database. The data period is from January 1, 2000 to December 31, 2022. Data cleaning shall be carried out in the following situations:(1) The data of venture capital with missing main information shall be deleted, including the data of "non-disclosure", "non-public investors" and other specific investment subjects which cannot be known; (2) The transaction nature of venture capital events is diverse. Non-venture capital events such as "mature" stage are deleted, and the research target is focused on venture capital; (3) Excluding investment events from individual investors. The processed dataset contains 142,485 investment events. Considering that venture capital exit events usually take 5–7 years, in order to fully screen successful startups, investment events that occurred during 2016–2017 were selected as experimental objects, with a total of 26,603 venture capital events. This paper selects two successful exit methods commonly found in existing studies, IPO exit and M&A exit [3], as the signs of startup success.

4.2 Feature Engineering

Startup Characteristics. To evaluate the characteristics and potential of startup companies, this paper constructs the characteristics of integrated enterprise nodes. For a startup v_p, feature vector $X_p = [X_p^{round}; X_p^{stage}; X_p^{type}; X_p^{area}; X_p^{ind}]$. Among them, the region and industry attributes of each enterprise are static and invariant, so unique heat coding is used to extend them, and finally 32-dimensional features were constructed. As shown in Table 1.

Table 1. Startup characteristics table

Property symbol	Meaning	Type
Round	The investment round of the enterprise	numeric type
Stage	The investment stage of the enterprise	numeric type
Type	The investment type of the enterprise	numeric type
Area	The location of the enterprise	literal type
Industry	The industry of the enterprise	literal type

Institutional Characteristics. For an investment institution v_q, feature vector $X_q = [X_q^{exp}; X_q^{reg}; X_q^{ind}; X_q^{sta}]$, the combination of four aspects of information can fully reflect the specific attributes and background of each institution. Further, the four feature vectors of investment experience, region attribute, industry attribute and stage attribute are expanded and taken as a set of node features of venture capital institutions. A total of 22-dimensional features of venture capital institutions are added. The specific features are given in Table 2, and all features are numerical data.

Table 2. Institutional characteristics table

Feature	Property symbol
Investment experience	Age, Amount, Firms
Region attribute	Provinces, YRD, PRD, BTH, Other Area
Industry attribute	Computer, Medicine, Biotech, Semicon, Media, Other Industry
Stage attribute	Stages, Seed, Initiation, Growth, Rounds, A, B, C

4.3 Experiment Settings

The total number of startups in the experimental interval is 9,192, and the ratio of the number of startup successes to startup failures according to the definition of startup success is approach 1:36. Due to the serious imbalance in the ratio of positive and negative samples, in order to ensure the training effect of the model, the negative samples are randomly sampled using down-sampling, and the ratio of the positive and negative samples is 1:10. Since this paper is based on the investment relationship modeling of companies, the 2016–2017 investment network is reconstructed after resampling. The final experimental data contains 6714 investment events and 9273 co-investment events. The remaining samples are divided into training set, validation set and test set according to the ratio of 6:2:2. To ensure the robustness of the experimental results, the experiments were randomly repeated 50 times.

The model constructed in this paper is implemented based on the PyTorch framework, and the detailed hyperparameter settings are shown in Table 3. The model performs best when number of hidden channels is set to 16. The number of output channels was set to 2, which meets the requirements of the binary classification task. The learning rate was set to 0.01, the dropout rate was set to 0.4 to reduce the risk of model overfitting, the epoch was 200, and the optimizer was Adam.

Table 3. Model Basic Settings

Hyper parameterization	Value
Hidden channels	16
Output channels	2
Learning rate	0.01
Dropout rate	0.4
Epoch	200
Optimizer	Adam

4.4 Results

The experiments use Precision, Recall, and F1-score as the model evaluation indexes, and the results were averaged to obtain the evaluation index scores, with the standard deviation in parentheses. The model order was sorted according to the F1-score, and the comparison of the classification performance of different models is shown in Table 4. From the results, it can be seen that the VC-HCNN model constructed in this paper outperforms all the baseline models, and the F1 score of VC-HGCN is 73.98% significantly better than the other models, which indicates the effectiveness of the proposed method for the prediction of startups success potential, and our results achieve a satisfactory performance. In addition to the graph convolutional network model, random forest also achieves better results with an F1 score of 68.42%. It is worth mentioning that nearly 20% of the successful startups in the experimental sample were only invested once. Such startups are difficult to predict through co-investment information, so even with the VC-HGCN model, the F1-score can only reach 73.98%.

4.5 Interpretability

As the performance of the random forest model is the best among machine learning methods, in order to enhance the interpretability of the model, this paper uses the Shapley value to evaluate the importance of the features of random forest model. The main goal of the Shapley value is to explain how much each feature contributes to the prediction of the model. The average value of the feature Shapley values was calculated for all samples in the test set, and the bar chart of Shapley values was obtained, as shown in Fig. 2. Figure 3 shows the colony graph, showing the distribution of Shapley values for important features in actual predictions. It can be found that investment in the growth

Table 4. Comparison of the different algorithms for predicting the success of startups

Model	Precision	Recall	F1-score
VC-HGCN	71.15% (0.0148)	77.43% (0.0132)	73.98% (0.0128)
GCN	67.76% (0.0117)	69.86% (0.0161)	69.70% (0.0135)
Random Forest	75.21% (0.0147)	64.95% (0.0071)	68.42% (0.0080)
SVM	75.75% (0.0201)	64.21% (0.0076)	67.99% (0.0090)
Naive Bayes	69.61% (0.0230)	63.71% (0.0144)	65.93% (0.0159)
Decision Tree	64.51% (0.0123)	60.22% (0.0117)	61.81% (0.0121)

stage of enterprises has a significant impact on predicting the success of startups. On the one hand, the startup can obtain more sources of capital, which is conducive to the growth of the enterprise, and on the other hand, the increase of investment in the startup means that the startup itself has a high potential for success.

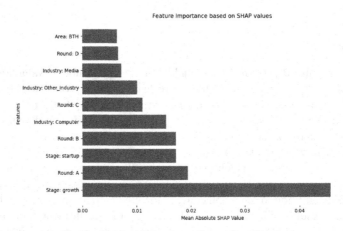

Fig. 2. Shapley feature map for random forests

After removing this feature and re-experimenting with VC-HGCN, it can be seen that the predictive capacity of VC-HGCN-del decreases, proving the importance of this feature (Table 5).

4.6 Robustness Analysis

This study further designs three sets of experiments with three training set sample ratios to ensure the robustness of the model on different samples. As can be seen from Table 6, the model in this paper has good robustness.

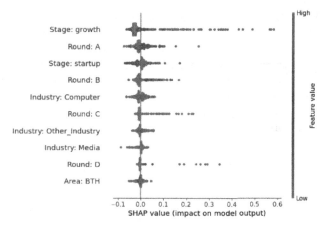

Fig. 3. The colony graph for random forests

Table 5. Comparison table before and after deletion of features

Model	Precision	Recall	F1-score
VC-HGCN	71.15% (0.0148)	77.43% (0.0132)	73.98% (0.0128)
VC-HGCN-del	67.32% (0.0178)	72.05% (0.0095)	69.23% (0.0107)

Table 6. Robust results of the training set sample proportion

Experimental	Setting	Precision	Recall	F1-score
Sample ratio	5:3:2	72.07% (0.0121)	76.32% (0.0083)	73.92% (0.0094)
	7:2:1	74.49% (0.0124)	79.84% (0.0200)	76.78% (0.0143)
	8:1:1	73.73% (0.0154)	76.75% (0.0168)	75.06% (0.0131)

5 Conclusion

In this paper, we propose a model VC-HGCN for predicting the success potential of startups using a sample of investment events from Chinese VCs to realize the processing of heterogeneous networks. Experimental results on the China 2016–2017 VC dataset show that the model constructed in this paper outperforms multiple classification machine learning methods commonly used for startup success prediction. In the VC-HGCN model, we pay special attention to two types of networks: one is the investment relationship network between investment institutions and startups, and the other is the co-investment network between investment institutions. Unlike traditional methods that rely only on node attributes or local network structures, VC-HGCN considers a wider range of network environments and deeper structural features, which is particularly important in the prediction task in the venture capital field.

However, the model in this paper needs to be combined with a theory-driven approach to feature construction, as it relies on feature extraction. In future work, we plan to further explore the potential of the model. For example, by validating it on larger data sets, and considering more complex network dynamics and investment behavior patterns, to continuously improve the accuracy and interpretability of venture capital success predictions, thereby creating greater value for investors and entrepreneurs.

Acknowledgement. This research was supported by the NSSF 22FGLB056, the National Statistical Science Foundation of China Project number 2023LY078, Program for innovation Research in CUFE, and the Emerging Interdisciplinary Project of CUFE.

References

1. Luger, M.I., Koo, J.: Defining and tracking business start-ups. Small Bus. Econ. **24**, 17–28 (2005)
2. Zider, B.: How venture capital works. Harv. Bus. Rev. **76**(6), 131–139 (1998)
3. Hochberg, Y.V., Ljungqvist, A., Lu, Y.: Whom you know matters: venture capital networks and investment performance. J. Financ. **62**(1), 251–301 (2007)
4. Krishna, A., Agrawal, A., Choudhary, A.: Predicting the outcome of startups: less failure, more success. In: 2016 IEEE 16th International Conference on Data Mining Workshops (ICDMW), pp. 798–805. IEEE (2016)
5. Kerr, W.R., Nanda, R., Rhodes-Kropf, M.: Entrepreneurship as experimentation. J. Econ. Perspect. **28**(3), 25–48 (2014)
6. Gompers, P., Kovner, A., Lerner, J.: Specialization and success: evidence from venture capital. J. Econ. Manage. Strategy **18**(3), 817–844 (2009)
7. Bargagli-Stoffi, F.J., Niederreiter, J., Riccaboni, M.: Supervised learning for the prediction of firm dynamics. In: Consoli, S., Reforgiato Recupero, D., Saisana, M. (eds.) Data Science for Economics and Finance, pp. 19–41. Springer, Cham (2021). https://doi.org/10.1007/978-3-030-66891-4_2
8. Gruber, M., MacMillan, I.C., Thompson, J.D.: Look before you leap: market opportunity identification in emerging technology firms. Manage. Sci. **54**(9), 1652–1665 (2008)
9. Wang, D., Pahnke, E.C., McDonald, R.M.: The past is prologue? Venture-capital syndicates' collaborative experience and start-up exits. Acad. Manag. J. **65**(2), 371–402 (2022)
10. Ling, L., Li, Y., Long, D., et al.: Does syndicating bring syndicating? An exploration targeting ECF based on social structure by complex network analysis. Soc. Networks **70**, 228–239 (2022)
11. Yankov, B.: Overview of success prediction models for new ventures. In: International Conference Automatics and Informatics, vol. 12, pp. 13–16 (2012)
12. Li, H.: How does new venture strategy matter in the environment–performance relationship? J. High Technol. Managem. Res. **12**(2), 183–204 (2001)
13. Brown, R., Rocha, A.: Entrepreneurial uncertainty during the Covid-19 crisis: mapping the temporal dynamics of entrepreneurial finance. J. Bus. Ventur. Insights **14**, e00174 (2020)
14. Weibl J, Hess T. Finding the next unicorn: When big data meets venture capital[J]. 2019
15. Wu, Z., Pan, S., Chen, F., et al.: A comprehensive survey on graph neural networks. IEEE Trans. Neural Networks Learn. Syst. **32**(1), 4–24 (2020)
16. Kipf, T.N., Welling, M.: Semi-supervised classification with graph convolutional networks. arXiv preprint arXiv:1609.02907 (2016)

17. Yang, H., Zhuang, Z., Pan, W.: A graph convolutional neural network for gene expression data analysis with multiple gene networks. Stat. Med. **40**(25), 5547–5564 (2021)
18. Zhu, J., Yan, Y., Zhao, L., et al.: Beyond homophily in graph neural networks: current limitations and effective designs. Adv. Neural. Inf. Process. Syst. **33**, 7793–7804 (2020)

The Influence of Algorithmic Control on Gig Drivers' Coping Behavior in Ride-Hailing Platforms

Yize Li[1], Jian Tang[1], Xuefeng Li[1]([✉]), and Xinxue Zhou[2]

[1] School of Information, Central University of Finance and Economics, Beijing, China
lixuefeng@cufe.edu.cn
[2] School of Business, Guangxi University, Nanning, China

Abstract. The use of algorithmic control is commonplace in gig economy platforms. Algorithms may direct, evaluate, or discipline gig workers to enforce their compliance, or conversely, trigger their reactance. This paper explores the impact of algorithmic control on ride-hailing drivers' coping behavior. Based on the legitimacy process model, we develop a research model that links perceived algorithmic control to gig drivers' compliance and workaround behaviors. Using survey data from 197 ride-hailing drivers, we find that perceived algorithmic control positively affects fairness and privacy judgment. Fairness judgment has a positive impact on compliance behavior, and privacy judgment has a negative impact on workaround behavior. The paper discusses theoretical and practical implications.

Keywords: Gig Economy · Algorithmic Control · Ride-hailing Platforms · Mixed Research Method

1 Introduction

With the exponential advancement of information technology and digital algorithms, the gig economy has emerged and rapidly developed into a new force driving economic growth. Gig platforms extensively use intelligent technologies to reshape organizational control. Algorithmic control (AC) is defined as leveraging the power of advanced digital technologies and smart algorithms to prompt workers to act in ways that align with organizational expectations [4]. AC can automate the managerial control process and enable effective business operations. In this process, the impact of algorithmic control on gig workers and platforms is worth exploring to ensure the responsible use of algorithmic control and promote the harmonious and stable development of the gig economy. A typical example is the ride-hailing service platforms, such as DiDi and Uber, which use app-based AC systems to control millions of gig drivers.

Despite gig drivers' freelancer status, their labor processes are under the surveillance of algorithms. According to labor process theory, traditional companies obtain the desired behaviors from their employees through three mechanisms, namely guidance, evaluation, and restraint. Prior research shows that AC implements more comprehensive control over gig workers through the above three control mechanisms. Among them, "guidance" informs employees of the work to be done and the corresponding guidelines; "evaluation" requires the review of employees to correct mistakes and evaluate performance; and "restraint" includes penalties and rewards for workers to motivate them to comply with the employer's instructions on the labor process.

The paradox of an independent workforce and tight algorithmic control raises questions about how the use of AC may affect gig drivers' judgments and their coping behaviors. Existing research focuses on the impact of AC on the emotions and perceptions of gig drivers, such as anxiety, job insecurity, privacy concerns, etc., as well as the impact of algorithmic control on drivers' turnover intentions, which are mostly negative [11, 13]. Only a few research explore the coping behaviors that workers might follow AC if they decide to stay on the platform. We argue that even though drivers follow the instructions of AC, their behaviors can be differentiated as compliance behavior or workaround behavior. Compliance behavior refers to gig drivers fully complying with the work instructions given by the AC, while workaround behavior is defined as conscious adaptations of work activities that are not expected to be changed in this manner.

As such, micro-level legitimacy judgments [3] – broadly defined as an individual's assessment that the actions of an entity (i.e., a ride-hailing platform) are desirable, proper, or appropriate – may help link gig drivers' perceptions of AC to their coping behavior [15]. Examining legitimacy-related issues in the context of the gig platform economy is interesting because AC changes the control relationship from "human-to-human" to "algorithms-to-human". In the context of our study, three dimensions of legitimacy judgment are most relevant to gig work: autonomy, fairness, and privacy [15]. Understanding what factors contribute to compliance or workaround behavior can provide nuanced insights into gig drivers' coping behaviors.

Against this backdrop, this study builds on a theory of micro-level legitimacy [3], which points out that the formation process of micro-level legitimacy judgments goes through three stages: perception, judgment, and action, to develop a research model focusing on two questions: (1) How does the use of AC relate to gig drivers' legitimacy judgments? (2) How are such judgments related to gig drivers' compliance and workaround behaviors? To answer these questions, this paper focuses on the ride-hailing industry, which is a typical case of the application of AC [13]. The structure of this paper is as follows: First, we review the research related to AC on gig platforms and workers' coping behaviors. Next, we develop our research model and research hypotheses. Then, we describe our research methodology and present empirical results. Finally, we discuss the theoretical contributions and practical significance of this paper, as well as the main limitations and direction for future research.

2 Related Work

2.1 Algorithmic Control

Organizations use algorithms and digital technologies to ensure that worker behavior aligns with organizational goals and interests [4, 11, 13]. In this process, AC serves as a proxy for human managers, typically driven by massive data and executing automated decisions. On gig platforms, algorithms are not just an auxiliary tool but a control means that can fully replace human managers.

Scholars commonly regard AC in gig platforms as an organizational control practice encompassing multiple control mechanisms. In recent years, research on AC in gig economy has gradually enriched both theoretically and empirically. These researches are mostly based on the labor process theory [11, 12], which emphasizes that control systems in work settings contain three elements: direction, evaluation, and discipline (see Table 1) [5]. Some studies also categorize specific mechanisms based on the different purposes or functions of AC [15]. However, the current research on algorithm control dimensions is based on multiple scenarios, many of which are not suitable for ride-hailing platforms. Therefore, it is necessary to delve into the dimension division and specific mechanisms of AC on ride-hailing platforms.

Table 1. Basic forms of algorithmic control (AC).

Form	Definition	Illustrative examples in ride-hailing platforms
Direction	The mechanism and method by which employers specify labor tasks, organize labor orders, determine production accuracy, and arrange labor time	Platforms assign orders in real-time based on drivers' personal circumstances, automatically providing drivers with the information they need
Evaluation	The supervision and evaluation procedures by which employers correct mistakes in the production process, evaluate workers' labor performance	Platforms monitor drivers and evaluate drivers with performance metrics (e.g., average customer ratings, ride acceptance, and completion rates)
Discipline	The mechanism that employers use to reward and punish workers to achieve productive cooperation and force workers to comply with the labor process	Platforms provide drivers with dynamic rewards and penalties, which can be expressed in various forms, such as driver scores, bonuses, or fines

2.2 Worker Coping Behaviors Under Algorithmic Control

Organizational rules dictate the expected employees' behaviors, which normally adhere to the organizations' benefits. Similarly, gig platforms also expect workers to comply with AC to standardize their services and enhance platform benefits. Therefore, we believe that GIG drivers' compliance with AC means that they need to complete their work in the manner and process expected by the platform, rather than just obtaining the results of their work. Previous studies have shown that control elements (norms, evaluations, and rewards), information quality, and individual perceptions such as threat assessment, and normative beliefs, affect workers' compliance behavior. Information systems (IS) scholars have explored information technology compliance in traditional corporate organizations, but there is little research on the compliance of gig workers under the emerging AC.

Non-compliance might be a multidimensional concept, including non-use, workaround, and misuse [10]. Among these, a workaround is a goal-driven adaptation or alteration of the existing work system, intended to overcome or minimize obstacles or impacts caused by managerial constraints [1]. When the control of IT is not in the interests of employees, employees may "workaround" by deviating from established procedures. Such workaround methods might pose risks, be inefficient or erroneous, and can impact subsequent work activities. Because AC in gig platforms completely replaces traditional organizational control to regulate the entire working process, algorithms are no longer just auxiliary controls like IT, and non-use or misuse of AC is unlikely to happen for gig workers under AC. Therefore, this paper focuses on the workaround behavior.

On gig platforms, workers' workaround behavior is directed against AC, i.e., using workaround methods to circumvent obstacles set by algorithms [1], typically associated with maximizing personal benefits or not wanting to blindly follow algorithms in executing work [13]. For example, experienced gig drivers take advantage of system vulnerabilities to induce passengers to cancel orders they did not want to complete. Qualitative studies have pointed out that the tension between gig drivers and ride-hailing platforms in terms of work autonomy and compensation will lead them to adopt workaround behavior [13], but relevant empirical studies are relatively scarce.

3 Research Model and Hypotheses

This study focuses on the impact of ride-hailing drivers' perceived AC on two key coping behaviors, which are compliance and workaround behavior, and further investigates the mediating role of micro-level legitimacy judgments. Micro-level legitimacy judgment, as an individual subjective perception, refers to an evaluator's approval of the organization, its actions, or its practices as desirable and appropriate.

In traditional "human-to-human" control relationships, the legitimacy of control usually originates from social power, such as a manager's formal position in the organizational hierarchy or legal contract. However, in ride-hailing platforms, algorithms replace human managers to exert direct control over workers, transforming the control relationship into "algorithm-to-human". Workers' legitimacy judgments of AC may change accordingly. Therefore, it's necessary to explore how AC affects gig drivers' micro-level legitimacy judgments and how these judgments influence drivers' coping behaviors. This study draws on past research to conceptualize micro-level legitimacy judgment into three dimensions most relevant to gig work: autonomy, fairness, and privacy [15].

To summarize, this paper builds the research model based on the legitimacy process model [3]. This model suggests that the micro-level legitimacy judgment formation process goes through three stages: perceptions, judgments, and actions, which provides an important theoretical foundation for our study. In the following, we will detail the research hypotheses demonstrated in Fig. 1.

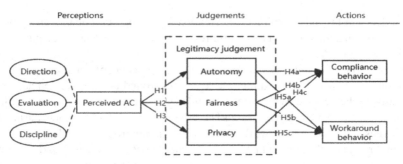

Fig. 1. Research model

3.1 Perceived AC and Micro-level Legitimacy Judgment

In the literature on AC, the mainstream view discusses scholars mainly focusing on the negative impact of AC on gig workers, suggesting that AC intensifies the "exploitation" of workers by gig platforms. We believe that although the complete replacement of human managers by AC may have increased complaints such as constant surveillance, limited transparency, and dehumanization, the certain negative effects, its powerful technological advantages provide workers with personalized support and efficient working advice, enabling platform work based on internet applications.

Flexibility in working hours and locations and the possibility gig drivers autonomously arrange their work are among the most prominent features of the ride-hailing platforms. Past research indicates that gig drivers do not perceive AC as leading to the loss of work autonomy, because they can flexibly plan and adjust their work schedules [13]. Fully automated AC breaks through the limitations of the traditional working environment, allowing gig drivers to freely enter and exit the platform and choose when and where to work. Specifically, relying on AC, the platform can recruit new workers more quickly on a larger scale, thus eliminating the need to sign employment contracts with drivers [13]. At the same time, AC's powerful computing power can integrate supply and demand resources in real-time, eliminating the need to require drivers to work all day. Hence, AC is an important basis for the autonomous work, we hypothesize:

H1: Gig drivers' perceived AC is positively related to autonomy judgment.

In traditional work environments, employees may receive unfair treatment due to the personal biases of managers. However, AC does not differ among individual drivers. Research shows that adherence to a set of unified rules of automated control can increase transparency, thereby leading to a sense of fairness among gig drivers [14]. AC can rationally and fairly allocate work tasks, provide information support, and implement consistent monitoring, reward, and punishment rules for all drivers. Therefore, gig drivers' perceived AC leads to stronger fairness judgment, and we hypothesize:

H2: Gig drivers' perceived AC is positively related to fairness judgment.

Ride-hailing platforms monitor drive behavior and collect personal data at a granular level [4]. Different from human supervisors, AC can integrate data from different sources, including drivers, customers, and other sensors, thereby reaching a comprehensive data record. Smartphones can record drivers' physical movements and conversations, providing evidence of drivers' adherence to or deviation from work requirements. At the same time, AC has lower transparency, and the algorithms used for data collection and analysis are usually secretive [11]. Therefore, gig drivers may find it difficult to fully understand when, where and what kind of information about them is being collected by algorithms. The panoramic monitoring of AC intensifies drivers' privacy concerns, weakening their privacy legitimacy judgment of perceived AC. Therefore, we hypothesize:

H3: Gig drivers' perceived AC is negatively related to privacy judgment.

3.2 Micro-level Legitimacy Judgment and Worker Coping Behavior

When employees believe organizational rules and authority are legitimate, they are more willing to comply with organizational rules and authority [2]. Regarding autonomy, a major reason driver is attracted to ride-hailing platforms is their flexibility in terms of time and a relatively stable hourly wage that doesn't fluctuate much with the number of working hours. This allows drivers to independently decide when to start working and how long to work. Similarly, previous research has found that organizational processes (including management control processes) judged by employees as fair help to build trust and commitment and encourage voluntary cooperation with the company. Employees who believe they are treated fairly are more likely to comply with company policies and are less likely to engage in counterproductive work behaviors. In terms of privacy, gig drivers are usually well aware of the platform's monitoring capabilities, but if drivers believe that the platform's monitoring is necessary and does not violate their privacy, they typically choose to comply with regulations. Hence, this paper proposes the following hypotheses:

H4a: Gig drivers' autonomy judgment is positively related to compliance behavior.
H4b: Gig drivers' fairness judgment is positively related to compliance behavior.
H4c: Gig drivers' privacy judgment is positively related to compliance behavior.

Workers' judgments on the legitimacy of AC can reduce their workaround behavior [15]. Conversely, when workers are guided by algorithms they perceive as unfair, it may undermine their sense of morality and increase their willingness to engage in unethical behaviors. For example, if drivers believe the platform's AC is unfair, they might try to manipulate their use of the platform's app, such as turning off the app after a long drive to avoid being too far from home [9]. If employees feel their privacy is violated, continuous tracking and close monitoring can lead to feelings of anxiety and tension [9, 14]. The resulting tension may lead drivers to adopt certain workaround methods to protect their autonomy and privacy [13]. Therefore, when organizational and individual interests align, AC deemed legitimate may lead to reduced workaround behavior. Given the above perspectives, this paper believes:

H5a: Gig drivers' autonomy judgment is negatively related to workaround behavior.
H5b: Gig drivers' fairness judgment is negatively related to workaround behavior.
H5c: Gig drivers' privacy judgment is negatively related to workaround behavior.

4   Research Method

4.1   Data Collection and Sample Characteristics

This study collected data using a questionnaire survey. There are three main ways to obtain samples: cooperation with research companies, online recruitment, and snowball sampling. Drivers recruited by the Internet need to provide relevant proof (such as screenshots or screen recordings of ride-hailing apps with real-time time), and then these drivers invited the researchers into WeChat group chats for snowball sampling. A total of 260 questionnaires were distributed in this study, and 197 were valid. Due to the lack of supervision by a third-party questionnaire platform, the drivers were not all serious about filling out the questionnaire, and those questionnaires that failed the attention test and took less than 2 min to answer or longer than 10 min were deleted. In our sample, the number of women and men was 50 and 147 respectively. 106 participants were 34 years old or younger, and 91 participants were older than 35 years. 114 participants had an education level of high school or below, 39 and 41 participants had a college or bachelor's degree, respectively, and only 3 people had a master's degree.

4.2   Measurements

This study adapted measures from existing studies (see Table 2). Perceived AC was adapted based on labor process theory [5] and the scales by Pei [12]. Labor process theory emphasizes that control systems in work settings contain three elements: guiding workers' work, evaluating workers' performance, and constraining workers through reward and punishment mechanisms. To contextualize the understanding of the use of AC in ride-hailing platforms, we conducted 12 semi-structured interviews with ride-hailing drivers. Each interview lasted about 40 min. The interview data were analyzed to help refine the measurements used in the study.

We modelled perceived AC as a three-dimensional second-order construct, using a reflective-formative (type II) specification [7]. The main reason for this specification is that we view direction, evaluation and discipline as the three key mechanisms of AC based on the labor process theory, as opposed to more concrete manifestations of this construct. Modeling perceived AC as a second-order construct also allowed us to reduce the number of structural relationships, making the model more parsimonious, while increasing the bandwidth of content covered [7].

Moreover, the control variables included gender, age, years of employment, annual household income, overall job satisfaction, and whether ride-hailing was the only source of income. Measurement items were all scored on a seven-point Likert scale. Before the main survey, we conducted three pre-tests, with 39, 30, and 50 respondents, respectively. Data collected from the pre-tests were used to assess the reliability and validity of the instrument.

4.3   Assessment of Measurement Model

Since this study measures the relationship between multiple latent variables, and our model has two dependent variables, we chose to use structural equation models for

Table 2. Operationalization of focal study constructs.

Construct		Reference(s)	Items
Perceived algorithmic control	Direction	Adapted from Pei et al. (2021) [12]	The system has assigned me a work task
			The system has given me work instructions
			The system provided me with information support
			The system helped me plan the work tasks
	Evaluation		The system tracks my location in real-time
			The system keeps following up on my work progress
			The system monitors my conversations with passengers in real time
			The system monitors my driving behavior in real-time
			The system automatically evaluates the quality of my work
	Discipline		The system will automatically calculate my rating
			The system will automatically reward or punish me
			The system will automatically increase or decrease the quality of orders assigned to me
			The system will automatically increase or decrease the number of orders assigned to me

(continued)

Table 2. (*continued*)

Construct		Reference(s)	Items
			The system will dynamically adjust the reward or penalty for me
Legitimacy judgment	Autonomy	Wiener et al. (2023) [15]	I can decide my own work schedule
			I don't think it's affected by the system
			I have the flexibility to organize my work
	Fairness		The rules of the system are fair
			The system enforces the relevant rules fairly for all drivers
			The system requires the same for all drivers
			The system is consistent in enforcing the rules
	Privacy		I feel that the system's monitoring of me violates my privacy. [R]
			The personal information collected by the system makes me feel uncomfortable. [R, D]
			The way the system monitors my behavior makes me uncomfortable. [R]
			I feel that the way the system collects information violates my privacy. [R]
Coping strategies	Compliance	Liang et al. (2013) [10]	I comply with the requirements of the system for my work
			I obey the system's schedule for my work

(*continued*)

Table 2. (*continued*)

Construct	Reference(s)	Items
		I follow the work instructions given to me by the system
Workaround	Laumer et al. (2017) [8]	I will find a way to avoid using the work guide given to me by the system
		I often use alternatives rather than just using the work guidelines the system gives me
		I will not rely entirely on the work instructions given to me by the system
		I will use "clever" methods to make the system lose control of me

[R]Reverse-coded item; [D]Deleted based on item-validation process.

data analytics. Compared to its covariance-based alternative (CB-SEM), partial least squares structural equation modeling (PLS-SEM) can readily handle both reflective and formative constructs, including second-order constructs of a reflective-formative type [6]. Since our research model includes a reflective-formative second-order construct (perceived AC), we employed the two-stage approach [7]. This approach draws on the repeated-indicators approach to obtain latent variable scores for the lower-order constructs (i.e., direction, evaluation, and discipline AC), and then uses these scores as manifest variables to measure the higher-order construct (i.e., perceived AC).

Specifically, in the first stage, we evaluated the reliability and validity of the measurement model as follows. To ensure item reliability, we analyzed the outer loadings of each item. (As noted above, all first-order constructs were measured reflectively with multiple items.) On this basis, we dropped one privacy item (see Table 2). The outer loadings of all remaining items are above the threshold of 0.7, except for one evaluation AC item being slightly below the threshold (0.679). In terms of composite reliability (CR) and average variance extracted (AVE), all constructs exceed the suggested thresholds of 0.7 and 0.5, respectively, indicating construct reliability and convergent validity [7] (see Table 3). Further, the square root of each construct's AVE was greater than the highest correlation with any other construct (see Table 3) and the loadings of each construct's assigned items were greater than cross-loadings, establishing discriminant validity for all constructs. In addition, all HTMT values are below the threshold value of 0.9 [7].

In the second stage, we re-evaluated our measurement model and were able to re-establish item reliability, construct reliability, as well as convergent and discriminant validity for all reflective constructs. We then assessed our formative construct (i.e., perceived AC) in terms of potential collinearity issues and the significance of outer weights and loadings [7].

Table 3. Convergent and Discriminant Validity Analyses

	DIR	EVA	DIS	AJ	FJ	PJ	COM	WU	CR	AVE
DIR	**0.800**								0.813	0.639
EVA	0.520	**0.723**							0.777	0.523
DIS	0.614	0.650	**0.806**						0.877	0.649
AJ	0.160	0.185	0.100	**0.865**					0.850	0.748
FJ	0.453	0.295	0.368	0.412	**0.820**				0.912	0.672
PJ	0.281	0.202	0.337	0.114	0.517	**0.927**			0.925	0.859
COM	0.495	0.179	0.257	0.160	0.444	0.318	**0.865**		0.851	0.749
WU	−0.300	−0.141	−0.330	−0.079	−0.363	−0.480	−0.313	**0.846**	0.880	0.716

DIR = Direction AC, EVA = Evaluation AC, DIS = Discipline AC, AJ = Autonomy judgment, FJ = Fairness judgment, PJ = Privacy judgment, COM = Compliance, WU = Workaround behavior. Diagonal cells (bold) show square root of AVE.

First, all (item-level) variance inflation factor (VIF) values are below the most conservative threshold of 2.1, suggesting that collinearity is unlikely to be an issue. Second, while the outer weight of two items was not significant (evaluation: $\beta = 0.047$, t = 0.155, ns; discipline: $\beta = 0.363$, t = 1.018, ns), the outer loadings of all three items are significant (direction: $\beta = 0.951$, t = 8.940, p < 0.001; evaluation: $\beta = 0.812$, t = 5.236, p < 0.001; discipline: $\beta = 0.650$, t = 3.727, p < 0.001). On this basis, and given the three items' theoretical relevance [11], we decided to retain all of them [7].

Moreover, to analyze the strength of construct intercorrelations, the VIF values for all constructs and control variables included in our research model are clearly below the threshold of 5. Finally, we mitigate the risk of common method bias (CMB). The highest correlation between constructs was 0.71, which is considerably lower than the threshold of 0.90. Second, we conducted Harman's single-factor test. Neither did one general factor account for more than 50% of the total variance nor did a single factor emerge from an exploratory factor analysis (one factor explained at most 29.33% of the variance in the data).

5 Results

In line with established guidelines, we used a bootstrap size of 5,000 subsamples [6]. H1, H2 and H3 refer to the relationships between gig workers' perceived AC, on one hand, and workers' autonomy (H1), fairness (H2) and privacy (H3) judgments, on the other hand. The first hypothesis (H1) was not supported. As hypothesized, perceived AC is significantly and positively related to fairness (H2). One hypothesis (H3) was found to be supported in the inverse of the predicted direction, indicating that perceived

AC positively influenced privacy judgments. H4 and H5 pertain to the effects of ride-hailing drivers' legitimacy judgements on their compliance and workaround behavior, respectively. As anticipated, fairness judgement is found to have a significantly positive effect on compliance (H4b) and privacy judgement has a significantly negative effect on workaround behavior (H5c), offering support for H4b and H5c, while four other hypotheses (H4a, H4c, H5a, H5b) were not supported (Table 4).

Table 4. Hypothesis test results.

Hypotheses		β (t-value)	Supported?
H1:	Gig drivers' perceived AC is positively related to autonomy judgment	0.158(1.439)	No
H2:	Gig drivers' perceived AC is positively related to fairness judgment	**0.458(4.585)*****	Yes
H3:	Gig drivers' perceived AC is negatively related to privacy judgment	**0.329(4.307)*****	Inverse
H4a:	Gig drivers' autonomy judgment is positively related to compliance behavior	−0.005(0.066)	No
H4b:	Gig drivers' fairness judgment is positively related to compliance behavior	**0.243(2.105)***	Yes
H4c:	Gig drivers' privacy judgment is positively related to compliance behavior	0.055(0.435)	No
H5a:	Gig drivers' autonomy judgment is negatively related to workaround behavior	0.030(0.460)	No
H5b:	Gig drivers' fairness judgment is negatively related to workaround behavior	0.002(0.019)	No
H5c:	Gig drivers' privacy judgment is negatively related to workaround behavior	**−0.300(3.237)*****	Yes

Notes: N = 197 ride-hailing drivers. Significant effects are in bold. *$p < 0.1$, **$p < 0.01$, ***$p < 0.001$; two-tailed test.

To analyze the mediation effects of gig workers' legitimacy judgments, we tested the significance of the direct effects (between perceived AC and coping behaviors) and the indirect effects (via fairness/privacy judgments). The test results show that both two indirect effects are significant since none of the 95% confidence intervals includes zero, whereas only one direct effect is significant (see Table 5). The results thus suggest that fairness judgments partially mediate the relationship between perceived AC and compliance. Further, they indicate that privacy judgments fully mediate the links between perceived AC and workaround behavior.

Table 5. Analysis of mediation effects.

	Direct effects			Indirect effects			Analysis results
Path	ß (t-value)	CI^a		ß (t-value)	CI^a		
AC → COM	**0.303(2.368)***	**[0.028, 0.527]**	via FJ	**0.083(1.882)***	**[0.005, 0.177]**	Partial mediation
AC → WU	−0.048(0.495)	[−0.213, 0.153]	via PJ	**−0.094(2.724)****	**[−0.171, − 0.037]**	Full mediation

Notes: N = 197 ride-hailing drivers. Significant effects are in bold. * p < 0.1, ** p < 0.01, *** p < 0.001; two-tailed test. a = Bias-corrected 95% confidence interval (5,000 bootstrap samples).

6 Discussion

6.1 Conclusion

This study explores the impact mechanism of drivers' perception of AC on their coping behaviors. Specifically, we adapt the scale of perceived AC to make it more applicable to ride-hailing platforms using data from semi-structured interviews. Using survey data from 197 ride-hailing drivers, we find that perceived AC positively affects fairness and privacy judgments. Fair-ness judgment has a positive impact on compliance behavior, and privacy judgment has a negative impact on workaround behavior. This view is consistent with recent findings suggesting that technologically advanced AC can both enhance managerial authority, while also providing benefits to workers [4].

Interestingly, perceived AC was found to positively influence privacy judgments. Differences in privacy between East and West may be one reason. Chinese workers generally believe that monitoring is a necessary process to complete work, which is common and legal in society. At the same time, in the context of the digital age, there may be blurred boundaries between data and privacy. In our interviews, drivers generally reported a more positive attitude towards monitoring, believing that algorithms accessing their information are necessary to support their work. They denied claims that AC violated privacy.

6.2 Theoretical and Practical Implications

This paper has theoretical implications for research related to AC on ride-hailing platforms. First, our study lies in presenting theoretical arguments and empirical evidence that counter the generally negative rhetoric surrounding the adoption of AC systems, thereby pointing to the need for a more balanced view of AC. Second, this paper depicts the coping behaviors of gig workers from two aspects: compliance and workaround use, constructing a model for the impact of gig drivers' perception of AC on their coping behaviors. Last but not least, our study offers empirical support for multi-dimensional conceptualization of micro-level legitimacy attuned to the gig economy work context. To sum up, this study responds to calls for attention to how gig workers cope with AC [11] and may provide novel insights for future works at the intersection of AC, organizational legitimacy, and gig work.

In practice, this paper provides insights for managers and algorithm designers of gig platforms. First, contrary to the previous popular belief that AC exploits workers, our research findings support the continued use of AC by ride-hailing platforms. By enhancing drivers' perception of organizational fairness and privacy protection, gig platforms can contribute to the cultivation of a more committed workforce. Platforms should more actively respond to workers' concerns about AC mechanisms. For example, platforms can emphasize fairness and privacy protection in AC rules, as well as alert drivers before monitoring and collecting information. Second, although autonomy is one of the prominent features of gig work, this study finds no evidence of the impact of autonomy judgment. It is worth discussing whether this control mechanism undermines the autonomy of drivers and deviates from the original purpose of the gig economy.

6.3   Limitations and Future Research

This study is subject to several limitations. First, our study focuses on the perspective of gig workers and the data is cross-sectional. Second, although ride-hailing platforms are a typical case, the extension migration and differences in the research results across different other platform (e.g., loosely controlled platforms, high-skilled job intermediaries' platforms, etc.) are worth exploring. For future research, we plan to conduct an interview study to further explain the findings of this study. What gig drivers think may help us find an entry point to understanding the problem.

Acknowledgment. This work is supported by the Social Science Fund Research Base Project of Beijing (19JDGLB029).

References

1. Alter, S.: Theory of workarounds. Commun. Assoc. Inf. Syst. **34**, 1041–1066 (2014). Article 55
2. Bijlsma-Frankema, K.M., Costa, A.C.: Consequences and antecedents of managerial and employee legitimacy interpretations of control: a natural, open system approach. Organ. Control, 396–434 (2010)
3. Bitektine, A., Haack, P.: The "macro" and the "micro" of legitimacy: toward a multilevel theory of the legitimacy process. Acad. Manag. Rev. **40**(1), 49–75 (2015)
4. Cram, W.A., Wiener, M., Tarafdar, M., et al.: Examining the impact of algorithmic control on Uber drivers' technostress. J. Manag. Inf. Syst. **39**, 426–453 (2022)
5. Edwards, R.: Contested terrain: the transformation of the workplace in the twentieth century. Sci. Soc. **46**(2), 237–240 (1982)

6. Hair, J.F., Ringle, C.M., Sarstedt, M.: PLS-SEM: indeed a silver bullet. J. Market. Theory Pract. **19**(2), 39–152 (2011)
7. Hair, J., Hair, J.F. Jr., Sarstedt, M., Gudergan, S.P., et al.: Advanced Issues in Partial Least Squares Structural Equation Modeling. Sage (2018)
8. Laumer, S., Maier, C., Weitzel, T.: Information quality, user satisfaction, and the manifestation of workarounds: a qualitative and quantitative study of enterprise content management system users. Eur. J. Inf. Syst. **26**(4), 333–360 (2017)
9. Lee, M.K., Kusbit, D., Metsky, E., et al.: Working with machines: the impact of algorithmic and data-driven management on human workers. In: Proceedings of the 33rd Annual ACM Conference on Human Factors in Computing Systems, pp. 1603–1612 (2015)
10. Liang, H., Xue, Y., Liansheng, W.: Ensuring employees' IT compliance: carrot or stick? Inf. Syst. Res. **24**(2), 279–294 (2013)
11. Kellogg, K.C., Valentine, M.A., et al.: Algorithms at work: the new contested terrain of control. Acad. Manag. Ann. **14**(1), 366–410 (2020)
12. Pei, J., Liu, S., Cui, X., Qu, J.: Perceived algorithmic control of gig workers: conceptualization, measurement and verification the impact on service performance. Nankai Bus. Rev. **24**(06), 14–27 (2021)
13. Möhlmann, M., Zalmanson, L., Henfridsson, O., Gregory, R.W.: Algorithmic management of work on online labor platforms: when matching meets contorl. MIS Q. **45**(4), 1999–2022 (2021)
14. Möhlmann, M., Zalmanson, L.: Hands on the wheel: navigating algorithmic management and Uber drivers' autonomy. In: Proceedings of the International Conference on Information Systems (ICIS), Seoul, South Korea, pp. 10–13 (2017)
15. Wiener, M., Alec Cram, W., Benlian, A.: Algorithmic control and gig workers: a legitimacy perspective of Uber drivers. Eur. J. Inf. Syst. **32**(3), 485–507 (2023)

Research on the Influence Mechanism of Perceived Customer Service Quality on Consumers' Purchase Decisions on E-commerce Platforms

Limeng Wang, Li Li[(✉)], and Ying Chen

School of Economics and Management, Nanjing University of Science and Technology,
Nanjing 210094, China
lily691111@126.com

Abstract. In the competitive e-commerce market, it is important to understand how perceived customer service quality affects consumer purchase decisions. This study analyses the effects of service quality, information quality, waiting time, and system quality on purchase decisions using logistic regression. The analysis is based on actual business data from an insurance company. The study confirms that all four dimensions of perceived quality significantly impact consumers' purchase decisions. To explore the influence path of perceived quality on consumers' purchasing decisions, we constructed a structural equation model through a questionnaire survey. The results verified the degree of influence of perceived quality on consumers' purchasing decisions, as well as the mediating role of perceived value. This finding offers a strategic foundation for enterprises to enhance their online customer service platforms, improve their customer service capabilities, and refine their performance appraisal systems. This will help to improve the perceived quality of e-commerce customer service and further enhance consumers' purchase decisions.

Keywords: Perceived Quality · Perceived Value · Purchase Decision

1 Introduction

The rapid development of e-commerce platforms has made online shopping a common phenomenon among consumers. However, due to the lack of direct face-to-face contact, customer service on e-commerce platforms has become particularly important. Customer service not only provides products and services but also meets consumers' needs at the right time and place, at a price and in a manner that satisfies them [1]. Providing real-time dialogue for customer service enhances consumers' willingness to shop, reduces uncertainty about product information, and increases consumer satisfaction and loyalty. High-quality customer service is essential for establishing good communication between enterprises and consumers, and it is also necessary for achieving the long-term development of enterprises. There may be differences in the quality of service provided by customer service teams on e-commerce platforms, leading to inconsistencies in the perceived quality of customer service by consumers, and thus differences in the impact on purchase intentions.

Previous research has indicated that consumers' purchasing decisions are influenced by factors such as perceived quality and perceived value. However, these studies have primarily relied on subjective questionnaire data, which may be limited in scope. In the current big data environment, e-commerce enterprises have access to a wealth of user data, allowing for a more comprehensive analysis. Therefore, this study utilizes real transaction data to investigate the impact of perceived quality of customer service on purchase decisions. The study investigates the influence of customer service perceived quality on purchasing decisions, using questionnaire data and analyzing the influence of consumers' perceived quality dimensions on purchasing behavior after chatting with customer service. The paper reviews the current status of related research to improve the credibility and relevance of the study.

Subsequently, the questionnaire survey is combined to investigate the causal relationship between consumers' perceived quality and perceived value of customer service. Based on the research findings, management recommendations and future research directions are suggested. These results offer practical guidance for e-commerce enterprises to enhance the quality of customer service and foster long-term growth.

2   Literature Review

Perceived quality refers to a consumer's evaluation of a product or service based on their own purpose and demand, and analysis of information obtained from formal or informal channels. The perceived quality of customer service on e-commerce platforms is subjective and based on overall feelings and evaluation. Previous research has demonstrated that consumers' purchasing intentions are influenced by their perception of quality, and they are more likely to shop on platforms that offer higher levels of customer service.

Perceived quality is a complex, hierarchical structure consisting of various dimensions, each with its own set of measurement items. When evaluating service quality, customers first assess the quality of interactions with service providers at the individual attribute level, then evaluate the quality of interactions at the dimension level, and finally assess the perceived quality at the overall service level [2]. This is as important as product quality for consumers.

DeLone and McLean's [3] information systems success model outlines that information quality is a crucial component of information systems success. The main objective of web-based customer service chat tools is to provide customers with relevant information related to their inquiry [4]. High-quality information is considered to be clear, up-to-date, accurate, complete, and reliable.

According to the five dimensions model of service quality, responsiveness is a crucial factor that affects the quality of customer service. Responsiveness refers to the ability to respond quickly and timely to customer needs and the willingness to provide service [5]. Once consumers opt for online customer service, the initial step is to wait for a response. It is expected that customer service will promptly and accurately address their needs, as prolonged waiting times may result in negative emotions.

In recent years, the development of information technology has led to increasingly powerful information systems. These systems not only produce and provide information but also offer guidance services to users. Therefore, some scholars have suggested that measuring the quality of system services should be included as an indicator of information systems. Therefore, based on previous research and the characteristics of the customer service system, we categorize perceived quality into four dimensions: service quality, information quality, system quality, and waiting time.

3 Influencing Factors of Consumer Purchasing Behavior Based on Perceived Quality of Customer Service

To confirm the impact of the four dimensions of perceived service quality, information quality, waiting time, and system quality on consumers' purchasing decisions, this study uses user characteristic data, transaction data, and customer service chat data from the actual business of the enterprise to extract specific measurement characteristic variables of perceived quality. Logistic regression is then applied to analyze the degree of influence of perceived quality on users' purchasing behaviors. Finally, a heterogeneity analysis of the samples is conducted from the perspective of gender to improve the robustness of the study.

3.1 Data

The data used in this study were obtained from a domestic online insurance service website. The data extracted included user characteristics, transaction data, and customer service chat data from January 1, 2019, to January 1, 2021. All of the data were obtained from the underlying database of this e-commerce enterprise. The purchase and access data were raw log record data, which required further processing to obtain the data format suitable for model building. The data processing involves cleaning, identifying users, slicing sessions, and extracting features. The processed data table contains information on 68,976 newly registered users, 6,136 new user purchase data, and 1,889 customer service data. The subsequent experiments use the available processed data list.

3.2 Variables

The purchase decision is the explained variable. A value of 1 is assigned if the user purchases the product, and 0 if they do not.

The explanatory variable chosen is perceived quality, divided into four dimensions. To measure service quality, we extracted objective indicators such as fun, empathy, and service depth from customer service conversations. Information quality was measured by detail, and system quality was measured by satisfaction rating. The consumer demographic characteristics of age and gender are used as control variables. Specific variable indicators and descriptive statistics analyses are shown in Table 1.

Table 1. Specific variable indicators and descriptive statistics analysis results

Variable Type	Dimension	Variable Name	Variable Explanation	Min	Max	Means
Explained Variable	-	$Purchase_i$	Whether the user purchases or not	0	1	0.627
Explanatory Variable	Service Quality [6]	$Emoji\_num_i$	Number of emoticons	0	10	0.161
		$Recomm\_num_i$	Number of times customer service recommended	0	7	0.308
		CS_num_i	Total number of customer service speeches in a session	1	56	9.326
		CS_word_i	Total number of words spoken by customer service in a session	4	3483	129.818
	Information Quality [7]	Num_ratio_i	Number of user speeches/number of customer service speeches	0.167	8	1.388
		$Word\_ratio_i$	Words spoken by users/Words spoken by customer service	0.055	41.5	2.419
		$Conti\_time_i$	Duration of a session	12	6908	546.077
	Waiting Time	$Wait\_time_i$	First reply time	0	1007	23.143
	System Quality	CSI_i	User satisfaction rating	0	1	0.343
Control Variable	Consumer information	$Gender_i$	Gender	0	1	0.526
		Age_i	Age	16	84	35.132

3.3 Model

This study constructs a logistic regression model to study the mechanism equation of the influence of customer service quality on consumer purchase decisions as shown in Eq. (1), where $\omega_0 - \omega_{11}$ is the vector of coefficients to be estimated, and μ_1 is the random perturbation term.

$$logit\left[P(Purchase = 1|X_i)\right] = \omega_0 + \omega_1 Emoji\_num_i + \omega_2 Recomm\_num_i + \omega_3 CS\_num_i$$
$$+ \omega_4 CS\_word_i + \omega_5 Num\_ratio_i + \omega_6 Word\_ratio_i + \omega_7 Conti\_time_i$$
$$+ \omega_8 Wait\_time_i + \omega_9 CSI_i + \omega_{10} Gender_i + \omega_{11} Age_i + \mu_1$$

$$(1)$$

3.4 Result

The results presented in Table 2 were obtained by importing the data into STATA. The logistic regression model's generalization ability for studying factors that influence consumer purchasing behavior based on perceived customer service quality is assessed using the ROC curve and AUC value, which are commonly used evaluation indexes for binary classifiers. The logistic regression model achieves an AUC value of 0.83, and the average values of accuracy, precision, recall, F1 value, and the ten-fold cross-validation score are all greater than 0.8, indicating good classification performance with accurate results.

Table 2. Logistic regression model analysis results

Variable Type	Dimension	Variable Name	Coef.	St. Err.	t	P
Explanatory Variable	Service Quality	$Emoji\_num_i$	0.587	0.140	4.180	***
		$Recomm\_num_i$	0.968	0.158	6.130	***
		CS_num_i	0.129	0.023	5.570	***
		CS_word_i	0.006	0.002	3.930	***
	Information Quality	Num_ratio_i	0.829	0.121	6.840	***
		$Word\_ratio_i$	−0.109	0.033	−3.240	***
		$Conti\_time_i$	−0.001	0.000	−3.640	***
	Waiting Time	$Wait\_time_i$	−0.003	0.001	−2.670	***
	System Quality	CSI_i	0.365	0.120	3.030	***
Control Variable	Consumer information	$Gender_i$	−0.005	0.111	−0.040	0.965
		Age_i	−0.010	0.006	−1.770	*
Constant	–	–	−1.752	0.264	−6.640	***

Note: ***, ** and * indicate significance at 1%, 5% and 10% levels respectively.

On the service quality dimension, the number of customer service emoticons and purchase decision are positively correlated, indicating that the number of customer service using emoticons will bring positive emotions to consumers, positively affecting the consumer's willingness to buy; customer service according to the needs of consumers personalized recommendation times and purchase decision also presents a significant positive correlation, and the coefficient of influence is the largest compared to the rest of the factors, indicating that the customer service from the point of view of the consumer, personalized Provide product recommendations will, to a certain extent, improve the consumer's purchase decisions. The degree of detail of customer service response also positively affects consumers' purchasing behavior, and deep-level communication will increase the probability of consumers' purchasing. Therefore, perceived service quality positively affects consumers' purchase decisions.

On the information quality dimension, the ratio of the number of sessions between customer service and consumers is positively correlated with the purchase decision, i.e., the more the number of speeches of customer service compared to the number of consumers, the easier it is to increase the consumers' willingness to buy; the ratio of the number of words in the session is highly negatively correlated with the purchase decision. The length of single communication between consumers and customer service is negatively related to purchase decisions, which may be due to the fact that long communication time will wear out the patience of customer service or consumers. Therefore, the quality of information also significantly affects consumers' purchasing decisions.

Consumers' waiting time for customer service is negatively correlated with purchase behavior, indicating that the longer the customer service waits after the consumer initiates a session, the lower the probability that the consumer will make a purchase, and the waiting time has a significant negative impact on the consumer's purchase decision.

On the system quality dimension, the positive correlation between consumers' satisfaction evaluation of customer service and purchase decision at the 1% level indicates that the higher consumers' evaluation of customer service, the more likely they are to generate purchase behavior, and therefore perceived system quality significantly and positively affects consumers' purchase decision.

Among the control variables, the age of the user shows a negative correlation with the purchase decision at the 10% level, indicating that the younger the age of the user, the higher the probability of purchasing, the situation may be related to the fact that the object of study in this section is insurance, and the nature of the insurance product will limit the age of the consumer to a certain extent.

In summary, the four dimensions of perceived service quality, perceived information quality, waiting time, and perceived system quality all affect consumers' purchasing decisions to some extent.

3.5 Heterogeneity Analysis

Logistic regression analyses were conducted using gender as the basis for grouping. The results showed that, in the female sample, the word count of customer service did not significantly affect consumers' purchase decisions in terms of service quality. This may be because women place more importance on the content of the chat and the number of messages replied to. Waiting time did not significantly affect consumers' purchase decisions in the male sample. This may be because men have a higher level of patience than women or because men care less about waiting time. There were no differences in the other indicators across genders, which is consistent with the results and further demonstrates the robustness of the model.

4 Research on the Influence of Path of Perceived Quality of Customer Service on Consumers' Purchase Intention

The impact of perceived quality of customer service on consumers' purchasing behavior has been confirmed through the study of actual business data of enterprises, but the path of the impact of perceived quality on purchasing behavior is still unclear to us. In fact, in the actual shopping process, the customer's purchasing behavior is not only affected by the perceived quality of customer service, but also the perceived value of the user in the process of chatting with customer service will also affect their subsequent purchasing behavior, and these variables are difficult to be described objectively with the actual business data of the enterprise, therefore, in this chapter, we will use a questionnaire to investigate the subjective perceived value, perceived cost and other factors of the customers in the process of the most recent chatting conversation with customer service, and construct a structural equation model. Value and other factors to construct a structural equation model to explore the specific path of the influence of perceived quality of customer service on consumers' purchase intention.

4.1 Hypotheses

Perceived value is a fundamental motivation for consumers to shop online. It is no longer solely based on the actual use value of the goods, but also on the pleasure and relaxation experienced during the shopping process. Mathwick [8] and others have identified two dimensions of perceived value that influence consumers' willingness to buy and, ultimately, their purchasing behavior: entertainment value and utility value.

Entertainment value refers to the fun and pleasure that consumers feel when using a customer service system, which comes from the feeling of relaxation and happiness during the shopping process. Utility value refers to the degree to which consumers perceive that the use of customer service can help them solve problems and thus improve the efficiency of the purchase, from the usefulness of the product or service or the utility of obtaining more product-related information.

When consumers perceive an increase in the entertainment value of a product or service, their satisfaction and happiness will increase accordingly. This positive emotional experience affects consumers' overall evaluation of the product or service and positively influences utility value. Therefore, the following hypothesis is proposed:

H1: Entertainment value has a positive effect on utility value.

Agarwal [9] et al. discovered that a consumer's perceived value is a subjective expectation probability. This is determined by comparing the quality of products on a specific shopping platform with the consumer's desired quality. If the actual quality is higher than the expected quality, the perceived value is higher, and the consumer's willingness to buy is stronger. This relationship between perceived value and willingness is promoted [10]. Thus, this paper proposes the following hypotheses:

H2a: Entertainment value has a positive impact on purchase intention;

H2b: Utility value has a positive impact on purchase intention.

User-perceived service quality has an important impact on purchase decisions because it affects consumers' purchase value, satisfaction and repurchase behavior [11].

Information quality refers to whether the content of information acquired by customers meets their needs [12], under the e-commerce environment, users need to obtain the information they need from a large number of commodity information, the higher the quality of the information fed back to the user by the customer service system, the higher the perceived value of the user [13]. Waiting time is an important factor of user experience, consumers will pay attention to the waiting time when shopping online, the shorter the waiting time, the higher the user's shopping experience and perceived value [14]. System quality is also an important aspect of user-perceived service quality; high-quality customer service systems are easy to use and have higher utility and utilization rates, whereas low-quality systems undermine user trust and lead to reluctance to use them. Ease of use and entertainment of customer service systems also affect the perceived value of users. Therefore, the following hypothesis is proposed:

H3a: Customer service quality has a positive effect on entertainment value;

H3b: Customer information quality has a positive effect on entertainment value;

H3c: Customer waiting time has a negative effect on entertainment value;

H3d: Customer service system quality has a positive effect on entertainment value;

H4a: Customer service quality has a positive effect on utility value;

H4b: Customer service information quality has a positive effect on utility value;

H4c: Customer waiting time has a negative effect on utility value;

H4d: Customer service system quality has a positive effect on utility value.

In the previous hypotheses, the influence of four variables, namely service quality, information quality, waiting time, and system quality, on perceived value was first proposed; subsequently, it was proposed that perceived value also significantly affects users' purchase intention. The stimulus-organism-response process proposed by the SOR model [15] suggests that in the process of users using the customer service system, service quality, information quality, waiting time and system quality are the external stimuli. After being exposed to these stimuli, the organism produces the perceived value and finally shows the corresponding response, which is the purchase intention. Accordingly, the study proposes the following mediation hypothesis:

H5a: Entertainment value mediates a significant effect between service quality and purchase intention;

H5b: Entertainment value mediates a significant effect between information quality and purchase intention;

H5c: Entertainment value mediates a significant effect between waiting time and purchase intention;

H5d: Entertainment value mediates a significant effect between system quality and purchase intention;

H6a: Utility value mediates a significant effect between service quality and purchase intention;

H6b: Utility value mediates a significant effect between information quality and purchase intention;

H6c: Utility value has a significant mediating effect between waiting time and purchase intention;

H6d: Utility value mediates a significant effect between system quality and purchase intention;

H7: Utility value mediates a significant effect between entertainment value and purchase intention.

4.2 Model

The conceptual model of the impact of perceived quality of customer service on consumers' purchase intention is constructed based on the previous literature review and research hypotheses, as shown in Fig. 1. The four dimensions of perceived quality will affect the user's entertainment value and utility value respectively, which in turn affects the user's purchase intention. The perceived value has a mediating effect between perceived quality and purchase intention.

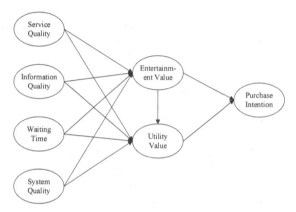

Fig. 1. Structural equation modeling diagram

4.3 Data

The model validation is based on questionnaire data. The questionnaires were distributed from 24th July to 30th August 2022 and 405 questionnaires were returned, resulting in a valid sample of 352 questionnaires.

This study used SPSS to conduct the reliability analysis of the sample data, and the seven latent variables included in this study: service quality, information quality, waiting time, system quality, entertainment-based value, utility-based value, and purchase intention, with corresponding Cronbach's alpha coefficients of 0.845, 0.832, 0.873, 0.868, 0.880, 0.857, and 0.826 respectively, all of which are greater than 0.7, and the overall Cronbach's α coefficient of the scale is 0.937, which is greater than 0.9 and close to 1, indicating that the whole scale has good internal consistency.

The discriminant and convergent validity between the model variables was tested by using AMOS software. The fit index $\chi^2/df = 2.367$ and RMSEA $= 0.062$, in addition, the values of GFI and AGFI were greater than 0.8, and the values of CFI, IFI, and TLI were greater than 0.9, which indicated that the model was well fitted overall. Meanwhile, the standardized factor loadings were greater than 0.5, the combined reliability CR was greater than 0.7.

4.4 Result

According to the model assumptions, the data were imported into AMOS for fitting, and the fitting yielded GFI = 0.836, AGFI = 0.803, CFI = 0.905, and RMSEA = 0.067, all of which are in line with the basic prescribed standards, indicating that the research model is relatively well fitted and that the demonstration of the assumptions related to structural equation modeling can be carried out. Next, each path is tested to determine the significance of each path, and the model path coefficients and significant levels are shown in Table 3.

The quality of information has a positive impact on the entertainment value for users. This means that the more complete, accurate, and popular the information is, the more pleasant the user's experience will be when using the customer service system. On the other hand, waiting time has a negative effect on the entertainment value. This means that the longer the waiting time, the worse the user's mood becomes, and they are unable to enjoy the process of chatting with the customer service representative. However, it appears that service quality and system quality do not significantly affect entertainment value. This suggests that users' moods are not influenced by factors such as customer service reliability, security, system operating speed, and interface.

On the other hand, customer service quality, information quality, and system quality have a positive impact on utility value. Waiting time, however, does not affect utility value. This indicates that users perceive customer service as stable, reliable, and tailored to their needs and that the system interface is clear, well-organized, and user-friendly. These factors contribute to users' perception of the value of the customer service system, which can enhance their shopping experience and improve shopping efficiency. Additionally, the entertainment value has a significant positive impact on users' purchase intention. Users may develop a sense of dependence on customer service and enhance their goodwill towards it, leading to increased purchases. Additionally, the perceived utility value of customer service has a positive effect on purchase intention. In other words, the more helpful users find customer service to be during the shopping process, the stronger their intention to make a purchase.

The study employed the Bootstrap sampling method to obtain multiple sample data through independent sampling. The standardized Bootstrap intermediate effects test was conducted using AMOS, with the number of repetitive samples set to 2000 and 95% confidence intervals selected.

According to the test criteria for mediating effects, entertainment value is not significant between service quality and purchase intention, system quality and purchase intention, utility value is not significant between perceived waiting time and purchase intention, and the rest of the mediating effects of the path from perceived quality to purchase intention are tested. Therefore, information quality and waiting time will affect users' willingness to purchase through the mediation of entertainment-based value; service quality, information quality, and system quality will affect users' willingness to purchase through the mediation of utility-based value. We therefore accept hypotheses H5b, H5c, H6a, H6b, H6d, H7 and reject hypotheses H5a, H5d, H6c.

Table 3. Structural equation model analysis results

Path	Coef.	S.E.	C.R.	P	Hypotheses
Entertainment Value → Utility Value	0.218	0.045	3.505	***	Accept H1
Service Quality → Entertainment Value	0.131	0.132	1.495	0.135	Reject H3a
Entertainment Value → Purchase Intention	0.446	0.055	6.945	***	Accept H2a
Utility Value → Purchase Intention	0.294	0.077	4.583	***	Accept H2b
Information Quality → Entertainment Value	0.328	0.127	3.593	***	Accept H3b
Waiting Time → Entertainment Value	0.229	0.104	2.727	**	Accept H3c
System Quality → Entertainment Value	0.070	0.108	0.809	0.419	Reject H3d
Service Quality → Utility Value	−0.253	0.089	−3.086	**	Accept H4a
Information Quality → Utility Value	0.340	0.089	3.832	***	Accept H4b
Waiting Time → Utility Value	0.119	0.070	1.511	0.131	Reject H4c
System Quality → Utility Value	0.451	0.075	5.354	***	Accept H4d

This study uses structural equation modeling to examine the relationships between perceived quality, perceived value, and purchase intention. The aim is to understand how perceived quality affects consumers' purchasing decisions and provide useful insights for enterprises to improve their customer service systems.

5   Conclusion

This study examines how the perceived quality of customer service on e-commerce platforms affects consumers' purchasing decisions. The investigation is based on questionnaire survey data and actual business data from enterprises. This paper analyses chat data between users and customer service to derive four characteristic variables of perceived quality. The logistic regression method is used to analyse the influencing factors of consumers' purchasing behaviour. The study concludes that factors such as fun, personalization, and interactivity of the customer service system's service quality have an impact on consumers' purchasing behaviour. Additionally, the level of detail in the information provided also affects purchasing behaviour. Finally, the study finds that longer waiting times increase the likelihood of customers making a purchase. The influence of perceived quality on consumers' purchasing decisions exists. The likelihood of customers' purchasing behaviour decreases with longer waiting times. Additionally, customers are more likely to purchase when they are satisfied with the quality of the customer service system.

This paper also constructs a research model to analyse the influence of perceived customer service quality on consumers' purchase intention. The structural equation model is analysed using SPSS, AMOS and other software to explore the specific path of this influence. The study concludes that the quality of information has a positive influence on users' entertainment value, while waiting time has a negative influence on entertainment value. Additionally, the quality of service, information, and system positively affect utility value. Perceived value also has a significant mediating effect on most of the factors of perceived quality in consumer purchase decisions.

The quality of customer service has a significant impact on purchase decisions. Therefore, e-commerce companies need to optimise the customer service system. Firstly, companies should improve the business skills of customer service staff. This includes improving their communication skills, industry knowledge and service attitude. In addition, enterprises should optimise their customer service platforms, which can be achieved by improving online chat tools, using shortcuts and emoticons, and other similar measures to improve customer service efficiency and consumer satisfaction. Companies should also strengthen their performance appraisal systems to incentivise customer service agents to deliver better service. By implementing these measures, companies can improve the perceived quality of customer service. Promote consumer purchase intention and behavior, and ultimately increase the order conversion rate of e-commerce stores. In addition, we only study the insurance industry, and the empirical results may be limited.

Acknowledgement. This research was supported by the National Natural Science Foundation of China under Grant 71771122.

References

1. Blanding, W.: Practical Handbook of Customer Service Operations. Springer, US (1989). https://doi.org/10.1007/978-1-4613-1645-9
2. Clemes, M.D., Brush, G.J., Collins, M.J.: Analysing the professional sport experience: a hierarchical approach. Sport Manag. Rev. **14**(4), 370–388 (2011)
3. Delone, W.H., Mclean, E.R.: Information systems success: the quest for the dependent variable. Inf. Syst. Res. **3**(1), 60–86 (1992)
4. Hernandez, B., Jimenez, J.M., Martin, J.: Key website factors in e-business strategy. Int. J. Inf. Manage. **29**(5), 362–371 (2009)
5. Parasuraman, A., Zeithaml, V.A., Malhotra, A.: E-S-QUAL a multiple-item scale for assessing electronic service quality. J. Serv. Res. **7**(3), 213–233 (2005)
6. Luor, T., Wu, L.L., Lu, H.P., et al.: The effect of emoticons in simplex and complex task-oriented communication: an empirical study of instant messaging. Comput. Hum. Behav. **26**(5), 889–895 (2010)
7. Guo, X., Ling, K.C., Liu, M.: Evaluating factors influencing consumer satisfaction towards online shopping in China. Asian Soc. Sci. **8**(13), 40 (2012)

8. Mathwick, C., Malhotra, K., Rigdon, E.: The effect of dynamic retail experiences on experiential perceptions of value: an Internet and catalog comparison. J. Retail. Consum. Serv. **78**(1), 51–60 (2002)

9. Agarwal, R., Prasad, R.: Are individual differences germane to the acceptance of new information technologies? Decis. Sci. **30**, 361–391 (1999)

10. Babin, J., Darden, R., Griffin, M.: Work and/or fun: measuring hedonic and utilitarian shopping value. J. Consum. Res. **20**(4), 644–657 (1994)

11. Jeyaraj, A.: DeLone & McLean models of information system success: critical meta-review and research directions. J. Manag. Inf. Syst. **54**(3), 102139 (2020)

12. Chen, C.C., Tseng, Y.D.: Quality evaluation of product reviews using an information quality framework. Decis. Support. Syst. **50**(4), 755–768 (2011)

13. Verhagen, T., Van Nes, J., Feldberg, F., et al.: Virtual customer service agents: using social presence and personalization to shape online service encounters. J. Comput.-Mediat. Commun. **19**(3), 529–545 (2014)

14. Mclean, G., Wilson. A.: Evolving the online customer experience … is there a role for online customer support? Comput. Hum. Behav. **60**, 602–610 (2016)

15. Mehrabian, A., Russell, J.A.: An Approach to Environment Psychology. MIT, Cambridge (1974)

Signaling Theory Application in Online Healthcare Community: A Systematic Review

Shanshan Guo[1], Lizhen Yang[1], and Yuanyuan Dang[2(✉)]

[1] Shanghai International Studies University, Shanghai, China
[2] South China University of Technology, Guangzhou, China
dyy777@scut.edu.cn

Abstract. In the context of online healthcare community, signaling theory has been widely applied in literature to overcome information asymmetry and reduce uncertainty. Especially in evaluating various information signals, the aim is to convey the quality of healthcare service and influence patient's decision-making. However, the existing literature on signals in online healthcare communities is facing certain challenges. The range of various studies involves the interaction between different signals and patient's decision-making. The classification of these signals is arbitrary, fragmented, and has not formed a common concept. This situation may affect the further development of the field. In order to establish a common foundation for scholars, we conducted a systematic literature review and summarized 63 articles in online healthcare signaling, providing a more comprehensive framework. This helps to establish an evidence-based knowledge system on the impact of online healthcare signals on patient's decision-making. This framework also clarifies signal construct, exploring its boundary, signals relationship, and mechanism. Finally, we identify gaps in existing literature and provide valuable suggestions for future research direction.

Keywords: Literature Review · Online healthcare community · Signals · Signaling Theory

1 Introduction

Over the past decade, online healthcare communities (OHCs) have experienced significant growth. These communities offer remote online medical consultation services, facilitating rapid and diverse transmission of information. Despite the expeditious development of OHCs, patients may experience negative outcomes with information asymmetry within communities. Physicians have information advantage due to their extensive medical training and expertise compared to patients. To comprehend how information asymmetry affects patients and determine how signals can reduce uncertainty, researchers have begun exploring OHCs by extending signaling theory.

Early research primarily aimed to address information asymmetry between physicians and patients using signaling theory, exploring effective signal categories such as physicians' basic information (e.g., physicians' titles, hospital levels, ratings, work experience), third-party certification (e.g., badges, qualifications), and the normativity of communities (e.g., privacy security, information quality). Additionally, the OHCs provide more attributes to physicians, offering patients more information about physicians' behaviors on the community (e.g., bundled service, timeliness of reply, recommend value) [1], which contributes to well-minimizing information symmetry and providing a better physician-patient interaction community.

However, with the development of OHCs, the mechanisms of physician-patient interaction in OHCs have become more complex. The role of signaling theory has expanded due to the abundance of signals, the diversity of influencing factors, and the increasing number of stakeholders. Meanwhile, the theory extends the scope beyond simple effective signals to encompass understanding the mechanisms of information transmission within the physician-patient relationship [2], the potential impact of the physician's image of benevolence on the patient, and so on. For instance, cumulative patient reviews and physician-patient interaction records in OHCs can be considered as physicians' reputation signals, conveying their capabilities and kindness; the physicians' initiative to provide free consultation services to patients or share health knowledge for free can be regarded as the physicians' benevolence signals, which conveys the kind and warm images, potentially influencing the patient's affective commitment. Furthermore, more influencing factors such as the physician's colleagues' reputation, the severity of patients' illnesses, patients' health information literacy, and the competitive intensity among physicians in the same disease sub-market have also been explored as signaling mechanism in physician-patient interaction.

According to the wide variety of signals, the increasing body of knowledge lacks an integrative framework for organizing these findings. To fill this gap, our review seeks a deep understanding of signal constructs, which provide clarity and a common comprehend of signal classification, signal characteristic and key elements in signaling theory. We present the state of the application of signaling theory in OHCs and propose a signaling framework, which could contribute to resolving isolated views within signaling research. Furthermore, previous researches on signaling pay less attention to information processing under the potential assumption that individuals are able to analyze all available signals in OHCs. This systematic review includes a discussion of signaling mechanisms to explain how individuals receive and interpret diverse signals based on the assumption of limited rationality, expanding traditional signaling theory.

2 Signaling Theory

Spence indicated the signaling theory resulted from the study of market economic transactions in the midst of information asymmetry [3]. Information asymmetry occurs when various parties involved in the transaction have different information. Signaling theory acknowledges that signalers as a sender (insiders) possess more information about unobservable quality of products and services, while receivers (outsiders) lack access to this information. Signals are valuable in shaping behavior and reducing information asymmetry between different parties. According to the review of previous literature, Connelly et al. [4] classified the key elements: **signaler**, **signal**, **signal receiver** and **environment**, as shown in Fig. 1. Their work provides the framework of the signaling process, which has been widely cited in other literature, indicating its crucial role in the advancement of signaling theory. This framework helps explain foundational signaling relationships and extends the boundaries of signaling.

In the context of OHCs, researchers have extended signaling theory to investigate various signals which reflect the physicians (signalers)' reputation, credibility and quality to minimize information asymmetry. However, prior researchers pay less attention to signal receivers and signaling environment, both of which play important roles in signaling process. This limited focus has resulted in a current state of research on signaling mechanism is not thoroughly explored. Accordingly, signaling theory should be expanded to explore a comprehensive understanding of signals based on the signaling process framework and signaling mechanism in field of OHCs.

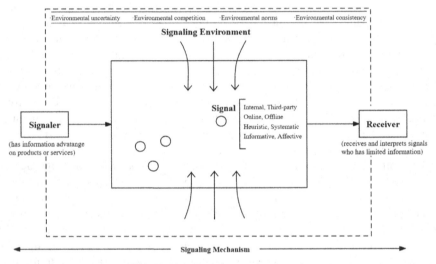

Fig. 1. Signaling process framework

3 Method

To identify suitable studies to include in the review, we follow best practices for data collections in systematic reviews(e.g., Denyer & Tranfield, 2009) [5]. First, to collect the relevant literature, we systematically searched the following electronic databases between 2010 and 2024: Web of Science, Science Direct, and Wiley Online Library, Springer. We used the Boolean search term "signal*" and five key words: "online health*", "online medical", "m-health", "mobile health", "virtual health" in the field of abstracts, titles and keywords. The systematic searches returned 341 articles, respectively. In order to expand the scope of literature search, we also used the Boolean search term "signaling theory*" in full-text.

Second, after reading all abstract, titles and articles' content, we excluded 291 studies that did not refer to signaling or did not deal with online healthcare.

Finally, we carefully reviewed the reference of the remaining articles, and added 11 relevant publications and 1 relevant conference article that did not appear in our database search because their text focuses on "signals" or other search terms, but those words did not appear in the title, abstract, or keywords. The relevant conference article is from the Thirty Sixth International Conference on Information Systems. It proposes an important concept and has been repeatedly cited in some literature.

The final sample thus contained 63 studies, published in 7 FT50 and 56 non-FT50 journals, which reflects provide an account of current knowledge and application of signaling theory to OHC.

4 Signaling Process Framework in OHC

4.1 Signalers and Receivers

Signalers, as insiders, hold information about individuals, products, services or platforms and organizations that is not to accessible to outsiders. Insiders decide whether and how to convey it to the outsiders. Typical signal providers in online healthcare community include physicians and platforms.

Characteristic of the signalers is related to their signaling strategy and credibility. Trust theory points out that source of trust, as an determining factor in establishing trust, can be divided into three dimensions: *integrity*, *benevolence*, and *competence* [6]. These three dimensions portray physicians' personal quality and characteristic in OHC. *Integrity* means the extent to which the signaler actually has the underlying quality associated with the signal. Physicians with integrity send signals consistent with their unobservable quality. Since signalers are often of varying competence and ability, inferior signalers have incentive to deceive or confuse and send false signals, attempting to make themselves appear similar to high-quality signalers so that receivers will select them. In this situation, physicians characterized by integrity are willing to disclose more detailed truth signals. *Benevolence* refers to the extent to that signalers are willing to do something beneficial to others, rather than focusing on self-centered profit motive. Benevolent physicians prioritize the interests of patients and send altruistic signals, which implies that physicians do not care about the cost they pay for transmission. If patients perceive that a physician's signaling is driven by self-interest, the patient will develop distrust and be unwilling to establish a long-term trusting relationship with the physician. *Competence* represents the skills or knowledge possessed by signalers in a certain field. A physician's competence will affect his own strategy for signaling. Physicians with low competence tend to disclose standardized information to imitate physicians with high competence, thereby influencing patient decision-making.

Additionally, the platform itself also convey signals, shaping them within an institutional environment where norms, requirements and regulations are embedded. Unlike individuals, platforms' characteristics can be categorized into *presentation quality* and *privacy*. *Presentation quality* can be further divided into information quality and functional quality. The reliability of information resource sources, the truthfulness of information disclosure content, advertising policies and website attributes are crucial criteria that reflect the quality of platform information. The webpage design, navigation design, visual design preferences, and page presentation style of OHCs reflect the functional quality of the platform, impacting perceived utility and patients' trust. The protection of personal *privacy* by the platform ensures security in the signaling process, promoting active signaling transmission among various parties on the platform. For example, protecting the privacy of patients' sensitive information can help increase enthusiasm and trust between physicians and patients in information exchanges. Therefore, when physicians and platforms possess these characteristics, they are more likely to gain the trust of patients, thus promoting the choices of patients.

Receivers, generally outsiders possessing limited information, are willing to receive it to alleviate information asymmetry. Recent researchers have found that the signaling effectiveness is determined, in part, by the characteristics of the receivers.

Patients' individual characteristics, including *disease type* and *ability*, impact the interpretation of signals. *Disease type* shapes patients' preferences and attention toward signals. For example, current literature indicate disease severity is a crucial factor influencing patients' choices. For patients with high-severity illnesses (e.g., tumors or heart disease), they are more prone to feel pain and anxiety, and be under greater psychological and physical suffering. These patients prioritize physicians' professional abilities, such as certification, titles, and hospital ranks, as indicators of their likelihood to aid in medical recovery. On the contrary, patients with low-severity diseases (e.g., headache or gastritis) need the support of friendly service attitude and pleasant communication rather than high-level medical skills [7]. Thus, service feedback signals which conveying other patients' experiences and recommendations become more significant in their decision-making.

Regarding to *ability*, it influences the extent to which receivers understand signals. Patients who have different knowledge, background and experience exhibit diverse evaluation capability, motives and expectation. Patients with a high level of *disease knowledge* are more likely to rely on service quality which reflects the truth treatment effect rather than online Word-of-Mouth (eWOM). In critical disease categories (e.g., cancer, internal medicine), patients grapple with a large amount of complex medical information. They often struggle to discern the quality of medical advices, resulting in minimal distinction between high and low-quality signals. Additionally, patients who have a high level of *health information literacy* will be able to use health-related information (not only about disease knowledge) resources. They rely more on established criteria to evaluate online health signals. As people age, they often take longer to process online information due to physical and cognitive impairments, worse numerical abilities, and decreased information processing capabilities. Consequently, individuals with poor health information literacy tend to pay more attention to less informative signals, such as pictures and simplified text signals.

4.2 Signals

Signals are informational cues sent out by signalers to receivers in order to influence desired behavior. Studies in OHC have examined multiple distinct signals: physicians' titles, hospital levels, self-introduction, valence of review, feedback from patients, to list a few. In the above literature review, we find that the stakeholders in signaling process are relatively simple: physicians, patients and platforms, with signals flowing among physician-patient, patient-patient, and platform-patient interactions. Typically, patients are influenced by the signals of various participants in the information flow. However, few studies offer a conceptual distinction among the various types of signals in OHCs. We classify signals based on their characteristics as list in Table 1.

Signal source describes various parties involved in signal generation process, including *internal-party signaler* and *third-party*. Common internal-party signals about healthcare providers include the physician's service price, response to question, sharing knowledge, interaction record, photo or video image and so on [8]. These signals tend to be determined by internal providers themselves without third-party certification. Third-party signals about providers include the physician's title, hospital level, Graduate university, Experience, Certification, Sanctions, Registration duration [8]. For example, physician's title, certification and hospital level rely on the rigorous professional evaluation and verification from official medical associations, which reflect technical competency and qualifications of physicians. Compared to internal-party signals, third-party signals seem more objective. One reason is that the involving and supervising of non-stakeholders reduces the likelihood of false signals being sent.

Signal Medium. Signal medium pertains to the way of signal transmission, which distinguishes between *online* and *offline* signals.

Patients generally have experience in offline hospitals, which means they understand the evaluation system and internal organizational structure of offline hospitals. Patients usually make offline consultation decisions based on the signals of physicians' titles, hospital rank and certifications. These signals, rooted in common sense from offline medical experiences, instill trust in certified online physicians. Therefore, offline signals are more easily understood and trust by patients. Physicians in OHCs generate online signals that reflect their online behavior. These signals tend to demonstrate online consultation service quality and their willingness to take extra effort online. Examples of online signals include badges of service star granted by the platform, prosocial behavior (e.g., knowledge sharing, free contribution), joining a healthcare team, and so on [9]. These signals provide a richer and more detailed picture of the physician's online behavior, and also convey their service orientation by going beyond patients' expectation, such as paid gift by patients.

Signal Processing. According to Chaiken's research on information processing, we categorize signals based on the distinction between *heuristic* signals and *systematic* signals [10]. *Systematic* signals involve detailed and comprehensive processing of judgment-relevant information. *Heuristic* signals involve simplified and quick processing of source reliability and the presentation of information, using intuitive judgment without deep analysis. Heuristic cues generally pertain to simple rules known as knowledge structures, learned and stored in memory. Examples of heuristic signals in OHC include conveying a kind and professional self-image through photo or video to facilitate a positive first impression; expressing affect in linguistic signal; providing free consultations, health knowledge and Q&A voluntarily to help patients. These signals convey common information not directly relevant to consultation service quality.

Examples of *systematic signals* include physician's professional background, crucial for providing accurate medical advice and diagnosis; feedback from thank-you letters and gifts, implying that medical service quality exceeds other patients' expectation; price as necessary factor in decision making process; and a badge granted by community to

Table 1. Signal classification.

Signaler-Receiver	Signal	Source	Medium	Processing	Affect	References
Physicians-Patients	Physician title	Third-party	Offline	Systematic	Informative	Yang (2018), Zhou (2022)
	Hospital level	Third-party	Offline	Systematic	Informative	Li (2019), Fan (2023)
	City	Third-party	Offline	Heuristic	Informative	Yang (2021),
	Experience	Third-party	Offline	Heuristic	Informative	Khurana (2019), Li (2019)
	Certification	Third-party	Offline	Systematic	Informative	Shah (2019)
	Service price	Internal	Online	Systematic	Informative	Yang (2018), Wu (2021), Wu (2018)
	Response to question	Internal	Online	Systematic	Informative, Affective	Zhou (2023), Khurana (2019), Zhang (2019), Zhou (2022)
	Sharing knowledge	Internal	Online	Heuristic	Informative	Li (2019), Ma (2022), Zhang (2019), Chen (2015)
	Self-representation	Internal	Online	Heuristic	Informative, Affective	Li (2019), Ouyang (2022)
	Free consultation	Internal	Online	Heuristic	Informative	Yan (2022), Chen (2015), Jiang (2021)
	Group Joining	Internal	Online	Systematic	Informative	Qiao (2021), Han (2021)
	Bundled service	Internal	Online	Systematic	Informative	Yin (2023)
	Photo/ video image	Internal	Online	Heuristic	Affective	Ouyang (2022), Shan (2019), Tan (2023)
	Linguistic signal	Internal	Online	Heuristic, Systematic	Informative, Affective	Liu (2023)
	Sanctions	Third-party	Offline	Systematic	Informative	Shah (2019)
Patients-Patients	Valence of review	Internal	Online	Systematic	Informative	Wang (2020), Chen (2015), Wu (2016), Lu (2018)
	Volume of review	Internal	Online	Systematic	Informative	Li (2019), Huang (2022), Shah (2022)
	Affect in review	Internal	Online	Heuristic	Affective	Shah (2019), Saifee (2020)
	Feedback	Internal	Online	Systematic	Informative	Yang (2021), Yang (2019)

(continued)

Table 1. (*continued*)

Signaler-Receiver	Signal	Source	Medium	Processing	Affect	References
	Linguistic signal in post	Internal	Online	Heuristic, Systematic	Informative, Affective	Chen (2020)
Platform-Patients	Registration duration	Third-party	Online	Systematic	Informative	Ma (2022), Yin (2023)
	Respond speed	Third-party	Online	Heuristic	Informative	Yang (2015), Guo (2022)
	Log-behavior	Third-party	Online	Heuristic	Informative	Chen (2021)
	Recommend value	Third-party	Online	Systematic	Informative	Qin (2022)
	Service star badge	Third-party	Online	Systematic	Informative	Cao (2017)

indicate online effort and service competence. These signals are strongly related to the quality information of medical consultation services, and receivers tend to rely on a deep and comprehensive analytical processing when receiving these signals. This distinction between systematic signals and heuristic signals helps us understand how signals generate persuasion, reaction, and influence receivers' decision-making.

Signaling Affect. *Informative signals* involve accurate information to reduce information asymmetry, emphasizing cognition of information. *Affective signals* are distinction from informative signals because they elicit affect or empathy to motivate action and influence decision-making [11]. Researchers have become increasingly interested in affective signal. Affective heuristics is the tendency of individuals in judgment and decision making based on the emotional status at the time. Although cognition is certainly important in some decision-making process, reliance on affect and emotion is a quicker, easier, and more efficient way to action in complex and uncertain situation.

In OHCs, signals predominantly engage cognitive mechanisms, directly or indirectly reflecting physicians' competence and service quality through factors like hospital level, work experience, certification, popularity, registration duration, and response speed. Affective signals, such as responses to questions, self-introductions, community posts, and expressions of affect in reviews, offer emotional support to patients and invoke responses. However, most of these affective signals are linguistic, which express emotion in words. There is limited research on the role of non-linguistic affective signals (such as emoticons in patient reviews, images and pictures on the platform, badges, etc.) in evaluation and decision process. Ouyang found that smiles in physicians' photos provide emotional support and positively influence patients' choice [12]. It seems to be a problem in the field of OHC that few researches on non-linguistic affective signals.

4.3 Signaling Environment

Signalers transmit signals inside a specific environment, whereas receivers receive and interpret these signals. Although some studies emphasize the significance of the signaling environment in influencing signal outcomes, there is a lack of clear definitions regarding environmental characteristics. We suggest classifying signaling environment according to environmental uncertainties, environmental competition, environmental norms and environmental consistency, as listed in Table 2.

Environmental uncertainties constitute all the diverse contextual factors that have the potential to impact the information symmetry between signalers and receivers. The signaling environment provides quality information about products and services. Delivering services in a high-quality hospital enables physicians to signal their commitment to high standards, positively influencing patient decisions. Additionally, when patients choose physicians, they actually enter different submarkets and cannot cross the market to choose physicians. The variations in perceptions of diseases among submarkets and the current development of medical technology contribute to different levels of uncertainty.

Environmental competition characterizes an intense setting in which multiple signalers compete simultaneously by transmitting numerous signals. In a highly competitive environment, patients receive numerous similar signals simultaneously. The effectiveness of identical signals diminishes, while signals that differ from those of other signalers become more impactful.

Environmental norms provide a detailed account of the order and regulations within the environment, including various patterns, rules, and organized factors. Such norm to a certain extent determines the interpretation and decision-making processes of receivers in response to signals. Patients are concerned about the platform's regulations and its ability to safeguard their privacy. This directly influences their trust in online physicians. Furthermore, the credibility of a signal can be enhanced by its widespread presence in the market, and signals linked to only one or a few products are insignificant [13].

Environmental consistency pertains to the degree of similarity or congruence between signals and the overall environmental context [14]. This suggests that some elements of the signals share differences or congruence with the environment, which can impact the recipient's interpretation. The reputation signal of a physician on OHCs is affected by the reputation of their peers in the same environment. When patients perceive high reputation of the colleagues, they have a higher level of expectations for the focus physician. The reputation signal displayed by the focus physician is inconsistent with the expected level, and the impact of the reputation signal decreases. Similarly, when the environment deviates from a patient's previous experience with other communities, the patient is required to invest additional cognitive effort to comprehend the motives behind the unusual setting. The process of understanding these motives generates distrust and feelings of insecurity in the patient, leading to distrust. Another example of what is meant by environmental consistency is that in the context of medical Q&A sites, environmental consistency refers to congruence between the content of an answer and its contextual cues, especially on language attributes. The congruence plays an indispensable role in signal receivers' value evaluation [14].

4.4 Signaling Mechanism

Rationality. The majority of research on signaling theory tends to investigate how a positive and isolated signal impacts the decision-making. Much of the existing literature on signaling concerns to investigate the impact of a specific signal on patients' choices, perceived helpfulness and satisfaction. Researchers emphasize the credibility of signals, which includes factors such as signal cost and observability. According to this perspective, the effectiveness of a signal is strengthened when one of cost and observability is increased. This perspective operates on the assumption of rationality, positing that

Table 2. Signaling environment in OHC

Construct	Variable	Content	References
Environmental uncertainty The diverse contextual factors that have the potential to impact the information symmetry between signalers and receivers	Organization reputation	A good organizational reputation has a positive effect the physicians within the organization, decreasing patients uncertainty	Liu (2016)
	Disease uncertainty	In the OHC, patients entering distinct sub-markets while selecting doctors face limitations in cross-market choices	Li (2019), Shah (2022), Ouyang (2022), Shah (2021), Wu (2021), Shah (2023),
		Disease perceptions vary within the current development of medical technology	Shah (2021), Wu (2021), Shah (2023)
	Volume of review	Potential patients perceive that the multitude of opinions from other users reduces their uncertainty	Xia (2023)
Environmental competition An intense setting in which multiple signalers compete simultaneously by transmitting numerous signals	Competition Intensity	In a highly competitive environment, patients receive numerous similar signals simultaneously. The effectiveness of identical signals diminishes, while signals that differ from those of other signalers become more impactful	Zhou (2023), Fang (2022)
Environmental norms The order and regulations within the environment, including various patterns, rules, and organized factors	Privacy	Patients are concerned about the platform's regulations and its ability to safeguard their privacy	Xue (2023)

(*continued*)

Table 2. (*continued*)

Construct	Variable	Content	References
	Consideration set size	The credibility of a signal can be enhanced by its widespread presence in the market, and signals linked to only one or a few products are insignificant. When only a few products receive ratings in a given market, patients do not perceive signals as systematic and reliable indicators of quality	Shukla (2021)
Environmental consistency The degree of similarity or congruence between signals and the overall environmental context	Colleagues' reputation	The reputation signal of a physician on OHCs is correlated with the reputation of their peers in the same environment	Wu and Liu (2016), Yin (2022)
	Content-Context Congruence	The congruence between the content of an answer and its contextual cues plays an indispensable role in signal receivers' value evaluations, especially on language attributes	Peng (2020)
	Situational abnormality	The environment deviates from a patient's previous experience with other platforms, the patient is required to put extra cognitive effort to comprehend the unusual setting	Xue (2023)

individuals can process all information highly rationally, and the quality of information is a key factor influencing the effectiveness of signals.

Information Processing. As we discussion above, prior studies have demonstrated that signal receivers' characteristics and the signaling environment affect the receiver's attention and interpretation of the signal, and further decision-making. This implies that

Individuals are often constrained by bounded rationality, unable to process all available data at the same time when making judgments and decisions. Researches in other fields are beginning to challenge the assumptions of traditional signaling theory.

Insights derived from cognitive science could help revise these assumptions by embracing the dual-process approach, which has proven as a valuable framework for complex decision environment [10]. In OHCs, the abundance of signals may lead to information overload, constraining decision-making with bounded rationality. We expect that this revision can be extended to the context of OHCs. Rooted on Elaboration likelihood model, individuals who process information through the peripheral route pay less attention to the quality of the information itself and rely heavily on the credibility of the source and the environmental characteristics of the information to judge the credibility of the information. The signals conveying information about service quality, such as the number of current patients who repeatedly interact with physician, last online time, physicians' title, introduction and so on, are central cues. The signals of online word of mouth, such as patient's votes, thank-you letters, gifts, the recommendation hotness are defined as peripheral cues. In addition, research has revealed that the central cue interaction quality has a stronger impact on new customers, while the peripheral cue has a stronger influence on non-new customers.

Affective Information Processing. Research on decision-making typically includes both cognition and affect, with affect recognized as an important part of human judgement and decision-making in many behavioral theories. Zajonc [15], an early advocate of the significance of affect, argued that affective reactions to stimuli are typically the first responses, occurring automatically and subsequently guiding information processing. Based our review on the section of signals, we note the emergence of the concept of affective signal in OHCs, which may be a novel research branch in signaling theory. While signal theory initially focused on rationality, recent research in cognitive science has expanded to include signal interpretation. In this paper, we suggest that affective signals can influence individuals' decision process.

Prior studies found that physicians' positive affective expression when responding to questions can directly alleviate patients' negative emotion and establish a certain physician-patient trust relationship at the initial stage. When patient's attention is first captured by the emotion support, they tend to prioritize the processing of emotional information, and easily influenced by the emotion orientation. However, it is crucial to note that these findings primarily pertain to emotional information conveyed through text and language, leaving a limited exploration of non-linguistic emotional cues. One relevant research explored that non-linguistic affective signals, such as a smile in a physician's photo, may contribute significantly to creating a positive first impression on patients and influence their choice of physicians.

5 Discussion and Directions for Future Research

In this work, we conducted a systematic review to identify, organize, and interpret the multiple insights provided by the different literature streams on signaling theory in OHC. In doing so, we have provided a comprehensive overview of the signalers, receivers, distinct signals, signaling environment, as well as signaling mechanism, that have been investigated and offered a pertinent perspective for future signaling research in online community. Moreover, we outline the significant issues that have not been considered and studied in OHCs for further research.

First, we recommend further exploration that signaling rests on mechanisms derived from cognitive psychology. It can be claimed that by further building on the work of Connelly et al., This review emphasizes the necessity to divert the attention towards the cognition of receivers and signaling environment, which can be the important gap in the body of literature on signaling in OHC.

Second, we argued that signaling theory researchers should keep their eye on affective signals, especially non-linguistic affective signals. The mechanism underlying the impact of affective signals on decision-making differ from those associated with informative signals. Research on these distinctions contributes to enhancing the diverse signals operation of online communities.

Finally, we need a better understanding of the link between affective signals and environment, that is, signaling mechanism, as individual cognition is assumed to be with the experience of affect. We expect that affective signals are more susceptible to signaling environment.

This study has some limitations. Although this study we executed the literature search for relevant articles with great care, we recognize that alternative sampling criteria could have been used, potentially enlarging or shrinking the size of our sample. Additionally, while we believe that our categorization approach for the articles in our sample was academically rigorous and practically useful, we acknowledge the existence of alternative methods. Despite these potential limitations, we think our review provides a new perspective on signaling theory in the context of OHC.

Acknowledgement. This research was funded by the National Natural Science Foundation of China (72171152 and 72101090), the Fundamental Research Funds for the Central Universities (2023TD003), and Shanghai International Studies University Tutor Academic Guidance Program.

References

1. Fan, W., Zhou, Q., Qiu, L., Kumar, S.: Should doctors open online consultation services? An empirical investigation of their impact on offline appointments. Inf. Syst. Res. **34**, 629–651 (2023)
2. Liu, H., Zhang, Y., Li, Y., Albright, K.: Better interaction performance attracts more chronic patients? Evidence from an online health platform. Inf. Process. Manage. **60**, 103413 (2023)
3. Spence, M.: Job market signaling. Uncertainty Econ., 281–306 (1973)
4. Connelly, B.L., Certo, S.T., Ireland, R.D., Reutzel, C.R.: Signaling theory: a review and assessment. J. Manag. **37**, 39–67 (2011)
5. Denyer, D., Tranfield, D.: Producing a systematic review. In: The Sage Handbook of Organizational Research Methods, pp. 671–689. Sage Publications Ltd., Thousand Oaks, CA (2009)
6. McKnight, D.H., Cummings, L.L., Chervany, N.L.: Initial trust formation in new organizational relationships. Acad. Manag. Rev. **23**, 473–490 (1998)
7. Lu, S.F., Rui, H.: Can we trust online physician ratings? Evidence from cardiac surgeons in Florida. Manage. Sci. **64**, 2557–2573 (2018)

8. Khurana, S., Qiu, L., Kumar, S.: When a doctor knows, it shows: an empirical analysis of doctors' responses in a Q&A forum of an online healthcare portal. Inf. Syst. Res. **30**, 872–891 (2019)

9. Yan, Z., Kuang, L., Qiu, L.: Prosocial behaviors and economic performance: evidence from an online mental healthcare platform. Prod. Oper. Manag. **31**, 3859–3876 (2022)

10. Chaiken, S.: Heuristic versus systematic information processing and the use of source versus message cues in persuasion. J. Pers. Soc. Psychol. **39**, 752 (1980)

11. Chen, L., Baird, A., Straub, D.: A linguistic signaling model of social support exchange in online health communities. Decis. Support. Syst. **130**, 113233 (2020)

12. Ouyang, P., Wang, J.-J.: Physician's online image and patient's choice in the online health community. Internet Res. (2022)

13. Shukla, A.D., Gao, G., Agarwal, R.: How digital word-of-mouth affects consumer decision making: evidence from doctor appointment booking. Manage. Sci. **67**, 1546–1568 (2021)

14. Peng, C.-H., Yin, D., Zhang, H.: More than words in medical question-and-answer sites: a content-context congruence perspective. Inf. Syst. Res. **31**, 913–928 (2020)

15. Zajonc, R.B.: Feeling and thinking: preferences need no inferences. Am. Psychol. **35**, 151 (1980)

Multi-criteria Health Science Short Video Recommendation Inspired by Heuristic Optimization

Shuang Geng, Chao Fu, Rui Wang$^{(\boxtimes)}$, Yuefeng Qian, and Yanghui Li

College of Management, Shenzhen University, Shenzhen 518060, China
wangrui.2002@foxmail.com

Abstract. An increasing number of people are obtaining healthcare and disease prevention-related knowledge through health science short videos, guiding their own health behavior habits in recent years. However, users may face the information overload problem in their searching process. Personalized recommendation can provide users with information related to their interaction history. Traditional personalized recommendation methods originate from e-commerce applications. Their excessive pursuit of click-through rates limits their usefulness over the health science short video platforms. Therefore, this study proposes a multi-criteria recommendation model that balances multiple recommendation goals. Specifically, we propose an item graph searching and updating encoding scheme that utilizes the relationships between discrete items to enhance the solution searching efficiency and the performance robustness. Results on real world data show that the proposed search scheme can effectively achieve multiple recommendation goals simultaneously.

Keywords: Multi-criteria Recommendation · Search Scheme · Short-video Recommendation

1 Introduction

Short-video platforms have become an increasingly popular media for disseminating health information [1]. However, the rapidly expanding number of short videos may overwhelm users, making it difficult for them to quickly find the content that meets their specific preferences. Recommendation systems can effectively solve the dilemma of information overload and provide personalized items that meet users' preferences, greatly saving users' information retrieval time and improving transaction efficiency [2]. However, traditional personalized recommendation methods mostly originate from the e-commerce field, and their excessive pursuit of click-through rates limits their usefulness in the health science short video recommendation field. Traditional recommendation systems predict users' preferences based on explicit or implicit interaction information between users and items, and provide the optimal recommendations [3]. Although existing methods can achieve high prediction accuracy for users' specific preferences, they

Y. P. Tu and M. Chi (Eds.): WHICEB 2024, LNBIP 517, pp. 372–381, 2024.
https://doi.org/10.1007/978-3-031-60324-2_31

often recommend a large number of similar items. In fact, recommending similar contents will lead users to the personal "interest trap" and gradually impair user interest in the recommended content [4, 5]. Moreover, existing recommendation algorithms that focus only on improving accuracy may fall short to recommend long-tail items. In the healthcare short video platforms, the vast majority of items in the dataset are less popular contents, with a very small number of popular contents [6]. By contrast, platform owners also generate considerable profits or click rates from these cold contents.

Multi-objective recommendation systems (MORSs) aim to optimize the system performance in terms of multiple evaluation criteria, although improving the system diversity and novelty may undermine the system accuracy performance. Therefore, MORSs can meet people's various requirements for recommendation systems, and have important theoretical and practical significance [7]. The existing MORSs mainly adopt two types of approaches: the scalarization method and population-based heuristic method [8]. The scalarization method converts multiple objectives (MO) into a single objective, which can be solved by single objective optimization strategies. Population-based heuristic algorithms use evolutionary or swarm intelligence algorithms to generate a Pareto optimal set that contains multiple recommendation solutions with dominant performance for at least one evaluation criteria. Compared to the scalarization method, swarm or evolutionary optimization based approach provides more solution choices and is able to solve non-convex problems. Nevertheless, swarm or evolutionary optimization based recommendation systems also face several performance challenges: (1) different recommendation criteria may conflict with each other, such as the trade-off between accuracy and diversity, making it difficult to find a balance point that maximizes all criteria simultaneously [9]. (2) MORSs typically rely on user behavioral data, which are often sparse [10], resulting in decreased accuracy of results. These limitations need to be carefully considered in multi-criteria recommendation methods to guarantee the system performance and practicability.

Therefore, this study proposes a solution to the aforementioned problems and makes the following contributions:

(1) The recommendation of health science video content is actually a discrete optimization task. To tackle the data sparsity and discrete optimization difficulty, we develop an item graph searching and updating based encoding scheme to smooth the heuristic optimization process.
(2) We evaluate the effectiveness of the proposed scheme on a real-world recommendation task. The results demonstrate that the proposed recommendation framework can achieve excellent balance between multiple evaluation criteria. The multi-criteria recommendation system is built on SPEA2 [16], which proves to converge to a better Pareto frontier.

2 Preliminaries

2.1 Recommendation Objectives

The multi-criteria health science short video recommendation problem is transformed into a multi-objective optimization problem, defined by three criteria functions - accuracy, diversity, and novelty. Accuracy is calculated using graph convolutional neural network model to evaluate the match between recommended videos and user preferences. Diversity is assessed by feature entropy to evaluate the richness of content in the recommended videos. Novelty is defined as the reciprocal of the popularity of the videos.

Accuracy. For the list of items to be recommended, accuracy is defined as the average predicted rating of items in the recommended list, and its calculation formula is as follows:

$$Accuracy(L) = \frac{1}{|L|}\left(\sum_{i=1}^{|L|} r_{ui}\right) \tag{1}$$

where L is the length of the recommendation list, and r_{ui} represents the predicted rating of item i by user u. For unrated items, LightGCN [11] is employed to estimate the r_{ui}. LightGCN is a graph-based recommendation algorithm that uses a simplified graph convolutional network to learn user and item embeddings by propagating information through the user-item interaction matrix. Its advantages include good scalability, simplicity, and high recommendation accuracy, especially in sparse data scenarios.

Diversity. In recommender systems, entropy is commonly used to evaluate the diversity of item combinations, such as by calculating the entropy of the number of items in each category or the distribution of item components. This study proposes to use the item embedding produced by LightGCN to evaluate the diversity of the recommendation list. Given the embedding of an item ed with d dimensions, it is assumed that each position in the embedding d_i^e follows a Gaussian distribution. For a list of items, the mean and standard deviation of their d_i^e are used to calculate the average differential entropy, which measures the diversity of the candidate item set, as in Eq. (2) and (3).

$$Div_i = \frac{1}{2}\log_2 \pi e\sigma_d^2 \tag{2}$$

$$Diversity(L) = \sum_{d=1}^{D} Div_i \tag{3}$$

where σ_d^2 represents the variance of the embeddings for a recommendation list with k items.

Novelty. Novelty is an important criterion in recommendation systems because it can help users discover new and interesting items that they may not have been aware of. We consider highly reviewed items as popular items, and items with less interactions as more novel items. The novelty in this study is calculated as follows:

$$Novelty(L) = \sum_{i=1}^{|L|} \log_2\left(\frac{C}{c_i}\right) \tag{4}$$

where L is the total number of all items in the data set. C is the total number of comments of all items, and c_i is the number of comments of candidate recommended item i.

2.2 Heuristic Optimization Algorithms

Compared to traditional algorithms such as the weighted coefficient method, multi-objective Heuristic algorithms are simple, versatile, robust, and possess advantages such as parallel processing mechanisms and global optimization. They are widely applied to solve multi-objective optimization problems. This category of algorithms includes Improved Strength Pareto Evolutionary Algorithm (SPEA2) [12], Multiobjective Evolutionary Algorithm based on Decomposition (MOEA/D) [13] and Improved Non-dominated Sorting Genetic Algorithm (NSGA2) [14], among others. In this study, the effectiveness of the proposed search framework is verified by using the above three multi-objective heuristic algorithms, which will be briefly introduced in the following paragraphs.

SPEA2. SPEA2 is a mature multi-objective genetic algorithm, representing an enhancement and extension of SPEA, designed for solving multi-objective optimization problems. This algorithm effectively manages the population of solutions by introducing the concepts of strength Pareto evolution and external archive, maintaining a uniformly distributed Pareto front during the solution of multi-objective problems. Key features of SPEA2 include control of external population size through pruning operations, fast computation speed, robustness, and the generation of a diverse solution set. The improvements in SPEA2 are primarily manifested in the optimization of individual evaluation and selection processes. Through these enhancements, SPEA2 can efficiently handle multi-objective optimization problems, identifying the Pareto-optimal solution set.

MOEA/D. The MOEA/D algorithm introduces the decomposition method into multi-objective evolutionary computation in a simple and effective manner. It explicitly breaks down the multi-objective optimization problem into N single-objective optimization subproblems. During each iteration, the population comprises the most optimal solutions identified thus far for each individual subproblem. The "neighborhood relationship" among subproblems is established based on the proximity of their aggregation coefficient vectors. This guarantees that optimal solutions for adjacent subproblems are closely situated to one another. When optimizing each subproblem, only relevant information from a few neighboring subproblems is utilized. This approach allows the algorithm to concurrently evolve solutions for all subproblems, enhancing the efficiency of solving multi-objective optimization problems.

NSGA2. NSGA2 represents an advancement from the initial non-dominated sorting genetic algorithm, with a specific emphasis on enhancing three crucial aspects. Primarily, it introduces an efficient non-dominated sorting algorithm to diminish computational complexity and unify parent and offspring populations. This enables the selection of the next generation's population from an expanded space, preserving all the best individuals. Secondly, it integrates an elite strategy to safeguard specific outstanding individuals within the population from being discarded throughout the evolutionary process, thereby improving optimization accuracy. Finally, it adopts crowding distance and crowding comparison operators, overcoming the drawback in NSGA of needing manually specified sharing parameters. These operators serve as the criteria for comparing individuals in the population, ensuring individuals in the approximate Pareto front evenly expand to the entire Pareto front and maintaining population diversity.

3   The Proposed Content Search Scheme

The overall recommendation framework is shown in Fig. 1.

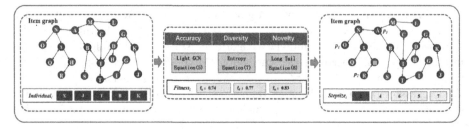

Fig. 1. Framework of the search scheme

The items to be recommended are organized in the form of an item-item graph. A recommendation list is composed of multiple items in the graph. In the heuristic optimization algorithm, an individual solution is a recommendation list, which is evaluated by the fitness value built on accuracy (Eq. 1), diversity (Eq. 3), and novelty (Eq. 4). In the content searching space, solutions on the optimal Pareto front are the final recommendation results.

Item relations are crucial for measuring item similarities in recommendation [15]. To explore the relationships between items and conduct a more organized search, we organize the items in the form of an item-item graph and design a graph-based random walk coding scheme. The item-item graph can be an interaction graph, a relationship graph similar to a knowledge graph, or an aggregation of several graphs.

3.1 Solution Encoding

Solution encoding plays a crucial role in guiding the search behavior of evolutionary algorithms and obtaining high-quality recommendation results. Based on graph structure, we design an appropriate encoding scheme using a trend-based strategy. The individual encoding consists of three components: The search step size in the item graph, the candidate items, and the fitness values on each criterion. Figure 2 illustrates an example of the encoding for a single individual. Different uppercase letters are used to differentiate the recommended items. The length of the item set represents the length of the recommendation list, which depends on the requirements of the recommendation system. The step size is a continuous vector, with each element corresponding to a candidate item, reflecting the performance of the current item in the recommendation list. Finally, the fitness values include accuracy evaluation (f_a), diversity evaluation (f_d), and novelty evaluation (f_n) values.

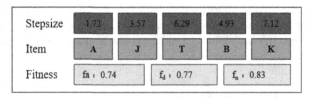

Fig. 2. The coding of individual bacteria

3.2 Graph Walking Scheme

Each value in the step size vector (Fig. 2) reflects the performance of the corresponding item in the current candidate item set. A smaller value indicates a higher probability of being replaced for the corresponding item, providing greater motivation to explore items further away, and vice versa. Figure 3 illustrates an example of random walking and item updating. First, the individual updates its step size vector using multi-objective algorithms and calculates the integer step size through rounding. Then, each item element randomly walks in the video item network based on its corresponding step size. For example, if the first element in the candidate item set is A and its step size is 2, a random walk point in the video item network starts at position A and walks 2 steps along adjacent edges. Following the path A → N → P, it arrives at a new position P, and the corresponding item A is updated to P. When the length of the candidate item set is L, L random walk points concurrently traverse the graph, and after the candidate item set is updated, the corresponding fitness values are calculated.

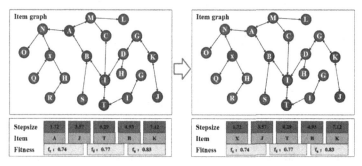

Fig. 3. Item update process diagram

3.3 Graph Node Selection

In the process of graph walking, the selection of nodes is very important to the search efficiency of recommendation lists. We conduct pre-sampling to reduce the redundant calculation. Specifically, the criteria for the node selection are divided into static criteria and dynamic criteria. Accuracy and novelty belong to the static criteria, as they are determined once the candidate items and the target user are defined. The accuracy and novelty criteria values for each item in the item network can be pre-calculated. Diversity criteria is the dynamic criteria, as the diversity of the candidate item set depends on the dissimilarity between the content of the item lists, which is influenced by the positions of nodes in the graph.

We let the walking node randomly selects the current objective among the three objectives randomly with equal probability (e.g., 1/3 in this study). Several neighboring nodes are randomly sampled, and we calculate the change in the selected criteria (i.e. accuracy) using Eq. (5) to Eq. (9). Nodes with an increase in the criteria will be added to the pre-sampled node set. The change in criteria accuracy, diversity, and novelty are calculated as follows, respectively:

$$\Delta_{accuracy} = ReLU\left(r_{uj} - r_{ui}\right) \tag{5}$$

$$e_{centre} = \frac{\sum_{k \in L/i} e_k}{|L| - 1} \tag{6}$$

$$\Delta_{diversity} = ReLU\left(\|e_j - e_{centre}\| - \|e_i - e_{centre}\|\right) \tag{7}$$

$$\Delta_{novelty} = ReLU\left(nol_j - nol_i\right) \tag{8}$$

$$ReLU(x) = \begin{cases} x, x > 0 \\ 0, x \le 0 \end{cases} \tag{9}$$

where $item_i$ represents the current item. $item_j$ represents the adjacent item. r_{ui} is the predicted rating of user u for $item_i$. nol represents the novelty of the current item. L represents the set of candidate items or nodes. e_i is the feature representation vector of the $item_i$.

$$c_i = c_{i-1} + \frac{\Delta_i^m}{\sum \Delta^m} \tag{10}$$

Assuming k pre-sampled nodes have a relative change in the selected criterion m denoted as $\Delta^m = \left\{\Delta_1^m, \Delta_2^m \ldots \Delta_k^m\right\}$. The probability threshold c for the pre-sampling is calculated using (Eq. 10). Then, a random number p is generated uniformly between 0 and 1, and the largest value of i satisfying $p < c_i$ is found. At last, the i-th pre-sampled item is selected as the next searching item.

4 Experiment

4.1 Dataset

In this study, we construct a health science short video dataset, which contains 2,946 health science videos created by 3,333 posters between November 2022 and January 2023 over the Tiktok platform, by using the Selenium tool. The dataset also contains 88,586 comments from 64,586 users, with an average of 1.33 comments per user. The data sparsity is 99.95%.

This study first used word2vec [16] to convert user comments into vector representations to preprocess the LightGCN model and improve the quality of vector representations. Then, the model was trained on the collected health science short video dataset, and the results were saved after the model converged.

4.2 Application Algorithms

The short video recommendation experiment compares the performance of our proposed model with popular algorithms, including MOEA/D, NSGA2 and SPEA2. The settings of the parameters are shown in Table 1. In the experiment, a maximum iteration count of 100 was set, and each algorithm was independently run 30 times to obtain stable average performance results. The experiment was conducted using random users for testing, and the values of the accuracy measure (Eq. 1), diversity measure (Eq. 3), and novelty measure (Eq. 4) obtained from the Pareto-optimal set generated by each algorithm were used as comparison metrics.

Table 1. Parameters Setting

Parameter	Meaning	Value
N	Population Size	100
G	Maximum Iterations	100
L	Recommended List Length	5–20
α	Response Amplitude Control Constant	1
β	Historical Amnesia Factor	0.5
K	External Archive Size	100
Pc	Crossover Probability	0.9
Pm	Mutation Probability	0.1

4.3 Results

The experimental results are presented in Table 2, with bold font highlighting the optimal evaluation metric values for all comparative algorithms in the recommendation problem. In terms of accuracy criteria, MOEA/D achieved the best results, followed by SPEA2. NSGA2 shows strong potential in novelty. In terms of the diversity criterion, SPEA2 demonstrates impressive convergence ability and consistently achieves the best results in terms of the mean value.

Table 2. Experiment Result

Accuracy	NSGA2	MOEA/D	SPEA2
l = 5	0.702	**0.754**	0.738
l = 10	0.673	**0.729**	0.710
l = 15	0.629	**0.704**	0.673
l = 20	0.634	**0.676**	0.631
Diversity	NSGA2	MOEA/D	SPEA2
l = 5	1.330	1.670	**2.150**
l = 10	1.760	1.850	**2.260**
l = 15	1.720	1.850	**2.190**
l = 20	1.730	1.840	**2.130**
Novelty	NSGA2	MOEA/D	SPEA2
l = 5	**4.190**	3.510	2.950
l = 10	**4.120**	3.590	3.110
l = 15	**4.210**	3.670	3.260
l = 20	**4.260**	3.710	3.400

5   Conclusion

This study proposes a graph based multi-criteria recommendation system to address the limitations of current multi-criteria recommendation problems and provides methodology support for health science short video recommendation. It transforms the multi-criteria recommendation problem into a multi-objective optimization problem that considers accuracy, diversity, and novelty. The items to be recommended are aggregated in an item-item graph, and a corresponding encoding and search scheme is designed. Experiment results show that the proposed multi-criteria recommendation scheme provides a reasonable solution to the urgent problems in the current multi-criteria recommendation, offering valuable insights for content resource management. Consequently, this approach can boost the ecological development of health-related short video creation and dissemination platforms, providing users with an enhanced health knowledge learning experience. In addition, the proposed method can be applied to recommendation algorithm research in various types of data and application scenarios and has strong practicality and promotion value.

Acknowledgement. This study was supported by the National Natural Science Foundation of China (71901150 and 72334004), Guangdong Basic and Applied Basic Research Foundation (2022A1515012077), Guangdong Philosophy and Social Science Planning Project (GD23XGL113), and Guangdong Province Innovation Team (2021WCXTD002).

References

1. Tan, Y., Geng, S., Chen, L., et al.: How doctor image features engage health science short video viewers? Investigating the age and gender bias. Ind. Manag. Data Syst. **123**(9), 2319–2348 (2023)
2. Chiang, J.-H., Ma, C.-Y., Wang, C.-S., Hao, P.-Y.: An adaptive, context-aware, and stacked attention network-based recommendation system to capture users' temporal preference. IEEE Trans. Knowl. Data Eng. **35**(4), 3404–3418 (2023)
3. Geng, S., Tao, B., Liang, G., et al.: Temporal knowledge graph attention network for online doctor recommendation. In: Proceedings of the 2023 8th International Conference on Intelligent Information Processing, pp. 277–282 (2023)
4. Li, P., Tuzhilin, A.: Learning latent multi-criteria ratings from user reviews for recommendations. IEEE Trans. Knowl. Data Eng. **34**(8), 3854–3866 (2022)
5. Geng, S., He, X., Wang, Y., et al.: Multicriteria recommendation based on bacterial foraging optimization. Int. J. Intell. Syst. **37**(2), 1618–1645 (2022)
6. Qian, T., Liang, Y., Li, Q., et al.: Intent disentanglement and feature self-supervision for novel recommendation. IEEE Trans. Knowl. Data Eng. (2022)
7. Geng, S., He, X., Liang, G., et al.: Accuracy-diversity optimization in personalized recommender system via trajectory reinforcement based bacterial colony optimization. Inf. Process. Manage. **60**(2), 103205 (2023)
8. Zheng, Y., Wang, D.X.: A survey of recommender systems with multi-objective optimization. Neurocomputing **474**, 141–153 (2022)
9. Alhijawi, B., Fraihat, S., Awajan, A.: Multi-factor ranking method for trading-off accuracy, diversity, novelty, and coverage of recommender systems. Int. J. Inf. Technol. **15**(3), 1427–1433 (2023)
10. Zhao, M., Huang, X., Zhu, L., et al.: Knowledge graph-enhanced sampling for conversational recommendation system. IEEE Trans. Knowl. Data Eng. (2022)
11. He, X., Deng, K., Wang, X., et al.: LightGCN: simplifying and powering graph convolution network for recommendation. In: Proceedings of the 43rd International ACM SIGIR Conference on Research and Development in Information Retrieval, pp. 639–648 (2020)
12. Zitzler, E., Laumanns, M., Thiele, L.: SPEA2: improving the strength Pareto evolutionary algorithm. TIK-report, vol. 103 (2001)
13. Zhang, Q., Li, H.: A multiobjective evolutionary algorithm based on decomposition. IEEE Trans. Evol. Comput. (2006)
14. Deb, K., Pratap, A., Agarwal, S., et al.: A fast and elitist multiobjective genetic algorithm: NSGA-II. IEEE Trans. Evol. Comput. **6**(2), 182–197 (2002)
15. Zhu, T., Sun, L., Chen, G.: Graph-based embedding smoothing for sequential recommendation. IEEE Trans. Knowl. Data Eng. **35**(1), 496–508 (2023)
16. Mikolov, T., Sutskever, I., Chen, K., et al.: Distributed representations of words and phrases and their compositionality. In: Advances in Neural Information Processing Systems, vol. 26 (2013)

Research on University Students' Information Security Behavior: The Moderating Effect of Disciplinary Background

Jingtong Xu and Nan Zhang[✉]

Harbin Institute of Technology, No. 92, Xidazhi Street, Harbin, Heilongjiang, People's Republic of China
andyzhang@hit.edu.cn

Abstract. While social networking sites (SNSs) provide university students with more diverse channels for information transfer, they also pose certain risks to their personal information security. Previous studies suggested that users' information security behavior is an effective way to prevent information security risks. Based on Technology Threat Avoidance Theory (TTAT), this study constructs a model to explore the influencing factors of information security behaviors of university students in SNSs. Specifically, this study focuses on the moderating effect of disciplinary background in the proposed model. An empirical study was conducted to verify the model. Consistent to the previous literature, the results show that self-efficacy and response efficacy have positive effects on perceived avoidability; perceived threat and perceived avoidability have positive effect on information security behavior. Further, disciplinary backgrounds moderate the relationship between perceived threat and perceived avoidability on information security behavior. Specifically, perceived threat motivates students in soft disciplines to take information security behaviors more than it motivates students in hard disciplines, while perceived avoidability motivates students in hard disciplines to take information security behaviors more than it motivates students in soft disciplines. Based on this, we put forward the information security protection countermeasures.

Keywords: Information Security Behavior · Technology Threat Avoidance Theory · Disciplinary Background · Social Networking Site

1 Introduction

With the advent of the information age, social networking sites (SNSs) have become the main source of information and the main platform for social activities. Moreover, the increasing social and economic reliance on SNSs for working from home has become part of the "new normal" since the start of the global COVID-19 pandemic. However, while people benefit from using SNSs, some hidden dangers affecting user information security also gradually emerge. As of June 2023, 37.6% of SNSs users had encountered cybersecurity problems in the past six months while surfing the Internet [1]. In terms

Y. P. Tu and M. Chi (Eds.): WHICEB 2024, LNBIP 517, pp. 382–395, 2024.
https://doi.org/10.1007/978-3-031-60324-2_32

of the various types of security problems encountered by SNSs users, the proportion of personal information leakage was the highest, at 23.2% [1]. The proportion of networking fraud was the second highest, at 20.0% [1]. The security management of SNSs is faced with an increasingly complex new situation. Among the many factors that affect information security, the insecure information behavior of SNSs users is one of the main reasons that leads to security breaches. Instances of information security breaches arising from unreliable user behaviors in SNSs outnumber incidents linked to systemic technology [2]. Considering that university students are a large group of SNSs users, the current status of university students' information security behavior and its influencing factors need to be further explored.

We take university students with different disciplinary backgrounds as the research subject, and explore the influencing factors of their information security behavior through empirical analysis. Specifically, we try to answer the following two research questions: (1) What are the influencing factors of university students' information security behavior in SNSs? (2) How the disciplines backgrounds moderate the effects of the factors identified in the RQ1 on the information security behavior? This paper introduces and tests a theoretical model based on the Technology Threat Avoidance Theory (TTAT). Our study helps to identify the influencing factors of university students' security behavior in SNSs and examine the moderating effect of disciplinary backgrounds. In addition, the exploration of the moderating effect of disciplinary backgrounds can help to provide suggestions for university students in different disciplines to keep their information security. This is of practical significance for the effective maintenance of cyberspace security.

2 Theoretical Background

Information security research is a broad field encompassing technical, behavioral, managerial, and organizational security approaches, where behavioral information security is a subarea that focuses on individual security behaviors. Insights from previous studies that based on Theory of Planned Behavior, Protection Motivation Theory, and Social Control Theory have enriched the understanding of organizational security behaviors in the workplace. Technology Threat Avoidance Theory (TTAT) can well explain the individual voluntary security behavior of SNSs users in the face of information security threats. Thus, we attempt to apply TTAT to the field of individual information security behaviors of university students.

TTAT explains why and how individuals avoid IT threats in voluntary environments, and describes the process and influencing factors of IT users' threat avoidance behavior [3]. Liang and Xue developed TTAT by integrating literature in a series of fields such as psychology, healthcare, risk analysis and information system [4]. The basic premise of TTAT is that when individual users perceive information technology threats, they will take security measures to avoid the threats actively if they believe the threats is avoidable; if users think the threat cannot be addressed by taking security measures, then they would resort to emotion-focused coping activities passively [3].

TTAT develops a general theoretical framework to explain SNSs user's security behavior. The theory is essentially based on two cognitive appraisal processes – perceived threat and perceived avoidability [5]. According to Liang and Xue (2009), TTAT "delineates the avoidance behavior as a dynamic, positive feedback loop in which users go through the two cognitive processes to decide how to cope with IT threats [3]." Perceived threat and perceived avoidability constitute the antecedents of coping behaviors. Also, TTAT proposes that individual users' perceived avoidability is contingent upon the response efficacy and costs of the security measure and the self-efficacy of applying the security measure. It is confirmed that both self-efficacy and response efficacy in TTAT can influence users' security behavior [3, 4].

In previous studies, TTAT has been applied and extended in various security scenarios, including spyware [4, 6], mobile security [7], and Internet security [5, 8]. The previous security studies often revolve around the mandate and structural security environments in the workplace, whereas individual voluntary security behaviors in daily life are less understood [5]. TTAT is very effective in explaining voluntary security behavior when information security is not mandatory. Therefore, it is argued that TTAT is suitable for investigating the information security behavior of SNSs users as well [6].

With the arrival of the knowledge economy era, SNSs provide a brand-new way for university students to exchange information, and university students have become the main force in using SNSs [9]. However, the impact of disciplinary differences on the information security behavior of university student users remains largely overlooked by researchers [10]. Therefore, it is of research significance to explore differences in information security behaviors of university students from different disciplinary backgrounds. In order to enrich the theoretical foundation of the research topic, we add disciplinary background as a moderating variable to TTAT and construct the research model. We conducted an empirical study to investigates the influence of perceived threat and perceived avoidability on university students' information security behaviors using disciplinary background as a moderating variable.

3   Research Hypotheses and Theoretical Model

3.1   Research Model

Based on TTAT, university students' information security behavior is predicted by perceived threat and perceived avoidability, while university students' perceived avoidability is predicted by response efficacy and self-efficacy. In addition, this study assessed the moderating effect of university students' disciplinary background. The research model and hypotheses are depicted in Fig. 1.

3.2   Research Hypotheses

Liang and Xue (2009) delineated perceived threat as the proximity between users' current and undesired end states and defined perceived threat as "the extent to which an individual perceives malicious IT as dangerous [3]." In the context of SNSs, perceived threat refers to the cognitive assessment when users perceive the existence of information security threats in the process of use. Perceived threat is a crucial factor affecting the behavioral intention of SNSs users [11].

According to the TTAT, if a user can foresee information security risks and believes that such risks may threaten his or her interests, then the user will engage in information

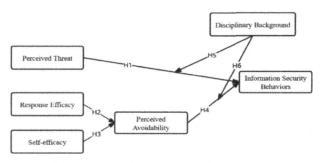

Fig. 1. Research Model

security protection behavior. However, if the user is unable to perceive, or does not believe that the risk will have serious consequences, then the user will likely not engage in information security protection behavior [12]. Hence, we argue that when university student users perceive that there is a risk in the SNSs they use and that this risk is likely to infringe on their interests, they tend to generate information security behavior to protect their personal information security. Perceived threat influences university students' information security behaviors. Thus, we propose that:

H1: In SNSs, perceived threat positively influences information security behavior of university users.

According to TTAT, coping appraisal refers to the cognitive assessment of the effectiveness of information security strategies, including response efficacy and self-efficacy. Response efficacy refers to users' subjective perception of the effectiveness of their behaviors. The assessment of response efficacy is a cognitive process in which individuals continually contemplate the effectiveness of the measures to respond to a threat. The ultimate perception of the effectiveness of safety measures determines how they will respond to the threat [3]. High response efficacy leads individuals to believe that taking risk avoidance measures is effective, which in turn positively influences information security protection behavior [13].

In the context of SNSs, if users believe that the security measures they take are effective, then they will take such security measures. University students will develop perceived avoidability only if they believe in the usefulness of risk aversion and believe that the measure is beneficial in reducing information risk. If university students do not believe that security behavior is effective, they may not develop perceived avoidability even if they are concerned about information risk. Thus, we propose that:

H2: In SNSs, response efficacy positively influences perceived avoidability of university users.

According to TTAT, self-efficacy is the degree to which a user is confident that he or she can use skills to accomplish a task. The results of numerous studies have shown that self-efficacy can influence users' avoidance and information security behaviors to a certain extent. For example, workman et al. argued that as the level of self-efficacy increases, users are more inclined to perform information security behaviors [14]. Chen et al. found that self-efficacy affects protective motivation by affecting perceived avoidability [13].

When SNSs users take security protection measures, they need to assess their ability to act on potential problems [15]. SNSs users will predict the outcome of their behaviors by evaluating their self-efficacy. Those with higher degree of self-efficacy are mostly confident in the security behaviors they adopt and believe that they can avoid information risks. For university students, they are more likely to develop perceived avoidability if they are confident in their ability to protect their information security. Thus, we propose that:

H3: In SNSs, self-efficacy positively influences perceived avoidability of university users.

According to TTAT, perceived avoidability is defined as an individual's perception of the likelihood that she will be able to avoid malware or its negative consequences by using certain safeguarding measures [5]. Coping appraisal includes response efficacy and self-efficacy. The result of coping appraisal is to achieve avoidability, that is, the possibility of eliminating or avoiding information security risks by applying security behaviors [3]. When individuals take security behavior, they need to assess their ability to take action on potential problems [15]. Once the individuals believe that the implementation of information security strategy is conducive to avoiding information security risks, they will be more likely to generate information security behavior.

In SNSs, when university students think that the security measures implemented is likely to avoid information security risks, they will be more inclined to produce information security behavior. Oppositely, they will reject information security behavior if they do not believe they have enough safeguarding measures to avoid the threat. Thus, we propose that:

H4: In SNSs, perceived avoidability positively influences information security behavior of university users.

For each discipline of higher education, discipline culture refers to a special and common code of conduct and values formed among discipline members [16]. According to Biglan (1973), academic disciplines can be classified by the dimension of "hard versus soft". It distinguishes disciplines with a clearly defined ordering of knowledge (such as physics) versus disciplines lacking such agreed ordering (such as sociology). Specifically, hard disciplines refer to natural sciences while soft disciplines refer to social sciences and humanities [17].

University students of different disciplines have different educational ideas, different lifestyles, and different behaviors in the face of information security problems. They also have different perceptions of information security threats and different perceptions of their own ability to avoid information risks. Hard disciplines require students to use more technology than soft disciplines because technology use is inherent in the nature of the discipline. Hence, students of hard disciplines are more inclined to use technology to maintain their own information security. When they believe that they can effectively deal with information security risks with practical technology, they are more likely to generate information security behaviors. Students of soft disciplines mainly focus on hot social phenomena and cases, and are more sensitive to the information risks. Hence, they are more likely to find the hidden information security threats in SNSs, which leads to their information security behaviors. Thus, we propose that:

H5: Disciplinary background moderates the relationship between perceived threat and information security behavior. Specifically, students of soft disciplines are more likely to produce information security behavior when perceiving information threat.

H6: Disciplinary background moderates the relationship between perceived avoidability and information security behavior. Specifically, students of hard disciplines are more likely to produce information security behavior when perceiving the avoidability of the threat.

4 Empirical Study

4.1 Scale Development

The measurement scales for the constructs in the research model were developed based on an extensive literature review. As the survey data were collected in China, one professor and two doctoral students in the information systems field who were proficient in both Chinese and English translated the questionnaire items with precision. Further, to ensure content validity, we conducted a focus group discussion and a pilot study. Two professors and three doctoral students were invited to review the quality of the questionnaire, such as the wording, legibility, and suitability of the items. The questionnaire was modified according to the panel experts' advice to ensure that the items would be clear and precise.

The questionnaire chooses the Likert 5-level scale as the design criteria. We conducted a pretest to further examine the applicability of the questionnaire. The pretest involved 20 participants, recruited at a Chinese university. Half of these 20 students are from hard disciplines (e.g., physics, engineering) and half are from soft disciplines (e.g., sociology, humanities). The instrument went through minor revisions after the pilot test.

4.2 Sample Data

A web-based survey was administered in China. Participants were students in undergraduate and graduate classes in some Chinese universities. Based on wjx.com and WeChat, 270 survey requests were sent out, which resulted in 243 responses. The response rate was a respectable 90%. We set a one-time limit on the IP addresses of respondents in order to ensure that each participant could only answer the questionnaire once. In order to ensure the validity of responses, we examined and cleansed the data in two rounds. First, we removed records in which many questions were not answered. Then, we examined the respondents' time spent to complete the survey. Our pretests had shown that to answer the survey carefully, a minimum of five minutes was needed. We therefore removed all observations that were completed in less than five minutes. This was done to ensure that the sample represented thoughtful and careful responses. The final data set had a total of 214 usable observations. The demographic statistics of the sample are reported in Table 1.

As shown in Table 1, the number of female respondents is higher, accounting for 66.36%, while male respondents are only 33.64%. In terms of grade distribution, senior students accounted for about half of the respondents at 50.93%, and master's and doctoral students were involved. In terms of disciplinary background, the proportion of soft

Table 1. Descriptive Statistics of Survey Sample

Statistics		Frequency	Percentage
Gender	Male	72	33.64%
	Female	142	66.36%
Grade	Freshman	16	7.84%
	Sophomore	25	11.68%
	Junior	42	19.63%
	Senior	109	50.93%
	Grade 1 master	8	3.74%
	Grade 2 master	2	0.93%
	Grade 3 master	10	4.67%
	PhD	2	0.93%
Disciplinary background	Soft disciplines	120	56.07%
	Hard disciplines	94	43.93%
Frequency of using social networking sites per day	0 times	4	1.87%
	1–2 times	13	6.07%
	3–4 times	38	17.76%
	5–6 times	27	12.62%
	7 times or more	132	61.68%

disciplines is larger at 56.07%, and the proportion of hard is smaller at 43.93%. The number of questionnaires for the two types of disciplines is more or less equal, so it is of research significance for subsequent analysis.

4.3 Measurement Model

The samples were checked in accordance with methodologies recommended in the literature. All the Cronbach alpha values exceeded the cutoff value of 0.70, the composite reliability (CR) values were above the threshold of 0.70, and the average variance extracted (AVE) values were above the cutoff value of 0.50 (see Table 2). Hence, the reliability checks supported construct reliability in the samples. We then checked the convergent and discriminant validity. As shown in the correlation matrix (Table 3), for each construct, the square root of AVE was greater than the correlation values with other constructs. These results supported the discriminant validity. Table 2 reports factor loadings and p-values for the items in the measurement model. All the factor loadings were greater than 0.60 with significant p-values, indicating item significance and supporting convergent validity. The measurement model was estimated in AMOS 24.0. As Table 4 shows, the fit indices of the measurement model had satisfactory fit.

Table 2. Results of Confirmatory Factor Analysis

Construct	Items	FL	P	CR	AVE	Cronbach's α
Perceived Threat (PT)	Q1 I think using social networking sites may put me at risk for security attacks	.782	***	.858	.602	.857
	Q2 I think information security risks in social networking sites may cause me to suffer losses	.842	***			
	Q3 I think the security risks of the Internet will affect how much I worry about social networking sites	.751	***			
	Q4 I think that there is a problem with the security scanning software that may threaten the security of my information	.723	***			
Response Efficacy (RE)	Q5 I think the protection I put in place can be effective against the security attacks in social networking sites	.779	***	.805	.580	.805
	Q6 I think learning more knowledge about social networking sites will help to protect personal information security	.708	***			
	Q7 I think security scanning software can effectively protect the information security of social networking sites users	.795	***			

(*continued*)

Table 2. (*continued*)

Construct	Items	FL	P	CR	AVE	Cronbach's α
Self-efficacy (SE)	Q8 I think my knowledge of information risk prevention is sufficient for me to handle security attacks in social networking sites	.782	***	.845	.646	.841
	Q9 I think I am capable of taking relevant protective measures to deal with security attacks in social networking sites	.846	***			
	Q10 I think I have the ability to make full use of technology to protect personal information security	.781	***			
Perceived Avoidability (PA)	Q11 I think security software can be used to reduce the risk of leakage of personal information	.812	***	.749	.502	.724
	Q12 I think the probability of information security incidents can be greatly reduced by security settings	.622	***			
	Q13 I think the penetration of information risks can be prevented by implementing security protection measures	.677	***			
Information Security Behavior (ISB)	Q14 I will update my information security scanning software frequently	.799	***	.818	.531	.813

(*continued*)

Table 2. (*continued*)

Construct	Items	FL	P	CR	AVE	Cronbach's α
	Q15 I often use security scanning software to monitor risks in social networking sites	.732	***			
	Q16 I will not easily click on unsafe links or download unsafe content in social networking sites	.649	***			
	Q17 I am willing to actively use information security technology to protect the information security	.726	***			

Notes: ***P < .001; FL: factor loading; CR: composite reliability; AVE: average variance extracted.

Table 3. Results of Discriminant Validity

	PT	RE	SE	PA	ISB
PT	**.776**				
RE	.001	**.762**			
SE	.049	.665	**.804**		
PA	.014	.583	.598	**.709**	
ISB	.213	.433	.362	.443	**.729**

Notes: Diagonal Values: the square roots of AVE values of each construct; Off-diagonal Values: the correlation coefficients between constructs.

Table 4. Fit Indices

Fit Index	χ^2/df	GFI	AGFI	PGFI	RMR	RMSEA	NFI	IFI	TLI	CFI
Measurement Model	1.764	.905	.866	.639	.048	.060	.901	.955	.942	.954
Structure Model	1.720	.903	.865	.649	.049	.059	.903	.955	.943	.954
Standard	1–3	>.9	>.8	>.5	<.05	<.08	>.90	>.90	>.90	>.90

Also, we assessed common method bias. We performed Harman's (1976) single-factor test – with the first factor explaining 35.89% of the variance (less than 50% threshold), indicating no single factor contributing to the majority of the variance.

4.4 Structure Equation Model

The Structure Equation Model (SEM) was estimated by using AMOS 24.0. The fit indices (reported in Table 4) indicated satisfactory fit for the estimated model. Table 5 shows the estimation results. All path coefficients were significant, providing a strong support for all hypothesized paths in H1–H4. The influence hypothesized in H1 was supported at p < 0.01, showing that perceived threat has a significant positive effect on information security behavior. The influence hypothesized in H2 was supported at p < 0.001, showing that response efficacy has a significant positive effect on perceived avoidability. The influence hypothesized in H3 was supported at p < 0.001, showing that self-efficacy has a significant positive effect on perceived avoidability. The influence hypothesized in H4 was supported at p < 0.001, showing that perceived avoidability has a significant positive effect on information security behavior.

Table 5. Path Coefficients of Model

Y	←	X	S.E.	C.R.	P	Std PC
ISB	←	PT	.063	2.760	.006	.207
PA	←	RE	.079	3.381	***	.259
PA	←	SE	.086	9.008	***	.811
ISB	←	PA	.069	5.678	***	.441

Notes: ***P < .001; S.E.: standard error; C.R.: critical ratio; Std PC: standardized path coefficient.

4.5 Moderating Effect

We use the method proposed by Keil to test the moderating effect of disciplinary background of university students [18]. The samples were divided into two groups according to the disciplinary background, that is hard disciplines and soft disciplines. We test the moderating effect on each path respectively. The results are shown in Table 6.

The differences between hard disciplines and soft disciplines make the moderating effects of both paths significant. The results show that the disciplinary background plays a moderating role in the relationship between perceived threat, perceived avoidability and information security behavior. Perceived threat motivates students in soft disciplines to take information security behaviors more than it motivates students in hard disciplines. While, perceived avoidability motivates students in hard disciplines to take information security behaviors more than it motivates students in soft disciplines. Hypotheses H5 and H6 are both verified.

Table 6. Results of Moderating Effect

Moderating Variable		Path	PC1	PC2	△PC	△CMIN	P	Hypothesis
Group1	Group2							
Hard Disciplines	Soft Disciplines	PT → ISB	0.054	0.369	0.315	4.071	0.044	H5 True (soft > hard)
		PA → ISB	0.634	0.228	0.406	4.534	0.033	H6 True (hard > soft)

Notes: PC1: Path coefficient of group1; PC2: Path coefficient of group2. △PC: Difference between the path coefficients of the two groups. △CMIN: Difference between the Chi-square of the two groups. P: Significance of the difference between the two groups.

In the higher education system, students majoring in hard disciplines learn mainly technical courses, and often use the technology to solve problems in life and study. Therefore, when they encounter information security problems in SNSs, they are more inclined to avoid information risks by implementing security measures. While the courses of soft disciplines emphasize more on the cultivation of students' logical thinking. Teachers often use real cases to guide students to discover and solve problems independently, so that students can solve various problems in real life by using sociology methods. Therefore, their perception ability is more sensitive, and they are more likely to perceive the threat of information security and generate information security behavior.

5 Discussions and Conclusions

Based on TTAT, we draw the following conclusions through the theoretical analysis and empirical research on the influencing factors of university students' information security behaviors in SNSs: self-efficacy and response efficacy have positive effects on perceived avoidability; perceived threat and perceived avoidability have positive effects on information security behaviors; and the disciplinary background has a moderating effect on the relationship between perceived threat, perceived avoidability, and information security behaviors.

Based on the results of this study, we propose the following information security protection countermeasures. Firstly, SNSs users, including university students, should know more about the cases of information security leakage and regularly learn information security protection methods. In this way, they can form the awareness of personal information security protection. Secondly, SNSs should notify users of their information security status on the platform and the importance of information security protection, so that users can realize that information security behavior is conducive to the protection of personal information security. Thirdly, in order to improve the information security behavior of university students from different disciplinary backgrounds, it is recommended that students from hard disciplines should be introduced to practical information security precautions, while students from soft disciplines can focus on improving their perceived sensitivity to information risks in SNSs.

The innovation of this paper is to separately explore the factors that influence the information security behaviors of university students from different disciplinary backgrounds. Furthermore, this paper has theoretical significance as it applies TTAT to the field of individual information security behaviors of university students in SNSs. This paper explores the individual voluntary security behavior of SNSs users in the face of information security threats and proposes information security protection countermeasures for university students from different disciplinary backgrounds.

However, there are still some research limitations of this paper. Firstly, the subjects are mostly domestic university students, and fewer foreign students are involved. Secondly, academic disciplines can also be classified by the dimension of "pure versus applied" and the moderating effect of this dimension has not been explored. Therefore, in the follow-up study, we will expand the scope of questionnaire distribution to explore the moderating effect of pure discipline and applied discipline on information security behavior, so as to conduct a more in-depth research and analysis.

Acknowledgement. This research was supported by the National Natural Science Foundation of China under Grant 72371083, 72121001 and 72131005 and Shanghai Pudong Development Bank under Project No.spdbheb-20220415.

References

1. CNNIC. https://www.cnnic.cn/n4/2023/0828/c88-10829.html. Accessed 28 Aug 2023. (in Chinese)
2. Abraham, S., Indushobha, C.S.: An overview of social engineering malware: trends, tactics, and implications. Technol. Soc. **32**(3), 183–196 (2010)
3. Liang, H., Xue, Y.: Avoidance of information technology threats: a theoretical perspective. MIS Q. **33**(1), 71–90 (2009)
4. Liang, H., Xue, Y.: Understanding security behaviors in personal computer usage: a threat avoidance perspective. J. Assoc. Inf. Syst. **11**(7), 394–413 (2010)
5. Chen, D.Q., Liang, H.: Wishful thinking and IT threat avoidance: an extension to the technology threat avoidance theory. IEEE Trans. Eng. Manage. **66**(4), 552–567 (2019)
6. Young, D.K., Carpenter, D., McLeod, A.: Malware avoidance motivations and behaviors: a technology threat avoidance replication. AIS Trans. Replication Res. **2**(1), 1–17 (2016)
7. Xin, T., Siponen, M., Chen, S.: Understanding the inward emotion-focused coping strategies of individual users in response to mobile malware threats. Behav. Inf. Technol. **41**(13), 2835–2859 (2022)
8. Chen, Y., Zahedi, F.M.: Individuals' Internet security perceptions and behaviors: poly-contextual contrasts between the United States and China. MIS Q. **40**(1), 205–222 (2016)
9. Chen, Q., Xiong, H.X., Dai, Q.Q., Gu, J.Y.: Research on evaluation and improvement strategies of college students' network information security literacy ability from the perspective of platform society. Libr. Inf. Serv. **66**(7), 75–87 (2022). (in Chinese)
10. Smith, G.G., Heindel, A.J., Torres-Ayala, A.T.: E-learning commodity or community: disciplinary differences between online courses. Internet High. Educ. **11**(3–4), 152–159 (2008)
11. Zhao, P., Zhang, J.C.: Research on continual usage intention of online storage service–a perspective of user satisfaction and perceived risk. J. Inf. Resource Manag. **5**(2), 70–78 (2015). (in Chinese)

12. Wang, X., Li, Y., Khasraghi, H.J., Trumbach, C.: The mediating role of security anxiety in internet threat avoidance behavior. Comput. Secur. (134), 103429 (2023)
13. Chen, H., Li, W.L.: An empirical study of information security protection behavior: mediating effect of emotion. Sci. Res. Manag. **39**(6), 48–56 (2018). (in Chinese)
14. Workman, M., Bommer, W.H., Straub, D.: Security lapses and the omission of information security measures: a threat control model and empirical test. Comput. Hum. Behav. **24**(6), 2799–2816 (2008)
15. Johnston, A.C., Warkentin, M.: Fear appeals and information security behaviors: an empirical study. MIS Q. **34**(3), 549–566 (2010)
16. Pumptow, M., Brahm, T.: Higher education students differ in their technology use. Comput. Educ. Open (5), 100149 (2023)
17. Biglan, A.: The characteristics of subject matter in different academic areas. J. Appl. Psychol. **57**(3), 195–203 (1973)
18. Keil, M., Tan, B.C., Wei, K.K., Saarinen, T., Tuunainen, V., Wassenaar, A.: A cross-cultural study on escalation of commitment behavior in software projects. MIS Q. **24**(2), 299–325 (2000)

To Err is Bot, Not Human: Asymmetric Reactions to Chatbot Service Failures

Aibo Tan[1], Caihong Jiang[1(✉)], and Yan Zhu[2]

[1] Key Laboratory of Brain-Machine Intelligence for Information Behavior (Ministry of Education and Shanghai), School of Business and Management, Shanghai International Studies University, Shanghai, China
02743@shisu.edu.cn

[2] Department of Electronic Commerce, School of Electronic Commerce, Hefei Vocational College of Finance and Economics, Hefei, Anhui, China

Abstract. The reaction of individuals to AI failures is a complex and controversial topic that remains widely debated. Existing research on this issue is fragmented and inconclusive, with multiple perspectives and conflicting findings. To further explore this issue, we conducted a study examining how customers respond to service failures committed by chatbots and human employees. We used an online vignette-based method to assess participants' emotional, cognitive, and behavioral intentions following such failures.

A total of 307 people participated in this study and the results indicated that participants were more tolerant of chatbot failures. They exhibited fewer negative emotions and were more likely to forgive erring chatbots. These results were moderated by service failure type. This study provides a more comprehensive understanding of how people respond to AI errors in service context, offering a more nuanced perspective than previously available in the literature.

Keywords: Chatbots · Service Failure · Customer Reactions

1 Introduction

The use of artificial intelligence (AI) in marketing is more and more prevalent, companies utilize AI to enhance customer experiences. Among all of applications of AI, the deployment of chatbots has been pretty frequent. Chatbots can talk to customers in many areas such as customer service encounters and online shopping platforms. Undoubtedly chatbots are replacing human employees because of their low cost and high efficiency. It is predicted that chatbots will power 95% of consumer interactions by 2025 (Microsoft 2017). Despite the booming development of chatbots, this technology has never been perfect. Chatbots are still incapable of understanding human's complex input messages or dealing with complicated customer services. There have been plenty of cases about

This research was supported by grants from the National Natural Science Foundation of China (Grant No. 71942005) and Open Research Fund of Key Laboratory of Brain-Machine Intelligence for Information Behavior (Ministry of Education and Shanghai) (2021KFKT011).

failing service chatbots (Jiang et al. 2023). Even ChatGPT, the most advanced AI tool at the moment, would make mistakes (Digital Trends 2023). Given that chatbot's error or failure is inevitable, it is crucial to disclose its impact on customers and companies.

To understand this problem, we address the following research questions in service failure context: how do customers react to chatbot's error? Are there any differences between the influence of chatbot's error and human employee's error?

We test our hypotheses in the context of online shopping in which participants read vignettes about two types of service failure, which made by either chatbots or human employees. We find that participants have asymmetric reactions to chatbot's failure compared to human's failure, that is, participants are more tolerant of chatbot's failure. Furthermore, we find that chatbot's failure has spillover effect on the platform, that is, participants would attribute the mistakes of chatbot to platform. We also find that the heterogeneous reactions to different types of service failure.

2 Theoretical Development and Hypotheses

2.1 Reactions to Chatbot Failures vs. Human Failures

There are two streams of related researches on AI' failures. The first has documented that people are more averse to AI-made failure comparing to human's failure, which is called "algorithm aversion" (Dietvorst et al. 2015). These studies compared negative feelings, trust and behavioral intentions before and after seeing AI/humans err. After seeing AI/humans fail or give incorrect advice, reliance and trust in AI decrease significantly more for AI compared to humans. Another is called "algorithm appreciation", which means people show more positive attitude toward AI compared to human (Logg et al. 2019). People are more tolerant when AI's failures lead to brand scandals (Srinivasan and Sarial-Abi 2021). These findings are consistently showing that an AI-made error is more forgivable and blamed less than the same human error. Additionally, the erring robot triggered more positive feelings than the flawless one (Mirnig et al. 2017). People are more likely to conform to incorrect algorithmic recommendations than identical recommendations from human (Liel and Zalmanson 2022).

Further focused on researches in service arena, service agent type is an important antecedent to customers' reactions (Liu et al. 2023). Previous studies have also found contradictory results. Compared to human staff, customers were more dissatisfied and angrier with machine's mistake, and show less forgiveness to machines (Sands et al. 2022). However, customers blamed service robots less than human employees following service failure (Leo and Huh 2020).

What's more, existing work has revealed that people's responses to AI's failures to a great extent depend on the domain of use. For instance, when contexts are more objective, or not involved in self-identity, people prefer AI to humans (Morewedge 2022). A meta-analysis also revealed that domain of use was an important factor influencing algorithmic preferences (Kaufmann et al. 2023). Therefore, our study chose a daily-life context (i.e. online shopping), in which customers are pretty familiar with chatbot use in this context, and know the capabilities of chatbots and human employees, i.e. what they can do and cannot do. In this context, customers may have higher expectations for human employees than chatbots, consequently, when a human employee makes mistake, customers may experience greater expectation disconfirmation. Hence, we propose that customers would show more negative reactions to human employee's failures versus chatbot's failures.

H1: Following the same service failure, customers will be more tolerant of chatbots versus human employees. Specifically, customers will have less trust in human employees than chatbots (H1a); have fewer negative feelings (anger and disgust) towards chatbots versus human employees (H1b); blame chatbots less than human employees (H1c); lastly, customers' continuous usage intentions (for service agent and platform) will be lower for human employees versus chatbots (H1d).

2.2 Moderating Role of Service Failure Type

Traditional marketing literatures have found that service failure can be categorized into process failure, which refers to deficiencies in service delivery, and outcome failure, which occurs when basic or core service cannot be performed. Extending to AI-made service failures, process failure occurs when the service delivery by chatbots is deficient, such as rudeness and unreliability (Choi et al. 2021). One common example is that a chatbot gives wrong answers, which leads to poor interaction quality (Wang et al. 2021). This type of failure occurs before the core services, and customers can attribute accurately the failure to service agent (Wang et al. 2021). Outcome failure means chatbots did not perform basic or core services, for example, "incorrect responses to customers' core service" (Choi et al. 2021), such as cannot provide answers that customers need. Based on our research context, we wonder whether and how different types of service failure interact with service agent type. Prior works provided some indirect evidences. Choi et al. (2021) found that following process failure, customers are less satisfied with more humanoid robots (vs. mechanical robots), however, after the outcome failure, customers have similar level of dissatisfaction with different service agents. Sands et al. (2022) investigated customers' responses to different service agents in two separate contexts, they found that customers responded more negatively with a virtual agent following a process failure, yet more negatively with human agent following an outcome failure. Hence, it is possible that customers hold different perceptions and expectations about interaction targets under different contexts, and we hypothesize that customers are stricter with human employees' service than chatbots following process failure than outcome failure.

H2: The main effects of service agent type on customers reactions are moderated by service failure type. Customers will be more tolerant of chatbots' mistakes (vs. human) following process failure, such differences will not happen in outcome failure.

3   Methodology

3.1 Design and Procedure

A 2 (service agent type: human vs. chatbot) × 2 (service failure type: process failure vs. outcome failure) between-subject design was conducted on Credamo. A total of 307 adults participated in exchange of payment (female 59.3%; age: 18–60; chatbot group = 160).

First, participants read introduction to AI service and rated their preferences for service agents in daily life:

Customer service improves customers' satisfaction by providing advice and support to customers and helping them solve problems. Customer service can be delivered by humans or through automated tools, such as intelligent customer service. Intelligent customer service can interact with users through voice, such as voice assistants; it can also communicate with users through text. Intelligent customer service has the agile conversational capability and has a significant efficiency advantage in performing objective, analytical, and procedural tasks.

Then, participants were randomly assigned to one of the four conditions. In process failure condition, participants were instructed to imagine a scenario in which they bought earphones online. In outcome failure condition, they were asked to imagine a scenario in which they asked about the logistic of products. We designed cover stories and pictures of conversations between customers and service agents. Both the scenarios were adapted from (Wang et al. 2021). We manipulated service agent type using different customer service agent (i.e. either human or chatbot). To ensure the consistency of experimental manipulation, the cover story and pictures are the same in both human and chatbot groups, except the identity of service agents.

In process failure condition, participants read:

You need to buy a pair of Bluetooth headphones on an online platform, which is provided by human customer service [chatbot service], you want to know what is the difference between different versions of headphones. At first the service agents gave an incorrect answer, and you repeated your question, the service agents finally understood and responded to you accurately. Next, you want to know about delivery, however, the customer services gave wrong answers at first, and after you repeated your question, the customer services eventually solved your query.

In outcome failure condition, participants read:

The weather is hot and the refrigerator in your house is broken, you desperately need to buy a refrigerator. After ordering on an e-commerce platform, you find that the logistics has been delayed, and then ask the customer service. The e-commerce platform uses human customer service [chatbot services] to provide post-sale consulting services. After you asked the question, the service agents quickly replied with logistic details and official regulations, but could not explain the cause and solution of the delay.

Next, dependent variables were measured. We then asked participants to finish two attention check items, participants who did not pass the attention checks or in an unrealistic length of completion time were excluded from data analyses. Additionally, participants rated two manipulation checks. Finally, we measured online shopping experience and demographics.

3.2 Measures

Trust. Participants were asked to evaluate their subjective trust ($\alpha = 0.944$), perceived competence($\alpha = 0.946$) and warmth ($\alpha = 0.921$) (Cheng et al. 2022).

Negative Feelings. We rated participants' angry and disgusted feelings with two seven-point Likert items ("The extent to which you are angry/disgusted with service failure", 1 = not at all, 7 = very likely) (Wang et al. 2021).

Attribution of Responsibility. Participants were asked to indicate attribution of service failure on two seven-point Likert items ("the platform/service agents was responsible for this service failure", 1 = strongly disagree, 7 = strongly agree) (Leo and Huh 2020).

Continuous Usage Intentions. We assessed the continuance intention to use service agent ($\alpha = 0.924$) and platform with seven-point Likert items ($\alpha = 0.955$) (Venkatesh et al. 2003).

Attention checks. Participants were asked to recall who served for them (two options: human service agent, chatbot) and whether the service agent solved their questions (two options: solved, unsolved).

Manipulation checks. We measured realism of scenarios with two seven-point Likert items ("In real life, how likely are you to encounter a situation similar to this scenario?", "Can you imagine yourself as the customer in the scenario?", 1 = not at all, 7 = very likely). We assessed perceived severity with one item ("To what extent do you think the severity of service failure is", 1 = not at all, 7 = very severe) (Wang et al. 2021).

Control variables. We assessed preference for service agent ("Do you prefer to be served by human or chatbot in daily life", 1 = definitely human, 7 = definitely chatbot) (Hou et al. 2021) and online shopping experience with seven-point Likert items ("The extent to which you perceive severity of this service failure", 1 = not at all, 7 = very likely) (Fig. 1).

Fig. 1. Examples of experimental scenarios (left: service agent-human, service failure type-process failure; right: service agent-chatbot, service failure type-outcome failure)

4 Results

4.1 Manipulation Checks

Realistic check showed that the scenarios were perceived as realistic (M = 6.138, SD = 0.64). Results of perceived severity showed that there were no significant differences between human and chatbot (F (1, 298) = 0.000, p = 0.995), the difference between process and outcome failure was significant (F (1, 298) = 74.914, p < 0.001). Participants rated that outcome failure was more severe than process failure ($M_{process}$ = 3.55, SD = 1.260; $M_{outcome}$ = 4.87, SD = 1.375).

4.2 Trust and Negative Feelings

Trust. We tested our hypotheses using ANCOVA with controlling sex, age, education, shopping experience and service preference. The ANCOVA results (Table 1) revealed significant main effects of service agent type (F (1, 298) = 4.089, p = 0.044) and service failure type (F (1, 298) = 223.234, p < 0.001) on trust. However, the interaction effect of service agent type × service failure type on trust was insignificant (F (1, 298) = 0.264, p > 0.05). We still ran pairwise comparisons, the results showed that in the process failure condition, participants trusted human less than they trusted chatbots (M_{human} = 4.618, SD = 1.410; $M_{chatbot}$ = 4.997, SD = 1.057; F (1, 298) = 2.996, p = 0.085); the same holds true in the outcome failure (M_{human} = 2.622, SD = 1.094; $M_{chatbot}$ = 2.854, SD = 1.198; F (1, 298) = 1.241, p = 0.266). Therefore, H1a was supported, whereas H2 was not supported.

Negative Feelings. In this study, we mainly investigated two specific negative feelings, which are anger and disgust. Results (Table 1) indicated a significant main effect of service agent type (F (1, 298) = 6.589, p = 0.011) and service failure type (F (1, 298) = 178.552, p < 0.001) on disgust. However, the interaction effect of service agent type × service failure type on disgust was insignificant (F (1, 298) = 2.802, p = 0.095). Pairwise comparisons showed that following the process failure, participants were more significantly disgusted with human than chatbots (M_{human} = 2.938, SD = 1.657; $M_{chatbot}$ = 2.154, SD = 1.396; F (1, 298) = 8.364, p = 0.004); following the outcome process failure, there was no significant effect of service agent type on disgust, but participants were also more disgusted with human than chatbots (M_{human} = 5.012, SD = 1.487; $M_{chatbot}$ = 4.841, SD = 1.629; F (1, 298) = 0.441, p = 0.507).

Regarding angry feeling, the main effect of service agent type on anger was not significant (F (1, 298) = 2.899, p = 0.09), the main effect of service failure type on anger was significant (F (1, 298) = 164.755, p < 0.001), and the interaction effect of service agent type × service failure type on anger was insignificant (F (1, 298) = 0.014, p > 0.05). Although not significant, after the process failure, participants were angrier with human than chatbots (M_{human} = 3.092, SD = 1.608; $M_{chatbot}$ = 2.782, SD = 1.364; F (1, 298) = 1.172, p = 0.28); as well as in the outcome failure condition, participants were angrier with human than chatbots (M_{human} = 5.305, SD = 1.358; $M_{chatbot}$ = 4.963, SD = 1.688; F (1, 298) = 1.803, p = 0.18). Overall, the study partially supported H1b and did not support H2 (Fig. 2).

Table 1. Effects of service agent type and service failure type on trust and negative feelings

| | Trust and Negative Feelings | | | | | | | | |
| | Trust | | | Disgust | | | Anger | | |
	F	p	$\eta^2 p$	F	p	$\eta^2 p$	F	p	$\eta^2 p$
SAT	4.089	0.044*	0.014	6.589	0.011*	0.022	2.899	0.090	0.010
SFT	223.234	<.001***	0.429	178.552	<.001***	0.375	164.755	<.001***	0.356
SAT × SFT	0.264	0.608	0.001	2.802	0.095	0.009	0.014	0.905	0.000
Sex	0.018	0.894	0.000	0.862	0.354	0.003	4.130	0.043*	0.014
Age	0.066	0.797	0.000	0.009	0.925	0.000	0.452	0.502	0.002
Education	1.545	0.215	0.005	1.426	0.233	0.005	0.196	0.658	0.001
Shopping Experience	0.003	0.956	0.000	0.726	0.395	0.002	0.002	0.961	0.000
Service Preference	5.625	0.018*	0.019	2.378	0.124	0.008	1.839	0.176	0.006

SAT: service agent type; SFT: service failure type.
* $p < .05$. ** $p < .01$. *** $p < .001$.

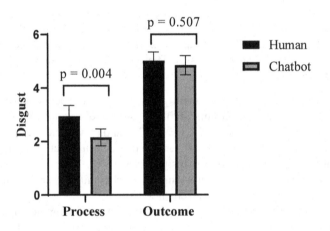

Fig. 2. Effects of service agent type and service failure type on disgust

4.3 Attribution of Responsibility

With regard to attribution of responsibility, we examined two dimensions respectively: attribution to service agent and attribution to platform (Table 2). The main effect of service agent type on attribution to service agent was insignificant (F (1, 298) = 0.709, p = 0.40), the main effect of service failure type on attribution to service agent was significant (F (1, 298) = 15.257, p < 0.001). Importantly, we found a significant interaction effect of service agent type × service failure type (F (1, 298) = 7.861, p = 0.005). A simple effects test showed that following the process failure, participants blamed human more than chatbots (M_{human} = 5.554, SD = 1.250; $M_{chatbot}$ = 4.936, SD = 1.560; F (1, 298) = 6.161, p = 0.014); following the outcome failure, service agent type had no significant effect on attribution, but participants blamed chatbots more than human (M_{human} = 4.427, SD = 1.826; $M_{chatbot}$ = 4.756, SD = 1.241; F (1, 298) = 2.065, p = 0.152).

There was a significant main effect of service agent type (F (1, 298) = 8.846, p = 0.003) and service failure type (F (1, 298) = 21.016, p < 0.001) on attribution to platform. However, the interaction effect of service agent type × service failure type was not significant (F (1, 298) = 1.535, p = 0.216). Although insignificant, pairwise comparisons showed that after the process failure, participants blamed platform more in the chatbot condition versus human condition (M_{human} = 2.969, SD = 1.500; $M_{chatbot}$ = 3.769, SD = 1.528; F (1, 298) = 6.161, p = 0.004); after the outcome failure, participants blamed platform more in the chatbot condition versus human condition (M_{human} = 4.000, SD = 1.587; $M_{chatbot}$ = 4.329, SD = 1.633; F (1, 298) = 1.648, p = 0.200). Overall, the results partially supported H1c and H2 (Figs. 3 and 4).

Table 2. Effects of service agent type and service failure type on attribution of responsibility

| | Attribution of Responsibility | | | | | |
| | Attribution to Service Agent | | | Attribution to Platform | | |
	F	p	$\eta^2 p$	F	p	$\eta^2 p$
SAT	0.709	0.4	0.002	8.846	0.003**	0.029
SFT	15.257	<.001***	0.049	21.016	<.001***	0.066
SAT × SFT	7.861	0.005**	0.026	1.535	0.216	0.005
Sex	1.157	0.283	0.004	3.022	0.083	0.010
Age	1.273	0.260	0.004	0.371	0.543	0.001
Education	5.292	0.022*	0.017	2.148	0.144	0.007
Shopping Experience	0.091	0.763	0.000	0.554	0.457	0.002
Service Preference	0.003	0.957	0.000	2.264	0.133	0.008

SAT: service agent type; SFT: service failure type.
* $p < .05$. ** $p < .01$. *** $p < .001$.

4.4 Continuous Usage Intentions

We didn't find the significant main effect of service agent type on continuous usage intention for customer service (F (1, 298) = 0.752, p = 0.387). The main effect of service failure type on continuous usage intention for customer service was significant (F (1, 298) = 135.059, p < 0.001). The interaction effect of service agent type × service

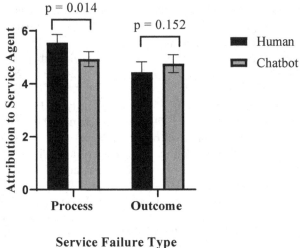

Fig. 3. Effect of service agent type and service failure type on attribution to service agent

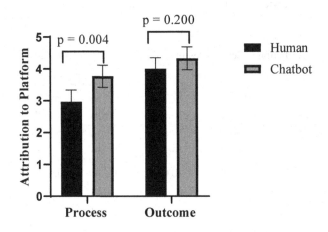

Fig. 4. Effect of service agent type and service failure type on attribution to platform

failure type was not significant (F (1, 298) = 1.515, p = 0.219). Both in the process and outcome failure conditions, service agent type had no significant effects on continuous usage intention for customer service, but participants had higher willingness to continue using chatbots than human employee's service in the process failure condition (M_{human} = 4.385, SD = 1.690; $M_{chatbot}$ = 4.795, SD = 1.361; F (1, 298) = 2.043, p = 0.154); and higher willingness to continue using human employee's service than chatbots in the outcome failure condition (M_{human} = 2.701, SD = 1.390; $M_{chatbot}$ = 2.665, SD = 1.386; F (1, 298) = 0.070, p = 0.792).

The main effect of service agent type on continuous usage intentions for platform was significant (F (1, 298) = 5.959, p = 0.015). As well, the main effect of service failure type on continuous usage intentions for platform was significant (F (1, 298) = 112.188, p < 0.001). Yet, the interaction effect of agent type × service failure type was not significant (F (1, 298) = 0.113, p = 0.736). There was a marginal significant effect of service agent type on continuous usage intentions for platform after the process failure (M_{human} = 4.692, SD = 1.675; $M_{chatbot}$ = 5.197, SD = 1.276; F (1, 298) = 3.599, p = 0.059); however, the effect of service agent type on continuous usage intentions for platform was insignificant after the outcome failure (M_{human} = 2.959, SD = 1.432; $M_{chatbot}$ = 3.313, SD = 1.578; F (1, 298) = 2.411, p = 0.122). Hence, both H1d and H2 were partially supported (Table 3).

Table 3. Effects of service agent type and service failure type on continuous usage intentions

| | Continuous Usage Intentions | | | | | |
| | Customer Service | | | Platform | | |
	F	p	$\eta^2 p$	F	p	$\eta^2 p$
SAT	0.752	0.387	0.003	5.959	0.015*	0.020
SFT	135.059	<.001***	0.312	112.188	<.001***	0.274
Agent Type × Service Failure Type	1.515	0.219	0.006	0.113	0.736	0.000
Sex	0.246	0.620	0.015	0.001	0.379	0.000
Age	4.050*	0.045	0.367	0.419	<.001***	0.001
Education	0.275	0.601	0.001	2.939	0.088	0.010
Shopping Experience	1.355	0.245	0.005	3.279	0.071	0.011
Service Preference	1.802	0.181	0.006	0.253	0.071	0.000

SAT: service agent type; SFT: service failure type.
* $p < .05$. ** $p < .01$. *** $p < .001$.

5 Discussion and Conclusion

The current study investigated customer reactions to chatbot's failure in a daily context. We mainly focused on customers reactions to chatbot versus human service failure, in a more nuance pattern. In addition, we tested the effect of service failure type.

Out results showed that customers react to erring chatbot and human asymmetrically, when encountering service failure, customers were more tolerant of chatbots and harsher on human employees, which is contrary to previous work suggested that people are more averse to algorithmic error (Dietvorst et al. 2015). Possible explanation is that reactions to AI depend on different agent types and domains of use (Kaufmann et al. 2023). Customers have different expectations of different agents and domains. In online shopping context, customers are familiar with both humans and chatbots, which leads to different performance expectations of humans and chatbots. Consequently, when failures occur, customers could experience more negative violation with human employees and more averse to failing humans. More importantly, the asymmetric reactions are moderated by service failure type.

It is noted that there are several limitations in present study. First, one might question that vignette is too experiential and lack of reality. Another issue was that in our experiment, we utilized products with different attributes in scenarios, which could affect customers' perceptions. Future research needs to be conducted with more realistic way, such as real interaction with chatbots. In addition, the product type should be considered to control the differences due to product attributes. Moreover, future research needs to explore other mechanisms behind this phenomenon such as mental models about algorithm and chatbots, such as mediators like mind perception and expectation disconfirmation. Last but not least, future researches are needed to investigate other types of service failure, since the development of AI are more and more frequent in human's daily life, there exists other kinds of error or mistake, such as social errors (Honig and Oron-Gilad 2018).

References

Cheng, X., Zhang, X., Cohen, J., Mou, J.: Human vs. AI: understanding the impact of anthropomorphism on consumer response to chatbots from the perspective of trust and relationship norms. Inf. Process. Manag. **59**, 102940 (2022)

Choi, S., Mattila, A.S., Bolton, L.E.: To err is human(-oid): how do consumers react to robot service failure and recovery? J. Serv. Res. **24**, 354–371 (2021)

Dietvorst, B.J., Simmons, J.P., Massey, C.: Algorithm aversion: people erroneously avoid algorithms after seeing them err. J. Exp. Psychol. Gen. **144**, 114–126 (2015)

Digital Trends: The 6 biggest problems with ChatGPT right now. https://www.digitaltrends.com/computing/the-6-biggest-problems-with-chatgpt-right-now/

Honig, S., Oron-Gilad, T.: Understanding and resolving failures in human-robot interaction: literature review and model development. Front. Psychol. **9**, 861 (2018)

Hou, Y., Zhang, K., Li, G.: Service robots or human staff: how social crowding shapes tourist preferences. Tour. Manag. **83**, 104242 (2021)

Jiang, Y., Li, Q., Liu, H., Guo, Q., Miao, M.: Although pitiless, yet moving? The effect of apology subject on consumer forgiveness when AI enabled robot service failed. Nankai Bus. Rev., 1–24 (2023)

Kaufmann, E., Chacon, A., Kausel, E.E., Herrera, N., Reyes, T.: Task-specific algorithm advice acceptance: a review and directions for future research. Data Inf. Manag. **7**, 100040 (2023)

Leo, X., Huh, Y.E.: Who gets the blame for service failures? Attribution of responsibility toward robot versus human service providers and service firms. Comput. Hum. Behav. **113**, 106520 (2020)

Liel, Y., Zalmanson, L.: Turning off your better judgment -conformity to algorithmic recommendations. In: Academy of Management Proceedings, vol. 2023 (2022)

Liu, D., Li, C., Zhang, J., Huang, W.: Robot service failure and recovery: literature review and future directions. Int. J. Adv. Robot. Syst. **20**, 1–18 (2023)

Logg, J.M., Minson, J.A., Moore, D.A.: Algorithm appreciation: people prefer algorithmic to human judgment. Organ. Behav. Hum. Decis. Process. **151**, 90–103 (2019)

Microsoft: How AI is powering the future of the customer experience. https://news.microsoft.com/europe/features/ai-powering-customer-experience/

Mirnig, N., Stollnberger, G., Miksch, M., Stadler, S., Giuliani, M., Tscheligi, M.: To err is robot: how humans assess and act toward an erroneous social robot. Front. Robot. AI **4**, 21 (2017)

Morewedge, C.K.: Preference for human, not algorithm aversion. Trends Cognit. Sci. **26**, 824–826 (2022)

Sands, S., Campbell, C., Plangger, K., Pitt, L.: Buffer bots: the role of virtual service agents in mitigating negative effects when service fails. Psychol. Mark. **39**, 2039–2054 (2022)

Srinivasan, R., Sarial-Abi, G.: When algorithms fail: consumers' responses to brand harm crises caused by algorithm errors. J. Mark. **85**, 74–91 (2021)

Venkatesh, V., Morris, M., Davis, G., Davis, F.: User acceptance of information technology: toward a unified view. MIS Q. **27**, 425–478 (2003)

Wang, H., Xie, T., Zhan, C.: When service failed: the detrimental effect of anthropomorphism on intelligent customer service agent avatar—disgust as mediation. Nankai Bus. Rev. **24**, 194–206 (2021)

Constructing Policy Domain Dictionary Generated by DTM-Embeddings to Identify Policy Response Features of Listed Companies in Electric Vehicle Industry

Yintong Liu, Runyi Yan, Qi Qi, and Zhen Zhu[✉]

School of Economics and Management, China University of Geosciences, Wuhan 430074, China
zhuzhen2008@gmail.com

Abstract. New technology industry policies play an important role in stimulating organizational transformation and motivating their strategic actions in responding to the policies. By developing an integrated method of dynamic topic modeling (DTM) and word embedding from BERT (referred to herein as DTM-EM), this study constructs a domain-specific dictionary to measure policy response in Electric Vehicle (EV) industry. The study initially employs dynamic topic modeling to extract key terms representing various themes in policy texts. Subsequently, utilizing similarity measures, it identifies synonymous terms corresponding to the key terms in the policy text, forming a word set for the policy text. Finally, utilizing similarity measures once again, it derives synonymous terms from the annual reports that is associated with the key words in the word set for the policy text to constructs a domain-specific dictionary. Furthermore, this study evaluates the accuracy of the dictionary for measure response dimension and features of Chinese publicly listed companies from 2009–2023.

Keywords: DTM-EM · EV · listed companies · response feature · policy domain dictionary

1 Introduction

To achieve carbon peaking and carbon neutrality goals, the Chinese government has placed high importance on the development of electric vehicles (EV) industry, and launched a series of policies aimed at propelling the advancement. Favorable policy implementation results not only depend on the policy makers' abilities but also rely on the behavior of those responding to the policies [1]. Therefore, this study aims to measure the response features of publicly listed companies in the EV industry to governmental policies.

Policy response plays an important role in translating policy objectives into tangible outcomes. Identifying policy responses of companies entails measuring the implementation effects of industrial policies from a microlevel perspective, enabling a better understanding of companies' behavioral and strategic effectiveness in response to policies.

Y. P. Tu and M. Chi (Eds.): WHICEB 2024, LNBIP 517, pp. 408–420, 2024.
https://doi.org/10.1007/978-3-031-60324-2_34

Existing research has been devoted to exploring the response behavior and influencing factors of these companies using econometric models or case study. However, these methods have certain limitations. For instance, research on company response identification primarily relies on indirect indicators such as R&D investment and output data of listed companies, which makes it challenging to achieve a detailed characterization of the spatiotemporal relationship between enterprise response behaviors and policy implementation. The use of multiple case study methods is mainly based on questionnaire content, which suffers from issues such as low response rates and subjective cognitive bias in the responses [2].

To depict the response behaviors of listed companies in a detailed and direct manner, this study adopts the DTM-Embeddings (DTM-EM) model to analyze the text. Historically, numerical information has primarily reflected a company's past operational performance, making it challenging to directly discern the company's responsive behaviors. In contrast, textual disclosure in annual reports offers researchers a tool to assess managerial behavior biases and understand corporate actions [3]. In terms of understanding textual disclosures, algorithmic analysis is more efficient and objective compared to traditional manual collection and reading.

2   Related Work

The study will conduct a comprehensive literature review from two distinct perspectives: organizational response and method construction.

2.1   Organizational Response Research

Scholars predominantly examine the determinants of corporate response behaviors and strategic changes from two primary perspectives: the external environmental perspective and the internal decision-maker perspective. Studies rooted in the external environmental perspective argue that companies must formulate distinct strategies in response to varying external environments [4]. In addition, research from the internal decision-maker perspective indicates that decision-makers often rely on their own cognitive frameworks [5] to formulate different strategic response plans.

From the external environmental perspective, Li et al. present a path criticality model and carry out an empirical study to analyze the effect of policy factors on action paths and responses [6]. Yuan et al. constructed extended CDM model to study the effects of environmental regulation on industrial innovation and productivity, by using 28 manufacturing industry panel data [7]. To investigate how strong market reactions are to FIT policies and what forms of policies are more effective, Liu et al. use an event study approach [8].

From the perspective of internal decision-makers, drawing upon the upper echelons and attention-based view of the firm, Wu et al. examine the relationship be-tween top management team attention and firms' diversification strategy through building regression models [9]. Building on signaling theory and the attention-based view of the firm, Sergej et al. examine organizational response behavior to customer complaint messages that differ in their value signaled to the firm [10]. The DTM-EM model in this study identifies the focal points disclosed by managers in annual reports, and thus, the study is conducted from the perspective of internal decision-makers.

2.2 Methodological Construction

Currently, in the field of research on the response behaviors of publicly listed companies, methods such as econometric models and case discussions are prevalent. Li et al. use the double difference method for empirical estimation and analyze the impact of green credit policy on the growth of energy firms based on the data of Chinese listed companies from 2009 to 2019 [11]. Zhou et al. conducts generalized impulse response analysis to estimate the scale and leverage of the response of thermal power enterprises to the unexpected positive impact on renewable power enterprises' scale and leverage using a VAR-based model [12]. Tian et al. use the multi-case study method and grounded theory to explore the mechanism of how tech firms respond to the innovation policies made by governments at the central, provincial, municipal, and district/county levels in China [13]. However, these methods generally suffer from limitations such as coarse granularity and the inability to reflect longitudinal time features. Therefore, this study adopts the DTM-EM method to construct a policy domain-specific dictionary for identifying policy response features of publicly listed companies in the electric vehicle sector.

The DTM model is a dynamic model capable of topic exploration, computing topic relevance, and analyzing the evolution paths of topics. For example, Denter et al. employ DTM to investigate the most suitable method for examining the diffusion of technology in a time-oriented and highly automated manner [14]. Distributed representation can transform the words in the word list into fixed length, low-dimensional dense vectors, that is, word vectors or word embed-ding. Word vector has good semantic features, which can be used to judge the similarity of words [15]. When utilizing the BERT model to generate word vectors, not only word embed-dings are marked, but also segment embeddings and position embeddings are employed, enhancing the semantic accuracy represented by the word vectors. This study combines the DTM model with Word Embedding to conduct text analysis on the annual reports of publicly listed companies, providing a more intuitive and detailed exploration of the implicit response behaviors of listed companies in Chinese texts.

3 Data

3.1 Data Acquisition and Processing

This study primarily focuses on the identification and measurement of response features of listed companies to government policies. Therefore, the sample data mainly includes policy texts and publicly disclosed annual report texts of listed companies.

For the policy samples, this study focused on national policies. Firstly, national policies offer a holistic perspective to reflect the overall changes in EV, considering that regional policies in various provinces and cities may exhibit certain specificity. Secondly, the study emphasizes the evolution of policies rather than conducting comparisons of policy differences among provinces and cities.

To collect relevant policies, this study employed Python technology to retrieve and gather policies related to themes such as "EV" and "charging stations" from the official websites of the central government and PKU Law from 2009 to 2023. The data collection continued until April 20, 2023, resulting in a total of 430 collected policies. For text data processing, policies with low relevance to "EV" were manually excluded, resulting in a cleaned set of 192 policy texts. Subsequently, the text data underwent tokenization, stop-word removal, and vectorization.

For the annual reports of listed companies, this study collected data from the Cninfo website covering the years 2009 to 2023 for China A-shares listed companies involved in the EV sector. Companies classified as ST, with less than 1 year of listing, terminated listings, and those with partially missing data were excluded. The final sample includes data from 280 listed companies in the electric vehicle industry and its associated industry chain. The "Management's Discussion and Analysis" section of the annual reports was chosen to measure managerial response features. Text data were processed through tokenization, stop-word removal, and vectorization.

3.2 Division of EV Policy Development Stages

In China, industrial economic development is often adjusted through government macro-control. The response of these companies to policy changes varies depending on the government's regulatory focus and methods. To better identify and measure the evolving features of companies responses, this study segments policy phases for detailed analysis. This study categorizes the collected policy texts pertaining to EV into three distinct temporal stages, based on their publication dates (Table 1).

Table 1. Policy Stages Segmentation

Time Period	Amount	Content	Policy
2009–2015	64	Enhance consumer acceptance of electric vehicles, and opening up the market through policies that incentivize consumption	New Energy Automobile Industry Development Plan
2016–2019	60	Through point-based management, standardizing the behaviors of both the government and enterprises	Dual Credit Policy
2020–2023	68	While phasing out subsidies, simultaneously enhancing infrastructure and optimizing dual credit management	Opinion on Accelerating the High-quality Development of the NEV

4 Method

4.1 Methodology Design

To achieve the identification of responses by listed companies, this study relies on policy texts related to the development of the EV industry issued by the government, as well as annual reports from EV listed companies. Employing the DTM-EM method, a policy domain-specific dictionary is constructed. Initially, DTM is used to extract keywords from policy texts. Subsequently, leveraging the word embeddings of a finetuned BERT model, the study obtains vectors corresponding to words in the policy and the keywords, extracting similar words from the policy text keywords using vector similarity. This process forms the basis of the policy text dictionary. Then using the embeddings from the fine-tuned Fin-BERT model which is trained on financial texts and more suitable to annual report, it obtains vectors for words in the annual report text corresponding to those in the policy text dictionary. Once again utilizing vector similarity, the study extracts similar words, resulting in the construction of a dictionary specific to the policy domain of the EV industry. This dictionary facilitates the measurement of listed companies' response behaviors. Methodology design are shown in Fig. 1.

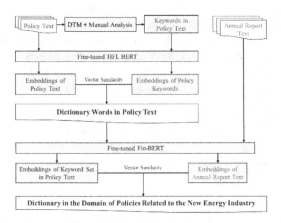

Fig. 1. Technology Roadmap

4.2 Topics and Topic Words

DTM Structure. Topic modeling is a statistical framework designed to extract topic information from textual data. Wellknown models include Latent Dirichlet Allocation (LDA) and Dynamic Topic Models (DTM), which are dynamic models that treat the posterior distributions of model parameters in the current time window as the conditional distributions of the model parameters in the next time window. DTM increases the temporal dimensions of LDA, and is therefore suitable for thematic evolution analysis [16]. In this study, the DTM model is chosen to elucidate the stage characteristics of listed companies' policy responses.

Determination of Optimal Number of Topics. For topic models, the choice of the number of topics determines the quality of the model results. In this study, we determine the optimal number of topics by calculating perplexity and coherence across different numbers of topics. The ideal value for perplexity is lower, indicating better model performance. The results are illustrated in the Fig. 2. For coherence, a higher value is preferable, and the coherence results are presented in the Fig. 3. Combining the outcomes of both metrics, we determine the optimal number of topics as seven.

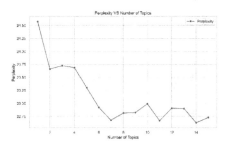 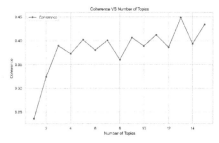

Fig. 2. Perplexity   **Fig. 3.** Coherence

Keywords. Through the training of the model on policy texts from the three distinct stages, we generate a stage-specific "Topic-Word Matrix" pertinent to EV policies. For each topic, we select the top 30 words by weight and then discard those without substantive meaning. The retained words constitute the key terms for each topic. The table below presents the final results (Table 2).

Topic Popularity. Topic heat reflects the degree of attention a specific theme receives across different time periods.

Figure 4 reveals that Themes One and Five have consistently maintained a high trend, indicating the Chinese government's sustained attention to green development and infrastructure construction. Theme Two, 'Technological Innovation,' peaked in popularity during the second phase, attributed to the government's intention to drive substantial innovation in EV companies through a dual credit policy. Theme Three, 'Regulatory Framework,' mirrors the trajectory of Theme Two, owing to the introduction of standards for point calculation and conversion during this phase, aimed at standardizing the innovative activities and point exchange behaviors of vehicle companies. The declining trend in Theme Four, 'Promotion and Application,' reflects the increasing public recognition of EV and their successful entry into the domestic market. The heightened prominence of Theme Six, 'Guided Development,' in the second phase correlates with the implementation of the dual credit policy, steering the healthy development of enterprises. Theme Seven, 'Fiscal and Tax Support,' demonstrates a steady upward trend, highlighting the government's ongoing commitment to refining fiscal and tax support policies.

Table 2. Themes as Keywords

No.	Topic	Keywords
1	Low-carbon emission	Green, Energy, Photovoltaic, Low-carbon, Resources, Clean, Optimization, Energy conservation, Driving, Emission Reduction, Environmental protection, Electricity, Power circulation, Ecological environment, Emissions, Wind power, Carbon reduction, Transformation, Breakthrough
2	Innovation	Innovation, R&D, Batteries, Automotive Industry, Encouragement, Performance, Tackling Key Issues, Integration, Intelligent, Development, Big Data, Artificial Intelligence, Testing, Modules, Nets Union, Shortcoming Communication
3	Licensing and Control	Access, Standard, Regulation, Review, Management, Safety, System, Declaration, Inspection, Specialized, Testing, Rule, Production Capacity
4	Reform and Demonstrations	Demonstration, Promotion, Subsidy, Incentive, Standardization, Development, Pilot, Reform, Implementation, Technology, Industry, Key Point, Assessment, Fiscal, Passenger Transport, Energy Conservation, Public, Public Transportation
5	Infrastructure investment	Charging, Infrastructure, Urban, Operation, Public Transportation, Charging Pile Battery Swapping, Parking, Electric Vehicle, Supporting, Government, Construction, Planning, Road, Service Communication, Region, Residential Area, Rural, Construction
6	Standards and Guidance	Consumption, DualCredits, Catalog, Informatization, Model, Scrap, Accounting, Testing Regulations, Credit Pool, Market
7	Subsidies and Tax support	Subsidy, Funds, Support, Awarding Subsidy, Sales, Central Finance, Vehicle Model, Local, Departments, Investment, Production, Consumers, Purchase Tax, Loans, Taxpayer

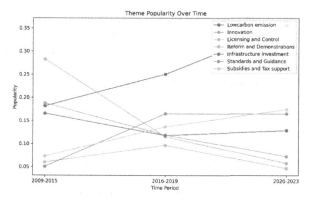

Fig. 4. Theme Popularity Over Time

4.3 BERT

BERT Architecture. BERT (Bidirectional Encoder Representations from Transformers), initially introduced by Google in 2018, stands as a groundbreaking language model, showcasing unparalleled performance across a myriad of Natural Language Processing (NLP) tasks.

The input for the BERT model typically comprises the summation of three preprocessed vectors: initial word embeddings, segment embeddings, and positional embeddings. The initial embeddings encapsulate information pertaining to the current word, while segment embeddings elucidate the positional context of the word within its sentence. Simultaneously, positional embeddings capture the semantic nuances inherent in words at distinct positions within the text. The input text is delineated with [CLS] and [SEP] serving as commencement and termination tokens. As [CLS] lacks explicit semantic information, it consolidates varied details from the associated sentence, rendering the resulting vector essential for downstream tasks.

Word Embedding Generation. BERT diverges from traditional word2vec models by dynamically enriching semantic information for each word during the processing of the input vocabulary. This dynamic enrichment empowers the model to thoroughly comprehend the contextual nuances, alleviating the limitation of associating each word solely with a fixed vector representation. The specific steps are outlined as follows:

Initially, the pertinent vocabulary undergoes processing in the BERT model, which computes vector encodings for each Chinese word. Following this, for every word, the final layer of one of the 12 encoders is extracted. At this juncture, leveraging the earlier mentioned information amalgamation, we utilize the [CLS] vector from this hidden layer to represent the word vector for the current word. Ultimately, the words and their corresponding 768-dimensional encodings are systematically stored, establishing the foundation for subsequent similarity calculations.

Model Training and Fine-Tuning. This study conducted two separate BERT training and fine-tuning procedures, focusing on the textual content of policies and annual reports from listed companies. The goal was to improve the model's accuracy in recognizing and encoding input words, ultimately refining task specificity.

For the initial fine-tuning, the chosen model was the Chinese-Bert-wwm-ext, released by the Harbin Institute of Technology and iFLYTEK Joint Laboratory (HFL). The pre-training corpus for this model encompassed Chinese Wikipedia and general data, with a total word count of 5.4 billion.

During the training and fine-tuning phases, a subset of the THUCNews classification dataset from the Tsinghua NLP Group was utilized. Original policy texts were introduced as a new category. Subsequent downstream tasks were structured to bias the model toward recognizing policy texts more effectively, bolstering its resistance to interference from irrelevant content. Comparative to the same pre-trained model without fine-tuning, the accuracy of policy text recognition witnessed an improvement of nearly 10% after fine-tuning.

The second selected model was FinBERT, a financial domain pre-trained model released by Value Simplex AI Lab. Its pre-training corpus comprised three themes related to finance and economics: financial and economic news, listed company announcements, and financial encyclopedia entries.

During the fine-tuning process, an additional subset of the news dataset was once more utilized. This subset included supplementary sections derived from annual reports, which were obtained through web crawling. Tasks were devised to guide the model in excluding interference from other corpora during training, specifically honing in on the identification of annual report texts. Our model's accuracy in recognizing annual report texts experienced an 8% increase compared to the same model without fine-tuning.

Model Application. In this phase, policy texts and textual keywords were initially fed into the fine-tuned HFL BERT model to generate their respective word vectors. Subsequently, similarity was computed based on these vectors. After manual screening and expert evaluation, a policy text dictionary comprising seven themes was compiled. Following this, the formed dictionary, in conjunction with annual report from listed companies, underwent input into the fine-tuned FinBERT to obtain their respective vector representations. Subsequent vector similarity calculations were conducted, and after thorough screening and evaluation of the final results, a policy domain dictionary was synthesized, encompassing 872 words. This comprehensive dictionary not only incorporates essential keywords from policy and annual report texts but also accounts for their interconnectedness. It serves the purpose of identifying policy response features in the annual reports of listed companies.

5   Assessment

To ascertain the efficacy and precision of the dictionary, two distinct application scenarios are employed. The initial scenario focuses on theme feature recognition, whether there is a differentiation of themes in the annual report for a given company at a given time. The second scenario centers on stage feature recognition, evaluating the changes in thematic popularity of a company throughout three distinct stages.

5.1 Topic Feature Identification

In terms of dimension recognition, this study selected eight representative publicly listed companies in the EV sector based on the industrial chain. The selected companies are listed in the table below (Table 3).

Table 3. Representative enterprises and their positions within the industry value chain

Industry Chain	Scope	Listed Companies
Upstream	Raw Material Components Batteries Motors Electronic Control	EVE Energy Co., wolong-electric, broad-ocean, Zhejiang, Grandwall Electric Science
Focal firm	Complete Vehicle Manufacturing	BYD
Downstream	Charging Piles Market Services	Pret, Meichen Ecology

Applying the policy domain dictionary, we conducted a thematic word frequency calculation on the annual reports of the aforementioned listed companies for the year 2021. Subsequently, the relative word frequency was computed based on the number of words in each theme.

$$R_i = \frac{n_i}{s_i}, i = 1, 2, \ldots 7 \tag{1}$$

In this context, R_i represents the relative word frequency of the i-th theme, n_i denotes the absolute word frequency of the i-th theme, and s_i signifies the number of themes in the dictionary corresponding to the i-th theme.

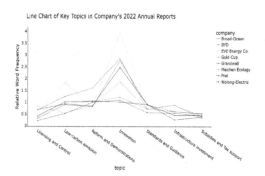

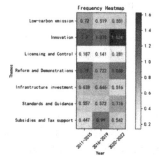

Fig. 5. Line Chart Topics in Company's 2022 Annual Report

Fig. 6. Frequency Heatmap

The line chart (Fig. 5) of themes and word frequencies reveals that (1) the new energy vehicle industry belongs to the high-tech industry. As shown in the chart above, the relative word frequencies of technological innovation and green low-carbon are higher, indicating that enterprises pay more attention to these two themes. (2) The downstream listed companies, Meichen Ecology, which is mainly focused on the charging pile sector, and Prite, which is mainly involved in the research and service of raw materials. Compared to each other, Meichen Ecology has a higher degree of policy response to policies related to infrastructure, which is more closely related to its business, while Prite has a higher degree of policy response to green innovation policies that are more closely related to green research and development of raw materials. This is due to the differences in the main business areas of the companies. The accurate identification of the response characteristics of listed companies at various stages of the new energy vehicle industry chain to different themes demonstrates the effectiveness and accuracy of the new energy vehicle policy domain dictionary established in this paper.

5.2   Feature Identification in Three Stage of Policy Systems

In the analysis of stage-specific features, BYD was selected to conduct a comprehensive examination of both horizontal and vertical response features. Employing the policy domain dictionary, a comparative analysis is conducted on the annual reports of BYD from 2011 to 2022, calculating the theme word frequencies. Subsequently, relative word frequencies are computed based on time and the number of theme words.

$$n_i^t = \frac{N_i^t}{s_i}, t = 1, 2, 3 \tag{2}$$

Here, n_i^t represents the relative word frequency of the i-th theme in the t-th stage, N_i^t denotes the absolute word frequency of the i-th theme in the t-th stage, and s_i signifies the number of themes in the dictionary corresponding to the i-th theme.

From the heatmap (Fig. 6) of phases, themes, and word frequencies, it can be observed that (1) the theme of technological innovation of BYD, a listed company, has the highest relative frequency in all three phases, indicating a higher response to technology innovation policies, which is consistent with BYD's long-standing public strategy of valuing technological innovation; (2) BYD has the smallest relative frequency of themes related to regulatory compliance in all three stages, reflecting that, as a listed company, BYD focuses more on responding to market changes rather than to government macro-control measures. (3) In the first phase, the relative frequency of the theme "promotion and application" is second only to technological innovation, in the second phase, the theme "financial and tax support" has a relatively high frequency, and in the third phase, the themes "promotion and application" and "guidance for development" have higher frequencies. This is consistent with the characteristics of the three stages of policies for new energy listed companies mentioned earlier, indirectly proving the accuracy of this paper's designed words for identifying corporate response features.

6   Conclusion

Utilizing DTM-EM technology, this study investigated the response features of listed companies to government policies. The primary objective was to identify policy responses and establish a policy domain dictionary to facilitate assessing response levels across different enterprises. By amalgamating the dictionary derived from this study with the annual reports of listed companies, the word frequency partially reflects the policy response features of these companies. Furthermore, the construction method of this dictionary can be extended to various industry domains. This study is limited by the insufficient volume of annual report data, and future studies will extend the analysis timespan to address this limitation effectively.

Acknowledgement. This research was supported by the National Natural Science Foundation of China under Grant 72293572.

References

1. Li, C., Qiu, Z., Fu, T.: The role of policy perceptions and entrepreneurs' preferences in firms' response to industry 4.0: the case of Chinese firms. J. Sustain. **13**(20), 11352–11352 (2021)
2. Hu, N., Xue, F., Wang, H.: Does managerial myopia affect long-term investment? – based on text analysis and machine learning. J. Manag. World **37**(05), 139–156+11+19–21 (2021). (in Chinese)
3. Li, F.: Textual analysis of corporate disclosures: a survey of the literature. J. Account. Lit. **29**, 143–167 (2010)
4. Wan, H., Zhong, X., Peng, Q.: Respond to change with change? Study on the impact of economic policy uncertainty on enterprise strategic change. J. Ind. Eng. Manag. **35**(05), 52–63 (2021). (in Chinese)
5. Lv, H., Cheng, M., Liu, H.: An empirical study on the driving factors of strategic complexity in transitional period: the analysis from managers' cognitive perspective. J. Ind. Eng. Manag. **27**(02), 54–64+53 (2013). (in Chinese)
6. Li ,C., Zhang ,Y.: A study of the industrial cluster technology S.&T. policy total factor critical paths and firm response effect. Manag. Rev. **27**(02), 145–157 (2015). (in Chinese)
7. Yuan, B., Zhang, K.: Can environmental regulation promote industrial innovation and productivity? Based on the strong and weak Porter hypothesis. Chin. J. Popul. Resour. **15**(04), 322–336 (2017)
8. Liu, C., Liu, L., Zhang, D., Fu, J.: How does the capital market respond to policy shocks? Evidence from listed solar photovoltaic companies in China. Energy Policy **151**, 112054 (2021)
9. Lanzhou, U.L.M.O.S.W.J., Lanzhou, U.L.M.O.S.Z.Y.C.: China: the impact of top management team attention on diversification strategy of firms. In: Proceedings of 2012 IEEE 5th International Conference on Management Engineering Technology of Statistics, pp. 431–435(2012)
10. Sergej, J.V., Andreas, P., Sabine, K.: Do they see the signs? Organizational response behavior to customer complaint messages. J. Bus. Res. **137**, 116–127 (2021)
11. Li, C., Feng, X., Li, X., Zhou, Y.: Effect of green credit policy on energy firms' growth: evidence from China. Econ. Res. Ekonomska istraživanja **36**(2), 2177701 (2023)
12. Zhou, D., Wu, C., Wang, Q., Zha, D.: Response of scale and leverage of thermal power enterprises to renewable power enterprises in China. Appl. Energy **251**, 113288 (2019)
13. Tian, Z., Chen, L., Taieb, H., Gu, J.: Corporate response strategy and behavior under the Chinese government Innovation policy system: a multi-case study based on grounded theory. J. Manag. Rev. **33**(12), 87–99 (2021). (in Chinese)
14. Denter, N., Caferoglu, H., Moehrle, M.G.: Applying dynamic topic modeling for understanding the evolution of the RFID technology. In: PICMET, pp. 1–9 (2019)

15. Sun, G., Cheng, Y., Zhang, Z., Tong, X., Chai, T.: Text classification with improved word embedding and adaptive segmentation. Expert Syst. Appl. **238**, 121852 (2024)
16. Gao, Q., Huang, X., Dong, K., Liang, Z., Wu, J.: Semantic-enhanced topic evolution analysis: a combination of the dynamic topic model and word2vec. J. Scientometrics **127**(3), 1543–1563 (2022)

Tourism Demand Forecasting with Multi-terminal Search Query Data and Deep Learning

Zhongyi Hu[1]([✉]), Xue Li[1], and Mustafa Misir[2]

[1] Wuhan University, Wuhan 430072, China
Zhongyi.hu@whu.edu.cn
[2] Duke Kunshan University, Suzhou 215316, Kunshan, China

Abstract. This study aims to explore the effectiveness of multiple devices' search query in tourism demand forecasting. Accordingly, this study collects search data from computer and mobile devices, and proposed a hybrid deep learning model, namely MUL-CNN-LSTM, with improved structure accordingly. In the model, a dual CNN module is employed to extract deep features of search queries from multi-devices. Subsequently, the LSTM is applied to generate the prediction of tourism demand. By taking JiuZhaiGou Valley as a case, the empirical results of three groups of comparisons demonstrate that the proposed deep learning model, along with the multi-terminal search query data, significantly enhances forecasting performance.

Keywords: Tourism demand forecasting · Deep learning · Search query data

1 Introduction

The tourism industry has made positive contributions to a country's GDP and employment. Accurate prediction of tourism demand is crucial for policymakers to effectively allocate limited resources. With the rapid development of Internet technology, search queries, as a representative form of big data, have been widely used in previous studies for tourism demand forecasting [1]. By recording retrieval times when tourists search with certain keywords, search queries provide valuable information about searchers' travel intentions and enhance the predictability of their travel behavior [1–3]. Consequently, tourism demand forecasting using search query data has become an emerging research trend [4].

Existing research has demonstrated that utilizing search data from multiple search engines can enhance forecasting results. However, they ignored the complexity of search data across different devices, which may possess distinct behavioral characteristics and intention trends. Therefore, it is important to investigate tourism demand forecasting using search query data from different devices and determine if incorporating multi-terminal search data can improve forecasting performance.

Multi-terminal search data with large volume often exhibits rich data characteristic, requiring strong capabilities for feature extraction and model learning. By automatically extracting deep features layer-by-layer from massive data, deep learning models have shown excellent forecasting performance. Thus, to address above issues, the study proposes an improved deep learning model for tourism demand forecasting with multi-terminal search data.

As one of the earliest attempts to utilize multi-terminal search data for tourism demand forecasting, the study aims to explore the effects of different search queries on improving forecasting performance. Additionally, the paper proposes a hybrid deep learning model called Mul-CNN-LSTM with an improved structure to enhance feature extraction. Through three groups of comparisons, experimental results confirm that the proposed model exhibits outstanding performance in forecasting tourism demand with multi-terminal search queries.

The rest of the paper is organized as follows. Section 2 reviews related research. Section 3 provides details of the proposed model. In Sect. 4, the data and experimental settings are described. Section 5 presents the empirical results and analysis. Finally, the conclusions and future work are discussed in Sect. 6.

2 Related Work

Search query data refers to the recorded number of instances in which individuals search for specific keywords to obtain relevant information. These records serve as a quantitative measure of users' interest in a particular keyword during a given time period and contribute to enhancing prediction performance of tourism demand [5]. According to Li et al.'s [6], the research process can be categorized into two main stages, that is search data analysis and model selection.

Google Trends has been commonly utilized for predicting overseas tourist arrival, whereas the Baidu Index has been employed for predicting tourism at domestic tourist attractions. Also, some studies have extended their data collection to encompass over search engines, such as 360 and Sougou, when conducting tourism demand forecasting. These studies have confirmed that utilizing multiple search query data from different search engines can enhance forecasting performance [7]. However, the increasing complexity of search engine data sources has introduced another significant consideration—the proliferation of multiple device sources with the widespread use of mobile devices. For instance, individuals may use a personal computer (PC) to conduct detailed trip planning searches, while casual travel-related searches may be conducted using portable mobile devices, potentially introducing more noise into the data. Therefore, the recorded search data from different devices may possess diverse influences on forecasting performance due to the underlying behavioral characteristics, warranting further attention. However, only few studies have explored the impact of multiple device sources of search query data [8], which adopted traditional time series models and shallow machine learning models to construct prediction models.

Apart from search query analysis, choosing forecasting models also has a great influence on tourism demand forecasting results. According to Li et al. [6], tourism demand forecasting methods with search data could be divided into five types: time series methods, econometric methods, machine learning methods, deep learning methods and hybrid models. While time series models greatly rely on consistent historical pattern [9], shallow learning methods lack the capacity of automatically extracting features and learn the long-term dependencies of tourist flow time series [10, 11]. The explosive growth of data has impeded the efficacy of traditional machine learning methods in both model training and forecasting performance when handling massive datasets.

In response to these challenges, deep learning models, such as recurrent neural networks (RNN) and long and short-term memory networks (LSTM), have demonstrated distinct advantages in forecasting by effectively capturing long-term dependencies within search data [12]. LSTM could effectively extract dynamic features and exhibits strong generalization and forecasting capabilities, thereby garnering increasing attention from researchers [11]. Furthermore, hybrid models combining different single models, es have been employed to address specific issues in tourist flow forecasting. In particularly, the combination of convolutional neural network (CNN) and LSTM, has gained traction in several studies. For example, *Lu et al.* [13] applied CNN-LSTM to predict the daily tourist flow of Huangshan mountain, employing CNN for feature extraction and LSTM for forecasting, while also integrating genetic algorithm for model parameter optimization. Results indicated that the proposed GA-CNN-LSTM model outperformed BPNN, CNN and LSTM. In conclusion, the aggregation of deep learning models has proven instrumental in enhancing forecasting performance compared to individual models [14].

3   MUL-CNN-LSTM Prediction Model

The paper highlights the challenge of combining search query data from different devices to improve the performance of tourism demand forecasting. This is a complex task that requires handling large volumes of data with complex characteristics. By leveraging the ability of deep learning models to automatically extract features and capture long-term dependencies within data, this study proposes a hybrid deep learning model, namely MUL-CNN-LSTM, to effectively combine search query data from different devices to improve tourism demand forecasting accuracy.

As depicted in Fig. 1, the proposed model consists of two main modules: feature extraction module utilizing CNN and tourist demand forecasting module employing LSTM. The feature extraction module extracts deep features, which are subsequently integrated and used as input for the tourist demand forecasting module. To better capture deep features from search query data originating from two distinct devices, the model was adapted to independently learn features from search queries associated with different devices.

3.1   Feature Extraction Module

Generally, to predict the tourist demand by using search query data, we can define the input features by a three-dimensional matrix X_d^{s*t*k}, where $d \in \{pc, mobile\}$ denotes the search query data from PC or Mobile, s denotes sample size, t denotes time steps, and k denotes the initially identified keywords.

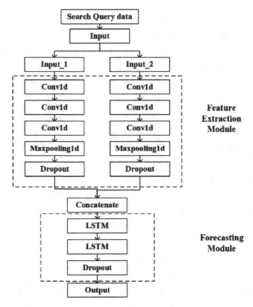

Fig. 1. Structure of MUL-CNN-LSTM

Considering the search query data from PC and Mobile may exhibit different patterns, a dual CNN is used in the feature extraction module. Each CNN consists of three convolution layers, one pooling layer and one dropout layer. The one-dimensional convolution layer, with the convolution kernel moving in the time direction, is used to extract features. Subsequently, the information contained within search data is gradually extracted, and the feature fusion process is gradually accomplished during the convolution process.

The extraction results are then transmitted to the MaxPooling1D pooling layer to reduce the dimensionality of features. To void overfitting of the prediction, the Dropout layer is further applied. Finally, the Concatenate layer is employed to combine the features extracted from the search query data of both PC and Mobile devices.

3.2 Forecasting Module

After the feature extraction and data reduction process through three convolution layers, the extracted features are passed on to the forecasting module. In this module, the time sequence characteristics of the search data are learned using a two-layer LSTM (Long Short-Term Memory) network.

The concept behind LSTM is that it incorporates three gates at each time step to regulate the flow of information along the sequences, enabling accurate capture of long-range dependencies. At each time step t in the LSTM, the hidden state h_t is updated based on the current input x_t, the hidden state at the previous time step h_{t-1}, the input gate i_t, the forget gate f_t, the output gate o_t, and the memory cell c_t. Among them, the forget gate is responsible for discarding irrelevant information and selecting relevant information to be retained in the long-term state of the current layer. The input gate determines which information should be updated in the cell through an activation function. The updated cell state is calculated by combining the old state (weighted by the forget gate) and the new state (weighted by the input gate). Finally, the output gate adjusts the range of the output cell state using the tanh function to determine the output information of the cell. The equations used for these calculations are represented as follows.

$$f_t = \sigma(W_f * [h_{t-1}, x_t] + b_f) \tag{1}$$

$$i_t = \sigma(W_i * [h_{t-1}, x_t] + b_i) \tag{2}$$

$$\tilde{C}_t = \tanh(W_c \cdot [h_{t-1}, x_t] + b_c) \tag{3}$$

$$C_t = C_{t-1} \cdot f_t + \tilde{C}_t \cdot i_t \tag{4}$$

$$O_t = \sigma(W_O * [h_{t-1}, x_t] + b_O) \tag{5}$$

$$h_t = O_t \cdot \tanh(C_t) \tag{6}$$

while W represents the weight matrix, b represents the bias, σ and tanh are activation functions, and the dot represents the inner product of vectors. Each neuron updates and transmits the cell state through the 'gate' structure, and the output from the previous layer serves as the input of the next layer. In this way, the LSTM model can capture the long-term dependencies of the input signals.

The results obtained from the LSTM are then passed through a Dropout layer and a fully connected Dense layer in sequence. The outputs of the Dense layer represent the daily prediction of tourist flow.

4 Empirical Study

4.1 Data Preparation

Data Collection. To evaluate the performance of proposed model, Jiuzhaigou Valley Scenic in China is selected as a case study. Due to the earthquake on 8 August 2017 and the outbreak of COVID-19 since 2020, the daily volumes of tourists from 1 January 2013 to 7 August 2017 are collected for evaluation purpose. The daily search query data related to the scenic is collected from Baidu Index (https://index.baidu.com) by focusing on specific search keywords and search devices.

Keyword Selection. To select the keywords used for search query selection, we initially select eight seed keywords covering fundamental elements of tourism. They are tourism, destination, accommodation, transportation, scenic spot, diet, shopping, and weather. Then, 35 search keywords were acquired according to the related word recommendation from Baidu. To filter out irrelevant search queries, the Pearson correlation analysis is applied to calculate the correlation between keywords and tourist volumes. The finally selected 25 keywords with correlation coefficient larger than 0.5 are shown in Table 1.

Table 1. Correlation analysis between search volumes and daily tourist volumes

Keyword	Cor	Keyword	Cor
Map	0.8388	Tourist map	0.6589
Huanglong	0.7875	Route	0.6485
Guide	0.7541	Weather forecast	0.6432
Hotel (Jiu Dian)	0.7496	Scenery	0.6257
Scenic map	0.7427	Airport	0.6599
Ticket	0.7288	Location	0.6240
Accommodation	0.7278	Pictures	0.5911
Attractions	0.7158	Hotel (Bin guan)	0.5830
Jiuzhaigou	0.7078	Self-help tour	0.5649
Free travel	0.7039	Transportation	0.5249
Travelogue	0.6961	Beauty	0.5122
Tourism	0.6669	Huanglong airport	0.5060
Airport	0.6599		

Notes: the keywords will be combined with Jiuzhaigou to get the search queries.

Data Cleaning. Data cleaning primarily involves handling outliers and missing values. When dealing with search data from multiple devices, which often exhibit complex descriptive patterns and do not adhere to a normal distribution, boxplot analysis is the most suitable method for identifying outliers. Values that fall beyond the bounds of the boxplot are identified as outliers. Once identified, these outliers are assigned a value of zero and converted into missing values for further processing.

In the case of search query data and tourist volumes, where the data is arranged in chronological order, directly deleting items with missing values may disrupt the overall sequence. Conversely, filling in missing values with specific values can maintain the original internal logic and preserve data information to a greater extent. Given that search query data and tourist volumes commonly exhibit fluctuations, it is decided to first fill in missing values with the preceding value and, if necessary, with the subsequent value. This strategy ensures that both outliers and missing values are effectively handled. By addressing outliers and missing values through appropriate techniques, the dataset can be cleaned and prepared for further analysis.

Lag Selection. Considering that tourists often search for relevant information days prior to their actual trip, it is important to consider the lagged values when analyzing search query data for tourist flow forecasting.

To determine the relevance between the forecasted variables and the search queries of keywords with different lags, a Pearson cross-correlation analysis was conducted. Search queries with lags of 1 day, 2 days, 15 days, 3 days, 1 week, 1 month was analyzed, and the results are presented in Table 2. Based on the analysis, a lag period of 2 days was deemed suitable for total and PC device, while a lag period of 1 day was found to be optimal for mobile device. Therefore, the lag period of search data is set to 2 days.

Table 2. Correlation analysis between daily tourist flow and search keywords in different lag

Lag	1	2	3	7	15	30
AGG	0.6865	0.6923*	0.6898	0.6662	0.6608	0.5569
PC	0.5369	0.5395*	0.5348	0.5483	0.5407	0.4759
WISE	0.6795*	0.6730	0.6666	0.6478	0.6323	0.5068

4.2 Experimental Setup

Experimental Setting. The full dataset consists 1680 samples. After being normalized and dimension conversion for model input, the dataset was split into two groups, the training set (the first 70%) and the test set (the last 30%). Additionally, 20% of the training set was separated for use as a validation set.

To evaluate the forecasting performance of different models, three evaluation metrics were applied. They are correlation coefficient (R^2), root mean square error (RMSE) and mean absolute percentage error (MAPE). The training and forecasting process were repeated 50 times for each round, and the averaged results were compared.

Model Implementation. In the proposed MUL-CNN-LSTM model, the input requires for four dimensions, namely Sample number, Timestep, Feature and Channel number. The Channel refers to terminal types, specifically PC and wise in this research. The model input is obtained by combining the search data from two different terminals with three dimensions.

The mean square error (MSE) is chosen as the loss function as it is commonly use in regression research to measure the error between the real value and the forecasted value. The Adam algorithm is selected as the optimization algorithm due to its widespread use in deep learning research. The hyperparameters in the model are configured based on preliminary experiments. Finally, the number of convolution layer is set as 3, the LSTM layer is set as 2. The Dropout layer is employed to randomly drop out some layers to simplify the network and avoid overfitting of the model. The batch size of each round for data sample was set as 50. The training epoch is set as 30. The early stopping mechanism stops the learning progress if the forecasting error fails to decrease for more than 10 consecutive times, with a tolerance set as 10.

Benchmark Models. To compare the forecasting performance with different search data, two different types of input are considered, i.e., single-terminal search data and multiple-terminal search data. Single-terminal search data includes PC index and WISE index, presenting search data generated from PC or Mobile device, respectively. Multiple-terminal search data includes aggregated search data and combined search data.

The aggregated search data adds up the volume of each terminal's keywords, which is commonly used in previous studies without considering the variety of search devices. The combined search data simply concatenates the search data matrix of each single terminal, increasing the dimension of search data. To sum up, the four search indexes are presented as input in Table 3.

Table 3. Different search data with their composition

Search Index	Data Source	Composition
PC Index	computer equipment	/
Wise Index	mobile devices	/
Agg Index	calculation results	add the corresponding value of PC index and Wise index terminal on keywords
Cob Index	calculation results	concatenate the search data matrix of PC index and Wise index

Regarding the prediction models, in addition to our proposed MUL-CNN-LSTM, a series of benchmark models are introduced for comparisons. They are time series models (AR and ARIMA), machine learning model (random forest), neural network models (Multilayer Perceptron and LSTM). The inputs for these benchmark models are presented in Table 4.

Table 4. Different models and their inputs

Category	Model	Inputs
time series model	AR and ARIMA	PC index, Wise index, Agg index, Cob index
machine learning model	RF	PC index, Wise index, Agg index, Cob index
neural network models	MLP and LSTM	PC index, Wise index, Agg index, Cob index
hybrid model	CNN-LSTM	PC index, Wise index, Agg index, Cob index
proposed model	MUL-CNN-LSTM	PC index and Wise index as dual inputs

5   Experiments and Results

5.1   Forecasting Results of Different Search Data

In this section, the study aims to examine the forecasting performance of different sources of search data. Specifically, it investigates whether certain types of search data consistently have a significant impact on forecasting results across different models. The results are presented in Table 5.

Table 5. Forecasting performance of different models with different search data

Input	Evaluate	AR	ARIMA	RF	MLP	LSTM	CNN-LSTM
PC Index	R^2	0.4678	0.3970	0.8249	0.8341	0.6816	0.8124
	RMSE	0.1789	0.1904	0.1019	0.0990	0.1372	0.1052
	MAPE (%)	44.5545	109.2966	147.0847	149.0235	28.0370	24.2612
Wise Index	R^2	0.5470	0.6161	0.8654	0.0792	0.6727	0.7536
	RMSE	0.1650	0.1519	0.0893	0.1102	0.1389	0.1200
	MAPE (%)	39.8138	41.4069	168.8084	170.3561	39.1538	34.6932
Agg Index	R^2	0.7357	0.7973	0.8438	0.8394	0.8442	0.8648
	RMSE	0.1261	0.1104	0.0962	0.0972	0.0960	0.0893
	MAPE (%)	32.3908	26.1497	169.1095	172.9710	24.9435	22.3832
Cob Index	R^2	0.3445	0.5242	0.8302	0.8257	0.7563	0.8497
	RMSE	0.2843	0.1692	0.1002	0.1008	0.1195	0.0941
	MAPE (%)	69.4012	51.7182	168.3313	167.3447	30.1935	23.2114

RF and MLP models exhibit considerable instability, which are disregarded due to their poor forecasting results. Among the four other models, the aggregated index consistently demonstrated the best forecasting performance, while the other three indexes showed varying degrees of fluctuations. As the model complexity increased, the forecasting performance of the combined index gradually improved, from the worst by AR to the best by CNN-LSTM. Conversely, the forecasting performance of the wise index gradually fell to the worst.

Regarding search data from individual devices, the forecasting performance did not consistently indicate one type of data being superior to another. For example, the PC index performed worse than the Wise index in AR and ARIMA models but outperformed the Wise index in the LSTM and CNN-LSTM models. Moreover, the relationship between the two indexes changed with the complexity of the model, suggesting that data features of the PC index might be better captured by models with more complex structures. Hence, it can be concluded that search data obtained from different devices contain distinct search characteristics and may be revealed to varying degrees in different forecasting models.

The improvement of the combined index and PC index can be attributed to the excellent feature learning and tourist flow forecasting capabilities of CNN-LSTM, as observed in previous studies and experiments. CNN-LSTM can effectively extract implicit features and learn more valuable information from combined and PC search data, resulting in higher forecasting performance compared to the WISE index. Search data may exhibit enhanced forecasting performance in hybrid neural networks, providing a fundamental basis for developing the MUL-CNN-LSTM with its modified structure.

5.2   Forecasting Results of Proposed Model with Multiple Search Data

After exploring the forecasting performance of multiple models and multiple search data obtained from different devices, the MUL-CNN-LSTM model with improved structure is proposed for further improvement. The modified CNN module is designed to learn distinct features from PC index and Wise index, enabling it to fully extract inherent and hidden information from search queries. The input of proposed model is similar as the combined index. Thus, its forecasting results are presented in the column of Cob Index with those of other related models, as shown in Table 6.

Table 6. Forecasting performance of the proposed model MUL-CNN-LSTM

Input	Metric	LSTM	CNN-LSTM	MUL-CNN-LSTM
Agg Index	R^2	0.8442	**0.8648**	
	RMSE	0.0960	**0.0893**	
	MAPE (%)	24.9435	**22.3832**	
Cob Index	R^2	0.7563	0.8497	**0.8747**
	RMSE	0.1195	0.0941	**0.0860**
	MAPE (%)	30.1935	23.2114	**20.9453**

By comparing the experimental results of three relevant models, it can be clearly concluded that CNN-LSTM performed better than LSTM, while MUL-CNN-LSTM demonstrated superior performance to CNN-LSTM. The introduction and the structural design of CNN module both focus on extracting features from search query data, yielding significant improvements in forecasting performance.

Notably, MUL-CNN-LSTM exhibited clear advantages in forecasting performance. Its RMSE of 0.0860 improved by 9.61%, and MAPE of 20.9453% increased by 2.2% compared to CNN-LSTM with Cob index, and significantly surpassed the best results obtained with Agg index.

6   Conclusions

Although previous studies have confirmed the effectiveness of search query data in predicting tourism demand, limited studies have considered the involvement of search query data from different devices. To this end, this study proposed a hybrid deep learning model, named MUL-CNN-LSTM. Two CNN were employed to extract deep features of multi-terminal search queries, followed by the LSTM for prediction of tourism demand. The experimental results clearly demonstrate that search queries via different search devices present varying forecasting performance, and the proposed MUL-CNN-LSTM model significantly improves forecasting performance when applied to multi-terminal search query data. These findings enrich the existing literature on search query data-based tourism demand forecasting and provide valuable insights into the influence of search patterns on forecasting accuracy.

Acknowledgement. This research was supported by the National Key Research and Development Program of China (2019YFB1405600), National Natural Science Foundation of China (72171183), National Natural Science Foundation of Hubei China (2021CFB481), and the 2022 WHU-DKU Joint Seeding Program (XXWHUDKUZZJJ202303).

References

1. Yang, X., Pan, B., Evans, J.A., Lv, B.: Forecasting Chinese tourist volume with search engine data. Tour. Manag. **46**, 386–397 (2015)
2. Oender, I., Gunter, U.: Forecasting tourism demand with google trends for a major European city destination. Tour. Anal. **21**, 203–220 (2016)
3. Xie, G., Qian, Y., Wang, S.: Forecasting Chinese cruise tourism demand with big data: an optimized machine learning approach. Tour. Manag. **82**, 104208 (2021)
4. Liu, H., Liu, Y., Wang, Y., Pan, C.: Hot topics and emerging trends in tourism forecasting research: a scientometric review. Tour. Econ. **25**, 448–468 (2019)
5. Li, S., Chen, T., Wang, L., Ming, C.: Effective tourist volume forecasting supported by PCA and improved BPNN using Baidu index. Tour. Manag. **68**, 116–126 (2018)
6. Li, X., Law, R., Xie, G., Wang, S.: Review of tourism forecasting research with internet data. Tour. Manag. **83**, 104245 (2021)
7. Fu, T., Wang, Z., Wang, T.: Research on application of a new algorithm based on multi-source data in tourism flow forecasting. In: Emrouznejad A. (ed.) ACM International Conference Proceeding Series. Association for Computing Machinery (2018)
8. Hu, M., Xiao, M., Li, H.: Which search queries are more powerful in tourism demand forecasting: searches via mobile device or PC? Int. J. Contemp. Hosp. Manag. (2021)
9. Song, H., Li, G.: Tourism demand modelling and forecasting—a review of recent research. Tour. Manag. **29**, 203–220 (2008)
10. Zhang, B., Pu, Y., Wang, Y., Li, J.: Forecasting hotel accommodation demand based on lstm model incorporating internet search index. Sustainability **11** (2019)
11. Zhang, B., Li, N., Shi, F., Law, R.: A deep learning approach for daily tourist flow forecasting with consumer search data. Asia Pac. J. Tour. Res. **25**, 323–339 (2020)
12. Law, R., Li, G., Fong, D.K.C., Han, X.: Tourism demand forecasting: a deep learning approach. Ann. Tour. Res. **75**, 410–423 (2019)
13. Lu, W., Rui, H., Liang, C., Jiang, L., Zhao, S., Li, K.: A method based on GA-CNN-LSTM for daily tourist flow prediction at scenic spots. Entropy **22**, 261 (2020)
14. Wu, X., Blake, A.: Does the combination of models with different explanatory variables improve tourism demand forecasting performance? Tour. Econ., 135481662211326 (2022)

Research on Blockchain Enabled Supply Chain Financing Under Option Contracts

Ke Yang, Jing Huang$^{(\boxtimes)}$, and LiHao Chen

University of Shanghai for Science and Technology, Shanghai 200093, China
huangjing@usst.edu.cn

Abstract. The development of enterprises can not be separated from the support of the financial industry, SMEs financing process is difficult, financing difficulties are many SMEs in the reality of the problem faced in the operation, due to many SMEs own credit is low, it is difficult to finance loans from banks and other third-party institutions, resulting in SMEs because of the lack of funds can not be production and business operations, affecting the development of SMEs, and the core business can provide trade credit financing to solve the financing difficulties of SMEs. Consider a secondary supply chain consisting of well-funded suppliers and capital-constrained retailers, with the suppliers as the leaders of the stackelberg game and the retailers as the followers. When the retailer is capital constrained, the supplier can provide trade credit financing for it, and the introduction of blockchain technology can facilitate the increase of market demand to some extent. In this paper, we study the retailer's optimal decision-making and the impact of blockchain technology on the profits of both parties by simultaneously introducing option contracts and establishing two models of traditional financing and blockchain financing.

Keywords: option contracts · blockchain technology · commercial credit financing

1 Introduction

The 20th Party Congress pointed out that we should insist on putting the focus of economic development on the real economy, and supporting the development of small, medium and micro enterprises will have an important and far-reaching positive impact on the future of the majority of small, medium and micro enterprises [1]. In the cruel market competition, the abundance of liquid capital is especially critical for enterprises, and the contradiction between development opportunities and capital constraints faced by small and medium-sized enterprises (SMEs) is particularly significant. Although these enterprises are not as rich as large enterprises in terms of financial resources, they play a role in the supply chain structure that cannot be ignored. Despite their enormous growth potential, they are often unable to meet their operational needs due to financing difficulties, which constrains their development and thus affects the overall supply chain operation, and thus solving their financing problems has become a task of great urgency.

In the face of financial constraints faced by SMEs, many scholars have studied the use of external financing methods that utilize loans from third-party financial institutions, such as accounts payable financing, inventory pledge financing, etc., to alleviate the problem of difficult cash flow for enterprises. However, some SMEs may find it difficult to apply for financing directly from third-party financial institutions due to their low credit history. At this time, the enterprises will use other methods, such as deferred payment and option purchasing, to minimize the expenditure of funds and alleviate the pressure on funds [2]. Fewer scholars have studied the optimal decision of retailers and suppliers in order pricing using trade credit under option contracts. In the case where the downstream retailers are SMEs, the supplier can increase the sales volume of goods by providing them with commercial credit financing, thus improving profits. When accepting trade credit from the supplier, the retailer can get the goods from the supplier first, at which time it does not have to pay cash immediately, but can delay payment until it realizes sales in the market, and then pay the supplier for the goods. Option contracts are derivative products originating from the financial sector that reduce the risks faced by companies such as the risk of demand uncertainty and the risk of market volatility. In the academic field, Ritchken and Tapiero firstly introduced option contracts into enterprise inventory management, which is used to cope with the risk of future changes in product prices and demand quantities [3]. Under the option contract, the buyer can ensure the availability of orders and determine the corresponding price in advance, while the option contract also gives the buyer some flexibility, according to the observed market demand, the buyer can execute part of the option or all of the option according to the actual needs, which can avoid the inventory backlog due to the uncertainty of demand. Since option contracts can increase retailers' ordering elasticity and effectively reduce the risk caused by demand uncertainty, this paper introduces option contracts with the expectation of enabling firms to make optimal ordering decisions.

The complexity of supply chain management is becoming more and more significant under the rapid development of the global economy and the gradual fierce competition in the market. In the traditional supply chain financing model, information asymmetry is more common, and decision makers lack a global perspective and are often unable to make optimal decisions. In addition, the mismatch between supply and demand caused by market fluctuation and information asymmetry is common in the supply chain. Under such circumstances, transaction costs rise significantly, including logistics costs, warehousing expenditures, and credit risks, which not only increase the operating costs of enterprises, but also have a considerable impact on the effectiveness and competitiveness of the entire supply chain [4]. Blockchain technology, as an emerging technology, is developing rapidly around the world. With the features of decentralization, high transparency, tampering, traceability and smart contract, blockchain can make up for the shortcomings of the traditional supply chain financing model.

2   Literature Review

The research related to this paper focuses on the following three areas.

One is the research related to supply chain commercial credit financing. Casey argued that trade credit financing was more flexible in terms of borrowing and lending methods and had relatively lower borrowing and lending risks compared to bank financing [5]. Chen Xiangfeng pointed out that suppliers were willing to provide delayed-payment trade credit for capital-constrained retailers, and through the establishment of a trade credit financing model between retailers and suppliers, it was pointed out that suppliers can promote capital-constrained retailers to take higher order quantities and create new value for the supply chain through trade credit [6]. Wang analyzed the optimal ordering strategy and commercial credit period for perishable goods under the commercial credit financing model [7]. Jim Jizhou pointed out that suppliers provided commercial credit period to increase the order quantity of retailers, and stated that the larger the commercial credit period was, the more order quantity the retailers would take [8].

Wang et al. studied the option decision of retailer-guided supply chain with risk sharing, and considered both option and strike price to get the option coordination contract, and finded that the option contract was better than the traditional price contract [9]. Li et al. concluded that when there was information asymmetry among supply chain members, the option contract was significantly better than other contracts [10]. Li et al. Hu, Benyong et al. studied that under the option contract, when the seller faced the constraint of purchasing budget, the supply chain coordination can be realized by adjusting the parameters of supplier's wholesale price, option purchasing price and execution price, and the option contract was better than the traditional price contract [11]. Wu, Yingjing et al. studied the optimal financing strategies of retailers under put option, call option and two-way option contracts, as well as retailers' selection strategies for option contracts [12]. Hua Shengya pointed out that suppliers could provide option contracts for retailers of startups to purchase products, and finded that suppliers slightly reduce the option price or loan interest rate, which could make the retailer obtain positive expected profits, when the retailer's purchasing volume will converge to a fixed value [13]. Dehghan et al. compared revenue-sharing contracts with call option contracts and finded that suppliers were more willing to offer option contracts in response to fluctuations in market demand [14].

Thirdly, supply chain operation management under blockchain technology. Treleaven argued that blockchain, when applied to the financial sector, could simplify operational business processes and also securely preserve the original records of transactions [15]. OmarAli et al. argued that blockchain technology can ensure data security, and digital service platforms cannot be built without these emerging technologies [16]. LiuLu et al. solved the optimal solution under traditional financial model and blockchain financial model, and concluded that blockchain finance can create more value for supply chain [17]. Choi argued that the application of blockchain can shorten the time needed for luxury goods testing and evaluation, guarantee the authenticity of luxury goods, and thus increase market demand [18]. Wang et al. constructed a blockchain-based supply chain finance platform and found that SMEs can obtain financial support from banks and other financial institutions through the blockchain platform, and the problem of financing constraints is alleviated to some extent [19]. Wang Daoping et al. established the traditional supply chain financing model and the blockchain supply chain financing model, analyzed the ordering and pricing strategies of suppliers and retailers under the two modes, and found that the application of blockchain technology can avoid the risk of delayed repayment of the enterprise, improve the market demand, and shorten the period of commercial credit through comparison [20]. The comparison reveals that the application of blockchain technology can avoid the risk of delayed repayment, improve market demand, and shorten business credit period.

Based on the above analysis, this paper focuses on a secondary supply chain system in which suppliers act as leaders and retailers as followers in a stackelberg game. This paper introduces the option contract and discusses the ordering and pricing decisions as well as the profits of supply chain firms under the traditional financing model and blockchain financing model. Considering the common interests of retailers and suppliers, it gives the option strategy of supply chain financing methods.

3 Model Description

This paper considers a secondary supply chain consisting of a supplier and a retailer. The supplier is the leader and the financially constrained retailer is the follower.

Prior to the start of the selling season, a retailer takes out trade credit financing from a supplier, receives the product without paying for it at the time of ordering, and then repays the supplier with the proceeds of the sale of the product over the course of a sales cycle. If the retailer's proceeds are insufficient to repay the supplier, the supplier receives all of its revenue and the retailer's proceeds are zero; if the retailer's proceeds are greater than the purchase price and interest, the retailer can repay the loan at a profit. The retailer orders q units of physical product at price w and q_0 units of option product at price w_0.

At the beginning of the selling season, the retailer decides how much of the option to execute at price we based on observed market demand x and the quantity of physical product ordered q. The maximum number of options to be executed cannot exceed q_0. Assume that one unit of option represents the right to purchase exactly one unit of physical product, and the retailer sells the purchased product in the final product market at price p. The supplier provides commercial credit financing to the retailer for the period (T, M). The supplier provides commercial credit financing to the retailer. Within (T, M), the retailer uses the sales proceeds to invest and earns an opportunity return, and the supplier incurs an opportunity cost during the commercial credit period. When $x < q$, the retailer does not execute the option, when $q \leq x < q + q_0$, the retailer executes a portion of the option $(x - q)$, and when $x \geq q + q_0$, the retailer executes the full option q_0 (Fig. 1).

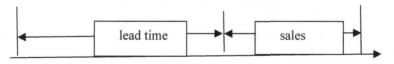

Fig. 1. Decision-making timeline

In the blockchain environment, after the supply chain enterprises put into use the blockchain, consumers can obtain the whole process information of production, transportation and sales of the products through the blockchain, which effectively improves the credibility of the product information, and then improves the market demand. The market demand is represented by a random variable x, and its corresponding probability density function and distribution function are f(x) and F(x), respectively, assuming that both functions are continuous and F(x) is differentiable.

This paper considers two modes of traditional supply chain financing and blockchain supply chain financing, analyzes the impact of blockchain-introduced technology on supply chain ordering and pricing decisions in the traditional mode, and provides a comparative analysis of the two financing modes (Table 1).

Table 1. Model Parameters and Meaning

Notation	Hidden meaning
x	market demand
q	Retailers' orders for physical products
q_0	Retailers' orders for option products
w	Wholesale prices of physical products from suppliers
w_0	Wholesale price of supplier option products
w_e	Option strike price
p	Selling price of the product
c	Unit production costs of suppliers
M	Commercial credit period for retailers
T	Retailer's sales cycle
r	Suppliers' opportunity cost ratio
α	Opportunity rate of return per unit of product per unit of time for retailers
θ	Rate of increase in market demand after the application of blockchain
c_B	Cost per unit of blockchain product usage
Π_s	Expected benefits for suppliers
Π_r	Expected benefits for retailers

The relevant assumptions are as follows:

H1: The product has no salvage value, i.e. the output of the product is equal to the market demand

H2: The supplier's commercial credit period is not less than one sales cycle of the retailer, i.e., $M \geq T$

H3: $0 < w < w_e + w_0$, the total cost of ordering and executing a unit of the option product is higher than the cost of ordering a unit of the physical product, the retailer buys the option will make the supplier bear some of the risk of changes in the market demand, the supplier will be willing to provide options when the total cost of buying and executing the option is greater than the cost of ordering.

H4: $0 < w_0 + w_e < p$, the total cost of ordering and executing one unit of the optioned product is lower than the market price of selling one unit of the physical product, guaranteeing that the purchase of the option will be profitable for the retailer

H5: $0 < w < p$, the wholesale price per unit of product is less than the market price per unit of product.

3.1 Ordering Model in Traditional Mode

At the beginning of the sale, the retailer applies for a trade credit facility from the supplier and orders a certain quantity of physical products and option products. After the supplier gives the retailer a wholesale price and a commercial credit period, the retailer orders the quantity of physical products q and the quantity of option products q_0 as well as the amount of financing $(wq + w_0q_0)$. The supplier receives the retailer's product order and signs a payment agreement to ship the product to the retailer. At the end of the selling season, the retailer realizes the return of funds based on the actual market demand for sales. When the retailer's closing cash flow is sufficient to repay the supplier's trade credit loan, the retailer pays off the loan and earns a residual profit; if the retailer's closing cash flow is insufficient to repay the supplier's loan, the retailer declares bankruptcy, the supplier receives all of the retailer's sales proceeds, and the supplier bears the residual loss (Fig. 2).

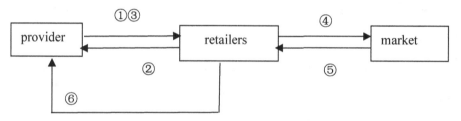

Fig. 2. Trade Credit Financing Process

The meaning of each process is as follows:

①: Suppliers set wholesale prices and provide retailers with commercial credit periods
②: the retailer determines the physical product order q and the option product order q0 and the financing amount based on the wholesale price of the product $(wq + w_0q_0)$
③: Agreement between supplier and retailer and supply of products
④: Retailers sell their products to the marketplace
⑤: Retailers receive funds for sales
⑥ If the retailer's combined sales returns and investment income are greater than the loan, the loan provided by the supplier can be repaid in full; if the retailer's combined sales returns and investment income are less than the loan, the income will go to the supplier and the loan will be partially repaid.

Retailer's profit function:

$$\Pi_{R1}(q, q_0) = p[1 + \alpha(M - T)] min(x, q + q_0) - w_0 q_0$$
$$- wq - w_e min[(x - q)^+, q_0] \qquad (1)$$

From the retailer's profit function, the retailer's return is the difference between sales and investment income and the cost of ordering and option execution, and as the market demand increases, the retailer's option execution will increase accordingly, and thus the cost of option execution increases. When $0 < x < q$, the retailer does not execute the option, at which time the retailer's profit is the difference between the sum of sales revenue and investment income px $[1 + \alpha(M - T)]$ and the cost of ordering physical and option products $wq + w_0 q_0$; when $q < x < q + q_0$, the retailer executes part of the option $x - q$, and the retailer's borrowing cost increases to $wq + w_0 q_0 + w_e (x - q)$, and the profit is the difference between the revenue and cost; when $x > q + q_0$, the retailer executes the full option, and the total revenue is $p(q + q_0) [1 + \alpha(M - T)]$, the cost is $wq + w_0 q_0 + w_e q_0$, and the profit is the difference between revenue and cost.

$$E\Pi_{R1}(q, q_0) = p[1 + \alpha(M - T)] \int_0^{q+q_0} \overline{F}(x) \, dx$$
$$+ w_e \int_q^{q+q_0} F(x) \, dx - w_0 q_0 - wq - w_e q_0 \qquad (2)$$

Apply partial derivatives to q and q_0 and construct the Hessian matrix H =

$$\begin{bmatrix} \frac{\partial E\Pi_{R1}}{\partial q^2} & \frac{\partial E\Pi_{R1}}{\partial q \partial q_0} \\ \frac{\partial E\Pi_{R1}}{\partial q \partial q_0} & \frac{\partial E\Pi_{R1}}{\partial q_0^2} \end{bmatrix}$$

$|H| = -w_e f(q + q_0)\{-p[1 + \alpha(M - T)]f(q + q_0) + w_e f(q + q_0)\} > 0$, so therefore therefore $E\Pi_{R1}(q, q_0)$ is a concave function with respect to (q, q_0) for which there exists a unique maximal value.

$$\text{Find } q* = F^{-1}(\frac{w_e - w + w_0}{w_e}), q_0* = F^{-1}(\frac{w_e + w_0}{w_e - p[1 + a(M - T)]}) - q*$$

Under the option contract, there exists a unique optimal physical product ordering quantity and option product ordering quantity for the retailer to satisfy its own interest maximization. The retailer's physical product is related to the supplier's wholesale price, and the option ordering quantity is related to the commercial credit period and the wholesale price of the product, and the supplier can control the retailer's product ordering quantity by adjusting the wholesale price and the commercial credit period. As shown by the physical product ordering volume, the retailer's ordering volume is inversely related to the supplier's wholesale price because as the supplier's wholesale price increases, the retailer's ordering cost also increases, which causes a decrease in the physical product ordering volume. The retailer's option product ordering volume increases as the commercial credit period increases.

Under a trade credit contract, if the retailer's final revenue is greater than the loan, the supplier can recover the loan in full, and if the retailer's final revenue is less than the loan, the supplier recovers a portion of the loan, so the supplier's profit function:

$$\Pi_{s1}(q, q_0) = w_0 q_0 + wq + w_e min[(x - q)^+, q_0] - c(q + min[(x - q)^+, q_0])$$

$$-Mrp(q + min[(x - q)^+, q_0]) \qquad (3)$$

From the supplier's revenue function, the supplier's revenue is the difference between the sum of the supplier's revenue from option sales, revenue from product sales, and revenue from option execution, and the cost of product production, and the opportunity cost incurred by the supplier over the commercial credit period. When $0 < x \le q$, the retailer does not execute the option, the supplier's revenue is the retailer's order of physical products and option products $wq + w_0q$, the cost is the cost of production of the product and the opportunity cost incurred in the period of commercial credit $cq + rMpq$; when $q < x \le q_0 + q$, the supplier's revenue increases the retailer's revenue from the execution of the option, the amount of the option to be executed for the $x - q$, the unit price of the w_e; when $x > q_0 + q$, the retailer executes the full option and the supplier's revenue from option execution is w_eq_0, and the cost is $(c + Mrp)(q_0 + q)$.

3.2 Ordering Model for Blockchain Financing Models

Under the blockchain financing model, the decentralization of the blockchain allows the various nodes within the system to engage in equal and free data exchanges without being restricted to a single central node. After the introduction of blockchain technology, the data on the chain is completely open and shared, and all the information of the retailer, such as basic information, business status, asset status, credit status, etc., will be stored and transmitted through the blockchain, which reduces the possibility of the retailer's default on repayment. All data information and transactions between suppliers and retailers, such as trade, financing, logistics, etc., will also be recorded on the chain, and the information of each link in the transaction process will be visible at any time. All data information cannot be changed after it is uploaded to the chain, which can ensure the security of all information in the supply chain. Since blockchain makes product information highly transparent and all members on the chain can view the relevant information, retailer companies can provide information on the source of ingredients and the place of origin of the products to increase the trust of consumers in the market, thus stimulating the rise of market demand. In addition, the blockchain's smart contract technology is an automated, digitized and irreversible contract that can automatically complete tasks such as payment, settlement and financial reconciliation of funds, which saves time and costs and is more secure and reliable than traditional contracts, thus increasing the trust between suppliers and retailers and improving the efficiency of the transactions between the two parties. The introduction of blockchain technology can ensure the authenticity of enterprise information, improve consumer trust, thus stimulating the increase of market demand, while the application of blockchain technology can save the transaction time between the two sides, reduce the retailer's commercial credit period [20], so that the supplier can recover the account within the agreed period.

Along with the introduction of blockchain, this paper proposes additional hypotheses. H6: In the blockchain financing model, both the supplier and the retailer pay the blockchain usage cost per transaction, and both parties pay the same amount of fees.

Retailer's profit function:

$$\Pi_{R2}(q, q_0) = p[1 + \alpha(M - T)]min[x(1 + \theta), q + q_0] - w_0q_0 - wq$$

$$- w_e min[((1 + \theta)x - q)^+, q_0] - c_B(q + min[((1 + \theta)x - q)^+, q_0]) \quad (4)$$

With the introduction of blockchain, the retailer's profit when is the difference between the sum of market sales revenue and sales investment revenue and the sum of option subscription costs, product subscription costs, option fulfillment costs, and blockchain application costs. If market demand $0 < x(1 + \theta) \leq q$, the retailer does not execute the option at this point and sells x products, the opportunity income from investing with the sales revenue is $px(1 + \theta)\alpha(M - T)$ and the cost is the sum of the option ordering cost and the product ordering cost and the blockchain usage cost $w_0 q_0 + wq + cq$; when market demand $q < x(1 + \theta) \leq q + q_0$, the retailer executes part of the option, the cost increases by the option execution cost $w_e[x(1 + \theta) - q]$, the cost of applying the blockchain is $c_B x(1 + \theta)$, when the market demand after applying blockchain $x(1 + \theta) > q + q_0$, the retailer executes all options, the revenue is the sum of sales revenue and investment income $p(q + q_0)[1 + \alpha(M - T)]$. The cost is the sum of option and product purchase cost and option execution cost and blockchain application cost $w_0 q_0 + wq + w_e q_0 + c_B(q + q_0)$.

$$E\Pi_{R2}(q, q_0) = -p[1 + \alpha(M - T)](1 + \theta) \int_0^{\frac{q+q_0}{1+\theta}} F(x)\,dx$$

$$+ (w_e + c_B)(1 + \theta) \int_{\frac{q}{1+\theta}}^{\frac{q+q_0}{1+\theta}} F(x)\,dx + p(q + q_0)[1 + \alpha(M - T)] - w_0 q_0 - wq - w_e q_0 \quad (5)$$

Construct the Hessian matrix to find

$$q^b* = (1 + \theta)F^{-1}(\frac{w_e - w + w_0}{w_e + c_B}),$$

$$q_0^b* = (1 + \theta)F^{-1}\frac{w_e + w_0}{w_e - p[1 + \alpha(M - T)] + c_B} - q^b*$$

Supplier's profit function

$$\Pi_{s2}(q, q_0) = wq + w_0 q_0 + w_e min[((1 + \theta)x - q)^+, q_0]$$

$$- c_B(q + min[((1 + \theta)x - q)^+ q_0]) - c(q + min[((1 + \theta)x - q)^+, q_0])$$

$$- Mrp(q + min[((1 + \theta)x - q)^+, q_0]) \quad (6)$$

From the supplier's revenue function, the supplier's revenue after the introduction of the blockchain is the difference between the sum of the supplier's revenue from the sale of options, revenue from the sale of products, revenue from the execution of options and the cost of production of the products, the opportunity cost incurred by the supplier during the commercial credit period and the cost of the blockchain application. The supplier's fixed revenue is the sum of product and option purchase costs $wq + w_0 q_0$. The supplier's option execution revenue as well as costs increase as the volume of sales in the market increases.

4 Comparison of Operational Decisions Such as Pricing and Ordering and Profitability Between the Two Models

Based on the analysis of the decision-making of retailers and suppliers as well as the profit function in the traditional financing model and the blockchain financing model, this section studies the changes in the decision-making and revenues of suppliers and retailers under the two models, and analyzes the impact of blockchain technology on the revenues of both parties.

Under the traditional supply chain financing model, suppliers are willing to provide trade credit financing to retailers only if they receive positive returns.

Supply chain enterprises will actively choose to introduce blockchain technology only when the expression of supply chain enterprise profit function after the introduction of blockchain technology is better than the expression of supply chain enterprise profit function under the traditional financing model. Analyzed according to different ranges of market demand: the relationship between blockchain unit cost and its positive utility.

When $x < q$, $\Pi_{R2} > \Pi_{R1}$, i.e. $px(1 + \theta)[1 + \alpha(M - T)] - w_0q_0 - wq - c_Bq > px + \alpha(M - T)pq - w_0q_0 - wq$. When $x < q$, the simplification is $px\theta[1 + \alpha(M - T)] - c_Bq > 0$, and $c_B < \frac{px[1 + \alpha(M - T)]\theta}{q}$. When $x < q$, the retailer will actively choose to introduce the blockchain technology; $\Pi_{s2} > \Pi_{s1}$, according to the supplier's benefit function, it can be seen that when the blockchain is introduced the supplier only increases the cost and does not increase the revenue, therefore, when $x < q$, the supplier will not consider invoking the blockchain technology.

When $q < x \leq q + q_0$, $\Pi_{R2} > \Pi_{R1}$, when $px[1 + \alpha(M - T)] - w_0q_0 - wq - w_e(x - q) < px(1 + \theta)[1 + \alpha(M - T)] - w_0q_0 - wq - w_e[x(1 + \theta) - q] - c_Bx(1 + \theta)$ i.e., when $c_B < \frac{(p - w_e)[1 + \alpha(M - T)]x\theta}{1 + \theta}$, the retailer will take the initiative to introduce blockchain technology; $\Pi_{s2} > \Pi_{s1}$, the $w_0q_0 + wq + w_e(x - q) - cx - rMpx < wq + w_0q_0 + w_e(x(1 + \theta) - q) - (c + c_B + Mrp)x(1 + \theta)$, we get $w_ex\theta - cx\theta + rMpx\theta > c_Bx(1 + \theta)$, i.e. $c_B < \frac{(w_e - c + Mrp)\theta}{1 + \theta}$, the supplier is willing to introduce blockchain technology.

When $x > q + q_0$ If $\Pi_{R2} > \Pi_{R1}$ is to be satisfied, the inequality does not hold. $p(q + q_0)[1 + \alpha(M - T)] - w_0q_0 - wq - w_eq_0 < p(q + q_0)[1 + \alpha(M - T)] - w_0q_0 - wq - w_eq_0 - c_B(q + q_0)$, the inequality does not hold, for the retailer to introduce blockchain technology only increases the cost of blockchain application, but does not increase the retailer's income, at this time, the introduction of blockchain is not beneficial to the retailer, so when $x > q + q_0$ retailer will not introduce blockchain. If to satisfy $\Pi_{s2} > \Pi_{s1}$, $w_0q_0 + wq + w_eq_0 - c(q + q_0) - rMp(q + q_0) < wq + w_0q_0 + w_eq_0 - (c + c_B + Mrp)(q + q_0)$, for the supplier to introduce blockchain technology only increases the cost of blockchain application, but does not increase the revenue, at this time the introduction of blockchain is not beneficial to the supplier, therefore, the supplier will not introduce blockchain when $x > q + q_0$ the supplier will not introduce blockchain. Therefore when the market demand $x > q + q_0$ When, neither suppliers nor retailers will consider introducing blockchain technology.

5 Risk Assessment

The introduction of blockchain technology may face the following risks for suppliers and capital-constrained retailers:

Cost risk: Blockchain technology is still at a relatively early stage, so the introduction of blockchain technology requires suppliers and retailers to pay higher costs, including blockchain operation costs, technology costs, labor costs, capital costs, etc. If the introduction of blockchain technology does not bring positive benefits to retailers and suppliers, it will cause huge losses to them.

Technical and security risks: Both suppliers and retailers need to have the appropriate technical capabilities and resources to introduce blockchain technology, including blockchain development team costs, server rental costs, etc. It is also necessary to consider the risks that may be encountered during the blockchain development process, which may lead to the failure of the project if the technical team's operating technology is not mature. In addition, since the blockchain system is open and transparent and the information on the chain cannot be changed, user privacy may be compromised in the event of security problems.

When introducing blockchain technology, suppliers and capital-constrained retailers need to carefully assess the above risks and take corresponding preventive measures, such as strengthening the awareness of risk prevention, evaluating and screening high-quality blockchain team members, enhancing the detection of security vulnerabilities, and complying with blockchain-related laws and regulations, in order to reduce the likelihood of risks occurring.

6   Conclusion

This paper addresses the problem of retailers as small and medium-sized enterprises (SMEs) facing financing difficulties, and the supplier provides them with commercial credit financing to meet their ordering needs. Option contracts are introduced to control the risk of retailers when facing uncertain market demand, hoping that options can bring higher returns for both parties. In this paper, by introducing blockchain technology and option trade model, it can facilitate the flow of credit in the supply chain, improve the efficiency of capital utilization, and reduce the idle and wasteful capital in the supply chain. By analyzing the transaction information of each participant in the supply chain, it can provide more accurate supply chain credit decisions for both parties in the supply chain, reduce the cost and retailer default risk, and improve the operational efficiency of the supply chain. Due to the highly transparent characteristics of blockchain technology, it can increase consumer trust and thus enhance market demand. This paper studies the profit changes of suppliers and retailers under the traditional model and under the blockchain supply chain financing model, and analyzes the circumstances under which suppliers and retailers are willing to introduce blockchain technology. However, due to the lack of technical ability, the impact of blockchain technology and option contract on the operation of both parties is not studied in depth, and in the future, the coordinating role of option contract on both parties of the supply chain can be studied under blockchain technology.

Acknowledgement. This research was supported by the National Natural Science Foundation of China under grant numbers 72101150.

References

1. Zhang, T., Hu, Y.: Research on advanced manufacturing supply chain management under blockchain technology based on green finance background. Bus. Obs. **10**(03), 81–84 (2024). (in Chinese)
2. Liu, Y.: Optimal combination purchasing strategy of option and physical products considering credit financing. Control Decis. Mak 31(09), 1561–1568 (2016). (in Chinese)
3. Ritchken, P.H., Tapiero, C.S.: Contingent claims contracting for purchasing decisions in inventory management. Oper. Res. **34**(6), 864–870 (1986)
4. Liu, C., Chen, A.: Innovation of "double-chain" model to alleviate financing difficulties of small and micro enterprises. Finance Account. Mon. **44**(22), 112–118 (2023). (in Chinese)
5. Casey, E., O'Toole, C.M.: Bank lending constraints, trade credit and alternative financing during the financial crisis: evidence from European SMEs. J. Corp. Finance, 173–193 (2014)
6. Chen, X.: Decision-making and value of trade credit contracts in a capital-constrained supply chain. J. Manag. Sci. (12), 13–20 (2013). (in Chinese)
7. Wang, W.-C., Teng, J.-T., Lou, K.-R.: Seller's optimal credit period and cycle time in a supply chain for deteriorating items with maximum lifetime. Eur. J. Oper. Res. (2), 315–321 (2014)
8. Jim, J., Lu, R.: Research on selection strategy of supply chain financing methods under retailers' purchasing capital constraints. J. Manag. Eng. (03), 106–113 (2016). (in Chinese)
9. Wang, X., Liu, L.: Coordination in a retailer-led supply chain through option contract. Int. J. Prod. Econ. (1), 115–127 (2007)
10. Li, H., Ritchken, P., Wang, Y.: Option and forward contracting with asymmetric information: valuation issues in supply chains. Eur. J. Oper. Res. (1), 134–148 (2008)
11. Hu, B.-Y., Peng, Q.-Y., Wang, S.-Y.: Supply chain option flexibility contract considering purchasing capital constraints. J. Manag. Sci. (06), 62–71 (2009). (in Chinese)
12. Wu, Y.J., Li, Y.J., Zhang, L.H.: Research on the optimal strategy of retailer financing based on option contract. Manag. Rev. (10), 197–208 (2014). (in Chinese)
13. Huashengya, Zhai, X.: Considering supply chain financing and option trading strategies for startups. China Manag. Sci. (02), 80–90 (2020). (in Chinese)
14. Dehghan-Bonari, M., Bakhshi, A., Aghsami, A., Jolai, F.: Green supply chain management through call option contract and revenue -sharing contract to cope with demand uncertainty. Clean. Logist. Supply Chain (2021)
15. Treleaven, P., Gendal Brown, R., Yang, D.: Blockchain technology in finance. Computer **50**(9), 14–17 (2017)
16. The state of play of blockchain technology in the financial services sector: a systematic literature review. Int. J. Inf. Manag. (2020)
17. Liu, L., Li, Y., Jiang, T.: Supply chain financing strategy based on blockchain credit transfer function. Syst. Eng. Theory Pract. (05), 1179–1196 (2021). (in Chinese)
18. Business Division, Institute of Textiles and Clothing, The Hong Kong Polytechnic University, Hung Hom, Kowloon, Hong Kong Blockchain- technology-supported platforms for diamond authentication and certification in luxury supply chains. Transp. Res. Part E, 17–29 (2019)
19. Wang, R., Lin, Z., Luo, H.: Blockchain, bank credit and SME financing. Qual. Quant. (3), 1127–1140 (2019)
20. Wang, D., Zhu, M., Dong, H.: Research on supply chain operation decision-making based on blockchain technology under capital constraint. China Manag. Sci., 1–13 (2023). (in Chinese)

A Multi-objective Particle Swarm Optimization Framework for Operations Management

Julian Sengewald$^{(\boxtimes)}$ and Richard Lackes

Technische Universität Dortmund, Otto-Hahnstr. 12, 44227 Dortmund, Germany
julian.sengewald@tu-dortmund.de

Abstract. There is ongoing research on the problem of how to best combine predictive modeling and optimization. This is especially important in operations management, where there are complex business processes to be optimized. We propose a framework based on evolutionary computing with multi-objective particle swarm optimization and on the design of the fitness function according to the business operations to be optimized. By doing so, one can optimize a range of interesting problems using neural networks that would be otherwise hard to handle with classically supervised learning.

Keywords: gradient-free optimization · multi-objective neural network

1 Introduction

1.1 Predictive Machine Learning and Neural Networks

The use of machine learning (ML) in operations management is growing [1]. For example, ML helps fast-food and retail organizations adjust staffing levels based on expected customer demand. This avoids overstaffing and understaffing. In predictive maintenance, companies use ML to predict potential component failures and ensure timely repairs. This can result in significant cost savings. All these applications share the common characteristic of predicting quantities before they occur, allowing the organization to take appropriate action in a timely manner. This approach addresses operations management issues through the "predict first, optimize later" paradigm, using various machine learning methods [1].

The *"predict first, then optimize"-paradigm* bases optimization on predictions, obtained from analyzing data for predictive patterns between input features and the outcome using ML. A common ML technique are deep neural networks (DNN) [2]. DNN have neurons as their basic units. These neurons are arranged in layers and connected through links. Each link has weights $w_{i,j}$ connecting layers i and j. The first layer of a network carries the input data. The last layer is the output layer, representing the prediction of the DNN. These two layers are connected via one or more hidden layers. Each layer consists of a fixed number of neurons m_i in layer i. The hidden layers process the output from their preceding layer, wherein each neuron receives $n_j = act\left(\sum_{i=1}^{m_i} \cdot w_{i,j} n_i\right)$ as input. Here, $act()$ is a non-linear function referred to as the activation function. Training a DNN requires solving an optimization problem by adjusting the weights $w_{i,j}$ such that the network's prediction matches the observed data.

Y. P. Tu and M. Chi (Eds.): WHICEB 2024, LNBIP 517, pp. 444–455, 2024.
https://doi.org/10.1007/978-3-031-60324-2_37

1.2 Supervised Learning and Its Limitations for Operations Management Problems

Supervised learning algorithms, such as DNN, have limitations when it comes to solving operations management problems [1, 3]. For example, the current use of ML and DNN provides solely predictive information and lacks the full capability of managerial decision-making [2]. Organizations often have different downstream implications arising from predictions, rendering a mismatch between the loss function used in training and the true optimization objective of the business operations [1, 3]. Many supervised prediction applications in operations management omit to include the uncertainty associated with decision-making [2].

Gradient descent is a common method for training DNNs [2]; its success in solving an ML problem largely depends on the availability of labeled training data and whether the loss function used accurately reflects the intended optimization objective. In contrast, in the context of operations management problems, loss functions often fail to sufficiently capture the true optimization objective mathematically. For instance, in regression tasks, a common choice for the loss function is mean squared error $L(y, \hat{y}) = \frac{1}{2N} \sum_i^N (y_i - \hat{y}_i)^2$. Optimizing for this loss function helps the DNN get closer to the conditional expectation of the target y_{target} given the input, since errors that are equally far above or below the prediction are given the same amount of weight. Yet, the implications of prediction errors for the interlinked decision problem are not necessarily symmetric. We call this *complication 1.* In personalized pricing, for example, a high prediction error is worse than a low one, while a slightly lower price leaves some margin, albeit slightly reduced. Hence, the quadratic loss function wrongly reflects the preferences of the business owner.

An approach to overcome these limitations is to design asymmetric losses. For example, the loss function could be adjusted so that it penalizes positive prediction errors more than negative prediction errors: $0.5(y_{target,i} - y_{prediction,i})^2$ if $y_{target,i} > y_{prediction,i}$ and $0.5(y_{target,i} - y_{prediction,i})^2 \cdot 2$ if $y_{target,i} < y_{prediction,i}$. This loss function penalizes positive prediction errors twice as much as negative prediction errors. Yet, there are a few more factors to consider in practice: i) the weights that were attached to the loss need to be known; ii) the same is true for the actual label, the reservation price, such that the prediction error can be calculated. While both may be addressed by using some suitable proxies that can be used instead of the principal quantities [1], the overall quality of the solution depends on how well using the proxy approximates the overall problem when the principal quantities would have been available. We call this complication 2, the proxy approximation challenge. Instead of using proxies, if they exist at all, a more straightforward approach would be to simulate business operations and optimize an ML model based on the repercussions of its prediction. This method does not require knowing the weights attached to the loss or the actual label.

Training a DNN with a simulation of business operations comes with its intricacies, especially when feeding the simulation output into the network. One way to address this challenge is to use a normal gradient-based predictive model and adjust the network architecture according to the simulation performance. In other words, the simulation is only used to tune the hyperparameters of the network. However, this method has drawbacks. First, it may result in suboptimal performance and inaccurate predictions since the network is not directly optimized for the actual objective at the level of the weights. Second, it may not be suitable for multi-objective problems where it is difficult to assign weights to each objective, linearize the problem, or apply the ϵ-constraint method. Therefore, not all objectives can be accurately optimized.

Overall, we conclude that there are four common edge cases for supervised learning algorithms where the prediction task is either not well-defined, not well-aligned with the business objective, or not well-measurable (see Table 1). These edge cases pose challenges for designing supervised learning models. As we have discussed above, there are many compromises to take to make supervised learning feasible in such circumstances; see also Table 1.

Table 1. Edge Cases for Supervised Learning Algorithms

Problem	Description	Examples
Complication 1	No natural quantity to predict	no label; sequential problems
Complication 2	Prediction errors are costly and imprecisely measurable	time lags, guesstimates, unreliable data
Complication 3	Ill-defined loss function	complex relationship between ML prediction and business outcome
Complication 4	Multiple objectives to optimize	multi-objective problem, trade-offs

Accordingly, we suggest that training NNs with gradient descent and standard loss functions may not optimally solve operations management problems involving complex consequences of prediction errors. In the next section, we explore alternative optimization methods that could overcome these limitations.

1.3 Case Study

We discuss the application of our optimization framework in the context of supporting procurement processes. The case study is based on the problem of sourcing suppliers and procuring items from them. The problem is that this overall process should be cost-efficient. We based our study on a dataset from the author's previous research [4].

The cost of total procurement includes the direct purchase cost of the item and the procurement process costs of sourcing suppliers. Supplier sourcing is costly in an industrial environment because it involves the working time of procurement staff in locating and contacting suppliers, as well as activities such as evaluating bids and the technical qualifications of items. All this processing can add up to a significant amount. When sourcing suppliers for many related items regularly, supporting the buyer with an intelligent decision support system can make the whole process more cost-effective. This is because information can be used to guide the sourcing process. For example, with the help of such an intelligent system, the agent can decide whether it is worthwhile to conduct further research and obtain additional quotes (lower purchasing costs) or not. One difficulty with process costs is that they may be difficult to quantify, and the buyer may wish to minimize the total number of suppliers contacted to avoid contacting too many suppliers unnecessarily (optimization problem). Therefore, I investigate how purchases can optimize their decisions when purchasing items from different suppliers. Overall, this case study presents all the features of the complications referred to before (see Table 1). There is no natural quantity to predict because the purchasing agent needs to find a low-priced supplier while balancing the purchase costs (Complication 1). One may use the average price of quotations for similar items as a rough guiding point. However, using the average as a stopping price may not provide the best approach to the underlying optimization problem. Therefore, I propose a method that models the consequences of the prediction so that one does not need to specify a label. Predicting an above-average market price could lead to the purchasing agent wrongly rejecting over-average offers, while underestimating may lead to wrongly accepting over-average offers. Which error is preferable is only decidable once the prediction errors are quantifiable (Complication 2). Yet, these prediction errors are not directly linked to the actual optimization objective, which consists of trading off low purchases with overall process costs, which cannot easily be represented by a standard loss function (Complication 3) and is multi-objective (Complication 4).

1.4   Related Literature

As our case study is based on procurement, we briefly review the status of ML applied to procurement and purchasing. We then summarize the relevant literature on ML and operations management.

Purchasing has increasingly turned to the use of AI [5]. Examples of potential uses of AI in purchasing include automation of repetitive tasks, process monitoring, supplier selection through matching systems, and decision support [5]. Prior review research combines academic literature and industry surveys to explore procurement analytics solutions from both the supply (vendor) and demand (user) sides [8]. By contrasting existing solutions from academic literature and industry with the needs identified by procurement professionals, the research aims to identify gaps and opportunities for improvement in current procurement analytics practices. This effort is particularly relevant when examining the sourcing phase, which, according to prior literature, consists of five steps: 1. specification definition; 2. supplier identification; 3. requests for quotation; 4. negotiation and selection; and 5. contracting [6]. Each of these phases has received varying levels of support from sourcing analytics solutions. For example, while there are several solutions for supplier selection and negotiation, both in the academic literature and in industry software [5], there is a lack of tools to support purchases in the activities preceding these steps. Some tools support the process of supplier discovery, also known as supplier scouting, by focusing on advanced AI-based search (e.g., incorporating unstructured data) [7]. The ability of these tools to control search costs and gather critical supplier data supports their effectiveness. These tools can help streamline the supplier-sourcing process. In addition, analytical support for supplier prequalification aids in tactical decisions [7]. In contrast, practitioners highlight the critical role of price benchmarking and the value of improved market intelligence as valuable insights [8]. Overall, the literature emphasizes the need for solutions that support purchasers at the operational level [7] and provide procurement intelligence [8].

ML for Operations Management. First, data in operations management typically has many categorical features, which can pose challenges for gradient descent optimization used in DNN due to discontinuities when using one-hot encoding [2]. Custom preprocessing via embeddings provides a better solution for handling categorical features, which are relevant for many applications in operations management [2]. Another line of literature revolves around the predict-then-optimize framework. In operations management, decision-making should account for outcome uncertainty due to outcome variability. However, many supervised ML methods discard this information for decision-making by predicting only the conditional expectation [9]. An approach that makes better use of the available data is to use a weighted expectation of the cost of a decision, where the weights are learned from relevant covariates associated with the outcome [9]. Alternatively, if the objective function is linear, there exists a surrogate loss function that can be used to incorporate decision error into training [3]. Another strategy is to construct weighted versions of conventional loss functions (e.g., weighted cross-entropy) that are differentiable and thus can be used by conventional ML methods [1].

1.5 Summary of Contribution

In summary, supervised learning via DNNs can be challenging in certain edge cases (see Table 1). Overall, resorting to standard gradient-based optimization for DNNs may lead to many compromises when using a standard DNN training procedure. In the following sections, we describe that these compromises are not necessary with a gradient-free optimization method: Particle Swarm Optimization (PSO). We also show that it is straightforward to optimize for multiple objectives using the PSO method. By doing so, we extend previous approaches towards combining prediction and optimization simultaneously for the actual optimization objective 1) with an additional procedure that doesn't need an explicit label and 2) is also able to optimize multiple objectives. We also explain when this is the case, such as when there is no natural label to predict, and one seeks to optimize many objectives. Finally, we illustrate our approach using a case study in procurement, which draws from previous research [4].

2   Description of Framework: Concepts and Measures in Multi-objective Optimization

2.1   Multi-objective Optimization

Balancing Cost and Efficiency in Supplier Search. Multi-objective optimization (MOO) involves optimizing multiple objectives simultaneously. For example, one might want to optimize purchase costs and procurement process costs simultaneously. When evaluating suppliers, minimizing direct purchase costs requires assessing a large pool, while minimizing procurement process costs involves keeping the supplier pool small (e.g., less effort on supplier qualification). Formally, this problem can be represented as $argmin_s = (Q(s), s)$ where $Q(s) = min\{p_1, \cdots, p_i, \cdots, p_s\}$, and s is the number of suppliers contacted, with p_i being the corresponding price offer from the i th supplier. In multi-objective optimization, considering multiple dimensions is necessary, unlike in single-objective optimization where sorting by objective value suffices for ranking. For this, the concept of Pareto optimality is used. Pareto-optimal solutions are those in which no other solution dominates them.

Pareto-Optimal. Formally, a solution x is Pareto optimal if there is no other solution x' such that x' is better than x in all objectives and strictly better in at least one objective. Because an increase in one objective value can make up for a decrease in another, there are multiple optimal solutions available to the decision-maker. The collection of all such solutions that are not subject to dominance by any other solution is known as the Pareto-optimal front.

Pareto-Front. The set of all Pareto-optimal solutions is called the Pareto-front. Formally, the Pareto-front is the set of all solutions that cannot be improved on one objective without worsening at least one other objective. All points on the Pareto-front are equally good; yet several such Pareto-fronts can be computed by an algorithm depending on how they were parametrized. The hyper-volume indicator, for instance, indicates that when ranking two Pareto-fronts produced by various algorithm configurations of the architecture of a DNN, the Pareto-front with a higher volume has a better ranking because it contains solutions that dominate another Pareto-front.

Hyper-Volume Indicator. The hyper-volume indicator is a measure to compare Pareto-fronts. It is the volume of the area where the Pareto-front dominates, and the volume is calculated relative to a pessimistic reference point [10].

2.2 Gradient-Free Multi-objective Optimization with Particle Swarm Optimization

Particle Swarm Optimization (PSO) is a heuristic optimization technique. In PSO, a population of potential solutions (called particles) moves around the search space, and each particle's movement depends on both its own trajectory and the trajectory of the swarm. The position of the best solution so far and the best position in the particle's trajectory both affect the trajectory of the particle (candidate solution). Approaching the best solution found is analogous to gradient descent: pointing in the direction of the optimum. However, instead of the gradient, a swarm is used to explore the location of the optimum in the solution space. The role of the swarm itself is both to explore new solution areas and to exchange information with other particles, allowing them to converge on the optimum solution.

There are several extensions of the single-objective algorithm that can extend PSO to the multi-objective case [11]. First, rather than a multidimensional gradient, the particles will naturally gravitate toward the Pareto-optimal set, which is the best solution so far. Since there are several such solutions, the challenge is to determine which one to choose to determine the direction in which an individual particle must move. For determining the global best solution, a leader selection mechanism must be applied [12]. This can be done using sigma scaling, which finds the particle in the Pareto optimal set that is closest to the particle in terms of the outcome space [13]. Sigma scaling also moves the particles closer to the Pareo-front [13]. The formula for sigma scaling:

$$\sigma = \frac{o1^2 - o2^2}{o1^2 + o2^2},$$

where $o1$ and $o2$ are the outcomes of the two objectives. The particle with the highest σ value is the one closest to the particle in the outcome space [13].

An archive stores the solutions generated by the continually evolving swarm, which are then utilized to construct the Pareto-front [12]. During each iteration, a comparison is made between all the solutions in the archive and the current set of solutions. If a new solution dominates a solution in the archive, a particle from the archive is updated with that solution from the current swarm [12].

3 Application to Case Study

3.1 Description of Methodology

To evaluate our approach, we apply our methodology to a real procurement dataset.

Features and Data Used. The data source is the same as in previous research by the authors [4]. The data is a collection of technical items, electrical resistors, which can be described according to a technical standard but are produced and sold by different suppliers. The data contains thus the technical features, which are common among all resistors. The resistor takes different specifications over the common attributes, such as resistance, wattage, or form factor which allows engineering features that can be used to predict quantities for new resistors (see description of decision modeling below).

The data also contains the price of the resistors from different suppliers. The suppliers themselves are not characterized further. The data is split into a training (n = 400) and a testing set (n = 200). Train and testing data set have no overlap in terms of the part number of the item. The testing dataset thus comprises the scenario of procuring completely new items from (unknown) suppliers. The features have undergone the same processing as in (previous research by authors blinded for review). For usage in the DNN, the features are normalized to the interval [0, 1] by dividing by the maximum value of the feature. In total, after pre-processing categorical features by one-hot-encoding, the data contains 20 features. The features are the resistance, wattage, tolerance, temperature coefficient, form factor (area and volume), material (4 types), resistance, wattage, tolerance (3 levels) and additional five derived by relating wattage and resistance to the size and volume of the resistor. To each resistor that has been PartNumber belongs a set of prices from different suppliers, which have adjusted for inflation for better comparability because the source data stems from different years.

We use a *deep neural network* with the technical specifications of each part number as input features. This input is propagated through the DNN in a forward pass. In contrast to conventional DNNs, a particle swarm optimization algorithm adjusts the weights.

Decision Modeling. The DNN predicts a stopping price that if undercut leads to the stopping of further searches for suppliers. After a stoppage has occurred, the lowest-priced supplier so far will be chosen to procure from. This price thus determines the purchase costs. Naturally, the lowest purchase price will be the offer that led to the stopping, but not the predicted price itself. Also, the number of searches performed will determine the process costs.

The tuning of the DNN consisted, firstly, of tuning the architecture of the network (size of hidden layers). Secondly, different parameter values were also tested for the underlying MO-PSO algorithm, as its optimization capacities are the primary research question of this paper.

Objective/Fitness Function. The *fitness function* simulates the repercussions of DNN prediction on operational outcomes. The DNN produces in the forward pass a stopping price for each part number p_i. Using this stopping price, the quotation prices are sampled randomly and sequentially from the database of historical prices. Then, if the obtained price is lower or equal to the stopping price, the process stops. Then the purchase costs are the lowest price of all offers obtained so far before the stopping price was reached. Necessarily, the purchase price is the last price obtained. The process costs reflect the stopping index, which is, the number of offers that were seen until the stopping price was reached. Both quantities, purchase and process costs, yield a tuple $(PartNumber: p_{purchase}, p_{process})$. This tuple represents the quality of a particular solution. The above calculations are repeated ten times for each PartNumber and averaged to account for randomness in the ordering of price quotations. By doing so, we obtain the expected performance of the stopping process obtained from the DNN. The overall algorithm that calculates the fitness of a solution is depicted in Algorithm 1.

Network Architecture and Training. We used a DNN consisting of two hidden layers and one output layer. The number of neurons in the hidden layers is a hyperparameter of the model. We tested $m_1 \in (18,8)$ and $m_2 \in (8,5)$ for the number of neurons in the first and second layer. The output layer consists of a single neuron. The activation function of the hidden layers is the leaky rectified linear unit (leakyReLU) and the output layer is linear. The output layer thus predicts a continuous value. The training procedure of the DNN was governed by the MO-PSO. Here we used for the cognitive parameter $c1 \in \{1, 2, 3\}$ and for the social parameter $c2$ the same values as for the cognitive. Setting social and cognitive parameter equal provides the optimizer with an equal opportunity for exploration and exploitation. For the inertia, we used $w \in \{0.9, 0.7\}$, and for the number of iterations maxits $= \{50, 250, 500\}$. We used a random grid search on the grid spanning these hyperparameters using 16 evaluations, which was the number of evaluations performed after running the experiment for 10 h.

Weight Initialization. We use the "he" initialization for the weights of the DNN [2]. In this initialization, the weights are drawn from a normal distribution with mean 0 and variance 2/n, where n is the number of neurons in the previous layer [2]. These weights represent the initial solution for the DNN. By randomly sampling the weights according to the initializer, each individual in the swarm represents a different initial solution for the weights of different DNNs. Note that each individual represents the same architecture of the DNN, but different weights that are optimized by the MO-PSO algorithm.

The forward pass of the DNN must also be self-implemented. A separate backward pass is not necessary as it is replaced by the MO-PSO algorithm. The MO-PSO algorithm was self-implemented in R using the methodology described in the literature [11, 12]. An external R package, EOF, was used to compute the hypervolume. The EMOA package was used to compute Pareto dominance.

Algorithm 1.
1. **For** each partNumber $\in$ E do
2. $p_{stop} \leftarrow$ get stopping price from DNN for f
3. **For** rep $\in 1,...,5$ do
4. $q_1 \leftarrow$ obtain the first offer randomly
5. $s \leftarrow 1$
6. $Q \leftarrow q_1 \cup Q$
7. $bestOffer \leftarrow \min(Q)$
8.   **While** $bestOffer \geq p_{stop}$ Do
9. $q_s \leftarrow$ get next offer
10. $Q \leftarrow q_s \cup Q$
11. $bestOffer \leftarrow \min(Q)$
12. $s \leftarrow s + 1$
13.   **End While**
14.   Append named tuple $(partNumber, rep: s, bestOffer)$ to temp results
15.   **End For**
16. $(partNumber, bestOffer) \leftarrow$ average temp results over reps $1,...,5$
17. Append named tuple $(partNumber, bestOffer)$ to result.
18. **End For**
19. Return(result)

3.2 Results

First, we compute performance metrics for each model. Each model is evaluated based on the training and test sets. The model differs depending on the architecture of the DNN (i.e., the number of neurons in the hidden layer) and the hyperparameters of the MO-PSO learning procedure (i.e., $c1$, $c2$, and w). The performance metrics are the RMSE and the hypervolume of the Pareo-front. The hypervolume is computed using the eof R package.

In Table 2, we show the top 4 models by hypervolume on the training set. Sorting by hypervolume on the train set corresponds to the usual procedure of hyperparameter tuning and picking the best model, which is then evaluated on the test set. Using hypervolume as a metric for model selection allows for multi-objective optimization of the model selection process.

Since the hypervolume indicator is a multi-dimensional metric characterizing a whole solution space, we also plot the Pareo-front, which visually depicts each solution in the archive. The Pareo-front is plotted in the search and purchase cost spaces (see Fig. 1). The search cost is the number of episodes the agent has to search for a product before purchasing it. The purchase cost is the price of the product. Both are averaged over different items in the testing set. The Pareo-front is plotted for the top 3 models by hypervolume on the training set and their resulting performance on the testing set. The result for the static search strategy is also plotted. The static search strategy is a simple heuristic that always searches for the product in the first three episodes and purchases

Table 2. Top 4 models by train hyper-volume

Parameters					Hypervolume		RMSE		
c1	c2	w	its	architecture	Train	Test	Train	Test	#solutions
2	2	1	50	18-5-1	349	340	6	7	59
1	1	1	250	8-8-1	349	270	20	21	100
2	2	1	500	8-5-1	349	270	318	318	69
2	2	1	50	18-8-1	349	340	3	3	56
Keras				8-5-1			1	2	

the cheapest found after three quotations have been seen. The static search strategy is used as a benchmark for the performance of the MO-PSO models.

Performances (Algorithm 1) on testing set. Pareto fronts for top 3 models in terms of hypervolume during training. Heuristic I is a static search strategy (search = 3). Heuristic II label is $y_i = \frac{1}{S} \sum_{s=1}^{S} p_{i,s}$ trained by MSE loss.

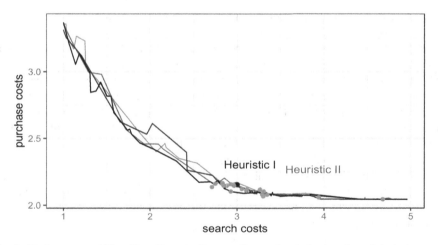

Fig. 1. Performances (Algorithm 1) on testing set. Pareto fronts for top 3 models in terms of hypervolume during training. Heuristic I is a static search strategy (search = 3). Heuristic II label is $y_i = \sum_{s=1}^{S} p_{i,s}$ trained by MSE loss.

In Fig. 1, we compare the MP-PSO algorithm with two other benchmark strategies, Heuristic I and Heuristic II. The static search strategy is a simple heuristic (Heuristic I) which always searches for three episodes and purchases the cheapest offer found after three quotations have been seen. Overall, we see in Fig. 1 that, using our approach, we can find solutions that are better than the Heuristic I strategy (marked in red). We also see that there are different Pareto-fronts produced by differently configured models, as these Pareto-fronts are shifted in the search and purchase cost space. Finally, we see solutions produced by the Keras model (green) that are clustered around Heuristic I.

We also see that the solutions produced by Keras using MSE loss and average price as labels are not diverse, as they barely vary in their objective values. Overall, low diversity is expected, as each of the 20 models produced by Keras is trained to predict the same label. We apply the Keras model to the test data, so some variation in the predicted labels is expected, and therefore, these different stopping prices also lead to different search costs.

4 Discussion

The use of machine learning in organizational operations is growing in popularity. Predictive analytics used in operations management often follows a "predict first, then optimize"-pattern. This means that businesses use past data to construct a predictive ML model. This approach works well when there is a specific quantity, such as demand or component failures, that can be accurately predicted. By accurately predicting this quantity, businesses can efficiently plan and react to operational needs. However, not all problems fit neatly into this pattern, and it may not be clear what to optimize if there is no naturally linked quantity to the operational outcome.

In this paper, a framework based on evolutionary computing is proposed that can be used for problems that do not fit into the above "predict first, then optimize"-pattern. Similarly, as with supervised learning, this approach utilizes historical data and develops an ML solution. The framework involves training a DNN based on simulating the effects of its predictions. We illustrate this framework by applying it to the domain of procurement, where organizations aim to optimize for conflicting objectives: purchase costs and process costs. To achieve this, we train a DNN to predict stopping prices using Multi-Objective Particle Swarm Optimization (MO-PSO). This means that instead of following the traditional 'predict first, then optimize' paradigm, we can directly optimize for the desired outcome. This approach also allows for the handling of multi-objective optimization problems. Furthermore, an explicit label is unnecessary, and it suffices to model the decision problem. By modeling the actual business problem as the target of the training procedure, we may also achieve better results after the model has been deployed. This approach not only increases the transparency of the DNN model but also allows the system's logic to be transparent to the user, as the system minimizes errors associated with its decision.

As with every research, there are limitations. First, the framework was only tested with one case study, and in other optimization problems, the results may be different. Second, it is not said that the presented approach cannot be improved by further research, e.g., turning the learning problem into a sequential one where past price quotations are also used for learning.

In sum, the proposed framework offers several advantages. First, it allows for the handling of multi-objective optimization problems (e.g., purchase costs and process costs). This is difficult to achieve with conventional supervised machine learning algorithms. Second, the approach eliminates the need for an explicit label and models the decision problem directly. This not only simplifies the training procedure but also increases the alignment of the predictions to the actual optimization problem and transparency of the DNN model. Lastly, by modeling the actual business problem as the target of the training procedure, we may achieve better results after the model has been deployed. This is because the model incorporates the entire decision-making process into the training procedure, allowing for more accurate and optimized predictions.

References

1. Vanderschueren, T., Verdonck, T., Baesens, B., Verbeke, W.: Predict-then-optimize or predict-and-optimize? An empirical evaluation of cost-sensitive learning strategies. Inf. Sci. **594**, 400–415 (2022)
2. Kraus, M., Feuerriegel, S., Oztekin, A.: Deep learning in business analytics and operations research: models, applications and managerial implications. Eur. J. Oper. Res. **281**(3), 628–641 (2020)
3. Elmachtoub, A.N., Grigas, P.: Smart "predict, then optimize." Manag. Sci. **68**, 9–26 (2022)
4. Sengewald, J., Lackes, R.: Prescriptive analytics in procurement: reducing process costs. In: Wirtschaftsinformatik 2022 Proceedings (2022)
5. Allal-Chérif, O., Simón-Moya, V., Ballester, A.C.C.: Intelligent purchasing: how artificial intelligence can redefine the purchasing function. J. Bus. Res. **124**, 69–76 (2021)
6. Spreitzenbarth, J.M., Bode, C., Stuckenschmidt, H.: Artificial intelligence and machine learning in purchasing and supply management: a mixed-methods review of the state-of-the-art in literature and practice. J. Purch. Supply Manag., 100896 (2024)
7. Guida, M., Caniato, F., Moretto, A., Ronchi, S.: The role of artificial intelligence in the procurement process: state of the art and research agenda. J. Purch. Supply Manag. **29**, 100823 (2023)
8. Handfield, R., Jeong, S., Choi, T.: Emerging procurement technology: data analytics and cognitive analytics. IJPDLM **49**, 972–1002 (2019)
9. Bertsimas, D., Kallus, N.: From predictive to prescriptive analytics. Manag. Sci. **66**, 1025–1044 (2020)
10. Zitzler, E., Thiele, L., Laumanns, M., Fonseca, C.M., da Fonseca, V.G.: Performance assessment of multiobjective optimizers: an analysis and review. IEEE Trans. Evol. Comput. **7**, 117–132 (2003)
11. Coello, C.C., Lechuga, M.S.: MOPSO: a proposal for multiple objective particle swarm optimization. In: Proceedings of the 2002 Congress on Evolutionary Computation. CEC 2002 (Cat. No. 02TH8600), pp. 1051–1056. IEEE (2002)
12. Kruse, R., Mostaghim, S., Borgelt, C., Braune, C., Steinbrecher, M.: Computational swarm intelligence. In: Kruse, R., Mostaghim, S., Borgelt, C., Braune, C., Steinbrecher, M. (eds.) Computational Intelligence. Texts in Computer Science, pp. 343–369. Springer, Cham (2022). https://doi.org/10.1007/978-3-030-42227-1_14
13. Mostaghim, S., Teich, J.: Strategies for finding good local guides in multi-objective particle swarm optimization (MOPSO). In: Proceedings of the 2003 IEEE Swarm Intelligence Symposium. SIS 2003 (Cat. No. 03EX706), pp. 26–33. IEEE (2003)

Author Index

Y. P. Tu and M. Chi (Eds.): WHICEB 2024, LNBIP 517, pp. 457–460, 2024.
https://doi.org/10.1007/978-3-031-60324-2

Printed in the United States
by Baker & Taylor Publisher Services